AN INDEX TO

WISDEN

CRICKETERS' ALMANACK

1864-1984

AN INDEX TO

WISDEN

CRICKETERS' ALMANACK

1864-1984

COMPILED BY DEREK BARNARD

Macdonald
Queen Anne Press

A **Queen Anne Press** Book

Original Wisden Material (c) John Wisden & Co Ltd
Additional introductory material (c) Derek Barnard
This Index (c) Queen Anne Press

First published in 1985 by Queen Anne Press,
a division of Macdonald & Co (Publishers) Ltd
Maxwell House, 74 Worship Street, London EC2A 2EN
A BPCC plc Company

British Library Catalogue in Publication Data

An Index to Wisden cricketers' almanack
1864-1984.
1. Wisden cricketers' almanack—Indexes
2. Cricket—Yearbooks—Indexes
I. Barnard, Derek
016.79635'8'05   GV925.W5

ISBN 0 356 10240 8

Typeset by Regent Typesetting, 123 High Street, Odiham, Hampshire

Printed in Great Britain at the University Press, Oxford

Dedicated to
my Parents, who have Always
Encouraged me in every Aspect of Life

ACKNOWLEDGEMENTS

I am eternally grateful to John Collinson of the Crowborough Cricket Club who awakened my interest in *Wisden* in 1981. In the preparation of this book I have received special assistance from Graeme Wright, Deputy Editor of *Wisden Cricket Monthly*, Celia Kent, Caroline North and Pamela Dix of Queen Anne Press, and Valerie Thorpe of the Tunbridge Wells Grammar School for Boys Secretarial Staff. Many people have offered help and advice along the way, but I have to single out one group: my family. Sheila, Alison, Helen and Ian left me to work when other matters seemed more important.

PREFACE

On a dark October evening in 1982 I decided to relive my boyhood cricketing days by following the progress of my hero Colin Cowdrey in the cricketers' bible: *Wisden*. Several questions came to mind. When did Colin score his hundredth hundred and against whom? How could I find out whether or not *Wisden* had produced a Special Article on Colin? Where did he hit his highest score of 307? After much random searching I came up with the answers but the above queries had necessitated the removal of at least twenty *Wisdens* from the shelf.

I glanced further along the shelf. Yes, in 1944 Rex Pogson had provided an *Index to Wisden 1864-1943*. But nobody had bothered to keep it up to date. Why not? Surely with the upsurge of cricket interest since Botham's exploits of 1981 and the ever increasing demand for the back copies of *Wisden*, the time had come for a new Index. 1985 would be the ideal time as the new Index would represent an Index to the first 121 issues of Wisden. That Index is now offered.

The contents of *Wisden* fall into two categories – the match reports and scores of the previous season (the Kent v Sussex match of 1983 will be found in the 'Kent in 1984' section), and the Book Reviews, Five Cricketers of the Year, Obituaries, Photographs and Special Articles. It is the second category of topics that often cannot be readily associated with any particular year.

This index is therefore concerned with those items that are not easily indentified with a particular issue. In most cases I have adhered to the view that an index of this size must concentrate upon first class cricket only, but personalities and feats outside the first class game (e.g., limited over cup competitions) have been included where they are thought to be of particular interest.

From 1864 to 1886 the page numbering began at 1; in 1887 the general information containing Special Articles and Obituaries was contained in the first part of the book and Roman numerals were employed. Part II was the Leading Counties performances which were numbered with Arabic numerals. From 1908 to 1937 (with the exception of the period 1916 to 1919) the book was divided into two parts, with each part beginning at page 1. Items during these years are shown with the figure I or II to indicate the part following the year and preceeding the page numbers. In 1938 the logical step was taken to number the book throughout from page 1 so that today *Wisden* amounts to about 1300 pages each year.

Each individual person indexed has his surname followed by the initials he used during his playing career. Then follows school, club, university, county, country, journalist, writer, etc. (Wellington after a player's entry indicates Wellington Public school and not Wellington, New Zealand. Where the entry is for Wellington, New Zealand it will be readily apparent.) All of the photographs appearing in *Wisden* have been indexed, including the head and shoulder portraits that were a feature of the County Sections from 1950 to 1982. Where possible Test Players have been identified if referred to in the Public Schools Article which is a feature of each *Wisden*. Readers should note that

Career Figures for players are often given at the end of an obituary. Many players also attained ranks in the Armed Forces during the two World Wars and often the Obituary entry will reflect this and hence they are given military ranking in the Index.

A word of warning needs to be given about double-barrelled names. For example, N. S. Mitchell-Innes, who played in one test match for England in 1935, will be found under Mitchell. The golden rule is to take the first surname.

The Cricketers of the Year from 1889 to 1940 will be found in the Index under the subheading Portrait and Biography, as this was how they were described in *Wisden*. From 1947 onwards separate entries under Cricketer of the Year and Photograph will be found.

The Book Reviews, which began in the 1950 issue, include all major Tour Accounts, Biographies and the County Histories. The majority of these Book Reviews have also been cross referenced. Tours are indexed under the country or county of origin: the Australians in England 1981, for example, will be found in the Australia section of the Index. Overseas tours have not always been of first class status but are still included. Where a country has changed its name recently the new name has been used, e.g., Zimbabwe for Rhodesia, Guyana for British Guiana, and Sri Lanka for Ceylon. However, if a player only played under the old name for his country then that old name has been retained under his entry.

Benefit Matches have only been included where *Wisden* makes a definite mention of them. Some matches have been for benefit purposes, but unless *Wisden* states this to be the case then the match has been excluded. Plans of the County Grounds are included when they first occur in *Wisden*.

The Records Section has been the most difficult to index. Individual feats with bat and ball and outstanding performances by fielders and wicket-keepers have been included. However, Bill Frindall's excellent publication, *The Wisden Book of Cricket Records*, provides the statistician with all the facts quickly. All schoolboys scoring in excess of 1000 runs in a season, or taking 75 or more wickets, have been included as these were thought to be a good criteria by which schoolboy superstars could be measured.

Readers will note two Appendices. Appendix A lists all the photographs appearing in *Wisden* except the Individual Photographs and the County Team Portraits which were a feature of the 1970s. Appendix B is a complete list in chronological order of all the Special Articles, excluding the Portraits and Biographies and Cricketers of the Year.

Above all I have attempted to achieve a reasonable standard of accuracy, but in dealing with 121 issues of the world's most famous cricket book it is possible that errors have occurred. I only hope that my readers will indicate them to me.

This Index was conceived as a hobby. It became an obsession. Its aim is to help the serious and not so serious students of the game to understand the wealth of material inside the covers of the world's finest cricket reference book.

DEREK BARNARD
CROWBOROUGH 1984

Abberley, R. N. (Warwickshire)
    Photograph   1967   *599*

Abbey, E. A. (President Artists C.C.)
    Obituary   1912/I   *162*

Abbott, 2nd Lieut. L. P. (Exeter College, Oxford)
    Obituary   1917   *161*

Abdul Aziz (Karachi)
    Obituary   1960   *949*

Abdul Hafeez   See also Kardar, A. H.
    'Growth of Pakistan Cricket'   1954   *97*

Abdul Qadir (Lahor; Habib Bank; Pakistan)
    Photograph   1983   *Plate*

Abel, R. (Surrey; England)
    Benefit Match   1896   *20*
    In First Class Cricket   1905   *cxvii*
    Obituary   1937/I   *263*
    Portrait and Biography   1890   *xxxiv*
    'Bobby Abel Professional Batsman 1857-1936'
    D. Kynaston Book Review   1983   *1307*

Abel, W. J. (Surrey)
    Obituary   1935/I   *259*

Abercrombie, Lieut. C. H. (Royal Navy; Hampshire)
    Obituary   1917   *161*

Aberdare, 3rd Baron (Winchester; Oxford University; Middlesex)
    Obituary   1958   *955*

Abergavenny, 1st Marquess of (President Kent C.C.)
    Obituary   1916   *140*

Abinger, 2nd Lieut. B. R. (South America)
    Obituary   1916   *140*

Aboriginal Australians in England 1868   1869   *108*

Abraham, Dr. A. (Leinster C.C.; Durham; Northumberland)
    Obituary   1923/I   *285*

Abraham J. (Northants)
    Obituary   1915/I   *211*

Abrahams, Dr. B. L. (Hon Sec Buckinghamshire)
    Obituary   1909/I   *131*

Absolon, C. (Middlesex)
    Obituary   1908/I   *156*
    and   1909/I   *149*
    Testimonial to   1875   *15*

Acfield, D. L. (Brentwood; Cambridge University; Essex)
    Photographs   1974   *383*
                                    1978   *371*
                                    1982   *386*

Acheson, Hon. Major E. A. B. (Harrow)
    Obituary   1922/I   *245*

Ackerman, H. M. (Border; N. E. Transvaal; Natal; Northamptonshire)
Photograph 1970 *497*
Ackroyd, A. (Uppingham; Yorkshire)
Obituary 1929/I *261*
Adam, Lieut. F. D. (Leys School)
Obituary 1919 *164*
Adam, J. (New York)
Obituary 1906 *lxxxvii*
Adam, 2nd Lieut. J. R. (County High School, Isleworth)
Obituary 1917 *161*
Adam, Gen. Sir R. F. Bart (President M.C.C.)
Obituary 1983 *1240*
Adam, 2nd Lieut. R. W. (Leys School)
Obituary 1918 *168*
Adam, W. (American Club Cricket)
Obituary 1910/I *150*
Adams, C. J. N. (King's, Canterbury)
Obituary 1920/I *151*
Adams, D. (Surrey)
Obituary 1978 *1084*
Adams, F. (New South Wales)
Obituary 1912/I *162*
Adams, 2nd Lieut. F. L. (Whitgift Grammar)
Obituary 1919 *164*
Adams, Sir G. H. (Barbados)
Obituary 1972 *1046*
Adams, 2nd Lieut. G. H. C. (Radley)
Obituary 1917 *161*
Adams, Sub-Lieut. G. J. (Bishop's Stortford C.C.; Hertfordshire)
Obituary 1943 *361*
Adams, J. C. (Surrey Club Cricket)
Obituary 1917 *237*
Adams, Lieut. H. (St.Lawrence College; Ramsgate; Winnipeg C.C.)
Obituary 1919 *164*
Adams, P. W. (Cheltenham)
Portrait 1919 *150*
Public School Cricketer of Year 1919 *156*
Adams, T. (Kent)
Obituary 1895 *xxxvii*
Adamson, Capt. C. Y. (Durham School; Durham; Queensland)
Obituary 1919 *164*
Adamson, 2nd Lieut. G. A. (Ardrossan Academy)
Obituary 1918 *168*
Adamson, J. (Durham)
Obituary 1933/I *261*

2

Adamson, W. M. (Brooklyn C.C.; New York)
Obituary   1919   *213*

Adcock, Rev. J. M. (Warwickshire Club Cricket)
Obituary   1915/I   *211*

Adcock, N. A. T. (Transvaal; Natal; South Africa)
Cricketer of the Year   1961   *83*
Photograph   1961   *95*
Visitor's Award   1961   *252*

Addenbrooke, Capt. A. (Warwick School; Oxford University)
Obituary   1917   *162*

Addison, V. (Writer)
with B. Bearshaw 'Lancashire Cricket at the Top'
Book Review   1972   *1096*

Adey, F. (Bristol Umpire)
Obituary   1947   *687*

Adhikari, Col. H. R. (Gujerat; Baroda; Services; India)
Photograph   1953   *53*

Adlard, Capt. G. H. (Highgate School)
Obituary   1942   *347*

Advisory County Committee
Prospects for Reform of Cricket after
World War II   1946   *117*
Replaced by Test and County Cricket Board   1969   *1019*

Aftab Baloch (National Bank of Pakistan; Pakistan International Airways; Pakistan)
428 runs v Baluchistan   1975   *196,1021*

Agar, Hon. H. W. E. (Harrow)
Obituary   1903   *lxxxii*

Agatha Christie Series
(England v West Indies U19)   1979   *638*

Aggregates for Four Consecutive Innings   1940   *83*

Agnew, C. M. (Rugby)
Obituary   1933/I   *261*

Agnew, J. (Leicestershire; England)
Whitbread Award   1979   *82*

Ahl, F. D. (Worcestershire)
Obituary   1968   *998*

Ainscough, Lieut. C. (Ampleforth; Ormskirk C.C.)
Obituary   1916   *140*

Ainscough, T. (Lancashire)
Obituary   1928/I   *275*

Ainslie, Ven. Archdeacon A. C. (Somerset)
Obituary   1904   *lxxxii*

Ainslie, Canon R. M. (St. Peter's, York)
Obituary   1925/I   *255*

3

Ainsworth, J. L. (Marlborough; Lancashire)
Obituary   1925/I   28.

Ainsworth, Lt-Cmdr. M. L. Y. (Shrewsbury; Worcestershire)
Obituary   1979   107.

Aird, Major R. (Eton; Cambridge University; Hampshire; Secretary M.C.C.; President M.C.C.)
Note on   1952   9
Presentation by M.C.C.   1965   32
Retirement   1963   143,33
Speech to County Secretaries   1956   101
Tributes to: K. Duleepsinhji   1960   95
           D. R. Jardine   1959   93.
           H. Preston   1961   16

Airey, Col.R. B. (Tonbridge; Hampshire)
Obituary   1934/I   25

Airey, Brig. R. M. (Kent Committee)
Obituary   1955   93

Airth, Lieut. R. A. (Leys School)
Obituary   1918   16

Aitken, A. A. (Melbourne C.C. Committee)
Obituary   1919   20.

Aitken, H. M. (Eton; Oxford University)
Obituary   1916   14

Aitken, J. (President; Victoria Cricket Association)
Obituary   1907   c

Aitken, Canon J. (Eton; Oxford University)
Obituary   1909/I   13.

Aitken, 2nd Lieut. J. I. M. (Edinburgh Academy)
Obituary   1919   16

Akers–Douglas, I. S. (Eton; Kent)
Obituary   1953   93.

Akroyd, B. N. (Radley; Surrey)
Obituary   1927/I   27.

Akroyd, S. H. (Radley; Surrey)
Obituary   1926/I   26.

Alanbrooke, Field Marshall Viscount (Life Member M.C.C.)
Note on   1947   20.

Alcock, C. W. (Secretary Surrey; Editor; Cricket)
In Surrey Cricket   1946   54
Obituary   1908/I   13.
Photograph   1980   107
'The Man who made all Seasons'
B. Easterbrook   1980   10

Alcott, C. F. W. (or Allcott, C. F. W.)(Hawkes Bay; Auckland; Otago; New Zealand))
Obituary   1975   107(

4

Alderman, A. E. (Derbyshire; Umpire)
Obituary   1966   *1010*

Alderman, T. (Western Australia; Australia)
'Alderman carried off injured'   1984   *Plates*
Cricketer of the Year   1982   *84*
Photograph   1982   *71*
42 wkts in England Test Series   1982   *222,237*

Alderson, Capt. A. E. (Dover College)
Obituary   1919   *164*

Alderson, Capt. R. (St. Bees School)
Obituary   1919   *164*

Aldridge, J. (Winchester)
Obituary   1918   *220*

Alexander, E. B. (Forest School)
Obituary   1956   *967*

Alexander, F. C. M. (Cambridge University; Jamaica; West Indies)
Retirement   1962   *922*
Tribute to O. G. Smith   1960   *956*

Alexander, G. (Victoria; Australia)
Obituary   1931/I   *247*

Alexander, Lieut. H. (Uppingham)
Obituary   1917   *222*

Alexander, Field Marshal Sir H. (President M.C.C.)
Obituary   1970   *1016*

Alexander, H. R. T. (Harrow)
Obituary   1921/I   *222*

Alexander, Capt. R. (Ireland)
Obituary   1944   *304*

Alford, F. S. (Hampstead C.C.)
Obituary   1907   *cv*

Alington, Rev. E. H. (Westminster)
Obituary   1939   *906*

Alington, Rev. H. G. (Rugby; Oxford University; Lincolnshire)
Obituary   1929/I   *241*

Alison, Capt. G. N. (Incogniti)
Obituary   1917   *162*

Allan, D. W. (Barbados; West Indies)
Pen Picture   1963   *90*

Allan, F. E. (Victoria; Australia)
Obituary   1918   *220*

Allan, J. M. (Edinburgh Academy; Kent; Warwickshire)
Photograph   1956   *404*
Schools Note   1950   *716*
85 wkts Schools Averages   1950   *745*

Allan, P. J. (Queensland; Australia)
10 wickets in Innings   1968   *210,863*

Allcock, Rev. A. E. (King Edward's, Birmingham; Staffordshire)
Obituary 1925/I 25

Allcock, C. H. (King Edward's, Birmingham; Cambridge University)
Obituary 1948 77

Allen, B. O. (Clifton; Cambridge University; Gloucestershire)
Obituary 1982 119

Allen, C. (Gloucestershire)
Obituary 1959 92

Allen, L/Cpl. C. B. (Lancaster Grammar; Lancaster C.C.)
Obituary 1917 16

Allen, D. A. (Gloucestershire; England)
Benefit Match 1973 41
Photographs 1960 39
1964 39
1967 40
Young Cricketer of the Year 1961 25

Allen, D. R. (Writer)
'Sir Aubrey' Book Review 1983 1316

Allen, Pte. E. D. (Cricket Reporting Agency)
Obituary 1916 140

Allen, F. (Derbyshire Physiotherapist)
Obituary 1981 373

Allen, G. O. B. (Eton; Cambridge University; Middlesex; England)
'G. O. Allen – Mr. Cricket' I. Peebles 1977 122
'A Case for more Natural Wickets' 1938 52
Career Figures 1977 129
'Fifty Years on' 1930 – 1980 Tests' 1981 107
'My Seven Year Stretch' 1962 118
Photographs 1938 52
1977 123
Schools Notes 1920/I 265
1921/I 249
1922/I 280/284
10 wkts in Innings 1930/II 231

Allen, J. (New York Clubs)
Obituary 1918 221

Allen, M. H. J. (Northants)
Photograph 1959 472

Allen, R. (Yorkshire)
Obituary 1966 962

Allen, R. C. (New South Wales; Australia)
Obituary 1953 937

Allen, Sir R. W. (Bedfordshire)
Obituary 1956 967
Views on Second Class Counties and
the LBW Rule 1903 lxii

6

Allen, Lieut. S. H. H. (Berkhampstead School)
Obituary 1919 *164*

Allen, S. R. (Secretary, Sussex)
Obituary 1977 *571*

Allen, W. R. (Yorkshire)
Obituary 1951 *917*

Alletson, E. B. (Nottinghamshire)
Incredible Hitting 1912/II *225*
'Alletson's Innings'. J. Arlott
Book Review 1958 *1023*
Obituary 1964 *945*

Alley, W. E. (New South Wales; Somerset; Umpire)
Brylcream Prize 1962 1963 *924*
Cricketer of the Year 1962 *104*
'My Incredible Innings' Book Review 1970 *1066*
Note on 1945 *50-51*
Photographs 1958 *523*
1962 *94*
1963 *574*
1965 *538*
1969 *551*
Retirement 1961 *498*
Testimonial

Alleyne, H. L. (Buckinghamshire; Worcestershire; Lincolnshire; Barbados)
Photograph 1981 *596*

Allin, A. W. (Glamorgan)
Photograph 1977 *395*
All India Schools Tour of U.K. 1967 1968 *825*
All India State Bank in Sri Lanka. 1966 1967 *894*
1968 1969 *923*

Allison, J. B. (Canada)
Obituary 1908/I *133*

Alliston, C. G. P. (Kent)
Obituary 1974 *1070*

Allo, A. W. (Otago)
Obituary 1951 *917*

Allom, Lieut. G. C. G. (Wellington College)
Obituary 1918 *168*

Allom, M. J. C. (Wellington College; Cambridge University; Surrey; England)
Records by 1941 *61*

Allott, P. J. W. (Lancashire; England)
Photograph 1982 *461*
Schools Notes 1976 *862*
1977 *809*

Allsop, G. (Transvaal)
Obituary	1928/I	*275*

Allsopp, Capt. Hon. F. E. (Cheltenham; Worcestershire)
Obituary	1929/I	*241*

Allsopp, Capt. Hon. H. T. (Cheltenham; Cambridge University)
Obituary	1921/I	*272*

Allsopp, Lt.-Col. J. B. (Stubbington House XI)
Obituary	1919	*165*

Allsopp, R. (Trent Bridge Groundsman)
Groundsman's Award	1978	*107*

Allsopp, T. A. (Umpire)
Obituary	1966	*961*

Allsopp, T. C. (Leicestershire; Norfolk)
Obituary	1920/I	*160*

All Rounders Note on
	1953	*79*
	1954	*81*

All Rounder's Strength Notes on
	1958	*73*

Almack, Rev. W. (Writer)
Obituary	1922/I	*245*

Almond, F. C. (Essex)
Obituary	1911/I	*136*

Almond, Dr. H. H. (l/c Loretto Cricket)
Obituary	1904	*lxxx*

Alpen, G. R. (Belgium)
Obituary	1917	*162*

Alston, G. H. (Marlborough)
Obituary	1920/I	*160*

Alston, R. (Broadcaster; Writer)
'Taking the Air' Book Review	1952	*1016*
'Test Commentary' Book Review	1957	*995*
'Over to Rex Alston' Book Review	1954	*982*

Alston, W. (Warwickshire)
Obituary	1918	*222*

Altham, H. S. (Winchester; Oxford University; Surrey; Hampshire)
Altham Committee	1950	*259,954*
'Cricket Thrives Here'	1961	*154*
'Cricket in War Time'	1940	*43*
'Evolution of the Laws'	1962	*153*
'Growth of Cricket Overseas'	1962	*156*
'Hampshire County Cricket' (with J. Arlott, D. Eagar, R. Webber) Book Review	1958	*1023*
'The Heart of Cricket – A Memoir of H. S. Altham' Ed. H. Doggart Book Review	1968	*1050*
Obituary	1966	*961*
Photograph	1961	*85*

'Some Dates in the History of Cricket'	1941 ad passim	*42*
Alva, B. C. (Madras; Mysore; Indian Clubs)		
Obituary	1984	*1195*
Alverstone, 1st Viscount (Charterhouse; President Surrey)		
Obituary	1916	*141*
Amar, Singh, L. (Nawanagar; India)		
Obituary	1941	*391*
America		
'Cricket in the West Indies and America'	1898	*lxx*
P. F. Warner		
'American Cricketers in the West Indies 1887–8'		
H. R. Holmes Book Review	1976	*1140*
American Baseball Players in England 1874	1875	*207*
Amarnath, L. (S.Punjab; Gujerat; Patiula; United Provinces; Railways; India)		
Benefit Match	1962	*863*
Photograph	1947	*39*
Amarnath, M. (Punjab; Delhi; India; Wiltshire)		
Cricketer of the Year	1984	*55*
Photographs	1984	*Plates*
Schools Note	1968	*761*
Amarnath, S. (Punjab; Delhi; India)		
Schools Note	1968	*760*
Amateur Status Definition	1963	*139*
Disappearance	1963	*137*
Examined	1958	*111*
Expenses – Test Matches 1947	1948	*816*
Ames, L. E. G. (Kent; England)		
Age and Cricket after the War Note on	1945	*47*
Benefit Matches	1938	*387*
	1949	*392*
'A Century of Centuries' with Figures		
V. G. J. Jenkins	1951	*91*
'Close of Play' Book Review	1954	*978*
Hundredth Hundred	1951	*392*
Photographs	1950	*376*
	1951	*90*
Portrait and Biography	1929	*271*
Tribute to J. M. Sims	1974	*1080*
Amin, Lakhari (Pakistan Universities)		
Double Hat Trick	1980	*972*
Amir, Elahi (Baroda; N. India; S. Punjab; India; Pakistan)		
Benefit Match	1954	*867*
Obituary	1982	*1193*

Amherst, Hon. J. G. H. (Harrow)
Obituary   1901   *li*
Amiss, D. L. (Warwickshire; England)
Action Photographs   1975   *82*
    1979   *57*
Benefit Match   1976   *596*
Cricketer of the Year   1975   *83*
'In Search of Runs' Book Review   1977   *1096*
Photographs   1973   *558*
    1975   *75*
    1980   *588*
Amor, S. L. (Somerset)
Obituary   1965   *963*
Amphlett, Judge R. H. (Patron of Worcestershire)
Obituary   1927/I   *294*
Anand, S. V. (Vizianagram Maharajah Kumar of) (United Provinces; India)
Obituary   1966   *973*
Vizzy Commemoration Souvenir
K. I. Dutt, K. V. G. Ratnam Book Review   1967   *1020*
Ancaster, Earl of (President M.C.C.)
Obituary   1912/I   *183*
Anderdon, H. E. M. (President Somerset)
Obituary   1923/I   *285*
Anderson, C. A. (Jack) (Journalist)
Obituary   1979   *1073*
'West Indies in Test Cricket'   1950   *119*
Anderson, Pte. D. (Stewart's College)
Obituary   1916   *141*
Anderson, Capt. D. K. (King's Canterbury)
Obituary   1918   *168*
Anderson, G. (Yorkshire)
Benefit Match   1871   *141*
Obituary   1903   *lxxx*
Anderson J. (Ceylon)
Obituary   1961   *943*
Anderson, J (Scotland)
Obituary   1962   *984*
Anderson, J. C. (Cricket Artist)
Obituary   1908/I   *133*
Anderson, 2nd Lieut. J. L. (Perthshire)
Obituary   1918   *168*
Anderson, Capt. R. C. (Army)
Obituary   1916   *141*
Anderson, 2nd Lieut. S. S. (George Heriot's)
Obituary   1917   *222*

Anderson, Rev. S. K. (Rugby)
Obituary   1975   *1070*
Anderson, T. (Merchiston Castle; Scotland)
Obituary   1939   *906*
Anderson, W. (Kincardineshire)
Obituary   1908/I   *133*
Anderson, W. B. (Middlesex)
Obituary   1949   *862*
Anderson, 2nd Lieut. W. H. (Leys School)
Obituary   1918   *168*
Anderson, W. McD. (Canterbury, New Zealand)
Obituary   1981   *1138*
Anderton, A. L. (Cleckheaton C.C.)
Obituary   1918   *221*
Anderton, Lieut. W. L. (Merchant Taylors; Cleckheaton C. C.)
Obituary   1916   *141*
Andreae, C. (Harrow)
Obituary   1943   *370*
Andreae, C. M. (Harrow)
Obituary   1971   *1023*
Andrew, Flt/Lieut. B. (Writer)
'Australians in English Club Cricket'   1944   *56*
Andrew, K. V. (Northamptonshire; England)
Benefit Match   1964   *507*
Photographs   1958   *482*
     1960   *499*
Retirement   1967   *510*
Andrew, W. (Hampshire)
Obituary   1912/I   *162*
Andrews, L. (Bankstown, Canterbury, New Zealand)
9 wkts as wicketkeeper Note on   1984   *977*
Andrews, N. P. (Northamptonshire)
Obituary   1972   *1046*
Andrews, O. (Rossall)
78 wkts Schools Averages   1895   *330*
Andrews, O. (Gentlemen of Ireland)
Obituary   1957   *942*
Andrews, T. J. E. (New South Wales; Australia)
Obituary   1971   *1023*
Testimonial Match   1935/II   *681*
Andrews, W. (Gentlemen of Ireland)
Obituary   1967   *962*
Andrews, W. H. (Radley; Sussex)
Obituary   1910/I   *150*

Andrews, W. H. R. (Somerset)
'The Hand that Bowled Bradman'
Book Review | 1974 | *1125*
Animals on the Field Note on | 1983 | *895*
Ansell, 2nd Lieut. A. G. (Solihull Grammar)
Obituary | 1919 | *165*
Anson, C. E. (Yorkshire)
Obituary | 1970 | *1016*
Anson, G. F. A. (Harrow; Cambridge University; Kent)
Obituary | 1979 | *1089*
Anson, 2nd Lieut. N. F. E. (Eton)
Obituary | 1919 | *197*
Anson, Hon. R. (Middlesex)
Obituary | 1967 | *962*
Anson, Rev. T. A. (Eton; Cambridge University)
Obituary | 1900 | *liv*
Anstruther-Duncan, Major A. W. (Sussex)
Obituary | 1904 | *lxxxvi*
Anthony, A. (Clydesdale C.C.; Canadian Clubs)
Obituary | 1921/I | *122*
Anthony, E (Author)
Obituary | 1920/I | *160*
Anthony, G. (Nottinghamshire)
Obituary | 1908/I | *133*
Anthony, Major P. (Dulwich, Herefordshire)
Obituary | 1917 | *162*
Anti-Aircraft Command Report on | 1945 | *121*
Apcar, Sir A. A. (Harrow)
Obituary | 1914/I | *177*
Aplin, Capt. E. S. (King's Rochester)
Obituary | 1919 | *165*
Appealing – Out of Control Note on | 1983 | *78*
| 1984 | *51*
Appleby, A. (Lancashire)
Obituary | 1903 | *lxxix*
Appleton, C. (Rossall; Yorkshire)
Obituary | 1926/I | *263*
Appleyard, 2nd Lieut. H. E. (Sedbergh)
Obituary | 1917 | *162*
Appleyard, J. (Patron of Cricket)
Hedley Verity Memorial Match | 1945 | *207*
Obituary | 1976 | *1092*
Appleyard, R. (Yorkshire; England)
Cricketer of the Year | 1952 | *81*
Photograph | 1952 | *73*
Testimonial | 1959 | *110*

12

Apted, S. (Oval Groundsman)
　Benefit Match　　　　　　　　　　　　　　1911/II　　　　*44*
　Obituary　　　　　　　　　　　　　　　　1917　　　　　*237*
Arber, G.(Worcestershire)
　Obituary　　　　　　　　　　　　　　　　1912/I　　　　*162*
Arbuthnot, Rear Admiral Sir R. K. (Navy)
　Obituary　　　　　　　　　　　　　　　　1917　　　　　*162*
Archer, A. G.(Worcestershire; Shropshire; England)
　Obituary　　　　　　　　　　　　　　　　1937/I　　　　*286*
Archer, 2nd Lieut. E. T. (Dewsbury and Saville C.C.)
　Obituary　　　　　　　　　　　　　　　　1918　　　　　*211*
Archer, Major H. (Blundells)
　Obituary　　　　　　　　　　　　　　　　1918　　　　　*168*
Archer, R. G. (Queensland; Australia)
　Action Photographs　　　　　　　　　　　1954　　　　*57,58*
Archer, Rev. W. W. (President Hampton Wick C.C.)
　Obituary　　　　　　　　　　　　　　　　1911/I　　　　*136*
Argall, P. (Umpire)
　Obituary　　　　　　　　　　　　　　　　1913/I　　　　*182*
Argentina in Brazil 1929　　　　　　　　　　1930/II　　　*719*
　　　　　Chile 1929　　　　　　　　　　　1930/II　　　*719*
　　　　　Cricket in 1967–68　　　　　　　1969　　　　　*928*
Argentina Elected Associate Member of I.C.C.　1975　　　　*1112*
Argyll G. H. Duke of (Patron of Cricket)
　Obituary　　　　　　　　　　　　　　　　1915/I　　　　*211*
Arif Butt (Lahore; Pakistan)
　Photograph　　　　　　　　　　　　　　　1968　　　　　*59*
Arkell, H. J. D. (Northamptonshire)
　Obituary　　　　　　　　　　　　　　　　1983　　　　　*1240*
Arkwright, C. L. (Harrow; Herefordshire)
　Obituary　　　　　　　　　　　　　　　　1928/I　　　　*275*
Arkwright, Lt–Col. F. G. B. (Eton; Hampshire)
　Obituary　　　　　　　　　　　　　　　　1943　　　　　*361*
Arkwright, H. A. (Eton; Oxford University; Essex)
　Obituary　　　　　　　　　　　　　　　　1943　　　　　*370*
Arlidge, J. (Journalist)
　'Tales of W.G. Grace'　　　　　　　　　　1977　　　　　*138*
　John Langridge Golden Jubilee　　　　　1979　　　　　*115*
Arlott, J. (Writer; Broadcaster)
　Book Reviewer Wisden 1950–1978 and 1981–84
　Articles in chronological order:
　'Cricket Literature of the Wisden Century'　1963　　　　*1077*
　'Neville Cardus'　　　　　　　　　　　　1965　　　　　*121*
　'M.C. Cowdrey Centurian and Captain
　Courteous'　　　　　　　　　　　　　　1969　　　　　*97*

'Lord Constantine – The Sportsman's Cricketer'	1972	*125*
'Sir Garfield Sobers: Cricket's most Versatile Performer'	1975	*106*
J.M. Brearley – Success through Perceptiveness'	1983	*87*
Book Reviews in chronological order:		
'Gone to the Test Match'	1950	*981*
'The First Test Match' with E.C. Brogden	1951	*989*
'Gone with the Cricketers'	1951	*1001*
'Maurice Tate'	1952	*1022*
'Days at the Cricket'	1952	*1022*
'Test Match Diary 1953'	1954	*987*
'Australian Test Journal'	1956	*1032*
'Hampshire County Cricket' (with H.S. Altham, D. Eagar, R. Webber)	1958	*1023*
'Alletson's Innings'	1958	*1023*
'Cricket Journal'	1959	*998*
'Cricket Journal 2'	1960	*1010*
'V.H.D. Cannings – An Appreciation'	1960	*1010*
'Cricket on Trial'	1961	*1006*
'J.R. Gray'	1961	*1006*
'The Australian Challange'	1962	*1050*
'Roy Marshall'	1962	*1050*
'A. Holt – An Appreciation'	1964	*1013*
'P. Sainsbury – An Appreciation'	1966	*1030*
'Fred : Portrait of a Fast Bowler'	1972	*1109*
'The Ashes 1972'	1973	*1066*
'The Young Cricketer's Tutor – J.Nyren. Ed'	1975	*1128*
'Jack Hobbs: Profile of the Master'	1982	*1278*
'A Word from Arlott'	1984	*1277*
Armistead, Rev. H. S. (Charterhouse; Free Foresters)		
Obituary	1913/I	*182*
Armistead, Canon J. R. (Cheshire)		
Obituary	1919	*202*
Armistead, Rev. W. G. (Westminster; Oxford University)		
Obituary	1908/I	*134*
Armitage, C. I. (Yorkshire)		
Obituary	1918	*222*
Armitage, Capt. E. L. (Hampshire)		
Obituary	1970	*1016*
Obituary correction	1971	*1034*
Armitage, Capt. F. R. (Oundle)		
Obituary	1918	*169*
Armitage, Sir S. C. (Rugby)		
Obituary	1963	*1032*

Armitage, T. (Yorkshire; England)
Obituary 1923/I *285*
Armitage, V. K. (Harrow; Cambridge University)
Obituary 1912/I *163*
Armitage, Lieut. W. H. (Wakefield Grammar School)
Obituary 1917 *162*
Armour, J. W. (Essex Scorer)
Obituary 1925/I *255*
Armstrong, G. D. (Glamorgan)
Photograph 1976 *391*
Armstrong, Major J. N. F. (Sydney Grammar School)
Obituary 1917 *162*
Armstrong, T. (Nottinghamshire)
Obituary 1939 *906*
Armstrong, U. (Detroit Club Cricket)
Obituary 1913/I *182*
Armstrong, W. W. (Victoria; Austrailia)
Obituary 1948 *779*
Portrait and Biography 1903 *1xxxvi*
'Warwick Armstrong's Australians'
R. Mason   Book Review 1972 *1094*
Army   1941 Team Portrait 1942 *28*
1944 Photograph of Flying Bomb 1945 *33*
Army v Civil Defence Services XI Team Portrait 1943 *25*
Team Portrait 1943 *25*
Arnall, P. J. (Thames Ditton C.C.)
Obituary 1919 *202*
Arnall-Thompson. H. T. (Rugby; Oxford University; Leicestershire)
Obituary 1917 *237*
Arneil, J. C. (Auckland, New Zealand)
Obituary 1939 *906*
Arnell, 2nd Lieut. R. B. (Berkhamsted School)
Obituary 1916 *141*
Arnold, 2nd Lieut. A. C. P. (Malvern; Cambridge University; Hampshire)
Obituary 1917 *163*
Arnold, C. (Cambridgeshire)
Throwing Record 1946 *94*
Arnold, Fl/Lt. C. V. (Dulwich)
Obituary 1918 *169*
Arnold, E. G. (Worcestershire; Devon; England)
Benefit Match 1912/II *167*
Obituary 1943 *370*
Arnold, G. G. (Surrey; Sussex; England)
Career Figures 1983 *711*
Cricketer of the Year 1972 *79*

Photographs	1972	*69*
	1976	*553*
Arnold, J. (Hampshire)		
Note on Age	1945	*47*
Arnold, W. (Tasmania)		
Obituary	1958	*955*
Arnott, T. (Glamorgan; Monmouthshire)		
Obituary	1976	*1092*
Arrowsmith, I. F. (Bohemian C.C.)		
Obituary	1956	*967*
Arrowsmith, J. W. (Publisher)		
Obituary	1914/I	*177*
Arrowsmith, R. L. (Writer)		
'Arthur Gilligan'	1977	*130*
'J. Gilman' Note on	1977	*141*
'The Great Years and Great Players		
of Kent'	1966	*138*
'Kent' Book Review	1972	*1095*
Memoir to F. Woolley	1979	*107*
Artificial Pitches Notes on	1951	*969*
	1967	*1066*
Art of Cricket Exhibition Note on	1983	*403*
Arundell, Rev.W. H. (Cheltenham; Devon; Cheshire)		
Obituary	1914/I	*198*
Ash, E. H. (Manager of W.W. Read's Team)		
Obituary	1912/I	*163*
Ash, Lt-Col. W. C. C. (Berkshire)		
Obituary	1917	*163*
Ashbolt, A. (Umpire)		
Obituary	1912/I	*163*
Ashbolt, F. (Wellington; North Island, New Zealand)		
Obituary	1941	*391*
Ashbridge, G. (Haverford College; Philadelphia)		
Obituary	1930/I	*268*
Ashburnham-Clement, Sir A. P. (President Sussex)		
Obituary	1936/I	*269*
Ashby, D. A. (Surrey; Canterbury, New Zealand)		
Obituary	1935/I	*259*
Ashby, W. G. (Treasurer Sussex)		
Obituary	1906	*lxxxvi*
Ashcroft, E. M. (Derbyshire)		
Obituary	1956	*967*
Ashcroft, Lieut. W. (Caius College, Cambridge)		
Obituary	1919	*165*

Ashdown, W. H. (Kent)
　Benefit match　　　　　　　　　　　1936/II　　　　*306*
　Obituary　　　　　　　　　　　　　1980　　　　　*1145*
Asher, Sir A. G. G. (Loretto; Oxford University; Oxfordshire)
　Obituary　　　　　　　　　　　　　1931/I　　　　　*247*
Ashes　　　Origin　　　　　　　　1945　　　　　　*59*
　　　　　　　　　　　　　　　ad passim
Ashfield Lieut L. A. (Marlborough)
　Obituary　　　　　　　　　　　　　1919　　　　　*165*
Ashley, C. H. (Journalist)
　Obituary　　　　　　　　　　　　　1915/I　　　　*211*
Ashley, Lt-Col. R. (Somerset)
　Obituary　　　　　　　　　　　　　1975　　　　　*1070*
Ashley-Cooper, F. S. (Writer)
　'F.S. Ashley-Cooper: The Herodutus
　　of Cricket' I. Rosenwater Book Review　1965　　　*1014*
　'England v Australia: A survey of 104 Matches'　1922/I　*227*
　'England v South Africa: A survey of 34
　　Matches'　　　　　　　　　　　　1924/I　　　　*219*
　Special Memoir of　　　　　　　　1933/I　　　　*237*
Ashton, C. T. (Atg. S.Ldr)(Winchester; Cambridge University; Essex)
　Obituary　　　　　　　　　　　　　1943　　　　　*361*
Ashton, G. (Winchester; Worcestershire)
　Obituary　　　　　　　　　　　　　1982　　　　　*1193*
Ashton, H. S. (President Essex, Father of G, C.T, H, Ashton)
　Obituary　　　　　　　　　　　　　1944　　　　　*310*
Ashton, Lt-Col. Sir H. (Winchester; Cambridge University, Essex)
　Obituary　　　　　　　　　　　　　1980　　　　　*1145*
　Portrait and Biography　　　　　　1922/I　　　　*276*
Ashton, Capt. P. (Essex)
　Obituary　　　　　　　　　　　　　1935/I　　　　*259*
Ashwell, A. T. (Rugby; Nottinghamshire)
　Obituary　　　　　　　　　　　　　1926/I　　　　*263*
Ashworth, P. (Harrow)
　Obituary　　　　　　　　　　　　　1938　　　　　*935*
Ashworth Lieut T. (St Edmunds C.C. of Toronto)
　Obituary　　　　　　　　　　　　　1919　　　　　*165*
Asian Cricket Conference　　　　　1949　　　*121,808*
Asif Iqbal (Hyderabad; Karachi; Pakistan International Airways; Kent; Pakistan)
　Career Figures　　　　　　　　　　1983　　　　　*711*
　Cricketer of the year　　　　　　　1968　　　　　*77*
　Photographs　　　　　　　　　　　1968　　　　　*69*
　　　　　　　　　　　　　　　　　1970　　　　　*436*
　　　　　　　　　　　　　　　　　1973　　　　　*431*
　　　　　　　　　　　　　　　　　1976　　　　　*441*

Askew, J. G. (Durham School; Durham)
Obituary   1943   *371*

Askham, 2nd Lieut. S. T. (Wellingborough Grammar; Northamptonshire)
Obituary   1917   *163*

Askham Capt W. (Wellingborough Grammar)
Obituary   1919   *165*

Aspden, Lieut F. F. (Chatham House Grammar)
Obituary   1919   *165*

Aspell. Pte. S. (Lynn Valley C.C. of Vancouver)
Obituary   1918   *169*

Aspinall, G. (Eton)
Obituary   1945   *327*

Aspinall, I. G. (Blackpool C.C.)
Obituary   1965   *963*

Asquith, F. (Yorkshire)
Obituary   1917   *238*

Asterley, R. N. (New York Club Cricketer)
Obituary   1911/I   *136*

Astill, W. E. (Leicestershire; England)
Benefit Matches   1923/II   *315*
  1932/II   *432*
Obituary   1949   *862*
Portrait and Biography   1933/I   *270*
'Study in Greatness' B. Easterbrook   1978   *156*

Astley, Lieut C. B. (Birkenhead School)
Obituary   1919   *165*

Aston, Capt F. M. (Shrewsbury)
Obituary   1916   *141*

Aston, R. L. (Tonbridge)
Obituary   1931/I   *248*

Aston, Lieut. R. M. (Rugby)
Obituary   1916   *142*

Astor, Col. J. J. (President M.C.C.)
Obituary   1972   *1046*

Atchison, Lt-Col. C. E. (United Services)
Obituary   1918   *169*

Atchison, 2nd Lieut. J. O. (Oratory School, Birmingham)
Obituary   1916   *142*

Atfield, A. J. (Gloustershire; London County)
Obituary   1950   *904*

Athawes, Rev. J. T. (Cambridge University)
Obituary   1916   *142*

Atherton, Corp. J. W. (Lancashire)
Obituary   1919   *165*

Atherton, T.(Vice President Lancashire)
Obituary   1976   *1104*

18

Athey, C. W. J. (Yorkshire; England)

Photograph	1980	*261*
Schools Note	1977	*809*
Whitbread Scholarship	1981	*645*

Athlumney, 2nd Lord (Harrow)

Obituary	1930/I	*245*

Atkinson, B. G. W. (Middlesex; Northamptonshire; Scotland)

Obituary	1967	*96*

Atkinson, C. R. M. (Somerset)

Photograph	1967	*545*
Retirement	1968	*550*

Atkinson, Rev. F. (Oxford University)

Obituary	1939	*906*

Atkinson, G. C. (Somerset; Lancashire)

Photographs	1959	*511*
	1961	*534*
	1962	*560*
	1966	*534*

Atkinson, Lieut. and Adjt. G. H. (Marlborough)

Obituary	1918	*169*

Atkinson, G. R. (Yorkshire)

Obituary	1907	*civ*

Atkinson, J. A. (Tasmania)

Obituary	1957	*942*

Atkinson, 2nd Lieut. M. L. (Fettes)

Obituary	1918	*169*

Atkinson, N. S. M. (Middlesex)

Obituary	1967	*962*

Atkinson-Clark, J. C. (Middlesex)

Obituary	1970	*1016*

Attenborough, T. (Derbyshire)

Obituary	1908/I	*134*

Attendances Notes on

	1948	*85*
	1958	*1006*
	1959	*977*
	1960	*989*
	1961	*121,986*
	1962	*1029*
	1964	*1006*
	1967	*1008*
	1968	*1041*
	1972	*913*

Atter, F. W. (Leicester C.C.)

Obituary	1919	*202*

Atterbury, Lieut. L. J. R. (Winnipeg C.C.)
Obituary 1917 163
Attewell, T. (Nottinghamshire)
Obituary 1938 935
Attewell, W. (Nottinghamshire; England)
Benefit Matches 1899 137
1904 9
Obituary 1928/I 275
Portrait and Biography 1892 xxxviii
Views on 'The Follow On' 1894 liii
Views on 'The Reforms of 1889' 1890 xxxviii
Views on 'Some Questions of the Day' 1890 xliv
Attey, R. (Durham)
Obituary 1917 238
Attfield, Dr. G. C. (Somerset; Surrey)
Obituary 1926/I 263
Attitude Wrong Note on 1954 79
Attractive Cricket, More Note on 1971 88
Aubrey-Fletcher, Major Sir H. L. Bt (Buckinghamshire)
Obituary 1970 1016
Auchinleck, Capt. D. G. H. (Winchester)
Obituary 1915/I 211
Auckland Scoreboard
Photograph 1956 49
Auden, B. (Uppingham)
Obituary 1950 904
Augustins, The of Malaya 1948 756
Austen, Dr. E. T. (Victoria)
Obituary 1984 1195
Austen-Leigh, C. E. (Harrow; Berkshire)
Obituary 1925/I 255
Austen-Leigh, E. C. (Eton)
Obituary 1917 238
Austin, Capt. G. (Charity Cricket Week Organiser)
Obituary 1904 lxxxvi
Austin, G. (Warwickshire Scorer)
Obituary 1964 945
Austin, H. J. (Hertfordshire; Bedfordshire; Buckinghamshire)
Obituary 1930/I 245
Austin, H. M. (Cambridge University; Victoria)
Obituary 1983 1240
Austin, H. P. (American Club Cricketer)
Obituary 1943 386
Austin-Leigh, Rev. A. H. (Cheltenham; Gentlemen of England)
Obituary 1918 222

Australia

Aboriginals in England 1868		1869	*108*
Cricket Walkabout D. J. Mulvaney		1969	*1023*
Book Review		1979	*965*
In Bermuda	1978	1979	*965*
In Canada and USA	1893	1894	*225*
	1912	1913/II	*573*
	1913	1914/II	*496*
	1932	1933/II	*689*
In England	1878	1879	*233*
	1880	1881	*215*
	1882	1883	*231*
	1884	1885	*249*
	1886	1887	*1*
	1888	1889	*130*
	1890	1891	*141*
	1893	1894	*166*
	1896	1897	*210*
	1899	1900	*256*
	1902	1903	*242*
Victor Trumper and the 1902 Australians			
L. H. Brown Book Review		1982	*1271*
	1905	1906	*1*
	1909	1910/II	*1*
	1912	1913/II	*24*
	1921	1922/II	*1*
Warwick Armstrong's Australians			
R. Mason Book Review		1972	*1094*
	1926	1927/II	*1*
	1930	1931/II	*1*
	1934	1935/II	*1*
	1938	1939	*195*
Team Portrait	1938	1939	*33*
	1948	1949	*204*
Team Portrait	1948	1949	*67*
Australians at Balmoral	1948	1949	*65*
Photograph			
'Gone to the Test Match'			
J. Arlott Book Review		1950	*981*
'Days without Sunset'			
D.Batchelor Book Review		1950	*977*
	1953	1954	*214*
Team Portrait	1953	1954	*55*
Action Photograph	1953	1954	*57*
'The Ashes Crown the Year'			
J.H. Fingleton Book Review		1954	*983*

'Behind the Tests' N. Cutler			
Book Review		1954	982
'The Book of the Tests'			
D. Batchelor Book Review		1954	983
'Cricket Triumph' B. Harris			
Book Review		1954	982
'The England Victory'			
C. White Book Review		1954	984
'Eyes on the Ashes'			
S. Barnes Book Review		1954	982
'The Fight for the Ashes'	1953		
R. Lester Book Review		1954	984
'Fight for the Ashes'			
P. West Book Review		1954	98.
'Gods or Flannelled Fools'			
K.R. Miller and R.S. Whittington Book Review		1955	99
'Over to Rex Alston'			
R. Alston Book Review		1954	982
'Test Match Diary'	1953		
J. Arlott Book Review		1954	987
'The Test Matches of 1953'			
E.W. Swanton Book Review		1954	948
	1956	1957	222
Team Portrait	1956	1957	47
Action Photograph	1956	1957	49-51
Australia Rebuilds Note		1957	69
'The Ashes'	1956		
J. Woodcock Book Review		1957	998
'The Ashes Retained'			
C. White/R. Webber Book Review		1957	999
'Australian Challenge'			
A.E.R. Gilligan Book Review		1957	997
'Behind the Australian Tests'	1956		
N. Cutler Book Review		1957	997
'Cricketers from Australia'			
G. Ross Book Review		1957	999
'Cape Summer and the Australians'			
A. Ross Book Review		1958	101
'Defending the Ashes'			
B. Harris Book Review		1957	997
'The Fight for the Ashes 1956'			
P. West Book Review		1957	998
'Operation Ashes' P. Landsberg, A. Morris			
Book Review		1957	997
'The Picture Post Book of the Tests'			
D. Batchelor Book Review		1957	997

22

'Test Commentary' R. Alston			
Book Review		1957	*995*
'Test Matches of 1956'			
E.W. Swanton. Book Review		1957	*997*
	1961	1962	*270*
Team Portrait	1961	1962	*86*
with Queen Photograph	1961	1962	*85*
Note on	1961	1961	*122*
'An Enjoyable Visit to England'			
J.H. Fingleton		1962	*126*
'A.B.C. Cricket Book – Australian Tour of UK			
in 1961'		1962	*1036*
Book Review			
'A Tale of Two Tests'			
R. Benaud Book Review		1963	*1108*
'Aussies and Ashes'			
W. E. Bowes Book Review		1962	*1138*
'The Australian Challenge'			
J. Arlott Book Review		1962	*1050*
'The Australians in England'			
C. Fortune Book Review		1962	*1038*
'The Australian Tour of 1961'			
J. Laker Book Review		1962	*1038*
'The Challenging Tests' R. Lindwall			
Book Review		1962	*1039*
'Cricketers from Australia' G. Ross			
Book Review		1962	*1036*
'The Fight for the Ashes in 1961'			
R. Lester Book Review		1962	*1039*
'The Fight for the Ashes in 1961'			
R. A. Roberts Book Review		1962	*1040*
'Meet the Stars' P. Morris and M. Cumming			
Book Review		1962	*1036*
'Rothmans Test Cricket Almanack' S. Smith			
Book Review		1962	*1036*
	1964	1965	*273*
Team Portrait	1964	1965	*70*
Grounds and Gate Receipts Note on		1965	*680*
'The 1964 Australians' G. Ross			
Book Review		1965	*1024*
'The Australians in England 1964'			
J. Clarke Book Review		1965	*1018*
'Denis Comptons Test Diary 1965'			
D. Compton Book Review		1965	*1020*
'Rothmans Test Cricket Almanack'			
England v Australia 1964 Book Review		1965	*1024*

Simpson's Australians: the English Tour 1964'			
E.M Wellings. Book Review		1965	*1020*
'The Test Matches of 1964' D. Batchelor			
Book Review		1965	*1018*
	1968	1969	*282*
Team Portrait	1968	1969	*55*
Action Photographs	1968	1969	*52,53*
'The A.B.C. Cricket Book – The Australian			
Tour of England 1968' A. McGilvray			
Book Review		1969	*1040*
'The Australians in England 1968'			
R.B. Simpson Book Review		1969	*1033*
'Rothmans/M.C.C. Cricket Almanack			
England v Australia 1968'			
Book Review		1969	*1039*
	1972	1973	*297*
Team Portrait	1972	1973	*62*
'Welcome Australia' E.R. Dexter		1972	*86*
Can England Keep the Ashes? Note on		1972	*91*
'The A.B.C. Cricket Book; Australian			
'Tour of England 1972'. A. McGilvray			
Book Review		1973	*1060*
'The Ashes' J. Arlott Book Review		1973	*1066*
World Cup Tournament	1975	1976	*300*
	1975	1976	*320*
'World Cup Runners–Up'			
Team Portrait	1975	1976	*37*
'Frindall's Scorebook			
England v Australia 1975'			
W. Frindall Book Review		1976	*1146*
	1977	1978	*306*
Team portrait	1977	1978	*83*
Action Photographs	1977	1978	*84,85*
'A.B.C. Cricket Book — The Australian Tour			
of England 1977' A.McGilvray Book Review		1978	*1127*
'The Ashes 77' G. Chappell, D. Frith			
Book Review		1978	*1124*
'Frindall's Scorebook – The Centenary Test and			
England v Australia 1977' W. Frindall			
Book Review		1978	*1124*
'The Jubilee Tests and the Packer Revolution'			
C. Martin–Jenkins. Book Review		1978	*1124*
'The Return of the Ashes' J.M. Brearley			
Book Review		1979	*1130*
World Cup Tournament 1979		1980	*297*
	1980	1981	*347*

Team Portrait	1980	1981	*71*
Centenary Test Photograph	1980	1981	*110*
	1981	1982	*306*
Team Portrait	1981	1982	*308*
Action Photograph	1981	1982	*66*
'A Summer to Remember' P. Eagar, A. Ross			
Book Review		1982	*1266*
'Australian Tour of United Kingdom'			
Ed. A. McGilvray. Book Review		1982	*1272*
'Botham Rekindles the Ashes' M. Melford			
Book Review		1982	*126*
'The Incredible Tests' I. Botham			
Book Review		1982	*1266*
'Phoenix from the Ashes' J.M. Brearley			
Book Review		1983	*1279*
World Cup Tournament	1983	1984	*293*
In Holland	1964	1965	*318*
In India	1935–36	1957/II	*688*
and Pakistan	1956	1957	*839*
	1959–60	1961	*832*
'Cricket Ups and Downs' Q. Butt			
Book Review		1961	*994*
	1964–65	1965	*843*
and Sri Lanka	1969–70	1971	*865*
and Pakistan	1979–80	1981	*967*
In New Zealand	1905	1906	*544*
	1910	1911/II	*521*
	1914	1915/II	*513*
	1921	1922/II	*637*
	1928	1929/II	*683*
First Test Match	1946	1947	*628*
First Test Recognised Note on		1948	*829*
	1950	1951	*828*
	1957	1958	*846*
	1960	1961	*847*
	1967	1968	*875*
	1969–70	1971	*904*
	1973–74	1975	*944*
	1976–77	1978	*946*
	1981–82	1983	*1003*
In Pakistan and India	1956–57	1957	*839*
	1959–60	1961	*832*
'Cricket Ups and Downs' Q. Butt			
Book Review		1961	*994*

'Cricket Cat and Mouse' Q. Butt
Book Review 1963 1109
 1964–65 1965 843
and India 1979–80 1981 986
 1982–83 1984 904
In South Africa 1902–03 1903 506
 1921–22 1922/II 588
 1935–36 1937/II 647
 1949–50 1951 773
'Cricket Caravan' K. Miller; R.S. Whitington
Book Review 1952 1012
 1957–58 1959 775
 1966–67 1968 828
'The Book of the Tests' E. Litchfield
Book Review 1968 1054
 1969–70 1971 884
'Cricket Grand Slam' E. Litchfield
Book Review 1971 1080
'The Book of the Tests' E. Litchfield
Book Review 1971 1081
In Sri Lanka (Ceylon) 1953 1954 860
 1964 1965 884,902
and India 1969–70 1971 865
 1981 1982 1137
 1982–83 1984 972
In USA 1896 1897 231
 and Canada 1893 1894 225
 1912 1913/II 573
 1913 1914/II 490
 1932 1933/II 689
In West Indies 1954–55 1956 861
'The Kangaroo Conquers' P. Landsberg
Book Review 1956 1028
 1964–65 1966 817
'The New Champions – Australia in the West Indies'
R. Benaud Book Review 1966 1010
'Rothmans Test Cricket Almanack:
West Indies v Australia 1965'
Book Review 1966 1024
 1972–73 1974 943
 1977–78 1979 944
Australian Air Force in England
 1944 1945 87-89,98
Team Portrait 1944 1945 34
Organization 1944 1945 107
Imperial Forces in England 1919 1920/II 348

'A.I.F. Cricket Team' R. Cordwell

Book Review		1982	*1263*
	1945	1946	*155*
Team portrait	1945	1946	*37*
In India	1945	1946	*356*
In South Africa	1919	1920/II	*477*
Old Collegians World Tour	1959	1960	*898*
	1972	1973	*898*
Schoolboys in India 1966–67		1968	*899*
Sri Lanka	1972	1973	*957*
Services in Australia	1946	1947	*626*
Women in England	1951	1952	*775*
	1963	1964	*890*
	1976	1977	*990*
Action Photograph	1976	1977	*89*
Young Cricketers in England	1977	1978	*839*
	1983	1984	*822*
In Zimbabwe	1983	1984	*1144*

Chronological List of Articles and Notes

'Australian Tours and their Management' (Sir F.C. Toone)	1930/I	*270*
'Australian Cricket: its Control and Organisation' (H.V. Evatt)	1935/I	*255*
'Australians in English Club Cricket' (Flt/Lt B. Andrew)	1944	*56*
'Australian Survey: Bradman – Past, Present, Future' (A.G. Moyes)	1945	*50*
'Australian Affection for Lord's'	1945	*58*
'Australia and England: Sidelights on the Tests' (V.G.J. Jenkins)	1948	*90*
Australia Retains the Ashes Note on	1951	*114*
Australian Reserves Note on	1953	*76*
'Australia Throws down the Gauntlet' (N. Cardus)	1953	*84*
Australian Recovery Note on	1956	*70*
'Two Eras of Australian Pace' (I.R. Peebles)	1956	*109*
Australia Regain the Ashes Note on	1959	*72*
'Cricket Alive Again' (J.H. Fingleton)	1961	*127*
'An Enjoyable Visit to England 1961' (J.H. Fingleton)	1962	*126*
'My Favourite Summer (1902)' (A.A. Thomson)	1967	*118*
'Notable Dates in Australian Cricket History' (R. Bowen)	1968	*144*
'Addenda and Corigenda (R. Bowen)'	1969	*1021*
'Watery Reflections From Australia' (J.H. Fingleton)	1969	*80*

'Australians in County Cricket' Note on	1969	*91*
'Welcome Australia' (E.R. Dexter)	1972	*91*
'Skills and Controversy' (R. Benaud)	1973	*97*
'Cricket Fever Hits Australia' (R.Benaud)	1974	*39*
'The Glorious Uncertainty' (R. Ryder)	1974	*117*
'The Greatest Centenary of Them All' (G. Ross)	1976	*96*
'From Spofforth to Lillee' (R. Benaud)	1977	*116*
'The Centenary Test – 1977' (R. Hayter)	1978	*130*
'Fifty Years on – 1930–1980 Tests v England' (G.O. Allen)	1981	*107*
'Australia – A New Era' (R.J. Parish)	1984	*69*
Auty, J. S. (Mill Hill School; Yorkshire)		
Obituary	1923/I	*286*
Auty, K. A. (Cricket Book Collector)		
Obituary	1960	*949*
Avebury, Lord (West Kent C.C.)		
Obituary	1914/I	*177*
Aveling, Dr. C. T. (Surrey)		
Obituary	1903	*lxxvii*
Aveling, Dr. E. B. (Author; Journalist)		
Obituary	1899	*xlviii*
Averages Lessons From	1983	*84*
Note on	1963	*144*
Avery, A. V. (Essex)		
Benefit Match	1951	*310*
Avory, H. K. (Surrey)		
Obituary	1919	*202*
Awdry, C. (Worcestershire; Wiltshire)		
Obituary	1913/I	*182*
Awdry, C. E. (Wiltshire)		
Obituary	1967	*975*
Awdry, C. S. (Winchester; Wiltshire)		
Obituary	1920/I	*151*
Awdry, H. (Winchester)		
Obituary	1911/I	*161*
Awdry, Col. R. W. (Wiltshire; Oxford University)		
Obituary	1950	*904*
Aworth, C. J. (Tiffin School Kingston; Cambridge University; Surrey)		
Photograph	1976	*553*
Babb, Comdr. B. O. (Secretary, Surrey)		
Obituary	1972	*1046*
Bache, Lieut. H. G. (King Edwards Birmingham; Cambridge University; Worcestershire)		
Obituary	1917	*164*
Backhouse, E. N. (Yorkshire)		
Obituary	1938	*948*

Bacon, F. H. (St Augustine's College, Canterbury; Warwickshire)
Obituary 1916 *142*
Bacon, F. W. (Felsted)
Obituary 1920/I *151*
Bad Behaviour Note on 1983 *76*
Photographs 1983 *Plate*
Badcock, C. L. (Tasmania; South Australia; Australia)
Obituary 1984 *1195*
Badcock, F. T. (Wellington College; Northamptonshire; Otago; Wellington; New Zealand)
Obituary 1984 *1195*
Schools Note 1916 *83*
Badenoch, Pte. G. H. (Indian Head C.C. of Saskatchewan)
Obituary 1918 *211*
Bader, Group Captain Sir D. (St. Edmund's, Oxford; Royal Air Force)
Obituary 1983 *1240*
Badham, P. H. C. (Winchester; Oxford University; Leicestershire; Buckinghamshire; Dorset)
Obituary 1984 *1195*
Badger, H. D. (Shrewsbury; Yorkshire)
Obituary 1976 *1092*
Bad Light Problem Note On 1951 *120*
Baerlin P/O. A. M. (Eton)
Obituary 1942 *347*
Baggallay, E. (Marlborough)
Obituary 1932/I *239*
Baggallay, Lt-Col. R. R. C. (Derbyshire)
Obituary 1976 *1092*
Bagge, Pte. S. C. J. (Westmount C.C. of Montreal)
Obituary 1918 *211*
Bagge, T. E. (Eton; Cambridge University; Norfolk)
Obituary 1909/I *131*
Bagguley, Lieut J. L. (Newcastle High School)
Obituary 1918 *169*
Bagnall, 2nd Lieut. G. B. (Norfolk Club Cricket)
Obituary 1918 *169*
Bagnall, H. F. (Cambridge University; Northamptonshire)
Obituary 1975 *1070*
Bagnall, T. (American Club Cricket)
Obituary 1928/I *277*
Bagot, 2nd Lieut. A. (Marlborough)
Obituary 1944 *309*
Bagshaw, H. (Derbyshire)
Obituary 1928/I *277*

Baig, A. A. (Hyderabad; Oxford University; Somerset; India)

Photograph	1960	92
Qualification	1962	1027
Visitor's Award	1960	250

Bailes, Gunner R. (Chickenley C.C.)

Obituary	1919	165

Bailey, Sir A. (Transvaal)

Obituary	1943	368

Bailey, G. H. (Elizabeth College, Guernsey; Tasmania)

Obituary	1927/I	271

Bailey, G. K. B. (Tasmania)

Obituary	1965	963

Bailey, J. A. (Christ's Hospital; Oxford University; Essex; Secretary M.C.C.)

Photograph	1955	310

Bailey, L. N. (Cricket Journalist)

Obituary	1971	1023

Bailey, N. C. (Westminster; Streatham C.C.)

Obituary	1924/I	253

Bailey, T. E. (Dulwich; Cambridge University; Essex; England)

Action Photograph	1954	56
Cricketer of the Year	1950	77
Note on	1946	199,291
	1962	112
Photographs	1950	72
	1952	310
	1953	316
	1957	325
	1964	67
	1969	129
Retirement	1968	380
Schools Notes	1940	643
	1942	240,242
		270
	1943	266,270
		271,294

'T. E. Bailey - Resolute and Impenitent' (With Career Figures).

J. Woodcock	1969	129
'Ray Illingworth; C.B.E'	1973	108
'The Helmet'	1981	123
'Sir Gary' Book Review	1977	1100

Bailie, Major-Gen.T. M. (Sandhurst)

Obituary	1919	202

Baily, E. P. (Harrow; Cambridge University; Middlesex; Somerset)

Obituary	1942	355

Baily, R. E. H. (Harrow; Cambridge University; Surrey)

Obituary	1974	1070

Bain, Capt. D. M. (Edinburgh Academy)
   Obituary   1916   *143*

Bainbridge, Rev. G. P. (Scarborough C.C.)
   Obituary   1905   *lxxxv*

Bainbridge, H. W. (Eton; Cambridge University; Surrey; Warwickshire)
   Obituary   1941   *391*
   Views on the Reforms of 1889   1890   *xxxix*
   Views on Some Questions of the Day   1890   *xli*
   Views on Throwing   1895   *lviii*

Bainbridge, P. (Gloucestershire)
   Photograph   1982   *415*

Bainbridge, Brig-Gen. P. A. (Wellington)
   Obituary   1935/I   *260*

Baines, Canon A. G. P. (Buckinghamshire; Berkshire)
   Obituary   1950   *904*

Baines, Dr. A. M. (Toronto C.C.)
   Obituary   1923/I   *286*

Baines, H. (Montgomeryshire; Cardiganshire; Merionethshire; Shropshire; Worcestershire)
   Obituary   1925/I   *256*

Baines, J. W. (Marlborough)
   Obituary   1925/I   *256*

Baines, M. T. (Harrow)
   Obituary   1926/I   *263*

Baird, Brig-Gen. A. W. F. (Eton)
   Obituary   1932/I   *239*

Baird, R. L. (Young America C.C.)
   Obituary   1922/I   *245*

Bairstow, D. L. (Yorkshire; England)
   Photographs   1971   *580*
                            1975   *614*
   Schools Note   1971   *786*

Baiss, R. S. H. (Kent)
   Obituary   1956   *967*

Bakelman, L. E. (Ceylon)
   Obituary   1966   961

Baker, A. (Surrey)
   Obituary   1949   *862*

Baker, Capt. C. D. (Sherborne)
   Obituary   1918   *169*

Baker, C. M. (Uppingham)
   Obituary   1905   *lxxxv*

Baker, C. S. (Warwickshire; Cornwall)
   Obituary   1977   *1037*

Baker, C. V. (Harrow; Middlesex)
   Obituary   1949   *872*

Baker, E. C. (Brighton College)
75 wkts Schools Averages   1912/II   *453*

Baker, G. C. (Writer)
Obituary   1978   *1068*

Baker, G. R. (Lancashire; Yorkshire)
Benefit Match   1899   *112*
Obituary   1939   *906*

Baker, Sir H. (Tonbridge)
Obituary   1947   *687*

Baker, J. C. (Otago)
Obituary   1940   *837*

Baker, P. C. (Kent)
Obituary   1940   *837*

Baker, R. (Scarborough C.C.)
Obituary   1897   *xi*

Baker, R. H. (Writer)
'Ashes Test Album 1954-55'
Book Review   1956   *1028*

Baker, R. L. (Sydney University)
Obituary   1954   *921*

Baker, R. P. (Surrey)
Photograph   1977   *554*

Baker, Lieut. S. (Saskatoon C.C.)
Obituary   1918   *169*

Baker, W. (Treasurer Surrey)
Note on   1946   *52*

Baker, W. A. (Wellington, New Zealand)
Obituary   1967   *962*

Baker, W. B. (Hertfordshire)
Obituary   1935/I   *276*

Bakewell, A. H. (Northamptonshire; England)
Obituary   1984   *1195*
Portrait and Biography   1934/I   *281*

Bakewell, Enid (Lady Cricketer)
Photograph   1970   *120*
'Enid Bakewell – Champion Woman Cricketer'
Netta Rheinberg'   1970   *119*

Balders, Capt. A. W. (Army)
Obituary   1916   *143*

Balderstone, J. C. (Yorkshire; Leicestershire; England)
Photograph   1974   *462*
      1980   *474*

Baldock, W. F. (Winchester; Somerset)
Obituary   1946   *434*

Baldwin, C. (Surrey; Suffolk)
Obituary   1948   *786*

Baldwin, H. (Hampshire)
  Benefit Match   1899   *195*
  Obituary   1936/I   *269*

Baldwin, H. G. (Surrey; Umpire)
  Obituary   1970   *1016*
  Photograph   1954   *56*

Baldwin, J. L. (IZingari)
  Obituary   1897   *xlii*

Baldwin, T. (Suffolk)
  Obituary   1908/I   *134*

Bale, E. (Surrey; Worcestershire)
  Obituary   1953   *937*

Balfour, Lieut. I. B. (Winchester; Oxford University)
  Obituary   1916   *143*

Balfour, R. D. (Westminster; Cambridge University)
  Obituary   1916   *143*

Balfour-Melville, E. S. (Grange C.C.)
  Obituary   1913/I   *183*

Balfour-Melville, Lieut. J. E. (Malvern; Grange C.C.; Scotland)
  Obituary   1916   *144*

Balfour-Melville, L. M. (Edinburgh Academy; Scotland)
  Obituary   1938   *935*
Ball Notes on   1955   *977*
                           1964   *94*
                           1966   *1009*
                           1967   *961*
                           1968   *515*
                           1970   *1046*
                           1971   *1066*
                           1973   *95*
                           1974   *69*
                           1980   *88*
                           1981   *474*
                           1982   *400*

Ball, E. W. (Gloucestershire Committee)
  Obituary   1918   *222*

Ball, W. (Midlands Clubs Professional)
  Obituary   1918   *222*

Ballance, Major T. G. L. (Uppingham; Oxford University; Norfolk)
  Obituary   1944   *304*

Ballantine, Capt. E. W. (Writer)
  Obituary   1940   *837*

Balmoral Australians at
  Photograph   1949   *65*

Baloo, P. (Indian Cricketer)
  Obituary   1956   *967*

Balshaw, 2nd Lieut. W. (Manchester Club Cricket)
  Obituary   1917   *222*

Balster, W. (Chicago C.C.)
  Obituary   1916   *144*

Bambridge, Capt. W. H. (Marlborough)
  Obituary   1918   *170*

Bamford, F. K. (Peninsula C.C. of Detroit)
  Obituary   1912/I   *183*

Bamford, J. (Cricket Supporter)
  Obituary   1919   *202*

Banbury, Capt.A. (Harrow)
  Obituary   1930/I   *245*

Bancroft, J. (Glamorgan)
  Obituary   1943   *371*

Bancroft, W. J. (Glamorgan)
  Obituary   1960   *949*

Banerjee, S. N. (Bengal; Bihar; Nawangar; India)
  Obituary   1981   *1138*
  Photograph   1947   *38*

Banes-Walker, 2nd Lieut. C. (Somerset)
  Obituary   1916   *144*

Bankier, A. A. (Winchester; Wiltshire)
  Obituary   1966   *961*

Bankier, Lieut. I. P. (Winchester)
  Obituary   1945   *319*

Banks, E. (Kent)
  Obituary   1911/I   *136*

Banks, Capt. N. B. (Cheltenham; Somerset)
  Obituary   1916   *144*

Banks, W. J. (Kent)
  Obituary   1902   *lviii*

Bannerman, A. C. (New South Wales; Australia)
  Obituary   1925/I   *256*

Bannerman, C. (New South Wales; Australia)
  Obituary   1931/I   *248*

Bannister, A. (Writer)
  'Cricket Cauldron' Book Review   1955   *991*
  'Bert Lock - King of Groundsmen'   1976   *141*
  'My Life Reporting Cricket'   1980   *113*

Bannister, H. M. (Leicestershire)
  Obituary   1961   *953*

Bannister, J. D. (Warwickshire)
  Benefit Match   1965   *602*
  Photographs   1956   *590*
                  1961   *591*
  Retirement   1970   *80*

34

Treasurer of Cricketers' Association | 1968 | *280*

Bapasola, N. C. (Parsis; All India)
Obituary | 1924/I | *253*

Bapty, J. (Journalist)
Obituary | 1977 | *1050*
'Yorkshire the Top County' | 1969 | *134*

Barbados   in England 1969 | 1970 | *776*

Barber, Dr. H. (Yorkshire)
Obituary | 1970 | *1016*

Barber, R. (Australian Writer)
Obituary | 1981 | *1138*

Barber, R. (Buckinghamshire)
Obituary | 1925/I | *257*

Barber, R. J. de C. (Nottinghamshire)
Obituary | 1976 | *1093*

Barber, R. W. (Ruthin; Lancashire; Warwickshire; England)
Cricketer of the Year | 1967 | *73*
Photographs | 1964 | *585*
| 1967 | *72*
Schools Notes | 1953 | *716*
| 1954 | *724*
| 1955 | *695*
1012 runs/108 wkts   Schools Averages | 1954 | *766*

Barber, W. (Yorkshire)
Obituary | 1969 | *978*

Barber, Col. W. D. (Nottinghamshire)
Obituary | 1972 | *1046*

Barber, W. H. (Warwickshire)
Obituary | 1982 | *1194*

Barbery, A. E. (Warwickshire)
Obituary | 1974 | *1070*

Barbour, Dr. E. P. (New South Wales)
Obituary | 1935/I | *260*

Barbour, C. Q. M. S, F. G. R. (Toowoomba Grammar School)
Obituary | 1918 | *170*

Barchard, E. (Winchester; Cambridge University)
Obituary | 1895 | *xlii*

Barclay, A. C. (Philadelphia)
Obituary | 1920/I | *160*

Barclay, C. (Harrow; Cambridge University)
Obituary | 1911/I | *137*

Barclay, J. R. T. (Eton; Sussex; Orange Free State)
Photographs | 1977 | *571*
| 1979 | *547*

Bardsley, R. V. (Oxford University; Lancashire)
Obituary | 1953 | *937*

35

Bardsley, W. (New South Wales; Australia)
Obituary	1955	92
Portrait and Biography	1910/I	157
Testimonial Match	1938	834

Bardswell, G. R. (Uppingham; Oxford University; Lancashire)
Obituary	1907	cv

Baring, F. A. (Victoria)
Obituary	1963	1038

Barker, A. H. C. (Winchester)
Obituary	1947	687

Barker, C. M. (Westminster)
Obituary	1911/I	137

Barker, Lieut. C. M. (Transvaal)
Obituary	1943	362

Barker, E. C. (Thames Ditton C.C.)
Obituary	1923/I	286

Barker, G. E. (Essex)
Photographs	1956	323
	1959	323
	1961	353
	1965	366
Testimonial	1971	127

Barker, 2nd Lieut. G. F (Brentwood C.C.)
Obituary	1918	170

Barker, J. S. (Writer; Journalist)
'Summer Spectacular' Book Review	1964	1000
:In the Main – West Indies v M.C.C. 1968.		
Book Review	1969	1032
With G. Sobers. 'Cricket in the Sun'.		
Book Review	1968	1040

Barker, K. E. M. (Uppingham; London County; Surrey)
Obituary	1939	906
Views on Second Class Counties and LBW Rule	1903	lxvii

Barker, M. M. (Radley)
Obituary	1955	926

Barker, R (Writer)
'The Cricketing Family Edrich' - Book Review	1977	1096

Barker, T. (Nottinghamshire)
Obituary	1878	202

Barker, W. W. (Leeds C.C.; Leamington C.C.)
Obituary	1913/I	202

Barling, T. H. (Surrey)
Benefit Matches:	1947	429
	1948	479

Barlow, A. (Lancashire)
Obituary	1984	119

Barlow, A. N. (Australian Umpire)
Obituary — 1962 — *984*
Barlow, C. S. (Clifton; Somerset)
Obituary — 1943 — *371*
Barlow, E. A. (Shrewsbury; Oxford University; Lancashire)
Obituary — 1981 — *1138*
Barlow, E. J. (Transvaal; Eastern Province; Western Province; Derbyshire; South Africa)
Action Photograph — 1971 — *69*
Photographs — 1966 — *58*
— 1977 — *361*
Barlow G. D. (Middlesex; England)
Photograph — 1977 — *490*
Schools Note — 1969 — *753*
Barlow, H. R. B. (Orange Free State)
Obituary — 1943 — *371*
Barlow, 2nd Lieut. L. H. (Merion C.C., Philadelphia)
Obituary — 1917 — *164*
Barlow, M. Y. (Harrow)
Obituary — 1937/I — *265*
Barlow, R. G. (Lancashire; England)
Benefit Match — 1887 — *162*
Career Figures — 1920/I — *162*
Obituary — 1920/I — *160*
Views on High Scoring and LBW Rule — 1899 — *lxxvi*
View on Reforms of 1889 — 1890 — *xxxix*
Views on Some Questions of the Day — 1890 — *xl*
Barmby, F. J. (Charterhouse)
Obituary — 1937/I — *265*
Barmby, Major J. (Oxfordshire)
Obituary — 1945 — *319*
Barnard, H. M. (Hampshire)
Testimonial — 1968 — *429*
Barnard, T. H. (Eton)
Obituary — 1917 — *238*
Barnard, Rev. W. (Winchester)
Obituary — 1910/I — *150*
Barnardo, Lieut. F. T. (Eton; Cambridge University)
Obituary — 1943 — *362*
Barnato, Capt. W. (Surrey)
Obituary — 1949 — *862*
Barnby, Col. A. C. (Royal Navy)
Obituary — 1939 — *920*
Barnes, A. (Australian Board of Control)
Tribute to Sir Frank Worrell — 1968 — *122*

Barnes, J. R. (Marlborough; Lancashire)

Obituary	1946	*436*

Barnes, Dr. S (President, Warwickshire)

Obituary	1956	*967*

Barnes, S. F. (Warwickshire; Staffordshire; Lancashire; England)

Obituary 'Sydney Francis Barnes' N. Cardus	1968	*110*
'S. F. Barnes - Master Bowler'		
L Duckworth.Book Review	1968	*1051*
'Giant of the Wisden Century' N. Cardus	1963	*106*
Barnes Ashes Note on	1969	*190*
Note on	1966	*82*
Photographs	1963	*107*
	1968	*111*
Portrait and Biography	1910/I	*158*
Records by	1941	*62*
Statistics	1968	*115*

Barnes, S. G. (New South Wales; Australia)

Obituary	1974	*1070*
Action Photograph	1949	*69*
'Eyes on the Ashes' Book Review	1954	*982*
'It isn't Cricket' Book Review	1954	*978*
'The Ashes Ablaze' Book Review	1956	*1025*

Barnes, T. (Father of W. Barnes)

Obituary	1898	*xlvi*

Barnes, W. (Nottinghamshire; England)

Benefit Match	1895	*125*
Obituary	1900	*1*
Portrait and Biography	1890	*xxxii*

Barnett, B. A. (Buckinghamshire; Victoria, Australia)

Obituary	1980	*1146*

Barnett, C. J. (Gloucestershire; England)

Benefit Match	1948	*316*
Portrait and Biography	1937/I	*297*
Tribute to W. Hammond	1966	*117*

Barnett, C. S. (Gloucestershire)

Obituary	1963	*1032*

Barnett, E. P. (Gloucestershire)

Obituary	1923/I	*286*

Barnett, K. J. (Derbyshire)

Whitbread Scholarship	1981	*645*

Barney, A. V. (Umpire)

Obituary	1905	*lxxxv*

Barnsby, W. H. (Birmingham League Cricket)

Obituary	1917	*239*

Baroda, The Gaekwar of (Oxford University; All India)

Obituary	1920/I	*163*

Barras, Fl/Off. A. E. (R.A.A.F)
Note on	1944	*58*

Barratt, E. (Surrey)
Benefit Match	1888	*28*
Obituary	1892	*xxxi*

Barratt, F. (Nottinghamshire, England)
Benefit match	1929/II	*162*
Obituary	1948	*781*

Barratt, J. (Lincolnshire)
Obituary	1946	*436*

Barrell, J. M. (Aldenham; Northern C.C.)
Obituary	1943	*363*

Barrett, Major A. G. (President Somerset)
Obituary	1955	*926*

Barrett, Capt. E. I. M. (Army; Hampshire)
Obituary	1951	*917*

Barrett, 2nd Lieut. J. A. (Merchant Taylors)
Obituary	1918	*170*

Barrett, Dr. J. E. (Victoria; Australia)
Obituary	1917	*239*

Barrett, J. S. (New Zealand Club Cricketer)
Obituary	1932/I	*239*

Barrick, D. (Northamptonshire)
Benefit Match	1961	*509*
Career Figures	1962	*696*
Photograph	1954	*478*

Barrie, Sir J. M. (Author)
Obituary	1938	*935*

Barrington, G. B. (Repton; Derbyshire)
Obituary	1943	*371*

Barrington, K. F. (Berkshire; Surrey; England)
'Ken Barrington - the Accumulator'		
J. Woodcock	1970	*106*
'Ken Barrington - An Appreciation'		
R. Marlar (Obituary)	1982	*93*
Benefit Match	1965	*570*
Career Figures	1969	*869*
	1970	*111*
	1982	*96*
Cricketer of the Year	1960	*112*
Photographs	1958	*544*
	1960	*86*
	1964	*67*
	1970	*107*
	1982	*93*
Retirement	1969	*94*

'Ken Barrington - A Tribute'.

B. Scovell Book Review	1983	*1308*
'Running into Hundreds' Book Review	1964	*1002*
'Playing it Straight' Book Review	1969	*1030*

Barrington, Hon. R. E. S. (Berkshire)
Obituary 1976 *1093*

Barrington, Viscount W. B. (Eton; Buckinghamshire; Devon)
Obituary 1934/I *254*

Barrow, G. S. (Tonbridge)
Obituary 1920/I *151*

Barrow, I. (Jamaica; West Indies)
Obituary 1980 *1146*

Barry, D. H. (Harrow)
Obituary 1946 *436*

Barrymore, 1st Lord (Warwickshire; Cheshire)
Obituary 1926/I *264*

Bartelt, Capt. F. (Bath College)
Obituary 1917 *164*

Bartholomew, A. C. (Marlborough; Oxford University; Devon)
Obituary 1941 *392*

Bartholomew, Capt. G. W. (Trinity College, Oxford)
Obituary 1917 *164*

Bartlett, E. L. (Barbados; West Indies)
Obituary 1978 *1068*
Notice of Obituary 1934/I *259*
Revision of Obituary 1935/I *277*

Bartlett, E. W. (Somerset)
Obituary 1943 *371*

Bartlett, F. E. (Yorkshire City C.C.)
Obituary 1903 *lxxiv*

Bartlett, Rev. G. H. (i/c Oundle Cricket)
Obituary 1959 *927*

Bartlett, H. T. (Dulwich; Cambridge University; Surrey; Sussex)
Portrait and Biography 1939 *34*

Bartlett, Capt. R. N. O. (King's School, Bruton)
Obituary 1917 *164*

Bartley, Comdr. E. L. D. (Royal Navy; Hampshire)
Obituary 1970 *1016*

Bartley, Lieut. F. J. (Brighton College)
Obituary 1918 *170*

Bartley, T. G. (Cheshire)
Obituary 1965 *963*

Barton, A. W. (Albion C.C. of New Jersey)
Obituary 1917 *239*

Barton, Major C. G. (Hampshire; Bombay Presidency)
Obituary 1920/I *163*

Barton, Rt. Hon. Sir E. (Australian Umpire)

Obituary   1921/I   *222*

Barton, Major-Gen. H. J. (Sussex)

Obituary   1923/I   *286*

Barton, H. G. M. (Hampshire; Buckinghamshire)

Obituary   1971   *1023*

Barton, V. A. (Kent; Hampshire; England)

Obituary   1907   *cvi*

Barton, W. E. (New Zealand Club Cricket)

Obituary   1944   *328*

Barwell, Capt. H. W. E. (Oundle)

Obituary   1919   *165*

Bashford, Rev. A. M. (Middlesex)

Obituary   1950   *904*

Bass, Hamer (Incogniti)

Obituary   1899   *xlv*

Bass, Harry (Kent; Kent Groundsman)

Obituary   1905   *lxxxv*

Bassett, H. (Oxford University; Oxfordshire)

Obituary   1944   *310*

Bastard, E. W. (Sherborne; Oxford University; Somerset)

Obituary   1902   *lviii*

Bastow, J. (Middlesex; Essex)

Obituary   1928/I   *277*

Bat   Notes on   1949   *122*

               1980   *87*

Batchelor, D. S. (Cricket Writer)

Obituary   1970   *1016*

'Days without Sunset' Book Review   1950   *977*

'C. B. Fry' Book Review   1952   *1018*

'The Book of the Tests' Book Review   1954   *983*

'The Picture Post Book of the Tests 1955'.

Book Review   1956   *1025*

'The Picture Post Book of the Tests 1956'.

Book Review   1957   *997*

'The Test Matches of 1964' Book Review   1965   *1018*

Batchelor, Capt. H. W. (Berkhamsted School)

Obituary   1919   *166*

Batchelor, Rev. W. J. (Warwickshire)

Obituary   1918   *222*

Bate, A. T. (Secretary Wellington Cricket Association)

Obituary   1923/I   *286*

Bate, Rev. T. P. (Canadian Club Cricket)

Obituary   1921/I   *222*

Bateman, Sir A. E. (Brighton College)

Obituary   1930/I   *245*

41

Bateman, E. L. (Marlborough; Oxford University)
Obituary   1910/I   *132*
Bateman-Champain, F. H. (Cheltenham; Oxford University; Gloucestershire)
Obituary   1943   *371*
Bateman-Champain, Rt. Rev. J. N. (Gloucestershire)
Obituary   1951   *917*
Bates, D. L. (Sussex)
Photographs   1961   *571*
                                                  1962   *601*
                                                  1963   *612*
                                                  1968   *583*
                                                  1970   *559*
Bates, F. S. (Marlborough; Hampshire)
Obituary   1970   *1017*
Bates, G. (Huntingdonshire)
Obituary   1919   *202*
Bates, J. (Warwickshire Groundsman)
Obituary   1938   *948*
Bates, L. A. (Warwickshire)
Benefit Match   1931/II   *416*
Obituary   1972   *1046*
Bates, R. (Lancashire Club Cricket)
Obituary   1910/I   *132*
Bates, Sgt. S. H. (Warwickshire)
Obituary   1917   *164*
Bates, T. H. (President New Zealand Cricket Council)
Obituary   1955   *926*
Bates, W. (Yorkshire; England)
Obituary   1901   *li*
Bates, W. E. (Yorkshire; Glamorgan)
Benefit Match   1931/II   *335*
Obituary   1958   *955*
Bateson, D. M. (Eton)
Obituary   1976   *1093*
Bath Plan of County Ground   1967   *546*
                                                  1970   *528*
                                                  1973   *518*
                                                  1976   *539*
Bather, E. W. (Shrewsbury; Shropshire)
Obituary   1931/I   *249*
Bathurst, Rev. Archdeacon F. Ven. (Winchester; Oxford University)
Obituary   1911/I   *137*
Bathurst, L. C. V. (Radley; Oxford University; Middlesex; Norfolk)
Obituary   1940   *837*
Bathurst, Rev. R. A. (Winchester; Oxford University)
Obituary   1907   *cvi*

42

Batsmanship Serious Decline in Note on	1973	*79*
Batsmen in County Cricket 1919-39	1941	*67*
Excell Note on	1948	*84*
Still Running Badly Note on	1945	*55*
Opening Notes on	1956	*70*
	1972	*87*
Reluctant Notes on	1954	*84*
'Batsmen must be bold' F. R. Brown	1954	*87*
'Batsmen must hit the ball again' D. Compton	1968	*96*
Battle, G. F. D. (Somerset Groundsman)		
Obituary	1972	*947*
Batson, 2nd Lieut. L. H. (Keble College, Oxford)		
Obituary	1917	*164*
Batten, J. M. (Haileybury; Devonshire)		
Obituary	1918	*222*
Battersby, 2nd Lieut. C. L. M. (King Edward's School; Sheffield)		
Obituary	1918	*211*
Battersby, J. L. (Malvern)		
Obituary	1956	*967*
Battersby, Major T. E. M. (Suffolk)		
Obituary	1973	*1004*
Batting Authoritative Note on	1967	*91*
Problems Note on	1973	*89*
and Fielding Note on	1959	*72*
Battock, O. G. (Buckinghamshire)		
Obituary	1971	*1023*
Batty, Lieut. C. F. (Mill Hill)		
Obituary	1917	*165*
Batty-Smith, H. (Journalist)		
Obituary	1928/I	*277*
Battye, Lieut. C. W. (Repton; Sandhurst; Berkshire)		
Obituary	1917	*165*
Battye, Lt-Col. C. W. (United Services)		
Obituary	1918	*170*
Baucher, R. H. (Harrow)		
Obituary	1975	*1070*
Bavin, Brig. A. J. W. (Incogniti)		
Obituary	1957	*942*
Bawtree, J. F. (Haileybury; Essex)		
Obituary	1939	*906*
Bax, C. (Writer)		
'W. G. Grace' Book Review	1953	*1000*
Baxter, H. W. (Glamorgan)		
Obituary	1963	*1032*
Baxter, Capt. W. H. B. (Merchiston Castle)		
Obituary	1918	*170*

Bayford, R. A. (Cambridge University; Middlesex; Surrey)
Obituary   1923/I   *287*
Bayley, J. (M.C.C.)
Obituary   1875   *145*
Bayley, Sir L. H. (Eton)
Obituary   1911/I   *138*
Bayley, M. (Surrey; Herefordshire)
Obituary   1927/I   *272*
Bayley-Laurie, Rev. Sir E. (Eton; Kent)
Obituary   1918   *223*
Bayly, H. V. (Tasmania)
Obituary   1904   *lxxix*
Bayly, S. J. H. (Border)
Obituary   1938   *935*
Baynton, R. G. (Warwickshire)
Obituary   1925/I   *258*
Bazalgette 2nd Lieut. W. T. A. (Blundell's School)
Obituary   1918   *170*
Beachcroft, Sir C. P. (Rugby)
Obituary   1928/I   *278*
Beadle, Lt-Comdr. S. W. (Royal Navy; Kent)
Obituary   1938   *935*
Beadle, Lt-Comdr. S. W. (Roual Navy, Hampshire)
Obituary   1939   *920*
Beal, C. W. (Manager Australian Teams 1882, 1888)
Obituary   1922/I   *245*
Beale, E. C. (New Zealand Club Cricket)
Obituary   1938   *935*
Beale, G. H. (Auckland Grammar School)
Obituary   1920/I   *151*
Beall, Pte. P. K. (Public Schools C.C., Vancouver)
Obituary   1918   *211*
Bean, E. E. (Victoria)
Obituary   1940   *837*
Bean, G. (Nottinghamshire; Sussex; England)
Benefit Matches   1899   *181*
    1922/II   *96*
Obituary   1924/I   *253*
Bean, J. (Sussex)
Obituary   1923/I   *287*
Bear, M. J. (Essex)
Photographs   1963   *392*
    1967   *370*
Retirement   1969   *366*
Beard, D. D. (Central Districts; Northern Districts; New Zealand)
Obituary   1983   *1240*

Beard, S. (Sussex Supporter)
Obituary 1911/I *161*
Beardmore, W. J. M. (Loretto; Scotland)
Obituary 1980 *1159*
Bearshaw, B. (Writer)
with Addison V. 'Lancashire Cricket at the Top'
Book Review 1972 *1096*
Beasley, 2nd Lieut. J. J. (Trinity College, Dublin)
Obituary 1916 *145*
Beasley, J. N. (Northamptonshire)
Obituary 1961 *943*
Beasley, Rev. R. N. (Northamptonshire)
Obituary 1967 *962*
Beatson, Lieut. R. S. M. (Rugby; British Columbia C.C.)
Obituary 1917 *165*
Beattie, G. N. (Scottish Cricket Union)
Obituary 1933/I *239*
Beatty-Pownall, Lt-Col. G. E. (St Paul's; Sandhurst)
Obituary 1919 *166*
Beauford, Major F. S. (Eton Ramblers C.C.)
Obituary 1960 *949*
Beaufort, Duke of (President Gloucestershire)
Obituary 1900 *li*
Beaumont, L/Cpl. F. (Chester C.C.)
Obituary 1918 *170*
Beaumont, J. (Yorkshire; Surrey)
Obituary 1921/I *223*
Views on the Reforms of 1889 1890 *xxxvii*
Views on some Questions of the Day 1890 *xli*
Beaumont, O. H. W. (Cricket Writer)
Obituary 1954 *921*
Beaumont-Checkland, Lieut. M. B. (Newton College)
Obituary 1918 *170*
Beaver, W. (Saltaire C.C.)
Obituary 1917 *239*
Becket, Major F. (Southport C.C.)
Obituary 1917 *165*
Beckford, W. G. (Jamaica)
Obituary 1960 *949*
Bedford, E. H. R. (Derbyshire)
Obituary 1978 *1084*
Bedford, P. I. (Woodhouse Grammar; Middlesex)
Career Notes 1948 *646*
Obituary 1967 *962*
Photograph 1962 *504*

Bedford, Col. R. B. R. (Free Foresters)
Obituary   1917   *239*
Bedford, Rev. W. C. R. (Free Foresters)
Obituary   1923/I   *287*
Bedford, Rev. W. K. R. (Founder of Free Foresters)
Obituary   1906   *lxxxvii*
Bedi, B. S. (Punjab; Delhi; Northamptonshire; India)
Photograph   1977   *506*
Retirement   1982   *1091*
Bedser, A. (Border)
Obituary   1982   *1194*
Bedser, A. V. (Surrey; England)
'Bowling for Surrey and England'   1961   *142*
'A. V. Bedser A Giant among Bowlers'
R. C. Robertson – Glasgow'   1953   *95*
'Another Record for Bedser' Action Photograph   1954   *58*
Action Photograph   1953   *59*
Benefit Match   1954   *551*
Career Figures   1953   *100*
     1960   *150*
     1961   *150,652*
Cricketer of the Year   1947   *45*
Notes on   1952   *97*
     1954   *81*
     1955   *80*
Photographs   1947   *40*
     1953   *98*
     1954   *537*
     1957   *533*
     1961   *143*
with Selectors   1963   *150*
Retires as Chairman of Selectors Note   1982   *91*
Tribute to W. R. Hammond   1966   *117*
With Bedser, E. A. 'Our Cricket Story'
Book Review   1952   *1017*
'May's Men in Australia' Book Review   1960   *998*
Bedser, E. A. (Surrey)
Benefit Match   1959   *546*
Career Figures   1962   *696*
Note on   1947   *45*
Photographs   1953   *527*
     1958   *544*
With Bedser, A. V. 'Our Cricket Story'
Book Review   1960   *998*
Bedwell, 2nd Lieut. V. L. S. (St John's; Leatherhead)
Obituary   1917   *165*

Beeching, Lt-Col. T. H. P. (Kent)
  Obituary   1972   *1047*
Beeson, F. E. (Buckinghamshire)
  Obituary   1984   *1197*
Beeson, Corp. N. W. (Malvern)
  Obituary   1945   *319*
Beet, G. (Derbyshire)
  Obituary   1947   *687*
Beevor, J. G. (Uppingham; Nottinghamshire)
  Obituary   1905   *ciii*
Begbie, Rev. A. J. (Harrow)
  Obituary   1924/I   *254*
Beisiegel, Air-Commodore W. K. (Leicestershire)
  Obituary   1974   *1071*
Belcher, Capt. G. (Brighton College; Cambridge University; Berkshire; Hampshire)
  Obituary   1916   *145*
Belcher, Major R. D. (Brighton College)
  Obituary   1918   *170*
Belcher, S. H. (New South Wales)
  Obituary   1921/I   *223*
Belcher, Rev. T. H. (Oxford University)
  Obituary   1920/I   *163*
Beldam, C. A. (Middlesex)
  Obituary   1941   *393*
Beldam, G. W. (Middlesex; London County)
  Obituary   1938   *935*
Belk, O. (Durham)
  Obituary   1927/I   *294*
Bell, A. K. (Perthshire)
  Obituary   1943   *372*
Bell, B. T. A. (Canada)
  Obituary   1905   *lxxxv*
Bell, C. L. (Marlborough)
  Obituary   1923/I   *309*
Bell, 2nd Lieut. C. M. (Birkenhead School)
  Obituary   1919   *166*
Bell, Lieut D. H. (Burrard C.C., Vancouver)
  Obituary   1918   *211*
Bell, E. (Chatham C.C., Ontario)
  Obituary   1923/I   *309*
Bell, Rt. Hon. Sir F. H. D. (President New Zealand Cricket Council)
  Obituary   1937/I   *265*
Bell, Rev. H. (Marlborough)
  Obituary   1920/I   *164*

Bell, L/Corp. J. (Ontario)
Obituary 1916 *145*
Bell, J. D. (Glenalmond)
Obituary 1920/I *151*
Bell, J. T. (Yorkshire; Glamorgan)
Obituary 1975 *1070*
Bell, Lieut. L. C. (Canada)
Obituary 1943 *363*
Bell, P. H. (Gloucestershire)
Obituary 1957 *942*
Bell, P. H. (Gloucestershire)
Obituary 1972 *1047*
Bell, R. M. (London County)
Obituary 1954 *921*
Bell, S. B. (Uppingham)
Obituary 1946 *436*
Bell, T. (Uppingham)
Obituary 1924/I *254*
Beloe, G. H. (Marlborough; Gloucestershire)
Obituary 1945 *327*
Beloe, H. W. (Chairman Gloucestershire)
Obituary 1926/I *264*
Belper, 2nd Lord (Harrow; President M.C.C.)
Obituary 1915/I *211*
Benaud, R. (New South Wales; Australia)
Cricketer of the Year 1962 *99*
'Fastest Hundred in Test Cricket' Note 1983 *108*
Photographs 1954 *56*
1962 *95*
Retirement 1965 *863*
'Skills and Controversy' 1973 *97*
'Cricket Fever Hits Australia' 1974 *39*
'Eleven West Indian Men of my Time' 1976 *67*
'From Spofforth to Lillee' 1977 *116*
'Effects of the Bumper – Has it Ruined
Batsmanship?' 1978 *148*
'Way of Cricket' Book Review 1962 *1034*
'A Tale of Two Tests' Book Review 1963 *1108*
'Benaud' A. G. Moyes Book Review 1963 *1110*
'Spin me a Spinner' Book Review 1964 *999*
'Bradman, Benaud, and Goddard's Cinderellas'
R.S. Whitington Book Review 1965 *1014*
Tributes to: A. T. W. Grout 1969 *981*
C. Taylor 1978 *1082*
Sir Frank Worrell 1968 *122*

Bencraft, Dr. R. (Hampshire)
  Views on some questions of the day   1890   *xlv*
  Later known as
Bencraft, Sir R. (Hampshire)
  Obituary   1944   *157,310*
Benefits Record ones See Cricket Records
Bendle, E. (Sedbergh; Cumberland)
  Obituary   1926/I   *264*
Bengal Silver Jubilee   1958   *858*
Bengough, C. S. (Marlborough; Gloucestershire)
  Obituary   1935/I   *260*
Benham, A. M. (Rugby)
  Obituary   1896   *xli*
Benham, Canon W. (Cricket Fanatic)
  Obituary   1911/I   *138*
Benka, H. F. (Middlesex)
  Obituary   1971   *1023*
Benjamin, R. B. (Manager Australian Team to U.S.A. 1913)
  Obituary   1927/I   *272*
Benn, Major A. A. (Wellington; Free Foresters)
  Obituary   1945   *319*
Bennett, A. C. L. (Northamptonshire)
  Obituary   1972   *1047*
Bennett, A. R. (Nottinghamshire)
  Obituary   1900   *lii*
Bennett, C. T. (Harrow; Cambridge University; Surrey; Middlesex)
  'When Three Day Cricket was Worthwhile'   1974   *130*
  Obituary   1979   *1073*
  Tribute to N. B. Sherwell   1961   *951*
Bennett, D. (Middlesex)
  Photograph   1954   *459*
Bennett, E. A. (East Gloucestershire C.C.)
  Obituary   1920/I   *192*
Bennett, Col. F. W. (Sherborne; Kent)
  Obituary   1931/I   *273*
Bennett, G. (Kent)
  Benefit Match   1874   *162*
Bennett, G. (American Club Cricket)
  Obituary   1919   *202*
Bennett, G. (Winchester; Oxford University)
  Obituary   1914/I   *177*
Bennett, Major G. G. M. (Berkshire)
  Obituary   1967   *963*
Bennett, Major G. M. (King's Bruton; Somerset)
  Obituary   1983   *1240*

Bennett, J. H. (Canterbury, New Zealand)
Obituary 1949 *872*
Bennett, M. V. (Lincolnshire)
Obituary 1942 *347*
Bennett, Capt. R. A. (Hampshire)
Obituary 1954 *921*
Bennett of Edgbaston, Lord (Chairman Warwickshire)
Obituary 1958 *955*
Bennett-Goldney, Major F. (Canterbury Cricket Week)
Obituary 1919 *166*
Bensimon, A. S. (Western Province)
Obituary 1978 *1068*
Benson, Lieut. C. S. (Pembroke College, Oxford)
Obituary 1918 *171*
Benson, E. T. (Oxford University; Gloucestershire)
Obituary 1968 *998*
Benson, 2nd Lieut. H. L. (Newcastle Club Cricket)
Obituary 1917 *165*
Benson, Capt. J. M. (Fettes)
Obituary 1919 *166*
Benson, J. P. (Winchester)
Obituary 1945 *327*
Benson, M. R. (Sutton Valence; Kent)
Photograph 1982 *445*
Schools Note 1978 *836*
1022 runs Schools Averages 1978 *885*
Whitbread Scholarship 1982 *354*
Benson, Lt-Col. Sir R. L. (Eton)
Obituary 1969 *978*
Benson and Hedges World Series Cup
1979-80 1981 *1018*
1980-81 1982 *984*
1981-82 1983 *1025*
1982-83 1984 *978*
Benthall, W. H. (Marlborough; Cambridge University; Devonshire;
Buckinghamshire; Middlesex)
Obituary 1910/I *132*
Bentinck, B. W. (Winchester; Hampshire)
Obituary 1932/I *239*
Benton, C. H. (Lancashire; Cheshire)
Obituary 1919 *203*
Benton, 2nd Lieut. F. (London County)
Obituary 1917 *165*
Benton, Capt. W. R. (Framlingham; Middlesex)
Obituary 1917 *165*

Beoku-Betts (Sierra-Leone)
   Obituary   1958   *956*

Bere, Rev. M. A. (Marlborough)
   Obituary   1948   *781*

Berens, A. A. (Northamptonshire)
   Obituary   1927/I   *272*

Berens, A. C. B. (Wellington; Kent)
   Obituary   1982   *1194*

Berens, R. B. (West Kent C.C.)
   Obituary   1917   *240*

Beresford, R. A. A. (Oundle; Cambridge University; Norfolk; Northamptonshire)
   Obituary   1942   *355*

Beresford, R. M. (Norfolk)
   Obituary   1969   *978*

Beresford, Hon. S. R. D. H. (Middlesex)
   Obituary   1929/I   *241*

Bergen, G. J. (Moorestown C.C, U.S.A.)
   Obituary   1919   *203*

Berger, Major-Gen. E. A. (Winchester)
   Obituary   1917   *240*

Bergin, S. F. (Ireland; Journalist)
   Obituary   1972   *1057*

Berkeley, G. F. H. (Oxford University; Oxfordshire)
   Obituary   1956   *967*

Berkeley, Capt. M. H. F. (A. S. C.)
   Obituary   1919   *166*

Berkeley, Capt. R. G. W. (Worcestershire)
   Obituary   1970   *1017*

Berkley, Rev. M. (Fettes)
   Obituary   1948   *781*

Berkley-Hill, P/O. O. W. H. (Hurstpierpoint)
   Obituary   1943   *363*

Bermuda   in England 1960   1961   *804*
          in England 1962   1963   *976*
   Bermuda Cricketers in England 1962
   E. Burn   Book Review   1963   *1113*

Bernard, A. C. (Eton)
   Obituary   1951   *917*

Bernard, C. A. (Somerset)
   Obituary   1955   *937*

Bernard, Dr. D. (West Gloucestershire C.C.)
   Obituary   1921/I   *224*

Bernau, E. H. L. (Wellington; New Zealand)
   Obituary   1967   *963*

Berressford, J. H. (Manhattan C.C.)
   Obituary   1922/I   *245*

Berridge, Dr. W. C. M. (Leicestershire)
Obituary | 1974 | *1071*
Berrington, Capt. C. D. (Wellington)
Obituary | 1917 | *166*
Berry, J. (Yorkshire)
Obituary | 1896 | *xxxix*
Berry, L. G. (Leicestershire)
Benefit Match | 1939 | *428*
Photograph | 1950 | *410*
Berry, R. (Lancashire; Worcester; Derbyshire; England)
Career Record | 1963 | *1042*
Three County Caps | 1962 | *726*
Berry, S. (Writer)
'Cricket in the Pacific' | 1981 | *119*
Cricket Wallah   Book Review | 1983 | *1307*
Besch, J. G. Q. (Metropolitan Club Cricket)
Obituary | 1930/I | *245*
Bessant, J. (Gloucestershire)
Obituary | 1983 | *1240*
Bessborough, Earl of (Harrow)
Obituary | 1896 | *xl*
Bessemer, H. D. (M. C. C.)
Obituary | 1969 | *978*
'Best Fast Bowler' (W. G. Grace Beard Incident)
Sir. S. Jackson | 1944 | *53*
Best, 2nd Lieut. F. R. (Preston C.C.)
Obituary | 1917 | *166*
Best, J. (Cornwall)
Obituary | 1906 | *lxxxvii*
Best, Dr. L. W. (New South Wales)
Obituary | 1926/I | *246*
Best, Lt-Col. T. A. D. (Sandhurst)
Obituary | 1918 | *171*
Best, W. F. (Kent)
Obituary | 1944 | *328*
Bestwick, W. (Derbyshire)
Obituary | 1939 | *907*
Beswick, J. (Lancashire)
Obituary | 1952 | *955*
Betham, J. D. (Writer)
Obituary | 1957 | *942*
Betham, W. D. (Sedbergh; Westmoreland)
Obituary | 1919 | *203*
Bethune, Major H. B. (Hampshire)
Obituary | 1913/I | *183*

Beton, W. (Dressing Room Attendant at Lord's)
Obituary   1941   *393*
Better Cricket Competition *Daily Express*   1964   *88*
Bettesworth, W. A. (Ardingly; Sussex; Journalist)
Obituary   1930/I   *245*
Bettington, Dr. R. H. B. (Oxford University; Middlesex; New South Wales)
Obituary   1970   *1017*
Bettison, H. (Forfarshire)
Obituary   1957   *942*
Betts, J. A. (Hertfordshire)
Obituary   1972   *1047*
Betts, M. P. (Middlesex; Kent; Secretary Essex)
Obituary   1915/I   *212*
Bevan, Lt-Col. T. (Eton)
Obituary   1943   *363*
Bevan, Venerable W. L. (Cricket Fanatic)
Obituary   1909/I   *132*
Beveridge, J. (Sydney Cricket Club)
Obituary   1917   *240*
Beves, G. (Leys School; Transvaal, Nottinghamshire)
Obituary   1928/I   *278*
Bevill, F. (Journalist)
Obituary   1912/I   *163*
Bevington, J. C. (Harrow; Essex; Middlesex)
Obituary   1935/I   *276*
Bevington, T. A. (Middlesex)
Obituary   1967   *963*
Bewicke, C. (Northumberland)
Obituary   1897   *xl*
Bezer, A. (Somerset)
Obituary   1945   *327*
Bharatan, R. (Journalist)
'Rivals in the Sun' Book Review   1954   *980*
Bhopal Nawab of (Mohomedan Anglo – Oriental College)
Obituary   1961   *943*
Bibliography of Cricket A. J. Gaston
  1892   *xlviii*
  1894   *lxiii*
  1900   *xc*
  1923/I   *255*
'Bibliography of Cricket' E. W. Padwick
Book Review   1978   *1117*
Bickmore, A. F. (Clifton; Oxford University; Kent)
Obituary   1980   *1146*
Biddle, L. (Gents of Philadelphia)
Obituary   1942   *355*

Biddle, Sir R. (Hampshire)
Obituary   1971   *1023*
Biddulph, A. J. (Trustee Cricketers' Fund)
Obituary   1896   *xliii*
Biddulph, S. (Nottinghamshire)
Obituary   1877   *200*
Big Hitting Note on   1946   *63*
Biggleston, Lieut. D. H. (Tonbridge)
Obituary   1944   *304*
Bignall, T. (Nottinghamshire)
Obituary   1899   *xlix*
Bignell, Lt-Col. G. N. (Hampshire)
Obituary   1966   *961*
Bignell, H. G. (Hampshire)
Obituary   1908/I   *134*
Bilbrough, J. G. P. (Eastern Province)
Obituary   1945   *327*
Billham, F. D. (Essex)
Obituary   1982   *1194*
Bingham, Capt, F. M. (St Peter's, York; Derbyshire)
Obituary   1916   *146*
Binks, J. G. (Yorkshire; Lincolnshire; England)
Benefit Match   1968   *645*
Cricketer of the Year   1969   *67*
Photographs   1961   *632*
      1963   *672*
      1967   *634*
      1969   *59*
Retirement   1970   *80,611*
Binney, E. J. (Victoria)
Obituary   1980   *1159*
Binyon, A. E. (Somerset)
Obituary   1949   *862*
Birch, A. E. (Kent)
Obituary   1937/I   *266*
Birch, Sir E. C. J. W. (Harrow)
Obituary   1931/I   *273*
Birch, J. D. (Nottinghamshire)
Photograph   1982   *525*
Birchall, Lt-Col. A. P. D. (Army)
Obituary   1916   *146*
Bircham, Lt-Col. A. H. (Treasurer, Incogniti)
Obituary   1901   *lit*
Bircham, Lt-Col. H. F. W. (Eton; Sandhurst)
Obituary   1917   *166*

Bircham, S. (Auditor M.C.C.)
Obituary   1924/I   *254*
Bird, A. (Warwickshire; Worcestershire)
Obituary   1928/I   *278*
Bird, Lt-Col. A. C. (Malvern)
Obituary   1939   *907*
Bird, Rev. F. N. (Gloucestershire; Northamptonshire; Buckinghamshire;
Devonshire; Suffolk)
Obituary   1966   962
Bird, Lieut. F. W. (Public Schools C.C., Vancouver)
Obituary   1918   171
Bird, G. (Middlesex; Lancashire)
Obituary   1931/I   *249*
Bird, H. D. (Yorkshire; Leicestershire; Umpire)
Photographs   1976   *41*
                                                        1978   *81*
'Not Out' Book Review   1979   *1132*
Bird, M. C. (Harrow; Surrey; Lancashire; England)
Obituary   1934/I   *259*
Note on   1946   *57*
Schools Notes   1906   *cxxi*
                                                        1907   *cxxxviii*
                                                                          cxxxix
                                                        1908/I   *117*
Bird, P. J. (Hampshire)
Obituary   1943   *372*
Bird, Lieut. W. C. (Kettering C.C.)
Obituary   1918   171
Bird, W. H. B. (Winchester)
Obituary   1936/I   *291*
Bird, Lieut. W. S. (Malvern; Oxford University; Middlesex)
Obituary   1916   146
Birkbeck, Capt. G. W. (Norfolk)
Obituary   1918   171
Birkbeck, H. (Norfolk)
Obituary   1931/I   250
Birkenshaw, J. (Yorkshire; Leicestershire; England)
Benefit Match   1975   706
Photographs   1969   *479*
                                                        1973   *459*
Birkett, Rt. Hon. Lord (Supporter of Cricket)
'The Love of Cricket'   1958   *68*
Obituary   1963   *1032*
Note on   1963   *143*
Birkin, Major P. A. (President Nottinghamshire)
Obituary   1952   955

55

Birkin, Sir T. I. Bart. (President Nottinghamshire)
Obituary   1923/I   *287*
Birley, F. H. (Winchester; Surrey; Lancashire)
Obituary   1911/I   *138*
Birley, L. (Uppingham)
Obituary   1952   *955*
Birmingham and District League
Views on the Laws   1957   *87*
Birmingham Festival   1944   *187*
                                                  1945   *199*
                                                  1946   *260*
Biron, Rev. H. B. (Kent)
Obituary   1916   *146*
Personal Recollections of J. Wisden   1913/I   *125*
Birrell, 2nd Lieut. H. A. (Repton)
Obituary   1917   *222*
Birrell, W. S. (Cupar C.C.)
Obituary   1956   *968*
Birtwell, Paym-Lt. A. J. (Lancashire; Buckinghamshire)
Obituary   1975   *1071*
Birtwhistle, Lieut. N. (Cheltenham)
Obituary   1920/I   *164*
Bisber, W. A. (Clifton)
Obituary   1920/I   *164*
Biscoe, Gen. W. W. (Winchester)
Obituary   1921/I   *224*
Bisgood, B. L. (Somerset)
Obituary   1969   *979*
Bishop, Lt-Col. B. F. (Repton)
Obituary   1919   *166*
Bishop, C. (Herefordshire; Carmarthenshire)
Obituary   1928/I   *278*
Bishop, Major C. G. (Uppingham)
Obituary   1918   *171*
Bishop, 2nd Lieut. K. F. (United Services College, Windsor)
Obituary   1917   *166*
Bishop, T. S. (Hampton School)
1004 runs Schools Averages   1979   *860*
Bispham, A. W. G. (Secretary New Jersey State Cricket League)
Obituary   1908/I   *134*
Bisset, G. F. (Griqualand West; South Africa)
Obituary   1966   *962*
Bisset, Sir M. (Western Province; South Africa)
Obituary   1932/I   *239*

Bissex, M. (Gloucestershire)
Photographs	1967	*406*
	1971	*368*

Bissley, 2nd Lieut. W. H. (Maidenhead C.C.)
Obituary	1917	*166*

Blaber, A. (Sussex)
Obituary	1906	*lxxxvii*

Black, A. E. (Toronto C.C.)
Obituary	1923/I	*264*

Black, Capt. J. N. L. (Malvern)
Obituary	1918	*171*

Black, Major M. A. (Rugby)
Obituary	1918	*171*

Black, Ft. Sub-Lt. N. (Christ's Hospital)
Obituary	1919	*197*

Black, T. H. (Yorkshire C.C.)
Obituary	1925/I	*258*

Blackburne, Lieut. J. (Giggleswick Grammar School)
Obituary	1918	*171*

Blackburn, Rev. W. (Repton)
Obituary	1921/I	*243*

Blackburne, Major J. G. (Charterhouse; Army)
Obituary	1916	*147*

Blackburne, Sir. K. (Jamaica)
Tribute to O. G. Smith	1960	*956*

Blacker, W. (Harrow; Oxford University; Ireland)
Obituary	1908/I	*135*

Blackett, B. J. (Eton; Hertfordshire)
Obituary	1928/I	*278*

Blackett, Capt. J. W. (Prince Alfred College, Adelaide)
Obituary	1917	*166*

Blackham, J. M. (Victoria; Australia)
Obituary	1933/I	*239*
Portrait and Biography	1891	*xxxiv*

Blackie, D. D. J. (Victoria; Australia)
Benefit Match	1935/II	*680*
Obituary	1956	*968*

Blacklidge, Sgt-Major. H. G. (Surrey)
Obituary	1918	*171*

Blacklock, A. (Wellington, New Zealand)
Obituary	1935/I	*260*

Blacklock, C. P. (Wellington)
Obituary	1925/I	*258*

Blacklock, J. P. (Wellington, New Zealand)
Obituary	1936/I	*270*

Blackman, A. (Surrey; Kent; Sessex)
Obituary   1909/I   132

Blackmore, 'David and Winnie' (Warwickshire)
Photograph   1973   128

Blackpool Plan of County Ground   1971   417

Blackton, W. R. (Derbyshire)
Obituary   1977   1037

Blackwell, T. G. (Harrow)
Bequest to Harrow   1944   125

Blades, Dr. C. C. (Surrey Committee)
Obituary   1917   240

Blades, C. E. (Barbados)
Obituary   1915/I   212

Blagg, P. H. (Shrewsbury; Oxford University)
Obituary   1946   434

Blagrave, H. H. G. (Cheltenham; Gloucestershire)
Obituary   1983   1241

Blaikie, T. (Cricket Coach Scotland)
Obituary   1905   lxxxv

Blair, A. E. (Radley)
Schools Note   1924/I   289,305
1011 runs Schools Averages   1924/II   570

Blair, Major-Gen. E. M. (Cheltenham; Kent)
Obituary   1940   838

Blair, Lieut. H. S. P. (Preston C.C.)
Obituary   1917   166

Blake, Capt. G. E. (Ridley College; Ontario)
Obituary   1917   166

Blake, G. F. (Norfolk)
Obituary   1922/I   244

Blake, Capt. J. P. (Cambridge University; Hampshire)
Obituary   1945   319

Blake, Lieut. M. F. (Military Cricket)
Obituary   1918   214

Blaker, R. N. R. (Cambridge University; Kent)
Obituary   1951   91

Blamires, Rev. E. O. (New Zealand Clubs)
Obituary   1964   943

Bland, C. H. G. (Sussex)
Obituary   1951   91

Bland, R. D. F. (Shrewsbury)
Schools Note: 1929/I   28.
76 wkts Schools Averages   1929/II   62

Bland, K. C. (Rhodesia; Eastern Province; Orange Free State; South Africa)
Action Photograph   1966   5
Cricketer of the Year   1966   7.

Photograph	1966	*62*
Blandford, J. A. R. (New Zealand Clubs)		
Obituary	1956	*968*
Blaxland, Capt. J. B. (Shrewsbury)		
Obituary	1918	*172*
Blaxland, L. B. (Shrewsbury; Derbyshire)		
Obituary	1978	*1084*
Bleackley, Major E. O. (Harrow; Lancashire)		
Obituary	1977	*1037*
Bleackley, H. W. (Author)		
Obituary	1932/I	*240*
Blease, Capt. H. (Sedbergh; Sefton Park C.C.)		
Obituary	1916	*147*
Blenkiron, T. W. (Charterhouse)		
Obituary	1935/I	*260*
Blenkiron, W. (Warwickshire)		
Photograph	1971	*546*
Bligh, A. S. (Somerset)		
Obituary	1953	*938*
Bligh, Capt. C. H. (Winnipeg C.C.)		
Obituary	1916	*147*
Bligh, Lieut. E. H. S. (Clifton; Cambridge University)		
Obituary	1916	*147*
Bligh, Hon. E. V. (Oxford University; Kent; Middlesex)		
'Cricket Centuries and L.B.W.'	1899	*lxvi*
	1900	*xcvii*
Obituary	1909/I	*132*
Bligh , Hon. Rev. H. (Kent)		
Obituary	1907	*cxvii*
Bligh, Hon. I. F. W. B. (See under Darnley, 8th Earl of)		
Bligh, L. E. (Kent)		
Obituary	1925/I	*258*
Blind Cricketers Festival	1983	*678*
Block, S. A. (Marlborough; Cambridge University; Surrey)		
Obituary	1980	*1147*
Blofeld, H. C. (Eton; Cambridge University; Writer; Broadcaster)		
'The Joy of Touring'	1975	*120*
'Welcome West Indies – How they rose to fame'	1976	*71*
'The Packer Affair' Book Review	1979	*1136*
Bloodworth, B. S. (Gloucestershire; Umpire)		
Obituary	1969	*989*
Bloomfield, H. O. (Surrey)		
Obituary	1974	*1071*
Blore, Rev. Canon G. J. (Charterhouse)		
Obituary	1917	*240*

Blore, W. P. (Marlborough)

Obituary   1949   *862*

Blount, Air Vice Marshall C. H. B. (Harrow; Royal Air Force)

Obituary   1941   *386*

Bloy, N. C. H. (Oxford University; I/C Clifton)

Views on Laws   1957   *83*

Blucke, Rev. R. S. K. (Leicestershire)

Obituary   1931/I   *250*

Blundell, Sir E. D. (Cambridge University)

Note on   1969   *95*

Blundell, N. (Secretary South Australian Cricket Association)

Obituary   1984   *1197*

Blunden, E. (Writer; Author)

Obituary   1975   *1071*

Blunt, R. C. (Canterbury; Otago; New Zealand)

Obituary   1967   *963*
Portrait and Biography   1928/I   *313*

Blyth, 2nd Lieut. A. F. (Radley)

Obituary   1918   *172*

Blyth, J. (President Sefton C.C.)

Obituary   1916   *147*

Blythe, C. (Kent; England)

Benefit Match   1910/II   *77*
Note on Bowling   1944   *50*
Obituary   1918   *172*
Portrait and Biography   1904   *xcvi*

Boal, Capt. J. K. (Campbell College, Belfast)

Obituary   1918   *175*

Board, J. H. (Gloucestershire; England)

Benefit Match   1902   *248*
Obituary   1925/I   *258*

Boddam, E. T. (Tasmania)

Obituary   1960   *949*

Boddam-Whetham, Lt-Col. A. C. (Eton Ramblers)

Obituary   1920/I   *164*

Boddam-Whetham, J. W. (Midland Club Cricket)

Obituary   1919   *203*

Boddington, R. A. (Rugby; Oxford University; Lancashire)

Obituary   1978   *1068*

Boden, Rev. C. A. (Christ's Hospital; Leicestershire)

Obituary   1982   *1194*

Boden, H. (Derbyshire)

Obituary   1909/I   *13.*

Boden, J. G. (Yorkshire)

Obituary   1929/I   *24.*

Boden, T. W. (Derbyshire)
Obituary   1970   *1017*
Boden, W. (President Derbyshire)
Obituary   1906   *lxxxvii*
Bodington, Capt. C. H. (King's Canterbury; Hampshire)
Obituary   1918   *175*
Body, Pte. H. (Wanderers C.C., Winnipeg)
Obituary   1918   *211*
Boger, A. J. (Winchester; Oxford University; Hertfordshire)
Obituary   1941   *393*
Bogle, Capt. G. V. (Edingburgh University)
Obituary   1917   *167*
Bogle-Smith, C. (Eton; Herefordshire)
Obituary   1918   *223*
Bohlen, F. H. (Philadelphia)
Obituary   1944   *328*
Boissier, A. P. (St. John's, Leatherhead)
Obituary   1954   *921*
Bokhari, I. A. (Cambridgeshire)
Wilfred Rhodes Trophy   1957   *682*
Boldero, Lt-Gen. G. N. (Harrow)
Obituary   1899   *xlv*
Boldero, Rev. H. K. (Harrow; Cambridge University)
Obituary   1901   *liv*
Boles, Lt-Col. D. C. (Eton)
Obituary   1959   *927*
Bolitho, W. E. T. (Harrow; Oxford University; Devonshire)
Obituary   1920/I   *164*
Bolland, Rev. W. E. (Marlborough)
Obituary   1920/I   *164*
Bolton, B. C. (Yorkshire)
Obituary   1911/I   *139*
Bolton, 2nd Lieut. C. A. (St. Paul's)
Obituary   1919   *166*
Bolton, D. H. W. (Haileybury)
Schools Note   1953   *717*
1067 runs Schools Averages   1953   *734*
Bolton, G. (Writer)
Obituary   1965   *963*
History of the Oxford University
'Cricket Club' Book Review   1963   *1104*
Bolton, H. (Aberdeenshire)
Obituary   1953   *938*
Bolton, J. T. (Cricket Journalist)
Obituary   1968   *998*

61

Bolton, L. H. (Rugby)
Obituary 1954 *921*
Bolton, R. (Thirsk C.C.)
Obituary 1920/I *164*
Bolton, Capt. R. H. D. (Hampshire)
Obituary 1965 *963*
Bolton, Lieut. S. (Cheltenham)
Obituary 1919 *166*
Bolton, W. S. (Harrow)
Obituary 1920/I *152*
Bolus, J. B. (Yorkshire; Nottinghamshire; Derbyshire; England)
Benefit Match 1972 *538*
Photographs 1965 *521*
1970 *513*
1973 *359*
1976 *360*
Bomb 'Scare Test' 1974 *348*
Bompass, H. S. (Winchester; Cambridge University)
Obituary 1945 *327*
Bonbright, W. P. (Haverford College)
Obituary 1910/I *133*
Bond, C. G. (Free Foresters)
Obituary 1916 *148*
Bond, Gen. F. H. B. (Toronto C.C.)
Obituary 1918 *211*
Bond, J. D. (Lancashire)
Cricketer of the Year) 1971 *75*
Note on 1973 *92*
Photographs 1962 *465*
1963 *483*
1969 *461*
1971 *74*
Testimonial Match 1971 *431*
'Jack Bond – The Little Giant'
Book Review 1971 *1088*
Bond, R. M. (Harrow)
Obituary 1946 *434*
Bone, D. D. (Journalist)
Obituary 1912/I *163*
Bonham-Carter, H. (Head of Family)
Obituary 1922/I *246*
Bonham-Carter, L. G. (Clifton; Hampshire)
Obituary 1928/I *278*
Bonham-Carter, Sir M. (Oxford University; Kent)
Obituary 1961 *943*

Bonham-Carter, 2nd Lieut. N. (Balliol College, Oxford)
Obituary   1918   *175*
Bonham-Carter, R. M. H. (Winchester)
Obituary   1916   *148*
Bonner, J. W. (Essex)
Obituary   1937/I   *266*
Bonner, Lt-Col. S. (Harrow House Matches)
Obituary   1918   *175*
Bonnor, G. J. (Victoria; New South Wales; Australia)
Fastest Test Hundred Note   1983   *106*
Obituary   1913/I   *183*
Bonser, Capt. W. J. (Westminster)
Obituary   1916   *148*
Bonsey, Rev. Canon F. R. (Forest School; Hertfordshire)
Obituary   1972   *1047*
Bonus Plan Prizes   1978   *796*
Booker, Rev. E. (City of London School)
Obituary   1920/I   *164*
Boosey, R. (Charterhouse; Kent)
Obituary   1974   *1071*
Booth, A. (Yorkshire)
Obituary   1975   *1071*
Booth, A. (Cricket Journalist)
Obituary   1958   *956*
Booth, B. J. (Lancashire; Leicestershire)
Photograph   1966   *466*
Booth, C. (Rugby; Cambridge University; Lincolnshire; Hampshire; Huntingdonshire)
Obituary   1927/I   *272*
Booth, C. L. (Marlborough)
Obituary   1927/I   *272*
Booth, F. S. (Lancashire)
Obituary   1981   *1138*
Booth, J. J. (Bradford Cricket League)
Obituary   1943   *373*
Booth, Major L. E. (R. M. A.)
Obituary   1919   *166*
Booth, P. (Leicestershire)
Photograph   1978   *458*
Booth, P. (Writer)
'Bert Sutcliffe's Book for Boys'
Book Review   1963   *1112*
Booth, R. (Worcestershire)
Benefit Match   1967   *625*

Photograph	1960	614
	1964	601
	1965	609
Retirement	1969	94

Booth, 2nd Lt-Major M. W. (Yorkshire; England)
Obituary	1917	167
Portrait and Biography	1914/I	237

Boothroyd, D.
'Half a Century of Yorkshire Cricket'
Book Review	1982	1255

Border, A. R. (New South Wales; Queensland; Australia)
Cricketer of the Year	1982	75
Photograph	1982	74

Bore, M. K. (Yorkshire; Nottinghamshire)
Photograph	1972	629

Borradaile, O. R. (Essex)
Obituary	1936/I	270

Borrett, R. (Cricket Writer; Norfolk)
Obituary	1948	78

Borrowes, Lt-Col. Sir K. D. Bart. (Cheltenham; Essex; Middlesex)
Obituary	1925/I	259

Borthwick, C. H. (Cambridgeshire; Norfolk; Kent)
Obituary	1979	1089

Borthwick, G. (Uppingham)
Obituary	1915/I	212

Borwick, E. G. (Umpire)
Obituary	1982	119

Bosanquet, B. J. T. (Eton; Oxford University; Middlesex; England)
'The Googly'	1925/I	22
Impressions of MCC Tour in Australia	1905	lxx
Obituary	1937/I	26
Portrait and Biography	1905	cx
Team in USA and Canada 1901	1902	52

Bosanquet, Lt-Col. B. T. (Father of 'B.J.T.')
Obituary	1911/I	13

Boscawen, Major G. E. (Woolwich; R. A.)
Obituary	1919/I	16

Boscawen, J. P. T. (Eton)
Obituary	1973	100

Boscawen, 2nd Lieut. Hon. V. D. (Eton)
Obituary	1915/I	21

Bose, M. (Cricket Writer)
'Keith Miller – A Cricketing Biography'
Book Review	1981	120

Boshier, B. S. (Leicestershire)
Photograph	1962	48

Bostock, H. (Derbyshire)

    Obituary 1955 *927*

Boswell, Capt. W. G. K. (Eton; Oxford University)

    Obituary 1917 *168*

Bosworth-Smith, B. N. (Harrow; Middlesex)

    Obituary 1948 *781*

Botejue, W. C. (Ceylon)

    Obituary 1911/I *162*

Botham, 2nd Lieut. A. F. (Merchant Taylors)

    Obituary 1918 *176*

Botham, I. T. (Somerset; England)

    Action Photographs 1979 *61,62*

    1980 *65*

    1982 *68*

    1983 *Plates*

    Cricketer of the Year 1978 *98*

    England's New Captain Note on 1981 *97*

    Fastest Test Double Note on 1980 *83*

    Like Jessop, Like Botham Note on 1982 *86*

    Notable Debut Note on 1978 *105*

    Photographs 1975 *533*

    1977 *537*

    1978 *90*

    1981 *72;73*

    'The Incredible Tests' Book Review 1982 *1266*

    'Ian Botham the Great All Rounder'

    D. Doust Book Review 1981 *1198*

    'Botham Down Under'

    Book Review 1984 *1262*

Bottings, S. (Kent)

    Obituary 1928/I *279*

Bottom, D. (Derbyshire; Nottinghamshire)

    Obituary 1938 *936*

Bottome, G. Mcd. (Tonbridge; Kent)

    Obituary 1973 *1004*

Bottomore, W. (Leicestershire)

    Obituary 1906 *lxxxviii*

Boucher, N. (Tonbridge)

    Obituary 1969 *979*

Boucher, Capt. S. (Kent)

    Obituary 1965 *972*

Boughey, J. F. (Eton)

    Obituary 1941 *386*

Boughton, W. A. (Gloucestershire)

    Obituary 1938 *948*

Boughty, Sir R. J. Bart. (Eton; Somerset)
  Obituary   1979   *1073*
Boult, Lieut. F. C. (Harrow; Oxford University)
  Obituary   1944   *304*
Boult, 2nd Lieut. R. H. S. (Liverpool C.C.)
  Obituary   1917   *168*
Boulter, Capt. H. S. (St. Albans School, Toronto)
  Obituary   1918   *176*
Boumphrey, D. (Cheshire)
  Obituary   1972   *1047*
Bouncers
  Notes on   1975   *96*
                                                1976   *62*
                                                1977   *111*
                                                1979   *79*
                                                1982   *91*
  Photographs   1979   *63*
                                                1983   *Plates*
Boundary   75 Yards Note on   1964   *93*
Boundy, G. O. (Somerset)
  Obituary   1965   *963*
Bourchier, 2nd Lieut. A. G. E. (Hertfordshire Club Cricketer)
  Obituary   1916   *148*
Bourchier, Rev. W. (Winchester)
  Obituary   1913/I   *184*
Bourdillon, Sir J. A. (Marlborough)
  Obituary   1914/I   *178*
Bourne, A. A. (Rugby; Cambridge University)
  Obituary   1932/I   *240*
Bourne, Lieut. H. H. (Ridley College, Ontario)
  Obituary   1917   *168*
Bourne, J. A. (Staffordshire)
  Obituary   1904   *lxxxiv*
Bournemouth Dean Park
  Plan of County Ground   1951   *361*
                                                ad passim
Bourns, Lieut. C. (Merchant Taylors)
  Obituary   1917   *222*
Bousfield, E. J. (Lancashire)
  Obituary   1896   *xliv*
Bousfield, R. (Durham)
  Obituary   1925/I   *260*
Bovill, B. (Harrow)
  Obituary   1946   *448*
Bovill, G. B. (Harrow)
  Obituary   1939   *907*

Bowbanks, J. S. (Ontario)
  Obituary   1927/I   *273*
Bowden, Rev. Father H. G. S. (Eton)
  Obituary   1921/I   *22*
Bowden, J. (Derbyshire)
  Obituary   1959   *927*
Bowden, M. P. (Dulwich; Surrey; Transvaal; England)
  Obituary   1893   *xxxiv*
Bowden, P. K. (Secretary, New South Wales Cricket Association)
  Obituary   1923/I   *287*
Bowden-Smith, E. (Rugby)
  Obituary   1946   *436*
Bowden-Smith, Rev. F. H. (Rugby; Oxford University)
  Obituary   1920/I   *165*
Bowden-Smith, G. (Rugby)
  Obituary   1924/I   *254*
Bowell, A. (Hampshire)
  Benefit Match   1915/II   *93*
  Obituary   1958   *956*
Bowen, E. E. (Harrow)
  Obituary   1902   *lix*
Bowen, M. (Lord's Printing Office)
  Obituary   1896   *xliv*
Bowen, R. (Writer; Researcher)
  Obituary   1979   *1073*
  'The County Championship in the
  Wisden Century'   1963   *366*
  'Cricket in the 17th and 18th Centuries'   1965   *135*
  'Dates in Cricket History'   1966   *144*
  'Dates of Formation of County Clubs
  now First Class'   1963   *370*
  'The Early County Champions'   1959   *91*
  'Notable Dates in Australian Cricket History'   1968   *144*
  'Some Dates in Indian Cricket History'   1967   *147*
  'Some Dates in Pakistan Cricket History'   1967   *157*
  'Notable Dates in South African
  Cricket History'   1970   *153*
  'Notable Dates in West Indian
  Cricket History'   1969   *151*
Bower, M. B. S. (Winchester; Dorset)
  Obituary   1976   *1093*
Bowers, Lieut. W. A. (Cricket Supporter)
  Obituary   1917   *168*
Bowes, W. E. (Yorkshire; England)
  Benefit Match   1948   *549*
  'Don't Tamper with the Laws'   1957   *78*

'Growing Pains of Cricket'	1956	*76*
'F. S. Trueman – Fiery Fred'	1970	*92*
Note on	1944	*192*
Portrait and Biography	1932/I	*274*
'Aussies and Ashes' Book Review	1962	*1038*
'Express Deliveries' Book Reviews	1950	*977*
	1955	*993*
Tributes to: J. H. Fingleton	1982	*1199*
W. R. Hammond	1966	*117*
D. R. Jardine	1959	*933*
H. Sutcliffe	1979	*98*
Bowes-Lyon. Capt. Hon. F. (Scottish Club Cricket)		
Obituary	1916	*148*
Bowie, W. (Kelburne C.C.)		
Obituary	1911/I	*139*
Bowlers 'in County Cricket 1919-1939'	1941	*68*
Bowlers of 100 wkts		
A. J. Gaston	1899	*xcvii*
Bowlers Notes on	1948	*83*
	1955	*78*
	1960	*122*
	1972	*88*
Bowles, H. (Witley C.C.)		
Obituary	1922/I	*246*
Bowles, J. J. (Gloucestershire; Worcestershire)		
Obituary	1978	*1084*
Bowley, E. H. (Sussex; Auckland; England)		
Benefit Match	1932/II	*178*
Obituary	1975	*1071*
Portrait and Biography	1930/I	*276*
Bowley, F. L (Worcestershire)		
Obituary	1944	*311*
Bowley, T. (Northants; Surrey; Dorset)		
Obituary	1940	*838*
Bowling		
'Bowling' Lohmann	1890	*xlvii*
'Bowling for Surrey and England' A.V. Bedser	1961	*142*
'Bowling Controversy, The'	1934/I	*328*
'Bowling Controversy, The Settlement of'	1935/I	*325*
'No Magic in Fast Bowling' (Kortright)	1948	*67*
Notes on	1967	*89*
	1974	*70*
	1984	*50*
Bowring, C. W. (Marlborough; American Club Cricket)		
Obituary	1941	*393*

Bowring, Major F. H. (Shrewsbury)
Obituary | 1919 | 167
Bowring, T. (Rugby; Oxford University)
Obituary | 1909/I | 133
Bowser, Pte. W. J. (Canadian Club Cricket)
Obituary | 1916 | 148
Bowyer, Capt. J. W. (Rugby)
Obituary | 1918 | 176
Box, F. M. (Christ's College, Finchley)
82 wkts Schools Averages | 1896 | 344
Boxall, J. (Mitcham C.C.)
Obituary | 1931/I | 250
Boxshall, C. (Canterbury, New Zealand)
Obituary | 1926/I | 287
Boyce, Pte. H. B. H. (Pickwick C.C., Barbados)
Obituary | 1918 | 176
Boyce, K. D. (Essex; Barbados; West Indies)
Cricketer of the Year | 1974 | 57
Photographs | 1968 | 380
| 1973 | 373
| 1974 | 53

Boycott, G. (Yorkshire; Northern Transvaal; England)
Action Photographs | 1974 | 49
| 1978 | 141
'Geoffrey Boycott' T. Brindle | 1978 | 140
Career Figures' | 1978 | 144
Cricketer of the Year | 1965 | 85
Hundredth Hundred | 1978 | 338
Photographs | 1964 | 619
| 1965 | 76
| 1976 | 620
| 1978 | 142
| 1980 | 621
Notes on | 1975 | 95
| 1976 | 1133
| 1978 | 105
'Boycott a Cricketing Legend'
J. Callaghan Book Review | 1983 | 1308
'The Geoffrey Boycott File'
S. Sheen Book Review | 1983 | 1308
'In the Fast Lane' Book Review | 1982 | 1266
'Opening Up' Book Review | 1981 | 1198
'Put to the Test' Book Review | 1980 | 1208
| 1981 | 1196
Boycott, Lieut. H. C. (Northamptonshire)
Obituary | 1919 | 167

69

Boyd, A. N. A. (Eton)
  Obituary 1941 *386*
Boyd, J. D. (New Jersey Athletic Club)
  Obituary 1906 *lxxxvii*
Boyd, Lieut. R. C. (Devon Dumplings C.C.)
  Obituary 1917 *168*
Boyes, G. S. (Hampshire)
  Benefit Match 1937/II *299*
  Obituary 1975 *107*
Boyington, F. (Scorer Surrey)
  Obituary 1928/I *279*
Boyle, Sir C. E. (Charterhouse; Oxford University)
  Obituary 1902 *lviii*
Boyle, Capt. C. W. (Clifton; Oxford University)
  Obituary 1901 *lii*
Boyle, H. F. (Victoria; Australia)
  Obituary 1908/I *135*
Boyson, Sir J. A. (Harrow)
  Obituary 1927/I *273*
Boyton, H. (Essex)
  Obituary 1910/I *133*
Boyton, 2nd Lieut. V. H. T. (King Edward's, Birmingham)
  Obituary 1918 *176*
Brabazon, Lieut. T. A. C. (King's, Rochester)
  Obituary 1917 *168*
Brabourne, C. M. Lord (Eton; Cambridge University)
  Obituary 1935/I *276*
Bracey, F. R. (Derbyshire)
  Obituary 1961 *944*
Bracher, Major F. V. (Secretary Glamorgan Wanderers C.C.)
  Obituary 1919 *167*
Bracher, 2nd Lieut. G. (Mote C.C.)
  Obituary 1917 *168*
Bradbeer, A. N. (Hertfordshire)
  Obituary 1959 *927*
Bradbury, 2nd Lieut. D. J. F. (Moravian School, Leeds)
  Obituary 1917 *168*
Bradby, Capt. D. E. (Rugby)
  Obituary 1918 *176*
Bradby, E. H. N. (Rugby)
  Obituary 1948 *781*
Bradby, H. C. (Rugby; Oxfordshire)
  Obituary 1949 *872*
Bradfield, A. (Essex)
  Obituary 1980 *1159*

Bradfield, D. (Wiltshire)
Obituary   1973   *1004*
Bradford, Lieut. A. R. (Bedford Grammar School)
Obituary   1917   *169*
Bradford, Sir E. R. 2nd Bart. (Hampshire)
Obituary   1915/I   *213*
Bradford League XI 1941
Team Portrait   1942   *30*
Views on Laws   1957   *86*
Bradford, Lt-Col. O. J. (Marlborough)
Obituary   1925/I   *260*
Bradford Park Avenue
Plan of County Ground   1951   *588*
    ad passim
Bradford, 2nd Lieut. P. (St Bees School)
Obituary   1918   *176*
Bradford, Brig-Gen. R. B. (Military Cricket)
Obituary   1918   *176*
Bradley, W. M. (Alleyn's; Kent; England)
Obituary   1945   *327*
Bradman, Sir D. G. (New South Wales; South Australia; Australia)
'Cricket at the Crossroads'   1939   *42*
'Views on the Growing Pains of Cricket'   1956   *82*
'Australian Survey – Bradman, Past, Present
and Future' A. G. Moyes   1945   *50*
'Bradman 1927-37' H. V. Evatt   1938   *57*
'Giant of the Wisden Century' N. Cardus   1963   *110*
'Sir Donald Bradman' R.C. Robertson-Glasgow   1949   *77*
'Sir Donald Bradman' Selector I. Rosenwater
    1972   *108*
'Bradman the Great' J. B. Wakely
Book Review   1960   *1002*
'Bradman, Benaud and Goddard's Cinderellas'
R. S. Whitington Book Review   1965   *1018*
'Brightly Fades the Don'
J. Fingleton Book Review   1950   *975*
'Don Bradman' P. Lindsey Book Review   1952   *1018*
'Sir Donald Bradman' A. Davies Book Review   1961   *998*
'Sir Donald Bradman A Biography'
I Rosenwater Book Review   1979   *1127*
'Bradman – The Illustrated Biography'
M. Page Book Review   1984   *1264*
'Farewell to Cricket' Book Review   1951   *994*
Fastest Hundred in Test Cricket
Note on   1983   *108*
1000 runs in May Note on   1974   *88*

Honour for Bradman		1949	87
Hundredth Hundred		1949	769
L.B.W. Law Change: Plea for		1954	84
Note on		1949	117
Photographs		1938	59
		1939	42
		1949	65,68,76
		1963	112
Portrait and Biography		1931/I	283
Records by		1941	62
Testimonial Matches		1939	810
		1950	843
Tributes or Appreciations:			
	A. T. W. Grout	1969	981
	W. R. Hammond	1966	118
	H. Sutcliffe	1979	98
	H. Verity	1944	50
	W. M. Woodfull	1966	975
	Sir F. Worrell	1968	122

Bradshaw, 2nd Lieut. H. J. (Bradfield)

Obituary		1918	176

Bradshaw, J. G. (Clifton)

Obituary		1932/I	240

Braimbridge, C. V. (Kenya)

Obituary		1965	963

Brain, B. M. (Worcestershire; Gloucestershire)

'Another Day, Another Match' Book Review		1982	1267
Photographs		1974	583
		1976	408

Brain, J. H. (Clifton; Oxford University; Gloucestershire; Glamorgan)

Obituary		1915/I	213
Views on Second Class Counties and L.B.W. Rule		1903	lxiv

Brin, J. H. (Tasmania)

Obituary		1962	984

Brain, Lieut. J. A. L. (Albion C.C. of British Columbia)

Obituary		1918	176

Brain, M. B. (Repton; Glamorgan)

Obituary		1972	1047

Brain, W. H. (Clifton; Oxford University; Gloucestershire)

'Hat Trick of Stumpings'		1894	163
Obituary		1935/I	260

Braithwaite, P. P. (Felsted)

Obituary		1919	167

Bramall, E. N. W. (Eton)

Obituary		1943	27

Bramall Lane Ground Sheffield
   'Farewell Bramall Lane'
   K. Farnsworth   1974   *135*
   Plan of Ground   1950   *573*
    ad passim
   Photograph of Ground   1974   *136*
Brampton, C. (Nottinghamshire)
   Obituary   1896   *xli*
Branch, F/O. G. R. (Eton)
   Obituary   1942   *351*
Brand, C. (Perthshire)
   Obituary   1903   *lxxv*
Brand, Rt. Hon. H. R. (Rugby; Sussex)
   Obituary   1907   *cvii*
Brann, G. (Sussex)
   Obituary   1955   *927*
Brann, W. H. (Eastern Province; South Africa)
   Obituary   1954   *921*
Brandt, Lieut. D. R. (Harrow; Oxford University)
   Obituary   1916   *148*
Brandt, F. (Cheltenham; Oxford University)
   Obituary   1926/I   *264*
Branston, G. T. (Oxford University; Nottinghamshire)
   Obituary   1970   *1017*
Brassey, Lt-Col. H. E. (Military Cricket)
   Obituary   1917   *169*
Brassington, A. J. (Gloucestershire)
   Holts Product Award   1981   *430*
   Photograph   1979   *390*
Braund, L. C. (London County; Somerset; Surrey; England)
   Benefit March   1909/II   *285*
   Obituary   1956   *968*
   Portrait and Biography   1902   *lxxxii*
   Testimonial Fund   1944   *178*
Bray, C. (Writer; Researcher)
   'Counties Reject the Clark Plan'   1967   *96*
   'Essex 1876-1960'   1960   *128*
   'Essex' Book Review   1951   *990*
   'The Story of New Zealand Cricket'   1958   *98*
Bray, Sir E. (Westminster; Cambridge University; Surrey)
   Obituary   1927/I   *273*
Bray, Sir E. H. (Cambridge University; Middlesex)
   Obituary   1951   *918*
Braybrooke, 6th Lord (Eton)
   Obituary   1905   *c*

Braybrooke, H. M. (Wellington; Cambridge University; Kent)

Obituary	1936/I	*270*
Brazil in Argentina 1967	1969	*928*

Breakwell, D. (Northamptonshire; Somerset)

Photographs	1970	*497*
	1977	*537*

Brearley, J. M. (City of London; Cambridge University; Middlesex; England)

'J. M. Brearley – Success through Perceptiveness'		
J. Arlott	1983	*87*
'John Murray M.B.E. Champion Keeper'	1976	*120*
'Some thoughts on Modern Captaincy'	1982	*109*
Career Figures	1983	*92*
Cricketer of the Year	1977	*102*
Notes on	1978	*103*
	1979	*77*
	1980	*83*
	1983	*82*
Photographs	1974	*482*
	1976	*490*
	1977	*90*
	1982	*110*
	1983	*86*
Schools Notes	1960	*745*
	1961	*743*
1015 runs Schools Averages	1960	*758*
Tribute to J. M. Sims	1974	*1080*
'The Return of the Ashes' Book Review	1979	*1130*
with D. Doust 'The Ashes Retained'		
Book Review	1980	*1214*
'Phoenix from the Ashes' Book Review	1983	*1297*

Brearley, W. (Lancashire; England)

Obituary	1938	*936*
Portrait and Biography	1909/I	*161*

Breed, G. (York C.C.)

Obituary	1918	*223*

Breed, G. W. (Durham C.C.)

Obituary	1916	*149*

Breeden, F. (Warwickshire)

Obituary	1941	*393*

Brentnall, A. C. (Vice President Derbyshire)

Obituary	1910/I	*133*

Brentwood County Ground

Note on	1969	*146*
Plan of Ground	1969	*367*

Brereton, H. E. (Victoria)

Obituary	1953	*951*

74

Breton, Major W. G. W. (Longton C.C.)
Obituary 1918 *176*
Brett, P. J. (Winchester; Oxford University)
Obituary **1983** *1241*
Brett, S. (Metropolitan Police)
Obituary 1917 *169*
Brettall, H. C. (Dudley C.C.)
Obituary 1916 *149*
Brewer, W. J. (Leyton Groundsman)
Obituary 1929/I *242*
Brewster, F. E. (Philadelphia)
Obituary 1940 *838*
Brewster, W. (Staten Island C.C.)
Obituary 1904 *lxxxii*
Briad, Lieut. E. F. V. (Felsted; Army)
Obituary 1917 *222*
Brice (Later Bruce) Col. E. A. (Cheltenham; Gloucestershire)
Obituary 1919 *203*
Brice, W. S. (New Zealand Club Cricket)
Obituary 1960 *949*
Brice-Smith, 2nd Lieut. J. K. (Cranleigh School)
Obituary 1916 *149*
Bricknell, G. A. (Western Province)
Obituary 1978 *1068*
Bridge, W. B. (Warwickshire)
Photograph 1962 *622*
Bridgeman, C. G. O. (Harrow)
Obituary 1936/I *292*
Bridgeman, Hon. Sir M. K. B. E. (Eton)
Obituary 1981 *1138*
Bridgeman, Viscount (Eton; Cambridge University; Staffordshire)
Obituary 1936/I *271*
Bridges, J. H. (Winchester; Surrey)
Obituary 1926/I *265*
Bridges, J. J. (Somerset)
Obituary 1967 *963*
Bridgman, H. H. M. (South Australia)
Obituary 1954 *922*
Brierley, E. (Rugby)
Obituary 1928/I *279*
Brierley, J. A. (Cricket Writer)
Obituary 1952 *955*
Briers, N. E. (Leicestershire)
Photograph 1979 *452*
Briggs, James (Father of J. Briggs)
Obituary 1900 *1*

Briggs, John (Lancashire; England)
Benefit match	1895	*84*
Bowling Record	1944	*50*
In the Cricket Field	1898	*lxxxix*
Obituary	1903	*lxx*
Portrait and Biography	1889	*xxx*
Views on 'The Follow On'	1894	*lii*

Briggs, Joseph (Nottinghamshire)
Obituary	1904	*lxxxvii*

Briggs, Canon R. (Winchester; Oxford University)
Obituary	1937/I	*269*

Bright, G. (Winchester)
Obituary	1918	*177*

Bright, Sir R. O. (Winchester)
Obituary	1897	*xlii*

Brinklow, P. F. (Cricket Journalist)
Obituary	1968	*998*

Brinkman, Sir T. E. W. (Eton Ramblers C.C.)
Obituary	1955	*927*
Team in Argentina 1937-38	1939	*819*

Brind, H. (Essex Groundsman)
Note on	1969	*96*

Brindle, T. (Cricket Writer)
'Geoffrey Boycott'	1978	*140*

Brindley, W. T. (Buckinghamshire; Ceylon)
Obituary	1959	*927*

Brinton, R. L. (Shrewsbury; Worcestershire)
Obituary	1981	*1138*

Brinton, R. S. (Worcestershire)
Obituary	1943	*372*

Briscoe, Capt. A. W. (Transvaal; South Africa)
Obituary	1942	*347*

Brisley, Major C. E. (Lancing)
Obituary	1919	*167*

Brissenden, S. (Transvaal)
Obituary	1962	*994*

Bristol Development of Ground
	1976	*1132*
Plan of County Ground	1950	*340*
	ad passim	

Bristow, M. (Mote C.C.; Kent Groundsman)
Groundsman's Award	1973	*296*

Bristow, M. G. (Ottawa C.C.)
Obituary	1921/I	*243*

Bristowe, O. C. (Oxford University; Essex)
Obituary	1939	*907*

British Empire XI

1940 Team Portrait	1941	*26*
1941 Team Portrait	1942	*27*
1943 Team Portrait	1944	*36*

British Public Schools Team in Canada

and U.S.A. 1939	1940	*610*

Brittain-Jones, Capt. J. (Indian Team Manager; Free Foresters)

Obituary	1976	*1093*

Britten-Holmes, E. (Oxford University Authentics)

Obituary	1916	*149*

Brittenden, R. T. (Cricket Journalist; Writer)

With R. J. Hadlee 'Hadlee' Book Review	1982	*1268*
'Red Leather and Silver Fern' Book Review	1966	*1014*
'Scoreboard 69' Book Review	1971	*1081*
'Silver Fern on the Veld' Book Review	1956	*1022*

Britton, C. H. (Warwickshire)

Obituary	1944	*187*

Britton, G. (Yorkshire)

Obituary	1911/I	*139*

Broad, Lieut. A. E. (Uppingham)

Obituary	1917	*169*

Broad, B. C. (Gloucestershire; Nottinghamshire; England)

Photograph	1981	*415*

Broadbent, R. G. (Caterham School; Worcestershire)

Schools Note	1942	*245,266*
	1943	*270,290*
80 wkts Schools Averages	1942	*295*
87 wkts Schools Averages	1943	*319*

Brockie, W. (Gentlemen of Philadelphia; U.S.A.)

Obituary	1911/I	*162*

Brocklebank, Sir J. M. Bart. (Cambridge University; Lancashire)

Obituary	1975	*1074*

Brocklebank, Sir T. A. L. Bart. (Eton)

Obituary	1954	*922*

Brocklehurst, E. T. (Buckinghamshire)

Obituary	1961	*944*

Brockwell, W. (Kimberley; Surrey; England)
'William Brockwell: His Triumph and Tragedy'

J. D. Coldham Book Review	1971	*1077*
Benefit Match	1901	*173*
Obituary	1936/I	*271*
Portrait and Biography	1895	*xlvii*

Brodhurst, Major B. M. L. (Clifton; Sandhurst)

Obituary	1916	*149*

Brodie, J. C. (Victoria)

Obituary	1913/I	*184*

Brodribb, G. (Writer)

'Fastest Hundreds in Test Cricket'		1983	*106*
'The Croucher' (G. L. Jessop)	Book Review	1975	*1120*
'Felix on the Bat'	Book Review	1963	*1102*
'Maurice Tate'	Book Review	1977	*1100*

Brogden, C. (Norfolk)

Obituary	1973	*1004*

Brogden, E. C. (Writer)
with J. Arlott 'The First Test Match'

(England v Australia) Book Review	1951	*989*

Bromhead, G. (Philadelphia)

Obituary	1922/I	*246*

Bromley, A. D. (Colston's School, Bristol)

Schools Notes	1976	*867*
	1977	*812*
75 wkts Schools Averages	1976	*878*
76 wkts Schools Averages	1977	*828*

Bromley, H. T. (Slough)

Obituary	1955	*927*

Bromley-Davenport, H. R. (Eton; Cambridge University; Middlesex; Cheshire; England)

Obituary	1955	*927*
Schools Notes	1888	*274*
	1889	*268*
	1890	*229*

Bromley-Davenport, Sir W. (Eton)

Obituary	1950	*904*

Bromley-Martin, E. G. (Eton; Worcestershire)

Obituary	1947	*687*

Bromley-Martin, G. E. (Eton; Oxford University; Worcestershire)

Obituary	1942	*355*

Brook, G. W. (Worcestershire)

Obituary	1967	*963*

Brooke, Lt-Col. F. R. R. (Lancashire)

Obituary	1961	*944*

Brooke, R. (Historian; Statistican)
'Warwickshire County Cricketers 1843-1973'

Book Review	1974	*1118*
Warwickshire Cricket Record Book		
Book Review	1983	*1302*

Brooke, Sub-Lt. R. C. (Rugby)

Obituary	1916	*149*

Brooke, Rev. R. H. J. (Oxford University; Buckinghamshire)

Obituary	1974	*1071*

Brooke-Smith, Pte. E. C. (Cowichan C.C.)

Obituary	1918	*211*

Brooke-Taylor, G. P. (Cheltenham; Cambridge University; Derbyshire)

Obituary	1969	*979*

Brookman, S. G. (Bristol Wayfarers C.C.)

Obituary	1956	*969*

Brookes, D. (Northamptonshire; England)

Benefit Match	1959	*486*
Cricketer of the Year	1957	*63*
Photographs	1953	*471*
	1956	*485*
	1957	*54*
Retirement	1960	*141*

Brookes, P. W. (Lord's Ground Staff)

Obituary	1947	*687*

Brookes, W. H. (Editor of Wisden 1936-1939)

Obituary	1956	*969*

Brookes, E. W. J. (Surrey)

Benefit Match	1939	*513*
Obituary	1961	*944*

Brooks, H. (Durham)

Obituary	1968	*998*

Brooks, R. (Cranleigh School; Surrey; London County)

Obituary	1928/I	*279*

Brothers, Twins 20 wickets

Schools Notes	1953	*717*

Brough, Rev. Major J. S. B. (Fettes)

Obituary	1919	*167*

Brougham, H. (Wellington, Oxford University; Berkshire)

Obituary	1924/I	*254*

Broughton, E. A. (Leicestershire)

Obituary	1983	*1241*

Broughton, Capt. Dr. N. W. (Sydney University)

Obituary	1917	*169*

Broughton, R. J. P. (Harrow; Cambridge University)

Obituary	1912/I	*163*

Broughton-Adderley, Capt. P. H. (Eton)

Obituary	1919	*167*

Brown, A. (Malton C.C.)

Obituary	1901	*lii*

Brown, A. (Kent; England)

Benefit Match	1972	*459*
Photograph	1961	*428*

Brown, A. S. (Gloucestershire)

Benefit-Note on	1977	*1117*
Benefit Match	1970	*416*

Photographs	1963	*428*
	1970	*405*
	1974	*409*
Brown, C. E. (Somerset)		
Obituary	1937/I	*269*
Brown, 2nd Lieut. C. W. (Merchiston Castle; Gala C.C.)		
Obituary	1918	*177*
Brown, D. C. (Harrow; Wiltshire)		
Obituary	1920/I	*152*
Brown, D. J. (Warwickshire; England)		
Benefit Match	1974	*577*
Photographs	1966	*58*
	1967	*599*
Brown, 2nd Lieut. F. H. (Felsted)		
Obituary	1918	*177*
Brown, F. R. (Leys; Surrey; Northamptonshire; England)		
'F. R. Brown – Leader of Men'		
V. J. G. Jenkins	1952	*100*
'Batsmen must be bold'	1954	*87*
'M.C.C. President – Note on'	1972	*88*
Photographs	1950	*443*
	1951	*453*
	1952	*102*
Portrait and Biography	1933/I	*266*
Retirement	1954	*86*
Schools Notes	1929/I	*291*
	1930/I	*298*
'Cricket Crusader' Book Review	1955	*994*
Brown, F. S. (Wigan C.C.)		
Obituary	1916	*149*
Brown, G. (Hampshire; England)		
Benefit Match	1929/II	*350*
Obituary	1965	*963*
Brown, H. A. (Nottinghamshire)		
Obituary	1975	*1075*
Brown, H. W. (Alameda C.C., America)		
Obituary	1914/I	*178*
Brown, J. (Staffordshire)		
Obituary	1911/I	*139*
Brown, J. (Sussex)		
Obituary	1917	*240*
Brown, J. A. T. (Scottish Cricket Union)		
Obituary	1978	*1068*
Brown, J. H. (Liverpool and District)		
Obituary	1916	*150*

Brown, J. T. (Yorkshire; England)

Benefit Match	1902	*21*
Fastest Hundred in Test Cricket Note on	1983	*106*
Obituary	1905	*lxxxv*
Obituary Correction	1906	*civ*
Portrait and Biography	1895	*xlviii*

Brown, J. J. (Yorkshire)

Obituary	1951	*918*

Brown, K. E. (Harrow)

Obituary	1920/I	*152*

Brown, L. H. (Writer)
'Victor Trumper and the 1902 Australians'

Book Review	1982	*1270*

Brown, L. S. (Transvaal; North–Eastern Transvaal; Rhodesia; South Africa)

Obituary	1984	*1197*

Brown, Capt. R. A. (St Andrew's College, Toronto)

Obituary	1919	*197*

Brown, R. G. (Peru)

Obituary	1948	*781*

Brown, Pte. R. R. (Point Grey C.C. of British Columbia)

Obituary	1918	*211*

Brown, S. M. (Middlesex)

Benefit match	1954	*463*
Photograph	1953	*452*

Brown, S. Van. N. (Western Province)

Obituary	1940	*838*

Brown, T. A. (Northamptonshire; Bedfordshire)

Obituary	1931/I	*250*

Brown, W. (Bedfordshire)

Obituary	1941	*393*

Brown, W. (Cricket Coach; Umpire)

Obituary	1970	*1017*

Brown, W. A. (New South Wales; Queensland; Australia)

Portrait and Biography	1939	*35*
Records by	1941	*62*

Brown, W. C. (Northamptonshire)

Tribute to A. H. Bakewell	1984	*1195*

Brown, W. D. G. (Gentlemen of Nottinghamshire)

Obituary	1925/I	*288*

Brown, 2nd Lieut. W. R. (Giggleswick Grammar School)

Obituary	1918	*177*

Brown, Capt. W. S. (Grange C.C.)

Obituary	1919	*167*

Brown, W. S. A. (Leys School; Gloucestershire)

Obituary	1953	*938*
80 wkts Schools Averages	1895	*328*

1032 runs Schools Averages   1897   *365*
Browne, C. R. (Barbados; British Guiana; West Indies)
Obituary   1965   *964*
Browne, C. R. (Sussex; Northamptonshire)
Obituary   1949   *862*
Browne, E. (Secretary Nottinghamshire)
Obituary   1905   *lxxxviii*
Browne, Rev. E. K. (Rugby; Hampshire; Gloucestershire)
Obituary   1916   *150*
Browne, Canon F. B. R. (Cambridge University; Sussex)
Obituary   1971   *1023*
Browne, F. D. (Dulwich; Kent)
Obituary   1947   *687*
Browne, Capt. H. V. (Wellington)
Obituary   1916   *150*
Browne, R. (Cartoonist)
Obituary   1970   *1018*
Browne, Major R. G. (Radley)
Obituary   1919   *167*
Browning, C. H. (Eton)
Obituary   1915/I   *214*
Browning, F. H. (Marlborough; Ireland)
Obituary   1917   *240*
Browning, Lt-Col. F. H. (Wellington)
Obituary   1930/I   *246*
Brownlee, L. D. (Oxford University; Gloucestershire)
Obituary   1956   *970*
Brownlee, W. M. (Biographer of W. G. Grace)
Obituary   1904   *lxxxiii*
Brownlee, W. M. (Clifton; Gloucestershire)
Obituary   1915/I   *214*
Brownlow, Brig-Gen. D. C. (Chairman Sussex)
Obituary   1939   *907*
Brownlow, Lt-Col. Hon. J. R. (Eton)
Obituary   1933/I   *241*
Brownrigg, Major J. H. T. (Oxfordshire)
Obituary   1945   *319*
Bruce, (Formerly Brice) Col. E. A. (Cheltenham; Gloucestershire)
Obituary   1919   *203*
Bruce, Hon. F. J. (Eton)
Obituary   1921/I   *224*
Bruce, Capt. G. J. (Winchester)
Obituary   1919   *167*
Bruce, W. (Victoria; Australia)
Obituary   1926/I   *265*

Bruce-Jones, Capt. (Charterhouse; Stirlingshire)
    Obituary   1945   *319*

Brumo, H. A. (New Jersey C.C.)
    Obituary   1916   *150*

Bruton, C. L. (Radley; Gloucestershire)
    Obituary   1970   *1018*

Brutton, C. P. (Winchester; Hampshire)
    Obituary   1965   *964*

Brutton, Rev. E. B. (Northumberland; Devon)
    Obituary   1923/I   *287*

Brutton, S. (Northumberland; Hampshire)
    Obituary   1935/I   *276*

Bryan, J. L. (Rugby; Cambridge University; Kent)
    Portrait and Biography   1922/I   *277*

Bryan, R. T. (Rugby; Kent)
    Obituary   1971   *1024*

Bryan-Brown, Rev. D. S. (Eastbourne College)
    Obituary   1961   *944*

Bryan-Brown, Rev. G. S. S. (Tonbridge)
    Obituary   1918   *177*

Bryans, 2nd Lieut. J. A. (Elstow School)
    Obituary   1918   *177*

Bryce-Smith, 2nd Lieut. N. (Cheltenham)
    Obituary   1919   *168*

Buccaneers   in 1944   1945   *232*
             in 1945   1946   *284*

Buccleuch, 6th Duke of (President M.C.C.)
    Obituary   1915/I   *215*

Buchan, C. M. (Durham)
    Obituary   1961   *944*

Buchanan, D. (Rugby; Cambridge University)
    Obituary   1901   *liii*
    'Views on High Scoring and L.B.W. Rule   1899   *lxxv*

Buchanan, J. H. (Charterhouse; Cambridge University; Buckinghamshire)
    Obituary   1970   *1018*

Buchanan, T. G. (Marlborough)
    Obituary   1928/I   *280*

Buck, Capt. G. S. (Winchester)
    Obituary   1919   *168*

Buckenham, C. P. (Alleyns; Essex; England)
    Obituary   1938   *936*

Buckingham, Lieut. P. E. (Churcher's College, Petersfield)
    Obituary   1919   *168*

Buckingham, W. (Harrow)
    Obituary   1897   *xxxix*

Buckland, A. V. (Marlborough)
Obituary   1920/I   *165*

Buckland, E. H. (Marlborough; Oxford University; Middlesex; Hampshire)
Obituary   1907   *cvii*

Buckland, F. M. (Eton; Oxford University)
Obituary   1914/I   *178*

Buckle, F. (New South Wales)
Obituary   1984   *1197*

Buckle, Rev M. B. (Bromsgrove Grammar)
Obituary   1916   *150*

Buckley, C. F. S. (Berkshire)
Obituary   1975   *1075*

Buckley, Capt. E. (Worksop College)
Obituary   1918   *177*

Buckley, Capt. E. C. G. (Liverpool C.C.)
Obituary   1917   *169*

Buckley, G. A. (Cheshire; Derbyshire)
Obituary   1936/I   *272*

Buckley, G. B. (Cricket Historian)
Obituary   1963   *1032*

Buckley, Capt. H. P. S. (St Bees School)
Obituary   1918   *177*

Buckley, Lieut. R. (Wanderers C.C. of Alberta)
Obituary   1918   *177*

Buckley-Johnson, Brig-Gen. C. B. (Military Cricket)
Obituary   1918   *177*

Bucknill, S. P. B. (Rugby; Warwickshire)
Obituary   1931/I   *250*

Bucknill, Sir T. T. (Supporter)
Obituary   1916   *151*

Buckston, Capt. G. M. (Eton; Cambridge University; Derbyshire)
Obituary   1943   *372*

Buckston, R. H. R. (Derbyshire)
Obituary   1968   *998*

Budd, Sir C. L. (Winchester)
Obituary   1946   *436*

Budd, E. H. (Middlesex)
Obituary   1876   *94*

Budd, H. H. (Secretary East Melbourne C.C.)
Obituary   1906   *lxxxviii*

Budge, Lt-Col. H. L. (Free Foresters)
Obituary   1917   *169*

Budge, Lieut. P. P. (Weymouth College)
Obituary   1919   *168*

Bull, Amy (Roedean School; Chairwoman Women's Cricket Association)
Obituary   1983   *1241*

Bull, A. S. (London Club Cricket)
  Obituary   1952   *955*
Bull, C. H. (Worcestershire)
  Obituary   1948   *788*
Bull, F. G. (Essex)
  Obituary   1911/I *139*
  Portrait and Biography 1898   *lv*
Bull, G. (Australian Journalist)
  Obituary   1917   *241*
Bull, G. (Northamptonshire)
  Obituary   1894   *xxxv*
Bull, H. E. (Westminster; Oxford University; Buckinghamshire; Oxfordshire)
  Obituary   1906   *lxxxviii*
Bull, H. E. (Buckinghamshire)
  Obituary   1923/I *288*
Bull, Major R. H. (Harrow)
  Obituary   1945   *319*
Bullen, Capt. R. E. (Leys School)
  Obituary   1917   *169*
Buller, C. F. (Harrow; Middlesex)
  Obituary   1907   *cviii*
Buller, L. M. (Eton House Matches)
  Obituary   1920/I *152*
Buller, J. S. (Yorkshire; Worcestershire; Umpire)
  Action Photograph   1966   *57*
  'Syd Buller' F. S. Lee Obituary 1971   *118*
  Photographs   1961   *116*
             1971   *119*
Buller-Leybourne-Popham, Capt. E. T. (Harrow; Devon)
  Obituary   1974   *1071*
Bullimer, L. (Scorer Northamptonshire)
  Obituary   1955   *928*
Bullock, B. W. (Surrey)
  Obituary   1956   *977*
Bullock, J. H. (Harrow)
  Obituary   1936/I *272*
Bullock, T. L. (Winchester)
  Obituary   1916   *151*
Bullock-Hall, H. W. (Rugby; Oxford University)
  Obituary   1905   *lxxxviii*
Bulmer, T. A. (Durham)
  Note on   1945   *82*
  Obituary   1947   *687*
Bulpett, C. W. L. (Rugby; Middlesex)
  Obituary   1940   *838*

Bumpers 'Effects of the Bumper

Has it ruined Batsmanship' R. Benaud 1978 *148*

Note on 1952 *98*

Bunbury, Lieut. H. St.P. (Eastbourne College)

Obituary 1918 *177*

Bunting, W. L. (Bromsgrove Grammar)

Obituary 1948 *781*

Bunyan, M. J. (Cricket Coach)

Obituary 1938 *937*

Burbidge, F. (Surrey)

Obituary 1893 *xxxvi*

Burbidge, 2nd Lieut. H. C. (Brough C.C.)

Obituary 1917 *170*

Burbidge, H. F. (Framlingham College)

82 wkts Schools Averages 1924/II *562*

Burbidge, T. (Surrey)

Obituary 1897 *xli*

Burbury, Lt-Col. F. W. (Shrewsbury)

Obituary 1920/I *165*

Burden, FL/Lt. C. E. (Upper Canada College)

Obituary 1919 *168*

Burdett, J. W. (Leicestershire)

Obituary 1975 *1075*

Burdett, T. (President Leicestershire)

Obituary 1926/I *266*

Burdon, Capt. R. (Eton)

Obituary 1918 *178*

Burge, G. R. (Marlborough; Middlesex; Hertfordshire; Bedfordshire)

Obituary 1934/I *260*

Burge, Rt. Rev. H. M. (Bedford Grammar School; Bedfordshire)

Obituary 1926/I *266*

Burge, P. J. P. (Queensland; Australia)

Cricketer of the Year 1965 *88*

Photograph 1965 *78*

Retirement 1968 *94*

Burge, T. J. (Australian Board of Control)

Obituary 1958 *956*

Burgess, G. F. (Hertfordshire)

Obituary 1933/I *262*

Burgess, G. I. (Somerset)

Photograph 1970 *527*

Testimonial Match 1978 *764*

Burgess, T. (Yorkshire)

Obituary 1923/I *288*

Burgoyne, T. (M.C.C.)

Obituary 1880 *108*

Burgoyne-Johnson, Capt. L. V. (Durham)
Obituary	1916	*151*

Burke, D. (Tasmania)
Obituary	1928/I	*280*

Burke, J. (New South Wales; Australia)
Cricketer of the Year	1957	*59*
Obituary	1980	*1147*
Photograph	1957	*52*

Burke, Major M. A. T. (St.Paul's)
Obituary	1944	*304*

Burlton, Lt-Col. A. T. (Worcestershire; Devon)
Obituary	1981	*1138*

Burls, C. W. (Surrey)
Obituary	1925/I	*288*

Burn, A. (Durham)
Obituary	1938	*937*

Burn, E. (Writer)
'Bermuda Cricketers in England 1962'
Book Review	1963	*1113*

Burn, E. H. M. (Canada)
Obituary	1970	*1018*

Burn, Capt. H. H. (Winchester)
Obituary	1917	*170*

Burn, K. E. (Tasmania; Australia)
Obituary	1957	*942*

Burn, Sir R. C. W. (Winchester, Oxford University)
Obituary	1956	*970*

Burnett, E. W. (Harrow)
Obituary	1933/I	*262*

Burnett, H. J. B. (Trinidad)
Obituary	1983	*1241*

Burnham, J. W. (Suffolk; Derbyshire)
Obituary	1915/I	*215*

Burns, J. (Essex)
Obituary	1958	*956*

Burns, J. N. (Staffordshire)
Obituary	1918	*223*

Burns, 2nd Lieut. W. B. (King's School, Ely; Staffordshire; Worcestershire)
Obituary	1917	*170*

Burnsfield, D. (Uddingston C.C.)
Obituary	1919	*203*

Burnup, C. J. (Malvern; Cambridge University; Kent)
Obituary	1961	*944*
Portrait and Biography	1903	lxxxv

Burr, Lieut. F. B. (Denstone)
Obituary	1918	*212*

Burra, Rev. T. F. (Tonbridge; Oxford University)
Obituary 1917 *241*
Burrell, Rev. H. J. E. (Essex; Norfolk; Cheshire; Oxford University; Hampshire)
Obituary 1950 *904*
Burrough, G. B. (Somerset)
Obituary 1966 *962*
Burrough, Rev. J. (Shrewsbury; Cambridge University)
Obituary 1923/I *288*
Burrough, Rev. J. W. (Gloucestershire)
Obituary 1970 *1018*
Burrow, Rev. J. A. (Shrewsbury)
Obituary 1920/I *165*
Burrows, Pte. A. (Lynn Valley C.C., Vancouver)
Obituary 1918 *178*
Burrows, A. (Winchester)
Obituary 1909/I *133*
Burrows, C. (Needham Y.M.C.; Massachusetts)
Obituary 1920/I *152*
Burrows, J. F. (Upper Canada College)
Obituary 1920/I *152*
Burrows, J. R. (Derbyshire)
Obituary 1955 *928*
Burrows, Lieut. L. R. (Charterhouse)
Obituary 1916 *151*
Burrows, Lieut-Gen. M. B. (Surrey; Oxfordshire)
Obituary 1968 *998*
Burrows, R. D. (Worcestershire)
Obituary 1944 *312*
Burrows, S. I. (Writer)
with Carneigie, J. A. 'George Headley'
Book Review 1972 *1100*
Burrows, T. E. (Chairman Lancashire)
Obituary 1979 *1073*
Burrup, J. (Secretary Surrey)
Obituary 1901 *liii*
Burrup, W. (Secretary Surrey)
Obituary 1902 *lix*
Burt, A. F. (Club Cricket Conference)
Obituary 1947 *688*
Burt, Lieut. O. L. (Felsted)
Obituary 1918 *178*
Burt, Lieut. W. J. (Felsted)
Obituary 1917 *171*
Burt-Marshall, Capt. W. M. (Rugby)
Obituary 1916 *151*

Burton, D. C. F. (Rugby; Yorkshire)		
Obituary	1972	*1047*
Burtob, G. (Middlesex)		
Benefit Matches	1893	*98*
	1906	*259*
Obituary	1931/I	*250*
Burton, G. H. (Colne C.C.)		
Obituary	1951	*918*
Burton, Lieut. G. W. M. (King's, Canterbury)		
Obituary	1917	*171*
Burton, Wing-Comdr. H. F. (Bedford School)		
Obituary	1945	*320*
Burton, R. C. (Malvern; Yorkshire)		
Obituary	1972	*1047*
Burton, R. H. M. (Warwickshire)		
Obituary	1981	*1139*
Burton, Major S. J. (Military Cricket)		
Obituary	1918	*178*
Burton-on-Trent Belvedre Road		
Plan of Ground	1967	*353*
	1971	*321*
Bury, 2nd Lieut. H. S. E. (Eton)		
Obituary	1916	*151*
Bury, L. (Eton; Cambridge University)		
Obituary	1937/I	*286*
Bury, Rev. Canon W. (Cambridge University; Northamptonshire)		
Obituary	1928/I	*280*
Busby, A. (Combe Village, Oxfordshire)		
Obituary	1954	*922*
Buse, H. T. F. (Somerset)		
Benefit Match	1954	*525*
Bush, A. J. (Gloucestershire)		
Obituary	1925/I	*260*
Bush, E. A. (Metropolitan Club Cricket)		
Obituary	1917	*241*
Bush, Col. H. S. (Dover College; Army; Surrey)		
Obituary	1943	*373*
Bush, R. E. (Gloucestershire)		
Obituary	1940	*838*
Bushby, H. (Imperial Cricket Conference)		
Obituary	1977	*1051*
Bushby, M. H. (Cambridge University; I/C Tonbridge)		
'Views on the Laws'	1957	*83*
Busher, S. E. (Lancing; Surrey; Worcestershire)		
Obituary	1956	*977*

Buss, A. (Sussex)
    Photographs   1964   567
     1967   581
Buss, M. A. (Sussex)
    Photographs   1967   581
     1972   578
Bussell, H. A. (Victoria)
    Obituary   1948   781
Buswell, W. A. (Northamptonshire)
    Obituary   1951   918
Butcher, A. R. (Surrey; England)
    Photographs   1975   549
     1979   531
Butcher, B. F. H. (Guyana; West Indies)
    Cricketer of the Year   1970   65
    Pen Picture   1963   90
    Photograph   1970   56
Butcher, Capt. C. L. (Kidderminster C.C.)
    Obituary   1917   171
Butcher, D. H. (Surrey)
    Obituary   1946   430
Butcher, R. O. (Middlesex; Barbados; England)
    John Player Batting Award   1982   72
    Photograph   1981   490
Butler, A. G. (Rugby)
    Obituary   1910/I   133
Butler, A. H. M. (Harrow)
    Obituary   1944   312
Butler, Lieut. Hon. B. D. (IZingari)
    Obituary   1917   171
Butler, C. (Vice-President Tasmanian Cricket Association)
    Obituary   1910/I   134
Butler, E. H. (Tasmania)
    Obituary   1929/I   24
Butler, E. M. (Harrow; Cambridge University; Middlesex)
    Obituary   1949   86
Butler, F. (Nottinghamshire; Durham)
    Obituary   1924/I   25
Butler, Lieut. G. L. (Haileybury)
    Obituary   1918   17
Butler, G. M. (Harrow)
    Obituary   1982   119
Butler, G. S. (Wiltshire)
    Obituary   1970   101
Butler, H. (Nottinghamshire)
    Obituary   1905   lxxxvi

Butler, Pte. H. B. (Five Ways C.C., Canada)
Obituary ... 1917 ... *222*

Butler, H. J. (Nottinghamshire; England)
Benefit Match ... 1951 ... *478*
Photographs ... 1951 ... *469*
... 1953 ... *490*

Butler, Dr. H. M. (Harrow)
Obituary ... 1919 ... *203*

Butler, R. (Nottinghamshire)
Obituary ... 1917 ... *241*

Butler, R. H. (Warwickshire)
Obituary ... 1964 ... *945*

Butler, S. E. (Eton; Oxford University)
Obituary ... 1904 ... *lxxxi*

Butler, S. P. (Rugby)
Obituary ... 1916 ... *152*

Butler, T. A. (American Club Cricket)
Obituary ... 1917 ... *242*

Butt, H. R. (Sussex; England)
Benefit Match ... 1901 ... *83*
Obituary ... 1929/I ... *242*

Butt, J. A. S. (Sussex)
Obituary ... 1967 ... *964*

Butt, Q. (Journalist; Pakistan)
'Pakistan on the Cricket Map' Book Review ... 1956 ... *1023*
'Cricket without Challenge' Book Review ... 1957 ... *994*
'Pakistan Cricket on the March' Book Review ... 1958 ... *1011*
'Cricket Wonders' Book Review ... 1960 ... *998*
'Cricket Ups and Downs' Book Review ... 1961 ... *994*
'Cricket Cat and Mouse' Book Review ... 1963 ... *1109*
'Playing for a Draw' Book Review ... 1964 ... *998*
'The Oval Memories' Book Review ... 1969 ... *1032*
'Sporting Wickets' Book Review ... 1971 ... *1080*

Butterworth, F. W. (Marlborough)
Obituary ... 1916 ... *152*

Butterworth, 2nd Lieut. H. M. (Marlborough; Oxford University; Wanganui)
Obituary ... 1916 ... *152*

Butterworth, H. R. W. (Rydal; Cambridge University; Lancashire)
Obituary ... 1960 ... *958*

Butterworth, P/O. R. E. C. (Harrow; Oxford University; Middlesex)
Obituary ... 1941 ... *386*

Butterworth, 2nd Lieut. W. C. (Milford C.C.)
Obituary ... 1917 ... *171*

Butterworth, W. S. (Lancashire)
Obituary ... 1909/I ... *134*

Buttery, J. A. (Journalist)
  Obituary   1907   cix
Button, L. P. (Vice President Hampshire)
  Obituary   1915/I   215
Buultjens, E. W. (Ceylon)
  Obituary   1981   1139
Buxton, Major A. (Harrow)
  Obituary   1971   1024
Buxton, A. R. (Harrow; Norfolk)
  Obituary   1946   448
Buxton, C. D. (Eton; Cambridge University; Essex)
  Obituary   1893   xxxiv
Buxton, E. G. (Norfolk)
  Obituary   1930/I   246
Buxton, E. N. (Norfolk; Essex)
  Obituary   1925/I   261
Buxton, I. R. (Derbyshire)
  Photographs   1962   354
     1968   362
     1971   319
Buxton, M. (Charterhouse)
  Obituary   1973   1004
Buxton, Lt-Col. R. V. (Eton; Oxford University; Middlesex)
  Obituary   1954   922
Buxton, S. G. (Norfolk)
  Obituary   1910/I   13
Buxton Snow in June   Photograph   1976   40
Buxton, Sir T. F. 3rd Bart. (Essex)
  Obituary   1916   15
'Buying Back One's Past' J. I. Marder   1975   14
Byass, R. W. (Eton)
  Obituary   1959   92
Byass, Sir S. H. 1st Bart. (Radley)
  Obituary   1930/I   24
'Bygone Phase of Cricket:
The Two Elevens'   1925/I   22
Byng, Capt. A. M. (Sandhurst; Hampshire)
  Obituary   1915/I   21
Byrne, G. R. (Warwickshire; Worcestershire)
  Obituary   1974   107
Byrne, J. F. (Warwickshire)
  Obituary   1955   92
Byrom. J. L. (Yorkshire)
  Obituary   1932/I   24
Byron, C. R. H. (Border)
  Obituary   1953   93

Cabot, A. S. Y. (Treasurer Philadelphia)
   Obituary   1917   *265*

Cadell, Lieut. A. R. (Hampshire)
   Obituary   1929/I   *243*

Cadman, S. (Derbyshire)
   Benefit Match   1923/II   *256*
   Obituary   1953   *938*

Cadogan, Earl (Eton)
   Obituary   1936/I   *292*

Cadogan, 5th Earl of (President M.C.C.)
   Obituary   1916   *152*

Cadogan, H. A., Viscount Chelsea (Eton)
   Obituary   1909/I   *134*

Cadogan, Major Hon. W. G. S. (Eton)
   Obituary   1915/I   *215*

Cadogan, P. J. (Glamorgan)
   Obituary   1919   *204*

Cadwalader, Dr. C. (Philadelphia)
   Obituary   1908/I   *137*

Cadwallader, H. G. (Journalist)
   Obituary   1898   *xlvi*

Caesar, J. (Surrey; All England)
   Benefit Match   1869   *55*

Café Royal Trophy Centenary   1968   *270*

Caffyn, W. (Surrey; New South Wales)
   Obituary   1920/I   *165*

Cahill, K. W. J. (Tasmania)
   Obituary   1967   *964*

Cahn, Sir J. Bart. (President Nottinghamshire; Leicestershire Committee)
   Obituary   1945   *328*
   Team in Argentina 1930   1931/II   *709*
   Team in Jamaica 1929   1930/II   *698*
   Team in U.S.A., Canada, Bermuda 1933   1934/II   *689*

Caine, C. S. (Editor of Wisden 1926 – 1933)
   Special Memoir of   1934/I   *25*

Cairns, A. S. (Scotland)
   Obituary   1945   *328*

Cairns, R. (Writer)
   'Glen Turner's Century of Centuries'
   Book Review   1984   *1268*

Cakobau, Sir E. R. (Auckland; Fiji)
   Obituary   1974   *1071*

Caldecott, W. (Central Lancashire League Cricket)
   Obituary   1947   *688*

Calder, H. L. (Cranleigh School)

Photograph	1918	150
Public School Bowler of the Year	1918	152

Caldera, Wing-Comdr. K. (Ceylon)

Obituary	1981	1139

Caldicott, W. (Worcestershire)

Obituary	1917	242

Caldwell, Rev. S. (Worcestershire)

Obituary	1965	964

Calendar

For 1963	1963	54

Call for Culture

'N. Cardus'	1952	88

Callaghan, J. (Writer)

'Boycott – A Cricketing Legend' Book Review	1983	1308

Callaway, H. (Carlton C.C., Sydney)

Obituary	1920/I	192

Callaway, J. (Carlton C.C., Sydney)

Obituary	1920/I	192

Callaway, S. T. (New South Wales; Queensland; Canterbury; Australia)

Obituary	1925/I	288

Callingham, T. (Thames Ditton C.C.)

Obituary	1920/I	170

Calloway, N. (New South Wales)

Record by	1941	62

Calthorpe, Hon. F. S. G. (Repton; Cambridge University; Sussex; Warwickshire; England)

Obituary	1936/I	27
Schools Notes	1911/I	12
	1912/I	21

Calthrop, Lt-Col. E. E. (Bradfield)

Obituary	1949	86

Calvert, C. P. (New South Wales)

Obituary	1946	43

Calvert, E. B. (St Lawrence, Ramsgate; Buckinghamshire)

Obituary	1981	113

Calvert, G. C. (Sedbergh)

Obituary	1920/I	15

Calvert, J. J. (President New South Wales Cricket Association)

Obituary	1917	24

'Cambridge Memories' A. G. Steel

	1891	xxxv

'Cambridge, My Years At'

G. H. Longman	1929/I	26

Cambridge University

Team Portraits	1901	1977	*139*
	1943	1944	*38*
	1981	1982	*645*
	1982	1983	*668*
	1983	1984	*626*

Cambridge University Past and Present
v Oxford University Past and Present   1970   *752*

Cameron, C. M. (Sedbergh)
Obituary   1919   *168*

Cameron, D. J. (Writer)
'Caribbean Crusade' Book Review   1974   *1124*

Cameron, E. J. (Manager Australian Imperial Forces)
Obituary   1948   *782*

Cameron, Sgt. E. S. (Blundells; Montreal C.C.)
Obituary   1916   *153*

Cameron, 2nd Lieut. F. B. (Rossall)
Obituary   1917   *·171*

Cameron, H. B. (Transvaal; Western Province; South Africa)
Obituary   1936/I   *273*
Portrait and Biography   1936/I   *295*

Cameron, J. H. (Taunton; Cambridge University; Somerset; West Indies)
Schools Notes   1931/I   *316*
    1933/I   *277*
    1934/I   *294,316*
91 wkts Schools Averages   1934/II   *634*

Cameron, Dr. J. J. (London County)
Obituary   1955   *928*

Cameron, R. M. (Toronto C.C.)
Obituary   1926/I   *287*

Cammell, G. H. (Eton)
Obituary   1905   *lxxxix*

Campbell, Major A. C. (Military Cricket)
Obituary   1919   *168*

Campbell, Lieut. C. (Weymouth C.C.; Nova Scotia)
Obituary   1918   *178*

Campbell, Brig-Gen. C. L. (Cheltenham)
Obituary   1919   *168*

Campbell, D. (New South Wales Juniors)
Obituary   1921/I   *224*

Campbell, Hon. E. O. (Military Cricket)
Obituary   1919   *168*

Campbell, Col. F. (IZingari)
Obituary   1927/I   *273*

Campbell, Rt. Hon. F. A. V. (President M.C.C.)
Obituary   1912/I   *164*

Campbell, Major Sir G. C. Bart. (Eton)
  Obituary   1961   94:
Campbell, Lieut. G. E. F. (Edinburgh Academy)
  Obituary   1916   15.
Campbell, G. F. (Fettes)
  Obituary   1934/I   26◂
Campbell, Lieut. G. H. (St. Andrews, Toronto)
  Obituary   1917   17'
Campbell, G. T. (Fettes)
  Obituary   1925/I   26
Campbell, G. V. (Eton; Surrey)
  Obituary   1952   96◂
Campbell, Lieut. I. M. (Mill Hill)
  Obituary   1919   16
Campbell, Col. I. M. (Middlesex; London County)
  Obituary   1955   92
  'Reminiscences of a Vintner' Book Review   1952   101
Campbell, I. P. (Canford School; Oxford University; Kent)
  Schools Notes   1946   290,29
              1947   56
  1027 runs Schools Averages   1946   3▮
  1277 runs Schools Averages   1947   58
Campbell, I. P. F. (Repton; Oxford University; Surrey)
  Obituary   1964   94
Campbell, G. J. (American Club Cricket)
  Obituary   1936/I   27
Campbell, Major R. C. (Devon; Secretary Minor Counties)
  Obituary   1945   32
Campbell, Rev. S. C. (Bury St.Edmunds School; Cambridge University)
  Obituary   1905   lxxx.
Campbell, T. (Transvaal; South Africa)
  Obituary   1925/I   2℃
Campbell, Lieut. T. C. (Ottawa C.C.)
  Obituary   1917   22
Campin, Sgt. K. C. (Bedfordshire)
  Obituary   1946   4.
Campion, Sir W. R. (President Sussex)
  Obituary   1952   9:
Canada
  In England   1887   1888   2'
              1922   1923/II   55
              1936   1937/II   5◂
              1954   1955   6◂
  Colts in England   1965   1966   7'
  Schoolboys in England   1939   1940   6
                               1959   1960   9.

Toronto Zingari in England   1910   1911/II   *468*

Canadian Cricket Association
  'Views on Laws'   1957   *87*

Cancellor, Lieut. D. B. (Radley)
  Obituary   1919   *168*

Candidates for Australian Tour
  Note on   1954   *82*

Candler, J. P. (Cambridge University)
  Obituary   1943   *373*

Cane, 2nd Lieut. M. (Victoria C.C., British Columbia)
  Obituary   1919   *197*

Cannings, V. H. D. (Hampshire)
  Benefit Match   1960   *425*
  Photographs   1953   *375*
                  1955   *366*
  Retirement   1960   *412*
  'V. H. D. Cannings – An Appreciation'
  J. Arlott   Book Review   1960   *1010*

Cannon, J. (Chief Clerk M.C.C.)
  Obituary   1950   *904*
  Retirement   1945   *49*

Canny, Sir G. B. (Malvern)
  Obituary   1955   *928*

Canterbury Plan of County Ground   1950   *377*
                  ad passim
  Note on Ground   1969   *148*

Cantley, F. D. (Pocklington)
  Obituary   1950   *905*

Cantley, Lieut. J. A. (Haileybury)
  Obituary   1943   *363*

Capes, C. J. (Malvern; Kent)
  Obituary   1934/I   *260*

Caple, S. C. (Writer)
  'History of the Gloucestershire Cricket Club'
  Book Review   1950   *973*
  with A. G. Powell 'The Graces'
  (E.M., W.G., G.F.) Book Review   1976   *1150*

Capp, E. (Singleton C.C.; New South Wales)
  Obituary   1917   *172*

Captaincy   Notes on   1950   *113*
                  1960   *125*
                  1961   *120*
                  1963   *137*
                  1972   *87*
  'Captaincy' A. R. Lewis   1979   *84*
  'Captaincy, The Gift of' N. Cardus   1964   *134*

'Modern Captaincy – Some Thoughts On'
J. M. Brearley 1982 *109*
Captains 'Captains Face the Camera'
Photograph 1983 *Plate*
'Captains and Googly Bowlers Retire'
E. M. Wellings 1958 *94*
Carbutt, Major N. J. O. (Army; Essex)
Obituary 1965 *965*
Cardew, A. E. (Repton)
Obituary 1973 *1004*
Cardiff – Arms Park   Plan of Ground 1950 *323*
ad passim
       Sophia Gardens   Plan of Ground 1968 *398*
ad passim
Cardus, Sir N. (Journalist; Writer)
'Neville Cardus' J. Arlott 1965 *121*
'Sir Neville Cardus' A. Gibson
Obituary Tribute 1976 *107*
Photographs 1965 *120*
1976 *108*
Articles in Chronological Order
'Fifty Years of Lancashire Cricket' 1951 *80*
'A Call for Culture' 1952 *88*
'Australia throws down the Gauntlet' 1953 *84*
'A. L. Hasslet: A Born Cricketer' 1954 *93*
'South Africa offers Serious Challenge' 1955 *88*
'Len Hutton: The Master' 1956 *91*
'C. B. Fry' 1957 *111*
'Laker's Wonderful Year' 1957 *91*
'Denis Compton – The Cavalier' 1958 *78*
'Charles Macartney and George Gunn' 1959 *87*
'Five Stalwarts Retire' (D. Brookes; T.G.
Evans; J.C. Laker; G. Tribe; C. Washbrook) 1960 *137*
'Hubert Preston' 1961 *157*
'Six Giants of the Wisden Century'
(S. F. Barnes; D. G. Bradman; W. G. Grace;
J. B. Hobbs; T. Richardson; V. Trumper) 1963 *92*
'Sir John Berry Hobbs' 1964 *97*
'The Gift of Captaincy' 1964 *134*
'Tom Graveney – A Century of Centuries' 1965 *113*
'Walter Reginald Hammond' 1966 *113*
'Sobers – The Lion of Cricket' 1967 *126*
'Sydney Francis Barnes' 1968 *110*
'The Modern Golden Age' 1968 *131*
'J. B. Stratham – Gentleman George' 1969 *114*
'Emmott Robinson' 1970 *82*

'Herbert Strudwick'	1971	*114*
'Percy Holmes – A True Yorkshireman'	1972	*130*
'Wilfred Rhodes – Yorkshire Personified'	1974	*92*
'Jack Gregory – Cricketer in Excelsis'	1974	*113*
'Old Trafford Humiliated'	1975	*102*
Books by List	1965	*126*
'Cricket all the Year' Book Review	1953	*993*

Cardwell, R. (Writer)

'Australian Imperial Forces Cricket Team'		
Book Review	1982	*1263*

Cardwell, Col. W. A. (Eastbourne Enthusiast)

Obituary	1917	*242*

Carew, D. C. (Journalist)

Obituary	1982	*1195*

Carew, M. C. (Trinidad; West Indies)

Pen Picture	1963	*90*

Carey, 2nd Lieut. A. J. E. (Malvern)

Obituary	1918	*178*

Carey, 2nd Lieut. L. A. (Christ's College, Finchley; American Club Cricket)

Obituary	1917	*172*

Carey, Lieut. W. V. (Trinity College School, Port Hope)

Obituary	1917	*172*

Carkeek, W. (Victoria; Australia)

Obituary	1938	*937*

Carless, J. (Hertfordshire)

Obituary	1910/I	*134*

Carless, W. (Hertfordshire)

Obituary	1930/I	*247*

Carlin, J. (Nottinghamshire)

Benefit match	1913/II	*172*

Carling, P. (Secretary Glamorgan)

'The Continuing Struggle for Survival'	1983	*100*
Carling Prize	1964	*682*
	ad passim	

Carlisle, D. (Winchester)

Obituary	1949	*872*

Carlisle, F. M. M. (Harrow)

Obituary	1974	*1071*

Carlisle, H. (Harrow; Cheshire)

Obituary	1929/I	*243*

Carlisle, K. M. (Harrow; Oxxford University)

Obituary	1968	*998*

Carlisle, K. R. M. (Harrow; Oxford University; Sussex)

Obituary	1984	*1197*

Carlisle, Lieut. M. M. (Harrow; Sandhurst)
Obituary   1907   *cix*
Carlyon, H. B. (Marlborough)
Obituary   1938   *937*
Carmichael, E. G. M. (Harrow; Worcestershire)
Obituary   1960   *950*
Carmichael, J. (Cranleigh School)
Obituary   1915   I   *215*
Carmody, P/O. D. K. (Royal Australian Air Force; Western Australia)
Obituary   1978   *1068*
Carneigie, J. S. (Writer)
with S. I. Burrows
'George Headley' Book Review   1972   *1100*
Carpenter, Capt. E. B. (Winchester)
Obituary   1916   *153*
Carpenter, H. (Essex)
Benefit Match   1902   *185*
Obituary   1934/I   *261*
Carpenter, R. (Cambridgeshire; All England XI)
Obituary   1902   *lix*
Views on 'The Follow on'   1894   *xlix*
Carpenter-Garnier, J. (Harrow; Oxford University; Devon; Cornwall)
Obituary   1927/I   *274*
Carr, A. M. (Eton; Worcestershire)
Obituary   1947   *688*
Carr, A. W. (Sherbourne; Nottinghamshire; England)
Obituary   1964   *945*
Portrait and Biography   1923/I   *312*
Schools Notes   1910/I   *126*
                                                            1911/I   *120,129*
Carr, B. (Yorkshire Supporter)
Obituary   1910/I   *134*
Carr, D. B. (Repton; Oxford University; Derbyshire; England)
Career Record   1963   *1042*
Cricketer of the Year   1960   *114*
Photographs   1956   *304*
                                                              1960   *89*
                                                              1962   *354*
                                                              1979   *83*
                                                              1943   *304*
Schools Notes   1944   *220,235*
                                                              1945   *236,254*
Tribute to C. Taylor   1978   *1082*
Carr, D. W. (Kent; England)
Obituary   1951   *918*
Portrait and Biography   1910/I   *161*

100

Carr, Lt-Gen. G. L. (Uppingham)
Obituary 1955 *928*
Carr, Fl-Lt. H. L. (Clifton; Glamorgan)
Obituary 1944 *304*
Carr, J. (Durham)
Obituary 1968 *999*
Carr, P. W. (President Nottinghamshire)
Obituary 1932/I *240*
Carr, Capt. V. F. (Durham)
Obituary 1919 *168*
Carr, Rev. W. A. (Gentlemen of Sussex)
Obituary 1916 *153*
Carr, Fl-Lt. W. C. (Clifton)
Obituary 1945 *328*
Carre, 2nd Lieut. G. T. (King's, Canterbury)
Obituary 1918 *178*
Carrick, J. S. (Scotland)
Obituary 1924/I *255*
Carrick, P. (Yorkshire; Eastern Province)
Photographs 1976 *620*
1981 *612*
Carrick, R. B. (Winchester)
Obituary 1946 *436*
Carrick-Buchanan, Col. Sir D. C. R. (Scotland)
Obituary 1905 *lxxxix*
Carris, H. E. (Mill Hill; Cambridge University; Middlesex)
Obituary 1960 *950*
Carroll, F. H. (Devon)
Obituary 1951 *919*
Carroll, T. D. (Tasmania)
Obituary 1958 *956*
Carruthers, Dr. J. F. (Fettes)
Obituary 1926/I *266*
Carson, H. A. H. (Journalist)
Obituary 1953 *939*
Carson, Fl-Lt. T. H. (Charterhouse)
Obituary 1944 *305*
Carson, W. N. (Auckland)
Obituary 1945 *320*
Carte, 2nd Lieut. A. S. (City of London School)
Obituary 1918 *178*
Carter, A. S. (East Melbourne C.C.)
Obituary 1921/I *224*
Carter, B. A. (Pallingswick C.C.)
Obituary 1917 *242*

Carter, C. A. (Surrey)
Obituary   1893   *xxxv*
Carter, C.C. (Lancing)
Obituary   1950   *905*
Carter, C. P. (Natal; Cornwall; South Africa)
Obituary   1953   *939*
Carter, Rev. E. S. (Oxford University; Victoria; Yorkshire)
Obituary   1924/I   *256*
Carter, 2nd Lieut. G. T. (Wellingborough Grammar School; Norfolk)
Obituary   1917   *172*
Carter, H. (New South Wales; Australia)
Obituary   1949   *863*
Carter, R. D. (Wellingborough; Norfolk)
Obituary   1970   *1018*
Carter, R. G. M. (Warwickshire; Worcestershire)
Photographs   1959   *570*
    1969   *620*
Carter, W. (Derbyshire)
Obituary   1976   *1093*
Cartland, Capt. G. T. (Greenjackets)
Obituary   1917   *172*
Cartman, W. (Yorkshire)
Obituary   1936/I   *273*
Cartmell, Lieut. G. M. (Rossall)
Obituary   1919   *169*
Cartwright, Lt-Col. G. H. B. M. (Writer; Eton; Oxford University)
Obituary   1977   *1037*
Cartwright, P. (Sussex)
Obituary   1956   *970*
Cartwright, T. (Warwickshire; Somerset; Glamorgan; England)
Benefit Match   1969   *614*
Photographs   1965   *590*
    1968   *602*
    1973   *516*
Cartwright, V. H. (Nottinghamshire)
Obituary   1966   *962*
Carver, Capt. W. L. (Hereford Cathedral School; Weston-Super-Mare C.C.)
Obituary   1918   *178*
Cary-Elwes, 2nd Lieut. W. G. (Downside)
Obituary   1918   *178*
'Case for More Natural wickets, A,'
G. O. Allen   1938   *52*
Case, C. C. C. (Somerset)
Obituary   1970   *1019*
Case, T. (Rugby; Oxford University; Middlesex)
Obituary   1926/I   *266*

Case, T. B. (Winchester; Oxford University)
   Obituary   1942   *355*
Case, W. S. (Winchester; Oxfordshire)
   Obituary   1923/I   *288*
Casey, Major W. A. (Victoria C.C.; British Columbia)
   Obituary   1919   *197*
Cass, G. R. (Worcestershire; Essex)
   Photograph   1971   *564*
Cassan, E. J. P. (Bruton School; Oxford University; Somerset)
   Obituary   1905   *lxxxix*
Cassatt, A. J. (President Merion C.C., Philadelphia)
   Obituary   1908/I   *155*
Cassels, Capt. W. G. (Trent College)
   Obituary   1917   *172*
Casswell, Lieut. E. D. S. (Tonbridge)
   Obituary   1919   *197*
Cassy, Lieut. M. J. W. (St. Dunstan's; Oxford University; Northamptonshire)
   Obituary   1945   *320*
Castens, H. H. (Rugby; Western Province)
   Obituary   1930/I   *247*
Castle, S. (Kent)
   Obituary   1939   *920*
Castor, B. K. (Essex)
Obituary   1980   *1148*
Caswall, A. J. (Colfe's School)
   Schools Note   1982   *859*
   1237 runs Schools Average   1982   *872*
Cat, Peter (Lord's Cat)
   Obituary   1965   *973*
Cater, C. A. (Harrow; Middlesex)
   Obituary   1893   *xxxiv*
Caterer, T. A. (South Australia)
   Obituary   1925/I   *262*
Cath, H. (Devon)
   Obituary   1957   *942*
Cator, Rev. W. (Oxford University)
   Obituary   1903   *lxxiv*
Catt, A. W. (Kent; Western Province)
   Photograph   1963   *466*
Catterall, R. H. (Natal; Orange Free State; Transvaal; South Africa)
   Obituary   1962   *985*
   Portrait and Biography   1925/I   *292*
Cattley, A. C. (Eton)
   Obituary   1896   *xliii*
Cattley, Major C.F. (Oxford Seniors)
   Obituary   1919   *197*

Cattley, G. W. (Eton)
  Obituary 1919 *204*
Cattley, S. W. (Eton; Surrey)
  Obituary 1926/I *267*
Cattley, W. (Treasurer Surrey)
  Obituary 1919 *204*
Catton, J. A. H. (Journalist)
  Obituary 1937/I *269*
Caulfield, F. (Orange Free State)
  Obituary 1937/I *270*
Caulfield, J. (Metropolitan Club Cricket)
  Obituary 1909/I *134*
Caunter, Dr. R. L. (Uppingham; Edinburgh University)
  Obituary 1920/I *192*
Causton, Rev. F. J. (Bradfield)
  Obituary 1933/I *241*
Caultley, Major W. O. (Bradfield)
  Obituary 1916 *153*
Cavaghan, H. (Sedbergh)
  Obituary 1945 *320*
Cavaliers in
  Jamaica 1964 1965 *845*
  South Africa 1963 1964 *881*
  West Indies 1965 1966 *854*
Cave, Lieut. A. D. (Brighton College)
  Obituary 1919 *169*
Cave, Sir B. S. (Merchant Taylors)
  Obituary 1934/I *279*
Cave, H. W. (Rugby)
  Obituary 1949 *863*
Cave, Gen. L. P. (New Zealand Club Cricket)
  Obituary 1919 *197*
Cave, W. F. (Eton; Gloucestershire)
  Obituary 1940 *838*
Cave, W. F. (Eton; Gloucestershire)
  Obituary 1947 *688*
Cawston, Sir. J. W. (Clifton)
  Obituary 1928 *280*
Cayley, D. (Yorkshire Gentlemen)
  Obituary 1913/I *184*
Cazalet, Major P. V. F. (Eton; Oxford University; Kent)
  Obituary 1974 *1072*
Cazalet, Col. V. A. (Eton)
  Obituary 1944 *305*
Cazenove, Canon (Oxford University)
  Obituary 1894 *xxxvii*

Cecil, Col. Lord W. (Eton)
Obituary   1944   *312*
Celebrations   Note on   1949   *123*
Centenary Test Group at Lords 1980
Photograph   1981   *110*
'Centenary Test Match, The' R. Hayter   1978   *130*
Centenary Test Match Fracas Note on   1981   *92*
Centenary Test Match 1980 Photograph   1981   *68*
Police Protection
Centenary Test Team – England 1980
Team portrait   1981   *70*
'Centenary of Trent Bridge' A. W. Shelton   1938   *461*
Central Mediterranean Force Note on   1946   *196*
Team Portrait   1946   *38*
Centuries By Licence Notes on   1951   *124*
'Centurions of 1977'
(J. H. Edrich; G. Boycott)   1978   *133*
J. H. Edrich – J. Woodcock   1978   *133*
G. Boycott – T. Brindle   1978   *140*
Ceylon Tea Centre Awards   1970   *278*
Chadwick, E. L. (Lancashire)
Obituary   1919   *204*
Chadwick, H. (American Journalist)
Obituary   1909/I   *134*
Chadwick, 2nd Lieut. R. M. (Rugby)
Obituary   1916   *154*
Chadwick, Rev. R. M. (Rugby; Dorset)
Obituary   1969   *979*
Chadwyck-Healey, H. P. (President Grasshoppers)
Obituary   1977   *1037*
Chalk, Fl-Lt. F. G. H. (Uppingham; Oxford University; Kent)
Obituary   1945   *320*
Challen, J. B. (Marlborough; Somerset)
Obituary   1938   *937*
Challenger, E. O. (American Club Cricket)
Obituary   1937/I   *287*
Challenor, Brig-Gen. E. L. (Army)
Obituary   1936/I   *274*
Challenor, G. (Barbados; West Indies)
Obituary   1948   *782*
Challenor, Lt-Col, G. R. (Army)
Obituary   1923/I   *288*
Chalmers, G. K. (Scotland)
Obituary   1947   *688*
Chalmers, T. (Scottish Clubs)
Obituary   1927/I   *274*

Chamberlayne, T. (Hampshire Patron)
  Obituary   1925/I   *262*
Chambers, 2nd Lieut. E. C. E. (Cock House, Marlborough)
  Obituary   1917   *172*
Chambers, F. S. (Canada)
  Obituary   1904   *lxxx*
Chambers, R. B. (Treasurer Derbyshire)
  Obituary   1930/I   *247*
Champian, Brig-Gen. H. F. B. (Cheltenham; Gloucestershire)
  Obituary   1934/I   *261*
Champion, A. (Yorkshire; Lancashire)
  Obituary   1910/I   *134*
Champion, 2nd Lieut. E. O. (Rugby)
  Obituary   1918   *178*
Chance, A. F. (Shrewsbury)
  Obituary   1935/I   *261*
Chancellor, Capt. R. A. B. (Harrow)
  Obituary   1917   *173*
Chandler, A. (Cheltenham; Surrey)
  Obituary   1928/I   *302*
Chandrasekar, B. S. (Mysore; India)
  Cricketer of the Year   1972   *81*
  Photograph   1972   *66*
  Retirement   1981   *1076*
Changes, Constant Note on   1967   *89*
Chant, Lieut. T. R. (University College School)
  Obituary   1919   *169*
Chapel, D. (Grange C.C.; Scotland)
  Obituary   1913/I   *184*
Chaplin, H. P. (Harrow; Sussex)
  Obituary   1971   *1024*
Chaplin, Col. R. S. (Harrow)
  Obituary   1941   *393*
Chapman, A. P. F. (Uppingham; Cambridge University; Kent; England)
  Obituary   1962   *985*
  Public School Cricketer of the Year   1919   *150*
  Photograph   1919   *151*
  Schools Notes   1918   *161*
     1919   *155,163*
     1920/I   *259,268*
  Tribute to S. J. Southerton   1936/I   *29*
Chapman, B. (Journalist)
  'Following Leicestershire'   1964   *150*
  Obituary   1980   *1147*
Chapman, Lt-Col. E. H. (Asygarth, United Services College)
  Obituary   1916   *154*

Chapman, H. W. (Natal; South Africa)
Obituary · 1943 · *386*

Chapman, J. (Nottinghamshire)
Obituary · 1897 · *xxxix*

Chapman, J. (Uppingham; Derbyshire)
Obituary · 1957 · *942*

Chapman, J. W. (Journalist; Assistant Secretary Sussex)
Obituary · 1964 · *946*

Chapman, T. A. (Leicestershire; Rhodesia)
Obituary · 1980 · *1147*

Chapman, W. W. (Sydney Club Cricket)
Obituary · 1933/I · *262*

Chappell, G. S. (South Australia; Queensland; Somerset; Australia)
Contract · 1976 · *1046*
Cricketer of the Year · 1973 · *82*
Photographs · 1969 · *550*
· 1973 · *69*
with D. Frith 'The Ashes 77' Book Review · 1978 · *1124*
'The 100th Summer' Book Review · 1978 · *1122*
with I. Chappell 'Cricket in our Blood'
Book Review · 1978 · *1124*

Chappell, I. M. (South Australia; Lancashire; Australia)
Contract · 1976 · *1046*
Cricketer of the Year · 1976 · *51*
Photographs · 1973 · *109*
· 1976 · *42*
'My World of Cricket' Book Review · 1976 · *1146*
with G. S. Chappell 'Cricket in Our Blood'
Book Review · 1978 · *1124*

Chappell, T. M. (New South Wales; Australia)
'Sneaky Chappell' Action Photograph · 1982 · *65*

Chapple, A. T. (Bedford School)
Obituary · 1918 · *178*

Charfield, K. M. (Marlborough)
Obituary · 1928/I · *280*

Charles, Prince of Wales
'Executes the Sweep' Action Photograph · 1969 · *51*

Charles, Lt-Col. S. F. (Harrow)
Obituary · 1951 · *919*

Charlesworth, A. P. (Yorkshire)
Obituary · 1927/I · *274*

Charlesworth, C. (Warwickshire)
Benefit match · 1921/II · *252*
Obituary · 1954 · *922*

Charlesworth, Rev. T. B. (Sedbergh; Worcestershire)
Obituary · 1918 · *223*

Charlton, Capt. A. N. (Westminster)
Obituary   1918   *179*

Charlton, M. T. (Journalist)
Obituary   1968   *999*

Charlton, Dr. P. C. (New South Wales; Australia)
Obituary   1956   *977*

Charlton, R. J. (Lincolnshire)
'Views on the Laws'   1957   *85*

Charlton, S. F. (Cranleigh School)
Obituary   1954   *922*

Charlton, W. T. (Durham)
Obituary   1968   *999*

Charlwood, H. (Sussex; England)
Benefit Match   1884   *230*

Charrington Trophy
    1966   *691*
    1967   *703*
    1968   *673*

Charsley, Major R. B. (Dover College; Military Cricket)
Obituary   1919   *197*

Chater, L. (Harrow)
Obituary   1933/I   *262*

Chatfield, K. M. (Marlborough)
Obituary   1928/I   *280*

Chatterton, Capt. R. L. (Bedford Grammar)
Obituary   1919   *169*

Chatterton, W. (Derbyshire; England)
Benefit Match   1897   *109*
Obituary   1914/I   *179*
'Views on the Reforms of 1889'   1890   *xxxix*

Chaytor, 2nd Lieut. A. K. (King's School; Worcester)
Obituary   1916   *154*

Chaytor, Capt. J. D. G. (Wellington)
Obituary   1938   *937*

Cheales, Rev. J. P. (Marlborough; Wiltshire; Lincolnshire)
Obituary   1949   *863*

Cheales, Col. R. D. (Harrow)
Obituary   1943   *373*

Cheating Note on   1977   *109*

Cheetham, J. E. (Western Province; South Africa)
'Caught by the Springboks'   Book Review   1955   *990*
'I Declare'   Book Review   1957   *995*
Obituary   1981   *1139*

Cheetle, G. A. (South African Journalist)
Obituary   1977   *1037*

Chelmsford, Lord (Winchester; Oxford University; Worcestershire; Middlesex)
    Obituary   1934/I   *262*
Chelmsford,   Plan of County Ground   1952   *311*
                                          ad passim

Cheltenham v Marlborough
    Centenary Match   1957   *790*
Cheltenham College   Plan of County Ground   1967   *407*
                                          ad passim

Cherry, Capt. A. D. (Dorset)
    Obituary   1918   *179*
Cherry-Downes, H. M. A. (Charterhouse; Lincolnshire)
    Obituary   1967   *964*
Chessman, W. E. F. (Sussex)
    Obituary   1946   *436*
Chester, A. (Surrey)
    Obituary   1916   *154*
Chester, F. (Umpire)
    Action Photograph   1953   *59*
    'How's That' Book Review   1957   *999*
    Obituary   1958   *956*
    Testimonial Fund   1948   *86*
    Thirty Years an Umpire – Chester's Unique
    Place in Cricket' V. J. G. Jenkins   1954   *103*
    Retirement from Umpiring   1956   *1017*
    'The Umpire's Point of View'   1933/I   *302*
Chester, J. (Yorkshire Committee)
    Obituary   1906   *lxxxix*
Chester, Lieut. J. L. (Birkenhead School)
    Obituary   1916   *154*
Chester, Lieut. R. H. V. (Merchant Taylors)
    Obituary   1919   *169*
Chester-Master, Major E. (Repton; Gloucestershire; Dorset)
    Obituary   1980   *1148*
Chesterfield, 10th Earl of (President M.C.C.)
    Obituary   1934/I   *262*
Chesterfield Queen's Park Note on Ground   1969   *143*
    Plan of County Ground   1951   *289*
                                          ad passim
Chetham-Strode, Capt. E. R. (St.Paul's)
    Obituary   1918   *179*
Chetham-Strode, R. W. (Sherborne)
    Obituary   1975   *1075*
Chetwynd, Sir G. Bart (Harrow)
    Obituary   1918   *223*
Chichester, 6th Earl of (Eton)
    Obituary   1927/I   *274*

Chichester, Rev. Father R. (Minehead C.C.; Somerset Stragglers C.C.)
Obituary 1915/I 216
Chichester, Constable-Brig. R. C. (Yorkshire)
Obituary 1964 946
Chidgery, H. (Somerset)
Obituary 1942 356
Chidson, Capt. L. D. (Dulwich College)
Obituary 1918 179
Chiesman, C. S. (Chairman Kent)
Obituary 1971 1034
Chignell, T. A. (Hampshire)
Obituary 1966 962
Chignell, Rev. W. R. (Writer)
'A History of Worcestershire County
Cricket Club' Book Review 1952 1016
'Worcestershire Cricket 1950-1968'
Book Review 1969 1024
Child, Sir J. Bart. (Eton)
Obituary 1972 1047
Childe-Pemberton, C. B. (Harrow)
Obituary 1901 lxii
Childs, J. H. (Gloucestershire)
Photograph 1982 415
Childs-Clarke, A. W. (Christ's Hospital School; Northamptonshire; Middlesex)
Obituary 1981 1139
Chile in Argentina 1929-30 1931/II 709
Chinese Year of the Cricket
Note on 1984 971
Chinnery, Capt. E. F. (Eton)
Obituary 1916 154
Chinnery, Lieut. H. B. (Eton; Surrey; Middlesex)
Obituary 1917 173
Chinnery, W. H. (Orsett C.C.; Essex)
Note on Performance 1945 105
Chinnery, W. M. (Surrey)
Obituary 1906 xc
Chitty, A. J. (Eton)
Obituary 1909/I 134
Chitty, J. M. (Eton)
Obituary 1920/I 152
Chitty, Lord Justice (Eton; Oxford University)
Obituary 1900 1
Cholmondeley, Lieut. H. P. G. (Harrow)
Obituary 1944 305
Choveaux, Lieut. N. (Victoria College, Jersey)
Obituary 1918 179

Christian, Lt-Col. H. K. (Surrey)
Obituary 1965 *972*
Christian, H. R. H. Prince of Schleswig – Holstein (President of Berkshire)
Obituary 1918 *224*
Christian, Victor Prince (Wellington)
Obituary 1901 *liv*
Christiani, C. M. (British Guiana; West Indies)
Obituary 1939 *908*
Christie, Pte. R. T. (Adelaide Club Cricket)
Obituary 1942 *347*
Christison, Lieut. Adj. F. J. (Edingburgh Academy; Oxford Univesity)
Obituary 1918 *212*
Christoffelsz, S. (Ceylon Club Cricket)
Obituary 1914/I *180*
Christopher, Rev. Canon A. M. W. (Cambridge University)
Obituary 1914/I *180*
Christopherson, C. (Brother of S. Christopherson)
Obituary 1926/I *268*
Christopherson, D. (Blackheath C.C.)
Obituary 1945 *328*
Christopherson, N. (Manager Kent)
Obituary 1973 *1004*
Christopherson, P. (Oxford University; Kent)
Obituary 1923/I *246*
Christopherson, S. (Member of Family)
Obituary 1917 *173*
Christopherson, S. (Kent; England; President M.C.C.)
Obituary 1950 *905*
Tribute to Sir Stanley Jackson 1948 *81*
Christy, 2nd Lieut. B. R. F. (Eton)
Obituary 1917 *173*
Christy, J. A. J. (Transvaal; South Africa)
Obituary 1972 *1047*
Chubb, G. W. A. (Border; Transvaal; South Africa)
Obituary 1983 *1241*
Chudleigh, 9th Baron of (Stonyhurst)
Obituary 1917 *243*
Church, Capt. H. (Marlborough)
Obituary 1917 *173*
Church, Sir W. S. Bart. (Harrow; Hertfordshire)
Obituary 1929/I *243*
Churchill, Rev. W. H. (Marlborough)
Obituary 1937/I *270*
Churchward, Capt. A. W. (Gentlemen of Kent)
Obituary 1930/I *247*

Chute, Rev. T. D. (Essex)
  Obituary   1927/I   275
Civil Defence Services   Team Portrait   1944   33
Clarendon, 5th Earl of (President Hertfordshire)
  Obituary   1915/I   216
Clark, A. G. F. (Sussex)
  Obituary   1929/I   243
Clark, C. R. (Felsted)
  Schools Note   1977   810
  1120 runs Schools Averages   1977   835
Clark, D. G. (Rugby; Kent)
  'Clark Committee on Future of County Cricket'   1966   87,101
Clark, E. (Rotherham C.C.)
  Obituary   1954   922
Clark, E. A. (Middlesex)
  Photograph   1966   483
Clark, E. W. (Northamptonshire; England)
  Obituary   1983   1242
Clark, G. M. (Bradfield)
  Obituary   1917   174
Clark, H. G. (Vice President Essex)
  Obituary   1969   990
Clark, H. P. (Club Cricket Conference)
  Obituary   1960   950
Clark, J. (Hunslett C.C.)
  Obituary   1916/I   216
Clark, Miss J. (England Women)
  Obituary   1971   1024
Clark, P. H. (Philadelphia)
  Obituary   1966   962
Clark, 2nd Lieut. R. (Edingburgh Academy)
  Obituary   1917   174
Clark, T. H. (Bedfordshire; Surrey)
  Benefit Match   1962   595
  Career Figures   1962   696
  Obituary   1982   1195
  Photograph   1955   505
  Retirement   1962   581
Clarke, Major A. C. K. S. (Scotland)
  Obituary   1954   922
Clarke, A. E. (East Melbourne C.C.)
  Obituary   1914/I   186
Clarke, A. T. (Berkshire)
  Obituary   1946   436

Clarke, 2nd Lieut. C. (St.Dunstan's)
    Obituary   1917   *174*

Clarke, C. F. C. (Berkshire; Surrey)
    Obituary   1932/I   *240*

Clarke, Lieut. C. G. (Bradfield)
    Obituary   1916   *154*

Clarke, Capt. E. C. K. (Westminster)
    Obituary   1919   *169*

Clarke, Capt. E. G. (Rugby)
    Obituary   1943   *363*

Clarke, Pte. E. J. (Edmonton C.C., Alberta)
    Obituary   1918   *212*

Clarke, F. H. (Editor 'American Cricketer')
    Obituary   1907   *cix*

Clarke, H. E. (U.S.A. Clubs)
    Obituary   1923/I   *288*

Clarke, J. (Journalist; Writer)
    'Challenge Renewed' Book Review   1964   *999*
    'Cricket with a Swing' Book Review   1964   *1000*
    'The Australians in England 1964' Book Review   1965   *1018*
    'With England in Australia' Book Review   1967   *1016*
    Obituary   1967   *964*

Clarke, P. (Middlesex; Ireland)
    Obituary   1916   *155*

Clarke, R. W. (Northamptonshire)
    Obituary   1982   *1195*

Clarke, Capt. S. H. (Marlborough)
    Obituary   1918   *179*

Clarke, S. T. (Barbados; Surrey; West Indies)
    Photograph   1980   *555*

Clarke, W. (Nottinghamshire)
    Obituary   1936/I   *274*

Clarke, W. A. F. (Surrey)
    Obituary   1936/I   *274*

Clarke, Lieut. W. A. S. (Uppingham)
    Obituary   1944   *305*

Clarke, W. B. (Nottinghamshire; Middlesex)
    Obituary   1903   *lxxv*

Clarke, 2nd Lieut. W. H. (Rugby)
    Obituary   1916   *155*

Clarkson, A. (Somerset)
    Photograph   1970   *527*

Clarkson, Capt. C. (King's Cross C.C., Yorkshire)
    Obituary   1918   *179*

Clarkson, Lieut. M. A. (Upper Canada College)
    Obituary   1918   *179*

Claughton, H. (Yorkshire)
Obituary | 1982 | *1195*
Clay, Gen. C. (Philadelphia)
Obituary | 1908/I | *137*
Clay, I. (Tasmania)
Obituary | 1959 | *927*
Clay, J. C. (Winchester; Glamorgan; England)
'Memoir to Maurice Turnbull' | 1945 | *41*
Note on Bowling | 1949 | *110*
Obituary | 1974 | *1072*
Schools Notes | 1916 | *75*
 | 1917 | *156*
Clayton, F. G. H. (Harrow; Northumberland)
Obituary | 1947 | *688*
'Views on Second Class Counties and
L.B.W. Rule' | 1903 | *lxiii*
Clayton, G. (Lancashire; Somerset)
Photographs | 1960 | *447*
 | 1964 | *446*
Clayton, J. G. (King's Bruton)
Obituary | 1917 | *174*
Clayton, R. (Yorkshire)
Benefit Match | 1893 | *184*
Obituary | 1902 | *lxii*
Clayton, Lieut. R. S. (Vancouver C.C.)
Obituary | 1917 | *174*
Clayton-Smith, H. H. (Pontefract C.C.)
Obituary | 1918 | *179*
Cleasby, R. D. (Eton; Cambridge University)
Obituary | 1910/I | *134*
Clegg, W. G. (Winchester)
Obituary | 1950 | *905*
Clement, Major R. A. (Rugby; Cambridge University)
Obituary | 1906 | *xc*
Cleminson, 2nd Lieut. R. (Ardingly)
Obituary | 1917 | *174*
Cleveland, 2nd Lieut. E. H. (Five Ways Old Edwardian C.C.)
Obituary | 1917 | *174*
Cliff, A. T. (Worcestershire)
Obituary | 1967 | *964*
Cliff, Major G. (Lincolnshire)
Obituary | 1919 | *169*
Cliff, Major H. T. (Yorkshire Gentlemen)
Obituary | 1915/I | *216*
Cliff, T. C. (President American Clubs)
Obituary | 1917 | *242*

Clift, 2nd Lieut. M. R. (Aldenham)
Obituary — 1917 — *174*

Clift, P. B. (Leicestershire; Natal; Rhodesia)
Photograph — 1977 — *475*

Clinton, G. S. (Kent; Surrey; Zimbabwe – Rhodesia)
Photograph — 1981 — *550*

Clissold, S. T. (Eton; Cambridge University)
Obituary — 1899 — *xlv*

Clixby, 2nd Lieut. E. D. (Berkhamsted School)
Obituary — 1916 — *155*

Cloete, Capt. P. H. B. (Western Province)
Obituary — 1943 — *363*

Cloete, W. B. (M.C.C.)
Obituary — 1916 — *155*

Close, D. B. (Yorkshire; Somerset; England)

Action Photograph	1977	*86*
Benefit Matches	1962	*680*
	1977	*753*
Cricketer of the Year	1964	*79*
Notes on	1967	*92*
	1975	*100*
	1977	111
Photographs	1950	*71*
	1953	*611*
	1959	*611*
	1963	*672*
	1964	*68*
	1972	*546*
Youngest English Test Player	1950	*240*
'Close on Cricket' Book Review	1967	*1020*
'Close to Cricket' Book Review	1969	*1030*
'The M.C.C. Tour of the West Indies 1968'		
Book Review	1969	*1032*
'I Dont Bruise Easily' Book Review	1979	*1132*

Close Fielding   Note on — 1950 — *117*

Close Finishes   Note on — 1948 — *85*

Clover-Brown, C. (Harrow; Buckinghamshire; All Ceylon)
Obituary — 1983 — *1242*

Club Cricket Conference
'Views on the Laws' — 1957 — *86*

Club Cricket Championship Note on — 1982 — *844*

'Club Cricketers Plea' (W. E. Bowes) — 1957 — *79*

Clutterbuck, Capt. T. R. (Harrow)
Obituary — 1936/I — *292*

Coaching at Schools   Note on — 1950 — *117*
'Coaching the School Boy' J. D. Eggar — 1950 — *103*

Coatbridge, G. (Durham)
   Obituary   1912/I   *165*
Coates, Lieut. A. D. (Tonbridge)
   Obituary   1916   *155*
Coates, J. (New South Wales)
   Obituary   1897   *xl*
Cobb, A. G. S. (Kent)
   Obituary   1973   *1004*
Cobb, C. E. (Rugby; Buckinghamshire)
   Obituary   1923/I   *288*
Cobb, H. E. (Rugby)
   Obituary   1932/I   *256*
Cobb, H. H. (Middlesex)
   Obituary   1950   *905*
Cobb, Capt. K. R. (Sedbergh)
   Obituary   1918   *212*
Cobbett, M. R. (Journalist)
   Obituary   1907   *cix*
Cobbold, J. D. (Suffolk)
   Obituary   1930/I   *247*
Cobbold, Lt-Col. J. I. C. (Eton)
   Obituary   1945   *321*
Cobbold, J. S. (Suffolk)
   Obituary   1973   *1004*
Cobbold, P. W. (Eton; Suffolk)
   Obituary   1946   *436*
Cobbold, W. N. (Charterhouse; Kent)
   Obituary   1923/I   *289*
Cobcroft, L. T. (New South Wales; Canterbury; Wellington(N.Z); Wairarapa)
   Obituary   1939   *908*
Cobden, F. C. (Harrow; Cambridge University)
   Obituary   1933/I   *241*
Cobham, Lord (C. G. Lyttleton) (Eton; Cambridge University; President M.C.C.)
   Obituary   1923/I   *289*
   Recollections of W. Caffyn   1920/I   *166*
Cobham, 9th Viscount (J. C. Lyttleton) (Eton; Worcestershire; President M.C.C.)
   Obituary   1950   *905*
Cobham, 10th Viscount (C. J. Lyttleton) (Worcestershire; President M.C.C.)
   Obituary   1978   *1068*
   'President Speaks'   1956   *72*
Cochran, D. G. (Aberdeenshire)
   Obituary   1973   *1005*
Cochrane, A. H. J. (Oxford University; Derbyshire; Northumberland)
   Obituary   1949   *863*
   Tribute to A. J. Webbe   1942   *353*

Cochrane, Sir C. A. (Sherborne)
  Obituary   1961   *945*

Cochrane, C. W. H. (Repton)
  Obituary   1933/I   *242*

Cockell, W. H. (Cambridgeshire)
  Obituary   1981   *1140*

Cockerell, Rev. L. A. (Rugby; Essex)
  Obituary   1930/I   *247*

Cockerham, J. W. (Vice President Yorkshire)
  Obituary   1916   *155*

Cockin, H. K. (Guelph C.C., Canada)
  Obituary   1918   *224*

Coe, S. (Leicestershire)
  Obituary   1956   *970*

Coen, S. K. (Western Province; Orange Free State; Griqualand West; South Africa)
  Obituary   1968   *999*

Coen, W. H. (President Chicago Cricket Association)
  Obituary   1909/I   *134*

Coghill, Lieut. N. H. (Cheltenham)
  Obituary   1919   *169*

Coghlan, J. C. (Kimberley)
  Obituary   1946   *437*

Coghlan, T. B. L. (I/C Rugby)
  'Views on Laws'   1957   *84*

Cohen, P/O. A. (Glamorgan Ground Staff; Secretary Welsh Schools)
  Obituary   1956   *970*

Cohen, S. (Sydney C.C.; New South Wales)
  Obituary   1905   *lxxxix*

Coker, Lieut. C. J. (Wellington College)
  Obituary   1918   *212*

Coker, Rev. J. (Winchester; Oxford University)
  Obituary   1902   *lxii*

Colah, S. H. M. (Western India; Nawanagar; India)
  Obituary   1952   *966*

Colahan, J. B. (President Belmont C.C., Philadelphia)
  Obituary   1921/I   *224*

Colbeck, 2nd Lieut. L. G. (Marlborough; Cambridge University; Middlesex)
  Obituary   1919   *169*

Colchester Castle Park
  Plan of County Ground   1953   *317*
                                                1965   *367*

Coldham, J. D. (Writer)
  'Northamptonshire Cricket' Book Review   1960   *995*

'William Brockwell –
His Triumph and Tragedy' Book Review 1971 *1077*
'German Cricket – A Brief History'
Book Review 1984 *1260*
'Lord Harris' Book Review 1984 *1268*
'Ups and Downs of Northamptonshire' 1958 *103*
Coldwell, Lt-Col. A. S. T. G. (Secretary Northamptonshire)
Obituary 1963 *1032*
Coldwell, L. J. (Worcestershire; Devon; England)
Benefit Match 1969 *628*
'Len Coldwell Souvenir Book' Book Review 1969 *1040*
Photograph 1963 *652*
Retirement 1970 *80,594*
Cole, D. H. (Devon)
Wilfred Rhodes Trophy Winner 1956 *75,696*
Cole, Rev. E. M. (Yorkshire Gentlemen)
Obituary 1912/I *164*
Cole, F. L. (Gloucestershire)
Obituary 1942 *356*
Cole, G. (Journalist)
Obituary 1915/I *216*
Cole, Canon G. L. (Hampshire)
Obituary 1965 *965*
Cole, 2nd Lieut. H. P. (Marlborough)
Obituary 1917 *174*
Cole, T. G. O. (Harrow; Cambridge University; Lancashire; Derbyshire;
Denbighshire)
Obituary 1945 *329*
Colebrooke, Rev. E. L. (Charterhouse; Oxford University)
Obituary 1940 *839*
Coleby, A. T. (Westminster)
Obituary 1951 *919*
Coleman, C. A. R. (Leicestershire)
Obituary 1979 *1074*
Coleman, Lieut. E. C. (Dulwich; Essex)
Obituary 1918 *179*
Coleman, Rt. Rev. L. (Union C.C., Philadelphia)
Obituary 1909 *152*
Coleman, W. E. (Hertfordshire)
Obituary 1961 *945*
Coleridge, A. D. (Eton; Cambridge University)
Obituary 1914/I *180*
Coleridge, Rev. F. J. (Eton; Oxford University)
Obituary 1907 *cx*
Coleridge, Capt. G. F. (Eton)
Obituary 1924/I *256*

Coles, P. (Rugby; Oxford University; Sussex)
Obituary   1921/I   *224*

Coley, E. (Secretary Northamptonshire)
Obituary   1958   *957*

Collard, A. (Derbyshire)
Obituary   1978   *1069*

Collett, W. E. (Surrey)
Obituary   1905   *xc*

Collette, H. E. (White Rose C.C., Winnipeg)
Obituary   1920/I   *193*

Colley, R. H. (Oxford University)
Obituary   1904   *lxxxvi*

Collier, Staff Sgt. C. G. A. (Worcestershire)
Obituary   1917   *175*

Collier, J. (Leicestershire)
Obituary   1936/I   *274*

Collin, E. W. (Eton)
Obituary   1945   *329*

Collins, A. (Sussex)
Obituary   1946   *437*

Collins, Lieut. A. E. J. (Clifton)
Obituary   1915/I   *216*

Collins, A. H. (Western Ontario)
Obituary   1914/I   *181*

Collins, B. A. (Malvern)
Obituary   1952   *955*

Collins, C. (Dunedin C.C.)
Obituary   1917   *243*

Collins, C. (Kent)
Obituary   1920/I   *170*

Collins, Dr. D. C. (Cambridge University; Wellington; New Zealand)
Obituary   1968   *999*

Collins, Lieut. F. B. (Victoria)
Obituary   1919   *198*

Collins, G. A. K. (Sussex)
Obituary   1969   *979*

Collins, G. C. (Natal)
Obituary   1957   *943*

Collins G. C. (Kent)
Benefit Match   1928/II   *120*
Obituary   1950   *906*

Collins, H. L. (New South Wales; Australia)
Obituary   1960   *950*
Testimonial Match   1935/II   *681*

Collins, I. G. (Harrow)
Obituary   1976   *1094*

Collins, Brig. L. P. (Marlborough; Oxford University)
  Obituary   1958   *957*
Collins, Capt. P. (Incogniti)
  Obituary   1916   *156*
Collins, T. (Cambridge University; Suffolk)
  Obituary   1935/I   *261*
Collins, Sir W. A. R. (Harrow)
  Obituary   1977   *1038*
Collins, W. E. (Cheltenham)
  Obituary   1935/I   *262*
Collins, W. E. W. (Radley; Shropshire)
  Obituary   1933/I   *242*
Collinson, J. (Middlesex; Worcestershire)
  Obituary   1984   *1197*
Collishaw, W. F. (Warwickshire)
  Obituary   1937/I   *270*
Collisson, Capt. Adj. E. R. (St. Edward's, Oxford)
  Obituary   1916   *156*
Collyer, W. R. (Rugby; Norfolk)
  Obituary   1929/I   *244*
Colman, C. (Surrey)
  Obituary   1914/I   *181*
Colman, 2nd Lieut. D. W. J. (Eton)
  Obituary   1943   *363*
Colman, Capt. G. R. R. (Eton; Oxford University; Norfolk)
  Obituary   1936/I   *274*
Colman, H. (Norfolk)
  Obituary   1896   *xl*
Colman, Sir J. (President Surrey)
  Obituary   1943   *373*
Colman, S. (Gentlemen of Norfolk)
  Obituary   1895   *xlii*
Colquhoun, J. C. (Glenalmond; Cornwall; Kent)
  Obituary   1978   *1069*
Colthurst, Sir G. St.J. 6th Bart. (Patron Irish Cricket)
  Obituary   1927/I   *294*
Coltman, F. J. (Eton)
  Obituary   1909/I   *134*
Colville, Rev. A. H. (Shropshire)
  Obituary   1919   *204*
Colwyn Bay Cricket Club
  Note on   1945   *105*
Comber, F. W. (Winchester)
  Obituary   1951   *919*
Comber, G. (Surrey)
  Obituary   1931/I   *273*

Comber, J. T. H. (Marlborough; Cambridge University)
    Obituary   1977   *1038*

Combey, J. (Durham)
    Obituary   1943   *374*

Commaille, J. M. M. (Western Province; Orange Free State; Guiqualand West; South Africa)
    Obituary   1957   *943*

Commandos Team   1946   *199*

Commercial Union N. A. Y. C.

Under 19 Championship   1983   *884*

Commonwealth Team
    in India 1949-50   1951   *801*
    in Ceylon/India 1950-51   1952   *836*
    Amendments   1953   *810*
    in India 1953-54   1955   *812*
    in India 1964   1966   *851*
    in Pakistan 1963   1965   *849*
    1968   1969   *870*
    1971   1972   *945*
    in South Africa 1959   1960   *898*
    in Rhodesia/South Africa 1960   1961   *893*

Compton, D. C. S. (Middlesex; England)
    Action Photograph   1951   *61*
    Benefit Match   1950   *435*
    Career Figures   1958   *81*
    Hundredth Hundred   1953   *461*
    Notable Achievements   1958   *93*
    Notes on   1944   *168*
                                      1947   *558*
                                      1948   *46,140,*
                                                      167,231
    Photographs   1948   *33*
                                      1950   *426*
                                      1968   *97*
    Portrait and Biography   1939   *37*
    'Batsmen Must Hit the Ball Again'   1968   *96*
    'Denis Compton – the Cavalier'
    N. Cardus   1958   *78*
    'Compton and Edrich' R.C. Robertson-Glasgow   1948   *45*
    'Compton's Record Season' B. Easterbrook   1972   *146*
    'Denis Compton' E. W. Swanton   1950   *979*
    Book Review
    'Denis Compton' I. A. R. Reebles
    Book Review   1972   *1100*
    'In Sun and Shadow' Book Review   1953   *1001*
    'End of an Innings' Book Review   1959   *988*

'Denis Compton's Test Diary 1964'   1965   *1020*
Book Review

Compton, E. D. (Lancing; Somerset; Oxfordshire)
Obituary   1941   *393*

Compton, L. H. (Middlesex)
Benefit Match   1955   *443*
Boundary Catch at Lords   1944   *64*

Comrie, Rifleman, J. M. (Wellington College, New Zealand)
Obituary   1917   *175*

Comyn, A. D. (Ireland)
Obituary   1950   *906*

Concrete Pitches
Note on   1948   *830*

Conder, W. S. (Statistican)
Obituary   1980   *1148*

Coney, J. V. (Wellington; New Zealand)
Action Photograph   1984   *Plates*
Cricketer of the Year   1984   *57*
Photograph   1984   *Plates*

Congdon, B. E. (Central Districts; Wellington; Otago; Canterbury; New Zealand)
Cricketer of the Year   1974   *65*
Photograph   1974   *50*

Congdon, Lt-Col. C. H. (Royal Navy)
Obituary   1959   *927*

Congdon, J. H. (Haverford College)
Obituary   1919   *204*

Conibere, W. J. (Somerset)
Obituary   1983   *1242*

Coningham, A. (Queensland; New South Wales; Australia)
Obituary   1940   *839*

Conmee, Lieut. J. A. (Catholic University School, Dublin)
Obituary   1918   *179*

Connaughton, J. M. (Oratory)
Schools Note   1938   *690*
79 wkts Schools Averages   1938   *750*

Connell, P. G. (Loretto)
Obituary   1908/I   *137*

Considine, Capt. H. J. (Beaumont College)
Obituary   1917   *175*

Considine, S. G. U. (Somerset)
Obituary   1951   *919*

Constable, B. (Surrey)
Benefit Match   1960   *560*
Photograph   1959   *531*

Constable, B. J. L. (Secretary Littlehampton C.C.)
Obituary   1916   *156*

Constantine, Sir L. N. (Lord) (Trinidad; West Indies)

Obituary 'Lord Constantine – The Spontaneous Cricketer' J. Arlott	1972	*125*
Honours Note on	1970	*80*
Photograph	1972	*126*
Portrait and Biography	1940	*34*
Tribute to W. Hammond	1966	*118*
Views on Growing Pains of Cricket	1956	*84*
'Cricket an Art not a Science'	1965	*108*
'How West Indies Cricket Grew up'	1957	*99*
'Sir Frank Worrell' Obituary Tribute	1968	*116*
'Welcome West Indies World Cricket Champions'	1966	*85*
'Cricket Crackers' Book Review	1951	*995*
'Learie Constantine' G. Howat Book Review	1976	*1148*

Constantine, L. S. (Trinidad)

Obituary	1943	*374*

Conway, A. J. (Worcestershire)

Obituary	1955	*928*

Conway, J. (Victoria)

Obituary	1910/I	*135*

Conway-Rees, J. (Carmarthenshire)

Obituary	1933/I	*242*

Conyers, 2nd Lieut. W. N. (Trinity College School, Port Hope)

Obituary	1917	*175*

Cooch, Behar Maharaja of (Indian Supporter)

Obituary	1924/I	*274*

Cooch, Behar Maharaja of (Indian Supporter)

Obituary	1912/I	*164*

Cooch, Behar Prince Victor of (Indian Supporter)

Obituary	1938	*938*

Coode, A. T. (Beccles School; Cambridge University; Middlesex)

Obituary	1941	*393*

Cook, Sqd. Ldr. A. E. (Bedford School; Bedfordshire)

Obituary	1945	*321*

Cook, B. (New South Wales)

Obituary	1982	*1195*

Cook, C. (Gloucestershire; England)

Benefit Match	1958	*379*
Photographs	1951	*342*
	1952	*345*
	1957	*364*
Retirement	1965	*401*

Cook, C. B. (St. Paul's; Devon)

Obituary	1966	*962*

Cook, Lieut. C. H. (Watson's College)
  Obituary   1918   179

Cook, G. (Northamptonshire; Eastern Province; England)
  Photographs   1976   506
                                                  1980   504

Cook, G. G. (Queensland)
  Obituary   1984   1198

Cook, 2nd Lieut. H. R. (Manchester Grammar School)
  Obituary   1918   180

Cook, J. G. (Bedford School; Bedfordshire)
  Obituary   1980   1148

Cook, L. (Lancashire)
  Benefit Match   1924/II   89
  Obituary   1934/I   262

Cook, N. G. B. (Leicestershire; England)
  Photograph   1981   475
  Whitbread Scholarship   1981   64

Cook, L/Cpl. P. H. (Liverpool C.C.)
  Obituary   1917   17

Cook, P. W. (Kent)
  Obituary   1967   96

Cook, R. (Committee Essex)
  Obituary   1909/I   13

Cook, T. E. R. (Sussex)
  Obituary   1951   91

Cook, Rt. Rev. T. W. (Lancing)
  Obituary   1929/I   24

Cook, W. (Groundsman Westcliff C.C.)
  Obituary   1913/I   18

Cook, W. (Lancashire)
  Obituary   1948   78

Cook, W. T. (Surrey)
  Obituary   1970   101

Cooke, E. J. (Umpire)
  Obituary   1958   95

Cooke, F. H. (Otago)
  Obituary   1934/I   26

Cooke, H. (Treasurer Sussex)
  Obituary   1915/I   21

Cooke, Capt. H. H. A. (Cambridgeshire)
  Obituary   1918   18

Cooley, B. C. (Natal)
  Obituary   1936/I   27

Coombes, M. J. (Tasamnia)
  Obituary   1984   119

Coope, M. (Somerset)
 Obituary 1976 *1104*
Cooper, A. V. (Essex)
 Obituary 1979 *1089*
Cooper, B. B. (Rugby; Middlesex; Kent; Victoria; Australia)
 Obituary 1915/I *217*
Cooper, C. J. H. (South East England Club Cricketer)
 Obituary 1910/I *135*
Cooper, C. O. (Dulwich; Kent)
 Obituary 1944 *312*
Cooper, E. (Worcestershire)
 Benefit Match 1952 *583*
 Obituary 1969 *979*
Cooper, F. J. (Essex)
 Obituary 1959 *927*
Cooper, G. C. (Sussex)
 Photograph 1969 *585*
Cooper, Sgt. H. A. (Eton)
 Obituary 1917 *175*
Cooper, H. P. (Yorkshire; Northern Transvaal)
 Photograph 1974 *598*
Cooper, K. E. (Nottinghamshire)
 Photograph 1977 *521*
Cooper, J. F. (Marlborough; Wiltshire; Shropshire)
 Obituary 1929/I *244*
Cooper, J. H. (President Leicestershire)
 Obituary 1907 *cx*
Cooper, J. W. (Yorkshire)
 Obituary 1910/ *135*
Cooper, L. H. (Buccaneers)
 Obituary 1973 *1005*
Cooper, W. H. (Victoria; Australia)
 Obituary 1940 *839*
Cooper, Pte. W. H. (Canada)
 Obituary 1918 *180*
Cooper, 2nd Lieut. W. M. (Reading School)
 Obituary 1918 *180*
Coote, C. (Cambridge University Groundsman)
 'Cyril Coote – A Cambridge Legend'
 J. G. W. Davis 1982 *123*
 Photograph 1982 *122*
Coote, E. (Cambridge University Groundsman)
 Obituary 1954 *922*
Coote, Lieut. G. B. (Radley)
 Obituary 1919/I *170*

Cope, G. A. (Yorkshire; England)
Photograph 1977 62

Cope, H. (Haverford College Groundsman)
Obituary 1925/I 262

Copeland, W. (Lancashire; Durham)
Obituary 1918 224

Copeman, Lieut. R. G. H. (Magdalen College, Oxford)
Obituary 1918 212

Copleston, Rev. J. H. (Winchester; Devon)
Obituary 1919 200
1920/I 193

Copinger, E. T. (Kent)
Obituary 1928/I 28

Coppinger, O. (Sussex Colts)
Obituary 1906 c

Copson, W. H. (Derbyshire; England)
Note on 1973 101
Obituary 1972 104
Portrait and Biography 1937/I 29
Studies in Greatness B. Easterbrook 1979 12

Corbett, A. M. (Yorkshire)
Obituary 1935/I 26

Corbett, B. O. (Derbyshire)
Obituary 1968 99

Corbett, L. J. (Gloucestershire; Journalist)
Obituary 1984 119

Corbett, P. T. (Worcestershire)
Obituary 1945 32

Corden, C. (Worcestershire)
Obituary 1925/I 26

Corder, Pte. A. (Sunderland C.C.)
Obituary 1916 15

Cordery, J. G. (Rugby)
Obituary 1901 8

Cordery, W. (Branshill C.C.)
Obituary 1916 15

Cording, G. E. (Glamorgan)
Obituary 1947 6

Cordingley, A. (Yorkshire; Sussex)
Obituary 1946 4

Cordle, A. E. (Glamorgan)
Benefit Match 1978 7

Corfield, 2nd Lieut. H. V. A. (St.Lawrence School, Ramsgate)
Obituary 1917 1

Corinthian Casuals Centenary 1983 10

Corke, M. D. (Suffolk)
'Views on the Laws' 1957

Cornell, P. P. (Suffolk)
  Obituary   1921/I   225
Cornford, W. L. (Sussex; England)
  Benefit Match   1935/II   146
  Obituary   1965   965
Cornhill Insurance
  'Case'   1984   953
  Sponsorship   1979   81
Cornwallis, Capt. O. W. (Hampshire)
  Obituary   1975   1075
Cornwallis, Rt. Hon. W. S. 2nd Baron (Kent)
  Obituary   1983   1242
Cornwell, T. E. (Bishop's Stortford College)
  Obituary   1916   156
Corrall, P. (Leicestershire; Services; Europeans)
  Benefit Match   1950   416
Corran, A. J. (Oxford University; Gresham's; Nottinghamshire)
  Photograph   1962   541
Cort, C. H. (Warwickshire)
  Obituary   1939   908
Cory-Wright, J. F. (Eton)
  Obituary   1946   433
Cosstick, S. (Victoria; New South Wales)
  Obituary   1897   xxxix
Costa, 2nd Lieut. L. G. (Dulwich)
  Obituary   1919   170
Costello, 2nd Lieut. A. G. (H.A.C.)
  Obituary   1917   175
Cotman, Capt. D. A. (Epsom College; Devon)
  Obituary   1976   1104
Cottam, R. M. H. (Hampshire; Northamptonshire; Devon; England)
  Photographs   1966   415
                                              1968   430
  Registration Details   1973   1044
Cutter, A. B. (New South Wales; Australia)
  Obituary   1919   198
Cotter, D. (Umpire)
  Obituary   1907   cxvii
Cotterill, Rev. G. E. (Brighton College; Cambridge University; Norfolk; Sussex; Cambridgeshire)
  Obituary   1914/I   181
Cotterill, Major. G. H. (Sussex; Brighton College; Cambridge University)
  Obituary   1951   920
Cotterill, Sir. J. M. (Sussex; Brighton College; Cambridge University)
  Obituary   1934/I   263
Cottesloe, 2nd Baron (Eton)
  Obituary   1919   205

Cotton, Rev. E. B. (Chatham House, Ramsgate; Essex)
Obituary 1920/I *170*
Cotton, J. (Leicestershire; Nottinghamshire)
Photographs 1961 *517*
1963 *556*
1966 *466*
Cotton, R. H. (Warwickshire)
Obituary 1980 *1148*
Cottrell, C. E. (Harrow; Middlesex)
Obituary 1898 *xliii*
Couchman, Rev. H. (Rossall)
Obituary 1923/I *293*
Coulson, H. (Cambridgeshire)
Obituary 1941 *393*
Coulson, S. S. (Leicestershire)
Obituary 1983 *1243*
Coulson, T. (Durham City)
Obituary 1920/I *170*
Coulter, Capt. W. M. (Glasgow High School)
Obituary 1918 *180*
Coulthurst, E. J. (Lincolnshire)
Obituary 1953 *939*
Coulthurst, J. (Lancashire)
Obituary 1971 *1024*
Council of Cricket Societies Note on 1970 *81*
Counties
Debt to M.C.C. 1953 *82*
Question to 1952 *93*
Postwar Plan 1944 *83*
'Reject Clark Plan' C. Bray 1967 *96*
Share Out £950,000 1977 *110*
Suffer 1950 *113*
County Champions
'The Early' R. Bowen 1959 *91*
'The Early – Postscript' R. Bowen 1960 *992*
County Championship
Attendance Figures Graph 1952 *85*
Count Victories Only 1955 *84*
Future of 1976 *64*
'In the Wisden Century' R. Bowen 1963 *366*
Increase in Clubs 1949 *123*
1950 *114*
Laws – Charges 1974 *69*
Monetary Awards 1974 *111*
'Mosts' E. L. Peake 1973 *356*

Only 20 Matches	1974	*89*
Pennant	1953	*988*
Reducing it	1971	*90*
'Reviewed' H. Preston	1942	*48*
County Clubs Members Needed	1945	*61*
'Dates of Formation of Clubs		
Now First Class' R. Bowen	1963	*366*
County Cricket		
Clark Committee's Report	1967	*101*
Dates in	1963	*369*
One Hundred Years of	1973	*94*
'Special Article on'	1889	*xxxii*
'Modern County Cricket'		
Col. R. S. Rait-Kerr	1952	*84*
County Histories in Wisden　List of	1967	*142*
County Ranking List 1919-1939	1941	*66*
Coupar, Capt. S. B. N. (Fettes)		
Obituary	1920/I	*152*
Couper, Major D. O. (Harrow)		
Obituary	1946	*434*
Couper, Major-Gen. Sir V. A. (Uppingham)		
Obituary	1939	*908*
Courage International Batsman of the Year	1980	*361*
Courthorpe, G. J. (Eton)		
Obituary	1911/I	*140*
Coutts, 2nd Lieut. P. C. (Clydesdale Club)		
Obituary	1919	*170*
Coventry, Col. Hon. C. J. (Worcestershire; England)		
Obituary	1930/I	*248*
Coventry, Hon. H. T. (Eton; Worcestershire)		
Obituary	1935/I	*262*
Coventry, Hon. J. B. (Eton; Worcestershire)		
Obituary	1970	*1019*
Coventry, 9th Earl of (Worcestershire)		
Obituary	1931/I	*251*
Coventry, Courtald's Ground		
Plan of County Ground	1953	*571*
	ad passim	
Coverdale, W. (Northamptonshire; Durham)		
Obituary	1973	*1005*
Covering Wickets		
Notes on	1959	*79*
	1981	*98*
Cowan, Capt. C. F. R. (Warwickshire)		
Obituary	1959	*928*

Cowan, S. (Masseur Sussex)
  Obituary   1965   *965*
Coward, C. (Lancashire; Umpire)
  Benefit Match   1879   *179*
  Obituary   1904   *lxxxiii*
Coward, E. (Preston C.C.)
  Obituary   1913   *185*
Coward, F. (Lancashire; Umpire)
  Obituary   1906   *xc*
Cowdrey, C. S. (Tonbridge; Kent; England)
  Photograph   1981   *446*
  Whitbread Scholarship   1981   *645*
Cowdrey, M. C. (Tonbridge; Oxford University; Kent; England)
  Action Photographs   1956   *50*
     1957   *50*
     1958   *47*
     1963   *152*
     1966   *58*
     1969   *52*
  All Round Performance at Lord's   1947   *217*
  Career Figures   1967   *103*
  C.B.E. Awarded   1972   *159*
  'County Cups' Special Award   1958   *216*
  Cowdrey and May   1955   *81*
  Cricketer of the Year   1956   *57*
  'Cricket Today' Book Review   1962   *1033*
  Hundredth Hundred   1974   *445*
  'M.C.C. The Autobiography of a Cricketer'
  Book Review   1977   *1096*
  'M. C. Cowdrey – Centurion and Captain
  Courteous' J. Arlott   1969   *97*
  Photographs   1956   *56*
     1964   *64*
     1968   *60*
     1969   *98,101*
     1974   *75*
  Schools Notes   1947   *560,575*
     1948   *661*
     1949   *689*
     1950   *713*
     1951   *704,723*
  1033 runs Schools Averages   1951   *752*
  'Time for Reflection' Book Review   1963   *1110*
  'The Incomparable Game' Book Review   1971   *1077*
Cowie, Capt. A. G. (Charterhouse; Cambridge University; Hampshire)
  Obituary   1917   *176*

Cowie, 2nd Lieut. G. (Rugby)
   Obituary   1919   *198*
Cowles, S. R. B. (Norfolk)
   Obituary   1939   *908*
Cowley, Lieut. J. L. (Harrow)
   Obituary   1944   *305*
Cowley, N. G. (Hampshire)
   Photograph   1978   *413*
Cowley, Capt. R. B. (Harrow)
   Obituary   1941   *394*
Cowpe, 2nd Lieut. G. B. (Burnley Grammar School)
   Obituary   1918   *180*
Cox, A. R. (Harrow; Cambridge University)
   Obituary   1951   *920*
Cox, Col. A. T. (Break O' Day C.C., Tasmania)
   Obituary   1908/I   *137*
Cox, Capt. E. R. A. C. (Bradfield)
   Obituary   1918   *180*
Cox, G. (Junior) (Sussex)
   Benefit Match   1952   *538*
   Photographs   1950   *514*
                                        1951   *525*
   Retirement   1956   *589*
Cox, G. R. (Senior) (Sussex)
   Benefit Match   1921/II   *154*
   Obituary   1950   *906*
Cox, M. (Northamptonshire)
   Obituary   1970   *1028*
Cox, Lieut. N. J. (Highgate; Hertfordshire)
   Obituary   1916   *156*
Cox, R. (King Edward Sixth School, Stratford-upon-Avon)
   10 wkts for 6 runs. Schools Note   1982   *901*
Cox, 2nd Lieut. R. W. T. (Merchant Taylors)
   Obituary   1917   *176*
Coxhead, Major M. E. (Eastbourne College; Middlesex)
   Obituary   1918   *180*
Coxon, H. (Journalist; Scorer Nottinghamshire)
   Obituary   1930/I   *248*
Coy, A. H. (Eastern Province)
   Obituary   1984   *1198*
Cozens-Hardy, A. W. (Kendall C.C.)
   Obituary   1926/I   *268*
Cozens-Hardy, F. (Norfolk)
   Obituary   1919   *205*
Crabtree, E. (Central Lancashire League)
   Obituary   1946   *437*

Crabtree, F. (Yorkshire; Lancashire)
  Obituary   1894   *xxxviii*
Crabtree, F. L. (Eton; Hertfordshire; Cambridge University)
  Obituary   1952   *955*
Crabtree, H. (Charterhouse)
  Obituary   1916   *156*
Crabtree, H. (Lancashire)
  Obituary   1952   *955*
Crabtree, H. P. (Essex; British Empire XI; St.Peter's, York)
  Obituary   1983   *1243*
Cracknell, R. (New England Club Cricket)
  Obituary   1914/I   *181*
Craddy, W. H. (Gloucestershire)
  Obituary   1980   *1148*
Craddock, T. T. (Transvaal; Natal)
  Obituary   1949   *863*
Cragg, Lieut. W. A. (Cheshire)
  Obituary   1919   *170*
Craig, A. ('Surrey Poet')
  Obituary   1910/I   *135*
Craig, E. J. (Charterhouse; Cambridge University; Lancashire)
  Schools Notes   1960   *743,745*
                                                    1961   *743*
  1079 runs Schools Averages   1960   *757*
  1106 runs Schools Averages   1961   *757*
Craig, J. (Scotland)
  Obituary   1911/I   *140*
Craig, J. D. (Shrewsbury)
  Obituary   1951   *920*
Craig, Lieut. J. M. (Westminster)
  Obituary   1916   *157*
Craigmile, Capt. A. M. (Sedbergh)
  Obituary   1919   *170*
Craik, Capt. J. B. (Blair Lodge School; Forfarshire; Calcutta C.C.)
  Obituary   1918   *180*
Crake, E. H. (Harrow; M.C.C.)
  Obituary   1949   *864*
Crake, Lt-Col. R. H. (Harrow)
  Obituary   1953   *939*
Crake, W. P. (Harrow)
  Obituary   1922/I   *246*
Cranfield, B. (Somerset; London County)
  Obituary   1910/I   *136*
Crankshaw, Sir E. N. S. (Eton; Gloucestershire)
  Obituary   1968   *1009*

Cranney, H. (New South Wales)
Obituary 1972 *1047*
Cranston, J. (Gloucestershire; Warwickshire; Worcestershire; England)
Obituary 1905 *xc*
Cranston, K. (Liverpool College; Lancashire, England)
Schools Notes 1934/I *292*
1935/I *298*
Cranstoun, Rev. J. P. (Shrewsbury)
Obituary 1922/I *271*
Crapp, J. F. (Gloucestershire; England; Umpire)
Benefit Match 1952 *349*
Note on 1945 *160*
Obituary 1982 *1195*
Photographs 1950 *339*
1954 *363*
Craven, N. (Writer)
'9, 10, Joker' Book Review 1974 *1122*
'To Gloucester with Thanks' Book Review 1970 *1073*
Glosters' Centenary Cricket Book Review 1971 *1083*
Crawford, A. (Club Cricketer)
Obituary 1927/I *275*
Crawford, Pte. A. (Galt C.C., Canada)
Obituary 1917 *223*
Crawford, Capt. A. B. (Oundle; Warwickshire; Nottinghamshire)
Obituary 1917 *176*
Crawford, Major F. F. (Kent)
Obituary 1902 *lxxii*
Crawford, H. L. (Ceylon)
Obituary 1932/I *241*
Crawford, Rev. J. C. (Kent; Leicestershire)
Obituary 1936/I *275*
Crawford, J. N. (Repton; Surrey; South Australia; Wellington; Otago; England)
Obituary 1964 *946*
Portrait and Biography 1907 *cxxiii*
Schools Notes 1904 *ci*
1905 *cxxi,cxxxiii,*
cxxxvi,cxxxiv
1906 *cxviii,cxxi*
75 wkts Schools Averages 1905 *452*
Crawford, Lt.-Col. P. E. P. (Sussex)
Obituary 1950 *906*
Crawford, R. T. (Leicestershire)
Obituary 1946 *437*
Crawford, S. J. (Northumberland)
Obituary 1923/I *293*

133

Crawford, T. A. (Tonbridge; Kent)
    Obituary   1981   *1140*
Crawford, V. F. S. (Whitgift Grammar; Surrey; Leicestershire)
    Obituary   1923/I   *293*
    Schools Note   1898   *lxviii*
    80 wkts Schools Averages   1897   *373*
    78 wkts/1340 runs Schools Averages   1898   *375*
Crawford, J. W. F. A. (Merchant Taylors; Oxford University; Ireland)
    Obituary   1940   *839*
    87 wkts Schools Averages   1897   *367*
    88 wkts Schools Note   1898   *lxvii*
Crawley, Canon A. S. (Harrow; Hertfordshire)
    Obituary   1949   *864*
Crawley, Rev. C. D. (Harrow)
    Obituary   1918   *240*
Crawley, Major E. (Harrow; Cambridge University; Hertfordshire)
    Obituary   1916   *218*
Crawley, H. E. (Harrow; Cambridge University)
    Obituary   1932/I   *241*
Crawley, K. E. (Harrow)
    Obituary   1982   *1196*
Crawley, L. G. (Harrow; Cambridge University; Worcestershire; Essex)
    Obituary   1982   *1196*
Crawley-Boevey, Capt. T. R. (Clifton)
    Obituary   1917   *176*
Crawshaw, E. E. (Christchurch High School, New Zealand)
    Obituary   1920/I   *153*
Crease Using it fully
    Photograph   1982   *63*
Creaton, Lieut. D. A. (Haileybury)
    Obituary   1945   *321*
Crebbin, Capt. W. A. (St Paul's)
    Obituary   1919   *170*
Creber, A. B. (Scotland)
    Obituary   1967   *964*
Creber, H. (Glamorgan)
    Obituary   1940   *839*
Creek, F. N. S. (Wiltshire; Dorset)
    Obituary   1981   *1140*
Creese, W. L. C. (Hampshire)
    Career Figures   1975   *1076*
    Obituary   1975   *1075*
Cregar, E. M. (Philadelphia)
    Obituary   1917   *243*
Crellin, Lt-Col W. A. (Military Cricket)
    Obituary   1919   *170*

Cremer, H. L. (King's Canterbury; Treasurer Kent)
   Obituary 1977 *1038*
Creswell, Capt. A. S. (East Kent Regiment)
   Obituary 1916 *157*
Creswell, Sgt. G. H. (Borlase School)
   Obituary 1919 *170*
Creswell, J. (Secretary; South Australian Cricket Association)
   Obituary 1910/I *136*
Creswell, J. (Warwickshire)
   Obituary 1933/I *242*
Cresswell, G. F. (Wellington; Central Districts; New Zealand)
   Obituary 1967 *964*
Crew, A. E. (Gloucestershire Scorer)
   Obituary 1956 *970*
Crichton, D. (Drumpellier C.C.)
   Obituary 1910/I *136*
Crichton, J. P. (Harrogate C.C.)
   Obituary 1918 *224*
Crichton, W. (Toronto Cricket Clubs)
   Obituary 1921/I *225*
Crick, Flt-Lieut. H. (Yorkshire)
   Obituary 1961 *945*
Cricket (Does not include Book Reviews)
   A Call for Strict Cricket 1948 *86*
   'Cricket – A Game – Not a Subject'
   A. D. G. Matthews 1966 *133*
   'Cricket Alive Again' J. H. Fingleton 1961 *127*
   'Cricket – an Enduring Art'
   Rt. Hon. Sir Robert Menzies 1963 *67*
   'Cricket an Art Not a Science'
   L. N. Constantine 1965 *108*
   'Cricket at the Crossroads'
   D. G. Bradman 1939 *42*
   'Cricket in the British Commonwealth'
   Rt. Hon. H. V. Evatt 1949 *111*
   Cricket and the War Effort (Cartoon) 1941 *25*
   'Cricketana – A Bull Market' D. Frith 1981 *127*
   Cricket Bibliography – see under Bibliography
   Cricket Book Reviews   1950-1978 J. Arlott
                          1979-1980 G. Ross
                          1981-1984 J. Arlott
   Cricket by Aeroplane 1948 *758*
   'Cricket Centuries and L.B.W.'
   Hon. E. V. Bligh 1899 *lxvi*
    1900 *xcvii*

'Cricket Conundrums' A. E. R. Gilligan	1939	48
Cricket Council: Statement on Discipline	1972	1086
Cricket Cup. K.O. Competition	1946	126
'Cricket Fever Hits Australia' R. Benaud	1974	39
Cricket for the million	1952	97
'Cricket, Growth of Overseas' H. S. Altham	1962	156
Cricket, In Honour of;		
Dinner at the Mansion House	1928/I	351
Cricket in Iceland	1944	62
'Cricket in the Pacific' S. Beny	1981	119
'Cricket in the 17th and 18th Centuries'		
R. Bowen	1965	135
'Cricket in the Sixties and at the Present Day'		
A. Lubbock	1909/I	109
'Cricket in the West Indies and America'		
P. F. Warner	1898	lxx
'Cricket in War Time' H. S. Altham	1940	43
Cricket Inquiry	1950	954
	1961	122
	1962	149
'Cricket Literature of the Wisden Century'		
J. Arlott	1963	1077
'Cricket, The Love of' Rt. Hon Lord Birkett	1958	68
Cricket Matches on the Ice. 1878-79	1880	17
Crickets Place in War Time	1944	59
'Cricket Reform' H. Trumble	1927/I	348
'Cricket Rhymester' B. Easterbrook	1977	142
Cricket Societies	1956	740
'Cricket Society Movement' R. Yeomans	1979	127
'Cricket Society Movement' Additional Note	1980	120
'Cricket's Strongest Wind of Change'		
G. Ross	1974	140
'Cricket Thrives Here'(Work of the M.C.C. Youth Cricket Association)		
H. S. Altham	1961	154
Cricket Umpires Association	1960	103
'Cricket Under the Japs' E. W. Swanton	1946	48
Cricket Welfare of First Class Counties	1957	70
Cricketer Cup	1970	864
Cricketers' Agents	1968	280
Cricketers Honoured	1975	101
	1980	91
'Cricketers of the Year' A. S. Dixon	1945	349
'Cricketers Past and Present'		
An Old Cambridge Captain	1895	lix
Cricketers' Peace Plan	1966	816
Cricketers' Salaries	1981	580

Crisp, R. J. (Rhodesia; Western Province; Worcestershire; South Africa)
Note on	1944	*58*
Records by	1941	*62*

Crockett, H. L. (President South African Cricket Association)
Obituary	1965	*965*

Crockett, R. W. (Umpire)
Obituary	1936/I	*276*

Croft, C. E. H. (Guyana; Lancashire; West Indies)
Action Photograph	1982	*63*

Crofts, Major D. D. (Charterhouse)
Obituary	1945	*321*

Croggon, Capt. J. F. S. (Mill Hill School)
Obituary	1919/I	*170*

Crole-Rees, A. (Charterhouse)
Obituary	1984	*1198*

Crommellin-Brown, J. L. (Winchester; Derbyshire)
Obituary	1954	*922*

Crompton, F. (Bedfordshire)
Obituary	1971	*1024*
Presentation to	1970	*160*

Crompton, Sqd Ldr. J. A. (Charterhouse)
Obituary	1945	*321*

Crook, R. (Wellington, New Zealand)
Obituary	1944	*305*

Crooke, A. R. (Cheshire)
Obituary	1977	*1051*

Crooke, F. J. (Winchester; Lancashire; Gloucestershire)
Obituary	1924/I	*256*

Croom, A. J. (Warwickshire; Berkshire)
Benefit Match	1937/II	*358*
Obituary	1949	*872*

Croome, A. C. M. (Wellington; Oxford University; Gloucestershire; Berkshire)
Obituary	1931/I	*251*

Crosby, A. B. (Sherborne; Durham)
Obituary	1933/I	*243*

Crosby, 2nd Lieut. A. B. L. (Sherborne)
Obituary	1918	*180*

Crosby, H. S. (Sherborne; Durham)
Obituary	1937/I	*270*

Crosfield, S. M. (Wimbledon School; Lancashire; Cheshire)
Obituary	1909/I	*135*

Cross, A. E. (Cranleigh School)
Obituary	1948	*782*

Cross, 2nd Lieut. F. A. (Birmingham Old Edwardians)
Obituary	1918	*180*

Crosse, E. M. (Cheltenham; Northamptonshire)
Obituary 1965 *972*
Crossland, A. (Yorkshire)
Obituary 1904 *lxxxvii*
Crossland, J. (Lancashire)
Obituary 1904 *lxxxiv*
Crossman, Capt. G. M. (Eton)
Obituary 1946 *434*
Crossman, Capt. R. D. (Eton)
Obituary 1919 *120*
Crouch, G. S. (Queensland)
Obituary 1953 *939*
Crow, J. (Kent Scorer)
Obituary 1940 *839*
Crowder, A. B. (Tasmania)
Obituary 1965 *965*
Crowds 'Great' 1948 *85*
Crowdy, Rev. J. G. (Rugby; Hampshire; Berkshire; Devon)
Obituary 1920/I *193*
Crowe, G. L. (Tonbridge; Westminster; Worcestershire)
Obituary 1977 *1038*
Crozier, Sgt. H. C. (Sheffield United C.C.)
Obituary 1917 *176*
Crozier, Lieut. W. M. (Repton; Dublin University)
Obituary 1917 *176*
Crumblehume, W. D. (President Lancashire)
Obituary 1982 *1197*
Cruickshank, S. (Trinity College, Glenalmond)
Schools Notes 1928/I *320,341*
76 wkts Schools Averages 1928/II *609*
Cruickshanks, Wg. Comdr. G. L. (Eastern Province)
Obituary 1943 *364*
Cruise, Sir R. R. (Harrow)
Obituary 1947 *688*
Crum, W. G. (Eton)
Obituary 1948 *782*
Crump, B. S. (Northamptonshire)
Photograph 1961 *499*
1964 *496*
1966 *500*
Crutchley, E. (Harrow; Oxford University; Middlesex)
Obituary 1983 *1243*
Crutchley, G. E. V. (Harrow; Middlesex; Oxford University)
Obituary 1970 *1019*
Crutchley, P. E. (Harrow)
Obituary 1941 *394*

Cudworth, H. (Lancashire)
Obituary   1915/I   *218*

Cuff, L. A. (Canterbury; Tasmania)
Obituary   1955   *928*

Cuffe, C. R. (Ireland)
Obituary   1974   *1084*

Cuffe, J. A. (New South Wales; Worcestershire)
Obituary   1932/I   *241*

Cullen, A. C. (Scotland)
Obituary   1923/I   *295*

Cullin, N. (Emerald Hill C.C., Victoria)
Obituary   1918   *224*

Cumberbatch, G. T. (Spartan C.C., Barbados)
Obituary   1913/I   *185*

Cumberland County Cricket Club
'A History' J. Hurst Book Review   1983   *1302*

Cumberlege, B. S. (Durham School; Cambridge University; Kent; Durham; Northumberland)
Obituary   1971   *1024*

Cumberlege, C. F. (Rossall; Wiltshire; Surrey; Northumberland)
Obituary   1930/I   *248*

Cumbes, J. (Worcestershire; Lancashire; Surrey; Warwickshire)
Career Figures   1983   *711*

Cumming, B. L. (Sussex; Oxford University)
Obituary   1969   *979*

Cumming, M. (Writer)
with P. Morris 'Meet the Test Stars'
Book Review   1962   *1036*

Cummings, J. (Pullman C.C., Illinois)
Obituary   1914/I   *181*

Cummins, Capt. H. C. B. (Tonbridge; Devon; Dorset)
Obituary   1917   *176*

Cummins, H. M. (Cricket Outfitter, Barbados)
Obituary   1913/I   *185*

Cundall, Capt. C. (Dover College)
Obituary   1918   *181*

Cuningham, Capt. C. A. (Sandhurst)
Obituary   1916   *157*

Cunliffe, Major Sir F. H. E. Bart. (Eton; Oxford University; Middlesex; Shropshire)
Obituary   1917   *177*

Cunningham, C. J. (Patron Scotland)
Obituary   1907   *cx*

Cunningham, E. (Northern Argentina; Brazil)
Obituary   1967   *964*

Cunningham, Capt. R. C. (Glenalmond)
Obituary   1918   *212*
Cunninghame, Capt. A. K. S. (Grenadier Guards)
Obituary   1917   *177*
    1918   *212*
Curgenven, G. (Repton; Derbyshire)
Obituary   1935/I   *263*
Curgenven, Capt. W. C. (Repton)
Obituary   1917   *223*
Curgenven, Dr. W. G. (Derbyshire)
Obituary   1911/I   *141*
Curle, G. (King Edward's Birmingham; Warwickshire)
Obituary   1978   *1069*
Curling, 2nd Lieut. D. L. (Eton)
Obituary   1942   *347*
Curran, W. (Umpire)
Obituary   1923/I   *309*
Currer, C. S. (Later C. S. Roundell)(Harrow; Oxford University)
Obituary   1907   *cx*
Currie, Sir D. (Donator of Currie Cup; South Africa)
Obituary   1911/I   *162*
Currie, Rev. Sir F. L. (Cambridge University)
Obituary   1902   *lxxii*
Curry, Atg-Major. W. E. (Upper Canada College)
Obituary   1918   *181*
Cursham, H. A. (Repton; Nottinghamshire)
Obituary   1942   *356*
Curteis, A. M. (Harrow)
Obituary   1923/I   *295*
Curteis, H. M. (Westminster; Oxford University; Supporter Sussex)
Obituary   1896   *xli*
Curteis R. M. (Westminster; Sussex)
Obituary   1928/I   *281*
Curteis, Rev. T. S. (Bury St.Edmunds Grammar; Cambridge University;
Norfolk; Suffolk; Cheshire)
Obituary   1915/I   *218*
Curtin, J. (Australian Prime Minister)
Obituary   1946   *437*
Curtis, C. B. (Essex)
Obituary   1900   *xlviii*
Curtis, J. S. (Leicestershire)
Obituary   1978   *1084*
Curtis, Major T. H. W. (Sussex)
Obituary   1968   *1009*
Curtler, W. H. R. (Marlborough)
Obituary   1926/I   *268*

Curwen, W. J. H. (Charterhouse; Oxford University; Surrey)
Obituary 1916 *157*
Curwen, Lieut. W. L. (Glenalmond)
Obituary 1918 *181*
Curzen, Major F. C. (Secretary Derbyshire)
Obituary 1919 *205*
Curzon, 1st Marquis (President Derbyshire)
Obituary 1926/I *268*
Cussen, Sir L. (President Melbourne C.C.)
Obituary 1934/I *263*
Cuthbert, D. C. (Break O' Day C.C., Hobart)
Obituary 1913/I *185*
Cuthbertson, Lieut. E. H. (Malvern; Cambridge University; Hertfordshire)
Obituary 1918 *181*
Cuthbertson, J. L. (Rugby; Oxford University; Surrey)
Schools Note 1961 *745*
1123 runs Schools Averages 1961 *785*
Cutler, E. (Eton)
Obituary 1917 *243*
Cutler, N. (Writer)
'Behind the Australian Tests'
Book Review 1957 *997*
'Behind the Tests' Book Review 1954 *982*
Cuttell, W. (Yorkshire)
Obituary 1897 *xl*
Cuttell, W. R. (Yorkshire; Lancashire; England)
Benefit Match 1904 *75*
Obituary 1930/I *265*
Portrait and Biography 1898 *liv*
Cutts, Capt. F. B. (Notts Forest C.C.)
Obituary 1917 *177*
Cyclone Disaster Relief Match in Pakistan 1972 *995*
Dacosta, D. C. (Supporter West Indies)
Obituary 1912/I *164*
Dacosta, G. M. (West Indies Board of Control)
Obituary 1969 *979*
Dacre, C. C. (Auckland; Gloucestershire)
Obituary 1977 *1051*
D'Aeth, E. K. H. (Haileybury; Oxford University)
Obituary 1924/I *257*
Daft, C. F. (Nottinghamshire)
Obituary 1916 *157*
Daft, C. F. (Nottinghamshire Club Cricket; Son of R. Daft)
Obituary 1919 *205*
Daft, C. F. (Nottinghamshire Club Cricket; Grandson of R. Daft)
Obituary 1919 *205*

Daft, F. (Leicestershire Scorer)
    Obituary   1907   *cx*
Daft, H. B. (Trent College; Nottingham ; Nottinghamshire)
    Obituary   1946   *437*
Daft, R. (Nottinghamshire; North of England; All England)
    Complimentary Dinner to   1878   *188*
    Complimentary Match   1877   *192*
    Obituary   1901   *liv*
    Team in U.S.A./Canada 1879   1880   *211*
    'Views on High Scoring and the L.B.W. Rule'   1899   *lxxxvii*
    Views on 'The Follow On'   1894   *xlviii*
    Views on Throwing   1895   *lvii*
Daft, R. P. (Nottinghamshire; Trent College)
    Obituary   1935/I   *263*
Daily, C. E. (Surrey)
    Obituary   1975   *1076*
Daily Express Better Cricket Competition   1964   *88*
Daines, Canon S. E. (Rugby)
    Obituary   1919   *205*
D'Albertanson, 2nd Lieut. R. (Sutton Valence)
    Obituary   1917   *177*
Dale, G. F. (Durham; Northumberland)
    Obituary   1952   *955*
Dale, H. A. (Journalist)
    'Cricket Crusader' Book Review   1953   *998*
    Obituary   1966   *963*
Dale, J. W. (Tonbridge; Cambridge University; Middlesex; Lincolnshire)
    Obituary   1896   *xl*
Dale, P. W. (Secretary Northamptonshire)
    Obituary   1912/I   *164*
Dales, H. L. (Middlesex; Durham)
    Obituary   1965   *966*
Dallas-Brooks, Gen. Sir R. A. (Dover College; Hampshire)
    Obituary   1967   *965*
Dalmeny, Lord (Eton; Oxford University; Middlesex)
    Obituary   1932/I   *242*
Dalton, E. L. (Natal; South Africa)
    Obituary   1982   *1197*
Dalton, G. L. (Natal)
    Obituary   1947   *688*
Daly, Col. D. N. (Downside)
    Obituary   1955   *929*
Daly, Hon. Sir M. B. (Canadian Club Cricket)
    Obituary   1921/I   *225*
Daly, Hon. T. M. (President Winnipeg Cricket Association)
    Obituary   1912/I   *16?*

Damian, Dr. O. J. (London County)
Obituary 1913/I *185*

Daniel, A. W. T. (Harrow)
Memorial to 1875 *58*

Daniel, Lt-Col. F. E. L. (Seaforth Highlanders)
Obituary 1917 *177*

Daniel, Rev. J. H. (Hereford C.C.)
Obituary 1951 *929*

Daniel, Capt. M. C. C. (Rugby)
Obituary 1943 *364*

Daniel, R. (Gault and Guelph Clubs)
Obituary 1920/I *153*

Daniel, T. H. (President Moseley C.C.)
Obituary 1917 *243*

Daniel, W. W. (Barbados; Western Australia; Middlesex; West Indies)
Photograph 1979 *467*

Daniell, J. (Clifton; Cambridge University; Somerset)
Obituary 1964 *947*

Daniels, A. N. (Congregational C.C.; Victoria; British Columbia)
Obituary 1920/I *153*

Danish XI in England 1953 1954 *683*

Danish Cricket Association
'Views on Laws' 1957 *87*

Dann, Rev. J. W. (Downend C.C.; Thornbury C.C.)
Obituary 1916 *158*

Danson, C. (Cheshire)
Obituary 1966 *963*

Danson, Lieut. F. R. (Trinity College, Oxford)
Obituary 1918 *212*

Dare, J. F. (West Indies Board of Control)
Tribute to O. G. Smith 1960 *956*

Dark, F. (Lord's Ground Staff)
Obituary 1907 *cx*

Dark, J. H. (Proprietor Lord's)
Obituary 1872 *71*

Darling, D. K. (Writer)
'Test Tussels on and off the Field'
Book Review 1971 *1070*

Darling, J. (South Australia; Australia)
Fastest Hundred in Test Cricket 1983 *106*
Obituary 1947 *688*
Portrait and Biography 1900 *lix*
'Test Tussels on and off the Field'
Book Review 1971 *1070*

Darling, Capt. R. C. (Upper Canada College)
Obituary 1917 *177*

143

Darlington, W. A. (Playwright)
Obituary 1980 *1148*
Darnley, 6th Earl of (Father of Ivo Bligh)
Obituary 1897 *xlii*
Darnley, 7th Earl of (Eton)
Obituary 1901 *lv*
Darnley, 8th Earl of (Hon. Ivo Bligh) (Eton; Cambridge University;
Kent; England)
Obituary 1928/I *281*
Recollections of F. R. Spofforth 1927/I *299*
Team in Australia 1882-83 1884 *17*
Tribute to the Hon. A. Lyttleton 1914/I *200*
Views on 'The Follow On' 1894 *xlix*
Views on the Reforms of 1889 1890 *xxxviii*
Views on Some Questions of the Day 1890 *xl*
Dartford Hesketh Park
Plan of County Ground 1972 *450*
Dartmouth, 6th Earl of (President M.C.C., Kent, Staffordshire)
Obituary 1937/I *271*
Dartmouth 7th Earl of (President M.C.C.)
Obituary 1959 *928*
Darwall-Smith, J. A. (Oxford University)
Obituary 1977 *1038*
Darwell, E. J. (U.S.A. Club Cricket)
Obituary 1919 *205*
Dashwood, T. H. K. (Wellington; Oxford University; Hertfordshire;
Cornwall; Hampshire)
Obituary 1930/I *248*
Dastur, M. P. (Parsis)
Obituary 1927/I *275*
'Dates in Cricket History' H. S. Altham 1953 *115*
ad passim
Dates in County Cricket 1963 *369*
**'Dates of Formation of First Class County
Clubs'** R. Bowen 1963 *370*
Daubeny, Rev. E. T. (Bromsgrove; Oxford University)
Obituary 1915/I *219*
Daughlish, Rev. A. F. (Harrow)
Obituary 1948 *789*
Dauglish, M. J. (Harrow; Oxford University; Middlesex; Berkshire)
Obituary 1923/I *295*
Davenport, Rev. E. (Rugby; Oxford University; Oxfordshire)
Obituary 1916 *158*
Davenport, G. (Cheshire)
Obituary 1903 *lxxix*

144

Davey, A. F. (Secretary Somerset)
  Obituary   1955   *929*
Davey, D. C. (Natal)
  Obituary   1912/I   *165*
Davey, J. G. (Sussex)
  Obituary   1879   *85*
Davey, W. (Assistant Secretary Kent)
  Obituary   1876   *80*
David, Major R. F. A. (Wellington; Glamorgan)
  Obituary   1970   *1019*
Davidson, A. K. (New South Wales; Australia)
  Cricketer of the Year   1962   *102*
  'Fifteen Paces' Book Review   1964   *1002*
  Photograph   1962   *93*
Davidson, 2nd Lieut. A. P. (Glenalmond)
  Obituary   1917   *178*
Davidson, G. (Derbyshire)
  Benefit match   1898   *224*
  Obituary   1900   *xlxi*
Davidson, J. (Harrow)
  Obituary   1899   *xliv*
Davidson J. (Derby)
  Obituary   1902   *lxiii*
Davidson, K. R. (Yorkshire)
  Obituary   1955   *929*
Davidson, Col. W. L. (Army)
  Obituary   1916   *158*
Davies, A. (Writer)
  'Sir Donald Bradman' Book Review   1961   *998*
Davies, D. (Glamorgan; Umpire)
  Benefit Match   1936/II   *364*
  'Dai Davies not out 78'
  J. Edwards   Book Review   1976   *1148*
  Obituary   1977   *1038*
Davies, E. (Glamorgan)
  Obituary   1976   *1094*
  Photograph   1951   *324*
  Records by   1976   *1095*
Davies, E. Q. (Eastern Province; North-Eastern Transvaal; Transvaal; South Africa)
  Obituary   1978   *1084*
Davies, 2nd Lieut. F. A. (Sefton Park C.C.)
  Obituary   1917   *178*
Davies, Lieut. F. L. (Haileybury)
  Obituary   1918   *181*

Davies, G. A. (Victoria)
Obituary   1958   *958*
Davies, Capt. G. B. (Rossall; Cambridge University; Essex)
Obituary   1916   *158*
Davies, Sub-Lt. G. L. (Eton)
Obituary   1916   *159*
Davies, G. W. (Gentlemen of Worcestershire)
Obituary   1911/I   *141*
Davies, 2nd Lieut. H. C. (Oundle)
Obituary   1917   *178*
Davies, H. D. (Lancashire)
Obituary   1959   *928*
Davies, H. G. (Glamorgan)
Benefit Match   1952   *341*
Career Figures   1959   *491*
Davies, Sir J. G. (Tasmania)
Obituary   1914/I   *182*
Davies J. G. W. (Tonbridge; Cambridge University; Kent)
'Cyril Coote – A Cambridge Legend'   1982   *123*
Davies, J. T. (Journalist)
Obituary   1904   *lxxxiv*
Davies, Capt. P. H. (Brighton College; Oxford University; Sussex)
Obituary   1931/I   *252*
Davies, V. L. G. (New Westminster C.C., British Columbia)
Obituary   1920/I   *153*
Davis, Pte. A. E. (Mill Hill School; Leicestershire)
Obituary   1917   *178*
Davis, 2nd Lieut. A. I. (Fettes)
Obituary   1919   *171*
Davis, A. T. (Berkshire)
Obituary   1980   *1159*
Davis, B. A. (Glamorgan; Trinidad; West Indies)
Photograph   1971   *351*
Davis, B. H. S. (Lancing; Berkshire)
Obituary   1978   *1069*
Davis, Lieut. C. (Farnborough School; Wellington College)
Obituary   1918   *181*
Davis, C. (Patron Australia)
Obituary   1923/I   *296*
Davis, I. R. (Young America C.C.)
Obituary   1915/I   *219*
Davis, J. (New South Wales)
Obituary   1912/I   *165*
Davis, J. G. (Chicago C.C.)
Obituary   1943   *375*

Davis, R. C. (Glamorgan)
Photographs   1972   *396*
                                                 1976   *391*

Davis, R. H. (Journalist)
Obituary   1917   *243*

Davis, S. (Writer)
'Hedley Venity' Book Review   1953   *1001*

Davis, T. (Nottinghamshire)
Obituary   1899   *xlv*

Davison, B. (Leicestershire; Rhodesia; Tasmania)
Career Figures   1984   *1250*
Photographs   1972   *481*
                                                 1975   *472*
                                                 1980   *474*

Davison, 2nd Lieut. C. M. (Newcastle Royal Grammar School)
Obituary   1919   *171*

Davison, I. (Nottinghamshire)
Photographs   1963   *556*
                                                 1965   *521*

Davison, R. W. J. (Yorkshire)
Obituary   1958   *958*

Davy, G. B. (Secretary Nottinghamshire)
Obituary   1909/I   *152*

Davy, Sir J. S. (Uppingham)
Obituary   1916   *159*

Daw, Lieut. H. B. (Trinity College School, Port Hope)
Obituary   1917   *178*

Dawkes, G. O. (Leicestershire; Derbyshire)
Career Records   1963   *1042*
Photograph   1956   *304*
Wicket Keeping Record Appearances   1962   *726*

Dawson, A. C. (Stowe; Leicestershire)
Obituary   1975   *1076*

Dawson, A. L. (Sydney University)
Obituary   1920/I   *193*

Dawson, E. W. (Eton; Leicestershire; Cambridge University; England)
Obituary   1980   *1148*
Schools Notes   1923/I   *327*
                                                 1924/I   *289,290*
                                                               293

Dawson, G. (Hampshire)
Obituary   1970   *1019*

Dawson, G. V. F. (Rugby)
Obituary   1929/I   *244*

Dawson, H. B. (Leeds C.C.)
Obituary   1969   *980*

Dawson, H. L. (Surrey)
Obituary   1911/I   *162*
Dawson, Major J. M. (Yorkshire Gentlemen)
Obituary   1949   *864*
Dawson, Capt. S. O. I. (Wellington)
Obituary   1944   *306*
Dawson, T. A. J. (Mill Hill School)
Schools Note   1982   *862*
79 wkts Schools Averages   1982   *887*
Dawson, W. A. (Marlborough; Yorkshire)
Obituary   1917   *243*
Dawson-Damer, 2nd Lieut. (Winchester)
Obituary   1918   *181*
Day, A. G. (Mill Hill School; Yorkshire)
Obituary   1909/I   *135*
Day, A. P. (Malvern; Kent)
Obituary   1970   *1020*
Portrait and Biography   1910/I   *163*
Day, Capt. D. A. S. (Tonbridge)
Obituary   1945   *321*
Day, H. L. V. (Bedford School; Bedfordshire; Hampshire)
'Happy Hampshire'   1962   *143*
Obituary   1973   *1005*
Tribute to A. S. Kennedy   1960   *953*
Day, S. E. (Malvern; Kent)
Obituary   1971   *1025*
Day, S. H. (Malvern; Cambridge University; Kent)
Obituary   1951   *920*
Deacon, Major W. J. (Peterborough Town C.C.)
Obituary   1919   *171*
Deacon, W. S. (Eton; Cambridge University; Kent)
Obituary   1905   *ciii*
Deakins, L. (Secretary Warwickshire)
Photograph   1973   *128*
Tribute to H. Preston   1961   *160*
Views on County Cricket   1968   *88*
Dealey, Lieut. T. S. O. (Stonyhurst College)
Obituary   1919   *171*
Dean, C. A. (Highgate School)
76 wkts Schools Averages   1954   *759*
83 wkts Schools Averages   1952   *724*
Dean, H. (Lancashire; Cheshire; England)
Benefit Match   1921/II   *65*
Obituary   1958   *958*
Dean, 2nd Lieut. L. L. (Keswick School)
Obituary   1919   *171*

Dean, Dr. W. E. (Canada)
  Obituary   1953   *940*
Deane, C. G. (Taunton School; Somerset)
  Obituary   1915/I   *219*
Deane, H. (New South Wales)
  Obituary   1923/I   *296*
Deane, Rt. Hon. Sir H. B. (Winchester)
  Obituary   1920/I   *170*
Deane, H. G. (Natal; Transvaal; South Africa)
  Obituary   1940   *839*
Dearden, J. (Ireland)
  Obituary   1973   *1005*
Dearlove, C. (Knaresborough C.C.)
  Obituary   1914/I   *182*
Dearnaley, I. (Derbyshire)
  Obituary   1966   *963*
De Bathe, Gen. Sir H. P. 4th Bart. (Old Stagers)
  Obituary   1908/I   *137*
De Bourbal, Capt. A. A. (Harrow)
  Obituary   1918   *224*
De Broke, Lord Willoughby (President Warwickshire)
  Obituary   1903   lxxxi
De Charleroy, M. (Hudson County, New York)
  Obituary   1913/I   *185*
Declarations:
  Controversial   1966   *81*
  First Day   1951   *966*
  Freak   1947   *67*
Decrespigny, P. A. C. (Hampshire)
  Obituary   1913/I   *184*
Deed, J. A. (Malvern; Kent)
  Obituary   1981   *1140*
Deedes, Gen. Sir C. P. (Hertfordshire)
  Obituary   1970   *1020*
Deeley, L/Cp. G. T. (Birmingham Cricket League)
  Obituary   1918   *181*
Deerhurst, Viscount (Chairman Worcestershire)
  Obituary   1928/I   *282*
De Gex, R. D. (Clifton)
  Obituary   1934/I   *263*
Deighton, J. H. G. (Denstone; Lancashire)
  Schools Notes   1939   *681,689*
  83 wkts Schools Averages   1939   *746*
De Klerk, T. (Western Province)
  Obituary   1983   *1243*

De Kretser, B. B. (Ceylon)
Obituary   1963   *1032*
De la Combe, W. B. (Bruton School; Derbyshire)
Obituary   1912/I   *165*
De La Motte, Capt. H. T. (Rossall)
Obituary   1919   *171*
Delany, V. B. (Lancashire)
Obituary   1981   *1140*
De Las Aux, R. A. (Kent)
Obituary   1915/I   *220*
De La Warr, 8th Earl (Cricket Supporter)
Obituary   1916   *159*
Delbridge, F. (Torquay C.C.)
Obituary   1911/I   *141*
De L'Isle, Rt. Hon. Lord (Beaumont School; Leicestershire)
'John Wisden's New Century'   1951   *126*
De Little, E. R. (Cambridge University)
Obituary   1927/I   *275*
Delme-Radcliffe, A. H. (Sherborne; Hampshire; Berkshire)
Obituary   1951   *920*
Delugo Señor, A. B. (Author Surrey)
Obituary   1908/I   *137*
De Mattos-Hooper, W. (Supporter U.S.A.)
Obituary   1913/I   *189*
De Mello, A. S. (Board of Control India)
Obituary   1962   *986*
De Montmorency, R. H. (St Paul's; Oxford University; Hertfordshire; Buckinghamshire)
Obituary   1939   *908*
Dempsey, Gen. Sir M. C. (Shrewsbury; Sussex; Berkshire)
Obituary   1970   *1020*
Dempster, C. S. (Leicestershire; Warwickshire; Wellington; Wanganui; Scotland; New Zealand)
Obituary   1975   *1076*
Portrait and Biography   1932/I   *272*
Dench, C. E. (Nottinghamshire; Umpire)
Obituary   1959   *928*
Denham, A. (Yorkshire Committee)
Obituary   1962   *986*
Denham, Lieut. A. C. (Student of Cricket)
Obituary   1916   *159*
Denison, Major H. (Eton House Matches)
Obituary   1918   *181*
Denison, W. E. (Military Cricket)
Obituary   1917   *244*
Denmark in England 1926   1927/II   *639*

Denne, H. (Band of Brothers)

Obituary	1909/I	*135*

Denne, Major W. H. (Cheltenham)

Obituary	1918	*181*

Denness, M. H. (Ayr Academy; Scotland; Kent; Essex; England)

Capped as Schoolboy by Scotland	1960	*686*
Cricketer of the Year	1975	*87*
'I Declare' Book Review	1978	*1124*
Note on	1974	*67*
Photographs	1966	*432*
	1968	*448*
	1972	*448*
	1975	*80*
Unlucky Denness	1975	*95*

Dennett, E. G. (Gloucestershire)

Obituary	1938	*938*

Denning, P. W. (Millfield; Somerset)

Photographs	1974	*525*
	1980	*537*

Dennis, Capt. J. E. W. (Exeter School)

Obituary	1917	*223*

Dennis, T. (Merchant Taylors)

Schools Note	1902	*ci*
1073 runs Schools Averages	1902	*455*

Denniss, Capt. T. V. B. (Elstree C.C.)

Obituary	1919	*171*

Dent, C. H. (Harrow)

Obituary	1939	*908*

Dent, Major W. H. (Harrow)

Obituary	1916	*160*

Denton, D. (Yorkshire; England)

Benefit Match	1908/II	*95*
In the Cricket Field Major R. O. Edwards	1923/I	*273*
Obituary	1951	*920*
Portrait and Biography	1906	*cxi*

Denton, J. S. (Wellingborough; Northamptonshire)

Obituary	1972	*1049*

Denton, W. H. (Northamptonshire)

Obituary	1981	*1140*

Deodhar, Prof. D. B. (Hindus; All India)

'I Look Back' Book Review	1967	*1018*

De Paravicini, H. F. (Harrow; Cambridge University; Middlesex)

Obituary	1943	*375*

De Paravicini, P. C. F. (Harrow; Buckinghamshire)

Obituary	1966	*970*

De Paravicini, P. J. (Eton; Cambridge University; Middlesex)
Obituary   1922/I   *266*
Views on Second Class Counties and
L.B.W. Rule   1903   *lxvi*
Derby, 16th Earl of (Vice President Lancashire)
Obituary   1909/I   *136*
Derby County Ground
Plan of County Ground   1950   *291*
                                   ad passim
Derbyshire County Cricket Club
Badge   1950   *290*
                                   ad passim
'Derbyshire County Cricket Club'
A Rippon and J. Grainger   Book Review   1983   *1300*
'Derbyshire Cricketers 1871-1981
– Association of Club Statisticians'
Book Review   1983   *1300*
'History of Derbyshire County Cricket Club
1870-1970' J. Shawcroft   Book Review   1973   *1050*
'History of Derbyshire Cricket'
W. T. Taylor   1953   *104*

Team Portraits	1974	1975	*368*
	1975	1976	*363*
	1976	1977	*364*
	1977	1978	*358*
	1978	1979	*346*
	1979	1980	*367*
	1980	1981	*373*
	1981	1982	*374*
	1982	1983	*374*
	1983	1984	*342*

De Robeck, Admiral Sir J. M. 1st Bart. (Devon)
Obituary   1929/I   *145*
De Rougemont, R. C. I. (Eton)
Obituary   1943   *364*
Desai, M. (Writer)
'India v England 1981-82 Bumper Cricket Souvenir'
Book Review   1983   *1316*
De Saram, F. C. (Oxford University; Hertfordshire; Ceylon)
Obituary   1984   *1198*
Desborough, Lord (Harrow)
Obituary   1946   *438*
Desert Air Force
Note on   1946   *199*
Team Portrait   1946   *39*

De Silva, D. H. L. (Board of Control Ceylon)
Obituary   1974   *1084*

De Silva, D. L. S. (Ceylon)
Obituary   1981   *1141*

De Silva, J. A. (Oxford University; Ceylon)
Obituary   1983   *1244*

De Soyres, Rev. J. (Brighton College)
Obituary   1906   *c*

De Soysa, Rt. Rev. C. H. (Royal College, Columbo)
Obituary   1972   *1048*

Detmold, Pte. P. W. (St.Judes C.C., Winnipeg)
Obituary   1918   *182*

De Uphaugh, R. G. (Harrow; Oxford University)
Obituary   1973   *1005*

'Development of Cricket, The'
Hon R. H. Lyttelton   1892   *xlii*

Devey, J. H. G. (Warwickshire)
Benefit Match   1907   *117*
Obituary   1941   *394*

Devonshire, 9th Duke of (President Derbyshire, M.C.C.)
Obituary   1939   *908*

Devonshire, 10th Duke of (President Derbyshire)
Obituary   1952   *966*

Dew, Pte. W. (Trinity College, Port Hope)
Obituary   1918   *182*

Dewar, Lieut. G. (Aberdeenshire)
Obituary   1917   *178*

Dewar, 2nd Lieut. L. J. A. (Oakham)
Obituary   1918   *182*

Dewdney, Capt and Adj. C. M. F. (Bromsgrove Grammar School)
Obituary   1919   *171*

Dewes, J. G. (Aldenham; Cambridge University; Middlesex; England)
Notes on   1944   *220*
     1946   *275*
Schools Notes   1942   *262*
     1943   *287*
     1945   *237,242*
'Views on the Laws'   1957   *84*

Dewfall, E. G. (Gloucestershire)
Obituary   1984   *1198*

Dewing, E. M. (Harrow; Cambridge University)
Obituary   1900   *liv*

Dewing, Lt-Col. R. E. (Haileybury; R.M.A.)
Obituary   1919/I   *171*

Dewinton, Major A. J. (Sherborne)
Obituary   1929/I   *245*

Dewinton, Capt. R. F. C. (Marlborough)
Obituary   1924/I   *257*
Dews, G. (Worcestershire)
Benefit Match   1961   *618*
Dewse, H. (Northumberland)
Obituary   1911/I   *141*
Dexter, E. R. (Radley; Cambridge University; Sussex; England)
Captaincy   1965   *102*
Cricketer of the Year   1961   *81*
Notes on   1961   *121*
   1979   *81*
Photographs   1961   *96*
   1965   *75*
Schools Notes   1951   *718*
   1953   *716,748*
   1954   *725*
'Ted Dexter's Book of Cricket' Book Review   1964   *1003*
'Ted Dexter Declares' Book Review   1967   *1018*
Tribute to Sir Frank Worrell   1968   *122*
'Welcome Australia'   1972   *91*
Dexter, J. (Leicestershire)
Obituary   1916   *160*
Dexter, R. E. (Nottingham High School; Nottinghamshire)
1230 runs Schools Averages   1975   *888*
Dezoete, H. W. (Eton; Cambridge University; Essex)
Obituary   1958   *958*
Dharmalingam, C. (Pakistan Clubs; Tamil Union Cricket; Trinity College, Kandy)
Obituary   1976   *1096*
Dhatigara, S. M. (Parsis)
Obituary   1929/I   *245*
Dickens, H. C. (M.C.C.)
Obituary   1967   *965*
Dickens, W. (Griqualand West)
Obituary   1952   *955*
Dickenson, G. (Canterbury, New Zealand)
Obituary   1914/I   *182*
Dicker, J. (Kent)
Obituary   1896   *x*
Dickinson, A. W. H. (Devon; Cornwall)
Obituary   1953   *940*
Dickinson, G. R. (Otago; New Zealand)
Obituary   1979   *1074*
Dickinson, P. J. (Kings College School, Wimbledon)
Schools Notes   1937/I   *317*
   1938   *677,687*

1061 runs Schools Averages	1938	*744*
Dickinson, S. P. (Haileybury; Derbyshire)		
Obituary	1976	*1104*
Dickinson, U. W. (Harrow)		
Obituary	1926/I	*268*
Dickson, M. R. (Marlborough; Scotland)		
Obituary	1941	*394*
Difford, Capt. A. (Western Province; Transvaal)		
Obituary	1919	*171*
Digby, Sir K. E. (Harrow; Oxford University; Norfolk; Oxfordshire)		
Obituary	1917	*244*
Personal Recollections of John Wisden	1913/I	*122*
Digby; R. (Harrow, Oxford University; Norfolk)		
Obituary	1928/I	*282*
Dillon, E. W. (Rugby; Oxford University; Kent; Laden County)		
Obituary	1942	*356*
Dillwyn-Venables-Llewelyn, Brig. Sir M. Bart. (Eton)		
Obituary	1977	*1039*
Dinan, 2nd Lieut. G. A. (Cork University)		
Obituary	1917	*178*
Dines, E. (Norfolk Club Cricket)		
Obituary	1918	*182*
Dipper, A. E. (Gloucestershire; England)		
Benefit Match	1927/II	*408*
Obituary	1946	*438*
Discipline Note on	1980	*89*
Disney, J. (Derbyshire; Cheshire)		
Obituary	1935/I	*263*
Disney, T. (Rossall)		
Obituary	1922/I	*247*
Disney-Roebuck, Col. F. H. A. (IZingari)		
Obituary	1920/I	*171*
Dissent-Unbridled Note on	1981	*90*
Photograph	1981	*67*
Diver, E. J. (Surrey; Warwickshire; Monmouthshire)		
Obituary	1925/I	*263*
Dixie-Smith, J. W. (Leicestershire)		
Obituary	1960	*950*
Dixon, A. L. (Kent)		
Benefit Match	1970	*447*
Photograph	1965	*436*
Dixon, A. S. (Writer)		
'Cricketers of the Year'	1945	*349*
Dixon, A. W. (Rugby; Yorkshire)		
Obituary	1936/I	*276*

Dixon, Lieut. C. M. (Bradfield)
   Obituary 1916 *160*
Dixon, Sub Lt. E. J. H. (St.Edward's, Oxford; Oxford University;
Northamptonshire)
   Obituary 1942 *347*
Dixon, J. A. (Nottinghamshire)
   Obituary 1932/I *242*
   Views on 'The Follow On' 1894 *xlix*
   Views on Throwing 1895 *lvii*
   Views on the Reforms of 1889 1890 *xxxvii*
   Views on Some Questions of the Day 1890 *xli*
Dixon, J. G. (Felsted; Essex)
   Obituary 1955 *929*
Dixon, J. W. (Secretary/Treasurer Manhattan C.C., New York)
   Obituary 1911/I *162*
Dixon, T. J. (Transvaal)
   Obituary 1916 *166*
Dixon, T. W. (Durham)
   Obituary 1937/I *271*
Dixon, W. (Rugby)
   Obituary 1960 *958*
Dobbie, Col. H. H. (Charterhouse)
   Obituary 1931/I *252*
Dobbie, Capt. J. S. (Canadian Schools)
   Obituary 1919 *198*
Dobson, A. (Yorkshire)
   Obituary 1934/I *279*
Dobson, B. P. (Stonyhurst College; Incogniti)
   Obituary 1938 *948*
Dobson, F. (Warwickshire)
   Obituary 1981 *114*
Dobson, K. W. (Derbyshire)
   Obituary 1961 *945*
Dobson, T. K. (1861-1921)(Durham City)
   Obituary 1923/I *310*
Dobson, T. K. (1901-1940)(Durham City)
   Obituary 1941 *394*
Dobson, Capt. W. J. (Toronto C.C.)
   Obituary 1917 *174*
Docker, C. T. (New South Wales; Australian Imperial Forces)
   Obituary 1976 *109*
Docker, Capt. G. A. M. (Highgate)
   Obituary 1915/I *22*
Docker, L. C. (Derbyshire; Warwickshire)
   Obituary 1941 *39*

Dodd, 2nd Lieut. E. J. (St Albans School; Hertfordshire)

Obituary   1918   *182*

Dodds, N. (Tasmania)

Obituary   1918   *240*

Dodds, T. C. (Essex)

Benefit Match   1958   *338*

'Hit Hard and Enjoy it'   Book Review   1977   *1096*

Photographs   1950   *306*

     1958   *325*

Dods, H. W. (Lincolnshire)

Obituary   1945   *321*

Dodson, M. (Berkshire; South Wales Clubs Professional)

Obituary   1957   *943*

Dodworth, M. J. (Vice President Yorkshire)

Obituary   1909/I   *136*

Doe, G. (Derbyshire)

Obituary   1902   *lxiii*

Doggart, A. G. (Bishop's Stortford College; Cambridge University; Middlesex; Durham)

Obituary   1964   *947*

Views on the Laws   1957   *83*

Doggart, A. P. (Winchester; Sussex)

Obituary   1966   *963*

Doggart, G. H. G. (Winchester; Cambridge University; Sussex; England)

'The Heart of Cricket – A Memoir of

H. S. Altham' Book Review   1968   *1050*

Schools Notes   1942   *242,286*

     1943   *311*

     1944   *181,240*

Doidge, F. C. (Devon Cricket Asssociation)

'Views on the Laws'   1957   *86*

Doig, J. (Southland, New Zealand)

Obituary   1952   *956*

Dolbey, H. O. (Dulwich; Surrey)

Obituary   1937/I   *271*

Dolding, D. L. (Middlesex)

Obituary   1955   *929*

Dolignan, Rev. J. W. (Eton)

Obituary   1897   *xl*

D'Oliveira, B. L. (Worcestershire; England)

Benefit Match   1976   *760*

Cricketer of the Year   1967   *75*

'D'Oliveira' Book Review   1969   *1030*

'The D'Oliveira Affair' Book Review   1970   *1066*

'The D'Oliveira Case' M. Melford   1969   *74*

Honoured   1970   *80*

157

Note on	1969	92
Photographs	1966	60!
	1967	7(
'Time to Declare' Book Review	1981	120.
Doll, M. H. C. (Charterhouse; Middlesex; Hertfordshire)		
Obituary	1967	96.
Doll, P. W. R. (Charterhouse)		
Obituary	1915/I	22(
Dollery, H. E. (Berkshire; Warwickshire; England)		
Benefit Match	1950	54
Cricketer of the Year	1952	76
Photographs	1950	53
	1952	7
	1953	57
	1954	58
	1955	54
Retirement	1956	61
Dolling, Dr. C. E. (South Australia)		
Obituary	1937/I	27
Dolman, E. C. (Monmouthshire; Wales)		
Obituary	1970	102
Dolphin, A. (Yorkshire; England; Umpire)		
Benefit Match	1923/II	4
Obituary	1943	3?
Dolphin, J. M. (Marlborough; Oxford University)		
Obituary	1900	xl
Dominions XI 1943		
Team Portrait	1944	
Domville, H. W. R. (Bradfield; Worcestershire; Shropshire)		
Obituary	1929/I	2
Donald, W. M. (President Staten Island C.C.)		
Obituary	1913/I	1
Donaldson, Canon A. E. (Breconshire)		
Obituary	1961	9
Donaldson, S. 2nd Lieut. (Edinburgh Royal Hill School)		
Obituary	1919	1
Donnelly, Sir A. T. (New Zealand Cricket Council)		
Obituary	1955	9
Donnelly, D. L. (Assam; British Empire XI)		
Obituary	1975	10
Donnelly, M. P. (Oxford University; Middlesex; Warwickshire; Canterbury; Taranaki; Wellington; New Zealand)		
Cricketer of the Year	1948	
Notes on	1946	63,2
Photographs	1948	
	1950	1

158

Donovan, J. (Glamorgan)
Obituary 1922/I *247*

Dooland, B. (Nottinghamshire; South Australia; Australia)
Benefit Match 1958 *515*
Career Figures 1958 *97*
Cricketer of the Year 1955 *74*
Obituary 1981 *1141*
Photographs 1954 *497*
1955 *66*
1957 *496*

Doran, R. (Queensland Club Cricketer)
Obituary 1917 *244*

D'Ornellas, F. A. (Ottawa C.C.)
Obituary 1920/I *153*

Dorling, Col. F. (Charterhouse)
Obituary 1945 *329*

Dorman, Rev. A. W. (Dulwich; Cambridge University)
Obituary 1915/I *202*

Dorning, H. (Argentine Cricket Association)
Obituary 1956 *970*

Dorning, N. (Cornwall)
Obituary 1971 *1025*

Dorrell, G. J. (President Worcestershire)
Obituary 1974 *1072*

Doubleday, Sir L. (President Kent)
Obituary 1976 *1096*

Double Wicket Competition 1968 1970 *946*

Douglas, Lieut. A. H. (Edinburgh Academy)
Obituary 1917 *178*

Douglas, Col. A. P. (Dulwich; Surrey; Middlesex)
Obituary 1954 *923*

Douglas, C. H. (Essex)
Obituary 1956 *977*

Douglas, C. N. (King's County C.C., Brooklyn, U.S.A.)
Obituary 1921/I *225*

Douglas, Rev. E. K. (Eton)
Obituary 1922/I *271*

Douglas, J. (Dulwich; Cambridge University; Middlesex)
Obituary 1959 *928*

Douglas, J. W. H. T. (Felsted; Essex; England)
'Johnny Won't Hit Today' D. Lemmon
Book Review 1984 *1264*
Obituary 1931/I *252*
Portrait and Biography 1915/I *201*
Schools Notes 1901 *xciii*
1902 *c,civ*

Douglas, L/Cpl. O. H. (Tasmania)
Obituary 1919/I 172

Douglas, Rev. R. N. (Dulwich; Cambridge University; Surrey; Middlesex)
Obituary 1958 958

Douglas, Capt. S. (Dulwich)
Obituary 1917 179

Douglas, S. (Yorkshire)
Obituary 1972 1049

Douglas-Hamilton, Canon Rev. H. A. (Wellington; Cambridge University)
Obituary 1930/I 248

Douglas-Home, Sir A. (U.K. Prime Minister)
Note on 1967 93
Photograph 1968 60

Douglas-Jones, Major S. D. (Army)
Obituary 1970 1020

Douglass, J. H. (Leicestershire Committee)
Obituary 1910/I 136

Doulton, H. V. (Dulwich)
Obituary 1942 353

Doust, D. (Writer)
'Ian Botham – The Great All Rounder'
Book Review 1981 1196
'The Return of the Ashes'
with J. M. Brearley Book Review 1979 1136
'The Ashes Retained'
with J. M. Brearley Book Review 1980 121

Douthwaite, H. (Lancashire)
Obituary 1973 100.

Dover Crabble Ground
Plan of County Ground 1956 40
1965 43
1967 44

Dovey, R. R. (Kent; Dorset)
Benefit Match 1955 39
Obituary 1976 110

Dow, Pte. A. T. (Canadian Club Cricket)
Obituary 1916 16

Dowding, A. J. C. (Winchester)
Obituary 1933/I 24

Dower, R. R. (Cape Colony; Eastern Province; South Africa)
Obituary 1965 96

Dowling, Capt. G. C. W. (Charterhouse; Sussex)
Obituary 1916 16

Down, M. (Writer)
'Archie: A Biography of A. C. Maclaren'
Book Review 1982 126

Downes, A. (Otago; New Zealand)		
Obituary	1951	*921*
Downes, F. (New South Wales)		
Obituary	1917	*244*
Downs, Dr. N. (German Town C.C.)		
Obituary	1917	*245*
Downton, P. R. (Sevenoaks; Kent; Middlesex; England)		
Photograph	1981	*490*
Schools Notes	1975	*853,856,*
	1977	*809*
Dowson, A. O. (Rugby)		
Obituary	1941	*395*
Dowson, E. (Shrewsbury; Surrey)		
Obituary	1923/I	*296*
Recollections of W. Caffyn	1920/I	*167*
Dowson, E. M. (Harrow; Cambridge University; Surrey)		
Obituary	1934/I	*263*
Dowson, Capt. H. (Uppingham)		
Obituary	1918	*212*
Dowson, J. (Durham)		
Obituary	1937/I	*271*
Dowty, Sir G. (President Worcestershire)		
Obituary	1976	*1097*
Doyle, Sir A. C. (Author)		
Obituary	1931/I	*255*
Doyle, Pte. C. (Orange Free State)		
Obituary	1943	*364*
D'Oyly, Sir W. H. Bart. (Haileybury; Dorset; Calcutta C.C.)		
Obituary	1922/I	*247*
Drag, The Photograph	1960	*96*
Dragging Still a problem	1972	*90*
Drake, A. (Yorkshire)		
Obituary	1920/I	*171*
Drake, Rev. E. T. (Westminster; Cambridge University; Oxfordshire; Buckinghamshire)		
Obituary	1905	*xci*
Drake, N. (Hampshire Scorer)		
Obituary	1974	*1072*
Draper, Major A. I. (Rossall)		
Obituary	1918	*182*
Draper, F. W. M. (Merchant Taylors)		
Schools Note	1902	*ci, cv*
91 wkts Schools Averages	1902	*455*
Draper, H. (Kent; Umpire)		
Obituary	1898	*xlvi*

Draper, Rev. W. H. (Oxford University; Herefordshire; Norfolk; Buckinghamshire)
Obituary   1927/I   275

Dredge, C. H. (Somerset)
Photograph   1979   514

Dresser, Major H. J. (Toronto)
Obituary   1920/I   153

Drewry, E. (Birmingham Club Cricket)
Obituary   1926/I   268

Driffield, 2nd Lieut. H. G. (Monkton Combe School)
Obituary   1918   182

Driffield, L. T. (St.John's, Leatherhead; Cambridge University; Northamptonshire)
Obituary   1918   224

Driver, Lieut. F. S. (Suffolk)
Obituary   1919   172

Driver, S. (Nelson C.C.; Keighley C.C.)
Obituary   1911/I   141

Druce, E. A. C. (Marlborough; Cambridge University; Kent)
Obituary   1935/I   263

Druce, N. F. (Marlborough; Cambridge University; Surrey; England)
Obituary   1955   929
Portrait and Biography   1898   lv
Schools Note   1892   271

Druce, W. G. (Marlborough; Cambridge University)
Obituary   1965   972

Drummond, Lieut. C. (Stirlingshire)
Obituary   1916   161

Drummond, Capt. G. H. (President Northamptonshire)
Obituary   1964   948

Drummond, F/Lt. L. (Upper Canada College)
Obituary   1918   182

Drummond, V. A. (Harrow; Buckinghamshire)
Obituary   1938   939

Dryden, Sir A. E. 8th Bart. (Winchester; Oxford University)
Obituary   1913/I   185

Dryden, C. H. (Wellington, New Zealand)
Obituary   1944   313

Drysdale, J. (Victoria)
Obituary   1924/I   257

Drysdale, Lt-Col. W. (Loretto; Sandhurst)
Obituary   1917   179

Duboulay-Brevet, Lt. Col. A. H. (Cheltenham; Kent; Army; Gloucestershire)
Obituary   1919   172

Du Boulay, Lieut. H. L. (Cheltenham)
Obituary   1917   179

Ducat, A. (Surrey; England)
Benefit Match	1924/II	*118*
Memoir (Obituary) H. Preston	1943	*42*
Photograph	1943	*29*
Portrait and Biography	1920/I	*254*

Duchesne, Lieut. R. E. (Bishop's Stortford College)
Obituary	1917	*179*

Duck, G. N. (Roxburgshire; Gentlemen of Yorkshire)
Obituary	1920	*171*
Duck Saved by Swallow	1970	*609*

Duckworth, G. (Lancashire; England)
Benefit Match	1935/II	*115*
Obituary	1967	*965*
Portrait and Biography	1929/I	*270*
Tributes to: A. P. F. Chapman	1962	*986*
Sir J. Hobbs	1964	*104*
W. R. Hammond	1966	*118*

Duckworth, Sir G. H. (Eton)
Obituary	1935/I	*263*

Duckworth, L. (Writer; Researcher)
'S. F. Barnes – Master Bowler' Book Review	1968	*1051*
'Holmes and Sutcliffe – Run Stealers' Book Review	1971	*1076*
'The Story of Warwickshire Cricket' Book Review	1975	*1116*

Dudlestone, B. (Leicestershire; Gloucestershire; Rhodesia)
Photographs	1970	*466*
	1973	*459*
	1975	*472*
Dudley Plan of County Ground	1971	*566*

Duff, Pte. J. (Calgary C.C., Alberta)
Obituary	1917	*223*

Duff, R. A. (New South Wales; Australia)
Obituary	1913/I	*202*

Duff, W. D. (Transvaal)
Obituary	1954	*923*

Duff, W. S. (Australian Club Cricket)
Obituary	1923/I	*310*

Duffield, L. T. (St.Johns, Leatherhead)
97 wkts Schools Averages	1900	*446*

Duffield, J. (Sussex)
Obituary	1957	*943*

Duffus, L. (Writer; Journalist)
'Play Abandoned' Book Review	1970	*1066*
'Ups and Downs on the Veld'	1951	*104*

Dugdale, J. S. (Warwickshire)
Obituary   1921/I   *225*

Duggan, Miss M. B. (Worcestershire Women; Yorkshire Women;
England Women)
Obituary   1974   *1072*

Duke, W. H. (Cricket Ball Manufacturer)
Obituary   1914/I   *182*

Duleepsinhji, K. S. (Cheltenham; Cambridge University; Sussex; England)
'Duleep, the Man and his Game'
Ed. V. Merchant Book Review   1964   *1003*
Obituary   1960   *950*
Portrait and Biography   1930/I   *275*
Schools Notes   1922/I   *280,293,294*
                                           1923/I   *334*
                                           1924/I   *288,289,290*
                                                     303

Dulwich College 1942
Team Portrait   1943   *28*

Duminy, Dr. J. P. (Transvaal; Oxford University; South Africa)
Obituary   1981   *1141*

Dunbavand, 2nd Lieut. H. (West Hartlepool C.C.)
Obituary   1917   *179*

Duncan, Lieut. D. C. (Aberdeen Grammar School)
Obituary   1919   *172*

Duncan, D. W. J. (Hampshire)
Obituary   1920/I   *172*

Duncan, H. (Otago)
Obituary   1965   *966*

Duncan, J. (Scotland)
Obituary   1900   *liii*

Duncan, 2nd Lieut. K. (Greenock Academy)
Obituary   1918   *182*

Duncan, W. (Sefton Park C.C.; Lancashire)
Obituary   1913/I   *185*

Dundas, Capt. H. L. N. (Eton)
Obituary   1919   *172*

Dundas, Rev. R. B. (Harrow)
Obituary   1913/I   *185*

Dundas, Sir R. W. Bart. (Glenalmond)
Obituary   1983   *1244*

Dunell, H. C. (Eton)
Obituary   1951   *921*

Dunell, O. R. (Eastern Province; South Africa)
Obituary   1930/I   *249*

Dunkerley, Capt. H. (Downing College, Cambridge University)
Obituary   1919   *172*

Dunlop, A. D. (Scotland)
  Obituary   1894   *xxxviii*
Dunlop, Lieut. B. E. (Charterhouse; Berkshire)
  Obituary   1945   *321*
Dunlop, C. E. (Merchiston Castle; Oxford University; Somerset)
  Obituary   1912/I   *166*
Dunlop, Capt. G. R. (Charterhouse)
  Obituary   1968   *999*
Dunlop, W. H. (Grange C.C., Scotland)
  Obituary   1914/I   *182*
Dunn, G. M. (Chicago C.C.)
  Obituary   1916   *161*
Dunn, Capt. J. (Harrow; Surrrey; Gentlemen of England)
  Obituary   1893   *xxxv*
Dunn, 2nd Lieut. J. H. M. (Eton Ramblers)
  Obituary   1917   *179*
Dunn, 2nd Lieut. M. (Montrose C.C.; Forfarshire)
  Obituary   1918   *182*
Dunning, E. (Auckland)
  Obituary   1938   *938*
Dunning, G. T. (Journalist)
  Obituary   1919   *205*
Dunning, J. A. (Oxford University; Otago; New Zealand)
  Obituary   1972   *1049*
Dupuis, Rev. G. R. (Eton; Cambridgeshire; Buckinghamshire)
  Obituary   1913/I   *186*
Durand, Rt. Hon. Sir H. M. (U.S.A. Club Cricket)
  Obituary   1925/I   *264*
Durand, Lieut. R. H. M. (Cheltenham)
  Obituary   1918   *182*
Durham, D. F. (Suffolk)
  Obituary   1975   *1077*
Durham Sands Race Course
  Note on   1972   *113*
Durlacher, P. N. (Wellington; Buckinghamshire; Middlesex)
  Obituary   1972   *1049*
Durrant, A. S. (New York Club Cricket)
  Obituary   1939   *909*
Durrant, 2nd Lieut. D. G. (Charterhouse)
  Obituary   1917   *179*
Durston, F. J. (Middlesex; England)
  Obituary   1966   *963*
Durston, T. J. (Middlesex; London Counties)
  Benefit Match   1930/II   *226*
Dury, Lt-Col. G. A. I. (Harrow)
  Obituary   1977   *1039*

Dury, T. S. (Harrow; Oxford University)
  Obituary   1933/I   *243*
Duthie, Col. A. M. (Hampshire)
  Obituary   1974   *1072*
Dutnall, F. (Kent)
  Obituary   1972   *1049*
Dutt, K. I. (Writer)
  with K. V. G. Ratnam
  'Vizzy Commemoration Souvenir' Book Review   1967   *1020*
Dwyer, E. A. (New South Wales; Australian Selector)
  Obituary   1976   *1097*
Dwyer, J. E. B. B. P. Q. C. (Sussex)
  Obituary   1913/I   *186*
Dye, J. C. (Kent; Northamptonshire)
  Photographs   1969   *442*
   1973   *488*
Dyke, Rev. Canon E. F. (Eton; Cambridge University)
  Obituary   1920/I   *172*
Dyke, Rt. Hon. Sir W. 7th Bart. (President M.C.C./Kent)
  Obituary   1932/I   *243*
Dymore-Brown, Lieut. H. P. (Reading College)
  Obituary   1920/I   *172*
Dyne, J. B. (Eton; Middlesex; Cambridge University)
  Obituary   1910/I   *137*
Dynes, Brig. E. D. (Army; Bedfordshire)
  Obituary   1969   *980*
Dyson, A. H. (Glamorgan)
  Benefit Match   1940   *300*
  Obituary   1979   *1074*
Eadie, W. S. (Derbyshire)
  Obituary   1915/I   *221*
Eady, C. J. (Tasmania; Australia)
  Obituary   1946   *439*
Eagar, E. D. R. (Cheltenham; Oxford University; Hampshire; Gloucestershire)
  Career Figures   1958   *97*
  'Growth of Hampshire Cricket'   1952   *117*
  with J. Arlott, H. S. Altham, R. Webber
  'Hampshire County Cricket' Book Review   1958   *1023*
  Obituary   1978   *1070*
  'Public School Cricket in the Wisden Century'   1963   *787*
Eagar, P. (Photographer)
  with A. Ross (all four entries)
  'A Summer to Remember' Book Review   1982   *1266*
  'Summer of the All Rounder' Book Review   1983   *1306*
  'Kiwis and Indians' Book Review   1984   *1262*
  'Summer of Speed' Book Review   1984   *1261*

Eagleton, Lieut. J. R. (Eastbourne College)
  Obituary   1919   *172*
Eakin, Capt. R. A. (Military Cricket)
  Obituary   1918   *183*
Ealand, V. F. (Surrey)
  Obituary   1954   *923*
Eales, C.C. (Northamptonshire)
  Obituary   1927/I   *276*
Eales, Lieut. C. W. (Weymouth College)
  Obituary   1919   *172*
Ealham, A. G. E. (Kent)
  Benefit Match   1983   *781*
  Career Figures   1983   *711*
  Photographs: 1971   *400*
                                                1979   *421*
Eardley-Simpson, Major L. E. (Secretary, Treasurer, Derbyshire)
  Obituary   1959   *928*
Earle, Rt. Rev. A. (Eton)
  Obituary   1920/I   *193*
Earle, G. F. (Harrow; Surrey; Somerset)
  Obituary   1967   *966*
Earle, Rev. W. (Uppingham)
  Obituary   1924/I   *274*
Early Finishes
  Note on   1952   *96*
Easby, J. W. (Kent)
  Obituary   1916   *161*
East, R. E. (Essex)
  'A Funny Turn' Book Review   1984   *1266*
  Photographs   1969   *365*
                                                1973   *373*
                                                1979   *359*
East, W. (Northamptonshire)
  Obituary   1928/I   *302*
East Africa World Cup Team 1975
  Team Portrait   1976   *304*
Eastbourne Saffrons Ground
  Plan of County Ground   1956   *569*
                                          ad passim
Easterbrook, B. (Writer; Journalist)
  'Compton's Record Season'   1972   *146*
  'The Cricket Rhymester'   1977   *142*
  'The Dreaded Cypher'   1971   *152*
  'Glen Turner Joins the Elite
  1000 Runs in May'   1974   *80*
  'The Greatly Praised – Hanif and his Brothers' 1976   *127*

'The Heritage of our Cricket Grounds'   1969   *142*

'The Man who made all Seasons
C. W. Alcock'   1980   *106*

'Norfolk and the Edrich Clan'   1973   *135*

'The Willing Work Horses of County Cricket'   1975   *150*

Three Studies in Greatness: W. E. Astill   1978   *156*

                             M. Turnbull   1978   *157*

                             J. C. White   1978   *159*

Three More Studies in Greatness:

                             T. Goddard   1979   *121*

                             W. H. Copson   1979   *122*

                             K. Farnes   1979   *125*

Easterbrook, Cpl. R. F. (Dulwich)

   Obituary   1920/I   *153*

Eastern Magic Photograph   1983   *Plate*

Eastman, L. C. (Essex; London Counties)

   Benefit Match   1940   *284*

   Obituary   1942   *357*

East Molesey Cricket Club Note on   1944   *60*

Eastmore, A. L. (President Church and Mercantile Cricket League, Toronto)

   Obituary   1920/I   *172*

Eastwood, D. (Yorkshire)

   Obituary   1904   *lxxxii*

Eastwood, Capt. F. A. J. (Sedbergh)

   Obituary   1918   *183*

Eastwood, J. E. (Huddersfield C.C.)

   Obituary   1913/I   *186*

Eaton, C. O. (Harrow)

   Obituary   1908/I   *137*

Eaton, Sir F. A. (Secretary Royal Academy)

   Obituary   1914/I   *182*

Eaton, G. H. (Manchester Club Cricket)

   Obituary   1918   *241*

Eaton, H. (Oratory School; Burghley Park)

   Obituary   1911/I   *141*

Eaton, J. (Sussex)

   Obituary   1973   *1006*

Eaton, Pte. J. C. (Staffordshire)

   Obituary   1918   *183*

Eaton, Lieut. J. N. (St.Johns C.C., Calgary)

   Obituary   1918   *183*

Ebbisham, 1st Baron (Lords and Commons; Surrey)

   Obituary   1954   *923*

Ebden, C. H. M. (Cambridge University; Sussex; Middlesex)

   Obituary   1950   *906*

Ebeling, H. I. (Victoria; Australia)

   Obituary   1981   *1141*

Eberle, V. F. (Clifton)
  Obituary   1975   *1077*
Ebery, J. (Nuneaton Town C.C.)
  Obituary   1919   *205*
Ebsworth, G. C. (Rossall; Cambridge University)
  Obituary   1905   *xcii*
Eccles, A. (Repton; Oxford University; Lancashire)
  Obituary   1920/I   *172*
Eccles, J. (Lancashire)
  Obituary   1936/I   *292*
Eccles, Capt. W. V. (Army)
  Obituary   1917   *245*
Eckersley, Lieut. P. T. (Rugby; Lancashire)
  Obituary   1941   *386*
Eckhoff, A. D. (Otago)
  Obituary   1950   *907*
Ede, E. E. (Journalist)
  Obituary   1970   *1020*
Ede, E. L. (Hampshire Scorer)
  Obituary   1909/I   *136*
Eden, E. (Journalist)
  Tribute to H. Preston   1961   *159*
Eden, E. Z. (Journalist)
  Obituary   1976   *1097*
Eden, F. M. (Oxford University)
  Obituary   1918   *225*
Eden, T. A. (Griqualand West)
  Obituary   1949   *864*
Edgar, A. (Bournemouth Festival)
  Obituary   1914/I   *182*
Edgar, Capt. J. M. (Stirlingshire)
  Obituary   1919   *172*
Edgbaston
  England Team at   1958   1959   *38*
                                      1961   1962   *87*
                                      1962   1963   *151*
                                      1978   1979   *58*
                                      1981   1982   *67*
  Plan of Ground   1950   *534*
                                            ad passim
  Test Cricket Again, Photograph   1958   *46*
  Turning Point at, Photograph   1982   *66*
Edge, Lieut. S. F. (Blackpool C.C.)
  Obituary   1918   *183*
Edgson, C. L. (Stamford School; Leicestershire)
  Obituary   1984   *1199*

Edinburgh, H. R. H. Duke of

Photographs	1950	*65*
	1975	*66,69*
'The Pleasures of Cricket'	1975	*67*

Editors of Wisden

W. H. Knight	1864 – 1879
G. H. West	1880 – 1886
C. F. Pardon	1887 – 1890
S. H. Pardon	1891 – 1925
C. S. Caine	1926 – 1933
S. J. Southerton	1934 – 1935
W. H. Brookes	1936 – 1939
H. Whitaker	1940 – 1943
H. Preston	1944 – 1951
N. Preston	1952 – 1980
J. Woodcock	1981 – 1984

Edkins, 2nd Lieut. H. (Dulwich)

Obituary	1917	*179*

Edlmann, Major E. E. (Leamington College)

Obituary	1916	*161*

Edmeades, B. E. A. (Essex)

Photographs	1967	*370*
	1974	*383*

Edmonds, P. H. (Cranbrook; Zambia Schools; Cambridge University; Middlesex; Eastern Province; England)

Dramatic Debut	1976	*62*
Photograph	1974	*482*
Schools Notes	1968	*827*
	1969	*755*

Edmondson, Sgt. J. H. (Point Grey C.C., British Columbia)

Obituary	1918	*183*

Edrich

'The Cricketing Family Edrich' R. Barker

Book Review	1977	*1096*

'Norfolk and the Edrich Clan'

B. Easterbrook	1973	*135*
Edrich Family Photograph	1948	*39*

Edrich, A. (Norfolk)

Obituary	1980	*1148*

Edrich, G. A. (Lancashire)

Benefit Match	1956	*435*

Edrich, J. H. (Norfolk; Surrey; England)

Career Figures	1978	*135*
Cricketer of the Year	1966	*65*
'John Edrich M.B.E.' J. Woodcock	1978	*133*

Family Group – Photograph	1978	*134*
Hundredth Hundred	1978	*547*
Photographs	1960	*554*
	1962	*581*
	1966	*64*
'Runs in the Family' Book Review	1970	*1067*

Edrich, W. (Father of W. J.; G.; E.; B.)
Obituary	1981	*1142*

Edrich, W. J. (Norfolk; Middlesex; England)
Career Figures	1959	*491*
'Cricketing Days' Book Review	1951	*995*
'Edrich and Compton'		
R. C. Robertson-Glasgow	1948	*45*
'1000 Runs in May'	1974	*91*
Photographs	1948	*33*
	1955	*435*
	1957	*458*
Portrait and Biography	1940	*36*
'Round the Wicket' Book Review	1960	*1000*

Edser, W. (Ripley C.C.)
Obituary	1916	*162*

Edward, VII, H. M. King
Obituary	1911/I	*136*

Edwards, A. (Writer)
'Milestones of Hampshire Cricketers' Book Review	1984	*1258*

Edwards, Capt. A. C. (Eton; Kent)
Obituary	1918	*212*

Edwards, Col. C. W. (Gloucestershire)
Obituary	1939	*909*

Edwards, F. (Buckinghamshire; Surrey)
Obituary	1971	*1025*

Edwards, Sir F. I. (Royal Engineers; Gentlemen of Kent)
Obituary	1911/I	*142*

Edwards, H. I. P. (Sussex)
Obituary	1947	*689*

Edwards, J. (Writer)
'Dai Davies: Not out 78' Book Review	1976	*1148*

Edwards, J. D. (Victoria; Australia)
Obituary	1912/I	*166*

Edwards, M. J. (Surrey)
Benefit Match	1975	*556*
Photograph	1967	*563*

Edwards, Major. R. O. (Norfolk; Cambridgeshire)
'G. Hirst in the Cricket Field'	1922/I	*308*
Obituary	1926/I	*269*

'J. T. Tyldesley and D. Denton in the Cricket
Field' | 1923/I | *273*
'Tom Hayward in the Cricket Field' | 1921/I | *264*
Edwards, Capt. W. (Bishop's Stortford School)
Obituary | 1919 | *173*
Edwards, 2nd Lieut. W. A. (Glamorgan)
Obituary | 1918 | *183*
Edwards, W. H. (Sussex Scorer)
Obituary | 1921/I | *225*
Egerton, Lt-Col. A. G. E. (Coldstream Guards)
Obituary | 1916 | *162*
Egerton, Major Hon. F. W. G. (Eton)
Obituary | 1949 | *864*
Egerton, Rev. P. R. (Winchester)
Obituary | 1912/I | *166*
Egerton-Green, Capt. J. W. (Essex Club Cricket)
Obituary | 1918 | *183*
Egerton-Warburton, J. (Eton)
Obituary | 1918 | *213*
Eggar, J. D. (Winchester; Oxford University; Hampshire; Derbyshire)
'Coaching the Schoolboy' | 1950 | *103*
Obituary | 1984 | *1199*
Eggleston, J. W. (Victoria)
Obituary | 1914/I | *198*
Eglington, R. (Sherborne; Surrey)
Obituary | 1980 | *1148*
Eglington and Winton, 15th Earl of (Scottish Patron)
Obituary | 1920/I | *173*
Ehrenfried, B. C. (Lincolnshire)
Obituary | 1966 | *975*
Eiloart, 2nd Lieut. C. H. (Uppingham)
Obituary | 1919 | *173*
Eiloart, R. E. (Harrow)
Obituary | 1932/I | *243*
Eisenhower, D. (President of U.S.A.)
Note on | 1961 | *631*
Elam, F. W. (Yorkshire)
Obituary | 1944 | *313*
Elborough, Capt. A. C. E. (Blair Lodge School)
Obituary | 1916 | *162*
Elcho, Lieut. Lord (Eton)
Obituary | 1917 | *179*
Elers, Major C. G. C. (Devon; Glamorgan)
Obituary | 1928/I | *283*
Elers, F. W. (Tonbridge)
Obituary | 1918 | *225*

Elford, L. H. (Umpire)
Obituary   1905   *xcii*

Elgin and Kincardine, 9th Earl of (Eton House Matches)
Obituary   1918   *225*

Eligon, D. (Trinidad)
Obituary   1938   *938*

Eliot, Lieut. W. L. (Exeter School)
Obituary   1917   *223*

Elizabeth II, Queen
Photographs at Lord's   1953   *53*
    1961   *85*
    1962   *85*
    1964   *61*
    1968   *59*
    at Oval   1956   *45*
    at Trent Bridge   1978   *81*

Ellershaw, Brig-Gen. (Woolwich Garrison)
Obituary   1917   *180*

Ellesmere, 3rd Earl of (Cricket Patron)
Obituary   1915/I   *221*

Ellesmere, 4th Earl of (Lord Brackley)
Obituary   1945   *329*
Team in West Indies 1905   1906   *514*

Elliot, E. W. (Wellington; Durham County)
Obituary   1932/I   *243*

Elliot, T. (Supporter Durham County)
Obituary   1914/I   *182*

Elliott, C. S. (Derbyshire)
Photograph   1952   *293*

Elliott, Capt. D. P. G. (Rugby)
Obituary   1945   *322*

Elliott, G. (Club Cricketer)
Obituary   1914/I   *198*

Elliott, G. F. (Kent; Surrey)
Obituary   1914/I   *182*

Elliott, H. (Derbyshire; England; Umpire)
Obituary   1977   *1039*

Elliott, H. D. E. (Newport Grammar; Essex)
Obituary   1974   *1073*

Elliott, J. (President Nottinghamshire)
Obituary   1981   *1142*

Elliott, 2nd Lieut. R. C. M. (Newport (Salop) Grammar School)
Obituary   1917   *180*

Ellis, B. (Old Carthusians C.C.)
Obituary   1925/I   *264*

Ellis, Lieut. B. H. (Shrewsbury)
Obituary   1916   *162*

173

Ellis, Comdr B. H. (University College School)
  Obituary 1919 173

Ellis, Lieut. C. B. (Beaconhurst C.C., New York)
  Obituary 1919 173

Ellis, Major G. A. (Sherborne)
  Obituary 1916 162

Ellis, H. V. (Rugby)
  Obituary 1920/I 173

Ellis, J. L. (Victoria)
  Obituary 1975 1077

Ellis, M. (Victoria)
  Obituary 1942 366

Ellis, Capt. R. A. (Wellington)
  Obituary 1919 173

Ellis, R. N. (Victoria)
  Obituary 1960 951

Ellis, V. (Rugby)
  Obituary 1930/I 249

Ellis, Lieut. Y. L. (Rossall)
  Obituary 1917 180

Ellison, Rev. C. C. (Gentlemen of Lincolnshire)
  Obituary 1913/I 187

Ellison, M. J. (President Yorkshire)
  Obituary 1899 x lvii

Ellwood, R. S. (Cumberland)
  Obituary 1959 928

Elmhirst, Rev. E. (Cambridge University; Leicestershire)
  Obituary 1895 xli

Elson, G. (Rydol)
  Schools Notes 1932/I 277
  81 wkts Schools Averages 1932/II 628

Eltham, Lieut. K. (Tasmania)
  Obituary 1918 213

Elwin, M. (Oxfordshire; Devon)
  Obituary 1974 1073

Elworthy, F. W. (Transvaal)
  Obituary 1979 1075

Emburey, J. E. (Middlesex; England)
  Cricketer of the Year 1984 5
  Photographs 1978 47
  1984 Plate

Emery, R. W. G. (Auckland; Canterbury; New Zealand)
  Obituary 1984 1199

Emery, T. (Northamptonshire)
  Obituary 1916 16

Emery, S. H. (New South Wales; Australia)
Obituary 1968 *999*
Emmett, B. (Yorkshire Club Cricket)
Obituary 1923/I *296*
Emmett, G. M. (Devon; Gloucestershire; England)
Benefit Match 1953 *371*
Obituary 1977 *1039*
Photograph 1954 *363*
1955 *347*
Emmett, T. (Yorkshire; England)
Benefit Match 1879 *194*
Biography 1878 *177*
Obituary 1905 *xcii*
Emu Club (New South Wales) in Malaya 1959 1960 *899*
Encouraging Signs 1952 *95*
Enfield, H. (Brighton College)
Obituary 1924/I *257*
Engel, M. (Journalist)
'M.C.C. and South Africa' 1984 *65*
Engineer, F. M. (Bombay; Lancashire; India)
Photograph 1976 *457*
England
Advance in Test Cricket 1958 *73*
Brilliant Fielding: Photographs 1978 *85*
1979 *61*
Captain Wanted 1950 *113*
Lean Period 1969 *92*
Prepare for Australia 1966 *76*
Preparing for Australia 1965 *103*
Problems 1962 *111*
1965 *102*
Rebuild for 1961 1960 *121*
Selectors: Photographs 1963 *150*
1984 *Plates*
England v Australia
Chance to Regain the Ashes 1953 *76*
'First Test Match' E. C. Brogden
and J. Arlott Book Review 1951 *989*
Reach the Crossroads 1954 *79*
'A Survey of 104 Matches' F. Ashley-Cooper 1922/I *227*
'Synopsis 1876-1938' 1939 *137*
Photographs of individual incidents will be found in the list of photographs in
the Appendix
v Australia – Team Portraits
Visiting Test Team 1945 1946 *36*
Team at Lord's 1948 1949 *66*

Winning Team at Oval	1953	1954	*55*
Team at Oval	1956	1957	*46*
Team at Edgbaston	1961	1962	*57*
Team at Leeds	1964	1965	*71*
Victorious Team at Oval	1968	1969	*54*
Team in First Test	1972	1973	*63*
Test Team	1975	1976	*38*
Team that won back the Ashes	1977	1978	*83*
Centenary Test Team	1980	1981	*70*
Fourth Test Team	1981	1982	*67*
England v Dominions XI			
Team Portrait	1943	1944	*34*
England v India (Team Portraits)			
Team at Oval	1946	1947	*34*
Team at Oval	1952	1953	*54*
Team at Old Trafford	1959	1960	*91*
Team at Lord's	1982	1983	*Plate*
England v New Zealand (Team Portraits)			
Team at Oval	1949	1950	*66*
Team at Edgbaston	1958	1959	*38*
Team at Trent Bridge	1969	1970	*51*
Team at Oval	1983	1984	*Plate*
England v Pakistan (Team Portraits)			
Winning Team at Nottingham	1954	1955	*60*
Team at Edgbaston	1962	1963	*151*
Team at Trent Bridge	1967	1968	*61*
Team at Headingley	1974	1975	*72*
Team at Edgbaston	1978	1979	*58*
England v Rest of the World			
Note on		1980	*90*
Team at Trent Bridge		1971	*66*
England v South Africa			
'A Survey of 34 matches'			
F. Ashley-Cooper		1924/I	*219*
'Survey of Matches' L. Duffus		1951	*104*
Team Portraits			
Team at Edgbaston	1924	1970	*126*
Team at Oval	1951	1952	*66*
Team at Lord's	1960	1961	*87*
Team at Trent Bridge	1965	1966	*56*
England v West Indies (Team Portraits)			
Team at Manchester	1950	1951	*59*
Team at Trent Bridge	1957	1958	*48*
Team at Lord's	1963	1964	*63*
Team at Oval	1966	1967	*63*
Team at Lord's	1976	1977	*85*

England In Australia (Tours with Test status)

and New Zealand	1876-77	1878	*15*
'The First Test Match' E. C. Brogden and			
J. Arlott Book Review		1951	*989*
and New Zealand	1878-79	1880	*22*
and New Zealand	1881-82	1883	*217*
and Ceylon	1882-83	1884	*17*
and Egypt	1884-85	1886	*17*
	1886-87	1888	*322*
	1887-88	1889	*306*
and Ceylon, Malta	1891-92	1893	*329*
and Ceylon	1894-95	1896	*367*
	1897-98	1899	*382*
	1901-02	1903	*479*
	1903-04	1905	*475*
'Impressions of M.C.C. in Australia'			
B. J. T. Bosanquet		1905	*lxxi*
	1907-08	1909/II	*490*
and Ceylon	1911-12	1913/II	*535*
and Ceylon	1920-21	1922/II	*596*
and Ceylon	1924-25	1926/II	*583*
and Ceylon	1928-29	1930/II	*653*
and Ceylon, New Zealand	1932-33	1934/II	*629*
'The Bodyline Controversy'			
L. Le Quesne Book Review		1984	*1261*
and Ceylon, New Zealand	1936-37	1938	*775*
and New Zealand	1946-47	1948	*707*
and Ceylon, New Zealand	1950-51	1952	*783*
'Ashes to Hassett' J. Kay Book Review		1952	*1011*
'Cricket all the Year' N. Cardus			
Book Review		1953	*993*
'Cricket Caravan' K. Miller and R. S. Whitington			
Book Review		1952	*1012*
'Cricket Task Force' W. J. O'Reilly			
Book Review		1952	*1013*
'Elusive Victory' E. W. Swanton Book Review		1952	*1013*
'The Fight for the Ashes 1950-51'			
A. G. Moyes Book Review		1952	*1013*
'In Sun and Shadow' D. Compton			
Book Review		1953	*1001*
'No Ashes for England' E. M. Wellings			
Book Review		1952	*1015*
'In Quest of the Ashes' B. Harris			
Book Review		1952	*1011*
Story of the Test Matches – *The Times*			
Book Review		1952	*1014*

and Ceylon, New Zealand	1954-55	1956	*812*
Team Portrait		1956	*48*
'The Ashes Ablaze' S. Barnes Book Review		1956	*1025*
'Ashes Triumphant' B. Harris Book Review		1956	*1025*
'The Ashes Retained' E. M. Wellings			
Book Review		1956	*1027*
'Australia 55' A. Ross Book Review		1956	*1027*
Australian Test Journal J. Arlott			
Book Review		1956	*1032*
'1954-55 Ashes Test Album' R. H. Baker			
Book Review		1956	*1028*
'Cricket Typhoon' K. Miller and R. S. Whitington			
Book Review		1956	*1025*
'England Keeps the Ashes' C. White and R. Webber			
Book Review		1956	*1028*
'The Fight for the Ashes 1954-55' A. G. Moyes			
Book Review		1956	*1026*
'Ian Peebles on the Ashes' I. A. R. Peebles			
Book Review		1956	*1026*
'The Long Hop' Margaret Hughes		1956	*1025*
Book Review			
'The Picture Post Book of the Tests' D. Batchelor			
Book Review		1056	*1025*
'The Urn Returns' A. E. R. Gilligan			
Book Review		1956	*1025*
'Victory in Australia' E. W. Swanton			
Book Review		1956	*1027*
and Ceylon, New Zealand	1958-59	1960	*807*
Note on		1959	*866*
'The Fight for the Ashes 1958-59' I. Peebles			
Book Review		1960	*1000*
'The Ashes Thrown Away' E. M. Wellings			
Book Review		1960	*1000*
'The Ashes Go Home' C. White and R. Webber			
Book Review		1960	*1000*
'Benaud and Company – The Story of the Tests			
1958-59' A. G. Moyes Book Review		.1960	*999*
'Cricket from the Grandstand' K. Miller			
Book Review		1960	*1001*
'Cricket Journal 2' J. Arlott			
Book Review		1960	*1010*
'England Down Under' J. Kay Book Review		1960	*999*
'Four Chukkas to Australia' J. H. Fingleton			
Book Review		1960	*999*
'May's Men in Australia' A. Bedser			
Book Review		1960	*998*

'Round the Wicket' W. J. Edrich			
Book Review		1960	*1000*
and Ceylon, New Zealand	1962-63	1964	*798*
'The Ashes in Suspense' E. W. Swanton			
Book Review		1964	*1000*
'Australia 63' A. Ross Book Review		1964	*1000*
'Challenge Renewed' J. Clarke		1964	*999*
Book Review			
'Dexter v Benaud' E. M. Wellings			
Book Review		1964	*1000*
'M.C.C. Tour of Australia 1962-63			
A.B.C. Cricket Book' Book Review		1963	*1114*
Rothmans Test Cricket Almanack 1962-63			
S. Smith Book Review		1963	*1114*
'Spin me a Spinner' R. Benaud Book Review		1964	*999*
'With the M.C.C. in Australia 1962-63'			
A. G. Moyes and T. Goodman Book Review		1964	*999*
and Ceylon, Hong Kong	1965-66	1967	*812*
and New Zealand			
'A.B.C. Cricket Book – M.C.C. Tour of Australia'			
Book Review		1967	*1021*
'Quest for the Ashes'			
K. Mackay Book Review		1967	*1021*
'Rothmans Test Cricket Almanack' S. Smith			
Book Review		1967	*1021*
'Time to Hit out' J. H. Parks Book Review		1968	*1052*
'With England in Australia' J. Clarke			
Book Review		1967	*1016*
and New Zealand	1970-71	1972	*891*
Team Portrait		1972	*59*
'Captain Outrageous'			
R. S. Whitington Book Review		1973	*1056*
and Hong Kong, New Zealand	1974-75	1976	*921*
'Test of Nerves' F. S. Tyson Book Review		1976	*1145*
and India, Sri Lanka 1976-77		1978	*895*
'The Centenary Test Match' R. Hayter			
Book Review		1978	*130*
'A.B.C. Cricket Book Australian Tour			
of England 1977' A. Mc Gilvray Book Review		1978	*1127*
'The Centenary Test' F. Tyson Book Review		1978	*1117*
'Frindall's Score Book' Jubilee Edition			
W. Frindall Book Review		1978	*1124*
'The 100th Summer' G. Chappell Book Review		1978	*1122*
'M.C.C. in India 1976-77' C. Martin-Jenkins			
Book Review		1978	*1122*
	1978-79	1980	*936*

Team Portrait		1980	*62*
'The Ashes 79' D. Frith Book Review		1980	*1204*
'The Ashes Retained' M. Brearley and D. Doust Book Review		1980	*1214*
'In Defence of the Ashes' C. Martin-Jenkins Book Review		1980	*1203*
'A. Pitch in Both Camps' A. Lee Book Review		1980	*1206*
'Put to the Test' G. Boycott Book Review		1980	*1208*
		1981	*1196*
and India 1979-80		1981	*923*
'Cricket Contest 1979-80. The Post Packer Tests' C. Martin-Jenkins Book Review		1981	*1198*
'Deadly Down Under' D. Underwood Book Review		1981	*1198*
'Frindall's Score Book; Australia v West Indies and England' W. Frindall Book Review		1981	*1196*
and New Zealand 1982-83		1984	*879*
'Botham Down Under' I. Botham Book Review		1984	*1262*
'The Captain's Diary' R. Willis Book Review		1984	*1268*
'Decision Against England' R. Marlar Book Review		1984	*1262*
'The Fight for the Ashes 1982-83' C. Harte Book Review		1984	*1262*
'Summer of Speed' P. Eagar and A. Ross Book Review		1984	*1261*
England in India (Tours with Test Status)			
	1933-34	1935/II	*631*
and Ceylon, Pakistan	1951-52	1953	*773*
'India v M.C.C. Tests' Prof. N. S. Phadre Book Review		1953	*998*
and Ceylon, Pakistan	1961-62	1963	*867*
	1963-64	1965	*800*
and Pakistan, Sri Lanka	1972-73	1974	*882*
and Australia, Sri Lanka	1976-77	1978	*895*
'M.C.C. in India 1976-77' C. K. Hakdates Book Review		1978	*1127*
'M.C.C. in India 1976-77' C. Martin Jenkins Book Review		1978	*1122*
and Australia	1979-80	1981	*940*
'Cricket Contest: The Post Packer Tests' C. Martin-Jenkins Book Review		1981	*1198*
and Sri Lanka	1981-82	1983	*947*
'Cricker Wallah' S. Berry Book Review		1983	*1307*

180

'India v England 1981-82 Bumper Cricket Souvenir'
M. Desai Book Review   1983   *1316*

England in New Zealand Tours with Test Status

and Australia, Ceylon	1929-30	1931/II	*642*
and Australia, Ceylon	1932-33	1934/II	*629*
and Australia	1946-47	1948	*707*
and Australia, Ceylon	1950-51	1952	*783*
and Australia, Ceylon	1954-55	1956	*812*
Team Portrait		1956	*48*
and Australia, Ceylon	1958-59	1960	*807*
and Australia, Ceylon	1962-63	1964	*798*
and Australia, Ceylon, Hong Kong	1965-66	1967	*812*
and Australia,	1970-71	1972	*891*
Team Portrait		1972	*59*
Preparing for		1970	*79*
and Australia, Hong Kong	1974-75	1976	*921*
and Pakistan	1977-78	1979	*896*

For Books on the above see England in Australia Section

England in Pakistan (Tours with Test Status)

and Ceylon, India	1961-62	1963	*867*
and Ceylon	1968-69	1970	*913*
and India, Sri Lanka	1972-73	1974	*882*
and New Zealand	1977-78	1979	*896*

England in South Africa (Tours with Test Status)

	1888-89	1890	*257*
	1891-92	1893	*352*
	1895-96	1897	*387*
	1898-99	1900	*466*
	1905-06	1907	*463*
	1909-10	1911/II	*484*
	1913-14	1915/II	*476*
	1922-23	1924/II	*589*
	1927-28	1929/II	*638*
	1930-31	1932/II	*64*
	1938-39	1940	*715*
	1948-49	1950	*758*

'Gone with the Cricketers' J. Arlott
Book Review   1951   *1001*
                                       1956-57   1958   *808*

'Cape Summer and the Australians'
A. Ross Book Review   1958   *1012*

'M.C.C. Tour of S.Africa'
C. Fortune Book Review   1958   *1013*

'Pitch and Toss' R. Mclean Book Review   1958   *1013*

'Report from South Africa'			
E. W. Swanton Book Review		1958	*1014*
'Sackcloth without Ashes'			
R. Mclean Book Review		1959	*987*
	1964-65	1966	*792*
'M.C.C. in South Africa 1964-65'			
C. Fortune Book Review		1966	*1016*
'Cricket Crisis' J. D. Mc Glew Book Review		1966	*1016*
England in Sri Lanka (Tours with Test Status)			
and India	1981-82	1983	*947*
England in West Indies (Tours with Test Status)			
	1929-30	1931/II	*672*
	1934-35	1936/II	*616*
	1947-48	1949	*739*
and Bermuda	1953-54	1955	*762*
'Cricket Cauldron' A. Bannister			
Book Review		1955	*991*
'West Indian Adventure' E. W. Swanton			
Book Review		1955	*991*
and Honduras	1959-60	1961	*805*
'Bowlers Turn' I. A. R. Peebles			
Book Review		1961	*993*
'Through the Carribean' A. Ross			
Book Review		1961	*993*
'West Indies Revisited' E. W. Swanton			
Book Review		1961	*994*
	1967-68	1969	*812*
'In the Main. West Indies v M.C.C. 1968'			
J. S. Barker Book Review		1969	*1032*
'The M.C.C. Tour of the West Indies 1968'			
D. B. Close Book Review		1969	*1032*
	1973-74	1975	*908*
'Testing Time: M.C.C.in West Indies 1973-74'			
C. Martin-Jenkins Book Review		1975	*1120*
'M.C.C. in Guyana' Book Review		1975	*1122*
	1980-81	1982	*907*
'Another Bloody Day in Paradise'			
F. Keating Book Review		1982	*1266*
'England v West Indies 1981'			
Ed. P. Smith Book Review		1982	*1266*
'In the Fast Lane'			
G. Boycott Book Review		1982	*1266*
England Teams Not Classified Elsewhere			
All England XI in U.S.A./Canada 1868		1869	*92*
England Amateurs in West Indies 1902		1903	*519*

England Young Cricketers in West Indies

| | 1972 | 1973 | 829 |

For all other Tours see under name of Tour Organiser especially M.C.C. section

Englehart, Sir J. G. D. (Rugby Sixth)
Obituary   1924/I   257
English, E. A. (Hampshire)
Obituary   1967   966
English Schools Cricket Association
Twenty One Years of Progress   1969   805
English Women in Australia and New Zealand
'Maiden Over' N. Joy Book Review   1951   999

| | 1957-58 | 1959 | 870 |
| | 1968-69 | 1970 | 871 |

U25 Women in India   1981   1982   1150
      in Jamaica   1971   1972   1000
      in South Africa 1960-61   1962   928
English Young Cricketers in West Indies

| | 1980 | 1981 | 1137 |

Enterprise, Spur to
Note on   1954   85
Entertainment Tax
Note on   1946   65
Enthoven, H. J. (Harrow; Cambridge University; Middlesex)
Obituary   1976   1097
Epping Foresters C.C.
Note on   1984   1079
Epsom Cricket Club in 1943   1944   211
Ernsthausen, A. C. E. Von (See Under **Howeson, A.C.E.**)
Erskine, Major-Gen. I. D. (Winchester)
Obituary   1974   1073
Erwood 2nd Lieut. C. V. (Bath Association C.C.)
Obituary   1918   183
Escolme, J. B. (Eastbourne College)
100 wkts Schools Averages   1899   357
Essex County Cricket Club
Badge   1950   306
                                           ad passim
'Essex 1876-1960' C. Bray   1960   128
'Essex' C. Bray Book Review   1951   990
Essex Champions   Note on   1984   52
'Essex County Cricket 1876-1975'
L. Newnham Book Review   1978   1118
'How Essex Rose to Glory' A. R. Lewis   1980   93
'Summer of Success – The Triumph of Essex County Club Cricket in 1980'
D. Lemmon Book Review   1981   1193

Triumphant at Last Note on		1980	*83*
Team Portraits	1974	1975	*383*
	1975	1976	*379*
	1976	1977	*382*
	1977	1978	*373*
	1978	1979	*361*
	1979	1980	*382*
	1980	1981	*387*
	1981	1982	*388*
	1982	1983	*390*
	1983	1984	*357*

Essington, Rev. R. W. (Eton)
Obituary 1908/I *137*

Esso Scholarships   List of 1983 *472*

Estridge, E. (Tonbridge)
Obituary 1920/I *173*

Ethelston, R. W. (Winchester)
Obituary 1915/I *221*

Ethiopia Cricket in   Note on 1965 *127*

Eton College
'R. A. H. Mitchell and Eton Cricket' 1899 *xci*
Team Portrait 1943 1944 *39*

Etting, N. (Philadelphia; U.S.A.)
Obituary 1915/I *221*

Evan, G. M. (President South Australian Cricket Association)
Obituary 1926/I *287*

Evans, A. (Merion C.C., U.S.A.)
Obituary 1926/I *269*

Evans, A. H. (Rossall; Clifton; Oxford University; Somerset; Hampshire)
Obituary 1935/I *263*

Evans, A. J. (Winchester; Oxford University; Hampshire; England)
Obituary 1961 *945*
Schools Notes 1908/I *116*
1909/I *119*

Evans, A. W. (West of Scotland)
Obituary 1910/I *137*

Evans, B. J. (Journalist)
Obituary 1954 *923*

Evans, B. T. H. (Journalist)
Obituary 1967 *966*

Evans, C. (Derbyshire)
Obituary 1957 *943*

Evans, Capt. D. (Sherborne; Dorset)
Obituary 1946 *434*

Evans, D. L. (Loretto; Gloucestershire; Somerset)
Obituary 1908/I *138*

Evans, Col. D. M. (Winchester; Hampshire)
  Obituary 1973 *1006*
Evans, E. (New South Wales; Australia)
  Obituary 1922/I *247*
Evans, E. N. (Haileybury; Oxford University)
  Obituary 1965 *966*
Evans, Canon Rev. F. R. (Rugby; Oxford University; Warwickshire; Worcestershire)
  Obituary 1928/I *283*
Evans, H. (Derbyshire)
  Obituary 1921/I *225*
Evans, J. (Hampshire)
  Obituary 1974 *1073*
Evans, J. B. (Glamorgan)
  Photograph 1961 *372*
Evans, R. (Western Australia)
  Obituary 1979 *1089*
Evans, R. (Merion C.C., U.S.A.)
  Obituary 1916 *163*
Evans, R. du B. (Winchester; Cambridge University; Hampshire)
  Obituary 1930/I *249*
Evans, R. G. (Bury St.Edmunds Grammar School; Cambridge University; Berkshire)
  Obituary 1982 *1197*
Evans, Lieut. R. J. (Border)
  Obituary 1944 *306*
Evans, T. G. (Kent; England)
  'Action in Cricket' Book Review 1957 *1000*
  Action Photographs 1950 *70*
   1960 *90*
  'Behind the Stumps' Book Review 1952 *1017*
  Benefit Match 1954 *416*
  Career Figures 1960 *143*
  Cricketer of the Year 1951 *69*
  'The Gloves are off' Book Review 1961 *996*
  Note on 1958 *75*
  Photograph 1951 *68*
  Retirement (N. Cardus) 1960 *137*
Evans, V. J. (Essex)
  Obituary 1978 *1084*
Evans, W. H. B. (Malvern; Oxford University; Worcestershire; Hampshire)
  Obituary 1914/I *183*
Evatt, Hon. Dr. J. H. V. (Journalist; Deputy Prime Minister, Australia)
  'Australian Cricket, its Control and Organisation' 1935/I *255*
  'D. G. Bradman 1927-37' 1938 *57*

'Cricket and the British Commonwealth' 1949 *111*
Obituary 1966 *963*
Evelyn, F. L. (Rugby; Oxford University; Herefordshire)
Obituary 1911/I *142*
Everard, Sir W. L. (Harrow; Leicestershire)
Obituary 1950 *907*
Everett, G. (Surrey Committee)
Obituary 1910/I *137*
Everett, S. C. (New South Wales)
Obituary 1972 *1057*
Everitt, R. S. (Worcestershire)
Obituary 1974 *1073*
Everitt, Capt. W. W. (Hertford Grammar)
Obituary 1919/I *173*
Evers, J. W. (Umpire)
Obituary 1909/I *136*
Evershed, E. (Derbyshire)
Obituary 1959 *959*
Evershed, F. (Amersham School; Oxford University; Derbyshire)
Presumed Obituary 1946 *439*
Correction – Still Alive! 1947 *697*
Obituary 1955 *929*
Evershed, S. (Vice President Derbyshire)
Obituary 1904 *lxxxv*
Evershed, S. H. (Clifton; Derbyshire)
Obituary 1938 *938*
Evershed, W. (Clifton; Derbyshire)
Obituary 1912/I *166*
Evetts, W. (Harrow; Oxford University)
Obituary 1937/I *271*
Ewbank, L. (Cambridge University Groundsman)
Obituary 1917 *245*
Ewbank, Rev. T. C. (Gentlemen of Sussex)
Obituary 1927/I *276*
Ewbank, W. A. (Gentlemen of Yorkshire)
Obituary 1918 *225*
Exham, P. G. (Repton; Cambridge University; Derbyshire)
Obituary 1923/I *297*
Exton, R. N. (Clifton; Hampshire)
77 wkts Schools Averages 1947 *585*
Eyer, J. H. (Parkdale C.C., Toronto)
Obituary 1921/I *226*
Eyre, Lieut. C. H. (Harrow; Cambridge University)
Obituary 1916 *163*
Eyre, Capt. H. W. (Westbury-on-Trym C.C.)
Obituary 1917 *180*

Eyre, J. (Winchester)
Obituary   1942   *358*

Eyre, M. C. (Staten Island C.C.)
Obituary   1917   *245*

Eyre, T. J. P. (Derbyshire)
Photograph   1970   *358*

Eytle, E. (Writer; Broadcaster; British Empire XI)
'Frank Worrell – The Career of a Great Cricketer'
Book Review   1964   *1004*
Obituary   1969   *980*

Faber, Canon A. H. (Winchester)
Obituary   1911/I   *142*

Faber, M. J. J. (Eton; Oxford University; Sussex)
Photograph   1975   *565*

Fabling, A. H. (Wellingborough; Warwickshire)
Obituary   1973   *1006*

Facey, P. (Secretary Tasmanian Cricket Association)
Obituary   1924/I   *258*

Fagg, A. E. (Kent; England; Umpire)
Benefit Match   1952   *382*
Career Figures   1978   *1071*
Double Hundred in Each Innings   1939   *321*
'Fagg Incident'   1974   *68*
Obituary   1978   *1070*
Photographs   1951   *378*
                                                              1952   *382*
                                                              1953   *395*

Fair, Major J. St. F. (Harrow)
Obituary   1951   *922*

Fair, J. T. (Treasurer Lancashire)
Obituary   1918   *225*

Fairbairn, G. A. (Cambridge University; Middlesex)
Obituary   1974   *1073*

Fairbairn, Capt. S. G. (Buckinghamshire)
Obituary   1944   *306*

Fairbairnes, Capt. A. (University College School)
Obituary   1919   *173*

Fairbanks, W. (Clifton; Gloucestershire)
Obituary   1925/I   *264*

Fairclough, H. D. (Devon Club Cricket Association)
'Views on the Laws'   1957   *85*

Fairclough, J. (Gentlemen of Lancashire)
Obituary   1909/I   *152*

Fairfax, A. G. (New South Wales; Australia)
Obituary   1956   *970*

Fairservice, W. J. (Kent; Middlesex; Northumberland)
　Benefit Match　　　　　　　　　　　　　　1922/II　　　　*165*
　Obituary　　　　　　　　　　　　　　　　　1972　　　　　*1049*
　Tribute to A. P. F. Chapman　　　　　　　　1962　　　.　*986*
Falcon, J. H. (Harrow; Cambridge University; Norfolk)
　Obituary　　　　　　　　　　　　　　　　　1951　　　　　*922*
Falcon, M. C. (Harrow; Cambridge University; Norfolk)
　Obituary　　　　　　　　　　　　　　　　　1977　　　　　*1040*
Faithful, H. M. (New South Wales)
　Obituary　　　　　　　　　　　　　　　　　1909/I　　　　*136*
Falklands, Cricket in　Note on　　　　　　　1984　　　　　*781*
Falkner, N. J. (Reigate Grammar School)
　Note on　　　　　　　　　　　　　　　　　1981　　　　　*859*
　1139 runs Schools Averages　　　　　　　　1981　　　　　*901*
Fallows, J. (Lancashire; Cheshire)
　Obituary　　　　　　　　　　　　　　　　　1975　　　　　*1077*
Fallows, J. C. (Treasurer Lancashire; Cheshire)
　Obituary　　　　　　　　　　　　　　　　　1949　　　　　*864*
Falmouth, Major-Gen. 7th Viscount (President Kent)
　Obituary　　　　　　　　　　　　　　　　　1919　　　　　*205*
Fane, F. L. (Charterhouse; Oxford University; Essex; England)
　Presumed Obituary　　　　　　　　　　　　1956　　　　　*977*
　Correction – Still Alive!　　　　　　　　　1957　　　　　*950*
　Obituary　　　　　　　　　　　　　　　　　1961　　　　　*945*
Fannelly, F. (Stonyhurst College)
　134 wkts Schools Averages　　　　　　　　1914/II　　　　*474*
Farebrother, Lieut. M. H. (Eton)
　Obituary　　　　　　　　　　　　　　　　　1945　　　　　*322*
Fargus, Rev. A. H. C. (Haileybury; Cambridge University; Gloucestershire)
　Obituary　　　　　　　　　　　　　　　　　1915/I　　　　*221*
　Correction　　　　　　　　　　　　　　　　1917　　　　　*227*
Farmer, Lieut. G. C. E. (Eton; Oxford University)
　Obituary　　　　　　　　　　　　　　　　　1917　　　　　*180*
Farmer, J. H. (Cricket Enthusiast)
　Obituary　　　　　　　　　　　　　　　　　1930　　　　　*240*
Farmer, Rev. M. S. (Eton)
　Obituary　　　　　　　　　　　　　　　　　1944　　　　　*31*
Farmer, W. (Barbados)
　Obituary　　　　　　　　　　　　　　　　　1977　　　　　*1040*
Farmiloe, 2nd Lieut G. F. (Hampstead C.C.)
　Obituary　　　　　　　　　　　　　　　　　1918　　　　　*18*
Farnes, P/O. K. (Royal Liberty School, Romford; Cambridge University; Essex;
England)
　Memorial Note　　　　　　　　　　　　　　1955　　　　　*32*
　Note on　　　　　　　　　　　　　　　　　1944　　　　　*24*
　Obituary　　　　　　　　　　　　　　　　　1942　　　　　*34*

Portrait and Biography	1939	*38*
Schools Note	1942	*240*
'Study in Greatness' B. Easterbrook	1979	*125*
Farnsworth, K. (Writer; Journalist)		
'Farewell Bramall Lane'	1974	*135*
'Story of Cricket at Bramall Lane'		
Book Review	1974	*1118*
Farquharson, Capt. L. S. (Charterhouse)		
Obituary	1916	*163*
Farquharson-Roberts. Capt. D. (Bedford Grammar; Bedfordshire)		
Obituary	1918	*183*
Farrands, F. H. (Nottinghamshire)		
Benefit Match	1882	*32*
Obituary	1917	*245*
Farrar, A. (Yorkshire)		
Obituary	1955	*930*
Farrar, Major H. W. F. B. (Bedford Grammar School; Dorset)		
Obituary	1919	*173*
Farrer, C. R. (Essex)		
Obituary	1951	*922*
Farrer, Capt. R. G. B. (Marlborough)		
Obituary	1929/I	*245*
Farrimond, W. (Lancashire; England)		
Benefit match	1940	*360*
Obituary	1981	*1142*
Farthing, F. H. (Journalist)		
Obituary	1930/I	*249*
Fast Bowlers ' From Spofforth to Lillee'		
R. Benaud	1977	*116*
Fast Hundreds		
'Fastest Hundreds in Test Cricket'		
G. Brodribb	1983	*106*
Faulkner, A. C. (Marlow C.C.)		
Obituary	1918	*225*
Faulkner, Major G. A. (Transvaal; South Africa)		
Obituary	1931/I	*255*
Fausset, 2nd Lieut. C. R. (Rathmines School; Dublin University)		
Obituary	1916	*163*
Fawcett, Capt. B. J. A. (Cheltenham; Ceylon)		
Obituary	1918	*184*
Fawcus, C. L. D. (Bradfield; Kent; Worcestershire; Dorset)		
Obituary	1968	*999*
Fawcus, Lt-Gen. Sir H. B. (Durham School; Durham University)		
Obituary	1949	*872*
Fawkes, Rev. W. H. (Uppingham)		
Obituary	1944	*313*

Fazal Mahmood (Northern India; Punjab; Pakistan)
Cricketer of the Year 1955 72
Photograph 1955 64
Fear, H. P. (Taunton School; Somerset)
Obituary 1944 313
Fearnley, M. C. (Yorkshire)
Obituary 1980 1149
Featherstone, N. G. (Middlesex; Glamorgan; Transvaal)
Photographs 1971 449
1979 467
1981 401
1982 403
Featherstone, Rev. S. W. (Secretary Devon County C.C.)
Obituary 1909/I 137
Featherstone, Lieut. W. (Redcar C.C.)
Obituary 1917 180
Fegan, J. H. (Cambridge Freshman)
Obituary 1950 90
Felix, N. (See under **Wanostrocht, N.**)
Fell, 2nd Lieut. M. H. (Scarborough C.C.)
Obituary 1917 180
Fellowes, Rev. E. L. (Oxford University)
Obituary 1897 x
Fellowes, Col. J. (Kent; Hampshire; Devon)
Obituary 1917 24
'Views on Second Class Counties
and the L.B.W. Rule' 1903 lxi
Fellows, H. W. (Eton)
Obituary 1908/I 13
'Views on High Scoring and L.B.W. Rule 1899 lxxv
Fellows, Rev. W. (Westminster; Oxford University)
Obituary 1903 lxxi
Felton, R. (St.Paul's; Middlesex)
Obituary 1983 124
Fender, P. G. H. (St.Paul's; Sussex; Surrey; England)
'P. G. H. Fender – A Biography'
R. Streeton Book Review 1982 126
Fastest Hundred in First Class Cricket
P. G. H. Fender's Account 1976 6
Portrait and Biography 1915/I 19
Schools Notes 1910/I 12
1911/I 13
Tribute to Sir J. Hobbs 1964 10
Fenner, F. P. (Groundsman)
Obituary 1897 xxx

Fenner, G. D. (Kent; M.C.C. Coach)
Note on	1962	*148*
Obituary	1972	*1050*

Fenwick, Major I. (Winchester)
Obituary	1945	*322*

Fenwick, Capt. R. C. (Harrow)
Obituary	1945	*322*

Fenwick, W. (New York Club Cricket)
Obituary	1918	*225*

Fenwick, W. (Ramsbottom C.C.)
Obituary	1951	*922*

Fereday, A. (Midlands Club Cricket)
Obituary	1914/I	*184*

Ferens, H. C. (Durham School; Durham)
Obituary	1976	*1097*

Ferguson, J. A. (Perthshire; Scotland)
Obituary	1948	*782*

Ferguson, Lieut. J. W. (Westminster)
Obituary	1916	*163*

Ferguson, W. H. (Scorer)
Retirement	1955	*86*
Obituary	1958	*958*

Ferguson-Davie, Lt-Col. A. F. (Sandhurst)
Obituary	1917	*180*

Fernandes, M. P. (British Guiana; West Indies)
Obituary	1982	*1198*

Fernandez, Rev. P. H. (Winchester)
Obituary	1933/I	*243*

Fernando, H. I. (Ceylon)
Obituary	1975	*1077*

Fernie, A. E. (Wellingborough; Cambridge University; Staffordshire)
Obituary	1961	*953*

Ferns, C. S. (Cricket Reporting Agency Journalist)
Obituary	1955	*930*

Ferrie, Capt. R. L. M. (Highfield School, Ontario)
Obituary	1919	*173*

Ferris, J. J. (New South Wales; South Australia; Gloucestershire; Australia; England)
Obituary	1901	*lv*
Portrait and Biography	1889	*xxix*

Festing, Brig-Gen. F. L. (Winchester)
Obituary	1949	*864*

Festival of Cricket   Note on
	1961	*804*

Fetherston, B. T. (Gentlemen of Warwickshire)
Obituary	1919	*206*

Feversham, Lt-Col. 8th Earl of (Patron Yorkshire)
    Obituary   1917   *180*
Fewin, H. (Queensland)
    Obituary   1983   *1244*
'Few Jottings, A' R. Thoms   1889   *xxxv*
'Few Words on Fielding' A G. A. Lohmann   1893   *xlix*
Ffolkes, 2nd Lieut. W. R. C. (Radley)
    Obituary   1919   *198*
Ffrench, 2nd Lieut. G. E. (Trent College)
    Obituary   1919   *173*
Ffrench-Blake, Lt-Col. A. O'B. (Free Foresters)
    Obituary   1974   *1073*
Fiddian-Green, C. A. F. (The Leys; Cambridge University; Warwickshire; Worcestershire)
    Obituary   1977   *1040*
Field, Lieut. D. H. (Wellington; Buckinghamshire)
    Obituary   1916   *163*
Field, E. (Clifton; Cambridge Univesity; Berkshire; Middlesex)
    Obituary   1948   *782*
Field, F. E. (Warwickshire)
    Benefit Match   1913/II   *241*
    Great Bowling Feat   1917   *270*
    Obituary   1935/I   · *264*
Field, 2nd Lieut. O. (Clifton)
    Obituary   1916   *164*
Field, T. (Yorkshire Club Cricket)
    Obituary   1918   *225*
Fielder, A. (Kent; England)
    Benefit Match   1912/II   *37*
    Obituary   1950   *907*
    Portrait and Biography   1907   *cxxvii*
Fielders, Too Many   Note on   1957   *7*
'Fielding, A Few Words on' G. A. Lohmann   1893   *xlix*
Fielding, Brilliant By England
    Photograph   1979   *6*
'Fielding in 1900' D. L. A. Jephson   1901   *lxxvi*
Fielding, Poor   Note on   1963   *13*
Fielding, F. (Malvern; Surrey)
    Obituary   1911/I   *14*
Fifoot, F. (Glamorgan)
    Obituary   1932/I   *24*
Fifties Fastest, Farcical   Note on   1966   *8*
'Fifty Years of Lancashire Cricket'
    N. Cardus   1951   *8*
'Fifty Years of Yorkshire County Cricket'
    Lord Hawke   1932/I   *25*

Fiji
'A Century in the Fiji Islands' P. Snow		1974	*123*
Fiji 1948 Team Portrait		1981	*121*
Fiji Tours List		1974	*129*
Fiji in Australia	1959-60	1961	*892*
Fiji in New Zealand	1954	1955	*868*
	1961-62	1963	*956*

Filgate, C. R. (Cheltenham; Gloucestershire)
Obituary	1931/I	*256*

Fillery, R. (Sussex)
Benefit Match	1881	*159*

Fillingham, G. H. (Harrow; Oxford University)
Obituary	1896	*xxxviii*

Filliston, J. W. (Staffordshire)
Obituary	1965	*966*

Financial Losses   Note on
	1975	*99*

Financial Worries   Note on
	1983	*84*

Finch, A. (Haileybury; Norfolk)
Obituary	1944	*313*

Finch, H. R. (Harrow)
Obituary	1937/I	*287*

Finch-Hatton, Hon. D. G. (Eton)
Obituary	1933/I	*262*

Findlay, W. (Eton; Oxford University; Lancashire; Secretary Surrey; Secretary M.C.C.)
Appreciation of Lord Harris	1933/I	*231*
Obituary	1954	*923*
Tributes to: C. S. Caine	1934/I	*27*
S. J. Southerton	1936/I	*30*

Fines for Slow Over Rates   Note on
	1975	*100*

Fine time for Test Team   Note on
	1982	*338*

Fingleton, J. H. W. (Journalist; New South Wales; Australia)
'An Enjoyable Visit to Britain'	1962	*126*
'The Ashes Crown the Year' Book Review	1954	*983*
'Batting from Memory - An Autobiography' Book Review	1982	*1268*
'Brightly Fades the Don' Book Review	1950	*975*
'Cricket Alive Again'	1961	*127*
'Four Chukkas to Australia' Book Review	1960	*999*
'The Greatest Test of All' Book Review	1962	*1038*
'The Immortal Victor Trumper' Book Review	1979	*1128*
Obituary	1982	*1198*
'Watery Reflections form Australia'	1969	*80*

Finishes – Arranged   Note on
	1953	*82*
– Tight Note on	1944	*65*

Finke, Capt. R. F. (Cheltenham)
Obituary 1916 *164*
Finlayson, Lieut. R. H. (Incogniti of Victoria, British Columbia)
Obituary 1919 *199*
Finney, Sir S. (Clifton)
Obituary 1925/I *264*
First Class Cricket – New Ideas 1984 *49*
– Note on 1970 *81*
– Reviving it 1957 *73*
'First Test Match' E. C. Brogden and J. Arlott
Book Review 1951 *989*
Firth, A. (Yorkshire)
Obituary 1928/I *284*
Firth, J. (Yorkshire; Leicestershire)
Benefit match 1959 *443*
Obituary 1982 *1200*
Firth, Rev. Canon J. D'E. E. (Winchester; Oxford University; Nottinghamshire)
Obituary 1958 *959*
Photograph 1918 *150*
Public School Bowler of the Year 1918 *152*
Firth, L/Cpl. R. B. (Dulwich)
Obituary 1918 *184*
Fischardt, C. G. (Orange Free State; South Africa)
Obituary 1924/I *258*
Fish, Ven. Preb. L. J. (Somerset Supporter)
Obituary 1925/I *264*
Fishbourne, Lt-Col. C. E. (Oakham)
Obituary 1917 *181*
Fisher, A. H. (Carisbrook C.C., Otago)
Obituary 1962 *986*
Fisher, P/O, B. M. (Eton)
Obituary 1941 *387*
Fisher, Lieut. C. D. (Westminster; Oxford University; Sussex)
Obituary 1917 *181*
Fisher, H. (Yorkshire)
Obituary 1975 *1078*
Fisher, Lt-Col. J. L. (Harrow)
Obituary 1954 *924*
Fisher, Lord (Archbishop of Canterbury)
Photograph 1962 *9*
Fisher-Rowe, Major C. V. (Eton)
Obituary 1924/I *258*
Fisher-Rowe, G. H. (Winchester)
Obituary 1947 *68*
Fishlock, L. B. (Surrey; England)
Benefit Match 1951 *51*

Cricketer of the Year	1947	*46*
Photographs	1947	*41*
	1950	*494*
	1951	*503*
Fishwick, T. S. (Warwickshire)		
Obituary	1951	*922*
Fison, T. A. (Mill Hill School; Hendon C.C.)		
Obituary	1912/I	*167*
Fitch, Rev. H. W. (Bury St.Edmunds Grammar School; Rutland)		
Obituary	1917	*246*
Fitzgerald, Lt-Col. A. E. (West Indies Club Cricket)		
Obituary	1917	*181*
Fitzgerald, G. A. R. (Sherborne)		
Obituary	1926/I	*269*
Fitzgerald, J. (Queensland)		
Obituary	1951	*922*
Fitzgerald, J. R. (Uppingham)		
Obituary	1929/I	*245*
Fitzgerald, M. O. (Uppingham)		
Obituary	1932/I	*243*
Fitzgerald, Brig-Gen. P. D. (M.C.C.)		
Obituary	1935/I	*276*
Fitzgerald, R. A. (Patron)		
Team in Canada and U.S.A. 1872	1873	*91*
Fitzgibbon, G. (New York Clubs)		
Obituary	1913/I	*187*
Fitzmaurice, D. M. J. (Victoria)		
Obituary	1983	*1244*
Fitzpatrick, C. W. (Cleveland, U.S.A.)		
Obituary	1920/I	*173*
Fitzroy-Newdegate, Comdr. Hon. J. M. (Later J. M. Fitzroy; Eton; Northamptonshire)		
Obituary	1977	*1040*
Fitzsimmons, E. (Wellington, New Zealand)		
Obituary	1943	*375*
Fixture Making Note on	1967	*88*
Flamson, W. H. (Leicestershire)		
Obituary	1946	*439*
Flannery, J. (Journalist)		
Obituary	1909/I	*137*
Flavell, J. A. (Worcestershire; England)		
Benefit Match	1964	*611*
Cricketer of the Year	1965	*83*
Photographs	1956	*612*
	1958	*610*
	1962	*644*
	1965	*79*

Fleetwood-Smith, L. O'B. (Victoria; Australia)
    Obituary   1972   *1050*
Fleming, A. J. (Leinster C.C.)
    Obituary   1916   *164*
Fleming, A. L. (Winchester)
    Obituary   1981   *1142*
Fleming, C. J. N. (Fettes)
    Obituary   1949   *864*
Fleming, J. M. (Scotland)
    Obituary   1963   *1032*
Flesher, 2nd Lieut. F. A. (Ripon Grammar School)
    Obituary   1917   *181*
Fletcher, D. G. W. (Surrey)
    Benefit Match   1958   *563*
    Photograph   1953   *527*
Fletcher, J. (Heywood C.C.)
    Obituary   1919   *206*
Fletcher, 2nd Lieut. J. H. (Haileybury; Sandhurst)
    Obituary   1919   *174*
Fletcher, K. W. R. (Essex; England)
    'Captains Innings' – An Autobiography
    Book Review   1984   *1266*
    Cricketer of the Year   1974   *55*
    Photographs   1964   *360*
    1968   *380*
    1974   *54*
    1982   *386*
Fletcher, Capt. M. (St.Edward's Canterbury)
    Obituary   1917   *181*
Fletcher, N. (Rugby)
    Obituary   1934/I   *264*
Fletcher, Capt. R. S. (Northumberland Fusiliers)
    Obituary   1916   *218*
Fletcher, T. (Derbyshire)
    Obituary   1955   *930*
Fletcher, W. (Yorkshire)
    Obituary   1936/I   *277*
Fletcher, 2nd Lieut. W. G. (Highgate School)
    Obituary   1917   *181*
Flett, Lieut. A. D. (The Leys)
    Obituary   1918   *184*
Fleuret, F. S. (Westminster)
    Obituary   1946   *439*
Flick, B. J. (Warwickshire)
    Photograph   1974   *567*

Flint, J. (Derbyshire)
   Obituary   1913/I   *187*
Flint, W. A. (Nottinghamshire)
   Obituary   1956   *971*
Flood, W. (Hayes C.C.)
   Obituary   1957   *943*
Floodlit Cricket   1978   *103*
Floodlit Cricket Competition   1982   *718*
Floquet, B. H. (Transvaal; South Africa)
   Obituary   1954   *924*
Flower, A. W. (Secretary Middlesex)
   Tribute to R. W. V. Robins   1969   *986*
Flowers, 2nd Lieut. H. (Eastbourne C.C.; Steyning C.C.)
   Obituary   1917   *181*
Flowers, 2nd Lieut. J. A. (Lancing)
   Obituary   1917   *182*
Flowers, W. (Nottinghamshire; England)
   Benefit Matches   1896   *208*
                        1900   *31*
   Obituary   1927/I   *276*
Floyd, W. E. (Birkenhead School)
   Obituary   1919   *174*
Fluke, Lieut. A. C. (King's Canterbury)
   Obituary   1916   *164*
Flux, Trooper J. (Colchester Grammar School)
   Obituary   1916   *164*
Flying Bomb Interrupts Innings Photograph   1945   *33*
Foat, J. C. (Gloucestershire)
   Photograph   1979   *390*
Foenander, S. P. (Journalist)
   Obituary   1968   *999*
Foley, Lt.-Col. C. P. (Eton; Cambridge University; Worcestershire; Middlesex)
   Obituary   1937/I   *272*
Foley, C. W. (Eton; Cambridge University)
   Obituary   1934/I   *264*
Foley, H. (Wellington; New Zealand)
   Obituary   1950   *915*
Foley, H. St. G. (Eton)
   Obituary   1905   *civ*
Foley, Canon The Rev. J. W. (Eton)
   Obituary   1927/I   *278*
Foley, P. H. (Worcestershire)
   Obituary   1929/I   *246*
Foljambe, Lt.-Col. G. S. (Nottinghamshire)
   Obituary   1921/I   *226*

Folkes, Capt. W. H. (President London Counties)
Obituary   1944   *313*
'Follow on',Discussion on the   1894   *xlvii*
Follows, D. (Football Association)
Tribute to A. G. Doggart   1964   *948*
Foord-Kelcey, W. (Chatham house, Ramsgate; Oxford University; Kent)
Obituary   1923/I   *297*
Foot, D. (Writer)
'Harold Gimblett – Tormented
Genius of Cricket' Book Review   1983   *1308*
Forbes, C. (Nottinghamshire)
Benefit Match   1970   *520*
Photographs   1966   *517*
                                                     1968   *533*
Forbes, C. W. (Stirling County)
Obituary   1949   *864*
Forbes, D. G. (Journalist)
Obituary   1904   *lxxix*
Forbes, D. H. (Eton; Oxford University)
Obituary   1902   *lxiii*
Forbes, Lt-Col. D. W. A. W. (Eton)
Obituary   1945   *326*
Forbes, J. (New Jersey Athletic Club)
Obituary   1921/I   *243*
Forbes, Col. O. B. (President Ceylon Cricket Association)
Obituary   1977   *1041*
Forbes, $\overline{\text{W. F.}}$ (Eton; IZingari)
Obituary   1934/I   *265*
Forbes-Adam, E. G. (Cambridge Seniors)
Obituary   1926/I   *269*
Ford, A. F. J. (Repton; Cambridge University; Middlesex)
Obituary   1932/I   *243*
Ford, 2nd Lieut. A. L. (Charterhouse; Durham County)
Obituary   1916   *164*
Ford, A. L. (Southgate C.C.)
Obituary   1925/I   *264*
Ford, Major C. G. (Harrow)
Obituary   1945   *322*
Ford, F. G. J. (Repton; Cambridge University; Middlesex; England)
Obituary   1941   *395*
Ford, F. W. J. (Repton)
Obituary   1921/I   *226*
Ford, H. J. (Repton)
Obituary   1942   *358*
Ford, J. P. (Manager Anglo American Team of 1879)
Obituary   1915/I   *222*

Ford, Very Rev. L. G. B. J. (Repton)
  Obituary   1933/I   *243*
Ford, P. H. (Gloucestershire)
  Obituary   1921/I   *226*
Ford, R. G. (Gloucestershire)
  Obituary   1983   *1244*
Ford, W. A. J. (Repton)
  Obituary   1939   *909*
Ford, W. J. (Repton; Cambridge University; Middlesex)
  Obituary   1905   *xciv*
Fordham, A. (Bedford Modern School)
  Schools Note   1983   *899*
  1042 runs Schools Averages   1983   *909*
Fordham, M. (Statistician; Writer)
  'The Career Figures of W. G. Grace'   1982   *127*
  Obituary   1983   *1244*
Fordon, A. E. (U.S.A. Club Cricket)
  Obituary   1926/I   *269*
Forester, T. (Warwickshire; Derbyshire)
  Obituary   1928/I   *284*
Forman, Rev. A. F. E. (Sherborne; Derbyshire; Dorset)
  Obituary   1906   *xc*
Forman, A. T. (Shrewsbury)
  Obituary   1928/I   *284*
Forman, F. G. (Derbyshire)
  Obituary   1961   *946*
  Amended Obituary   1962   *994*
Forman, H. (Shrewsbury; Cambridge University; Somerset)
  Obituary   1926/I   *287*
Forman, J. (Rugby)
  Obituary   1933/I   *262*
Forrest, A. J. (Cheltenham)
  Obituary   1937/I   *272*
Forsdike, A. W. (Haileybury; Burnley C.C.)
  Obituary   1983   *940*
Forster, H. W. (Lord of Lepe)(Eton; Oxford University; Hampshire)
  Obituary   1937/I   *272*
Forster, Major H. M. (Charterhouse)
  Obituary   1916   *165*
Forster, S. E. (Eton)
  Obituary   1951   *922*
Forster, T. H. B. (Winchester)
  Obituary   1928/I   *284*
Forster-Morris, 2nd Lieut. H. G. F. (Exeter School)
  Obituary   1916   *165*

Fort, J. A. (Winchester)
Obituary ... 1935/I ... *265*

Fortescue, Rev. A. T. (Oxford University)
Obituary ... 1900 ... *lv*

Fortune, C. (Writer; Journalist)
'The Australians in England' Book Review ... 1962 ... *1038*
'Cricket Overthrown' Book Review ... 1961 ... *994*
'The M.C.C. in South Africa 1964-65'
Book Review ... 1966 ... *1016*
'M.C.C. Tour of South Africa 1956-57'
Book Review ... 1958 ... *1013*

Fortune, Major-Gen. V. M. (Winchester)
Obituary ... 1950 ... *907*

Fosberry, Pte. S. I. (Five C's C.C.; Victoria; British Columbia)
Obituary ... 1918 ... *213*

Fosdick, Lieut. J. H. (Charterhouse)
Obituary ... 1916 ... *165*

Foster, B. S. (Worcestershire; Middlesex)
Obituary ... 1960 ... *951*

Foster, C. K. (Worcestershire)
Obituary ... 1972 ... *1050*

Foster, Major D. G. (Shrewsbury; Warwickshire)
Obituary ... 1981 ... *1142*

Foster, E. (Hastings C.C.)
Obituary ... 1905 ... *xcv*

Foster, F. R. (Solihull; Warwickshire; England)
'F. R. Foster – A Prince of the Golden Age'
R. Ryder ... 1976 ... *134*
Obituary ... 1959 ... *929*
Photograph ... 1976 ... *135*
Portrait and Biography ... 1912/I ... *191*

Foster, G. N. (Malvern; Oxford University; Worcestershire; Kent)
Obituary ... 1972 ... *1050*

Foster, H. K. (Malvern; Oxford University; Worcestershire)
Obituary ... 1951 ... *922*
Portrait and Biography ... 1911/I ... *167*

Foster, Capt. J. H. N. (Harrow; Kent)
Obituary ... 1977 ... *1041*

Foster, M. K. (Malvern; Worcestershire)
Obituary ... 1941 ... *396*

Foster, N. J. A. (Worcestershire; Federated Malaysian States)
Obituary ... 1979 ... *1075*

Foster, R. A. C. (Eton)
Obituary ... 1978 ... *1073*

Foster, R. E. (Malvern; Oxford University; Worcestershire; England)
'In the Cricket Field' ... 1913/I ... *169*

200

Obituary	1915/I	*222*
Portrait and Biography	1901	*lxix*
Schools Note	1897	*lxiv*
'South African Bowling'	1908/I	*106*

Foster, T. W. (Yorkshire)
Obituary	1948	*783*

Foster, W. (Warwickshire)
Obituary	1915/I	*224*

Foster, W. B. (Winchester)
Obituary	1946	*433*

Foster, W. L. (Worcestershire)
Obituary	1959	*930*

Foster-Jackson, Capt. S. (Shrewsbury)
Obituary	1916	*165*

Fothergill, A. J. (Northumberland; Somerset)
Benefit Match	1893	*58*

Foulke, W. (Derbyshire)
Obituary	1917	*246*

Foulkrod, W. W. (Frankford County C.C., Philadelphia)
Obituary	1911/I	*143*

Fowke, Major G. H. S. (Uppingham; Leicestershire)
Obituary	1947	*689*

Fowke, J. N. (Canterbury; Auckland)
Obituary	1939	*909*

Fowle, D. (Writer)
'Kent the Glory Years' Book Review	1975	*1115*

Fowle, Lieut. L. R. (Wellington)
Obituary	1916	*165*

Fowler, A. J. B. (Middlesex)
Obituary	1978	*1073*

Fowler, E. (Victoria)
Obituary	1910/I	*137*

Fowler, G. (Clifton; Oxford University; Essex; Somerset)
Obituary	1917	*247*

Fowler, G. (Lancashire; England)
Photograph	1981	*460*
Schools Notes	1976	*862*
	1977	*809,810*

Fowler, H. (Clifton; Oxford University; Essex)
Obituary	1935/I	*265*

Fowler, Sir R. H. (Winchester; Norfolk)
Obituary	1945	*329*

Fowler, Capt. R. H. (Ireland)
Obituary	1958	*959*

Fowler, Rev. R. H. (Worcestershire)
Obituary	1972	*1057*

Fowler, Capt. R. St. L. (Eton; Hampshire)
Obituary   1926/I   *270*

Fowler, T. F. (Uppingham; Cambridge University; Huntingdonshire)
Obituary   1916   *165*

Fowler, Cpl. T. H. (Lancing; Gloucestershire; Dorset)
Obituary   1916   *166*

Fowler, W. H. (Essex; Somerset)
Obituary   1942   *358*

Fox, C. J. M. (Westminster; Surrey; Kent)
Obituary   1902   *lxiv*

Fox, F. H. (Marlborough)
Obituary   1953   *940*

Fox, F. I. (Nottinghamshire)
Obituary   1936/I   *277*

Fox, H. F. (Clifton; Somerset; Oxfordshire; Suffolk)
Obituary   1927/I   *278*

Fox, J. (Warwickshire; Worcestershire)
Obituary   1962   *986*

Fox, J. H. (Clifton)
Obituary   1952   *956*

Fox, J. M. (Philadelphia)
Obituary   1919   *206*

Fox, Capt. R. H. (Haileybury; M.C.C.)
Obituary   1953   *940*

Fox, Lt-Col. R. W. (Wellington; Oxford University; Sussex)
Obituary   1949   *864*

Fox, W. V. (Worcestershire)
Obituary   1950   *907*

Foxton, Col. Hon. J. F. G. (Australian Cricket Board of Control)
Obituary   1917   *247*

Foy, P. A. (Bedford School; Bedfordshire; Somerset)
Obituary   1958   *960*

Frampton, Preb. C. T. (Harrow)
Obituary   1911/I   *162*

France-Hayhurst, Lt-Col. F. C. (Eton)
Obituary   1916   *166*

Francis, B. C. (Essex; New South Wales; Australia)
Photograph   1972   *380*

Francis, C. K. (Rugby; Oxford University; Middlesex)
Obituary   1926/I   *271*

Francis, G. (Gloucestershire)
Obituary   1949   *864*

Francis, G. H. (Chatham House School; Ramsgate)
123 wkts Schools Averages   1908/II   *458*

Francis, G. N. (Barbados; West Indies)
Obituary   1943   *375*

202

Francis, H. H. (Gloucestershire; Western Province; South Africa)
Obituary   1938   *948*

Francis, J. G. (Suffolk)
Obituary   1918   *225*

Francis, P. T. (Worcestershire; Suffolk)
Obituary   1965   *966*

Francis, T. E. S. (Tonbridge; Cambridge University; Somerset; Eastern Province)
Obituary   1970   *1020*

Francis, Dr. W. (Essex)
Obituary   1918   *226*

Francois, Air Sgt. C. M. (Griqualand West; South Africa)
Obituary   1945   *329*

Francois, H. A. (Border)
Obituary   1983   *1244*

Frank, J. (Yorkshire)
Obituary   1941   *396*

Frank, R. W. (Yorkshire)
Obituary   1951   *923*

Frank, W. H. B. (Transvaal)
Obituary   1946   *439*

Frankish, F. S. (Canterbury, New Zealand)
Obituary   1910/I   *137*

Franklin, C. F. (King's County, New York State)
Obituary   1920/I   *193*

Franklin, Lieut. L. W. (Dulwich)
Obituary   1919   *174*

Franklin, R. C. (Essex)
Obituary   1983   *1245*

Franklin, W. B. (Repton; Cambridge University; Buckinghamshire)
Obituary   1969   *980*

Franks, B. M. F. (Eton)
Obituary   1983   *1245*

Franks, F. H. (Malvern; Kent)
Obituary   1975   *1078*

Fraser, M. F. K. (Writer)
'Warwickshire's Ups and Downs'   1950   *88*

Fraser, Capt. R. (Merchiston Castle; Perthshire)
Obituary   1917   *182*

Fraser, Capt and Adjt. W. (Northern C.C.)
Obituary   1917   *182*

Fraser, Pte. W. (Galt C.C., Ontario)
Obituary   1917   *182*

Frazer, C. E. (Winchester; Oxford University)
Obituary   1972   *1051*

Frazer, J. E. (Winchester; Oxford University; Sussex)
Obituary   1928/I   *284*

Freak Declarations   Notes on   1947   *67*
                                Example   1947   *262*

Freakes, F/O. H. D. (Rhodes University; Grahamstown; Oxford University)
   Obituary   1943   *364*

Frederick, Capt. J. St. J. (Eton; Oxford University; Middlesex; Hampshire)
   Obituary   1908/I   *140*

Frederick, Capt. T. (Aldenham)
   Obituary   1918   *184*

Fredericks, R. C. (Guyana; Glamorgan; West Indies)
   Cricketer of the Year   1974   *60*
   Photographs   1972   *396*
                                     1974   *52*

Free Foresters   in Canada 1923   1924/II   *581*

'Free Foresters: Centenary of'
   Col. K. B. Stanley   1956   *126*

Freeman, A. J. (Essex)
   Obituary   1973   *1006*

Freeman, A. P. (Kent; England)
   Benefit Matches   1930/II   *276*
                                     1935/II   *211*
   Career Record   1966   *965*
   'Tich Freeman and the Decline of the Leg
   Break Bowler' D. Lemmon Book Review   1983   *1308*
   In the Cricket Field   1937/I   *257*
   Obituary   1966   *964*
   Photograph   1938   *41*
   Portrait and Biography   1923/I   *316*
   'Spin Bowling'   1938   *41*

Freeman, E. (Somerset)
   Obituary   1950   *915*

Freeman, E. C. (Essex; Essex Groundsman)
   Obituary   1940   *840*

Freeman, E. H. (Warwickshire Club and Ground)
   Obituary   1958   *960*

Freeman, E. J. (Essex; Dorset)
   Obituary   1965   *966*

Freeman, G. (Nottinghamshire)
   Obituary   1933/I   *262*

Freeman, G. (Yorkshire)
   Obituary   1896   *xliii*

Freeman, H. (Hertfordshire)
   Obituary   1917   *245*

Freeman, J. (Essex)
   Benefit Match   1927/II   *289*

Freeman, 2nd Lieut. J. R. (King's College, London)
   Obituary   1918   *184*

Freeman-Cowen, 2nd Lieut. C. (Felsted)
Obituary 1917 *182*
Freeman-Thomas, Lieut. Hon. G. F. F. (Eton)
Obituary 1918 *213*
French, B. (Nottinghamshire)
Photograph 1978 *506*
French, Lt-Col. Hon. E. G. F. (Wellington; Devon)
Obituary 1971 *1025*
French, S. (Writer)
'Francis "Mindoo" Phillip: A Portrait from Memory'
Book Review 1982 *1270*
French, 2nd Lieut. T. H. (King's Canterbury)
Obituary 1918 *184*
French, Rev. T. L. (Eton; Cambridge University; Suffolk)
Obituary 1910/I *138*
Frere, L. R. T. (Haileybury; Cambridgeshire; Norfolk)
Obituary 1937/I *273*
Frew, Capt. D. T. (Glasgow High School; Glasgow University)
Obituary 1917 *182*
Friend, Major-Gen. Rt. Hon. Sir L. B. (Cheltenham; Kent)
Obituary 1945 *330*
Frindall, W. H. (Statistician; Broadcaster)
'Frindall's Score Book: England v Australia 1975'
Book Review 1976 *1146*
'Frindall's Score Book: Australia v West Indies 1975-76'
Book Review 1977 *1094*
'Frindalls Score Book – Jubilee Edition'
Book Review 1978 *1124*
'Frindall's Score Book: Australia v England/West Indies 1979-80'
Book Review 1981 *1196*
Frisby, J. B. (Leicestershire)
Obituary 1979 *1089*
Frith, C. (Canterbury; Otago)
Obituary 1920/I *173*
Frith, C. W. (Leinster C.C.; Journalist)
Obituary 1919 *206*
Frith, D. (Writer; Journalist)
'The Ashes 77'
with G. S. Chappell Book Review 1978 *1124*
'The Ashes 79' Book Review 1980 *1204*
'The Archie Jackson Story' Book Review 1975 *1120*
'Cricketana – A Bull Market' 1981 *127*
'My Dear Victorious Stod' Book Review 1971 *1080*
Front Foot Experiment 1964 *93*
Frost, Lieut. A. B. (Whitgift Grammar)
Obituary 1919 *174*

Frost, G. (Derbyshire)
    Obituary   1914/I   *184*
Frowd, G. W. (Proprietor of James Lillywhite's Cricketer's Annual)
    Obituary   1915/I   *224*
Fry, Capt. C. A. (Staten Island)
    Obituary   1919   *174*
Fry, C. B. (Repton; Oxford University; Surrey; Sussex; Hampshire; England)
    'C. B. Fry' D. Batchelor Book Review   1952   *1018*
    'C. B. Fry' N. Cardus   1957   *111*
    'In First Class Cricket'   1902   *cvii*
    Obituary   1957   *943*
    Photograph   1957   *112*
    Portrait and Biography   1895   *xlv*
    Schools Notes   1890   *230*
                             1891   *301*
                             1892   *272*
    Tribute to G. Lohmann   1902   *liv*
Fry, K. R. B. (Cheltenham; Cambridge University; Sussex)
    Obituary   1950   *908*
Fry, S. (Hampshire)
    Obituary   1980   *1149*
Fryer, E. H. (Wellingborough; Berkshire)
    Obituary   1973   *1006*
Fryer, F. E. R. (Harrow; Cambridge University; Suffolk)
    Obituary   1918   *226*
Fryer, P. A. (Norfolk, Northamptonshire)
    Obituary   1951   *923*
Fryer, W. H. (Kent Umpire)
    Obituary   1920/I   *173*
Fulcher, E. A. (Devon)
    Obituary   1947   *689*
Fulcher, Major E. A. (Devon)
    Obituary   1974   *1073*
    Correction   1975   *1028*
Fulcher, Capt. E. J. (Radley; Norfolk)
    Obituary   1924/I   *25*
Fuller, D. M. (Wellington, New Zealand)
    Obituary   1937/I   *27*
Fuller, G. P. (Winchester; Oxford University)
    Obituary   1928/I   *28*
Fuller, J. M. (Marlborough; Cambridge University)
    Obituary   1894   *xxxv*
Fuller, Sir J. M. F. 1st Bart. (Winchester; Wiltshire)
    Obituary   1916   *16*
Fuller, L. G. (Orange Free State)
    Obituary   1947   *68*

Fuller-Maitland, W. (Harrow; Oxford Univesity; Essex)
Obituary 1933/I *243*
Furber, Capt. L. D. (Army)
Obituary 1913/I *187*
Furley, F. W. (Treasurer Kent)
Obituary 1923/I *297*
Furley, J. (Northamptonshire)
Obituary 1910/I *138*
Furness, F. (Lord's Pavillion Clerk)
Obituary 1893 *xxxiii*
Furness, T. S. (Young America C.C.)
Obituary 1925/I *288*
Furniss, A. E. (Sheffield Club Cricket)
Obituary 1911/I *143*
Furniss, H. (Caricaturist)
Obituary 1926/I *271*
Furse, Ven. Archdeacon C. W. (Eton)
Obituary 1901 *lv*
Furze, Capt and Adjt. A. (Bradfield)
Obituary 1917 *182*
Furze, 2nd Lieut. N. F. (Westminster)
Obituary 1918 *184*
Gaby, Family – 100 Years at Lord's
Note 1974 *71*
Gaby, G. (Joe)(Lord's Staff)
Obituary 1977 *1041*
Gaddum, F. D. (Rugby; Cambridge University; Lancashire)
Obituary 1901 *lvii*
Gadsdon, D. B. (Framlingham College)
76 wkts Schools Averages 1923/II *524*
Gaggin, W. W. (Victoria)
Obituary 1926/I *272*
Gainford, Lord (Durham)
Obituary 1944 *313*
Gale, D. (Dorset)
Obituary 1978 *1073*
Gale, F. ('Old Buffer') (Winchester; Kent)
Obituary 1905 *xcv*
Views on High Scoring and L.B.W. Rule 1899 *lxxvii*
Gale, H. F. (Journalist)
Obituary 1955 *930*
Gale, N. R. (Cricket Poet)
Obituary 1943 *376*
Gale, P. G. (London County)
Obituary 1941 *396*

Gale, R. A. (Bedford Modern School; Middlesex)
Photograph 1959 *454*
Gale, Capt. W. N. (Dover College)
Obituary 1920/I *153*
Galletly, Lieut. I. (Edinburgh Academy)
Obituary 1917 *182*
Gallichan, N. M. (Manawatu; Wellington; New Zealand)
Obituary 1970 *1021*
Galliher, L/Cpl. F. T. (Victoria C.C., British Columbia)
Obituary 1917 *223*
Galloway, 10th Earl of (Harrow; President M.C.C.)
Obituary 1902 *lxiv*
Galloway, 11th Earl of (Harrow)
Obituary 1921/I *226*
Galloway, J. O. (Royal Engineers)
Obituary 1967 *967*
Game, W. H. (Sherborne; Oxford University; Surrey)
Obituary 1933/I *245*
Gamesmanship Note on 1973 *96*
Games, The Thing Note on 1962 *111*
Gamlin, H. T. (Somerset)
Obituary 1938 *939*
Ganapathi Pillai, C. R. (Combined Madras)
Obituary 1955 *930*
Gandar-Dower, K. C. (Harrow)
Obituary 1946 *434*
Gandar-Dower, 2nd Lieut. L. L. F. (Brighton College)
Obituary 1919 *199*
Gange, T. H. (Gloucestershire)
Obituary 1950 *908*
Ganly, J. B. (Ireland)
Obituary 1978 *1085*
Gannon, Brig. J. R. C. (M.C.C.)
Obituary 1981 *1142*
Gardiner, Dr. I. B. (Western Province; Border)
Obituary 1952 *956*
Gardiner, 2nd Lieut. W. E. M. (Forest School)
Obituary 1917 *182*
Gardner, F. C. (Warwickshire)
Benefit Match 1959 *585*
'F. C. Gardner Benefit Souvenir'
Book Review 1959 *993*
Obituary 1980 *1149*
Photograph 1951 *548*
Gardner, H. (King's Canterbury; Army)
1166 runs Schools Averages 1909/II *459*

Gardner, H. W. (Rugby; Staffordshire)
Obituary   1925/I   *265*
Gardner, J. (Suffolk; Leicestershire)
Obituary   1911/I   *143*
Gardner, R. J. C. (President Border Cricket Union)
Obituary   1975   *1078*
Gardner, W. T. (Transvaal)
Obituary   1935/I   *277*
Garner, J. (Barbados; Somerset; West Indies; South Australia)
Cricketer of the Year   1980   *80*
Photograph   1980   *67*
Garnett, C. A. (Cheltenham; Oxford University)
Obituary   1920/I   *173*
Garnett, Capt. C. H. (Free Foresters)
Obituary   1918   *228*
Garnett, E. (Charterhouse; Berkshire)
Obituary   1951   *923*
Garnett, G. (Free Foresters)
Obituary   1930/I   *250*
Garnett, H. G. (Lancashire)
Obituary   1918   *184*
Garnett, Rev. L. (Eton)
Obituary   1913/I   *187*
Garnett, Lieut. L. H. (Radley)
Obituary   1918   *185*
Garnett, R. (Cheltenham)
Obituary   1922/I   *248*
Garnett, S. (Free Foresters)
Obituary   1922/I   *248*
Garnett, T. R. (Charterhouse; Somerset)
Schools Note   1934/I   *302*
1023 runs Schools Averages   1934/II   *596*
Garnier, Rev. E. S. (Marlborough; Oxford University)
Obituary   1939   *909*
Garnier, E. T. (Norfolk)
Obituary   1925/I   *265*
Garnier, G. R. (Sherborne)
Obituary   1949   *865*
Garnier, Rev. T. P. (Oxford University; Winchester; Hampshire)
Obituary   1900   *lv*
Garrard, W. R. (Auckland)
Obituary   1958   *967*
Garraway, 2nd Lieut. W. F. (Bedford Grammar School)
Obituary   1917   *182*
Garrett, Lieut. H. F. (Somerset)
Obituary   1916   *166*

Garrett, H. S. (Parkdale C.C., Toronto)
Obituary 1920/I *174*
Garrett, T. W. (New South Wales; Australia)
Obituary 1944 *314*
Garrett, W. T. (Essex)
Obituary 1954 *924*
Garrow, Sub-Lieut. I. P. (Winchester)
Obituary 1944 *309*
Garth, Rt. Hon. Sir R. (Eton; Oxford University)
Obituary 1904 *lxxx*
Garth, T. C. (Bramshill C.C., Hampshire)
Obituary 1908/I *140*
Gartley, Major J. D. E. (Transvaal)
Obituary 1943 *369*
Gaskell, 2nd Lieut. D. L. S. (Tonbridge)
Obituary 1917 *183*
Gaskin, B. M. (British Guiana; West Indies)
Obituary 1980 *1149*
Gasson, E. A. (Canterbury, New Zealand)
Obituary 1964 *954*
Gaston, A. J. (Cricketologist)
'Batsman of One Thousand Runs' 1897 *lxix*
'Bowlers of One Hundred Wickets' 1899 *xvcii*
'Bibliography of Cricket' 1892 *xlviii*
1894 *lxiii*
1900 *xc*
1923/I *255*
Obituary 1929/I *246*
'Alfred James Gaston – A Study in Enthusiasm'
I. Rosenwater Book Review 1976 *1143*
Gates, Lieut. A. F. (Ridley College, Ontario)
Obituary 1919 *199*
Gatting, M. W. (Middlesex; England)
Cricketer of the Year 1984 *61*
Photographs 1978 *474*
1984 *Plates*
Schools Note 1977 *809*
Gaukrodger, J. (Brooklyn C.C., U.S.A.)
Obituary 1937/I *273*
Gauld, Dr. G. O. (Nottinghamshire)
Obituary 1951 *923*
Gaunt, Rev. Canon H. C. A. (Tonbridge; Warwickshire)
Obituary 1984 *1199*
Gavaskar, S. M. (Bombay; Somerset; India)
Cricketer of the Year 1980 *71*
Outstanding Achievement 1984 *53*

Photographs	1980	*70*
	1981	*535*
'Sunny Days' Book Review	1977	*1098*
Gay, Major L. H. (Brighton College; Hampshire; Cambridge University; Somerset; England)		
Obituary	1959	*908*
Geary, A. (New South Wales)		
Obituary	1912/I	*167*
Geary, G. (Leicestershire; England)		
Benefit matches	1925/II	*297*
	1937/II	*395*
Obituary	1982	*1200*
Portrait and Biography	1927/I	*307*
Geddes, Capt. J. (Winnipeg Club Cricket)		
Obituary	1916	*167*
Gedge, Rev. H. T. S. (Loretto)		
Obituary	1945	*330*
Gee, H. (Journalist)		
Obituary	1977	*1041*
'Throw and Drag'	1960	*97*
Geen, 2nd Lieut. W. P. (Haileybury; Monmouthshire)		
Obituary	1916	*167*
Geeson, F. (Leicestershire)		
Obituary	1921/I	*226*
Gehrs, D. R. A. (South Australia; Australia)		
Obituary	1956	*978*
Gehrs, Capt. L. (Charterhouse)		
Obituary	1919	*199*
Genders, R. (Writer)		
'Worcestershire' Book Review	1953	*1000*
Gentlemen of Philadelphia in England 1908	1909/II	*350*
Gentlemen v Players Records	1940	*110*
	1963	*358*
150th Anniversary	1957	*298*
Gentlemen v Players Matches		
'W. G. Grace in'	1907	*cxxx*
Gentry, J. S. B. (Christ's Hospital; Hampshire; Surrey; Essex)		
Obituary	1979	*1075*
Geoghegan, J. P. A. (Glamorgan)		
Obituary	1917	*247*
Geoghegan, T. P. (Downside)		
Obituary	1922/I	*248*
George V, H. M. King		
Obituary	1937/I	*263*
George VI, H. M. King		
Death of	1952	*99*

Photograph	1947	*36*
George Tubow II, King of Tonga		
Obituary	1919	*206*
George, W. (Warwickshire)		
Obituary	1934/I	*265*
Georgetown Crowd Disturbance		
Photograph	1955	*63*
German, A. C. J. (Repton; Leicestershire)		
Obituary	1969	*980*
German, Major H. B. (Portsmouth Grammar School)		
Obituary	1919	*174*
'German Cricket: A Brief History'		
J. D. Coldham Book Review	1984	*1260*
Germantown C.C. (U.S.A.)		
in England 1911	1912/II	*423*
Gerrard, Major R. A. (Taunton; Somerset)		
Obituary	1944	*306*
Ghorpade, J. M. (Baroda; Maharashtra; India)		
Obituary	1979	*1075*
Ghulam, M. (Mohammadians)		
Obituary	1967	*967*
Gibb, Dr. J. M. (Kensington C.C., Jamaica)		
Obituary	1908/I	*140*
Gibb, P. A. (St.Edward's Oxford; Cambridge University; Yorkshire; Essex; England; Scotland)		
Career Figures	1979	*1090*
Obituary	1979	*1089*
Schools Note	1930/I	*302*
Gibbes, W. R. L. (Wellington, New Zealand)		
Obituary	1920/I	*193*
Gibbons, H. H. I. (Worcestershire)		
Benefit Match	1939	*565*
Obituary	1974	*1073*
Gibbons, Capt. T. P. (Radley)		
Obituary	1919	*174*
Gibbs, G. L. (British Guiana; West Indies)		
Obituary	1980	*1149*
Gibbs, J. A. (Eton; Somerset)		
Obituary	1900	*lii*
Gibbs, L. R. (Warwickshire; Guyana; South Australia; West Indies)		
Cricketer of the Year	1972	*71*
Photograph	1972	*70*
Gibbs, N. J. F. (Dover College)		
Schools Note	1934/I	*311*
78 wkts Schools Averages	1934/II	*598*

Gibbs, P. J. (Hanley High School; Oxford University; Derbyshire)
Photograph   1968   *362*

Gibbs, Lt.-Col. W. B. (Newton Abbot; Sandhurst; Wellington School)
Obituary   1917   *183*

Gibson, A. (Writer)
'Jackson's Year' Book Review   1966   *1011*
'A Mingled Yarn' Book Review   1977   *1098*
'Sir Neville Cardus – An Appreciation'   1976   *107*
'Mike Procter – A Great All-Rounder'   1982   *99*

Gibson, A. H. (Canada)
Obituary   1921/I   *227*

Gibson, A. L. (Winchester)
Obituary   1944   *315*

Gibson, C. H. (Eton, Cambridge University; Sussex)
Obituary   1977   *1041*
Photograph   1918   *150*
Public School Bowler of the Year   1918   *152*

Gibson, D. (Surrey)
Photographs   1960   *554*
    1961   *554*
    1966   *552*

Gibson, G. (Victoria)
Obituary   1911/I   *143*

Gibson, Sir H. Bart. (Uppingham)
Obituary   1933/I   *246*

Gibson, Dr. I. (Manchester Grammar School; Oxford University; Derbyshire)
Obituary   1964   *948*

Gibson, 2nd Lieut. J. G. (Glenalmond)
Obituary   1918   *185*

Gibson, J. M. (Treasurer New South Wales Cricket Association)
Obituary   1913/I   *188*

Gibson, Sir K. L. (Eton; Sussex)
Obituary   1968   *1000*

Gibson, 2nd Lieut. S. A. C. (Christ's Hospital)
Obituary   1918   *185*

Gibson, Lt.-Col. T. A. (Toronto Club Cricketer)
Obituary   1926/I   *272*

Giddy, L. L. (Eastern Province)
Obituary   1943   *376*

Giffard, W. J. F. (Harrow)
Obituary   1936/I   *292*

Giffard-Wood, 2nd Lieut. L. K. (Richmond School)
Obituary   1917   *223*

Giffen, G. (South Australia; Australia)
Obituary   1928/I   *285*
Portrait and Biography   1894   *xl*

Testimonial Match	1924/II	*651*
Giffen, W. F. (South Australia; Australia)		
Obituary	1950	*908*
Gifford, G. C. (Northamptonshire)		
Obituary	1973	*1006*
Gifford, J. (Buenos Aires C.C.)		
Obituary	1932/I	*244*
Gifford, Trooper J. D. (Denbighshire)		
Obituary	1918	*185*
Gifford, N. (Worcestershire; Warwickshire; England)		
Benefit Match	1975	*747*
Cricketer of the Year	1975	*92*
Photographs	1962	*644*
	1967	*617*
	1968	*620*
	1972	*613*
	1975	*79*
	1976	*602*
Gilbert, A. (Manchester Grammar School; Cheshire)		
Obituary	1984	*1199*
Gilbert, E. (Queensland)		
Obituary	1979	*1076*
Gilbert, G. (Gloucestershire; New South Wales)		
Obituary	1907	*cx*
Gilbert, H. A. (Charterhouse; Oxford University; Worcestershire; Monmouthshire; Radnorshire; Wiltshire)		
Obituary	1961	*946*
Gilbert, J. (Sussex)		
Obituary	1897	*xlii*
Gilbert, W. R. (Middlesex; Gloucestershire; Worcestershire; Northamptonshire)		
Obituary	1925/I	*265*
Gilchrist, R. (Jamaica; Hyderabad; West Indies)		
'Hit me for Six' Book Review	1964	*1003*
Giles, A. B. (Harrow)		
Obituary	1929/I	*246*
Giles, Sir C. T. (Harrow)		
Obituary	1941	*396*
Giles, R. J. (Nottinghamshire)		
Benefit Match	1960	*524*
Photograph	1956	*505*
Giles, W. (Treasurer Gloucestershire)		
Obituary	1956	*971*
Gill, Gnnr. F. (Yorkshire)		
Obituary	1918	*185*
Gill, G. C. (Somerset; Leicestershire; London County)		
Obituary	1938	*939*

Gill, Capt. K. C. (St.John's, Leatherhead)
Obituary   1919   *174*
Gill, 2nd Lieut. W. G. O. (Dulwich)
Obituary   1918   *185*
Giller, J. F. (Victoria)
Obituary   1948   *783*
Gillespie, A. (Canada)
Obituary   1913/I   *188*
Gillespie, D. W. (Uppingham; Cambridge University)
Obituary   1983   *1245*
Gillespie, H. D. (Auckland)
Obituary   1955   *930*
Gillespie-Stanton, R. W. (Harrow)
Obituary   1920/I   *193*
Gillett, Rev. E. A. (Radley; Leicestershire; Norfolk)
Obituary   1927/I   *278*
Gillett, Rev. H. H. (Winchester; Oxford University)
Obituary   1916   *167*
Gillette Connection   Note on   1981   *98*
'Gillette Cup Spans the World' A. Ross   1977   *156*
Gillhouley, K. (Yorkshire; Nottinghamshire)
Photograph   1962   *665*
Gilliat, I. A. W. (Charterhouse; Oxford University)
Obituary   1968   *1000*
Gilliat, O. C. S. (Eton)
Obituary   1915/I   *224*
Gilliat, R. M. C. (Charterhouse; Oxford University; Hampshire)
Benefit Match   1979   *719*
Note on   1979   *78*
Photograph   1970   *421*
   1973   *417*
   1975   *426*
Gilligan, A. E. R. (Dulwich; Cambridge University; Surrey; Sussex; England)
'And Gilligan Led them Out' R. Ryder   1970   *124*
'Arthur Gilligan' R. L. Arrowsmith   1977   *130*
'Australian Challenge' Book Review   1957   *997*
Career Figures   1977   *133*
'Cricket Conundrums'   1939   *48*
Photographs   1939   *48*
   1969   *57*
   1977   *131*
Portrait and Biography   1924/I   *280*
Schools Notes   1913/I   *219*
   1914/I   *223*
   1915/I   *178,194*
78 wkts Schools Averages   1915/II   *435*

'Sussex through the Years' 1954 *108*
Tributes to: S. F. Barnes 1968 *114*
        H. Strudwick 1971 *1032*
        M. Tate 1957 *949*
'The Urn Returns' Book Review 1956 *1025*
Gilligan, A. H. H. (Dulwich; Cambridge University; Sussex; England)
Career Figures 1979 *1077*
'Growth of New Zealand Cricket' 1949 *125*
Obituary 1979 *1076*
Schools Notes 1914/I *223*
  1915/I *194*
Tribute to H. Preston 1961 *160*
Gilligan, F. W. (Dulwich; Oxford University; Essex)
Obituary 1961 *946*
Gilligan, W. A. (Dulwich; Father of the Gilligan Brothers)
Obituary 1940 *840*
Gillingham, Canon F. H. (Dulwich; Essex)
Obituary 1954 *924*
Tribute to Sir S. Jackson 1948 *81*
Gillingham, Rev. G. W. (Secretary Worcestershire)
Obituary 1954 *924*
Gilman, J. (Writer)
Note on 1977 *141*
'Tales of W. G. Grace – Recalls the Past' 1977 *138*
Gilmour, Capt. A. K. (Westminster)
Obituary 1917 *183*
Gilmour, Lieut. H. J. G. (Gentlemen of Worcestershire)
Obituary 1916 *218*
Gilroy, Capt. G. B. (Winchester)
Obituary 1917 *183*
Gimblett, H. (Somerset; England)
Benefit Match 1953 *519*
Career Figures 1979 *1078*
Cricketer of the Year 1953 *71*
Obituary 1979 *1077*
Photographs 1950 *476*
  1951 *486*
  1953 *62*
  1954 *518*
'Harold Gimblett – Tormented Genius of Cricket'
D. Foot Book Review 1983 *1308*
Gimson, C. (Oundle; Cambridge University; Leicestershire)
Obituary 1976 *1098*
Girling, A. C. (Chairman Essex)
Obituary 1962 *986*

Gladwin, C. (Derbyshire)

Career Figures		1959	*491*
Photographs		1950	*290*
		1952	*293*
		1955	*291*

Gladwin, J. (Derbyshire)

Obituary		1963	*1032*

Glamorgan County Cricket Club

Badge		1950	*322*
		ad passim	
'Glamorgan's March of Progress'			
J. H. Morgan		1949	*107*
'Glamorgan – A Peep into the Past'			
J. H. Morgan		1970	*86*
'Glamorgan' J. H. Morgan Book Review		1953	*999*
'Glamorgan' W. Wooller Book Review		1972	*1095*
Glamorgan: Rise of Note		1949	*121*
Team Portraits			
Champion County	1948	1949	*70*
County Champions	1969	1970	*50*
	1974	1975	*398*
	1975	1976	*394*
	1976	1977	*398*
	1977	1978	*387*
	1978	1979	*377*
	1979	1980	*397*
	1980	1981	*403*
	1981	1982	*403*
	1982	1983	*406*
	1983	1984	*373*
in the West Indies	1970	1971	*926*

Glanvill, B. A. (President Surrey)

Obituary		1951	*923*

Glass, Pte. T. (West Toronto C.C.)

Obituary		1918	*185*

Gleed, 2nd Lieut. J. V. A. (Uppingham)

Obituary		1918	*185*

Glennie, Canon Rev. H. J. (Marlborough; Shropshire)

Obituary		1927/I	*278*

Glennie, Canon R. G. (Staffordshire)

Obituary		1954	*925*

Gloucestershire County Cricket Club

Badge		1950	*339*
		ad passim	
'Gloster's Centenary Cricket'			
N. Craven Book Review		1971	*1083*

'The Book of Gloucestershire County Cricket
Records from 1919 to 1960'
C. M. Plenty Book Review | | 1962 | *1034*
'Gloucestershire Road'
G. Parker Book Review | | 1984 | *1258*
'To Gloucester With Thanks'
N. Craven Book Review | | 1970 | *1073*
'The History of Gloucestershire Cricket Club'
S. C. Caple Book Review | | 1950 | *973*
'100 Years of Gloucestershire Cricket'
Gloucestershire C.C.C. Book Review | | 1971 | *1082*
'Great Men of Gloucestershire' F. H. Hutt | | 1957 | *104*
Gloucestershire Retain Holts Products Trophy | | 1981 | *430*

Team Portraits			
County Champions	1877	1971	*143*
Championship Runners-up	1947	1948	*35*
Championship Runners-up	1959	1960	*95*
Gillette Cup Winners	1973	1974	*48*
	1974	1975	*414*
	1975	1976	*411*
	1976	1977	*414*
	1977	1978	*401*
Benson and Hedges			
Cup Winners	1977	1978	*86*
	1978	1979	*392*
	1979	1980	*413*
	1980	1981	*417*
	1981	1982	*417*
	1982	1983	*423*
	1983	1984	*389*
in Zambia 1971-72		1973	*416*

Glover, A. C. S. (Repton; Staffordshire; Warwickshire)
Obituary | 1950 | *908*
Glover, E. R. K. (Sherborne; Glamorgan)
Obituary | 1968 | *1000*
Glover, G. K. (Griqualand West; South Africa)
Obituary | 1939 | *909*
Glover, Capt. R. B. G. (Uppingham)
Obituary | 1917 | *223*
Glyka, 2nd Lieut. A. L. (City of London School)
Obituary | 1917 | *183*
Goad, F. E. (Eton)
Obituary | 1952 | *956*
Goatly, E. G. (Surrey)
Obituary | 1959 | *930*

Goatman, S. (Kent Women; England Women)

England Captaincy Note	1983	*1194*

Godambe, S. R. (Bombay; Hindus)

Obituary	1971	*1034*

Godby, C. V. (Winchester)

Obituary	1920/I	*174*

Goddard, Sub-Lieut. F. M. J. (Winchester)

Obituary	1944	*306*

Goddard, T. (Natal; North East Transvaal; South Africa)
'The Trevor Goddard Story'

Book Review	1967	*1018*

Goddard, T. W. J. (Gloucestershire; England)

'Appreciation of Retirement' D. Moore	1952	*123*
Benefit Matches	1937/II	*175*
	1949	*353*
Bradford League Note	1944	*286*
Obituary	1967	*967*
Photograph	1950	*339*
Portrait and Biography	1938	*34*
'Study in Greatness' B. Easterbrook	1979	*121*
Tribute to W. R. Hammond	1966	*118*

Godfree, G. S. (President Sussex)

Obituary	1948	*783*

Godfrey, Rev. C. J. M. (Magdalen College School; Oxford University)

Obituary	1942	*359*

Godfrey, 2nd Lieut. F. (Grenadier Guards)

Obituary	1917	*183*

Godsal, Major W. H. (Military Cricket)

Obituary	1919	*174*

Godsell, R. T. (Clifton; Cambridge University; Gloucestershire)

Obituary	1956	*978*

Godward, 2nd Lieut. E. J. (Merchant Taylors)

Obituary	1917	*183*

Gold, Lieut and Adjt. C. A. (Eton)

Obituary	1917	*183*

Gold, P. H. G. (Harrow; Cambridge University)

Obituary	1956	*971*

Goldberg, 2nd Lieut. F. W. (University College, Oxford)

Obituary	1917	*184*

Goldie, Major K. O. (Wellington; Sussex; London County)

Obituary	1939	*909*

Golding, A. J. (Hertfordshire)

Obituary	1951	*924*

Goldman, J. W. (Author)

Obituary	1979	*1079*

Goldsmith, L. (Victoria)
  Obituary   1912/I   *167*
Gollar, W. (Otago)
  Obituary   1917   *248*
Gomes, H. A. (Trinidad; Middlesex; West Indies)
  Schools Note   1971   *786*
Gonsalves, D. (Civic and Wanderers C.C., Winnipeg)
  Obituary   1920/I   *194*
Gooch, C. W. (Blundells)
  Obituary   1919   *206*
Gooch, Rev. F. H. (Durham)
  Obituary   1932/I   *244*
Gooch, G. A. (Western Province; Essex; England)
  Action Photograph   1982   *63*
  Cricketer of the Year   1980   *75*
  'My Cricket Diary' Book Review   1983   *1310*
  Photographs   1977   *379*
                                      1980   *68*
                                      1981   *385*
  Schools Notes   1973   *826*
                                      1974   *828*
Goodall, A. W. (Vice President Lancashire)
  Obituary   1969   *980*
Goodden, C. P. (Harrow; Dorset)
  Obituary   1970   *1021*
Gooden, C. C. (South Australia)
  Obituary   1914/I   *184*
Gooden, J. E. (South Australia)
  Obituary   1914/I   *184*
Goodenough, W. S. M. (President Lansdown C.C.)
  Obituary   1914/I   *184*
Goodfellow, J. E. (South Australia)
  Obituary   1925/I   *266*
Goodhew, W. (Kent)
  Obituary   1898   *xlii*
Goodland, Major E. S. (Taunton School; Somerset)
  Obituary   1975   *1078*
Goodman, C. E. (Barbados)
  Obituary   1912/I   *16*
Goodman, Sir G. A. (Pickwick C.C.)
  Obituary   1922/I   *24*
Goodman, P. A. (Barbados)
  Obituary   1936/I   *27*
Goodman, S. (Pennsylvania University; Philadelphia)
  Obituary   1906   *x*

Goodman, T. (Journalist)
with A. G. Moyes
'With the M.C.C. in Australia 1962-63'
Book Review   1964   *999*
Goodrick, A. (Durham)
Obituary   1960   *951*
Goodridge, A. (Journalist)
Obituary   1971   *1034*
Goodwill, Spreading it   Note   1949   *120*
Goodwin, 2nd Lieut. H. J. (Marlborough; Cambridge University; Warwickshire)
Obituary   1918   *186*
Goodwin, H. S. (Gloucestershire)
Obituary   1956   *971*
Goodwin, R. (New York Veterans Association)
Obituary   1915/I   *224*
Goodwyn, Canon F. W. (Clifton; Gloucestershire)
Obituary   1933/I   *262*
Goodyear, 2nd Lieut. F. (University College School)
Obituary   1918   *186*
Goodyear, W. (Derby Groundsman)
Award to   1971   *596*
'Googly Bowlers and Captains Retire'
E. M. Wellings   1958   *94*
'Googly, The'
B. J. T. Bosanquet   1925/I   *225*
Goonaratne, Major L. V. (Secretary Ceylon Cricket Association)
Obituary   1972   *1051*
Goonerane, Major M. O. (Ceylon)
Obituary   1975   *1078*
Goonesena, G. (Cambridge University; Nottinghamshire; New South Wales;
Ceylon)
Photographs   1956   *505*
                                                         1959   *492*
Gordon, C. (Clapton C.C.)
Obituary   1900   *liii*
Gordon, 2nd Lieut. E. A. (Hillhead School, Glasgow)
Obituary   1919   *175*
Gordon, Capt. G. M. (Wellington; Dorset)
Obituary   1918   *186*
Gordon, H. P. (Worcestershire)
Obituary   1966   *965*
Gordon, Sir H. S. C. M. (Writer; Journalist)
Obituary   1957   *943*
'Sussex' Book Review   1951   *990*
Gordon, J. H. (Winchester; Oxford University; Surrey)
Obituary   1935/I   *277*

Gordon, Lieut. R. (Gala C.C.)
Obituary 1917 184

Gordon, Major R. E. (King's Canterbury)
Obituary 1919 174

Gordon, Major R. G. (Edinburgh Academicals)
Obituary 1919 174

Gordon-Lennox, Major Lord (Sandhurst; IZingari)
Obituary 1915/I 224

Gordon-Steward, Brig-Gen. C. S. (Marlborough; Victoria; Dorset; Gloucestershire)
Obituary 1931/I 257

Gore, A. C. (Eton; Army)
Photograph 1919 150
Public School Cricketer of the Year 1919 156

Gore, C. St. G. (Wellington, New Zealand)
Obituary 1915/I 248

Gore, S. W. (Harrow; Surrey)
Obituary 1907 cx

Gore-Brown, Major E. A. R. (Oundle)
Obituary 1919 175

Gorell, 3rd Lord R. Gorell-Barnes (Harrow; Oxford University; Suffolk)
Obituary 1965 972

Gornall, L/Cpl. J. F. (Liverpool Institute)
Obituary 1919 175

Gornall, J. P. (Navy; Hampshire)
Obituary 1984 1199

Gornell, Lieut. N. C. (Lancaster Royal Grammar School)
Obituary 1919 17.

Gorrell, Major Rt. Hon. Lord (Harvard University)
Obituary 1919 19

Gorrie, 2nd Lieut. A. K. (Watson's College)
Obituary 1917 18

Goschen, G. J. 1st Viscount (M.C.C.)
Obituary 1908/I 14

Gosford, 4th Earl of (Harrow)
Obituary 1923/I 29

Goslett, 2nd Lieut. J. S. (Bradfield)
Obituary 1917 22

Gosling, Major C. H. (Eton; Oxford University)
Obituary 1975 107

Gosling, Lieut. G. B. (Eton)
Obituary 1907 cx

Gosling, L. D. (Eton)
Obituary 1946 43

Gosling, R. C. (Eton; Cambridge University)
Obituary 1923/I 29

222

Gosling, Major W. S. (Eton)
Obituary   1953   *940*

Gossage, Major G. W .(Sedbergh)
Obituary   1918   *186*

Gostling, Col. E. V. (Framlington College)
Obituary   1924/I   *275*

Gothard, E. J. (Derbyshire; Staffordshire)
Obituary   1980   *1149*

Gothard, J. (Warwickshire Committee)
Obituary   1915/I   *224*

Goudge, Rev. W. H. (Navy; Wiltshire)
Obituary   1968   *1000*

Gough, W. H. (Shropshire)
Obituary   1918   *228*

Gould, E. (Umpire)
Obituary   1961   *946*

Gould, Capt. F. H. (Repton)
Obituary   1917   *224*

Gould, I. J. (Middlesex; Sussex; Auckland)
Photograph   1976   *490*

Gould, J. (New South Wales)
Obituary   1910/I   *150*

Gould, W. (Cheltenham Groundsman)
Obituary   1924/I   *258*

Goulding, W. (Middlesex)
Obituary   1879   *120*

Goulding, Sir W. B. (Ireland)
Obituary   1984   *1199*

Gouldsworthy, W. R. (Gloucestershire)
Obituary   1970   *1021*

Goulstone, J. (Writer)
'The 1789 Tour to France'
Book Review   1973   *1047*
'Early Kent Cricketers'
Book Review   1972   *1091*

Gouly, L. (Western Australia)
Obituary   1912/I   *168*

Gover, A. R. (Surrey; England)
Benefit Matches   1947   *429*
     1948   *479*
Note on   1944   *180*
Portrait and Biography   1937/I   *296*
'Views on the Growing Pains of Cricket'   1956   *88*

Gow, J. C. (Westminster)
Obituary   1930/I   *250*

Gow, Capt. R. G. A. (Winchester)
Obituary 1946 *435*
Gowans, Lt-Col. J. (Harrow)
Obituary 1937/I *273*
Gower, D. I. (King's Canterbury; Leicestershire; England)
Cricketer of the Year 1979 *69*
Photographs 1977 *475*
    1979 *68*
Schools Notes 1974 *831*
    1975 *855*
    1977 *809*
'With Time to Spare' Book Review 1981 *1202*
Gower, Dr. J. H. (Denver C.C.)
Obituary 1923/I *298*
Goy, H. (Lincolnshire)
Obituary 1973 *1006*
Graburn, W. T. (Repton; Surrey)
Obituary 1945 *330*
'The Graces (E.M.; W.G.; G.F.)'
A. G. Powell and S. C. Caple Book Review 1976 *1156*
Grace, Dr. A. (Gloucestershire Club Cricketer)
Obituary 1917 *248*
Grace, Dr. A. H. (Epsom College; Gloucestershire)
Obituary 1931/I *27*
Grace, Mrs. A. N. (Wife of W. G. Grace)
Obituary 1931/I *25*
Grace, C. B. (Son of W. G. Grace; Club Cricketer)
Obituary 1939 *91*
Grace, Capt. E. M. (Grandson of Dr. E. M. Grace; Wrekin College)
Obituary 1945 *32*
Grace, E. M. (Brother of W. G. Grace; Gloucestershire; England)
In the Cricket Field 1900 *lxxxv*
Obituary 1912/I *16*
Views on 'The Follow On' 1894 *xlv*
Views on High Scoring and the L.B.W. Rule 1899 *lxx*
Views on Some Questions of the Day 1890 *xli*
Views on Throwing 1895 *l*
Grace, Dr. E. M. (Son of E.M. Grace; Thornbury C.C.)
Obituary 1975 *107*
Grace, E. S. H. (Nephew of W.G. Grace)
Obituary 1954 *92*
Grace, Col. H. R. (Marlborough; President Kent)
Obituary 1983 *124*
Grace, Dr. H. (Gloucester C.C.)
Obituary 1896 *xi*

Grace, Capt. N. V. (Son of E.M. Grace; Nephew of W.G. Grace; Navy)
Obituary 1976 *1098*
Grace, Lieut. T. M. (Wellington, New Zealand)
Obituary 1917 *224*
Grace, Dr. W. G. (Gloucestershire; London County; England)
And the Surrey Club 1897 *liv*
Batting Averages in First Class Matches 1896 *lviii*
Beard Singed – Note 1959 *76*
'The Best Fast Bowler' Sir S. Jackson 1944 *53*
Birthday Celebration Match 1949 *278*
Bowling Averages in First Class Matches 1896 *lix*
'The Career Figures of W. G. Grace'
M. Fordham 1982 *127*
Centenary Match 1949 *355*
'Giant of the Wisden Century' N. Cardus 1963 *92*
'Dr Grace to Peter May' H. Strudwick 1959 *61*
'W. G. Grace' C. Bax Book Review 1953 *1000*
'W. G. Grace Centenary' H. Preston 1949 *101*
'W. G. Grace' Rev. A. N. B. Sugden
Book Review 1967 *1018*
'W. G. Grace' The Great Cricketer'
G. N. Weston Book Review 1976 *1148*
'W. G. – Cricketing Reminiscences and Personal Recollections'
Book Review 1981 *1202*
'W. G. Grace – His Life and Times'
E. Midwinter Book Review 1982 *1268*
W. G. Grace – Public House – Note on 1967 *94*
'The Great Cricketer'
A. A. Thomson Book Review 1958 *1015*
1969 *1032*
Hundreds 1903 *xciii*
Hundredth hundred 1896 *77*
In Gentlemen v Players Matches 1907 *cxxx*
In the Cricket Field 1916 *89*
Large Scores (Records) 1940 *84*
Memorial to 1922/I *315*
Personal Recollections of – Lord Harris and
A. G. Steel 1896 *xlix*
Photograph 1963 *93*
Portrait 1896 *xlvii*
Presentation to 1880 *84*
Records by 1941 *63*
Remembering W. G. Grace Note 1966 *83*
Scores of 100 and upwards in
First Class Matches 1896 *lvii*

'Shillings for W. G. – Looking Back Eighty Years'
Sir C. Mackenzie   1973   *103*
Special Memoir of (Obituary) S. H. Pardon   1916   *84*
'Tales of W. G. Grace – James Gilman Recalls the Past'
J. Arlidge   1977   *138*
Testimonial Fund   1873   *163*
1000 Runs in May   1974   *81*
Tribute – Lord Harris   1916   *68*
Views on Reforms of 1889   1890   *xxxviii*
Views on Some Questions of the Day   1890   *xl*
Views on Throwing   1895   *liii*
W. G.'s Beard   Note on   1975   *98*
Grace, W. G. (Junior) (Son of W. G. Grace; Clifton; Cambridge University;
Gloucestershire)

Obituary   1906   *xci*
Gracie, Col. A. (Staten Island)
Obituary   1914/I   *199*
Graham, A. L. (Scotland)
Obituary   1912/I   *170*
Graham, H. (Victoria; South Island; Otago; Australia)
Obituary   1912/I   *170*
Graham, J. (Marlborough; Cambridge University)
Obituary   1894   *xxxvii*
Graham, J. N. (Kent; Northumberland)
Benefit Match   1978   *441*
Photograph   1968   *448*
                                                         1974   *437*
Graham, Major J. P. A. (Winchester)
Obituary   1941   *387*
Graham, Capt. M. W. (Malvern)
Obituary   1916   *16?*
Grainger, C. E. (Marlborough; Cambridge University)
Obituary   1935/I   *26.*
Grainger, G. (Derbyshire)
Obituary   1978   *107.*
Grainger, J. (Writer)
and Rippon, A. (Writer)
'Derbyshire County Cricket Club' Book Review   1983   *130*
Grandage, F. W. (Manningham C.C.)
Obituary   1918   *22*
'Grange Cricket Club – Centenary'
W. Reid   1933/II   *63*
Grant, E. A. (Wiltshire; Somerset)
Obituary   1954   *92*

Grant, E. R. (New Jersey Athletic Club)
Obituary — 1922/I — *248*

Grant, G. C. (Cambridge University; Trinidad; West Indies)
'Jack Grant's Story' Book Review — 1981 — *1202*
Obituary — 1980 — *1159*
Record By — 1941 — *63*

Grant, R. S. (Cambridge University; Trinidad; West Indies)
Obituary — 1978 — *1073*

Grant, Capt. W. St. C. (Clifton)
Obituary — 1919 — *175*

Grant-Cook, A. J. (Ceylon Club Cricketer)
Obituary — 1913/I — *188*

Grant-Meek, A. (Harrow)
Obituary — 1918 — *228*

Grant-Peterkin, Col. M. J. (Charterhouse; North of Scotland)
Obituary — 1955 — *930*

Grant, 2nd Lieut. H. F. (Witham C.C.)
Obituary — 1916 — *168*

Grantham, Sir W. (Cricket Fanatic)
Obituary — 1913/I — *202*

Granville, R. St. L. (Warwickshire)
Obituary — 1973 — *1006*

Graveney, D. A. (Gloucestershire)
Photograph — 1977 — *411*

Graveney, T. W. (Bristol Grammar School; Gloucestershire; Worcestershire; Queensland; England)
Action Photograph — 1967 — *64*
Benefit Matches — 1960 — *401*
— 1970 — *603*
Career Record — 1966 — *853*
Career Statistics — 1965 — *116*
Cricketer of the Year — 1953 — *65*
'Cricket Over Forty' Book Review — 1971 — *1078*
'Cricket through the Covers'
Book Review — 1959 — *990*
'Tom Graveney – A. Century of Centuries'
N. Cardus — 1965 — *113*
'Tom Graveney on Cricket' Book Review — 1966 — *1018*
Tom Graveney's Farewell Photograph — 1971 — *63*
'Graveney's Majestic Return   Note on — 1967 — *91*
'The Heart of Cricket' Book Review — 1984 — *1266*
Hundredth Hundred — 1965 — *622*
Walter Lawrence Trophy — 1969 — *655*

Photographs	1951	*342*
	1952	*345*
	1953	*64*
	1957	*364*
	1965	*112*
Schools Note	1944	*223*
Graves, D. H. F. (Whitgift)		
Schools Notes	1938	*695*
75 wkts Schools Averages	1938	*760*
Graves, N. Z. (Philadelphia; U.S.A.)		
Obituary	1919	*206*
Graves, P. J. (Sussex; Orange Free State)		
Photographs	1970	*559*
	1973	*544*
	1975	*565*
Graves, P. P. (Haileybury)		
Obituary	1954	*925*
Gray, C. D. (Middlesex)		
Obituary	1970	*1021*
Gray, Lieut. E. T. (St.Johns, Leatherhead)		
Obituary	1916	*168*
Gray, Lieut. G. E. M. (Sherborne)		
Obituary	1917	*184*
Gray, Rev. H. (Perse School; Cambridge University; Devon; Cambridgeshire)		
Obituary	1939	*910*
Gray, Major J. F. (Military Cricket)		
Obituary	1919	*175*
Gray, J. R. (Hampshire)		
'J. R. Gray' J. Arlott Book Review	1961	*1006*
Photographs	1954	*382*
	1957	*384*
	1963	*447*
Gray, L. H. (Middlesex; Umpire)		
Benefit Match	1949	*432*
Obituary	1984	*1200*
Gray, Capt. M. (Winchester)		
Obituary	1919	*175*
Gray, Lieut. M. N. (Loretto)		
Obituary	1916	*168*
Greatorex, J. E. A. (Harrow)		
Obituary	1941	*397*
Greatorex, Rev. Canon T. (Harrow; Cambridge University; Middlesex)		
Obituary	1934/I	*265*
'Greatness, Three Studies in – W. E. Astill;		
M. J. Turnbull; J. C. White' B. Easterbrook	1978	*156*

'Greatness, Three More Studies in T. Goddard;
W. H. Copson; K. Farnes' B. Easterbrook   1979   *121*
Greaves, Dr. H. S. (Barbados)
    Obituary   1913/I   *188*
Greaves, W. A. (Journalist)
    Obituary   1933/I   *247*
Green, B. (Writer; Broadcaster; Critic)
    'P. G. Wodehouse: A Literary Biography'
    Book Review   1982   *1271*
Green, C. E. (Uppingham; Cambridge University; Middlesex; Sussex; Essex)
    Obituary   1917   *248*
Green, D. M. (Manchester Grammar School; Oxford University; Lancashire;
Gloucestershire)
    Cricketer of the Year   1969   *69*
    Photographs   1965   *453*
        1969   *61*
        1970   *405*
    'Zaheer Abbas – A Flourishing Talent'   1984   *76*
    (Twentieth Batsman to Reach 100 Hundreds)
Green, 2nd Lieut. F. (Wakefield Grammar School)
    Obituary   1917   *184*
Green, G. B. (Scotland Club Cricket)
    Obituary   1928/I   *287*
Green, H. (East Lancashire C.C.)
    Obituary   1956   *971*
Green, Lt-Col. H. W. (Charterhouse)
    Obituary   1920/I   *154*
Green, J. F. (Rugby)
    Obituary   1924/I   *259*
Green, J. P. (Philadelphia Cricket)
    Obituary   1925/I   *266*
Green, Col. L. (Bromsgrove School; Lancashire)
    Obituary   1964   *948*
Green, Brig. M. A. (Gloucestershire; Essex; Manager of M.C.C. Teams Abroad)
    Obituary   1972   *1051*
    'Sporting Campaigner' Book Review   1957   *1000*
Green, S. (M.C.C. Curator)
    '1884 – A Year to Remember'   1984   *81*
Green, S. S. (Eton)
    Obituary   1916   *218*
Green-Price, Rev. A. E. (Repton)
    Obituary   1941   *397*
Green-Price, Rev. H. C. (Radnorshire)
    Obituary   1920/I   *174*
Greene, A. D. (Clifton; Oxford University; Gloucestershire; Somerset)
    Obituary   1929/I   *246*

Greenfield, Rev. F. F. J. (Cambridge University; Sussex)
  Obituary   1902   *lxxii*
Greenhill, 2nd Lieut. F. W. R. (Merchant Taylors)
  Obituary   1918   *186*
Greenhill, Major H. M. (Sherborne, Hampshire; Dorset)
  Obituary   1927/I   *278*
Greenhough, T. (Lancashire; England)
  Benefit Match   1965   *462*
Greenidge, C. G. (Hampshire; Barbados; West Indies)
  Cricketer of the Year   1977   *99*
  Greenidge's Record   1976   *65*
  'The Man in the Middle'
  Book Review   1981   *1203*
  Photographs   1974   *423*
               1977   *93*
Greenidge, G. A. (Sussex; Barbados; West Indies)
  Photographs   1971   *531*
               1974   *553*
Greening, T. (Warwickshire)
  Obituary   1957   *943*
Greenlees, J. R. C. (Loretto)
  Obituary   1952   *956*
Greenlees, Lt-Col. W. L. (Oxford University)
  Obituary   1976   *1098*
Greenstock, W. (Fettes, Cambridge University)
  Obituary   1945   *330*
Greenwood, F. (Oundle; Yorkshire)
  Obituary   1964   *948*
Greenwood, H. W. (Sussex; Northamptonshire; Forfarshire)
  Obituary (but died 1979)   1984   *1200*
Greenwood, L. (Yorkshire; Umpire)
  Benefit Match   1875   *178*
  Obituary   1910/I   *138*
Greenwood, Major L. M. (British Guiana)
  Obituary   1919   *175*
Greenwood, L. W. (Winchester; Oxford University; Somerset; Worcestershire)
  Obituary   1983   *1245*
Greer, Lt-Col. E. B. G. (Military Cricket)
  Obituary   1918   *186*
Greetham, C. M. (Somerset)
  Photograph   1964   *530*
Greg, A. H. (Marlborough)
  Obituary   1948   *783*
Gregg, A. L. (Campbell College, Belfast)
  78 wkts Schools Averages   1913/II   *494*

Gregoire, J. M. (Trinity College, Glenalmond)

Schools Note	1935/I	*320*
75 wkts Schools Averages	1935/II	*617*

Gregory, A. H. (New South Wales)

Obituary	1930/I	*250*

Gregory, C. S. (New South Wales)

Obituary	1938	*949*

Gregory, C. W. (New South Wales)

Obituary	1911/I	*143*

Gregory, D. W. (New South Wales; Australia)

Obituary	1920/I	*174*

Gregory, E. J. (New South Wales; Australia; Custodian of Sydney Cricket Club Ground)

Obituary	1900	*li*

Gregory, F. E. (President Nottinghamshire)

Obituary	1977	*1042*

Gregory, J. C. (Surrey)

Obituary	1895	*xl*

Gregory, J. M. (New South Wales; Australia)

Career Figures	1974	*116*
Fastest Hundred in Test Cricket	1983	*108*
'Jack Gregory – Cricketer in Excelsis'		
Sir. N. Cardus	1974	*113*
Obituary	1974	*1073*
Photograph	1974	*114*
Portrait and Biography	1922/I	*275*
Testimonial Match	1938	*834*

Gregory, R. C. (Essex; Surrey; Club Cricket)

Obituary	1925/I	*266*

Gregory, Sgt. Obsv. R. G. (Victoria; Australia)

Obituary	1943	*364*

Gregory, R. J. (Surrey)

Benefit Match	1940	*455*
Obituary	1974	*1074*

Gregory, R. P. (Cambridgeshire)

Obituaries	1919	*175*
	1920/I	*194*

Gregory, S. E. (New South Wales; Australia)

Benefit Match	1908/II	*528*
Obituary	1930/I	*250*
Portrait and Biography	1897	*li*
Presentation to	1913/II	*534*

Gregory, T. (Hampshire)

Obituary	1915/I	*224*

Gregory, Major W. R. (Irish Club Cricket)

Obituary	1919	*175*

Gregson–Ellis, Lt-Col. G. S. (Charterhouse; Berkshire)
    Obituary   1970   *1021*
Gregson-Ellis, Capt. R. (Eton)
    Obituary   1918   *186*
Greig, A. W. (Border; Eastern Province; Sussex; England)
    Action Photograph   1975   *76*
    Cricketer of the Year   1975   *85*
    Greig Becomes Captain   1976   *61*
    Greig in Australia   1976   *62*
    Greig Inspires his Men   1977   *109*
    'My Story' Book Review   1981   *1203*
    Photographs   1968   *583*
                                        1971   *531*
                                      1975   *78*
Greig, I. A. (Border; Griqualand West; Cambridge University; Sussex; England)
    Obituary   1982   *573*
Greig, Canon J. G. (Hampshire)
    Obituary   1959   *930*
Greig, Major R. H. (Military Cricket)
    Obituary   1917   *184*
Greive, J. (Scotland)
    Obituary   1972   *1051*
Grell, Lieut. E. L. (Clifton; Trinidad)
    Obituary   1920/I   *154*
Grellet, Lt-Col. R. C. (Bedford Grammar School; Hertfordshire)
    Obituary   1949   *872*
Grenfell, Lt-Col. A. M. (Eton)
    Obituary   1960   *958*
Grenfell, Col. C. A. (Eton)
    Obituary   1925/I   *266*
Grenfell, Capt. F. O. (Eton)
    Obituary   1916   *168*
Grenfell, J. S. G. (Sherborne)
    Obituary   1928/I   *287*
Grenville-Grey, Lieut. W. H. (Wellington)
    Obituary   1916   *168*
Gresham, A. L. (Besonhurst C.C.)
    Obituary   1920/I   *175*
Gresson, C. R. H. (Lancing; Buckinghamshire)
    Obituary   1921/I   *227*
Gresson, F. H. (Winchester; Oxford University; Sussex)
    Obituary   1950   *908*
Greswell, W. T. (Repton; Somerset; Ceylon)
    Obituary   1972   *1051*
Grevett, W. S. G. (Eastbourne C.C.)
    Obituary   1968   *1006*

Grew, F. (Canada)
Obituary — 1938 — *939*

Grewcock, G. (Leicestershire)
Obituary — 1923/I — *298*

Grey, F. W. (Umpire)
Obituary — 1953 — *940*

Gribble, H. W. R. (Clifton; Gloucestershire)
Obituary — 1944 — *315*

Grierson, H. (Bedford; Cambridge University; Bedfordshire)
Obituary — 1973 — *1006*

Grieve, B. A. F. (Harrow; England)
Obituary — 1918 — *228*

Grieve, Lieut. W. (Scotland)
Obituary — 1919 — *175*

Grieve, L/Cpl. W. (Selkirk C.C.; Scotland)
Obituary — 1917 — *184*

Grieve, Lieut. W. R. (Scotland)
Obituary — 1918 — *186*

Grieves, K. J. (Lancashire; New South Wales)
Benefit Match — 1957 — *437*
Photograph — 1954 — *421*

Griffin, G. M. (Natal; Rhodesia; South Africa)
Action Photograph — 1961 — *89*

Griffith, C. C. (Barbados; West Indies)
'Chucked Around' Book Review — 1971 — *1078*
Cricketer of the Year — 1964 — *82*
Photograph — 1964 — *69*

Griffith, C. H. E. (Dulwich; American Club Cricket)
Obituary — 1928/I — *287*

Griffith, G. (Surrey; United England XI)
Benefit Match — 1873 — *136*
Biography — 1872 — *104*
Obituary — 1880 — *163*

Griffith, H. C. (Barbados; West Indies)
Obituary — 1981 — *1143*

Griffith, M. G. (Marlborough; Cambridge University; Sussex)
Photographs — 1969 — *585*
— 1972 — *578*
Schools Note — 1962 — *772*
1070 runs Schools Averages — 1962 — *808*

Griffith, S. C. (Dulwich; Cambridge University; Sussex; England; Secretary and President M.C.C.)
Backs the Club Cricketer — 1968 — *89*
Photograph — 1963 — *149*

Schools Notes	1931/I	*310*
	1932/I	*291*
	1933/I	*288,289*
	1934/I	*292*
		307
Tributes to: S. F. Barnes,	1968	*114*
A. P. F. Chapman	1962	*985*
A. G. Doggart	1964	*948*
A. T. W. Grout	1969	*981*
E. Hendren	1963	*1033*
S. McCabe	1969	*983*
Peter Cat	1965	*973*
R. W. V. Robins	1969	*986*
O. G. Smith	1960	*956*
H. Strudwick	1971	*1032*
M. Tate	1957	*949*
Sir F. Worrell	1968	*121*

Griffiths, B. J. (Northamptonshire)

| Photograph | 1979 | *482* |

Griffiths, B. L. (Wellington; Warwickshire)

| Obituary | 1984 | *1200* |

Griffiths, D. (Drumpellier C.C.)

| Obituary | 1910/I | *139* |

Griffiths, Capt. J. N. (Sydney Grammar School)

| Obituary | 1918 | *186* |

Griffiths, J. V. C. (Gloucestershire)

| Obituary | 1983 | *1245* |

Grimmett, C. V. (Victoria; South Australia; Wellington; Australia)

Career Record	1981	*106*
Obituary (by W. J. O'Reilly)	1981	*103*
Photograph	1981	*105*
Portrait and Biography	1931/I	*285*
Testimonial Match	1939	*810*

Grimsdale, T. B. (Uppingham)

| Obituary | 1937/I | *273* |

Grimsdell, A. (Hertfordshire)

| Obituary | 1964 | *949* |

Grimshaw, I. (Yorkshire)

| Obituary | 1912/I | *171* |

Grimshaw, J. W. T. (King Williams, Isle of Man; Cambridge University; Kent)

| Obituary | 1945 | *322* |

Grimshaw, Pte. S. (Yorkshire)

| Obituary | 1918 | *187* |

Grimston, W. E. (Harrow; Essex; Suffolk)

| Obituary | 1933/I | *247* |

Grinter, T. G. (Essex)
　Obituary　　　　　　　　　　　　　　　　　　1967　　　　968
Grisewood, F. H. (Radley; Worcestershire; Broadcaster)
　Obituary　　　　　　　　　　　　　　　　　　1973　　　　1007
Groom, H. R. (Croydon C.C.)
　Obituary　　　　　　　　　　　　　　　　　　1926/I　　　272
Gross, F. A. (Hampshire; Warwickshire)
　Obituary　　　　　　　　　　　　　　　　　　1976　　　　1098
Groube, T. U. (Victoria; Australia)
　Obituary　　　　　　　　　　　　　　　　　　1928/I　　　287
Grout, A. W. T. (Queensland; Australia)
　'My Country's Keeper' Book Review　　　　　　1966　　　　1018
　Obituary　　　　　　　　　　　　　　　　　　1969　　　　980
　Wicket Keeping Record, with Photograph　　　1962　　　　88
Grout, H. (Cambridgeshire; Essex)
　Obituary　　　　　　　　　　　　　　　　　　1897　　　　xli
Grove, C. W. (Warwickshire; Worcestershire)
　Benefit Match　　　　　　　　　　　　　　　　1952　　　　553
　Obituary　　　　　　　　　　　　　　　　　　1983　　　　1245
　Photograph　　　　　　　　　　　　　　　　　1953　　　　570
Grove, Lt-Col. L. T. (Army; Kent)
　Obituary　　　　　　　　　　　　　　　　　　1944　　　　306
Groves, G. J. (Nottinghamshire; Journalist)
　Obituary　　　　　　　　　　　　　　　　　　1942　　　　349
Groves, G. T. (Journalist)
　Obituary　　　　　　　　　　　　　　　　　　1917　　　　249
'Growth of Hampshire Cricket'
　E. D. R. Eagar　　　　　　　　　　　　　　　1952　　　　117
'Growth of New Zealand Cricket'
　A. H. H. Gilligan　　　　　　　　　　　　　　1949　　　　125
Grundy, Lieut. G. E. (Malvern)
　Obituary　　　　　　　　　　　　　　　　　　1916　　　　169
Grundy, G. G. S. (Harrow; Sussex)
　Obituary　　　　　　　　　　　　　　　　　　1946　　　　439
Grundy, J. (Nottinghamshire; United England XI)
　Biography　　　　　　　　　　　　　　　　　　1870　　　　61
Grundy, W. F. (Cricket Writer)
　Obituary　　　　　　　　　　　　　　　　　　1919　　　　206
Grylls, H. B. (Rugby)
　Obituary　　　　　　　　　　　　　　　　　　1937/I　　　274
Guard, D. R. (Winchester; Hampshire)
　Obituary　　　　　　　　　　　　　　　　　　1980　　　　1159
Guard, G. M. (Bombay; Gujerat; India)
　Obituary　　　　　　　　　　　　　　　　　　1979　　　　1079
Guggisberg, Brig-Gen. Sir F. G. (Overseas Club Cricketer)
　Obituary　　　　　　　　　　　　　　　　　　1931/I　　　257

Guild, A. (Northumberland)

Obituary	1915/I	*225*

Guilding, 2nd Lieut. S. C. L. (Epsom College)

Obituary	1919	*175*

Guillemard, A. G. (Butterflies C.C.)

Obituary	1910/I	*139*

Guise, C. A. L. (Winchester)

Obituary	1972	*1051*

Guiseppe, U. (Writer)

'Sir Frank Worrell' Book Review	1970	*1070*

Gull, Major F. L. (Army Cricket)

Obituary	1919	*175*

Gull, Capt. Sir R. C. Bart. (Eton)

Obituary	1961	*946*

Gulland, R. G. (Highgate)

Obituary	1982	*1201*

Gunasekara, Dr. C. H. (Middlesex; Ceylon)

Obituary	1970	*1021*

Gunasekera, L. D. S. (Ceylon)

Obituary	1975	*1079*

Gunary, W. C. (Essex)

Obituary	1970	*1021*

Gunn, A. (American Club Cricket)

Obituary	1931/I	*258*

Gunn, G. (Nottinghamshire; England)

Benefit Match	1926/II	*129*
'Charles Macartney and George Gunn'		
N. Cardus	1959	*87*
Obituary	1959	*930*
Portrait and Biography	1914/I	*233*

Gunn, G. V. (Nottinghamshire)

Obituary	1958	*960*

Gunn, J. (Nottinghamshire; England)

Benefit Match	1923/II	*75*
Obituary	1964	*949*
Portrait and Biography	1904	*xcii*

Gunn, 2nd Lieut. R. W. C. (Durham School)

Obituary	1918	*187*

Gunn, T. W. (Surrey)

Obituary	1909/I	*137*

Gunn, W. (Nottinghamshire; England)

Benefit Matches	1898	*171*
	1902	*33*
	1903	*48*
Obituary	1922/I	*248*
Portrait and Biography	1890	*xxx*

Gunner, Capt. J. H. (Marlborough; Hampshire)
Obituary | 1919 | *176*
Gurdon, His Hon. Judge C. (Haileybury)
Obituary | 1933/I | *263*
Gurdon, Rt. Rev. F. (Haileybury)
Obituary | 1931 | *273*
Gurney, W. S. (Haileybury; Norfolk; Suffolk)
Obituary | 1943 | *376*
Gurunathan, S. K. (Journalist)
Obituary | 1967 | *968*
Gustard, F. J. C. (Cricket Statistician)
Obituary | 1939 | *910*
Guthrie, Capt. R. F. (Loretto)
Obituary | 1917 | *184*
Gutteres, Rev. G. G. (Winchester)
Obituary | 1899 | *xliv*
Gutteridge, L. E. S. (Journalist; Writer)
'A. History of Wisden' | 1963 | *74*
Guttridge, F. H. (Nottinghamshire; Sussex; Umpire)
Obituary | 1919 | *207*
Guy, J. K. (Forest School; Essex)
Obituary | 1972 | *1052*
Guy, Rev. R. C. (Forest School; Essex)
Obituary | 1950 | *909*
Guy, Canon T. E. B. (Lancing)
Obituary | 1933/I | *247*
Guyana 'M.C.C. in Guyana'
Book Review | 1975 | *1122*
M.C.C. leaving Guyana – Photograph | 1982 | *64*
Gwyn, Capt. C. C. (Highfield School)
Obituary | 1918 | *187*
Gwynn, L. H. (Dublin University)
Obituary | 1903 | *lxxxi*
Gwynn, Rev. R. M. (Gentlemen of Ireland)
Obituary | 1964 | *953*
Habershon, Capt. K. R. (Wanderers C.C., Winnipeg)
Obituary | 1917 | *185*
Hack, A. T. (South Australia)
Obituary | 1934/I | *266*
Hacker, P. J. (Nottinghamshire; Derbyshire; Orange Free State)
Photograph | 1981 | *520*
Hacker, S. (Gloucestershire; Hereford; Glamorgan)
Obituary | 1926/I | *272*
Hackett, 2nd Lieut. E. A. N. (All Hallows School)
Obituary | 1917 | *185*

Hackett, W. W.. (President West Bromwich Dartmouth C.C.)
Obituary 1965 *966*
Haddington, 11th Earl of (Enthusiast)
Obituary 1918 *228*
Haden, F/O. F. S. (New Zealand Air Force)
Obituary 1944 *309*
Hadfield, J. (Journalist)
'A Wisden Century' Book Review 1951 *989*
Hadji, B. J. (Secretary Ceylon Cricket Association and Board of Control)
Obituary 1963 *1032*
Hadlee, R. J. (Nottinghamshire; Canterbury; Tasmania; New Zealand)
Cricketer of the Year 1982 *77*
'Hadlee' Book Review 1982 *1268*
Photograph 1982 *70*
Hadlee, W. A. (Canterbury; Otago; New Zealand)
'The Escalating Effects of Politics on Cricket' 1982 *106*
Hadley, Capt. P. S. (Charterhouse)
Obituary 1919 *176*
Hadow, A. A. (Harrow)
Obituary 1895 *xxxix*
Hadow, E. M. (Harrow; Middlesex)
Obituary 1896 *xxxviii*
Hadow, P. F. (Harrow; Middlesex)
Obituary 1947 *690*
Hadow, W. H. (Harrow; Oxford University; Middlesex)
Obituary 1899 *xlviii*
Haffenden, M. R. (New Jersey Cricket Clubs)
Obituary 1921/I *227*
Haig, N. E. (Eton; Middlesex; England)
with H. R. Murrell
'Middlesex County Cricket Club 1921-1947'
Book Review 1951 *989*
Obituary 1967 *986*
Haigh, D. (Yorkshire)
Obituary 1917 *249*
Haigh, H. L. (Yorkshire Club Cricket)
Obituary 1957 *944*
Haigh, J. (Lascelles Hall C.C.)
Obituary 1914/I *195*
Haigh, S. (Yorkshire; England)
Benefit Match 1910/II *110*
In First Class Cricket 1914/I *170*
Obituary 1922/I *252*
Portrait and Biography 1901 *lxxv*
Haigh, W. H. (North American and Yorkshire Club Cricketer)
Obituary 1906 *xc*

Haigh-Brown, Lt.-Col. A. (Pembroke College; Cambridge)
    Obituary   1919   *176*
Haigh-Brown, C. W. (Eton)
    Obituary   1945   *330*
Haigh-Smith, H. A. (Marlborough; Hampshire)
    Obituary   1956   *971*
Haileybury College 1941   Team portrait   1942   *31*
Hain, Capt. E. (Winchester)
    Obituary   1916   *169*
Haines, C. V. G. (King's Canterbury; Kent; Glamorgan)
    Obituary   1966   *964*
Haines, H. A. (Philadelphia; U.S.A.)
    Obituary   1973   *1014*
Hakdates, C. K. (Writer)
    'M.C.C. in India 1976-77' Book Review   1978   *1127*
Hake, H. D. (Haileybury; Cambridge University; Hampshire)
    Obituary   1976   *1098*
Hale, W. H. (Somerset; Gloucestershire)
    Obituary   1957   *944*
Hales, J. (Cambridge University)
    Obituary   1916   *169*
Halford, R. (President Nottinghamshire)
    Obituary   1911/I   *144*
Halfyard, D. J. (Durham; Northumberland; Cornwall; Kent; Nottinghamshire; Surrey)
    Photographs   1958   *403*
                                       1960   *429*
Hall, Lieut. A. B. (Uppingham)
    Obituary   1919   *199*
Hall, A. E. (Transvaal; Lancashire; South Africa)
    Obituary   1965   *967*
Hall, C. H. (Yorkshire)
    Obituary   1978   *1085*
Hall, D. (Derbyshire)
    Obituary   1984   *1200*
Hall, Lieut. D. A. (Oakham School)
    Obituary   1918   *187*
Hall, E. M. (Derbyshire)
    Obituary   1905   *xcvi*
Hall, Lieut. G. (Free Foresters)
    Obituary   1917   *185*
Hall, Capt. G. O. (Toronto C.C.)
    Obituary   1918   *187*
Hall, I. (Derbyshire)
    Photograph   1966   *348*

Hall, J. (Wetherby C.C.)
Obituary   1910/I   *139*
Hall, J. B. (Bloxham; Nottinghamshire)
Obituary   1980   *1149*
Hall, J. E. (Secretary Canadian Cricket Association)
Obituary   1943   *376*
Hall, J. W. (Worksop Town C.C.)
Obituary   1918   *228*
Hall, L. (Yorkshire)
Benefit Matches   1891   *68*
    1892   *142*
Obituary   1916   *169*
Portrait and Biography   1890   *xxxiii*
Views on High Scoring and the L.B.W. Rule   1899   *lxxvi*
Views on Reforms of 1889   1890   *xxxviii*
Views on Some Questions of the Day   1890   *xli*
Hall, M. (Cricket Supporter)
Obituary   1895   *xlii*
Hall, Rev. R. A. (Warwickshire)
Obituary   1918   *228*
Hall, Lieut. W. (Denstone)
Obituary   1917   *185*
Hall, Lieut. W. E. (Exeter School)
Obituary   1917   *224*
Hall, W. E. (U.S.A. Club Cricket)
Obituary   1923/I   *298*
Hall, W. W. (President Nottinghamshire)
Obituary   1904   *lxxxv*
Hall, W. W. (Queensland; Barbados; Trinidad; West Indies)
'Pace Like Fire' Book Review   1966   *1018*
Tribute to A. T. W. Grout   1969   *981*
Hallam, A. W. (Lancashire; Nottinghamshire)
Portrait and Biography   1908/I   *162*
Hallam, 2nd Lieut. H. (Moseley C.C.)
Obituary   1918   *187*
Hallam, M. R. (Leicestershire)
Benefit Match   1963   *516*
Photographs   1957   *440*
    1958   *444*
    1961   *465*
    1962   *485*
    1969   *479*
Hallam, T. H. (Derbyshire; Wellington; New Zealand)
Obituary   1960   *958*
Hallas, C. E. W. (Yorkshire)
Obituary   1910/I   *139*

Halley, R. (Canterbury)
Obituary   1910/I   *139*
Halliday, H. (Yorkshire)
Obituary   1968   *1000*
Halliday, J. A. (Harrow)
Obituary   1915/I   *225*
Halliday, Wing Comdr. J. G. (City of Oxford High School; Oxford University; Oxfordshire)
Obituaries   1946   *433*
                                                1948   *789*
Halliwell, E. A. (Middlesex; Transvaal; South Africa)
Obituary   1920/I   *175*
Portrait and Biography   1905   *cxii*
Hallows, C. (Lancashire; England)
Benefit Match   1929/II   *108*
Career Figures   1973   *1008*
Obituary   1973   *1007*
Portrait and Biography   1928/I   *310*
1000 Runs in May   1974   *87*
Hallows, J. (Lancashire)
Obituary   1911/I   *144*
Portrait and Biography   1905   *cxiv*
Halsey, Capt. Sir T. E. Bart. (Eton; Cambridge University; Hertfordshire)
Obituary   1971   *1025*
Hambling, M. L. (Somerset)
Obituary   1961   *946*
Hambro, Sir C. J. (Eton)
Obituary   1964   *949*
Hamer, A. (Yorkshire; Derbyshire)
Benefit Match   1959   *314*
Photographs   1954   *305*
                                                1957   *309*
                                                1960   *342*
Record of Service   1961   *652*
Hamer, W. (Committee Lancashire)
Obituary   1908/I   *140*
Hamilton, Major C. P. (Kent)
Obituary   1942   *349*
Hamilton, Lieut. E. P. (Transvaal)
Obituary   1945   *326*
Hamilton, F. T. (President Melbourne C.C.)
Obituary   1906   *xcii*
Hamilton, Lord G. F. (President M.C.C.)
Obituary   1928/I   *287*
Hamilton, W. D. (Haileybury; Oxford University)
Obituary   1915/I   *225*

Hamilton, W. R. (New Westminster C.C., British Columbia)
Obituary 1920/I *154*
Hamilton-Campbell, Lt-Col. W. K. (Sedbergh)
Obituary 1918 *187*
Hamilton-Fletcher, 2nd Lieut. G. (Eton)
Obituary 1916 *170*
Hamilton-Hoare, H. W. (Eton)
Obituary 1932/I *244*
Hammond, C. (Sussex)
Obituary 1902 *lxv*
Hammond, E. (Sussex)
Obituary 1922/I *254*
Hammond, E. R. (President South African Cricket Association)
Obituary 1978 *1073*
Hammond, G. W. (Club Cricket Conference; Middlesex)
Obituary 1944 *315*
Hammond, Lieut. L. (Tonbridge)
Obituary 1917 *185*
Hammond, Rev. O. (Uppingham; Cambridge University)
Obituary 1909/I *137*
Hammond, Lieut. R. M. (Tonbridge)
Obituary 1919 *176*
Hammond, W. R. (Cirencester Grammar School; Gloucestershire; England)
Benefit Match 1935/II *256*
Career Statistics and Achievements 1966 *118*
'Cricketer's School' Book Review 1951 *995*
'Cricket's Secret History' Book Review 1953 *1001*
Hammond's Ashes 1967 *423*
'Hammond the Sportsman' 1945 *63*
'Walter Hammond' R. Mason Book Review 1963 *1110*
'Walter Reginald Hammond' N. Cardus
(Obituary Tribute) 1966 *113*
Hundredth Hundred 1936/II *402*
'W. R. Hammond – In First Class Cricket'
R. C. Robertson-Glasgow 1942 *33*
Notes on 1944 *58*
1945 *159*
Photographs 1942 *32*
1966 *115,119*
Portrait and Biography 1928/I *309*
1000 Runs in May 1974 *85*
Hammond-Chambers, Capt. H. B. B. (Evans House XI; Eton)
Obituary 1917 *185*
Hampden, Brig-Gen. 3rd Viscount (Eton; Hertfordshire)
Obituary 1959 *931*

Hampden, 4th Viscount (Eton)
Obituary   1966   *965*

Hampden, 5th Viscount (Eton; Cambridge University)
Obituary   1976   *1098*

Hampshire County Cricket Club
County Badge   1950   *357*
    ad passim

'Growth of Hampshire Cricket'
E. D. R. Eagar   1952   *117*
'Hampshire County Cricket' H. S. Altham; E. D. R. Eagar; J. Arlott;
R. Webber Book Review   1958   *1023*
'Hampshire Cricketers' – 1800-1982'
Association of Cricket Statisticians
Book Review   1984   *1258*
Hampshire's Debt to R. Gilliat   1979   *78*
'Happy Hampshire' H. L. V. Day   1962   *143*
Initiative Note on   1959   *81*
'Milestones of Hampshire Cricket'
A. Edwards Book Review   1984   *1258*
Rise of Hampshire Cricket   Note on   1956   *74*
Team Portraits
Runners-up County
Championship   1958   1959   *43*
County Champions   1961   1962   *90*
County Champions   1973   1974   *46*
    1974   1975   *429*
John Player League Champions   1975   1976   *428*
    1976   1977   *429*
    1977   1978   *415*
    1978   1979   *407*
    1979   1980   *428*
    1980   1981   *433*
    1981   1982   *432*
    1982   1983   *440*
    1983   1984   *405*

Hampshire, J. H. (Tasmania; Yorkshire; Derbyshire; England)
'Family Argument' Book Review   1984   *1266*
Note on   1970   *79*
Photographs   1964   *619*
    1966   *624*
    1969   *637*
    1972   *629*
    1979   *595*

Hampson, Lieut. E. (Manchester Grammar School)
Obituary   1917   *185*

Hampson, W. (Yorkshire Club Cricket)
Obituary   1913/I   *188*
Hampton, W. M. (Clifton; Warwickshire; Worcestershire)
Obituary   1965   *967*
Hanbury, E. (Eton)
Obituary   1919   *207*
Hancock, H. B. (Cheshire Club Cricket)
Obituary   1924/I   *259*
Hancock, R. E. (Rugby; Somerset)
Obituary   1915/I   *225*
Hancock, W. C. (Secretary Staffordshire)
Obituary   1933/I   *247*
Views on Second Class Counties and the
L.B.W. Rule   1903   *lxviii*
Hancock, W. I. (Somerset)
Obituary   1911/I   *145*
Hand, C. R. (Natal; Transvaal)
Obituary   1935/I   *265*
Handford, A. (Nottinghamshire)
Obituary   1936/I   *277*
Handford, S. (Rushton C.C.; Ulster; Young America C.C.; Philadelphia)
Obituary   1917   *249*
Handley, M. (Midlands Cricket Professional)
Obituary   1934/I   *266*
Hands, K. C. M. (Oxford University; Western Province)
Obituary   1955   *930*
Hands, P. A. M. (Western Province; South Africa)
Obituary   1952   *956*
Hands, Capt. R. H. M. (Western Province; South Africa)
Obituary   1919   *176*
Hands, W. C. (Warwickshire)
Obituary   1975   *1079*
Hanham, C. S. (Gloucestershire Groundsman)
Obituary   1962   *986*
Hanif Mohammad (Bahawalpur; Pakistan International Airways; Kanachi; Pakistan)
Cricketer of the Year   1968   *74*
'The Greatly Praised – Hanif and his Brothers'
B. Easterbrook   1976   *127*
Photograph   1968   *68*
Record Individual Innings   1959   *108*
World Record Score   1959   *80*
Hanksley, Lieut. G. (Gresham's School)
Obituary   1919   *177*
Hannam, Capt. F. J. (President Bristol Cricket Association)
Obituary   1917   *185*

Hannam, R. P. (Eastern Province)
  Obituary   1953   *940*
Hannay, A. K. (Rugby)
  Obituary   1934/I   *266*
Hansard, H. H. (Malvern; Canada)
  Obituary   1932/I   *244*
Hansell, J. (Norfolk)
  Obituary   1901   *lviii*
Hansell, Lieut. K. J. N. (Charterhouse)
  Obituary   1919   *176*
Harben, Sir H. (President Sussex)
  Obituary   1913/I   *202*
Harben, Major H. E. S. (Eton; Sussex)
  Obituary   1972   *1052*
Harbord, Rev. H. (Marlborough)
  Obituary   1921/I   *227*
Hardcastle, Ven. E. H. (Winchester; Kent; Worcestershire)
  Obituary   1946   *440*
Hardcastle, F. (Lancashire)
  Obituary   1910/I   *151*
Hardie, B. R. (Essex; Scotland)
  Photographs   1975   *380*
       1981   *385*
Harding, B. (Felsted; American Club Cricket)
  Obituary   1931/I   *258*
Harding, Major C. E. H. (Army)
  Obituary   1918   *187*
Harding, P/O. D. R. (Salesian College, Farnborough)
  Obituary   1944   *309*
Harding, Lieut. E. S. M. (Cheshire; Secretary Birkenhead C.C.)
  Obituary   1918   *187*
Harding, F. G. (Islington Albion C.C.)
  Obituary   1915/I   *225*
Harding, K. (St.Edward's Oxford; Sussex)
  Obituary   1979   *1091*
Harding, N. W. (Reading School; Berkshire; Kent)
  Obituary   1948   *783*
Harding, R. (Western Australia)
  Obituary   1931/I   *258*
Harding, Capt. R. W. F. (St Pauls)
  Obituary   1918   *187*
Harding, W. E. (King's College, Cambridge)
  Obituary   1927/I   *295*
Hardinge, H. T. W. (Kent; England)
  Benefit Match   1924/II   *139*
  Obituary   1966   *965*

Portrait and Biography	1915/I	*203*
Hardinge, Lord of Penshurst (Harrow)		
Obituary	1945	*330*
Hardman, J. L. (American Club Cricket)		
Obituary	1909/I	*137*
Hardman, Lieut. W. F. K. (City of London School)		
Obituary	1918	*187*
Hardstaff, J. (Junior) (Nottinghamshire; Auckland; England)		
Benefit Match	1949	*470*
Note on	1944	*58*
Photograph	1950	*460*
Portrait and Biography	1938	*35*
Retirement	1956	*524*
Hardstaff, J. (Senior) (Nottinghamshire; England)		
Obituary	1948	*783*
Hardstaff, R. G. (Nottinghamshire)		
Obituary	1933/I	*247*
Hardwick, H. G. C. (Marlborough)		
Obituary	1928/I	*288*
Hardy, C. S. (President Kent)		
Obituary	1915/I	*225*
Hardy, Sir E. (President Kent)		
Obituary	1976	*1098*
Hardy, Pte. F. P. (Somerset)		
Obituary	1917	*250*
Hardy, Lieut. G. J. M. (Army; Oxford University Authentics)		
Obituary	1918	*188*
Hardy, N. (Somerset)		
Obituary	1924/I	*259*
Hardy, Major R. S. A. (Stonyhurst College; Staffordshire)		
Obituary	1984	*1201*
Hardy, S. (Nottinghamshire)		
Obituary	1907	*cxvii*
Hardy, Major W. E. (M.C.C. Committee)		
Obituary	1909/I	*137*
Hardy, W. E. (President Nottinghamshire)		
Obituary	1927/I	*279*
Hardyman, Major W. H. (Trinity College Dublin; Lansdown C.C.)		
Obituary	1908/I	*141*
Hare, C. F. A. (Winchester)		
Obituary	1929/I	*247*
Hare, J. H. M. (Uppingham; Oxford University; Norfolk)		
Obituary	1936/I	*277*
Hare, S. N. (Chigwell School; Essex)		
Obituary	1978	*1073*

Harford, H. M. (Hertfordshire)
  Obituary 1917 *250*
Harford, N. S. (Central Districts; Auckland; New Zealand)
  Obituary 1982 *1202*
Hargreave, S. (Lancashire; Warwickshire)
  Obituary 1930/I *252*
Hargreaves, J. H. (Hampshire)
  Obituary 1923/I *298*
Hargreaves, 2nd Lieut. J. P. (Leys)
  Obituary 1918 *187*
Hargreaves, R. G. (Hampshire)
  Obituary 1927/I *279*
Hargreaves, 2nd Lieut. S. J. (Eton House Matches)
  Obituary 1919 *176*
Hargreaves, T. K. (Yorkshire Council Cricket)
  Obituary 1956 *971*
Haridass, C. K. (Writer)
  'Pakistan in India 1979-80' Book Review 1981 *1206*
Harington, Gen. Sir C. (Cheltenham)
  Obituary 1941 *397*
Harkness, Capt. P. Y. (Malvern Link School)
  Obituary 1917 *185*
Harley, F. (Canada)
  Obituary 1922/I *272*
Harman, G. R. U. (Dublin University)
  Obituary 1978 *1085*
Harman, R. (Surrey)
  Photograph 1965 *554*
Harper, H. (Worcestershire)
  Obituary 1984 *1201*
Harper, L. V. (Rossall; Cambridge University; Surrey)
  Obituary 1925/I *267*
Harper, Surg. M. H. de J. (Trent College; Durham University)
  Obituary 1917 *185*
Harper, Judge, N. (Cloughton C.C.)
  Obituary 1968 *1000*
Harragin, Col. A. E. (Trinidad)
  Obituary 1943 *386*
Harrington, Dr. A. J. (St.Albans C.C., Toronto)
  Obituary 1938 *939*
Harrington, H. W. (Journalist)
  Obituary 1907 *cxi*
Harrington, J. (Proprietor of Hotel at Hove Ground)
  Obituary 1911/I *145*
Harrington, 2nd Lieut. P. W. (Dover College)
  Obituary 1918 *188*

Harris, B. (Writer; Journalist)
  'Ashes Triumphant' Book Review   1956   *1025*
  'Cricket Triumph' Book Review   1954   *982*
  'Defending the Ashes' Book Review   1957   *997*
  'In Quest of the Ashes' Book Review   1952   *1011*
  'West Indies Cricket Challenge' Book Review   1958   *1014*
Harris, C. (Northamptonshire)
  Obituary   1952   *956*
Harris, C. B. (Nottinghamshire)
  Benefit Match   1950   *470*
  Obituary   1955   *930*
Harris, D. F. (Warwickshire)
  Obituary   1961   *946*
Harris, Capt. E. (Christ's College; Christchurch, New Zealand)
  Obituary   1917   *185*
Harris, Lt-Col. F. (Southborough C.C.)
  Obituary   1958   *960*
Harris, H. E. (Hampshire)
  Obituary   1924/I   *259*
Harris, J. E. (Cambridge University; Cornwall; Suffolk)
  Obituary   1926   I   *272*
Harris, 4th Lord (Eton; Oxford University; Kent; England)
  And Umpire's Decisions   1923/I   *231*
  Appreciations of (Lord Hawke; W. Findlay;
  C. S. Caine)   1933/I   *229*
  'Appreciation of R. A. H. Mitchell'   1906   *lxxviii*
  'Lord Harris'
  J. D. Coldham Book Review   1984   *1268*
  Memoir of C. I. Thornton   1930/I   *316*
  'Modern Batting'   1910/I   *113*
  'Oxford Memories'   1928/I   *305*
  'Personal Recollections of W. G. Grace'   1896   *xlix*
  Photograph   1933/I   *229*
  'Recollections of F. R. Spofforth'   1927/I   *299*
  'Suggested Reforms'   1900   *lxvii*
  Team in Australia 1878-79   1880   *22*
  Tribute to W. G. Grace   1916   *68*
  Tribute to S. H. Pardon   1926/I   *30*
  Views on High Scoring and the L.B.W. Rule   1899   *lxxi*
  Views on the L.B.W. Rule   1888   *354*
  Views on Some Questions of the Day   1890   *xl*
Harris, M. J. (Middlesex; Nottinghamshire; Eastern Province; Wellington, New Zealand)
  Benefit Match   1978   *757*

Photographs	1967	*493*
	1970	*513*
	1974	*510*
	1980	*520*
Harris, N. (Writer; Journalist)		
'Turner Marches on'	1983	*93*
Harris, S. B. (Journalist)		
Obituary	1961	*947*
Harris, S. S. (Westminster; Cambridge University; Surrey; Gloucestershire; London County)		
Obituary	1927/I	*279*
Harris, W. (Essex Club Cricketer)		
Obituary	1911/I	*145*
Harrison, F. (King's College, London)		
Obituary	1924/I	*259*
Harrison, G. C. (Clifton; Oxford University)		
Obituary	1901	*lvii*
Harrison, G. P. (Yorkshire)		
Obituary	1941	*397*
Harrison, G. T. (Whitgift)		
78 wkts Schools Average	1924/II	*579*
Harrison, 2nd Lieut. H. (Clifton)		
Obituary	1918	*188*
Harrison, H. A. (Harrow)		
Obituary	1915/I	*248*
Harrison, H. S. (Surrey)		
Obituary	1972	*1052*
Harrison, I. M. (Nottinghamshire)		
Obituary	1910/I	*139*
Harrison, Lieut. J. A. (Cheshire)		
Obituary	1919	*176*
Harrison, J. W. (Whitgift Grammar School)		
84 wkts Schools Averages	1923/II	*539*
Harrison, L. (Hampshire)		
Benefit Match	1958	*401*
Photograph	1960	*411*
Harrison, Capt. M. C. (Army)		
Obituary	1917	*186*
Harrison, W. P. (Clifton)		
Obituary	1937/I	*274*
Harrison, W. P. (Rugby, Cambridge University; Kent; Middlesex)		
Obituary	1967	*975*
Harry, F. (Lancashire; Durham County)		
Obituary	1926/I	*272*
Harry, J. (Victoria; Australia)		
Obituary	1921/I	*243*

249

Harston, Capt. F. N. (Eastbourne College)
  Obituary   1919   *176*
Hart, Sub-Lieut. A. R. (London University)
  Obituary   1917   *186*
Hart, G. E. (Middlesex)
  Benefit Match   1940   *394*
Hart, H. B. (Cambridgeshire)
  Obituary   1942   *359*
Hart, Dr. J. R. (Merion C.C., Pennsylvania)
  Obituary   1968   *1000*
Hart-Davis, G. C. (Natal)
  Obituary   1943   *365*
Harte, C. (Writer)
  'The Fight for the Ashes' Book Review   1984   *1262*
Hartigan, G. P. D. (Border; South Africa)
  Obituary   1956   *972*
Hartigan, R. J. (New South Wales; Queensland; Australia)
  Obituary   1959   *93*
Hartington, H. E. (Yorkshire)
  Obituary   1951   *92*
Hartington, Lieut. J. E. (Bury Grammar School)
  Obituary   1918   *18*
Hartley, A. (Lightcliffe C.C.)
  Obituary   1974   *1074*
Hartley, Lieut. A. (Lancashire)
  Obituary   1919   *17*
  Portrait and Biography   1911/I   *16*
Hartley, C. R. (Lancashire)
  Obituary   1928/I   *28*
Hartley, F. (Oxford Parks Groundsman)
  Obituary   1944   *31*
Hartley, F. (Oxfordshire)
  Obituary   1966   *96*
Hartley, Col. J. C. (Tonbridge; Oxford University; Sussex; England)
  Obituary   1964   *94*
Hartley, Lieut. R. (Bromsgrove School)
  Obituary   1916   *17*
Hartley, S. N. (Yorkshire; Orange Free State)
  Photograph   1982   *61*
Hartley, T. (Harrow; Cumberland)
  Obituary   1930/I   *22*
Hartopp, E. S. (Eton; Cambridge University)
  Obituary   1895   *2*
Harvey, Capt. C. L. (Lincolnshire)
  Obituary   1918   *18*

Harvey, Preb. C. M. (Charterhouse; Oxford University)
Obituary   1918   *228*

Harvey, Rev. Canon F. C. (Marlborough)
Obituary   1923/I   *298*

Harvey, G. (Norfolk)
Obituary   1967   *969*

Harvey, R. N. (Victoria; New South Wales; Australia)
Cricketer of the Year   1954   *70*
'My World of Cricket' Book Review   1964   *1004*
Photograph   1954   *61*

Harvey, 2nd Lieut. R. de W. (Weymouth College)
Obituary   1917   *186*

Harvey, T. P. (Surrey Club Cricket)
Obituary   1924/I   *259*

Hasan, S. F. (President Pakistan Board of Control)
Obituary   1979   *1091*

Haslehurst, G. W. F. (Marlborough)
Obituary   1953   *940*

Haslip, S. M. (Rugby; Middlesex)
Obituary   1969   *981*

Hassall, A. E. (Derbyshire)
Obituary   1917   *250*

Hassan, S. B. (Nottinghamshire; Kenya; East Africa)
Benefit Match   1979   *749*
Photographs   1971   *482*
                                    1978   *506*

Hassett, A. L. (Victoria; Australia)
Cricketer of the Year   1949   *88*
'A. L. Hassett – A Born Cricketer'
N. Cardus   1954   *93*
'How Test Players are Raised'   1952   *107*
Photographs   1949   *71*
                                    1954   *92*
'The Quiet Australian'
R. S. Whitington Book Review   1970   *1067*

Hastilow, C. A. F. (Warwickshire)
Obituary   1976   *1098*

Hastings – Central Cricket Ground
Plan of County Ground   1950   *632*
                              ad passim

Hastings, A. G. (Winchester)
Obituary   1917   *250*

Hastings, E. P. (Victoria)
Obituary   1906   *xcii*

Hastings-Bass, Capt. P. R. H. (Stowe)
Obituary   1965   *967*

Hatfeild, Capt. C. E. (Eton; Oxford University; Kent)
  Obituary   1919   177

Hatfeild, Major H. S. (Eton; Harrow; President Kent)
  Obituary   1951   924

Hatfield, Lt-Col. E. J. (Devon)
  Obituary   1981   1143

Hathorn, C. M. H. (Transvaal; South Africa)
  Obituary   1921/I   227

Hattersley-Smith, Rev. P. (Gloucestershire)
  Obituary   1919   207

Hat Trick – Controversy
  Note on   1956   74

Hat Tricks
  In Test Matches – Table   1961   677

Haughton, M. G. (American Club Cricket)
  Obituary   1907   cx.

Havelock-Davies, P. (Brighton College; Oxford University; Sussex)
  Schools Notes   1913   206,220
  78 wkts Schools Averages   1913/II   494

Haverford College (U.S.A)
  in England   1896   1897   375
     1900   1901   424
     1904   1905   510
     1910   1911/II   46
     1914   1915/II   45

Haversham, 1st Lord (Eton)
  Obituary   1918   22

Havewalla, D. R. (Bombay)
  Obituary   1983   124.

Haviland, 2nd Lieut. J. B. (Marlborough; Northamptonshire)
  Obituary   1917   18

Hawarden, Lieut. 6th Viscount (Military Cricket)
  Obituary   1918   21.

Hawden, E. (Middleton Park C.C.)
  Obituary   1945   336

Hawke, A. W. (Staffordshire)
  Obituary   1923/I   29

Hawke, 7th Lord (Eton; Cambridge University; Yorkshire; President M.C.C. England)
  Appreciations of (Sir S. Jackson; Sir F. Lacey;
  H. Preston)   1939   6
  Appreciation of Lord Harris   1933/I   22
  'Fifty years of Yorkshire Cricket'   1932/I   25
  In The Cricket Field   1911/I   17
  Photograph   1939   6
  Portrait and Biography   1909/I   16

252

Obituary – See Appreciations of
Team in: India 1892-93 1894 *370*
     New Zealand
     and Australia 1902-03 1904 *439*
     South Africa 1895-96 1897 *387*
      1898-99 1900 *466*
     U.S.A. and
     Canada 1891 1892 *313*
      1894 1895 *374*
     West Indies 1897 1898 *387*
Tributes to: Sir S. Jackson 1932/I *257*
     1948 *78*
     S. H. Pardon 1926/I *30*
Views on the L.B.W. Rule 1888 *354*
Views on Throwing 1895 *liv*

Hawkins, Capt. C. V. T. (Leys School)
Obituary 1918 *188*

Hawkins, E. R. (Bedford Grammar School; U.S.A. Club Cricket)
Obituary 1917 *267*

Hawkins, G. W. (Victoria)
Obituary 1980 *1149*

Hawkins, Major H. (Northamptonshire)
Obituary 1931/I *258*

Hawkins, H. H. B. (Whitgift; Cambridge University)
Obituary 1934/I *266*

Hawksley, Lt-Col. J. P. V. (Military Cricket)
Obituary 1917 *186*

Hawkyard, B. (Flintshire)
Obituary 1951 *924*

Hawson, R. J. (Tasmania)
Obituary 1929/I *247*

Hawtin, A. P. R. (Northamptonshire)
Obituary 1976 *1099*

Hawtin, R. W. R. (Northamptonshire)
Obituary 1918 *229*

Hawtin, W. (Northamptonshire)
Obituary 1941 *387*

Hay, Lieut. D. A. (Trinity College School, Port Hope)
Obituary 1918 *213*

Hay, G. (Derbyshire)
Benefit Match 1903 *194*
Obituary 1914/I *184*

Hay, J. (Derbyshire Colts)
Obituary 1909/I *138*

Hay, Sgt. R. A. (Peterborough C.C., Ontario)
Obituary 1917 *186*

Hay, Lieut. R. B. (Blundells)
Obituary 1918 188

Hay, T. D. B. (Auckland)
Obituary 1968 1000

Hay, W. H. (Eton; Leicestershire)
Obituary 1926/I 273

Haycraft, J. S. (Middlesex)
Obituary 1943 376

Haydock, C. (Worksop Town C.C.)
Obituary 1922/I 254

Haye, J. C. (Cornwall)
Obituary 1941 387

Hayes, Capt. C. B. (Campbell College, Belfast)
Non-Obituary 1917 227

Hayes, E. G. (Surrey; Leicestershire; England)
Benefit Matches 1909/II 6
1909/II 38
Obituary 1954 92
Portrait and Biography 1907 cxxiv

Hayes, F. C. (Lancashire; England)
Photograph 1975 45
1978 44

Hayes, W. B. (Queensland)
Obituary 1928/I 30

Haygarth, A. (Harrow; Middlesex; Sussex; Cricket Historian)
Obituary 1904 lxxi

Haygarth, E. B. (Lancing; Hampshire; Gloucestershire)
Obituary 1916 17

Haygarth, Col. F. (Brother of A. Haygarth)
Obituary 1912/I 17

Haygarth, J. W. (Winchester; Oxford University)
Obituary 1924/I 20

Hayley, H. (Yorkshire)
Obituary 1923/I 29

Hayman, H. B. (Middlesex)
Obituary 1931/I 25

Hayman, Rev. Canon H. T. (Bradfield; Kent)
Obituary 1942 35

Haynes, R. W. (Gloucestershire; Oxfordshire)
Obituary 1977 104

Hayter, R. J. (British Empire XI; Writer; Journalist)
'The Centenary Test Match 1977' 1978 1

Hayter, W. L. (Highgate)
Obituary 1951 9

Hayter, Rev. W. T. B. (Charterhouse)
Obituary 1936/I 2

Hayward, A. (Cambridge University Groundsman)
Obituary	1906	*xcii*

Hayward, C. S. B. (Bradfield)
Obituary	1960	*951*

Hayward, D. (Surrey; Cambridgeshire)
Obituary	1911/I	*145*

Hayward, D. M. (Cambridgeshire; Fenner's Groundsman)
Obituary	1954	*926*

Hayward, F/O. D. R. (Harrow)
Obituary	1946	*433*

Hayward, 2nd Lieut. E. R. (Winchester)
Obituary	1917	*186*

Hayward, G. T. (American Groundsman)
Obituary	1914/I	*185*

Hayward, J. A. (Benefactor Hayward Hall)
Note	1978	*106*

Hayward, J. C. (Winchester)
Obituary	1913/I	*188*

Hayward, T. W. (Cambridgeshire; Surrey; England)
Benefit Match	1903	*75*
Hundred Hundreds	1914/I	*125*
Hundredth Hundred	1914/II	*59*
In First Class Cricket	1906	*cxv*
In the Cricket Field	1921/I	*264*
Obituary	1940	*840*
Portrait and Biography	1895	*xlix*
1000 Runs in May	1974	*84*

Haywood, R. (Metropolitan Club Cricket)
Obituary	1923/I	*299*

Haywood, R. A. (Northamptonshire)
Obituary	1943	*377*

Haywood, W. T. (Superintendent Southgate C.C. Ground)
Obituary	1921/I	*228*

Hazare, V. S. (Maharashtra; Baroda; Central India; India)
Benefit Match	1968	*870*
'Cricket Replayed' Book Review	1975	*1120*

Hazell, H. L. (Somerset)
Benefit Match	1950	*487*
Photographs	1950	*476*
	1953	*508*

Hazlerigg, Lord (Leicestershire)
Obituary	1950	*909*

Hazlitt, G. R. (Victoria; New South Wales; Australia)
Obituary	1916	*171*

Head, J. R. (Clifton; Middlesex)
Obituary	1950	*909*

Head, R. L. (Marlborough)
  Obituary   1923/I   299
Headingley
  England Team at Photographs   1964   1965   71
                                         1974   1975   72
  'Headingley' J. Marshall Book Review   1971   1070
  History at Headingley 1983
  (New Zealand's Win) Photograph   1984   Plate
  Pitch   Note on   1973   91
  Plan of Ground   1952   587
                              ad passim
  Scoreboard (Photograph)   1953   58
  Test Sabotage Note on   1976   345
  Vandals at Note on   1976   6.
Headlam, C. (Rugby; Oxford University)
  Obituary   1935/I   265
Headley, G. A. (Jamaica; West Indies)
  Awarded M.B.E. Note on   1956   75
  'George Atlas Headley'
  G. Headley and N. White Book Review   1976   1150
  'George Headley' S. I. Burrows and
  J. S. Carneigie Book Review   1972   1100
  Obituary   1984   1200
  Portrait and Biography   1934/I   28
Headley, R. G. A. (Jamaica; Worcestershire; Derbyshire; West Indies)
  Benefit Match   1973   580
  Photograph   1972   61.
Heal, 2nd Lieut. C. A. (Marlborough)
  Obituary   1916   17
Heale, Rev. W. H. (Harrow; Hertfordshire)
  Obituary   1908/I   14
Healing, J. A. (Clifton; Cambridge University)
  Obituary   1935/I   27
Healy, J. (Victoria)
  Obituary   1917   25
Heane, G. F. H. (Nottinghamshire; Lincolnshire)
  Obituary   1970   102
  Views on L.B.W. Experiment   1936/I   34
Heap, J. S. (Lancashire)
  Benefit Match   1922/II   18
  Obituary   1952   95
Hearn, W. (Hertfordshire; Umpire)
  Benefit Match   1898   14
  Obituary   1905   xc
Hearne, A. (Kent; England)

Benefit Matches	1899	*125*
	1914/II	*105*
Obituary	1953	*941*
Portrait and Biography	1894	*xliv*

Hearne, F. (Kent; Western Province; England; South Africa)
| Obituary | 1950 | *909* |

Hearne, G. (Middlesex; Buckinghamshire)
| Obituary | 1905 | *xcvii* |

Hearne, G. A. L. (Western Province; South Africa)
| Obituary | 1980 | *1159* |

Hearne, G. F. (Pavilion Clerk at Lord's)
| Benefit Match | 1895 | *297* |
| Obituary | 1932/I | *244* |

Hearne, G. G. (Kent; England)
Benefit Matches	1891	*53*
	1899	*17*
Obituary	1933/I	*248*
Views on Reforms of 1889	1890	*xxxix*
Views on Some Questions of the Day	1890	*xli*

Hearne, H. (Kent)
| Obituary | 1907 | *cxi* |

Hearne, J. T. (Middlesex; England)
Benefit Match	1901	*126*
Obituary	1945	*330*
Portrait and Biography	1892	*xxxvi*
Tribute to A. J. Webbe	1942	*354*

Hearne, J. W. (Middlesex; England)
Benefit Matches	1926/II	*166*
	1933/II	*314*
Obituary	1966	*966*
Portrait and Biography	1912/I	*192*

Hearne, T. (Buckinghamshire; Middlesex)
Benefit Match	1877	*50*
Biography	1876	*94*
Obituary	1901	*lviii*
Views on the Reforms of 1889	1890	*xxxviii*
Views on Some Questions of the Day	1890	*xliv*

Hearne, T. A. (Ground Superintendent Lord's)
| Obituary | 1911/I | *146* |

Hearne, W. (Kent)
| Obituary | 1926/I | *273* |

Hearne, W. (Winchester)
| Obituary | 1917 | *250* |

Hearne, W. (Father of J. T. Hearne)
| Obituary | 1909/I | *138* |

Hearne, W. H. (Umpire)
Obituary   1956   *972*
Hearson, H. F. P. (Uppingham)
Obituary   1933/I   *249*
Heaslip, J. G. (Hounslow C.C.; Gentlemen of Ireland)
Obituary   1967   *969*
Heasman, Dr. W. G. (Sussex; Berkshire; Norfolk)
Obituary   1935/I   *265*
Heath, Col. A. H. (Clifton; Oxford University; Gloucestershire; Middlesex; Staffordshire)
Obituary   1931/I   *259*
Views on Reforms of 1889   1890   *xxxix*
Heath, M. (Hampshire)
Photograph   1959   *380*
Heath, W. H. G. (Surrey)
Obituary   1966   *967*
Heathcoat-Amory, Sir J. Bart. (Eton; Oxford University; Devon)
Obituary   1973   *1009*
Heathcote, Lieut. J. S. (Indian Head C.C., Saskatchewan)
Obituary   1918   *188*
Heathcote-Amery, Major L. (Knightshayes C.C.)
Obituary   1919   *177*
Heatley, H. R. (Marlborough)
Obituary   1934/I   *266*
Heaton, 2nd Lieut. E. R. (Woking C.C.)
Obituary   1917   *186*
Heaton, H. (Lancashire League)
Obituary   1917   *251*
Heaton-Ellis, Lieut. C. E. R. (Highgate School)
Obituary   1917   *186*
Heavisides, M. (Stockton C.C.)
Obituary   1926/I   *273*
Hebden, G. L. (Middlesex)
Obituary   1947   *690*
Hedderwick, Lieut. R. Y. (Haileybury)
Obituary   1916   *172*
Hedges, B. L. (Glamorgan)
Benefit Match   1964   *387*
Photograph   1963   *409*
Hedges, L. P. (Tonbridge; Oxford University; Kent; Gloucestershire)
Obituary   1934/I   *266*
Public School Cricketer of the Year   1919   *155*
Photograph   1919   *150*
Schools Note   1920/I   *259,273*
1038 runs Schools Averages   1920/II   *344*

Hedges, Capt. W. H. (Moseley C.C.)
Obituary 1917 *186*

Hedley, H. W. (Journalist)
Obituary 1912/I *172*

Hedley, Col. Sir W. C. (Marlborough; Kent; Somerset; Devon; Hampshire)
Obituary 1938 *939*

Heesom, D. (Statistician)
Obituary 1980 *1150*

Heighington, Lieut. G. (Toronto C.C.)
Obituary 1920/I *154*

Hele, G. (Umpire)
Obituary 1983 *1246*

Helfrich, B. A. (Griqualand West)
Obituary 1939 *910*

Helm, G. F. (Marlborough; Cambridge University; Sussex)
Obituary 1899 *xliv*

'Helmet, The' T. E. Bailey 1981 *123*
Notes on 1979 *80*
1981 *97*

Helmet and Denis Amiss
Photograph 1979 *57*

Helmore, Lieut. F. C. (Christ's College, Christchurch, New Zealand)
Obituary 1918 *188*

Helmore, J. H. (Somerset)
Obituary 1955 *931*

Hemingway, G. E. (Uppingham; Gloucestershire)
Obituary 1908/I *141*

Hemingway, Capt. K. S. (Hereford Cathedral School)
Obituary 1919 *177*

Hemingway, 2nd Lieut. R. E. (Nottinghamshire)
Obituary 1916 *172*

Hemingway, W. M. G. (Uppingham; Cambridge University; Gloucestershire)
Obituary 1968 *1001*

Hemmant, Lieut. M. (Tonbridge School)
Obituary 1918 *188*

Hemmerde, C. L. (Winchester)
Obituary 1946 *440*

Hemmerde, E. G. (Winchester)
Obituary 1949 *865*

Hemming, Sir A. W. L. (Epsom College; Incogniti)
Obituary 1908/I *141*

Hemmings, E. E. (Warwickshire; Nottinghamshire; England)
Photographs 1975 *582*
1981 *520*

259

Helmsley, E. J. O. (Worcestershire)
Photographs   1970   594
                                                     1979   578
Hemus, 2nd Lieut. C. H. (Royal Grammar School, Worcester)
Obituary   1919   178
Hemus, L. G. (Auckland)
Obituary   1934/I   267
Henderson, A. (West of Scotland C.C.)
Obituary   1907   cxi
Henderson, Hon. A. (Wellington; Berkshire)
Obituary   1934/I   267
Henderson, Capt. A. (Forfarshire)
Obituary   1918   188
Henderson, 2nd Lieut. A. H. M. (Edinburgh University)
Obituary   1916   172
Henderson, Capt. E. B. (Trinity College, Port Hope)
Obituary   1920/I   154
Henderson, E. J. (Sutton Cricket Club)
Obituary   1983   1246
Henderson, M. (Wellington; New Zealand)
Obituary   1971   1025
Henderson, P. E. (Canadian IZingari)
Obituary   1935/I   266
Henderson, R. (Surrey)
Benefit Match   1898   39
Obituary   1932/I   244
Portrait and Biography   1890   xxx
Henderson, R. G. (Middlesex)
Obituary   1896   xli
Henderson, R. L. (Galashiels C.C.; President Scottish Cricket Union)
Obituary   1944   315
Henderson, S. (Grange C.C.)
Obituary   1907   cxi
Henderson, Dr. T. B. (Winchester, Oxford University)
Obituary   1921/I   228
Hendren, D. (Middlesex)
Obituary   1963   1033
Hendren, E. H. (Middlesex; England)
At Lords since the war   1923/I   281
Batting Summary 1907-1937   1938   429
Benefit Matches   1924/II   195
                                                     1932/II   325
'Patsy Hendren – The Cricketer and his Times'
I. A. R. Peebles Book Review   1970   1067
Hundredth Hundred   1930   664
Obituary   1963   1033

260

Photograph	1938	*47*
Portrait and Biography	1920/I	*254*
'Reflections'	1938	*47*
Tribute to M. W. Tate	1957	*949*
Hendren, Cpl. J. M. (Middlesex; Durham)		
Obituary	1917	*187*
Hendrick, M. (Derbyshire; Nottinghamshire; England)		
Cricketer of the Year	1978	*97*
Photographs	1973	*359*
	1975	*365*
	1978	*89*
Henery, P. J. T. (Harrow; Cambridge University; Middlesex)		
Obituary	1939	*910*
Henfrey, A. G. (Wellington Grammar School; Northamptonshire)		
Obituary	1930/I	*253*
Henley, F. A. H. (Forest School; Oxford University; Middlesex; Suffolk)		
Obituary	1964	*950*
Schools Note	1903	*cxiv*
75 wkts Schools Averages	1903	*456*
Henley, H. J. (Journalist)		
Obituary	1938	*939*
Henriques, D. J. Q. (Harrow)		
Obituary	1941	*387*
Henry, A. (Queensland)		
Obituary	1910/I	*140*
Henry, Capt. B. J. (Oxfordshire)		
Obituary	1952	*957*
Henry, Lieut. C. (Exeter College, Oxford)		
Obituary	1918	*213*
Henry, Dr. J. N. (U.S.A.)		
Obituary	1939	*910*
Henry, W. A. (Merchiston Castle; Canada)		
Obituary	1928/I	*288*
Henson, Lt-Col. H. A. (Secretary Gloucestershire)		
Obituary	1959	*932*
Henstock, Col. F. T. (Sandhurst)		
Obituary	1918	*229*
Henty, E. (Kent)		
Obituary	1901	*lvii*
Hepburn, Lieut. G. (Westminster)		
Obituary	1919	*178*
Hepton, Lieut. A. (Pocklington School)		
Obituary	1919	*178*
Hepworth, N. R. (Yorkshire Committee)		
Obituary	1915/I	*226*

Herbert, Dr. A. K. C. (American Club Cricket)
Obituary   1937/I   *274*
Herbert, E. J. (Northamptonshire)
Obituary   1964   *950*
Herbert, Dr. F. I. (Durham)
Obituary   1971   *1025*
Herbert, Hon. M. R. H. M. (Eton; Nottinghamshire; Somerset)
Obituary   1930/I   *253*
Hercy, J. E. (Writer)
Obituary   1951   *924*
Herdman, Lieut. J. (Edinburgh Institute)
Obituary   1918   *189*
Herford, Capt. G. M. I. (Fettes; Royal Navy)
Obituary   1915/I   *226*
Heriot, J. (Border District)
Obituary   1917   *187*
Herman, R. S. (Middlesex; Border; Griqualand West; Hampshire)
Photograph   1968   *500*
Hermon-Hodge, Capt. G. G. (Army)
Obituary   1917   *187*
Hertslet, 2nd Lieut. H. T. (Crescent Athletic C.C., New York)
Obituary   1918   *189*
Hervey, A. C. G. (Marlborough)
Obituary   1935/I   *266*
Hervey-Bathurst, Lt-Col. Sir F. T. (Eton)
Obituary   1901   *lii*
Heseltine, Lt-Col. C. (Hampshire)
Obituary   1945   *332*
Heselton, (Treasurer Yorkshire)
Obituary   1969   *981*
Heslop, Capt. G. H. (Lancing)
Obituary   1917   *187*
Hesmond-Halagh, Capt. L. J. (Rossall)
Obituary   1944   *306*
Heatherton, W. (Northumberland)
Obituary   1939   *910*
Heugh, W. (Transvaal)
Obituary   1920/I   *176*
Hever, H. L. (Kent)
Obituary   1972   *1052*
Correction   1973   *1015*
Hewetson, E. P. (Shrewsbury; Oxford University; Warwickshire)
Obituary   1979   *1091*
Hewett, H. T. (Harrow; Oxford University; Somerset)
Obituary   1922/I   *254*

Portrait and Biography	1893	*xlii*
Views on 'The Follow On'	1894	*xlix*

Hewett, Sir J. P. (Winchester)
Obituary — 1942 — *359*

Hewitt, C. de Lisle (Charterhouse)
Obituary — 1942 — *359*

Hewlett, W. O. (Harrow)
Obituary — 1913/I — *189*

Hewson, R. (Western Australia)
Obituary — 1974 — *1084*

Hey, S. (Uppingham; Secretary Dorset)
Obituary — 1978 — *1074*

Heygate, H. J. (Epsom College; Sussex)
Obituary — 1938 — *940*

Heygate, Rev. R. T. (Lancing)
Obituary — 1948 — *784*

Heymann, W. G. (Haileybury; Nottinghamshire)
Obituary — 1970 — *1022*

Heyworth, Brig-Gen. F. J. (Household Brigade)
Obituary — 1917 — *187*

Heyworth, 2nd Lieut. W. A. (Birkenhead School)
Obituary — 1917 — *187*

Hichens, J. K. J. (Winchester)
Obituary — 1909/I — *138*

Hickley, A. N. (Winchester; Middlesex)
Obituary — 1973 — *1009*

Hickley, C. L. (Winchester)
Obituary — 1936/I — *278*

Hickley, Lieut. R. T. (Winchester)
Obituary — 1919 — *178*

Hickling, 2nd Lieut. J. C. (Uppingham; Woking C.C.)
Obituary — 1917 — *187*

Hickling, S. (Leicestershire)
Obituary — 1974 — *1075*

Hickman, Lieut. A. K. (Clifton)
Obituary — 1917 — *188*

Hickmott, E. (Kent)
Obituary — 1935/I — *266*

Hickmott, Lieut. R. G. (Christchurch High School, Canterbury, New Zealand)
Obituary — 1917 — *188*

Hickmott, W. E. (Kent; Lancashire)
Obituary — 1969 — *981*

Hicks, J. (Yorkshire)
Obituary — 1913/I — *189*

Hickson, Lieut. H. G. (Royal Naval College, Eltham)
Obituary — 1916 — *173*

Hickson, O. S. (Northamptonshire)
Obituary   1945   *333*
Hickton, W. (Lancashire)
Obituary   1901   *lviii*
Hiddleston, J. S. (Wellington; Otago)
Obituary   1941   *397*
Hide, A. (Sussex)
Obituary   1937/I   *287*
Hide, J. B. (Sussex; South Australia; Cornwall)
Benefit Match   1895   *146*
Obituary   1925/I   *267*
Higginbotham, Major C. E. (Rugby)
Obituary   1916   *173*
Higgins, H. L. (King Edward's, Birmingham; Worcestershire)
Obituary   1980   *1150*
Higgins, J. (Yorkshire)
Obituary   1955   *931*
Higgins, J. B. (King Edward's, Birmingham; Worcestershire)
Obituary   1971   *1026*
Higgins-Bernard, Lt-Col. F. T. (Westminster)
Obituary   1936/I   *278*
Higgs, G. (Dulwich)
Obituary   1952   *957*
Higgs, K. (Lancashire; Leicestershire; England)
Action Photograph   1967   *65*
Benefit Match   1969   *472*
Cricketer of the Year   1968   *80*
Photographs   1961   *445*
    1966   *449*
    1967   *459*
    1968   *67*
Higgs, K. A. (Sussex)
Obituary   1960   *951*
Higgs-Walker, J. A. (Repton; Worcestershire)
Obituary   1980   *1150*
High Court Case
Note on   1966   *83*
High Scoring and the Law of Leg Before Wicket
A Discussion   1899   *lxv*
Hignell, A. J. (Denstone; Cambridge University; Gloucestershire)
Career Figures   1984   *1250*
Photograph   1981   *415*
Higson, T. A. (Rossall; Oxford University; Lancashire; Derbyshire; Cheshire)
Obituary   1950   *909*
Hilary, 2nd Lieut. H. J. (Tonbridge)
Obituary   1918   *189*

Hilary, R. J. (Tonbridge)
  Obituary   1938   *940*
Hilder, A. L. (Lancing; Kent)
  Obituary   1971   *1026*
Hilder, Capt. M. L. (Lancing)
  Obituary   1918   *189*
Hildyard, Rev. L. D'A. (Oxford University; Somerset; Lancashire)
  Obituary   1932/I   *245*
Hill, A. (Yorkshire, England)
  Benefit Match   1885   *163*
  Biography   1884   *268*
  Obituary   1911   *246*
Hill, A. (Derbyshire; Orange Free State)
  Photograph   1979   *344*
Hill, Col. A. (West Kent C.C.)
  Obituary   1951   *924*
Hill, A. J. L. (Marlborough; Wiltshire; Cambridge University; Hampshire; England)
  Obituary   1951   *925*
Hill, 2nd Lieut. A. L. (Radley)
  Obituary   1916   *173*
Hill, Capt. B. E. (Lichfield Grammar School)
  Obituary   1919   *178*
Hill, C. (South Australia; Australia)
  Obituary   1946   *440*
  Portrait and Biography   1900   *lxiii*
Hill, C. M. (Ireland)
  Obituary   1984   *1201*
Hill, Lt-Col. D. V. (Worcestershire)
  Obituary   1972   *1052*
Hill, E. (Somerset; Writer)
  'The Story of Somerset'   1959   *99*
Hill, E. (Dewsbury and Savile C.C.)
  Obituary   1917   *251*
Hill, Rev. E. H. (Malvern)
  Obituary   1916   *173*
Hill, Major E. T. (Winchester; Somerset)
  Obituary   1935/I   *277*
Hill, G. M. (Tonbridge)
  Obituary   1952   *957*
Hill, H. (Yorkshire)
  Obituary   1937/I   *287*
Hill, Lt-Col. H. (Army)
  Obituary   1917   *188*
Hill, H. G. (Warwickshire)
  Obituary   1914/I   *185*

Hill, H. J. (Brother of C. Hill; South Australia)
Obituary   1907   *cxi*
Hill, H. J. (Father of C. Hill; North Adelaide C.C.)
Obituary   1927/I   *279*
Hill, H. J. (Hertfordshire)
Obituary   1947   *690*
Hill, Col. J. (Northamptonshire)
Obituary   1919   *178*
Hill, J. C. (Victoria; Australia)
Obituary   1975   *1079*
Hill, J. E. (Warwickshire)
Obituary   1964   *950*
Hill, Pte. M. A. (Irish Club Cricket)
Obituary   1919   *178*
Hill, Lieut. M. C. (Rossall)
Obituary   1917   *188*
Hill, M. L. (Eton; Cambridge University; Somerset)
Obituary   1949   *865*
Hill, N. W. (Nottinghamshire)
Career Record   1963   *1042*
Photographs   1959   *492*
                                               1960   *517*
                                             1962   *541*
Hill, Capt. N. W. (Winchester)
Obituary   1918   *189*
Hill, R. H. (Winchester; Cambridge University; Middlesex; Journalist)
Obituary   1960   *952*
Hill, R. P. (Cartoonist **'Rip'**)
Obituary   1950   *910*
Hill, S. (Bristol C.C.)
Obituary   1946   *441*
Hill, V. T. (Oxford University; Somerset; Gloucestershire)
Obituary   1933/I   *249*
Hilleard, Rifleman. P. J. (Essex)
Obituary   1916   *173*
Correction   1917   *227*
Hilliard, H. (New South Wales)
Obituary   1915/I   *226*
Hillier, 2nd Lieut. C. A. H. (Cheltenham; Suffolk)
Obituary   1916   *173*
Hillier, Rt. Hon. W. (Vice-President Surrey)
Obituary   1912/I   *176*
Hillingdon, 2nd Lord (Uxbridge C.C.)
Obituary   1920/I   *176*
Hills, 2nd Lieut. A. H. (Aldenham)
Obituary   1919   *199*

Hills, 2nd Lieut. F. M. (Tonbridge)
  Obituary   1918   *189*
Hills, H. F. (Essex)
  Obituary   1931/I   *259*
Hills, J. J. (Glamorgan; Umpire)
  Obituary   1971   *1034*
Hills, R. W. (Kent)
  Photograph   1978   *428*
Hill-Wood, Sir B. S. (Eton; Derbyshire)
  Obituary   1955   *931*
Hill-Wood, D. J. C. (Eton; Oxford University; Derbyshire)
  Obituary   1983   *1246*
Hill-Wood, Sir S. (Derbyshire)
  Obituary   1950   *910*
Hill-Wood, Sir W. W. H. (Eton; Cambridge University; Derbyshire)
  Obituary   1981   *1143*
Hillyard, Rev. A. (Warwickshire)
  Obituary   1920/I   *176*
Hillyard, Comdr. G. W. (Middlesex; Hertfordshire; Leicestershire)
  Obituary   1944   *315*
Hillyard, Major J. M. (Harrow)
  Obituary   1984   *1201*
Hilton, C. (Lancashire; Essex)
  Photographs   1962   *465*
                     1963   *483*
Hilton, Rev. F. K. (Lancing)
  Obituary   1925/I   *288*
Hilton, M. J. (Lancashire; England)
  Benefit Match   1961   *459*
  Cricketer of the Year   1957   *65*
  Photograph   1957   *55*
Hilton, P. (Kent)
  Obituary   1907   *cxii*
Hilton, R. (Hove Ground Staff)
  Obituary   1906   *cii*
Hime, C. F. W. (Natal; South Africa)
  Obituary   1943   *386*
Hinchliffe, J. (Patron American Cricket)
  Obituary   1916   *174*
Hinchliffe, J. A. (Secretary Central Lancashire League)
  Obituary   1918   *229*
Hind, A. E. (Uppingham; Cambridge University; Nottinghamshire)
  Obituary   1948   *784*
Hind, 2nd Lieut. C. R. (Radley)
  Obituary   1917   *188*

Hinde, Brig. H. M. (Blundells; Berkshire; Egypt)
Obituary   1967   *975*
Hindlekar, D. D. (Bombay; India)
Obituary   1950   *910*
Hine-Haycock, R. W. (Devon)
Obituary   1927/I   *280*
Hine-Haycock, Rev. T. R. (Wellington; Oxford University; Kent; Devon)
Obituary   1954   *926*
Hine-Haycock, W. (Surrey)
Obituary   1904   *lxxvii*
Hingley, F/Sgt. L. G. H. (Rugby)
Obituary   1944   *306*
Hingston, A. (Devon)
Obituary   1954   *926*
Hinley, J. (Worcestershire)
Obituary   1908/I   *142*
Hint to League Players Note on   1945   *65*
Hinton, 2nd Lieut. W. R. (St.Dunstans)
Obituary   1917   *188*
'Hints from the Press Box'   1893   *xlv*
Hipkins, A. B. (Essex)
Obituary   1958   *960*
Hippisley, H. E. (King's Bruton; Somerset)
Obituary   1915/I   *226*
Hird, S. F. (New South Wales; Lancashire; Eastern Province)
Obituary   1982   *1202*
Hirsch, J. G. (London County)
Obituary   1959   *932*
Hirst, A. (Lascelles Hall)
Obituary   1914/I   *185*
Hirst, A. A. (Donator of Hirst Trophy)
Obituary   1922/I   *256*
Hirst, A. A. (Junior) (Merion C.C., Philadelphia)
Obituary   1908/I   *142*
Hirst, E. T. (Rugby; Oxford University; Yorkshire)
Obituary   1915/I   *226*
Hirst, G. H. (Yorkshire; England)
Benefit Match   1905   *42*
'Hirst and Rhodes'
A. A. Thomson Book Review   1960   *1003*
'In First Class Cricket'   1910/I   *165*
'In the Cricket Field'   1922/I   *308*
Obituary   1955   *931*
Portrait and Biography   1901   *lxxiii*
Presentation to   1945   *49*
Tribute to Sir S. Jackson   1948   *80*

Hirst, H. (Heckmondwike C.C.)
   Obituary   1918   *189*
Hirst, Lt.-Col. H. D. (Kent Supporter)
   Obituary   1919   *207*
Hirst, T. H. (Yorkshire)
   Obituary   1928/I   *289*
Hiscock, E. J. (South Australia)
   Obituary   1896   *xliv*
Historical Events
   Note on   1950   *118*
Hitch, J. W. (Surrey; England)
   Benefit Match   1922/II   *124*
   Obituary   1966   *967*
   Portrait and Biography   1914/I   *238*
Hitchcock, R. E. (Warwickshire; Canterbury)
   Benefit Match   1964   *595*
   Photograph   1956   *590*
                                        1961   *591*
Hitchcock, Col. T. B. (Winchester)
   Obituary   1910/I   *140*
Hitchman, E. F. (Canada)
   Obituary   1962   *986*
Hitchon, Dr. H. H. I. (President Lancashire)
   Obituary   1937/I   *274*
Hoar, A. E. (Durham)
   Obituary   1925/I   *267*
Hoare, Rev. A. R. (Eton; Norfolk)
   Obituary   1942   *359*
Hoare, Capt. C. A. R. (Kent; President Hampshire)
   Obituary   1909/I   *138*
Hoare, C. J. (Sussex)
   Obituary   1914/I   *185*
Hoare, C. S. (Tonbridge)
   Obituary   1918   *229*
Hoare, H. S. (Harrow)
   Obituary   1931/I   *260*
Hoare, Canon J. G. (Tonbridge)
   Obituary   1924/I   *260*
Hoare, R. B. (Harrow)
   Obituary   1932/I   *246*
Hoare, Sir R. H. (Eton)
   Obituary   1955   *933*
Hoare, Sir S. 1st Bart. (Harrow)
   Obituary   1916   *174*
Hoare, Major V. R. (Eton)
   Obituary   1916   *174*

Hoare, Rev. W. M. (Eton)
Obituary   1913/I   *189*
Hoare, Major W. R. (Eton; Norfolk)
Obituary   1942   *359*
Hobbs, 2nd Lieut. G. P. (Felsted)
Obituary   1918   *189*
'Hobbs Era, The'
Sir J. Hobbs   1935/I   *247*
Hobbs, Sir. J. B. (Cambridgeshire; Surrey; England)
Benefit Matches   1920/II   *97*
    1927/II   *208*
Career Statistics   1964   *104*
'Giant of the Wisden Century' N. Cardus   1963   *95*
'The Hobbs Era'   1935/I   *247*
'Jack Hobbs' R. Mason Book Review   1961   *999*
'Jack Hobbs – Profile of the Master'
J. Arlott Book Review   1982   *1278*
'Sir J. B. Hobbs' P. Landsberg
Book Review   1954   *978*
'Sir John Berry Hobbs' Obituary Tribute
N. Cardus   1964   *97*
Hobbs Hundreds   1953   *78*
Hundreds   1926/I   *293*
Hundredth Hundred   1924/II   *211*
Knighthood   1954   *85*
'A Lifetime with Surrey – Stealing Singles
With J. Hobbs' A Sandhan   1972   *114*
Notes on   1964   *95*
Photographs   1926/I   *293*
    1963   *95*
    1964   *96,101,105*
    1972   *114*
Portrait and Biography   1909/I   *157*
Special Article on   1926/I   *291*
Tributes to: A. P. F. Chapman   1962   *985*
    K. Duleepsinhji   1960   *951*
    C. B. Fry   1957   *116*
    E. Hendren   1963   *103:*
    D. R. Jardine   1959   *93:*
    G. Jessop   1956   *97:*
    C. G. Macartney   1959   *93:*
    H. Preston   1960   *160*
    S. J. Southerton   1936/I   *3(*
    M. Tate   1957   *94(*
'Twenty Five Years of Triumph'   1936/I   *26*
Views on Growing Pains of Cricket   1956   *8.*

Hobbs, J. W. (Patron)
    Obituary   1915/I   227
Hobbs, R. N. S. (Essex; Glamorgan;Suffolk; England)
    Hits Fastest Hundred   1976   64
    Photograph   1970   373
Hobbs, Lieut. V. W. J. (St.John's College, Cambridge)
    Obituary   1919   178
Hobday, Capt. V. M. (British Columbia)
    Obituary   1918   189
Hobson, Lieut. J. C. (Westminster)
    Obituary   1918   189
Hobson, J. I. (Canadian Cricket Club)
    Obituary   1938   940
Hobson, T. E. C. (Western Province)
    Obituary   1938   940
Hockaday, Capt. S. R. (Birmingham University)
    Obituary   1917   189
Hockyns-Abrahall, 2nd Lieut. B. E. (Repton)
    Obituary   1919   178
Hodder, Major Rev. C. W. (Somerset Committee)
    Obituary   1919   178
Hodder, Group Capt. F. S. (Free Foresters; R.A.F.)
    Obituary   1945   326
Hodges, E. (Gentlemen of Kent)
    Obituary   1908/I   142
Hodges, Capt. H. A. (Sedbergh; Nottinghamshire)
    Obituary   1919   178
Hodges, 2nd Lieut. H. W. (Epsom College)
    Obituary   1916   175
Hodgkin, Lieut. J. P. (Wyggeston Grammar School; Leicestershire)
    Obituary   1918   189
Hodgkins, A. R. (Nottingham High School)
    Schools Note   1975   853
    81 wkts Schools Averages   1975   888
Hodgkinson, Lieut. G. C. (Clifton)
    Obituary   1917   189
Hodgkinson, Capt. G. F. (Derbyshire)
    Obituary   1941   387
Hodgkinson, Rev. G. L. (Harrow; Oxford University; Middlesex)
    Obituary   1916   175
Hodgkinson, 2nd Lieut. G. S. (Radley)
    Obituary   1918   189
Hodgkinson, Wing-Comdr. G. W. (Somerset)
    Obituary   1961   947
Hodgson, A. (Northamptonshire)
    Photograph   1978   490

Hodgson, 2nd Lieut. C. F. (King's Canterbury)
Obituary   1918   *189*
Hodgson, D. (Writer)
'Cricket World Cup 83' Book Review   1984   *1262*
Hodgson, G. (Lancashire)
Obituary   1952   *957*
Hodgson, G. H. (Harrow)
Obituary   1918   *229*
Hodgson, Capt. R. D. (Radley)
Obituary   1919   *178*
Hodgson, Lieut. R. E. (Sherborne)
Obituary   1919   *178*
Hodgson, Rev. R. G. (Kent)
Obituary   1932/I   *246*
Hodgson, Rev. R. L. ('A County Vicar'; Journalist)
Obituary   1954   *931*
Hodson, 2nd Lieut. S. (Merchant Taylors)
Obituary   1919   *179*
Hogarth, Major J. U. (Harrow)
Obituary   1945   *322*
Hogg, Capt. H. M. (Sandhurst)
Obituary   1918   *190*
Hogue, T. (Western Australia)
Obituary   1957   *944*
Holbech, Lieut. W. H. (Warwickshire)
Obituary   1915/I   *227*
Holberton, Lt-Col. P. V. (Shrewsbury)
Obituary   1919   *179*
Holcombe, M. J. (Eltham College)
Schools Notes   1983   *900*
1039 runs Schools Averages   1983   *917*
Holcroft, 2nd Lieut. R. B. (Warwick School)
Obituary   1917   *189*
Holden, C. (Cheshire; Lancashire)
Obituary   1929/I   *247*
Holden, C. (Sussex Groundsman)
Obituary   1964   *950*
Holden, Capt. H. (Secretary Nottinghamshire)
Obituary   1901   *lix*
Holder, J. W. (Hampshire)
Photograph   1971   *385*
Holder, V. A. (Worcestershire; Shropshire; Barbados; West Indies)
Benefit Match   1980   *618*
Photograph   1971   *564*
                                                                1975   *598*

Holding, M. A. (Lancashire; Derbyshire; Tasmania; Jamaica; West Indies)
Action Photograph	1981	68
Cricketer of the Year	1977	97
Holding's Oval Record – Photograph	1977	87
Photograph	1977	92
Unbridled Dissent – Photograph	1981	67

Holdship, A. R. (Auckland)
Obituary	1924/I	260

Holdsworth, Lt-Col. A. M. (Berkshire)
Obituary	1917	189

Holdsworth, E. F. (Yorkshire)
Obituary	1954	926

Holdsworth, F. (Wellington; New Zealand)
Obituary	1943	386

Holdsworth, R. L. (Repton; Oxford University; Warwickshire; Sussex)
Obituary	1977	1042

Hole, W. J. (President Fairmount C.C., Philadelphia)
Obituary	1973	1014

Holegate, G. (Secretary Lancashire)
Obituary	1951	929

Holland
De Flamingos in England	1953	1954	671
	1966	1967	810
Gentlemen of England	1894	1895	361

Holland, 2nd Lieut. E. H. (Bedford Grammar School)
Obituary	1918	190

Holland F. C. (Surrey)
Benefit Match	1908/II	122
Obituary	1958	960

Holland, J. (Leicestershire; Lancashire; Cheshire)
Obituary	1915/I	227

Hollands, Eileen (Writer)
'Never Marry a Cricketer' Book Review	1975	1118

Hollands, R. L. (Journalist)
Obituary	1979	1080

Hollies, W. (Old Hill C.C.)
Obituary	1969	981

Hollies, W. E. (Warwickshire; Staffordshire; England)
Benefit Match	1949	534
Birmingham League Notes	1944	290
	1945	303
Career Figures	1958	97
Cricketer of the Year	1955	67
'I'll Spin you a Tale' Book Review	1956	1029
Obituary	1982	1202

Photographs | 1950 | *533*
  | 1951 | *548*
  | 1952 | *544*
  | 1954 | *580*
  | 1955 | *65*
  | 1957 | *578*

Hollingberry, Lieut. R. A. R. (Merchant Taylors)
  Obituary | 1917 | *189*
Hollings, H. J. B. (Winchester)
  Obituary | 1923/I | *299*
Hollingsworth, R. P. (Philadelphia C.C.)
  Obituary | 1906 | *xcii*
Hollings, Sir A. M. (Eton; Oxford University)
  Obituary | 1939 | *910*
Hollins, Capt. E. R. L. (Sussex Club Cricket)
  Obituary | 1917 | *189*
Hollins, Sir F. Bart. (President Lancashire)
  Obituary | 1925/I | *268*
Hollins, Sir F. H. (Eton; Oxford University; Lancashire)
  Obituary | 1965 | *973*
Hollins, S. (Cheshire; Lancashire Committee)
  Obituary | 1915/I | *227*
Holloway, Capt. B. H. (Leys; Cambridge University; Sussex)
  Obituary | 1916 | *175*
Holloway, G. J. W. (Clifton; Gloucestershire)
  Obituary | 1967 | *969*
Holloway, N. J. (Leys; Cambridge University; Sussex)
  Obituary | 1965 | *967*
Holloway, R. F. P. (Clifton; Gloucestershire)
  Obituary | 1980 | *1150*
Hollowood, B. (Staffordshire; Journalist)
  'Cricket on the Brain' Book Review | 1971 | *1070*
  Obituary | 1982 | *1203*
Holman, B. W. (Charterhouse)
  Obituary | 1897 | *xlii*
Holme, 2nd Lieut. G. W. (Pocklington School)
  Obituary | 1917 | *189*
Holme, P. A. T. (Winchester)
  Obituary | 1976 | *1099*
Holme, T. W. (Winchester)
  Obituary | 1929/I | *247*
Holmes, Group Capt. A. J. (Repton; Sussex)
  Obituary | 1951 | *925*
Holmes, Major E. R. T. (Malvern; Oxford University; Surrey; England)
  'Flannelled Foolishness'
  Book Review | 1958 | *1015*

Obituary	1961	*947*
Portrait and Biography	1936/I	*298*
Schools Notes	1922/I	*297*
	1923/I	*337*
		338
	1924/I	*289*
		291
		299
	1925/I	*298*
		309
		310
Views on L.B.W. Experiment	1936/I	*344*

Holmes, H. (Hampshire)

Obituary	1914/I	*185*

Holmes, H. R. (Journalist)

'The American Cricketers in the West Indies 1887-88'

Book Review	1976	*1140*

Holmes, Dr. J. B. (President Lancashire)

Obituary	1957	*944*

Holmes, J. H. (Umpire)

Obituary	1899	*1*

Holmes, J. R. R. (Repton; Sussex)

Obituary	1981	*1143*

Holmes, J. W. (Lancashire)

Obituary	1975	*1079*

Holmes, M. (Clifton; Manitoba)

Obituary	1928/I	*289*

Holmes, P. (Yorkshire; England)

Batting Summary 1913-33	1934/I	*245*
Benefit Match	1929/II	*185*
Career Figures	1972	*135*

'Holmes and Sutcliffe – Run Stealers'

L. Duckworth Book Review	1971	*1076*

'Percy Holmes – A True Yorkshireman'

Obituary N. Cardus	1972	*130*
Photograph	1972	*131*
Portrait and Biography	1920/I	*252*

Holmes, Rev. R. S. (Writer)

Obituary	1934/I	*267*

Holmes, Major T. K. (Old Stagers' Dramatic Company)

Obituary	1895	*xxxvii*

Holroyd, Sir E. D. (Winchester)

Obituary	1918	*241*

Holt, A. G. (Hampshire)

'A Holt – An Appreciation'

J. Arlott Book Review	1964	*1013*

Holt, G. L. (Richmond C.C.)
Obituary 1965 *967*
Holt, J. (Treasurer Lancashire)
Obituary 1907 *cxii*
Holt, J. K. (Senior) (Jamaica)
Obituary 1969 *981*
Holt, Sir S. (President Lancashire)
Obituary 1974 *1075*
Homer, H. W. (Staffordshire)
Obituary 1978 *1074*
Hone, Sir B. (Oxford University; South Australia; Wiltshire)
Honoured Note on 1970 *80*
Obituary 1979 *1080*
Hone, J. (Phoenix Park; Dublin C.C.)
Obituary 1909/I *138*
Hone, W. P. (Ireland)
Obituary 1977 *1042*
Hone-Goldney, G. H. (Eton; Cambridge University)
Obituary 1922/I *256*
Honey, 2nd Lieut. A. C. (Malvern)
Obituary 1919 *179*
Hong Kong in England 1976 1977 *792*
Honiball, R. D. (Jamaica)
Obituary 1908/I *142*
Honours
For Cricketers 1958 *77*
1979 *82*
1981 *367*
1983 *280*
1984 *270*
Honywood, Sir J. W. 8th Bart. (President Kent)
Obituary 1908/I *142*
Hood, Lt-Col. E. H. M. (Somerset; Army)
Obituary 1969 *981*
Hood, Rear Adm. Hon. H. L. A. (Cricket Enthusiast)
Obituary 1918 *213*
Hood, Rev. J. S. E. C. (Rugby; Cambridge University)
Obituary 1903 *lxxvi*
Hooker, J. E. H. (New South Wales)
Obituary 1983 *1246*
Hooker, R. W. (Middlesex; Buckinghamshire)
Benefit Match 1969 *504*
Photograph 1966 *483*
Hooman, C. V. L. (Charterhouse; Oxford University; Devon; Kent)
Obituary 1970 *1022*

276

Hooper, Rev. R. P. (Cambridge University; Norfolk)
Obituary   1919   207

Hope, A. (Victoria)
Obituary   1917   *251*

Hope, C. S. (Winchester)
Obituary   1917   *251*

Hopkins, A. J. Y. (New South Wales; Australia)
Obituary   1932/I   246

Hopkins, Dr. H. O. (St.Peters; Adelaide; Oxford University; Worcestershire)
Obituary   1973   *1009*

Hopkins, J. (Warwickshire; Hampshire)
Obituary   1931/I   260

Hopkins, J. A. (Glamorgan; Eastern Province)
Photograph   1979   *375*

Hopkins, W. R. I. (Stockton C.C.)
Obituary   1922/I   272

Hopkinson, E. (Pennsylvania University)
Obituary   1937/II   287

Hopley, F. J. (Harrow; Cambridge University)
Obituary   1952   *957*

Hopley, 2nd Lieut. G. W. V. (Harrow; Cambridge University)
Obituary   1916   *176*

Hopwood, J. L. (Lancashire)
Benefit Match   1939   *411*

Horan, T. P. (Victoria; Australia)
Obituary   1917   *251*

Horden, Dr. H. V. (Philadelphia; New South Wales; Australia)
Obituary   1939   *911*

Hore, Rev. A. H. (Tonbridge; Oxford University)
Obituary   1904   *lxxxi*

Horlick, Lt-Col. Sir J. N. Bart. (Eton; Oxford University; Gloucestershire)
                                                   1973   *1009*

Horlick, O. P. T. (Shrewsbury)
Obituary   1961   *948*

Horlicks Awards   1967   269
                                        ad passim

Horn, J. F. (U. S. A. Club Cricket)
Obituary   1939   *911*

Horn, W. B. (Lafayette C.C., New York)
Obituary   1913/I   *189*

Hornby, A. H. (Lancashire)
Obituary   1953   *942*

Hornby, A. N. (Harrow; Lancashire; England)
Obituary   1926/I   *274*

Hornby, Col. C. G. (Sandhurst)
Obituary   1920/I   *154*

Hornby, Dr. C. H. (President N.Y.C.C.)
Obituary 1935/I *266*

Hornby, C. L. (Harrow)
Obituary 1897 *xxxix*

Hornby, C. R. (Eton)
Obituary 1922/I *256*

Hornby, E. C. (Winchester; Lancashire)
Obituary 1923/I *299*

Hornby, E. G. S. (Eton)
Obituary 1924/I *260*

Hornby, G. (Lancashire Club Cricket)
Obituary 1906 *xcii*

Hornby, Dr. J. J. (Eton)
Obituary 1910/I *140*

Horne, Rev. E. L. (Shrewsbury; Cambridge University)
Obituary 1909/I *138*

Horne, 2nd Lieut. J. A. (Ashford Grammar School)
Obituary 1919 *179*

Horner, Lieut. B. (Stockport C.C.)
Obituary 1918 *190*

Horner, C. E. (Surrey)
Obituary 1926/I *276*

Horner, J. (Vice President Lancashire)
Obituary 1925/I *268*

Horner, M. (Eton)
Obituary 1938 *940*

Horner, N. F. (Warwickshire)
Benefit Match 1963 *644*
Photograph 1959 *570*

Hornibrook, P. M. (Queensland; Australia)
Obituary 1977 *1042*

Hornsby, J. H. T. (Fettes; Middlesex)
Obituary 1927/I *280*

Hornung, E. W. (Cricket Fanatic)
Obituary 1922/I *256*

Horridge, Capt. J. L. (Uppingham)
Obituary 1919 *179*

Horser, Capt. S. C. S. (Queen's College, Oxford)
Obituary 1918 *214*

Horsfall, 2nd Lieut. A. M. (Marlborough)
Obituary 1917 *224*

Horsfall, 2nd Lieut. B. A. (Borlase School, Marlow)
Obituary 1919 *179*

Horsfall, J. (Yorkshire)
Obituary 1931/I *260*

Horsfall, R. (Glamorgan; Essex)
    Obituary   1982   *1203*
    Photograph   1954   *323*
Horsfield, G. C. (New South Wales)
    Obituary   1983   *1247*
Horsham Plan of County Ground   1953   *550*
Horsley, A. B. (Leys; Durham)
    Obituary   1925/I   *289*
Horsley, J. (Nottinghamshire; Derbyshire; Aberdeenshire)
    Obituary   1977   *1043*
Horspool, E. (Auckland)
    Obituary   1959   *939*
Horton, H. (Hampshire; Worcestershire)
    Photographs   1960   *411*
                                1967   *424*
Horton, J. N. (President Queensland Cricket Association)
    Obituary   1928/I   *303*
Horton, J. R. (Victoria C.C., British Columbia)
    Obituary   1920/I   *154*
Horton, M. J. (Worcestershire; Northern Districts; England)
    Benefit Match   1966   *614*
    Photographs   1956   *612*
                                  1959   *591*
                                  1960   *614*
                                  1964   *601*
Horton, T. (Repton; Northamptonshire)
    Obituary   1933/I   *250*
Hosegood, 2nd Lieut. R. (Leys)
    Obituary   1917   *189*
Hosford, S. (President Manhattan C.C.)
    Obituary   1913/I   *189*
Hosie, A. L. (St.Lawrence College, Ramsgate; Hampshire)
    Obituary   1958   *961*
Hoskin, W. W. (Oxford University; Gloucestershire)
    Obituary   1957   *944*
Hoskin, Sgt. G. A. (Rossall; Cheshire)
    Obituary   1944   *307*
Hoskyns, Rt. Rev. E. (Haileybury)
    Obituary   1927/I   *295*
Hoskyns, Canon Sir J. L. Bart. (Rugby)
    Obituary   1913/I   *202*
Hotham, Adm. Sir A. G. (Hampshire; Devon)
    Obituary   1966   *967*
Hothfield, 1st Lord (President Kent)
    Obituary   1927/I   *280*

Hothfield, 2nd Lord (Kent)
Obituary 1953 *942*
Hot Tempered Test Crowd
Photograph 1955 *63*
Hough, Capt. G. G. (Brooklands C.C., Cheshire)
Obituary 1919 *179*
Hough, Capt. G. de Lisle (Winchester; Kent)
Obituary 1960 *952*
Houghton, Rev. E. J. (Rossall)
Obituary 1920/I *176*
Houghton, Lt-Col. N. (Glenalmond)
Obituary 1918 *190*
House, 2nd Lieut. M. H. (Rugby)
Obituary 1918 *190*
Household, 2nd Lieut. E. S. (Watford Grammar School; Hertfordshire)
Obituary 1918 *190*
Houston, R. (Victoria)
Obituary 1923/I *310*
Hove Plan of County Ground 1950 *515*
ad passim
Test Trial at 1973 *91*
'How Test Players are Raised'
L. Hassett 1952 *107*
Howard, A. (Haileybury)
Obituary 1924/I *261*
Howard, C. (Sussex)
Obituary 1930/I *253*
Howard, C. G. (Secretary Lancashire)
Team in India 1956-57 1958 *858*
Howard, H. C. (Western Australia)
Obituary 1962 *994*
Howard, J. H. (Kentish Association C.C., Winnipeg)
Obituary 1920/I *176*
Howard, N. D. (Rossall; Lancashire; England)
Obituary 1980 *1150*
Schools Notes 1942 *280*
1943 *268*
271
304
Howard, Major R. (Lancashire)
Obituary 1968 *1001*
Howard-Smith, Lieut. G. (Eton; Cambridge University; Staffordshire)
Obituary 1917 *189*
Howarth, G. P. (Surrey; Auckland; Northern Districts; New Zealand)
Photographs 1974 *539*
1977 *554*

Howarth, H. (Auckland; New Zealand)
Action Photograph 1974 *49*

Howat, G. (Writer)
'Cricket Militant – The Life of Jack Parsons'
Book Review 1981 *1203*
'Learie Constantine' Book Review 1976 *1148*

Howe, 4th Earl of (Eton)
Obituary 1930/I *253*

Howe, Lieut. G. (Wellington, New Zealand)
Obituary 1918 *190*

Howe, R. (Hertfordshire)
Obituary 1970 *1022*

Howell, Dr. C. M. H. (Marlborough)
Obituary 1961 *948*

Howell, G. (Christ's College, Brecon)
78 wkts Schools Averages 1912/II *455*

Howell, H. (Warwickshire; England)
Obituary 1933/I *250*

Howell, 2nd Lieut. J. (Repton)
Obituary 1916 *176*

Howell, L. S. (Winchester; Surrey)
Obituary 1896 *xli*

Howell, M. (Repton; Oxford University; Surrey)
Obituary 1977 *1043*

Howell, R. (Surrey)
Obituary 1913/I *189*

Howell, W. P. (New South Wales; Australia)
Obituary 1941 *398*

Howeson, A. C. E. (Formerly A. C. Von Ernsthausen; Uppingham; Oxford University; Surrey)
Obituary 1929/I *247*

Howitt, G. (Middlesex)
Benefit Match 1878 *184*

Howlett, Brig.B. (Army; Kent)
Obituary 1944 *307*

Howorth, R. (Worcestershire; England)
Benefit Match 1950 *555*
Obituary 1981 *1143*

Hoyer-Millar, E. G. (Harrow)
Obituary 1950 *910*

Hoyland, J. (Yorkshire Scorer)
Obituary 1922/I *256*

Hubband, G. D. (Winchester)
Obituary 1944 *315*

Hubband, R. C. (Winchester; Cambridge University)
Obituary 1965 *967*

281

Hubbard, Hon. E. (Radley)
  Obituary   1935/I   266

Hubbard, G. C. (Tonbridge; Kent)
  Obituary   1933/I   263

Hubble, J. C. (Kent)
  Benefit Match   1925/II   186
  Obituary   1966   968

Hubert, G. S. (Ceylon)
  Obituary   1975   1079

Huddleston, W. (Lancashire)
  Benefit Match   1915/II   20
  Obituary   1963   1034

Hudson, J. L. (Tasmania)
  Obituary   1962   986

Huggins, H. J. (Gloucestershire)
  Obituary   1943   372

Hughes, D. P. (Lancashire; Tasmania)
  Photographs   1971   41
   1974   45
   1982   46

Hughes, D. W. (North Wales Cricket Association)
  Obituary   1968   100

Hughes, Canon E. S. (Victoria Cricket Association)
  Obituary   1945   34

Hughes, H. G. S. (Rugby; Hertfordshire)
  Obituary   1927/I   28

Hughes, Capt. H. K. (Repton)
  Obituary   1917   22

Hughes, J. (Hertfordshire)
  Obituary   1908/I   14

Hughes, J. A. (Essex)
  Obituary   1954   92

Hughes, K. J. (Western Australia; Australia)
  Cricketer of the Year   1981   7
  Photograph   1981   7

Hughes, Margaret (Writer)
  'The Long Hop' Book Review   1956   102

Hughes, O. (Malvern; Cambridge University)
  Obituary   1973   100

Hughes, Capt. R. F. (St. Ignatius College, Sydney)
  Obituary   1917   19

Hughes, S. P. (Middlesex; Northern Transvaal)
  Photograph   1982   4

Hughes, T. B. (Winchester)
  Obituary   1941   3

Hughes, Capt. T. H. (Repton)
Obituary   1917   *224*

Hughes-Onslow, Major A. (Eton)
Obituary   1915/I   *227*

Hugonin, Lt-Col. F. E. (Eastbourne College; Essex; Army)
Obituary   1968   *1001*

Huish, F. H. (Kent)
Benefit Match   1906   *188*
Obituary   1958   *961*

Hull Plan of County Ground   1971   *582*

Hull, Surgeon, Rear Adm. H. R. B. (Royal Navy)
Obituary   1971   *1026*

Hull-Brown, Rev. R. A. (Gentlemen of Warwickshire)
Obituary   1918   *229*

Hulme, J. (Middlesex; London Counties)
Benefit Match   1940   *394*

Hulton, C. A. G. (Lancashire)
Obituary   1920/I   *177*

Human, J. H. (Repton; Cambridge University; Middlesex)
Note on   1944   *58*

Human, Capt. R. H. C. (Repton; Cambridge University; Berkshire; Oxfordshire; Worcesterhire)
Obituary   1943   *365*

Humble-Crofts, Capt. C. M. (Eastbourne College)
Obituary   1917   *190*

Humble-Crofts, Rev. Preb. W. J. (Derbyshire)
Obituary   1925/I   *268*

Hume, E. (Marlborough; Oxford University)
Obituary   1922/I   *256*

Hume, E. (New South Wales)
Obituary   1913/I   *190*

Humpage, G. W. (Warwickshire)
Photographs   1977   *588*
    1982   *588*

Humpherson, V. W. (Worcestershire)
Obituary   1979   *1080*

Humphrey, R. (Surrey)
Benefit Match   1886   *171*
Obituary   1907   *cxii*

Humphrey, S. H. G. (Oakham; Northamptonshire)
Obituary   1976   *1099*

Humphrey, T. (Surrey)
Benefit Match   1877   *153*
Biography   1874   *123*

Humphreys, E. W. (Harrow)
Obituary   1893   *xxxiv*

Humphreys, G. T. (Sussex)
  Obituary   1896   *xliv*
Humphreys, Capt. N. F. (Durham School)
  Obituary   1919   *179*
Humphreys, W. A. (Sussex; Hampshire)
  Obituary   1925/I   *268*
Humphreys, W. A. (Harrow)
  Obituary   1925/I   *269*
Humphries, D. J. (Leicestershire; Worcestershire)
  Photograph   1978   *584*
Humphries, E. (Kent)
  Obituary   1950   *914*
Humphries, J. (Derbyshire; England)
  Obituary   1947   *694*
Humphry, D. (Writer)
  'The Cricket Conspiracy' Book Review   1976   *113*
Humphrys, Sir F. H. (Shrewsbury; Oxford University)
  Obituary   1972   *105*
'Hundred Years of Surrey Cricket'
  H. D. Leveson Gower   1946   *5*
Hundreds in England Since 1935 Table   1959   *7*
'Hundreds, Fastest in Test Cricket'
  G. Brodribb   1983   *10*
Hundreds Fastest Note on   1966   *8*
Hunt, F. H. (Kent; Worcestershire)
  Obituary   1968   *1004*
Hunt, G. (Somerset)
  Obituary   1960   *95*
Hunt, H. R. (Uppingham)
  Obituary   1925/I   *26*
Hunt, J. H. (Middlesex)
  Obituary   1918   *21*
Hunt, Col. K. (Dover College; Gloucestershire)
  Obituary   1973   *100*
Hunt, R. N. (Middlesex)
  Obituary   1984   *120*
Hunt, W. H. (Marlborough)
  Obituary   1925/I   *27*
Hunte, C. C. (Barbados; West Indies)
  Cricketer of the Year   1964   *2*
  Photograph   1964   *2*
  'Playing to Win' Book Review   1972   *110*
Hunte, E. A. C. (Trinidad; West Indies)
  Obituary   1968   *1004*
Hunter, C. H. (Uppingham; Cambridge University; Kent)
  Obituary   1956   *9*

Hunter, D. (Yorkshire)
Benefit Match	1898	*76*
Obituary	1928/I	*289*

Hunter, G. J. (Reigate Priory; Essex)
Obituary	1944	*315*

Hunter, 2nd Lieut. H. M. (Winchester)
Obituary	1916	*176*

Hunter, J. (Yorkshire; England)
Obituary	1892	*xxxi*

Hunter, 2nd Lieut. J. G. (Gala C.C.)
Obituary	1918	*190*

Hunter, K. O. (Winchester)
Obituary	1961	*949*

Hunter, R. C. (Winchester)
Obituary	1922/I	*257*

Hunter, Capt. R. J. (Winchester)
Obituary	1919	*179*

Hunter, Sgt. W. J. (Coquitlam C.C., Vancouver)
Obituary	1918	*214*

Hunting, G. L. (Loretto; Northumberland)
Obituary	1967	*969*
Schools Note	1911/I	*134*
1081 runs Schools Averages	1911/II	*446*

Hurditch, C. P. (St.Pauls; Jamaica)
Obituary	1918	*229*

Hurlbutt, Capt. P. (Montgomeryshire)
Obituary	1920/I	*154*

Hurn, C. (Wiltshire)
Obituary	1944	*315*

Hurst, C. S. (Uppingham; Oxford University; Kent)
Obituary	1964	*950*

Hurst, J. (Writer)
'Cumberland County Cricket Club: A History'
Book Review	1983	*1302*

Hurst-Brown, 2nd Lieut. C. (Westminster)
Obituary	1916	*177*

Hurt, C. N. (Derbyshire)
Obituary	1973	*1009*

Hurt, S. F. A. A. (Harrow)
Obituary	1915/I	*228*

Hurwood, A. (Queensland; Australia)
Obituary	1984	*1202*

Husain, F. S. (Writer)
'Shabash! Pakistan' Book Review
	1956	*1023*

Husband, 2nd Lieut. D. I. (University College, London)
Obituary	1917	*190*

Husey-Hunt, J. H. (Marlborough)
  Obituary 1925/I 27(

Huskinson, Dr. E. C. (New York Club Cricket)
  Obituary 1926/I 27(

Huskinson, G. N. B. (Oundle; Nottinghamshire)
  Obituary 1983 124?

Huskisson, Major J. (Merchant Taylors)
  Obituary 1942 35(

Huson, A. C. (Winchester)
  Obituary 1942 35?

Hussain, Dr. D. (Central India; India)
  Obituary 1968 100

Hussain, S. M. (Hyderabad)
  Obituary 1983 124

Hustler, J. A. (Yorkshire Club Cricket)
  Obituary 1913/I 19

Hutcheon, J. S. (Queensland)
  Obituary 1958 96

Hutchings, F. V. (Tonbridge; Kent)
  Obituary 1936/I 29

Hutchings, Lieut. K. L. (Tonbridge; Kent; England)
  Obituary 1917 1?
  Portrait and Biography 1907 cx?
  Schools Notes 1902 xc?
    c?
    1903 ?

Hutchinson, D. J. M. (Loretto)
  Schools Note 1975 8?
  79 wkts Schools Averages 1975 8?

Hutchinson, Major C. K. (Eton)
  Obituary 1942 3?

Hutchinson, Lieut. D. H. (Merchiston Castle)
  Obituary 1916 1?

Hutt, H. F. (Writer)
  'The Great Men of Gloucestershire' 1957 1?

Hutton, C. F. (Harrow)
  Obituary 1939 9

Hutton, Sir L. (Yorkshire; England)
  Action Photographs 1951
    1953
  Benefit Match 1951 5?
  Bradford League Notes 1944 ?
    1945 ?
  Career Statistics 1956
  'Cricket is my Life' Book Review 1950 ?
  Hundredth Hundred 1952 ?

'Tribute to Hutton' V. G. J. Jenkins		1950	*93*
Hutton's Lean Time Note on		1955	*81*
Hutton and M.C.C. Note on		1956	*75*
'Hutton's Men Bring Home the Ashes' Note on		1955	*78*
Hutton's Reward		1950	*115*
'L. Hutton'			
L. Kitchin Book Review		1954	*978*
'Len Hutton – the Master' N. Cardus		1956	*91*
'Hutton and Washbrook' A. A. Thomson			
Book Review		1964	*1001*
Knighthood		1957	*68*
'Just My Story' Book Review		1957	*1000*
Notable Achievements		1956	*105*
Notes on		1944	*55*
			193
		1945	*205*
Photographs		1950	*92*
		1951	*587*
		1956	*92*
with G. Boycott; H. Sutcliffe		1978	*142*
Portrait and Biography		1938	*37*
Tributes to: C. B. Fry		1957	*116*
S. McCabe		1969	*983*
H. Sutcliffe		1979	*98*
'Victorious Captain' Photograph		1954	*53*
utton, N. H. (South Australia)			
Obituary		1983	*1247*
utton, R. A. (Repton; Cambridge University; Yorkshire; Transvaal; England)			
Hutton's Prize – Photograph		1962	*91*
Photograph		1971	*580*
Schools Note		1962	*772*
1036 runs Schools Averages		1962	*814*
utton, T. (Durham)			
Obituary		1937/I	*288*
de, Sir C. Bart. (President Warwickshire)			
Obituary		1943	*378*
de, Lord (Eton)			
Obituary		1936/I	*278*
derabad Blues			
in Ceylon	1967	1968	*943*
in Ceylon/S.E. Asia	1967-68	1969	*927*
met, F. (Victoria)			
Obituary		1920/I	*177*
land, F. J. (Hampshire)			
Obituary		1965	*967*

Hylton, 4th Baron (President Somerset)
  Obituary   1968   100

Hylton, L. G. (Jamaica; West Indies)
  Obituary   1956   97

Hylton-Stewart, B. D. (Somerset; Hertfordshire)
  Obituary   1973   100

Hyman, C. S. (Ontario Clubs)
  Obituary   1927/I   28

Hyman, W. (Somerset)
  Obituary   1960   95

Hyndman, H. M. (Cambridge University; Sussex)
  Obituary   1922/I   25

Hyndson, Capt. J. G. W. (Surrey)
  Obituary   1937   28

Hynes, Sir L. C. (New South Wales)
  Obituary   1978   107

Hysop, H. H. (Hampshire)
  Obituary   1921/I   22

I'Anson, J. (Lancashire)
  Obituary   1939   92

Ibadulla, K. (Lahore; Warwickshire; Tasmania; Otago; Pakistan)
  Benefit Match   1970   59
  Photographs   1958   5
                                    1965   5

Iceland Cricket in
  Note on   1944   6

Ice, Cricket Matches on the 1878-79   1880

Iceton, T. H. (New South Wales)
  Obituary   1909/I   1

Iddison, R. (Yorkshire)
  Benefit Match   1873   1
  Biography   1872   1

Iddon, J. (Lancashire; England)
  Benefit Match   1937/II   3
  Obituary   1947   6

Ikin, J. T. (Lancashire; Staffordshire; England)
  Action Photograph   1952
  Benefit Match   1954   4
  Career Figures   1958
  Photographs   1952   4
                                      1956   4

Ilford Valentines Park
  Plan of County Ground   1951   5
                                      ad passim

Illingworth, C. (Vancouver C.C.)

Obituary	1938	*940*

Illingworth, R. (Yorkshire; Leicestershire; England)

Benefit Match	1978	*742*
Captain of England Note on	1971	*91*
Career Figures	1973	*113*
Cricketer of the Year	1960	*117*
'Ray Illingworth C.B.E. Keeper of the Ashes'		
T. Bailey	1973	*108*
Illingworth Era Ends Note on	1974	*67*
Photographs	1954	*619*
	1957	*620*
	1958	*630*
	1959	*611*
	1960	*87*
	1965	*628*
	1973	*109*
	1976	*473*
'Spinner's Wicket' Book Review	1970	*1067*
'Yorkshire and Back' Book Review	1981	*1203*

Illman, J. C. (Lincolnshire)

Obituary	1960	*952*

Imlay, A. D. (Clifton; Cambridge University; Gloucestershire)

Obituary	1960	*952*

Imperial Cricket Conference

Photographs	1956	*51*
	1961	*88*

Imran Khan Niazi (Worcester Royal Grammar School; Lahore; Pakistan
International Airways; Worcestershire; Oxford University; Sussex; Pakistan)

Cricketer of the Year	1983	*65*
Outstanding Achievement Note on	1984	*53*
Photographs	1977	*605*
	1981	*566*
	1983	*Plate*
Schools Notes	1973	*827*

Incentives Note on

	1962	*116*

Inchmore, J. D. (Worcestershire; Northern Transvaal)

Photograph	1977	*605*

Incogniti

in Holland	1922	1923/II	*559*
in U.S.A.	1920	1921/II	*475*

India

in Australia	1947-48	1949	*761*
	1967-68	1969	*836*
	1977-78	1979	*923*

and New Zealand	1980-81	1982	*943*
'New Zealand and India in Australia'			
Ed. A. McGilvray Book Review		1982	*1272*
in East Africa	1967	1968	*871*
in England	1911	1912/II	*359*
	1932	1933/II	*1*
	1936	1937/II	*1*
	1946	1947	*154*
Team Portrait	1946	1947	*35*
Last Wicket Record Photograph		1947	*38*
at Hove Four Centuries Photograph		1947	*39*
	1952	1953	*213*
Team Portrait	1952	1953	*55*
Worst Start in Test Cricket Photograph		1953	*58*
Action Photographs		1953	*59*
'Rivals in the Sun' R. Bharatan			
Book Review		1954	*980*
	1959	1960	*263*
Team Portrait	1959	1960	*93*
'Cricketers from India' G. Ross			
Book Review		1960	*997*
	1967	1968	*281*
Team Portrait	1967	1968	*62*
	1971	1972	*319*
Team Portrait	1971	1972	*65*
	1974	1975	*300*
World Cup Tournament	1975	1976	*300*
Team Portrait	1975	1976	*303*
World Cup Tournament	1979	1980	*297*
	1979	1980	*328*
Team Portrait	1979	1980	*333*
'Diary of a Cricket Season' R. Willis			
Book Review		1980	*1212*
	1982	1983	*299*
Team Portrait	1982	1983	*300*
'Summer of the All Rounder' P. Eagar and A. Ross			
Book Review		1983	*1306*
World Cup Tournament	1983	1984	*293*
Team Portrait	1983	1984	*294*
'Moment of Triumph' Photograph		1984	*Plate*
in New Zealand	1967-68	1969	*852*
	1975-76	1977	*897*
and Australia	1980-81	1982	*943*

290

in Pakistan	1952	1953	*872*
	1954-55	1956	*878*
'Cricket Without Challenge' Q. Butt			
Book Review		1957	*994*
	1978-79	1980	*963*
	1982-83	1984	*923*
in Sri Lanka	1956-57	1958	*897*
	1974	1975	*970*
in West Indies	1952-53	1954	*820*
	1961-62	1963	*913*
	1970-71	1972	*922*
'India v West Indies 1971'			
S. Rajan Book Review		1972	*1100*
'Gone with the Indians'			
B. Jones Book Review		1973	*1056*
	1975-76	1977	*908*
	1982-83	1984	*954*
All India Schools Tour			
of the U.K.	1967	1968	*825*
'The Souvenir Programme of the All India Schools			
Cricket Tour of the U.K.' Book Review		1968	*1054*
All India State Bank in Ceylon	1966	1967	*894*
Indian Parsees in England	1886	1887	*285*
	1888	1889	*332*
Indian Schoolboys Tour			
in Britain	1973	1974	*833*
Indian Under 20 Team in			
Sri lanka	1980-81	1982	*1138*
Indian Young Cricketers in			
England	1981	1982	*847*
Chronological List of Articles and Notes			
'India – Twenty years of Test Cricket'			
V. Merchant		1952	*110*
'India be Bold' V. Merchant		1959	*82*
Distinction for India Note on		1962	*116*
'Indian Cricket – its Problems and Players'			
D. Rutnagur		1967	*143*
'Dates in Indian Cricket History' R. Bowen		1967	*147*
India – World Champions Note on		1972	*85*
India v Pakistan Exchange Note on		1975	*326*
'India 1932-1982' M. Melford		1982	*119*
India Win World Cup Note on		1984	*48*

'Individual Innings of 200 or More Runs'
W. H. Knight	1869	*98*
Indoor School at Lord's Note on	1977	*113*

Inge, Rev. F. G. (Charterhouse; Oxford University)
| Obituary | 1924/I | *261* |

Inge, Lt-Col. J. W. (Free Foresters)
| Obituary | 1920/I | *177* |

Inge, Rev. Dr. W. (Oxford University)
| Obituary | 1904 | *lxxxii* |

Ingelse, R. G. (Holland)
| Obituary | 1977 | *1044* |

Ingham, C. W. (Journalist))
| Obituary | 1970 | *1022* |

Ingle, 2nd Lieut. R. G. (King's School, Ely)
| Obituary | 1917 | *192* |

Ingleby, H. (Malvern)
| Obituary | 1927/I | *281* |

Ingleby-Mackenzie, A. C. D. (Eton; Hampshire)
'Many a Slip' Book Review	1963	*1110*
Photographs	1959	*380*
	1962	*426*

Ingles, Rev. G. L. (Toronto C.C.)
| Obituary | 1916 | *219* |

Ingleton, W. J. (South Melbourne C.C.)
| Obituary | 1924/I | *261* |

Inglis, G. (Writer)
| Obituary | 1925/I | *270* |

Inglis, R. (Durham; Minor Counties)
| Obituary | 1983 | *1247* |

Inglis, Rev. R. E. (Rugby; University College, Oxford)
| Obituary | 1917 | *192* |

Ingram, E. A. (Belvedere College, Dublin; Leinster; Ireland; Middlesex)
Obituary	1974	*1075*
Schools Notes	1929/I	*297*
1011 runs Schools Averages	1929/II	*605*
1008 runs; 85 wkts Schools Averages	1930/II	*622*

Ingram, F. M. (Winchester; Berkshire)
| Obituary | 1934/I | *267* |

In Honour of Cricket, Dinner at the Mansion House | 1928/I | *351* |

Inman, C. C. (Leicestershire; Ceylon)
Benefit Match	1971	*445*
Note on	1966	*81*
Photographs	1964	*464*
	1967	*475*
	1970	*466*

Inman, H. C. (Colombo Sports Club)
    Obituary   1970   *1028*
Inman, 2nd Lieut. L. Y. (Radley)
    Obituary   1917   *193*
Innes, G. A. S. (Western Province; Transvaal)
    Obituary   1983   *1247*
Inns, J. H. (Essex)
    Obituary   1906   *xciii*
Inskip, Major-Gen. R. D. (Framlingham; Suffolk)
    Obituary   1972   *1052*
Insole, D. J. (Cambridge University; Essex; England)
    'Cricket from the Middle' Book Review   1961   *997*
    Cricketer of the Year   1956   *67*
    Photographs   1950   *306*
         1951   *305*
         1952   *310*
         1955   *310*
         1956   *52*
         1963   *150*
    Tribute to R. W. V. Robins   1969   *986*
Insole, J. H. (Essex Committee)
    Obituary   1975   *1079*
International Cricket Conference Trophy
     1979   1980   *313*
     1982   1983   *347*
International XI
    in Africa and Asia   1968   1969   *864*
International Wanderers
    in Rhodesia   1975   1977   *960*
    South Africa   1974-75   1976   *988*
         1976   1977   *963*
International World Tour   1962   1963   *968*
Intikhab Alam (Karachi; Pakistan International Airways; Surrey; Pakistan)
    Benefit Match   1979   *763*
    Photographs   1973   *530*
         1982   *557*
Inverarity, R. J. (Western Australia; South Australia; Australia)
    Swallow Incident   1970   *609*
Inverarity, M. (Western Australia)
    Obituary   1980   *1150*
Irani, Z. R. (President Indian Board of Control)
    Obituary   1971   *1026*
Iredale, F. A. (New South Wales; Australia)
    Obituary   1927/I   *281*
    Testimonial Match   1923/II   *568*

Ireland
   in England   1902   1903   *377*

   in U.S.A./Canada   1892   1893   *369*

                             1973   1974   *880*

   'Tour of U.S.A. and Canada' Book Review   1974   *1128*

   Leprechaun's Influence Note on   1970   *870*

Ireland, J. F. (Marlborough; Cambridge University)
   Obituary   1971   *1026*

Ireland, M. W. (Norfolk)
   Obituary   1922/I   *257*

Iremonger, A. (Nottinghamshire)
   Obituary   1959   *932*

Iremonger, J. (Nottinghamshire)
   Obituary   1957   *945*

   Portrait and Biography   1903   *lxxxviii*

Ironmonger, H. (Victoria; Australia)
   Obituary   1972   *1052*

Irons, J. P. (New York Veterans Cricketers' Association)
   Obituary   1926/I   *276*

Ironside, F. J. (Sydney Supporter)
   Obituary   1914/I   *199*

Irvine, B. L. (Natal; Transvaal; Essex; South Africa)
   Photograph   1969   *365*

Irvine, Col. L. G. (Taunton; Cambridge University; Kent)
   Obituary   1974   *1075*

Irvine, 2nd Lieut. A. (Epsom College)
   Obituary   1919   *179*

Irving, R. L. G. (Winchester)
   Obituary   1970   *1022*

Irwin, Lieut. T. W. C. (Radley)
   Obituary   1919   *179*

Isherwood, Lt-Col. L. C. R. (Eton; Hampshire; Sussex)
   Obituary   1971   *1026*

'Israel, Cricket in' T. Prittie   1975   *157*

Israel in England   1970   1971   *846*

Issac, Lieut. A. W. (Worcestershire)
   Obituary   1917   *193*

Issac, Capt. D. C. (Merchant Taylors)
   Obituary   1918   *190*

Issac, Capt. J. E. V. (Worcestershire)
   Obituary   1916   *177*

Issac, V. (Writer)
   with P. Thorn 'Hampshire Cricketers 1800-1982'
   Book Review   1984   *1258*

Issacs, Wilfrid's South Africans
  in England 1966 1967 *809*
  1969 1970 *770*
Issacson, R. F. (Marlborough)
  Obituary 1930/I *254*
Iverson, J. B. (Victoria; Australia)
  Obituary 1974 *1075*
IZingari in Egypt 1914 1915/I *475*
  1946 1947 *555*
Jack, Major J. C. (Merchant Taylors)
  Obituary 1919 *179*
Jack, K. M. (Queensland)
  Obituary 1984 *1202*
Jack, Pte. W. E. (Central Park C.C., Vancouver)
  Obituary 1918 *190*
Jackman, D. (East Suffolk C.C.)
  Obituary 1908/I *143*
Jackman, R. D. (Surrey; Western Province; Rhodesia; England)
  Cricketer of the Year 1981 *81*
  Photographs 1971 *515*
  1974 *539*
  1981 *74*
Jackson, A. A. (New South Wales; Australia)
  'The Archie Jackson Story'
  D. Frith Book Review 1975 *1120*
Jackson, A. B. (Derbyshire)
  Photograph 1965 *349*
Jackson, A. K. (Warwickshire)
  Obituary 1973 *1014*
Jackson, A. L. S. (Cheltenham; South America)
  Obituary 1984 *1202*
Jackson, D. C. (Western Province; Transvaal)
  Obituary 1978 *1085*
Jackson, Major E. (Doncaster Grammar School)
  Obituary 1919 *180*
Jackson, E. A. (Marlborough)
  Obituary 1923/I *299*
Jackson, Rt. Hon. Sir F. S. (Harrow; Cambridge University; Yorkshire; England)
  Appreciation of Lord Hawke 1939 *65*
  'Sir Stanley Jackson' H. Preston
  (Obituary Tribute) 1948 *74*
  'Jackson's Year' A. Gibson Book Review 1966 *1011*
  Portrait and Biography 1884 *xlii*
  'The Best Fast Bowler' 1944 *53*

Schools Notes	1888	*274*
	1889	*266*
	1890	*229*
'Tribute to Ranjitsinhji'	1934/I	*251*
Views on High Scoring and L.B.W. Rule	1899	*lxxiv*
Views on 'The Follow on'	1894	*xlix*
Jackson, Capt. G. L. (Harrow; Derbyshire)		
Obituary	1918	*191*
Jackson, Lieut. G. O. (St.Judes C.C., Winnipeg)		
Obituary	1918	*191*
Jackson, Capt. G. R. (Harrow; Derbyshire)		
Obituary	1967	*969*
Jackson, H. (Burton C.C., Isle of Man)		
Obituary	1911/I	*147*
Jackson, H. (Ireland)		
Obituary	1982	*1203*
Jackson, H. L. (Derbyshire; England)		
Benefit Match	1958	*310*
Cricketer of the Year	1959	*57*
Photographs	1950	*290*
	1954	*305*
	1955	*291*
	1958	*307*
	1959	*45*
	1960	*342*
Jackson, H. L. C. (St Jude's C.C., Winnipeg)		
Obituary	1918	*191*
Jackson, J. (Nottinghamshire; All England)		
Benefit Match	1875	*159*
Obituary	1902	*lxvi*
Jackson, K. L. T. (Rugby; Oxford University)		
Obituary	1983	*1248*
Jackson, Capt. R. R. (Loretto)		
Obituary	1918	*191*
Jackson, S. R. (Yorkshire)		
Obituary	1942	*360*
Jackson, V. E. (Leicestershire; New South Wales)		
Benefit Match	1957	*454*
Obituary	1966	*968*
Photographs	1952	*417*
	1954	*439*
	1955	*419*
	1956	*445*
Jacobs, M. C. (Natal Club Cricket)		
Obituary	1915/I	*228*

Jacobson, H. (Journalist)
Obituary   1898   *xliii*
Jacques, 2nd Lieut. D. W. (Gresham's)
Obituary   1917   *193*
Jaffray, J. P. (Journalist; Canadian Club Cricket)
Obituary   1935/I   *266*
Jagger, S. T. (Malvern; Cambridge University; Worcestershire; Sussex; Bedfordshire; Denbighshire; Wales)
Obituary   1965   *968*
Jai, L. P. (Bombay; India)
'L. P. Jai: Memories of a Great Batsman'
V. Raiji Book Review   1977   *1098*
Jakeman, F. (Yorkshire; Northamptonshire)
Photograph   1952   *452*
Jamiaca
in Bermuda   1975   1976   *1026*
in England   1970   1971   *747*
James, A. (Chairman Glamorgan)
Obituary   1960   *952*
James, 2nd Lieut. B. G. (Gloucestershire)
Obituary   1916   *178*
James, 2nd Lieut. D. C. (Clifton)
Obituary   1917   *193*
James, Capt and Adj. E. G. (Cheltenham)
Obituary   1917   *193*
James, Lieut. G. B. L. (Rossall)
Obituary   1918   *191*
James, G. E. (Groundsman West Kent C.C.)
Obituary   1928/I   *289*
James, G. T. H. (Tasmania)
Obituary   1968   *1001*
James, K. C. (Wellington, N.Z.; Northamptonshire; New Zealand)
Obituary   1977   *1044*
James, Lord of Hereford (Rt. Hon. Sir H.; Cheltenham)
Obituary   1912/I   *172*
James, R. A. (Eton)
Obituary   1957   *945*
James, R. V. (New South Wales; South Australia)
Obituary   1984   *1202*
Jameson, J. A. (Taunton; Warwickshire; England)
Benefit Match   1975   *591*
Photograph   1966   *587*
                                                                 1972   *598*
                                                                 1975   *71*
                                                                                  582
Retirement   1977   *115*

Schools Note	1960	*745*
1031 runs Schools Averages	1960	*793*
Jameson, T. O. (Harrow; Hampshire; Ireland)		
Obituary	1966	*968*
Jamieson, D. J. T. (Fettes; Aberdeen)		
Obituary	1964	*950*
Janson, F. W. (Westminster)		
Obituary	1905	*civ*
Japan, Cricket in	1984	*1146*
Jaques, Capt. A. (Aldenham; Huntingdonshire)		
Obituary	1916	*177*
Jardine, D. R. (Winchester; Oxford University; Surrey; England)		
Obituary	1959	*932*
Portrait and Biography	1928/I	*312*
Schools Notes	1918	*156*
	1920/I	*260,263*
'Stuart Surridge – Surrey's Inspiration'	1957	*88*
Jardine, M. R. (Fettes; Oxford University; Middlesex)		
Obituary	1948	*784*
Jardine, Flt-Lt. R. G. (Ridley College, Ontario)		
Obituary	1919	*180*
Jarman, A. (Bradford C.C.)		
Obituary	1911/I	*148*
Jarman, B. N. (South Australia; Australia)		
Tribute to A. T. W. Grout	1969	*981*
Jarrett, H. H. (Warwickshire; Glamorgan)		
Obituary	1984	*1202*
Jarvis, A. H. (South Australia; Australia)		
Obituary	1934/I	*269*
Jarvis, C. J. E. (Harrow)		
Obituary	1894	*xxxv*
Jarvis, K. B. S. (Kent)		
Photographs	1977	*443*
	1982	*445*
Jarvis, L. K. (Harrow; Cambridge University; Norfolk)		
Obituary	1939	*911*
Jaswant, S. W. (Kenya)		
Obituary	1971	*1026*
Javed Miandad Khan (Karachi; Sind; Habib Bank; Sussex; Glamorgan; Pakistan)		
Cricketer of the Year	1982	*79*
Photographs	1981	*401*
	1982	*72*
		403
Jayasinghe, S. (Leicestershire; Ceylon)		
Photograph	1963	*503*

Jayasundera, D. S. (Ceylon)
Obituary   1965   *968*
Jayawardena, L. (St Joseph's, Colombo)
Obituary   1970   *1022*
Jayaweera, (Ceylon Colts)
Obituary   1969   *981*
Jayawickreme, S. S. (Ceylon)
Obituary   1984   *1202*
Jayes, T. (Leicestershire)
Benefit Match   1913/II   *305*
Obituary   1914/I   *186*
Jeacocke, A. (Surrey)
Obituary   1962   *987*
Jeanes, W. H. (Australian Board of Control)
Obituary   1959   *933*
Jeans, Canon G. E. (Cricket Fanatic)
Obituary   1922/I   *258*
Jeeves, P. (Warwickshire)
Obituary   1917   *193*
Jeeves, T. (Hertfordshire; Scotland)
Obituary   1908/I   *143*
Jeffries, L. Cpl. H. G. (Windsor Club Cricket)
Obituary   1916   *178*
Jeffrey, G. E. (Rugby; Cambridge University)
Obituary   1892   *xxxiii*
Jeffreys, Rt. Hon. A. F. (Hampshire)
Obituary   1907   *cxiii*
Jeffreys, H. (Scorer Glamorgan)
Obituary   1975   *1079*
Jelf, Comdr. H. F. D. (Derbyshire)
Obituary   1945   *333*
Jelf, R. H. (Eton)
Obituary   1941   *387*
Jellicoe, Admiral Earl (IZingari)
Obituary   1936/I   *278*
Jellicoe, Rev. F. G. G. (Haileybury; Oxford University; Hampshire)
Obituary   1928/I   *290*
Jenkin, Capt. L. F. (Dulwich)
Obituary   1919   *180*
Jenkins, Capt. E. K. (Army)
Obituary   1917   *194*
Jenkins, Lt-Col. L. (St.Bees)
Obituary   1920/I   *154*
Jenkins, 2nd Lieut. P. G. (Glenalmond)
Obituary   1918   *191*

Jenkins, R. O. (Worcestershire; England)
Benefit Match	1954	*613*
Cricketer of the Year	1950	*79*
Photographs	1950	*73*
	1951	*567*
	1953	*590*
	1957	*599*

Jenkins, V. G. J. (Llandovery College; Oxford University; Glamorgan)
'Leslie Ames – A Century of Centuries'	1951	*91*
Australia v England. Sidelights on the Test'	1948	*90*
'F. R. Brown – Leader of Men'	1952	*100*
'Thirty years an Umpire (F. Chester)'	1954	*103*
'Tribute to Hutton'	1950	*93*

Jenkins, W. H. P. (Free Foresters)
Obituary	1918	*241*

Jenner, F. D. (Sussex)
Obituary	1954	*926*

Jenner, 2nd Lieut. G. R. (Ardingly)
Obituary	1917	*194*

Jenner, Rev. H. L. (Harrow; Cambridge University)
Obituary	1899	*xlix*

Jenner, W. (Victoria College Jersey)
Schools Notes	1983	*906*
	1984	*837*
1227 runs Schools Averages	1983	*943*
1010 runs Schools Averages	1984	*870*

Jenner-Fust, H. (Eton; Cambridge University; Kent; President M.C.C.)
Obituary	1905	*xcvii*
'The Oldest Living Cricketer'		
S. H. Pardon	1898	*lix*

Jennings, C. B. (South Australia; Queensland; Australia)
Obituary	1951	*925*

Jennings, D. J. (Groundsman Marlborough)
Obituary	1939	*911*

Jennings, Cpl. D. W. (Kent)
Obituary	1919	*180*

Jennings, G. A. (Warwickshire)
Obituary	1960	*952*

Jennings, Capt. L. S. (Nelson College, New Zealand; Canterbury University, New Zealand)
Obituary	1917	*194*

Jennings, T. S. (Surrey; Devon)
Obituary	1973	*1010*

Jephson, D. L. A. (Cambridge University; Surrey)
'Fielding in 1900'	1901	*lxxvi*
'Leg-Break Bowling in 1901'	1902	*lxxxv*

Obituary	1927/I	*282*
'Play Back'	1904	*lxviii*
Tributes to: V. F. S. Crawford	1923/I	*294*
Gregor MacGregor	1920/I	*247*

Jepson, A. (Nottinghamshire; Umpire)

Benefit Match	1952	*481*

Jepson, Lieut. H. R. (Nanaimo C.C., British Columbia)

Obituary	1918	191

Jersey, 7th Earl of (President M.C.C.)

Obituary	1916	*178*

Jervis, Hon. W. M. (Derbyshire)

Obituary	1910/I	*140*

Jervis, Col. W. S. (Warwickshire)

Obituary	1921/I	*228*

Jerwood, Major J. H. (Oakham)

Obituary	1919	*180*

Jesson, 2nd Lieut. A (Witley C.C.)

Obituary	1917	*194*

Jesson, Major R. W. F. (Sherborne; Oxford University; Hampshire)

Obituary	1918	*191*

Jessop, G. L. (Beccles College Staff and Students; Cambridge University; Gloucestershire; London County; England)

'The Croucher' G. Brodribb Book Review	1975	*1120*
Fastest Hundreds in Test Cricket	1983	*107*
'Gilbert Jessop – The Most Exciting Cricketer of All'		
R. Ryder	1975	*137*
Obituary	1956	*972*
Photograph	1975	*138*
Portrait and Biography	1898	*lii*
1058 runs, 100 wkts Schools Note	1896	*341*

Jessop, H. (Gloucestershire)

Obituary	1926/I	*287*

Jessop, N. A. (Harrow; Oxford University; Norfolk)

Obituary	1979	*1091*

Jessop, O. W. T. (Cheltenham; Gloucestershire)

Obituary	1942	*360*

Jesty, T. E. (Hampshire; Border; Griqualand West; Canterbury)

Cricketer of the Year	1983	*67*
Photographs	1973	*417*
	1979	*405*
	1983	*Plate*

Jesuthasan, A. (Treasurer Ceylon Cricket Association)

Obituary	1963	*1034*

Jewell, Major A. N. (Felsted; Worcestershire; Orange Free State)

Obituary	1923/I	*300*

Jewell, 2nd Lieut. D. M. H. (Felsted)
Obituary   1917   *194*
Jewell, H. E. (Journalist)
Obituary   1923/I   *300*
Jewell, J. E. (Felsted; Orange Free State)
Obituary   1967   *969*
Jewell, J. M. H. (Worcestershire)
Obituary   1947   *691*
Jewell, Major M. F. S. (Worcestershire; Sussex)
Obituary   1979   *1080*
Jilani, M. B. (Northern India; India)
Obituary   1943   *387*
Jinkins, G. (Melbourne C.C.)
Bowling Feat   1960   *126*
Jobson, E. P. (Worcestershire)
Obituary   1910/I   *140*
Joel, J. (Eton Curator)
Obituary   1904   *lxxxiv*
John, G. (Trinidad)
Obituary   1945   *333*
Johns, A. E. (Victoria)
Obituary   1935/I   *266*
Johns, 2nd Lieut. B. C. (St.John's, Leatherhead)
Obituary   1919   *180*
Johns, D. F. V. (Buckinghamshire)
Obituary   1981   *1144*
Johnson, Capt. A. (Wellingborough Grammar School)
Obituary   1919   *180*
Johnson, Pte. B. A. (Uppingham)
Obituary   1917   *194*
Johnson, C. (Yorkshire)
Photograph   1974   *598*
Johnson, C. L. (Dublin University; Gentlemen of Ireland; Transvaal; South
Africa)
Obituary   1909/I   *139*
Johnson, Capt. D. C. (Malvern)
Obituary   1919   *180*
Johnson, F. (Surrey)
Obituary   1924/I   *26*
Johnson, Major-Gen. F. F. (Cheltenham)
Obituary   1932/I   *24*
Johnson, 2nd Lieut. F. L. (Upper Canada College)
Obituary   1918   *19*

Johnson, G. H. (Northamptonshire)
Obituary	1966	*968*

Johnson, G. R. (Bury St.Edmunds School; Cambridge University; Suffolk)
Obituary	1920/I	*177*

Johnson, G. W. (Kent; Transvaal)
Photographs	1971	*400*
	1976	*441*
	1979	*421*
'South Africa: Progress Towards Non-Racial Cricket'	1983	*104*

Johnson, H. L. (Derbyshire)
Photograph	1961	*337*

Johnson, I. W. (Victoria; Australia)
Awarded M.B.E.	1956	*75*
'Cricket at the Crossroads'		
Book Review	1958	*1016*
Tribute to Sir F. Worrell	1968	*122*
Views on Growing Pains of Cricket	1956	*85*

Johnson, J. (Secretary Nottinghamshire)
Obituary	1878	*202*

Johnson, K. O. E. (Australian Services Team Manager)
Message re 1945 Australian Team	1946	*157*
Obituary	1973	*1010*

Johnson, L. A. (Surrey; Northamptonshire)
Photograph	1967	*510*

Johnson, L. J. (Queensland; Australia)
Obituary	1978	*1074*

Johnson, P. D. (Nottingham High School; Cambridge University; Nottinghamshire)
Photograph	1976	*521*
Schools Notes	1969	*753*
	1970	*813*
1016 runs, 75 wkts Schools Averages	1969	*787*
1038 runs, 91 wkts Schools Averages	1970	*846*

Johnson, P. R. (Eton; Cambridge University; Somerset)
Obituary	1960	*953*

Johnson, R. B. (Forest School)
Obituary	1928/I	*290*

Johnson, S. (President Mount Vernon C.C., New York)
Obituary	1915/I	*228*

Johnson, Capt. S. F. (Westminster)
Obituary	1918	*192*

Johnson, T. (Grange C.C.)
Obituary	1919	*207*

Johnson, Major T. H. F. (Bradfield)
Obituary	1920/I	*177*

Johnson, W. J. (Australian Test Selector)
  Obituary   1942   *360*
Johnston, Col. A. C. (Winchester; Hampshire)
  Obituary   1953   *943*
Johnston, Major F. (Charterhouse)
  Obituary   1919   *180*
Johnston, R. H. (Clifton; Scotland)
  Obituary   1911/I   *148*
Johnston, W. (Otago)
  Obituary   1949   *872*
Johnston, W. A. (Victoria; Australia)
  Cricketer of the Year   1949   *96*
  Photograph   1949   *75*
Johnstone, C. P. (Rugby; Madras; Cambridge University; Kent)
  Obituary   1975   *1080*
Johnstone, Capt. F. J. L. (Eton)
  Obituary   1917   *194*
Jones, A. (Glamorgan; Western Australia; Northern Transvaal; Natal)
  Career Figures   1984   *1250*
  Cricketer of the Year   1978   *100*
  Photographs   1964   *376*
     1966   *381*
     1968   *397*
     1973   *387*
     1975   *395*
     1978   *91*
        385
     1984   *Plate*
Jones, A. K. G. (Bedford Modern School)
  Schools Notes   1982   *858*
  1022 runs Schools Averages   1982   *867*
Jones, 2nd Lieut. A. L. G. (Malvern)
  Obituary   1919   *181*
Jones, A. O. (Bedford Modern School; Cambridge University; Nottinghamshire; London County; England)
  Obituary   1915/I   *228*
  Portrait and Biography   1900   *lxiv*
Jones, B. (Journalist)
  'Gone with the Indians' Book Review   1973   *1056*
  'Gone with the Kiwis' Book Review   1973   *1056*
Jones, B. (New York Club Cricket)
  Obituary   1911/I   *148*
Jones, C. J. E. (Secretary and Founder London Counties C.C.)
  Obituary   1967   *96*
Jones, C. L. (Lancashire)
  Obituary   1905   *xcvii*

Jones, Lieut. D. W. L. (Bradfield)
    Obituary   1917   *195*

Jones, E. (South Australia; Australia)
    Obituary   1944   *316*

Jones, E. W. (Glamorgan)
    Photographs   1971   *351*
                                                1974   *396*
                                                1978   *385*

Jones, Lt-Col. F. A. (Old Lansdown C.C.)
    Obituary   1917   *195*

Jones, Capt. H. (Gloucestershire)
    Obituary   1919   *181*

Jones, H. V. (Gloucestershire; Journalist)
    Obituary   1921/I   *228*

Jones, I. J. (Glamorgan; England)
    Photographs   1964   *376*
                  1967   *388*

Jones, J. F. (Fettes; Scotland)
    Schools Note   1930/I   *284,305*
    1000 runs Schools Averages   1930/II   *630*

Jones, Capt. J. L. T. (Llangollen County School)
    Obituary   1918   *192*

Jones, 2nd Lieut. J. V. (King's Bruton)
    Obituary   1917   *195*

Jones, 2nd Lieut. J. Y. P. (Blundells)
    Obituary   1919   *181*

Jones, Hon. Sir L. M. (Toronto C.C.)
    Obituary   1918   *230*

Jones, L. N. (Cheshire)
    Obituary   1963   *1034*

Jones, Brig-Gen. L. O. W. (Winchester)
    Obituary   1919   *181*

Jones, M. (Harrow; Oxford University)
    Obituary   1906   *xciii*

Jones, P. H. (Kent; Suffolk)
    Photograph   1962   *448*

Jones, P. S. T. (Western Province; South Africa)
    Obituary   1955   *933*

Jones, R. S. (Chatham House, Ramsgate)
    Obituary   1936/I   *278*

Jones, R. T. (Eton; Oxford University; Shropshire; Staffordshire)
    Obituary   1941   *398*

Jones, Major R. W. F. (Ridley College, Ontario)
    Obituary   1919   *181*

Jones, S. P. (New South Wales; Queensland; Auckland; Australia)
Obituary 1952 *957*
Jones, T. A. (New Westminster C.C., British Columbia)
Obituary 1920/I *154*
Jones, W. E. (Cheshire)
Obituary 1958 *961*
Jones, W. E. (Glamorgan)
Benefit Match 1954 *357*
Career Figures 1959 *491* ·
Jones, W. L. (Midlands Club Cricket Conference)
Obituary 1974 *1075*
Jones, W. R. (Vice President Australian Board of Control)
Obituary 1933/I *251*
Jones, W. T. (Umpire)
Obituary 1970 *1022*
Jones-Bateman, Rev. J. B. (Cambridge University)
Obituary 1912/I *183*
Jordan, C. (West Indian Umpire)
Obituary 1983 *1248*
Jordan, Lt-Col. H. G. B. (Marlborough; Derbyshire)
Obituary 1982 *1203*
Jordan, Col. J. P. (Journalist)
Obituary 1957 *945*
Jordan, T. C. (U.S.A.)
Obituary 1926/I *277*
Jose, Dr. A. D. (Oxford University; Kent; South Australia)
Obituary 1973 *1010*
Jost, Lieut. N. R. M. (Wanderers C.C., Edmonton, Canada)
Obituary 1917 *195*
Jourdain, Capt. E. N. (Suffolk Regiment)
Obituary 1916 *178*
Jowett, C. J. C. (Christ's Hospital; Dorset)
Obituary 1967 *970*
Joy, F. D. H. (Winchester; Somerset)
Obituary 1967 *970*
Joy, Nancy (English Women's Cricket)
'Maiden Over' Book Review 1951 *999*
Joy, Rev. P. C. (Winchester)
Obituary 1923/I *300*
Joy, Col. R. C. G. (Winchester; Essex)
Obituary 1976 *1104*
Joyce, 2nd Lieut. E. G. (Framlingham)
Obituary 1917 *195*
Joice, R. (Bedford Grammar School; Oxford University; Leicestershire)
Obituary 1909/I *139*

Joynson, Lt-Col. W. O. H. (President Kent)
Obituary 1969 *982*
Jubilee Honours 1977 1978 *107*
Jubilee Test England v Australia at Lord's 1977
Photograph 1978 *84*
Scoreboard 1978 *324*
Juckes, 2nd Lieut. G. F. (King's, Canterbury)
Obituary 1916 *178*
Juckes, R. H. (King's, Canterbury; Sussex)
Obituary 1982 *1203*
Judd, F. S. H. (Eton)
Obituary 1936/I *292*
Judge, P. F. (St.Paul's; Middlesex; Glamorgan; Bengal)
Schools note 1934/I *307*
84 wkts Schools Averages 1934/II *615*
Judge, 2nd Lieut. W. S. (Rugby)
Obituary 1917 *195*
'Judge Hits Cricket Ban for Six' 1978 *128*
Jungkurth, A. G. (Philadelphia Club Cricket)
Obituary 1918 *230*
Jupp, A. D. (Tonbridge)
Obituary 1928/I *290*
Jupp, H. (Surrey; England)
Benefit Match 1882 *173*
Biography 1870 *84*
Presentation to 1877 *157*
Jupp, V. W. C. (Sussex; Northamptonshire; England)
Obituary 1961 *949*
Portrait and Biography 1928/I *311*
Kallicharran, A. I. (Guyana; Warwickshire; Queensland; Transvaal; West Indies)
Action Photograph 1976 *41*
Cricketer of the Year 1983 *69*
Photographs 1979 *563*
 1983 *Plate*
Kanga, P. D. (Parsees)
Obituary 1929/I *248*
Kanhai, R. B. (Trinidad; Western Australia; Tasmania; British Guiana; Warwickshire; West Indies)
Benefit Match 1978 *582*
'Blasting for Runs' Book Review 1967 *1019*
Cricketer of the Year 1964 *85*
Photographs 1964 *71*
 1969 *603*
 1972 *596*
Warwickshire's World Record Photograph 1975 *71*

'With Wisden Trophy' Photographs   1974 *43*
                 1976 *68*

Kannangara, R. L. (Wesley College, Ceylon)
 Obituary   1974 *1084*

Kapil, Dev (Haryana; Northamptonshire; North Zone; India)
 Cricketer of the Year   1983 *71*
 'Moment of Triumph' with World Cup Photograph 1984 *Plate*
 Photograph   1983 *Plate*

Kardar, A. H. (Formerly Abdul Hafeez; Oxford University; Warwickshire; India; Pakistan)
 'Green Shadows' Book Review   1960 *997*
 'Growth of Pakistan Cricket'   1954 *97*
 'Inaugural Test Matches' Book Review 1955 *990*
 'Test Status on Trial' Book Review   1956 *1023*

Karunaratne, E. (President Ceylon Cricket Association)
 Obituary   1978 *1085*

Kay, J. (Journalist; Writer)
 'Ashes to Hassett' Book Review   1952 *1011*
 'England Down Under' Book Review 1960 *999*
 'Lancashire' Book Review   1973 *1052*
 'Reshaping Lancashire Cricket'   1971 *93*

Kaye, Lt-Col. H. J. (Harrow; Yorkshire)
 Obituary   1954 *926*

Kaye, Dr. H. W. (Winchester)
 Obituary   1923/I *300*

Kaye, Lt-Col. J. L. (Winchester)
 Obituary   1918 *230*

Kaye, L. R. (Phoenix C.C., Halifax, Canada)
 Obituary   1915/I *230*

Kearsley, Col. A. H. C. (Buckinghamshire)
 Obituary   1968 *1001*

Keating, F. (Journalist)
 'Another Bloody Day in Paradise' Book Review 1982 *1266*

Keating, J. L. (Victoria)
 Obituary   1963 *1034*

Keatinge, Lieut. C. F. (Winchester)
 Obituary   1945 *322*

Keay, 2nd Lieut. R. N. (Perthshire)
 Obituary   1917 *195*

Keeble, F. H. G. (Staten Island C.C.)
 Obituary   1926/I *277*

Keely, E. R. P. (Shrewsbury)
 Obituary   1930/I *254*

Keenan, W. F. (U.S.A. Club Cricketer)
 Obituary   1935/I *267*

Keene, J. W. (Surrey; Worcestershire; Scotland)
Obituary	1934/I	*279*

Keeton, W. W. (Nottinghamshire; England)
Obituary	1981	*1144*
Photograph	1950	*460*
Portrait and Biography	1940	*41*

Keigwin, 2nd Lieut. H. D. (St.Paul's; Cambridge University; Essex; Scotland)
Obituary	1917	*195*

Keigwin, R. P. (Clifton; Cambridge University; Essex; Gloucestershire)
Obituary	1973	*1010*

Keir, 2nd Lieut. P. C. (Barnsley C.C.)
Obituary	1919	*181*

Keith, 2nd Lieut. D. H. (Glenalmond)
Obituary	1918	*192*

Keith, G. L. (Hampshire; Somerset; Western Province)
Obituary	1977	*1051*

Kekewich, Capt. J. (Eton; Sandhurst)
Obituary	1918	*214*

Kelaart, M. (Ceylon Club Cricket)
Obituary	1969	*982*

Kelaart, T. (Ceylon Club Cricket)
Obituary	1951	*925*

Kelleway, C. E. (New South Wales; Australia)
Obituary	1945	*333*
Testimonial Match	1935/II	*681*

Kellick, C. M. (New South Wales)
Obituary	1919	*207*

Kelly, F. F. (U.S.A.)
Obituary	1945	*334*

Kelly, Lt-Col. G. H. F. (Sandhurst)
Obituary	1916	*219*

Kelly, G. N. B. (Stonyhurst College; Ireland)
Obituary	1982	*1203*

Kelly, G. W. F. (Stonyhurst College; Oxford University)
Obituary	1953	*951*

Kelly, J. F. (Club Cricketer)
Obituary	1925/I	*289*

Kelly, J. J. (Victoria; New South Wales; Australia)
Benefit Match	1907	*498*
Obituary	1939	*911*
Portrait and Biography	1903	*lxxxix*

Kelly, J. M. (Lancashire; Derbyshire)
Benefit Match	1961	*346*
Obituary	1980	*1150*
Record of Service	1961	*652*

Kelly, T. J. D. (Victoria; Australia)
Obituary 1894 *xxxvii*
Kelly, W. (Victoria)
Obituary 1969 *982*
Kelson, G. M. (Kent)
Obituary 1921/I *229*
Kemble, A. T. (Lancashire; Cumberland)
Obituary 1926/I *277*
Kemble, Lt-Col. H. (Bath College)
Obituary 1918 *192*
Kemnitz, E. J. (Nelson, New Zealand)
Obituary 1930/I *254*
Kemnitz, J. (Albion C.C.)
Obituary 1917 *252*
Kemp, A. F. (Harrow; Kent)
Obituary 1941 *399*
Kemp, C. F. (President Kent)
Obituary 1908/I *143*
Kemp, C. W. M. (Harrow; Oxford University; Kent)
Obituary 1934/I *269*
Kemp, H. F. (Harrow)
Obituary 1943 *378*
Kemp, Sir K. H. 12th Bart. (Sandhurst; Norfolk)
Obituary 1937/I *274*
Kemp, M. C. (Harrow; Oxford University; Kent)
Obituary 1952 *958*
'Views on 'The Follow On' 1894 *l*
Views on Throwing 1895 *lv*
Kemp-Welch, Capt. G. D. (Charterhouse; Cambridge University; Warwickshire)
Obituary 1945 *323*
Kempe, W. J. (Bromsgrove School)
Obituary 1916 *178*
Kempis, G. S. (Transvaal)
Obituary 1949 *865*
Kempson, Rt. Rev. E. H. (Rugby)
Obituary 1932/I *247*
Kempson, S. M. E. (Cheltenham; Cambridge University)
Obituary 1895 *xxxix*
Kempster, J. F. (Ireland)
Obituary 1979 *1092*
Kempster, Major-Gen. W. F. H. (Cheltenham)
Obituary 1953 *943*
Kempton, A. (Surrey Colts)
Obituary 1958 *961*
Kendall, T. (Victoria; Tasmania; Australia)
Obituary 1925/I *270*

Kendle, Rev. W. J. (Sherborne; Hampshire)
  Obituary   1921/I   *229*
Kennard, Rt. Rev. Monsignor C. H. (University College, Oxford)
  Obituary   1921/I   *230*
Kennaway, Rev. C. L. (Norfolk)
  Obituary   1941   *399*
Kennaway, C. R. (Harrow)
  Obituary   1915/I   *230*
Kennedy, A. (Lancashire)
  Photographs   1976   *457*
                                                  1981   *460*
Kennedy, A. S. (Hampshire; England)
  Benefit Match   1927/II   *244*
  Obituary   1960   *953*
  Portrait and Biography   1933/I   *272*
Kennedy, C. M. (Sussex)
  Obituary   1907   *cxiii*
Kennedy, Sgt. D. (Uddington C.C., Scotland)
  Obituary   1918   *192*
Kennedy, H. L. (Haberdasher's Aske School)
  Schools Note   1942   *246*
Kennedy, 2nd lieut. T. C. (Edinburgh Academy)
  Obituary   1916   *179*
Kennerley-Rumford, R. G. M. (Eton)
  Obituary   1924/I   *262*
Kenney-Herbert, Brig.-Gen. A. R. (Rugby)
  Obituary   1917   *252*
Kenney-Herbert, E. M. (Rugby; Oxford University; Warwickshire)
  Obituary   1917   *252*
Kent County Cricket Club
  County Badge   1950   *376*
                                                  ad passim
'Early Kent Cricketers' J. Goulstone
  Book Review   1972   *1091*
  'The Great Years and Great Players of Kent
  R. L. Arrowsmith   1966   *138*
  in the U.S.A. 1903   1904   *461*
  'Kent' R. L. Arrowsmith Book Review   1972   *1095*
  'Kent – The Glory Years' D. Fowle
  Book Review   1975   *1115*
  'Kent's Triumphant Revival' D. Moore   1974   *74*
  Kent Win Two Titles Note on   1979   *78*
  'One Hundred Years of Kent Cricket 1870-1970'
  The Club Book Review   1971   *1082*
  'A Short History of Kent Cricket for the past 30 Years and More'
  G. Marsham   1907   *lxxxv*

311

'The Story of Canterbury Cricket Week'

H. W. Warner Book Review		1961	*992*
Survivors of Noted Victory Note on		1950	*118*
'The Tonbridge Nursery' W. McCanlis'		1907	*xcvi*
Team Portraits			
Gillette Cup Winners	1967	1968	*60*
County Champions	1970	1971	*64*
Dual Champions (John Player League			
and Benson and Hedges Cup)	1973	1974	*47*
Gillette Cup Winners	1974	1975	*444*
	1975	1976	*444*
	1976	1977	*446*
	1977	1978	*431*
	1978	1979	*423*
	1979	1980	*444*
	1980	1981	*448*
	1981	1982	*447*
	1982	1983	*458*
	1983	1984	*421*

'The White Horse and the Kangaroo'

C. Porter Book Review	1982	*1258*

Kent, Air-Com. H. R. H. Duke of

Obituary	1943	*365*

Kent, Lieut. E. (Borlase School, Marlow)

Obituary	1918	*192*

Kent, K. G. (King Edward's, Birmingham; Warwickshire)

Obituary	1976	*1104*

Kentfield, R. W. (Lancashire; Sussex)

Obituary	1905	*xcviii*

Kenworthy, Capt. S. (Edinburgh Nomads C.C.)

Obituary	1917	*196*

Kenyon, D. (Worcestershire; England)

Benefit Match	1958	*622*
Career Records	1966	*853*
Cricketer of the Year	1963	*161*
Photographs	1951	*567*
	1952	*566*
	1953	*590*
	1954	*600*
	1955	*569*
	1957	*599*
	1963	*160*

Kenyon, 2nd Lieut. J. de W. (Giggleswick School)

Obituary	1916	*179*

Kenyon, M. N. (Eton; Lancashire)

Obituary	1961	*949*

Kenyon-Slade, Rt. Hon. Col. N. S. (IZingari)
Obituary   1909/I   *140*

Kermode, A. (New South Wales; Lancashire)
Obituary   1935/I   *267*

Kerr, J. R. (Loretto; Scotland)
Obituary   1973   *1010*
Schools Notes   1899   *lxxxvi*
78 wkts Schools Averages   1899   *362*

Kerr, S. (St. George's College, Salisbury, Rhodesia; Gloucestershire)
Obituary   1975   *1080*
Schoolboy Prodigy   1973   *134*

Kershaw, P/O. A. (Rugby)
Obituary   1942   *350*

Kershaw, Capt. C. A. (Royal Navy)
Obituary   1973   *1010*

Kershaw, H. (Staten Island C.C.)
Obituary   1910/I   *151*

Kershaw, J. E. (Lancashire)
Obituary   1904   *lxxxvi*

Kershaw, R. (Yorkshire Committee)
Obituary   1926/I   *277*

Kerwood, Lieut. P. M. (Bromsgrove School)
Obituary   1916   *179*

Kettering   Note on County Ground   1969   *142*
         Plan of County Ground   1953   *47*
                              ad passim

Kettle, M. K. (Northamptonshire)
Photograph   1969   *516*

Kettlewell, Lt.-Col. H. W. (Eton; Somerset)
Obituary   1965   *973*

Key, 2nd Lieut. F. B. (Lichfield School; Lichfield C.C.)
Obituary   1917   *196*

Key, Sir K. J. Bart. (Clifton; Oxford University; Surrey)
Obituary   1933/I   *251*

Key, L. H. (Somerset)
Obituary   1972   *1053*

Keyser, C. E. (Hertfordshire)
Obituary   1930/I   *254*

Khan, G. M. (Journalist)
'The Rise of Cricket in Pakistan'   1967   *153*

Kidd, Capt. C. E. (Trinity College, Port Hope)
Obituary   1920/I   *155*

Kidd, Major G. E. (Army)
Obituary   1917   *196*

Kidd, Dr. P. M. (Uppingham; Kent)
   Obituaries   1944   *316*
                                     1945   *347*
Kidderminster
   Plan of County Ground   1968   *621*
                                     1974   *585*
Kiddle, P/O. H. P. H. (Dulwich)
   Obituary   1945   *323*
Kidson, P/O. M. W. T. (Lancing)
   Obituary   1943   *365*
Kiernan, C. (Victoria)
   Obituary   1927/I   *295*
Kilbracken, 1st Baron (Rugby)
   Obituary   1933/I   *246*
Kilburn, J. M. (Journalist; Writer)
   'A Century of Yorkshire Cricket'
   Book Review   1964   *997*
   'History of Yorkshire County Cricket 1924-1949'
   Book Review   1951   *989*
   'A History of Yorkshire Cricket'
   Book Review   1971   *1070*
   'Over 100 Years of Scarborough Festival'   1977   *151*
   'Statham and Trueman: An Appreciation'   1962   *134*
   'The Story of Yorkshire'   1955   *105*
   'Herbert Sutcliffe'   1979   *96*
   'Thanks to Cricket' Book Review   1973   *1056*
   Tribute to Sir F. Worrell   1968   *122*
Kilby, 2nd Lieut. J. (Bristol and District Cricket Association)
   Obituary   1917   *196*
Kilby, L. (Physiotherapist Kent)
   Obituary   1975   *1080*
Killick, E. H. (Sussex)
   Benefit Match   1911/II   *136*
   Obituary   1949   *865*
Killick, Rev. E. T. (St.Paul's; Cambridge University; Middlesex; England)
   Obituary   1954   *920*
   Schools Notes   1925/I   *319*
                                         1926/I   *302*
                                                      304
                                                     321
                                     1927/I   *312,333,334*
Kilner, N. (Yorkshire; Warwickshire)
   Benefit Match   1938   *547*
   Obituary   1980   *1154*
Kilner, R. (Yorkshire; England)
   Benefit Match   1926/II   *6*

Obituary	1929/I	*248*
Portrait and Biography	1924/1	*277*

Kinch, T. (Durham)

Obituary	1945	*334*

Kinder, Cpl. H. (Middleton C.C.)

Obituary	1919	*181*

King George VI at Oval Photograph 1947 *36*

King, B. P. (Worcestershire; Lancashire)

Obituary	1971	*1026*

King, Capt. C. E. D. (Wellington; Army)

Obituary	1917	*196*

King, C. J. S. (Felsted)

Obituary	1929/I	*250*

King, C. S. (Southern Tasmania)

Obituary	1960	*953*

King, D. (Secretary Canadian Cricket Association)

Obituary	1978	*1074*

King, E. H. (Warwickshire)

Obituary	1982	*1203*

King, 2nd Lieut. E. W. (Sherborne)

Obituary	1919	*181*

King, G. L. (Rugby; Sussex)

Obituary	1945	*334*

King, Sir H. C. (Marlborough; Madras Presidency)

Obituary	1921/I	*230*

King, H. D. (Middlesex)

Obituary	1975	*1080*

King, H. P. (Essex Committee; Clacton Festival)

Obituary	1969	*990*

King, J. (Scarborough C.C.)

Obituary	1917	*253*

King, J. B. (Philadelphia; U.S.A.)

Obituary	1966	*969*

King, J. H. (Leicestershire; England)

Benefit Matches	1911/II	*184*
	1924/II	*308*
Obituary	1947	*691*

King, 2nd Lieut. M. (Borlase School, Marlow)

Obituary	1918	*192*

King, P. (Scotland)

Obituary	1911/I	*148*

King, Lieut. R. H. (Mansfield C.C.; Nottinghamshire Colts)

Obituary	1918	*192*

King, S. (Groundsman Oxford University)

Obituary	1926/I	*277*

King, W. E. (Bedfordshire)
  Obituary 1963 1034

King-Turner, Dr. C. J. (Cheltenham; Gloucestershire)
  Obituary 1973 1011

Kingdom, 2nd Lieut. L. L. (Bishop's Stortford C.C.)
  Obituary 1917 196

Kingham, 2nd Lieut. L. A. (Oakham)
  Obituary 1918 192

Kingscote, Col. H. B. (Gloucestershire)
  Obituary 1916 179

Kingsley, D. C. (Beaumont College)
  Schools Note 1946 293
  81 wkts Schools Averages 1946 313

Kingston Festival 1947 1948 598

Kingston, F. W. (Cambridge University; Northamptonshire)
  Obituary 1934/I 276

Kingston, Rev. G. H. (Northamptonshire)
  Obituary 1960 95

Kingston, H. E. (Northamptonshire)
  Obituary 1956 974

Kingston, J. P. (Northamptonshire; Warwickshire)
  Obituary 1930/I 25

Kingston, W. H. (Northamptonshire)
  Obituary 1957 94

Kinloch, H. (Matabeland)
  Obituary 1895 xl

Kinnear, A. W. (Chicago Cricket Association)
  Obituary 1920/I 19

Kinneir, S. P. (Wiltshire; Warwickshire; England)
  Obituary 1929/I 25
  Portrait and Biography 1912/I 18

Kinsey, 2nd Lieut. T. (Bristol Grammar School)
  Obituary 1918 19

Kippax, A. F. (New South Wales; Australia)
  Obituary 1973 101
  Testimonial Match 1950 84

Kirby, H. R. (Malvern; Sussex)
  Obituary 1978 108

Kirchhoffer, Hon. J. N. (Canada)
  Obituary 1916 21

Kirk, E. C. (Surrey)
  Obituary 1933/I 25

Kirk, L. (Nottinghamshire)
  Obituary 1954 92

Kirkpatrick, Sir J. (Civil Service)
  Obituary 1900 l

Kirmani, S. M. H. (Mysore; India)
Schools Note   1968   *761*

Kirsten, P. N. (Western Province; Sussex; Derbyshire)
Photographs   1979   *344*
     1981   *371*

Kirton, H. O. (Warwickshire)
Obituary   1975   *1080*

Kirwan, Rev. J. H. (Eton; Cambridge University; Surrey)
Obituary   1900   *liii*

Kirwan, Rev. R. M. (Forest School; Incogniti)
Obituary   1917   *196*

Kissling, H. P. (Auckland)
Obituary   1930/I   *254*

Kitcat, S. A. P. (Marlborough; Gloucestershire)
Obituary   1943   *378*

Kitchen, M. J. (Somerset)
Photographs   1967   *545*
     1973   *516*
Testimonial Match   1974   *706*

Kitchin, Capt. E. H. (Bradfield)
Obituary   1917   *197*

Kitchin, L. (Journalist; Writer)
'L. Hutton' Book Review   1954   *978*

Kittermaster, F. J. (Shrewsbury)
Obituary   1953   *943*

Kittermaster, H. J. (Rugby)
Obituary   1968   *1002*

Knapp, C. A. (Wellington, New Zealand)
Obituary   1928/I   *290*

Knaresborough, 1st Lord (Eton)
Obituary   1930/I   *255*

Knatchbull, Col. N. (Marlborough)
Obituary   1923/I   *310*

Knatchbull-Hugessen, H. T. (President Kent)
Obituary   1923/I   *300*

Kneller, A. H. (Ardingly; Hampshire)
Obituary   1970   *1022*

Knight, A. E. (Leicestershire; London County; England)
Obituary   1948   *789*
Portrait and Biography   1904   *xcii*

Knight, A. T. (Mill Hill; Incogniti)
Obituary   1917   *197*

Knight, B. (Witney Town C.C.)
Obituary   1967   *970*

Knight, B. R. (Essex; Leicestershire; England)
Photographs   1960   *359*

		1961	*354*
		1963	*392*
		1964	*360*
		1966	*364*

Knight, D. J. (Malvern; Oxford University; Surrey; England)

Batting for Artists' Rifles C.C.	1917	*281*
Obituary	1961	*949*
Portrait and Biography	1915/I	*200*
Schools Notes	1910/I	*123*
	1911/I	*125*
	1912/I	*212*
	1913/I	*206*
		215
	1914/I	*206*
		218
		229

Knight, E. A. (Sussex Committee)

| Obituary | 1911/I | *165* |

Knight, 2nd Lieut. E. A. (City of London School; Bishop's Stortford C.C.)

| Obituary | 1918 | *192* |

Knight, G. (Sussex)

| Obituary | 1903 | *lxxxi* |

Knight, G. W. (Victoria College, Jersey)

| Schools Note | 1940 | *609* |
| 1250 runs, 89 wkts Schools Averages | 1940 | *70* |

Knight, 2nd Lieut. J. W. (Denstone)

| Obituary | 1918 | *192* |

Knight, Lieut. M. M. (Lancing)

| Obituary | 1920/I | *155* |

Knight, R. D. V. (Dulwich; Cambridge University; Surrey; Gloucestershire; Sussex)

Photographs	1972	*41*
	1975	*41*
	1977	*57*
	1979	*53*

Knight, R. F. (Wellingborough; Northamptonshire)

| Obituary | 1956 | *97* |

Knight, R. L. (Clifton; Oxford University)

| Obituary | 1939 | *91* |

Knight, T. H. (Scorer Somerset)

| Obituary | 1896 | *xl* |

Knight, W. H. (Editor of Wisden 1864-1879)

| 'Individual Innings of 200 or more runs' | 1869 | *9* |
| Obituary | 1880 | |

Knock Out Competition Plan | 1946 | *12* |

Knott, A. P. E. (Kent; Tasmania; England)

Action Photographs	1968	*64*
	1977	*88*
Benefit Match	1977	*454*
Cricketer of the Year	1970	*61*
Photographs	1966	*432*
	1970	*60*
	1981	*446*
'Stumpers View' Book Review	1973	*1058*

Knott, Pte. A. R. (Hillhurst C.C., Calgary)

Obituary	1918	*214*

Knott, C. J. (Hampshire)

Photograph	1951	*360*

Knott, 2nd Lieut. C. S. (Perse)

Obituary	1919	*181*

Knott, F. H. (Tonbridge; Oxford University; Kent)

Obituary	1973	*1011*
Schools Note	1911/I	*128*
1126 runs Schools Averages	1911/II	*456*

Knowles, 2nd Lieut. A. B. (Dulwich College)

Obituary	1917	*197*

Knowles, R. G. (Canterbury; Secretary New Zealand Cricket Council)

Obituary	1982	*1204*

Knowles, W. L. (Kent; Sussex)

Obituary	1944	*317*
Testimonial Fund	1944	*182*

Knox, N. A. (Dulwich; Surrey; England)

Obituary	1936/I	*279*
Portrait and Biography	1907	*cxxvii*
Schools Notes	1902	*c*
	1903	*cxi*
		cxii

Knox, Capt. W. J. (Scotch College, Melbourne)

Obituary	1918	*192*

Kortlang, B. J. (Wellington, New Zealand)

Obituary	1962	*987*

ortright, C. J. (Essex)

'No Magic in Fast Bowling'	1948	*67*
Obituary	1953	*943*

ortright, Lieut. M. C. W. (Harrow)

Obituary	1918	*193*

otelawala, Col. Rt. Hon. Sir J. L. (Royal College, Colombo; Indian Gymkhana)

Obituary	1981	*1145*

otze, J. H. (Western Province; Eastern Province; Transvaal; South Africa)

Obituary	1932/I	*247*

oyna Relief Fund Matches 1968 1969 *915*

Krause, R. W. (Germantown C.C., Philadelphia)
    Obituary   1912/I   *183*

Kreeft, C. V. (Wellington, New Zealand)
    Obituary   1925/I   *271*

Kyle, J. H. (Victoria)
    Obituary   1920/I   *178*

Kynaston, D. (Journalist)
    'Bobby Abel – Professional Batsman'
    Book Review   1983   *1307*

Kynaston, R. (Secretary, Treasurer M.C.C.)
    Obituary   1875   *91*

Labouchere, Major A. M. (Wellington)
    Obituary   1919   *181*

Lacey, Sir F. E. (Sherborne; Cambridge University; Dorset; Hampshire)
    Appreciation of Lord Hawke   1939   *67*
    'Lord's and the M.C.C. Thirty Years of History'   1931/I   *275*
    Obituary   1947   *691*
    Presentation to   1924/II   *654*
    Tribute to C. S. Caine   1934/I   *27*
    Tribute to S. H. Pardon   1926/I   *31*
    Views on Reforms of 1889   1890   *xxxix*
    Views on Some Questions of the Day   1890   *xl*

Lacy, G. (Writer)
    Obituary   1905   *xcvii*

Lacy, H. (Manager Australian Imperial Forces 1919)
    Obituary   1938   *940*

La Fontaine, W. E. J. (Harrow)
    Obituary   1949   *865*

Lagden, R. B. (Marlborough; Cambridge University)
    Obituary   1945   *334*

Lagden, Capt. R. O. (Marlborough; Oxford University)
    Obituary   1916   *17*

Laidley, J. E. (Scottish Club Cricket)
    Obituary   941   *399*

Laidley, W. J. (Grange C.C.)
    Obituary   1913/I   *19*

Laing, 2nd Lieut. D. (Loretto)
    Obituary   1919   *19*

Laing, J. M. (Canada)
    Obituary   1949   *87*

Laing, Lieut. R. M. (Dollar Academy; Clackmannanshire)
    Obituary   1917   *19*

Lainson, Major J. A. (Bury and West Suffolk C.C.)
    Obituary   1932/I   *25*

Laird, 2nd Lieut. A. D. (Glasgow Academy; West of Scotland; Glasgow Academicals)
Obituary	1917	*197*

Laithwaite, Lieut. J. (Denstone)
Obituary	1917	*197*

Lake, E. W. (Secretary Bury and West Suffolk C.C.)
Obituary	1923/I	*301*

Laker, J. C. (Surrey; Auckland; Essex; England)
Action Photographs	1957	*49,51*
'The Australian Tour of 1961' Book Review	1962	*1038*
Benefit Match	1957	*541*
Career Figures	1960	*143*
Cricketer of the Year	1952	*77*
'Laker's Wonderful Year' N. Cardus	1957	*91*
'J. C. Laker with Bat and Ball' S. Conder	1957	*93*
'Over to Me' Book Review	1961	*99*
	1962	*1032*
Photographs	1950	*494*
	1951	*503*
	1952	*75*
Presentation to Photograph	1957	*45*
Record Maker Note on	1957	*69*
Retirement N. Cardus	1960	*143*
'Spinning Round the World' Book Review	1958	*1016*
'Thrills of Sunday Cricket'	1971	*122*

Lakin, Lieut. C. (St.Catherine's College, Oxford)
Obituary	1918	*215*

Lamason, J. R. (Wellington, New Zealand)
Obituary	1962	*987*

Lamb, A. (Gloucestershire)
Obituary	1909/I	*140*

Lamb, A. J. (Northamptonshire; Western Province; England)
Cricketer of the Year	1981	*83*
Eligibility Question	1983	*79*
Photographs	1980	*504*
	1981	*76*

Lamb, Capt. R. S. (Kildare)
Obituary	1904	*lxxix*

Lamb, Hon. T. M. (Shrewsbury; Oxford University; Middlesex; Northamptonshire)
Photograph	1982	*510*

Lamb, Pte. W. (George Heriots)
Obituary	1916	*180*

Lambert, Capt. E. N. (Radley)
Obituary	1918	*193*

Lambert, G. (Club Cricket)
Obituary   1916   *180*

Lambert, G. E. (Gloucestershire; Somerset)
Benefit Match   1956   *376*
Photograph   1953   *355*

Lambert, Lieut. J. E. D. (Bedford Grammar School)
Obituary   1916   *180*

Lambert, R. E. (Harrow; Sussex)
Obituary   1969   *982*

Lambert, R. H. (Ireland; London County)
Obituary   1958   *967*

Lambert, S. J. (Otago)
Obituary   1917   *253*

Lambert, T. (Northumberland; Durham)
Obituary   1906   *xciii*

Lambert, W. (Middlesex; Hertfordshire)
Obituary   1928/I   *290*

Lambrick, Rev. C. M. (Winchester)
Obituary   1948   *784*

Lambrick, Preb. Rev. G. M. (Repton)
Obituary   1930/I   *255*

Lampard, F. J. F. (Gray's Inn C.C.)
Obituary   1918   *230*

Lancashire County Cricket Club
Centenary Celebration Match   1965   *470*
County Badge   1950   *393*
    ad passim
'Fifty Years of Lancashire Cricket'
N. Cardus   1951   *80*
'Lancashire' R. Pogson Book Review   1953   *1000*
'Lancashire County Cricket' A. W. Ledbrooke
Book Review   1955   *988*
'Lancashire Cricket at the Top'
V. Addison and B. Bearshaw Book Review   1972   *1096*
'Lancashire' J. Kay Book Review   1973   *1052*
'Re-Shaping Lancashire Cricket' J. Kay   1971   *93*
Team Portraits
Joint Champions   1950   1951   *61*
John Player League Winners   1969   1970   *54*
John Player League and
Gillette Cup Winners   1970   1971   *65*
Lancashire Retain the Gillette
Cup   1971   1972   *62*
Triple Winners of the Gillette
Cup   1972   1973   *64*
    1974   1975   *459*

Gillette Cup Winners		1975	1976	*460*
		1976	1977	*462*
		1977	1978	*446*
		1978	1979	*439*
		1979	1980	*461*
		1980	1981	*462*
		1981	1982	*463*
		1982	1983	*475*
		1983	1984	*438*

Lancashire Cricket League
  Views on the Laws   1957   87

Lancashire, O. P. (Lancing; Cambridge University; Lancashire)
  Obituary   1935/I   *267*

Lancashire, Rev. P. (Rossall)
  Obituary   1927/I   *283*

Lancashire, W. (Hampshire)
  Obituary   1983   *1248*

Lancaster, A. J. (Secretary Kent)
  Obituary   1937/I   *274*

Lancaster, 2nd Lieut. P. (Old Rossallians C.C.; Birkenhead Park C.C.)
  Obituary   1917   *197*

Lancaster, T. (Lancashire; Yorkshire)
  Obituary   1937/I   *288*

Lancaster, 2nd Lieut. T. E. (Highgate School)
  Obituary   1917   *197*

Landon, C. W. (Bromsgrove School; Lancashire; Yorkshire)
  Obituary   1904   *lxxx*

Landsberg, P. (Journalist)
  'Sir J. B. Hobbs' Book Review   1954   *978*
  'The Kangaroo Conquers' Book Review   1956   *1028*
  with A. R. Morris 'Operation Ashes'
  Book Review   1957   *997*

Lane, A. F. (Warwickshire; Worcestershire)
  Obituary   1949   *865*

Lane, Rev. C. G. (Westminster; Oxford University; Surrey)
  Obituary   1893   *xxxv*

Lane, Rev. E. B. (Bristol Club Cricket)
  Obituary   1917   *253*

Lane, G. (Nottinghamshire)
  Obituary   1918   *231*

Lane, J. C. (Treasurer Warwickshire)
  Obituary   1909/I   *140*

Lane, J. H. H. V. (Enthusiast)
  Obituary   1918   *230*

Lane, J. K. (Rossall; Nottinghamshire)
  Obituary   1959   *933*

Lane, S. (St.Patrick's College, New Zealand)
Fourteen Catches in a Match 1975 *816*
Lane-Fox, E. (Eton)
Obituary 1950 *911*
Lane-Joynt, Lieut. A. W. (Radley; Surrey)
Obituary 1917 *197*
Lang, A. (Journalist; Writer)
Obituary 1913/I *190*
Lang, 2nd Lieut. A. H. (Harrow; Cambridge University; Suffolk; Sussex)
Obituary 1916 *180*
Lang, Col. A. M. (Addiscombe C.C.)
Obituary 1917 *253*
Lang, G. L. (Harrow)
Obituary 1899 *xlv*
Lang, Major H. A. (Worcestershire Regiment)
Obituary 1916 *181*
Lang, Capt. J. (Loretto)
Obituary 1918 *193*
Lang, Rev. R. (Harrrow; Cambridge University)
Obituary 1909/I *140*
Lang, T. W. (Clifton; Oxford University; Gloucestershire)
Obituary 1903 *lxxiii*
Langdale, Capt. E. G. (Eastbourne College)
Obituary 1916 *181*
Langdon, Rev. G. L. (Sussex)
Obituary 1895 *xxxvii*
Langdon, Lieut. L. (Hampshire Hogs; Southampton Trojans C.C.)
Obituary 1917 *197*
Langdon, T. (Gloucestershire)
Obituary 1945 *335*
Langford, A. W. T. (Journalist)
'Arthur Langford: A Memoir'
I. Rosenwater Book Review 1978 *1124*
Obituary 1977 *1044*
'Sir Pelham Warner' (Obituary) 1964 *120*
Langford, B. A. (Somerset)
Photographs 1959 *511*
1961 *534*
1965 *538*
1969 *550*
Langford, W. (Hampshire)
Obituary 1958 *962*
Langham, F. N. (Eton)
Obituary 1918 *241*
Langham, J. (U.S.A. Club Cricket)
Obituary 1922/I *272*

324

Langley, C. K. (Radley; Warwickshire)

Obituary	1949	*866*

Langley, G. R. A. (South Australia; Australia)

Cricketer of the Year	1957	*61*
Photograph	1957	*53*

Langridge, James (Sussex; England)

Benefit Match	1948	*497*
Obituary	1967	*970*
Photograph	1952	*525*
Portrait and Biography	1932/I	*270*
Retirement Note on	1954	*86*

Langridge, John G. (Sussex; Umpire)

Benefit Match	1949	*518*
Career Statistics	1979	*119*
Cricketer of the Year	1950	*81*
'John Langridge – Golden Jubilee'		
J. Arlidge	1979	*115*
Photographs	1950	*76*
	1951	*525*
	1979	*116*
Retirement Note on	1956	*589*

Langton, Flt-Lt. A. B. C. (Transvaal; South Africa)

Obituary	1943	*365*

Lanham, Pte. A. E. (East Kildonan C.C., Winnipeg)

Obituary	1919	*199*

Lanigan, J. (Western Australia)

Obituary	1974	*1084*

Large Attendances and Gate Receipts –
See records section of most recent *Wisden*

Large, J. (Philadelphia)

Obituary	1904	*lxxix*

Larkin, G. M. (Western Province)

Obituary	1977	*1044*

Larkins, W. (Northamptonshire; Western Province; England)

Photograph	1977	*506*

Larrette, C. H. (Journalist)

Obituary	1914/I	*186*

Larter, J. D. F. (Northamptonshire; England)

Photographs	1961	*499*
	1962	*522*

Larwood, H. (Nottinghamshire; England)

Benefit Match	1937/II	*191*
'The Larwood Story' Book Review	1966	*1018*
Portrait and Biography	1927/I	*306*
Tributes to: W. Hammond	1966	*118*
H. Sutcliffe	1979	*98*

Lascelles, 2nd Lieut. J. F. (Winchester)
Obituary   1916   *181*
Lascelles Hall Note on   1944   *60*
Last Over Note on   1945   *62*
Last Wicket Records at the Oval
Photograph   1947   *38*
Latchman, H. C. (Middlesex; Nottinghamshire)
Photograph   1969   *498*
Latham, A. M. (Wellington; Cheshire)
Obituary   1935/I   *268*
Latham, Dr. C. (Supporter Cheshire)
Obituary   1908/I   *143*
Latham, F. H. (Winchester)
Obituary   1928/I   *291*
Latham, P. H. (Malvern; Cambridge University; Sussex)
Obituary   1923/I   *301*
Latham, T. (Winchester; Cambridge University; Cheshire)
Obituary   1927/I   *283*
Lathom, Lord (President M.C.C.)
Obituary   1899   *l*
Latter, A. (King's, Canterbury)
Obituary   1945   *335*
Latter, B. H. (King's, Canterbury; Bickley Park C.C.)
Obituary   1920/I   *178*
Lattimer, R. B. (Durham; Breconshire; Cumberland)
Obituary   1930/I   *255*
Laurie, A. G. (U.S.A.; South American Club Cricket)
Obituary   1938   *940*
Laurin, D. E. (Harrow)
Obituary   1903   *lxxxii*
Lavelle, 2nd Lieut. J. (Stonyhurst College)
Obituary   1916   *181*
Laver, F. (Victoria; Australia)
Obituary   1920/I   *178*
Laverton, G. A. (Harrow)
Obituary   1955   *933*
Lavis, G. (Glamorgan)
Obituary   1957   *946*
Law, A. (Warwickshire)
Obituary   1920/I   *179*
Law, 2nd Lieut. C. L. (Exeter School)
Obituary   1917   *224*
Law, J. P. (Lincolnshire)
Obituary   1930/I   *255*
Law, Rev. W. (Harrow; Oxford University)
Obituary   1894   *xxxviii*

326

Lawless, C. T. (Secretary Thames Ditton C.C.)
Obituary 1910/I *141*
Lawrence, Pte. A. E. (Calgary C.C.)
Obituary 1917 *224*
Lawrence, A. S. (Harrow; Cambridge University)
Obituary 1940 *842*
Lawrence, C. (Surrey; Middlesex; New South Wales; Ireland; Scotland)
Obituary 1918 *230*
Lawrence, Lt-Col. H. M. (Kent; Suffolk)
Obituary 1976 *1099*
Lawrence, J. (Somerset)
Benefit Match 1955 *494*
Photographs 1951 *486*
1955 *490*
Retirement Note on 1956 *524*
Lawrence, 2nd Lieut. J. R. M. (Haileybury)
Obituary 1917 *198*
Lawrence, Pte. R. (Cheltenham Grammar School)
Obituary 1917 *224*
Lawrence, Sir W. (Founder of Lawrence Trophy)
Obituary 1940 *842*
Lawrence Trophy See various Wisdens
Lawrie, C. D. (Fettes; Oxford University)
Obituary 1977 *1044*
Lawry, W. M. (Victoria; Australia)
Cricketer of the Year 1962 *97*
Photograph 1962 *96*
'Run Digger, His Own Story' Book Review 1967 *1019*
'Laws, Don't Tamper With W. E. Bowes 1957 *90*
'Laws, 200 Years of' G. Ross 1975 *128*
Laws – Experiment with L.B.W. at Lord's
Photograph 1964 *67*
Lawson, 2nd Lieut. C. D. N. (Haileybury)
Obituary 1916 *181*
Lawson-Smith, E. M. (Harrow)
Obituary 1943 *378*
Lawson-Smith, T. E. (Harrow)
Obituary 1915/I *231*
Lawton, A. E. (Derbyshire; Lancashire)
Obituary 1956 *974*
Lawton, J. C. (Warwickshire; Otago)
Obituary 1935/I *268*
Lax, S. K. (Leeds Grammar School)
Schools Note 1976 *866*
1126 runs Schools Averages 1976 *894*

Lay, A. T. (Fettes)
1259 runs Schools Averages   1920/II   *332*
Lay, G. (Hastings Priory C.C.)
Obituary   1966   *969*
Layne, O. H. (Barbados)
Obituary   1934/I   *279*
Layton, Lieut. F. P. H. (Lynne Valley C.C., British Columbia)
Obituary   1918   *215*
Le Couteur, P. R. (Oxford University; Victoria)
Obituary   1959   *933*
Le Fleming, J. (Tonbridge; Kent)
Obituary   1943   *379*
Le Fleming, Lt-Col. L. J. (Tonbridge; Kent)
Obituary   1919   *181*
Le Marchand, F. P. (Malvern; Devon)
Obituary   1934/I   *270*
Le Marchant, Dr. A. W. (Malvern)
Obituary   1924/I   *262*
Le Marchant, Capt. E. H. C. (Harrow)
Obituary   1917   *198*
Le Mesurier, Col. F. A. (Royal Engineers)
Obituary   1927/I   *283*
Le Quesne, L. (Journalist)
'The Bodyline Controversy' Book Review   1984   *1261*
Le Roux, F. L. (Transvaal; Eastern Province; South Africa)
Obituary   1965   *973*
Le Roux, G. S. (Sussex; Western Province)
Photograph   1982   *573*
Lea, Sir T. Bart. (Worcestershire)
Obituary   1903   *lxxii*
Leach, G. (Sussex)
Obituary   1946   *441*
Leach, H. (Marlborough; Lancashire)
Obituary   1929/I   *251*
Leach, W. E. (Marlborough; Lancashire)
Obituary   1933/I   *253*
Leadbeater, B. (Yorkshire)
Photograph   1970   *610*
Leadbeater, H. (Yorkshire)
Obituary   1929/I   *251*
Leadbeater, W. W. (Secretary Scarborough C.C.)
Obituary   1941   *399*
'Leaders of England and Australia'
N. Cardus   1964   *134*
Leaf, C. H. (Marlborough)
Obituary   1911/I   *148*

Leaf, F. W. (Harrow)
  Obituary   1945   *335*

Leaf, H. (Harrow; Surrey)
  Obituary   1937/I   *275*

Leaf, Major H. M. (Marlborough; Wiltshire; Essex)
  Obituary   1932/I   *248*

League Cricket Conference   1962   1963   *783*

League Cricket Conference   1963   1964   *736*

Leake, E. (Port Arthur C.C. of Ontario)
  Obituary   1920/I   *155*

Leake, W. M. (Rugby; Cambridge University)
  Obituary   1919   *207*

Leaney, E. J. (Kent)
  Obituary   1905   *xcviii*

Lear, Ven. F. (Winchester; Oxford University)
  Obituary   1915/I   *231*

Learmouth, Capt. I. D. (Sedbergh)
  Obituary   1944   *30*

Leary, S. E. (Kent)
  Benefit Match   1968   *459*
  Photograph   1961   *428*

Leatham, A. E. (Gloucestershire)
  Obituary   1949   *866*

Leatham, Major B. H. (Yorkshire Regiment)
  Obituary   1916   *181*

Leatham, C. (Yorkshire Colts)
  Obituary   1914/I   *186*

Leatham, G. A. B. (Yorkshire)
  Obituary   1933/I   *253*

Leatham, H. W. (Charterhouse)
  Obituary   1975   *1080*

Leather, R. S. (Marlborough; Yorkshire)
  Obituary   1914/I   *187*

Leatherbarrow, C. (Patron)
  C. Leatherbarrow's XI   Team Portrait   1944   *37*

Ledbrooke, A. W. (Journalist)
  'Lancashire County Cricket' Book Review   1955   *988*
  Obituary   1959   *934*
  'Old Trafford Centenary'   1957   *117*

Ledger, F. W. (Surrey)
  Obituary   1907   *cxiii*

Ledwidge, R. R. (Umpire)
  Obituary   1979   *1092*

Lee, A. (Journalist)
  'A Pitch in Both Camps' Book Review   1980   *1206*

Lee, Rev. A. G. (Westminster; Oxford University; Berkshire; Worcestershire; Suffolk)

Obituary	1926/I	*278*

Lee, Judge, A. M. (Winchester; Hampshire)

Obituary	1984	*1202*

Lee, C. (Derbyshire; Yorkshire)

Photographs	1957	*309*
	1959	*306*
	1964	*343*

Lee, E. C. (Winchester; Oxford University; Hampshire)

Obituary	1943	*379*

Lee, F. (Yorkshire)

Obituary	1897	*xli*

Lee, F. (Rugby; Cambridge University; Surrey)

Obituary	1923/I	*301*

Lee, F. H. (Marlborough; Suffolk)

Obituary	1925/I	*271*

Lee, F. S. (Middlesex; Somerset; London Counties; Umpire)

Benefit Match	1948	*463*
'Syd Buller – A Great Umpire'	1971	*118*
'Cricket Lovely Cricket' Book Review	1961	*997*
Obituary	1983	*1248*
Photograph	1971	*119*
Tribute to W. F. F. Price	1970	*1024*

Lee, G. (Umpire)

Obituary	1895	*xli*

Lee, Rev. G. B. (Winchester; Oxford University; Hampshire)

Obituary	1904	*lxxix*

Lee, G. M. (Nottinghamshire; Derbyshire; Umpire)

Obituary	1977	*1044*

Lee, H. (Yorkshire)

Obituary	1909/I	*142*

Lee, 2nd Lieut. H. D. (North Middlesex C.C.)

Obituary	1918	*193*

Lee, H. W. (Middlesex; England)

Benefit Match	1928/II	*226*
Obituary	1982	*1204*

Lee, J. F. (Balliol College, Oxford)

Obituary	1919	*181*

Lee, Rev J. M. (Oundle; Cambridge University; Surrey)

Obituary	1904	*lxxviii*

Lee, J. W. (Middlesex; Somerset; London Counties)

Obituary	1945	*323*

Lee, M. H. (Oxfordshire)

Obituary	1965	*968*

Lee, P. (Rugby)
  Obituary 1954 *932*
Lee, P. G. (Northamptonshire; Lancashire; Durham)
  Career Figures 1983 *711*
  Cricketer of the Year 1976 *49*
  Photographs 1974 *453*
   1976 *44*
Lee, P. K. (South Australia; Australia)
  Obituary 1981 *1145*
Lee, 2nd Lieut. R. (Haileybury)
  Obituary 1917 *225*
Lee, Pte. R. (Witley C.C.)
  Obituary 1917 *198*
Lee, R. (American Club Cricket)
  Obituary 1930/I *255*
Lee, S. C. B. (Oxfordshire)
  Obituary 1961 *950*
Lee, W. (Staffordshire)
  Obituary 1952 *958*
Leech, F. E. (Derby Committee)
  Obituary 1907 *cxiii*
Leeming, Capt. A. J. (Christ's Hospital)
  Obituary 1918 *193*
Leeming, Sgt. R. E. (St.Albans C.C, Christchurch, New Zealand)
  Obituary 1918 *193*
Lees, Major J. (Uppingham; Cambridge University; Cambridgeshire)
  Obituary 1936/I *280*
Lees, W. S. (Surrey; England)
  Benefit Match 1907 *64*
  Obituary 1925/I *271*
  Portrait and Biography 1906 *cxii*
Leese, C. M. (Winchester)
  Obituary 1923/I *310*
Leese, C. P. (Wellington; Oxford University; Lancashire)
  Obituary 1948 *784*
Leese, Sir J. F. (Lancashire)
  Obituary 1915/I *231*
Leese, Lt-Gen. Sir O. Bart. (Eton; President M.C.C.; President Shropshire; President Warwickshire; President Cricket Society)
  Obituary 1979 *1080*
Leese, T. (Winchester)
  Obituary 1917 *253*
Leese, V. F. (Winchester; Cambridge University; Devon)
  Obituary 1928/I *291*
Leese, Sir W. H. (Winchester)
  Obituary 1938 *940*

Leeston-Smith, F. A. (Christ College, Brecon; Breconshire; Somerset)
   Obituary   1905   *civ*
Left Hand Rivals Note on   1956   71
Legard, Sir C. Bart. (President M.C.C.)
   Obituary   1902   *lxviii*
L.B.W., 'Cricket Centuries' and
   Hon. E. V. Bligh   1900   *xcvii*
   'L.B.W. Discussion,' The   1888   354
   'L.B.W. Experiment, The Success of' 1936/I   341
   'L.B.W., High Scoring and the Law of' 1899   *lxv*
   'L.B.W., The Second Class Counties and' 1903   *lxii*
   L.B.W. The Law Notes on   1967   89
                             1970   76
                             1971   88
                             1972   90
Leg Break Bowling in 1901
   D. L. Jephson   1902   *lxxxvi*
Leggat, J. G. (Canterbury; New Zealand)
   Obituary   1974   1075
Leggat, 2nd Lieut. L. C. (Eton; Cambridge University)
   Obituary   1918   193
Leggatt, Lt-Col. W. M. (Winchester; Kent)
   Obituary   1947   692
Legge, Lieut. G. B. (Malvern; Oxford University; Kent; England)
   Obituary   1941   387
   Schools Notes   1922/I   297
                             1923/I   337
Legh, A. C. (Clerk to M.C.C. Committee)
   Obituary   1918   231
Legros, Lt-Col. P. W. (Rugby; Buckinghamshire)
   Obituary   1981   1145
Leicester – Grace Road
   Note on Ground   1969   145
   Plan of County Ground   1950   411
                           ad passim
Leicester, 2nd Earl of (Norfolk)
   Obituary   1910/I   141
Leicestershire County Cricket Club
   County Badge   1950   410
   'Following Leicestershire' B. Chapman 1964   150
   History of Leicestershire Cricket
   E. E. Snow Book Review   1950   973
   'Leicestershire Cricket 1949-1977'
   E. E. Snow Book Review   1978   1118
   'Leicestershire Cricketers' Association of
   'Cricket Statisticians' Book Review 1978   1118

'100 Years of Leicestershire Cricket'			
E. E. Snow		1978	*151*
Leicestershire in Zimbabwe 1980-81		1982	*1143*
Team Portraits:			
Leicestershire Win Benson and			
Hedges Trophy	1972	1973	*67*
Leicestershire: John Player			
League Champions	1974	1975	*475*
Leicestershire:			
County Champions	1975	1976	*64*
Benson and Hedges Cup Winners	1975	1976	*476*
	1976	1977	*477*
	1977	1978	*460*
	1978	1979	*454*
	1979	1980	*477*
	1980	1981	*477*
	1981	1982	*479*
	1982	1983	*491*
	1983	1984	*454*

Leigh, Rev. A. A. (Eton; President Cambridge University C.C.)
Obituary	1906	*xciii*

Leigh, Hon. Sir E. C. (Harrow; Oxford University; Oxfordshire)
Obituary	1916	*181*

Leigh, J. (Uppingham; Lancashire)
Obituary	1926/I	*278*

Leigh, S. A. (Harrow; Sussex)
Obituary	1914/I	*187*

Leiper, J. M. (Chigwell School; Essex)
Schools Note	1939	*683*
77 wkts Schools Averages	1939	*743*

Leiper, R. J. (Chigwell School; Essex)
Schools Note	1980	*868*
1031 runs Schools Averages	1980	*884*

Leitch, 2nd Lieut. G. F. (Clydesdale C.C.)
Obituary	1917	*198*

Lemmon, D. (Writer)
'Johnny Won't Hit Today'		
Book Review	1984	*1264*
'Summer of Success – The Triumph of Essex County Cricket Club in 1980'		
Book Review	1981	*1193*
'Tich Freeman and the Decline of the Leg Break Bowler'		
Book Review	1983	*1308*

Lemon, 2nd Lieut. L. E. T. (All Hallows School)
Obituary	1918	*193*

Lenham, L. J. (Sussex)
Photographs   1964   *567*
     1966   *569*
Lenham, N. J. (Brighton College)
Schools Note   1983   *899*
1076 runs Schools Averages   1983   *911*
Lennon, C. W. (President Wanderers C.C., Chicago)
Obituary   1907   *cxiii*
Lennox, C. (2nd Duke of Richmond)
'The Duke who Was Cricket' J. Marshall
Book Review   1962   *1040*
Lepper, Rev. Canon A. L. (Dublin University)
Obituary   1943   *379*
Lesley, R. W. (President Merion C.C.)
Obituary   1937/I   *288*
Leslie, C. F. H. (Rugby; Oxford University; England; Middlesex; Shropshire)
Obituary   1922/I   *258*
Leslie, Sir J. 1st Bart. (Oxford University)
Obituary   1917   *254*
Leslie-Jones, F. A. (Bromsgrove School)
Obituary   1947   *692*
Lester, J. A. (Haverford, Philadelphia)
Obituary   1970   *1023*
Lester, J. H. (Writer)
Obituary   1915/I   *231*
Lester, R. (Writer)
'The Fight For The Ashes 1953' Book Review   1954   *984*
'The Fight For The Ashes 1961' Book Review   1962   *1039*
Letcher, C. (East Melbourne C.C.)
Obituary   1918   *241*
Letts, P. E. (Christ's Hospital; Berkshire)
Obituary   1978   *1074*
Lever, J. K. (Essex; Natal; England)
Cricketer of the Year   1979   *76*
Photographs   1972   *380*
     1976   *376*
     1979   *64*
Surprises Indians Note   1977   *110*
Lever, P. (Lancashire; Tasmania; England)
Photograph   1970   *452*
Levers, W. C. S. (Wellington; Auckland; Hawkes Bay)
Obituary   1924/I   *275*
Leveson Gower, E. M. G. (Winchester)
Obituary   1939   *91*
Leveson Gower, Rev. F. A. G. (Winchester; Oxford University; Hampshire)
Obituary   1947   *692*

Leveson Gower, G. C. G. (Free Foresters; IZingari)
Obituary	1949	*866*

Leveson Gower, Sir H. D. G. (Winchester; Oxford University; Surrey; England)
'Hundred Years of Surrey Cricket'	1946	*52*
Obituary	1955	*933*
'Recollections of Oxford Cricket'	1937/I	*249*
Schools Notes	1891	*301*
	1892	*270*
		271
	1893	*300*
Team in Portugal 1934	1935/II	*640*
Tributes to: C. S. Caine	1934/I	*28*
Sir S. Jackson	1948	*80*
S. H. Pardon	1926/I	*31*
S. J. Southerton	1936/I	*30*

Levett, W. H. V. (Brighton College; Kent; England)
Schools Notes	1925/I	*324*
	1926/I	*328*
	1927/I	*328*

Levick, Capt. P. (Jesus College, Cambridge)
Obituary	1919	*182*

Levick, Capt. T. H. C. (Southgate C.C.)
Obituary	1958	*962*

Lewin, Major-Gen. E. O. (Winchester)
Obituary	1951	*925*

Lewington, P. J. (Warwickshire; Berkshire)
Photograph	1974	*567*

Lewis, A. E. T. (Somerset)
Obituary	1957	*946*

Lewis, A. H. (Hampshire; Berkshire)
Obituary	1981	*1145*

Lewis, A. R. (Neath Grammar School; Cambridge University; Glamorgan; England)
Benefit Match	1974	*661*
'Captaincy'	1979	*84*
'How Essex rose to Glory'	1980	*93*
Photographs	1967	*388*
	1970	*389*

Lewis, C. P. (Oxford University)
Obituary	1924/I	*262*

Lewis, E. B. (Warwickshire)
Obituary	1984	*1203*

Lewis, Sir E. R. (Rugby)
Obituary	1981	*1145*

Lewis, G. (Cameron C.C.)
Obituary	1922/I	*259*

Lewis, G. A. (Felsted; Suffolk)
Obituary   1927/I   *283*
Lewis, Lieut. G. L. (Harrow)
Obituary   1917   *198*
Lewis, Lt-Col. H. (Uppingham)
Obituary   1917   *198*
Lewis, H. L. (Berkshire)
Obituary   1979   *1081*
'Views on the Laws'   1957   *84*
Lewis, 2nd Lieut. H. L. (St Bees)
Obituary   1918   *193*
Lewis, Capt. J. D. G. (Shrewsbury)
Obituary   1919   *182*
Lewis, J. H. (New South Wales)
Obituary   1902   lxviii
Lewis, Major N. A. (Lancashire)
Obituary   1958   *962*
Lewis, P. (East Melbourne C.C.)
Obituary   1924/I   *275*
Lewis, P. T. (Western Province; South Africa)
Obituary   1977   1045
Lewis, Lt-Col. R. P. (Winchester; Surrey; Middlesex; Oxford University)
Obituary   1918   *193*
Lewis, V. (Journalist)
Obituary   1981   *1145*
Ley, Sir 1st Bart. (President Notts County C.C.)
Obituary   1917   *254*
Ley, 2nd Lieut. G. A. H. (St.Paul's)
Obituary   1918   *194*
Ley, W. H. (Winchester)
Obituary   1920/I   *179*
Leyland, F. D. (Harrow)
Obituary   1917   *254*
Leyland, M. (Yorkshire; Patiala; England)
Benefit Match   1935/II   *232*
'Maurice Leyland' R. C. Robertson-Glasgow   1943   *31*
'MauriceLeyland in First Class Cricket'   1968   *1003*
Obituary   1968   *1002*
Photograph   1943   *30*
Portrait and Biography   1929/I   *270*
Views on Growing Pains of Cricket   1956   *90*
Leyton   Plan of County Ground   1958   *326*
                 ad passim
Liardet, Col. C. A. (Madras)
Obituary   1904   *lxxix*

Lichfield, 3rd Earl of (Harrow)
  Obituary   1919   *208*
Liddell, A. G. (Northamptonshire)
  Obituary   1971   *1027*
Liddell, Major J. S. (Haileybury)
  Obituary   1935/I   *268*
Liddell, Capt. L. E. (Northumberland)
  Views on Laws   1957   *84*
Liddicut, A. E. (Victoria)
  Obituary   1984   *1203*
Liddle, J. R. (Eastern Province; Orange Free State; Western Province;
South Africa)
  Obituary   1960   *953*
Light, W. (Hampshire; Devon)
  Obituary   1931/I   *260*
Lightfoot, A. (Northamptonshire)
  Benefit Match   1971   *478*
Lightning Strikes Down Players
  Note on   1960   *882*
Lillee, D. K. (Western Australia; Australia)
  'Back to the Mark' Book Review   1976   *1150*
  Cricketer of the Year   1973   *76*
  Lillee and Thomson – the Attraction   1976   *60*
  Note on   1973   *372*
  Photographs   1973   *68*
                                                   1977   *119*
Lilley, A. A. (Warwickshire; London County; England)
  Benefit Match   1902   *95*
  Obituary   1930/I   *255*
  Portrait and Biography   1897   *xlv*
Lilley, A. R. (Natal; Transvaal)
  Obituary   1981   *1145*
Lilley, B. (Nottinghamshire)
  Benefit Match   1936/II   *199*
  Obituary   1951   *925*
Lilleywhite, F. (Sussex; Editor of Lillywhite's Guide to Cricketers)
  'English Cricketers Trip to Canada and U.S.A. 1859'
  Book Review   1981   *1193*
Lillywhite, H. F. (Son of 'W')
  Obituary   1919   *208*
Lillywhite, James (Junior) (Sussex; England)
  Benefit Match   1890   *271*
  Obituary   1930/I   *256*
  Views on 'The Follow On'   1894   *lii*

Lillywhite, John (Sussex; Middlesex)
  Benefit Match   1872   *133*
  Obituary   1875   *173*
Lincoln, R. (Lincolnshire)
  Obituary   1919   *208*
Lindley, T. (Nottinghamshire)
  Obituary   1941   *399*
Lindsay, Lieut. A. T. T. (Wellington)
  Obituary   1919   *182*
Lindsay, Major C. F. T. (Wellington)
  Obituary   1919   *182*
Lindsay, D. J. (Irish Club Cricket)
  Obituary   1925/I   *272*
Lindsay, Capt. G. W. T. (R.A.XI)
  Obituary   1918   *194*
Lindsay, N. V. (Transvaal; Orange Free State; South Africa)
  Obituary   1977   *1045*
Lindsay, P. (Writer)
  'Don Bradman' Book Review   1952   *1018*
Lindsay, R. M. (Forfarshire)
  Obituary   1957   *946*
Lindsay, W. (Winchester; Surrey)
  Obituary   1924/I   *262*
Lindsay, Sir W. O'B (Harrow; Oxford University; Kent)
  Obituary   1976   *1099*
Lindsey, G. G. S. (Upper Canada College XI)
  Obituary   1921/I   *230*
Lindwall, R. R. (New South Wales; Queensland; Australia)
  'The Challenging Tests' Book Review   1962   *1039*
  Cricketer of the Year   1949   *90*
  'Flying Stumps' Book Review   1955   *993*
  Photographs   1949   *73*
              1956   *108*
  'Two Eras of Australian Pace'
  I. A. R. Peebles   1956   *109*
Line, 2nd Lieut. J. Y. A. (Oundle)
  Obituary   1917   *198*
Line, Across the Note on   1982   *90*
Ling, Capt. F. G. (Bradfield)
  Obituary   1920/I   *155*
Lingwood, 2nd Lieut. E. St.H. (Woodbridge School)
  Obituary   1918   *194*
Linnell, H. J. (St.Lawrence, Ramsgate; Kent)
  Obituary   1969   *982*
Linnett, Prof. J. W. (Oxfordshire)
  Obituary   1976   *1099*

Linton, G. C. (Jamaica)
Obituary   1961   *950*
Lipscomb, Pte. C. H. P. (Cowichan C.C., Canada)
Obituary   1918   *194*
Lipscomb, R. (Kent)
Obituary   1896   *xxxviii*
Lipscomb, W. H. (Marlborough; Oxford University; Hampshire)
Obituary   1919   *208*
Lipscomb, W. P. (King's College, Wimbledon)
92 wkts Schools Averages   1906   *478*
Lissette, A. F. (Waikato; Auckland; Northern Districts; New Zealand)
Obituary   1974   *1076*
Listless Cricket Note on   1952   *92*
Litchfield, E. (Writer)
'Cricket Grand Slam' Book Review   1971   *1080*
'The Book of the Tests' Book Review   1971   *1081*
Obituary   1983   *1249*
Little, C. W. (Winchester; Kent)
Obituary   1923/I   *302*
Little, Rev. J. R. (Uppingham)
Obituary   1921/I   *230*
Little, W. (Stirlingshire)
Obituary   1976   *1099*
Littlehales, Rev. C. G. (Forest School; Essex)
Obituary   1946   *441*
Littlejohn, A. R. (Middlesex)
Obituary   1920/I   *179*
Littlewood, G. H. (Lancashire)
Obituary   1918   *231*
Liverpool, Aigburth
Plan of County Ground   1957   *423*
       ad passim
Livesay, Brig-Gen. R. O'H. (Wellington; Kent)
Obituary   1947   *692*
Livingstone, L. (New South Wales; Northamptonshire)
Career Figures   1958   *97*
Photographs   1951   *453*
       1955   *454*
       1957   *477*
Livingstone, D. A. (Hampshire)
Photograph   1965   *419*
Livock, A. H. D. (Cambridgeshire)
Obituary   1972   *1053*
Livsey, W. H. (Hampshire)
Benefit Match   1930/II   *337*
Obituary   1980   *1160*

Llewellyn, C. B. (Natal; Hampshire; South Africa)
    Benefit Match   1909/II   *166*
    Obituary   1965   *968*
    Portrait and Biography   1911/I   *172*
Llewlyn, Sir J. T. D. Bart. (Glamorgan; Breconshire; Camarthanshire)
    Obituary   1928/I   *291*
Llewlyn, W. D. (Eton; Oxford University; Glamorgan)
    Obituary   1894   *xxxvii*
Lloyd, B. J. (Glamorgan)
    Photograph   1982   *401*
Lloyd, C. H. (Guyana; Lancashire; West Indies)
    Action Photograph   1973   *61*
    Cricketer of the Year   1971   *77*
    'Living for Cricket' Book Review   1981   *1203*
    Photographs   1971   *73*
                                                        1972   *465*
    Single Wicket Champion   1980   *361*
    With World Cup 1975 Photograph   1976   *35*
Lloyd, Pte. C. H. (Vancouver C.C.)
    Obituary   1918   *215*
Lloyd, D. (Lancashire; England)
    Action Photograph   1975   *77*
    Career Figures   1984   *1250*
    'England's Find' Note on   1975   *99*
    Photographs   1970   *452*
                                                        1973   *446*
                                                        1979   *437*
Lloyd, E. W. M. (Rugby; Shropshire; Somerset)
    Obituary   1929/I   *251*
Lloyd, J. (Brecknockshire)
    Obituary   1916   *182*
Lloyd, N. (Yorkshire)
    Obituary   1983   *1249*
Lloyd, R. A. (Lancashire)
    Obituary   1952   *966*
Lloyd, Col. W. N. (Uppingham)
    Obituary   1936/I   *280*
Lloyd-Price, Lieut. J. E. (Wellingborough)
    Obituary   1944   *301*
Lloyds, J. W. (Blundells; Somerset)
    Photograph   1982   *541*
Loader, P. J. (Surrey; Western Australia; England)
    Benefit Match   1964   *562*
    Cricketer of the Year   1958   *63*
    Photographs   1955   *509*
                                                        1958   *52*

Lobb, B. (Warwickshire; Somerset)

Photograph	1956	*525*
Lobs Note on	1952	*96*

Lock, C. H. A. (Norfolk)

Obituary	1913/I	*203*

Lock, G. A. R. (Surrey; Leicestershire; Western Australia; England)

Action Photograph	1959	*39*
Benefit Match	1961	*561*
Cricketer of the Year	1954	*65*
Notes on	1953	*81*
	1956	*71*
Photographs	1952	*505*
	1954	*64*
	1968	*482*
'Put Lock on' K. Ward Book Review	1973	*1058*
'For Surrey and England' Book Review	1958	*1016*

Lock, H. C. (Surrey; Devon; Inspector of Pitches)

'Bert Lock – King of Groundsmen'		
A. Bannister	1976	*141*
Note on	1968	*1042*
Obituary	1979	*1081*
Photograph	1976	*145*
14 wkts in one innings	1976	*143*

Locker, W. (Derbyshire)

Obituary	1954	*932*

Lockett, A. (Staffordshire)

Obituary	1966	*969*

Lockhart, J. H. B. (Sedbergh; Cambridge University)

Obituary	1957	*946*

Lockhart, W. P. (North of England)

Obituary	1894	*xxxvii*

Lockton, J. H. (Dulwich; Surrey)

Obituary	1973	*1011*

Lockwood, E. (Yorkshire)

Benefit Match	1883	*165*
Obituary	1922/I	*259*

Lockwood, W. H. (Nottinghamshire; Surrey; England)

Benefit Match	1902	*124*
Obituary	1933/I	*253*
Portrait and Biography	1899	*lxi*

Loder-Symonds, Lieut. T. L. (Lancing)

Obituary	1916	*182*

Lodge, L. V. (Durham School; Durham; Hampshire)

Obituary	1917	*254*

Logan, C. J. (Canada)

Obituary	1908/I	*155*

Logan, Hon. J. D. (Patron South Africa)
Obituary 1921/I *230*

Logan, J. D. (Junior) (South African Cricket)
Obituary 1961 *950*

Lohmann, G. A. (Surrey; Western Province; Transvaal; England)
'A Few Words on Fielding' 1893 *xlix*
Benefit Match 1897 *73*
'Bowling' 1890 *xlvii*
'George Lohmann' (Obituary) 1902 *liii*
George Lohmann in First Class Cricket 1894 *lxviii*
Portrait and Biography 1889 *xxx*
Views on Some Questions of the Day 1890 *xliv*

Lomas, Lieut. H. (Wimbledon C.C.; Baltimore C.C.)
Obituary 1917 *198*

Lomas, J. M. (Charterhouse; Oxford University)
Obituary 1946 *441*

Londesborough, 1st Earl of (Yorkshire Patron)
Obituary 1901 *lix*

Londesborough, 2nd Earl of (President M.C.C.)
Obituary 1918 *231*

London Counties 1940 Team Portrait 1941 *27*
London Counties 1941 Team Portrait 1942 *27*
London County 1901 Team Portrait 1977 *139*

Londonderry, 9th Marquess of (President Durham)
Obituary 1916 *183*

London Schools in India and Ceylon 1965-66 1967 *903*

Lonergan, R. (South Australia)
Obituary 1957 *946*

Loney, E. F. (Derbyshire)
Obituary 1984 *1203*

Long, A. (Surrey; Sussex)
Benefit Match 1972 *575*
Photographs 1964 *548*
1969 *568*
1972 *562*
1976 *569*
Sussex Thrive under Long 1979 *78*

Long, Rev. F. E. (Eton; Cambridge University)
Obituary 1905 *civ*

Long, H. J. (Journalist)
Obituary 1965 *968*

Long, Lord of Wraxall (Harrow; Wiltshire; Devon)
Obituary 1925/I *272*

Long, R. (Surrey)
Obituary 1925/I *272*

Long, Brig-Gen. W. (Army)
    Obituary   1918   194
Long, W. T. (Philadelphia)
    Obituary   1973   1014
Longbottom, 2nd Lieut. R. (Wellington)
    Obituary   1916   183
Longbourne, Capt. H. R. (Repton)
    Obituary   1918   194
Longden, A. (Canterbury)
    Obituary   1925/I   273
Longe, F. D. (Harrow; Oxford University)
    Obituary   1911/I   148
Longfield, Wing-Comdr. G. P. (Aldenham; Kent)
    Obituary   1946   435
Longfield, T. C. (Aldenham; Cambridge University; Kent)
    Obituary   1982   1204
Longhurst, Rev. Canon W. H. R. (Marlborough)
    Obituary   1944   317
Longman, G. H. (Eton; Cambridge University; Hampshire)
    'My Years at Cambridge'   1929/I   263
    Obituary   1939   912
Longman, Lt-Col. H. K. (Eton; Cambridge University; Middlesex; Surrey)
    Obituary   1959   934
Longrigg, E. F. (Rugby; Cambridge University; Somerset)
    Obituary   1975   1080
Longrigg, J. F. (Shrewsbury; Kent)
    Obituary   1972   1053
Longton, 2nd Lieut. E. J. (Westminster)
    Obituary   1916   183
Longworth, T. (Journalist)
    Obituary   1974   1076
Lonsdale, Lieut. A. C. G. (Radley)
    Obituary   1916   183
Looker, S. J. (Journalist)
    Obituary   1966   969
Looking Ahead   Note   1970   75
Loraine, Sir P. L. 12th Bart. (Eton)
    Obituary   1962   987
Lord, A. (Leicestershire)
    Obituary   1970   1023
Lord, L. (Bacup C.C.)
    Obituary   1922/I   260
Lord's Cricket Ground
    Activity at Note on   1944   62
    and Australia Note on   1945   58

'And the M.C.C.: Thirty Years of History'
Sir F. E. Lacey		1931/I	*275*
Centenary Dinner		<u>1915/II</u>	*302*
Centenary Match		1915/II	*300*
Centenary Test Group at Photograph		1981	*110*
Changes at Note		1983	*81*
Drainage at Note		1965	*107*
Elizabeth II, Queen at	1952	1953	*53*
Photographs	1960	1961	*85*
	1961	1962	*85*
	1963	1964	*61*
	1967	1968	*59*
England Selectors at			
Photographs	1983	1984	*Plate*
England Team at Photographs	1948	1949	*66*
	1960	1961	*87*
	1963	1964	*63*
	1976	1977	*85*
	1980	1981	*70*
	1982	1983	*Plate*
Fine Catch at Photograph		1963	*152*
First Class Umpires at Photograph		1984	*Plate*
Flying Bomb stops Cricket at Photograph		1945	*33*
Four Stumps in Lord's Experiment			
Photograph		1964	*67*
Full House for Jubilee Test Photograph		1978	*84*
Hendren, E. at, Since the War		1923/I	*312*
Imperial Cricket Conference at Photograph		1961	*88*
Indoor School at Notes on		1977	*113*
		1978	*106*
'Lord's' J. Marshall Book Review		1970	*1060*
'Lord's 1946-1970' D. Rait-Kerr and			
I. A. R. Peebles Book Review		1972	*1094*
Old Timers at Photograph		1958	*45*
Paintings at Note on		1984	*51*
Personnel Charges at Note on		1974	*70*
Petition handed in at Note on		1984	*66*
Plan of Ground		1950	*427*
		ad passim	
Police Protection at Photograph		1981	*68*
Public Schools XI at 1942 Photograph		1943	*27*
Rest of the World Team at			
Photograph	1970	1971	*67*
Royal Australian Air Force at Photograph		1945	*34*
Square to be Relaid Note on		1972	*86*
Sunday Play at Note on		1966	*494*

Tavern Rebuilding Note on	1967	*324*
Test Match Saving Stand at Photograph	1954	*56*
'Two Chiefs at Lord's' (Duke of Norfolk and		
S. C. Griffith) Photograph	1963	*149*
Victory Calypso at Photograph	1951	*57*
Women Play at Photograph	1971	*89*
Loreburn, Lord (Cheltenham; Oxford University)		
Obituary	1924/I	*262*
Loudoun, G. M. (Essex)		
Obituary	1973	*1011*
Loudoun-Shand, Major S. W. (Dulwich)		
Obituary	1917	*198*
Loudspeaker Note on	1945	*62*
Loughery, W. G. R. (Ireland)		
Obituary	1978	*1074*
Loughnan, A. (Stonyhurst College; Melbourne C.C.; Victoria)		
Obituary	1928/I	*303*
Lovatt, C. (Staffordshire)		
Obituary	1953	*944*
Love, H. (Sussex)		
Obituary	1943	*379*
Love, H. S. B. (Victoria; New South Wales; Australia)		
Obituary	1970	*1023*
Love, J. (Nottinghamshire Club Cricket)		
Obituary	1907	*cxiii*
Love, J. D. (Yorkshire)		
Photographs	1977	*621*
	1982	*619*
Lovegrove, Lieut. E. W. (Cheltenham; Suffolk)		
Obituary	1941	*387*
Lovelace, 2nd Lieut. R. D. W. (Tonbridge)		
Obituary	1918	*194*
Lovell, 2nd Lieut. J. A. (Metropolitan Club Cricket)		
Obituary	1917	*199*
Lovell, Lieut. J. C. (Metropolitan Club Cricket)		
Obituary	1918	*194*
Lovell, L/Cpl. L. (Calgary C.C, Canada)		
Obituary	1917	*199*
Lovelock, O. H. (Western Australia)		
Obituary	1984	*1203*
Lovett, A. S. (Charterhouse)		
Obituary	1944	*307*
Lowe, F. S. (Kent)		
Obituary	1915/I	*231*
Lowe, Wing-Comdr, J. C. M. (Uppingham; Oxford University; Warwickshire)		
Obituary	1971	*1027*

Lowe, R. F. (Surrey)
Obituary   1961   950
Lowe, W. W. (Malvern; Cambridge University; Worcestershire)
Obituary   1946   442
Lowndes, Rev. Canon R. (Oxford University)
Obituary   1899   1
Lowndes, W. G. L. F. (Eton; Oxford University; Hampshire)
Obituary   1983   1249
Views on L.B.W. Experiment   1936/I   343
Lowry, T. C. (Hawkes Bay; Rangitikei; Wellington; Cambridge University; Somerset; New Zealand)
Obituary   1977   1045
Lowry, W. C. (Haverford College; U.S.A.)
Obituary   1920/I   180
Lowson, F. A. (Yorkshire; England)
Career Figures   1959   491
Photograph   1954   619
Lowson, Dr. J. A. (Hong Kong)
Obituary   1937/I   288
Lowth, Rev. A. J. (Winchester; Oxford University)
Obituary   1908/I   143
Lowther, Rt. Hon. W. (Patron Club Cricket)
Obituary   1913/I   19
Loyd, Gen. Sir H. (Army)
Obituary   1974   107
Lubbock, A. (Eton; Kent)
'Cricket in the Sixties and at the Present Day'   1909/I   109
Obituary   1917   25
Lubbock, A. B. (Eton)
Obituary   1945   33
Lubbock, E. (Eton; Kent)
Obituary   1908/I   14
Lubbock, H. J. (West Kent C.C.)
Obituary   1911/I   14
Lubbock, Dr. M. (Eton)
Obituary   1926/I   27
Lubbock, Sir N. (Eton; Kent)
Obituary   1915/I   23
Lubbock, R. (Eton)
Obituary   1900   lv
Lucan, Brig-Gen. Earl of (President M.C.C.)
Obituary   1950   91
Lucas, Rev. A. (Uppingham)
Obituary   1922/I   26
Lucas, A. P. (Uppingham; Cambridge University; Surrey; Middlesex; Essex; England)

Obituary	1924/I	*263*
Views on 'The Follow on'	1894	*xlviii*
Views on Throwing	1895	*lviii*

Lucas, C. E. (Eton; Sussex)
Obituary	1968	*1004*

Lucas, C. J. (Middlesex; Sussex)
Obituary	1929/I	*252*

Lucas, Major F. T. (Canada)
Obituary	1918	*195*

Lucas, M. P. (Sussex; Warwickshire)
Obituary	1922/I	*260*

Lucas, R. J. (Eton)
Obituary	1915/I	*232*

Lucas, R. S. (Merchant Taylors; Middlesex)
Obituary	1943	*379*
Team in West Indies 1895	1896	*400*

Lucas, Lieut. W. H. (Dover College)
Obituary	1917	*199*

Luckes, W. T. (Somerset)
Benefit Match	1938	*493*
Obituary	1983	*1249*

Luckhurst, B. W. (Kent; England)
Cricketer of the Year	1971	*79*
Luckhurst Stay with Kent Note on	1977	*115*
Photographs	1964	*429*
	1967	*441*
	1971	*70*
	1973	*431*
	1975	*441*

Luckie, M. M. F. (Wellington, New Zealand)
Obituary	1952	*958*

Luckin, M. W. (Transvaal)
Obituary	1938	*940*

Luddington, H. T. (Uppingham; Cambridge University; Cambridgeshire; Norfolk)
Obituary	1923/I	*302*

Luff, H. (Proprietor of Wisden)
Obituary	1911/I	*149*

Luff, J. M. G. A. (Durham)
Obituary	1919	*208*

Lugton, L/Cpl. F. (Victoria)
Obituary	1918	*215*

Lumb, E. (Yorkshire)
Obituary	1892	*xxxiii*

Lumb, R. G. (Yorkshire)
Photographs   1973   58&
    1975   61‹
Lumgair, Capt. R. R. M. (Uppingham; Peebleshire; Selkirk)
Obituary   1918   19:
Lumley, 2nd Lieut. F. W. (Royal High School; Edinburgh)
Obituary   1918   19·
Lund, V. (Buckinghamshire)
Obituary   1972   105
Lunnon, W. H. (Buckinghamshire)
Obituary   1912/I   17
Lunt, S. (Scorer Lancashire)
Obituary   1915/I   23·
Lupton, Major A. W. (Sedbergh; Yorkshire)
Obituary   1945   33·
Lusaka Nondescripts in Mauritius 1972   1973   96·
Lushington, Lt-Col. C. H. G. (Gentlemen of Worcestershire)
Obituary   1917   19·
Lushington, Capt. G. W. (M.C.C.)
Obituary   1917   1·
Lushington, Rev. T. G. L. (Rugby; Suffolk)
Obituary   1929/I   2·
Lusk, H. B. (Auckland; Canterbury; Wellington)
Obituary   1962   98·
Luther, Major A. C. G. (Rugby; Sussex)
Obituary   1962   98·
Lutter, F. (Denstone)
76 wkts Schools Averages   1920/II   3.
Luxmoore, Rt. Hon. Justice. (King's, Canterbury; President Kent)
Obituary   1945   3.
Luxton, Rev. C. H. (Exeter School; Cambridge University; Devon)
Obituary   1919   2·
Luxton, Rev. R. R. (Devon)
Obituary   1929/I   2.
Lyall, D. R. (Edingburgh Academy)
Obituary   1918   2.
Lydall, Rev. C. W. (Bradfield)
Obituary   1917   1
Lygon, Hon. R. E. (Chairman Worcestershire)
Obituary   1971   10·
Lyle, Lieut. A. J. (Greenock C.C.)
Obituary   1920/I   1
Lyle, Col. Sir A. M. P. (Fettes; Oxford University; Stirling; Scotland)
Obituary   1947   6
Lyle, Capt. I. A. de. H. (Eton)
Obituary   1943   3·

Lyle, Capt. R. C. (Felsted; Journalist)
Obituary   1944   *317*

Lyle, 2nd Lieut. T. B. (Merchiston Castle)
Obituary   1917   *225*

Lynch, 2nd Lieut. F. W. (Irish Club Cricket)
Obituary   1916   *183*

Lynch, Capt. J. (Dublin University)
Obituary   1916   *183*

Lynch, M. A. (Surrey; Guyana)
Photograph   1982   *557*

Lynden-Bell, Major-Gen. Sir A. (Kent Supporter)
Obituary   1944   *317*

Lynn, G. H. (Sussex)
Obituary   1922/I   *261*

Lyon, B. H. (Rugby; Oxford University; Gloucestershire)
Obituary   1971   *1027*
Portrait and Biography   1931/I   *289*

Lyon, Admr. Sir G. H. D'Oyly (Royal Navy; Hampshire)
Obituary   1948   *784*

Lyon, G. S. (Canada)
Obituary   1939   *913*

Lyon, H. (Winchester)
Obituary   1952   *958*
   1953   *944*

Lyon, J. (Lancashire)
Photograph   1978   *444*

Lyon, M. D. (Rugby; Cambridge University; Somerset)
Career Figure Amendment   1984   *1212*
Obituary   1965   *969*

Lyon, W. J. (Torquay; Cambridge University; Derbyshire; Staffordshire)
Obituary   1919   *208*

Lyons, A. T. (Eastern Province)
Obituary   1911/I   *149*

Lyons, J. J. (South Australia; Australia)
Obituary   1928/I   *291*

Lyttelton, Rt. Hon. A. (Eton; Cambridge University; Middlesex; England; President M.C.C.)
Obituary   1914/I   *187*
Tribute by Lord Darnley   1914/I   *200*
Views on High Scoring and L.B.W. Rule   1899   *lxxii*

Lyttelton, Rt. Rev. Hon. A. T. (Eton)
Obituary   1904   *lxxix*

Lyttelton, Rev. Hon. A. V. (Worcestershire)
Obituary   1929/I   *252*

Lyttelton, Rev. Hon. C. F. (Eton; Cambridge University; Worcestershire)
Obituary   1932/I   *248*

Lyttelton, Hon. C. G. See under Cobham, Lord
Lyttelton, Rev. Hon. Dr. E. (Eton; Cambridge University; Middlesex; Worcestershire)

Obituary	1943	38●
Views on High Scoring and the L. B. W. Rule	1899	lxxiv
Views on 'The Follow On'	1894	●

Lyttelton, Hon. G. W. (Eton)

Obituary	1963	103

Lyttelton, Hon. G. W. S. (Eton; Cambridge University)

Obituary	1914/I	18●

Lyttelton, Lieut. J. A. (Eton)

Obituary	1945	32●

Lyttelton, Gen. Rt. Hon. Sir N. G. (Eton; Worcestershire)

Obituary	1932/I	24●

Lyttelton. Hon. R. H. (Eton; Cricket Writer)

'The Development of Cricket'	1892	xl●
'Modern Batting and the L.B.W. Law'	1921/I	21●
Obituary	1940	84.
Tribute to A. G. Steel	1915/I	17●
Views on 'The Follow On'	1894	li●
Views on Throwing	1895	lv●

Lywood, L. W. (Surrey; Essex)

Obituary	1972	105.

McAlister, P. A. (Victoria; Australia)

Obituary	1939	91

McAllen, C. (Tasmanian Club Cricket)

Obituary	1925/I	27●

McAlpine, K. (Kent)

Obituary	1924/I	26●

Macan, G. (Harrow; Cambridge University)

Obituary	1944	3●

McArthur, H. D. (Winchester)

Obituary	1915/I	23●

Macartney, C. G. (New South Wales; Australia)

Benefit Match	1928/II	6●
'Charles Macartney and George Gunn'		
N. Cardus	1959	●
Obituary	1959	9●
Portrait and Biography	1922/I	2●

Macartney, I. (Journalist)

Tribute to H. Preston	1961	1●

Macaulay, C. H. (Yorkshire Club Cricket)

Obituary	1910/I	1●

McAulay, D. M. (Barbados)

Obituary	1913/I	1●

Macaulay, 2nd Lieut. G. C. G. (Rossall)
Obituary — 1918 — *195*

Macaulay, G. G. (Yorkshire; England)
Benefit Match — 1932/II — *111*
Obituary — 1941 — *388*
Portrait and Biography — 1924/I — *278*

Macaulay, T. (Rugby)
Obituary — 1898 — *xlvi*

McBain, A. (Aberdeenshire)
Obituary — 1955 — *934*

McBeath, D. J. (Otago; Canterbury; Scotland)
Obituary — 1964 — *950*

McBride, W. N. (Westminster; Oxford University; Hampshire)
Obituary — 1975 — *1081*

MacBryan, Lieut. E. C. (Oundle; Wiltshire)
Obituary — 1917 — *199*

MacBryan, J. C. W. (Exeter School; Cambridge University; Somerset; England)
Obituary — 1984 — *1203*
Portrait and Biography — 1925/I — *292*

McCabe, S. J. (New South Wales; Australia)
Fastest Hundred in Test Cricket — 1983 — *108*
Obituary — 1969 — *982*
Portrait and Biography — 1935/I — *282*
Testimonial Match — 1958 — *887*
Tribute to: W. Hammond — 1966 — *118*

McCaffrey, W. J. (Toronto Club Cricket)
Obituary — 1913/I — *191*

McCanlis, L. (Ducks C.C.)
Obituary — 1951 — *929*

McCanlis, Capt. W. (Kent)
Obituary — 1926/I — *279*
'The Tonbridge Nursery' — 1907 — *xcvi*

McCann, T. J. (Writer)
'Cricketer and the Sussex County by Election of 1741'
Book Review — 1978 — *1118*

McCarthy, Brig. C. H. F. D'Arcy (Rugby; Devon)
Obituary — 1978 — *1074*

McCaskie, N. (Winchester; Middlesex)
Obituary — 1969 — *983*

McCaughey, S. (Geelong; Cambridge University)
Obituary — 1956 — *974*

McConaghey, Lt-Col. M. E. (Clifton; Sandhurst)
Obituary — 1918 — *195*

McConchie, A. R. (Suffolk)
Obituary — 1922/I — *262*

McConnel, Major-Gen. D. F. (Winchester)
   Obituary   1962   98
McConnel, Major M. H. (Winchester)
   Obituary   1918   19
McConnon, J. E. (Glamorgan; England)
   Benefit Match   1962   39
   Photographs   1952   32
                                       1958   34
   Retirement Note   1956   56
McCool, C. L. (New South Wales; Queensland; Somerset; Australia)
   'Cricket is a Game' Book Review   1962   104
   Photographs   1957   51
                                     1960   53
   Record of Service   1961   65
McCorkell, N. T. (Hampshire)
   Photograph   1950   35
McCormack, V. C. (Jamaica)
   Obituary   1967   97
McCormick, E. J. (Sussex)
   Obituary   1943   38
McCormick, Rev. Canon J. (Bingley Grammar School; Ireland; Cambridge University)
   'Cricketers – Past and Present'   1895   li
   Obituary   1915/I   23
   Personal Recollections of John Wisden   1913/I   12
McCormick, Rt. Rev. Dr. J. G. (Devon; Norfolk)
   Obituary   1925/I   27
McCorquodale, E. G. (Harrow; Cambridge University)
   Obituary   1905   xc
McCosker, R. B. (New South Wales; Australia)
   Cricketer of the Year   1976   5
   Photograph   1976   4
McCraith, Sir D. (President Nottinghamshire)
   Obituary   1953   9
McCrudden, R. J. (Secretary Gloucestershire)
   Obituary   1968   100
McCubbin, Major G. R. (Transvaal)
   Obituary   1945   3
McCulloch, Capt. J. W. H. (Westminster)
   Obituary   1916   1
McCully, C. A. (Morris Park C.C., U.S.A.)
   Obituary   1923/I   3
McDonald, E. A. (Lancashire; Victoria; Australia)
   Benefit Match   1930/II   1
   Obituary   1938   9
   Portrait and Biography   1922/I   2

Macdonald, J. (Ireland)
Obituary   1970   *1023*
McDonald, J. A. (Derbyshire)
Obituary   1962   *988*
MacDonald, Lieut. M. D. (Rosedale C.C., Toronto)
Obituary   1916   *184*
MacDonald, Capt. Hon. R. I. (Radley)
Obituary   1919   *182*
McDonell, H. C. (Winchester; Cambridge University; Surrey; Hampshire)
Obituary   1967   *971*
MacDonnell, Lt-Col. Sir A. C. (Canadian Club Cricket)
Obituary   1943   *387*
McDonnell, P. S. (Victoria; New South Wales; Queensland; Australia)
Obituary   1897   *xli*
MacDonogh, Capt. J. J. (Philadelphia; U.S.A)
Obituary   1913/I   *190*
McEachern, Sir M. (Major of Melbourne)
Obituary   1911/I   *150*
McElhone, F. E. (New South Wales)
Obituary   1982   *1205*
McElhone, W. P. (Australian Cricket Board)
Obituary   1933/I   *255*
McElroy, C. E. (Canada)
Obituary   1908/I   *156*
McEntyre, G. A. (Cheshire)
Obituary   1977   *1051*
McEvoy, A. (Albion C.C.)
Obituary   1905   *xcix*
M'Evoy, F. E. (Victoria)
Obituary   1915/I   *248*
McEwan, J. W. (Middlesex)
Obituary   1904   *lxxxvi*
McEwan, K. S. (Essex; Eastern Province; Western Province; Western Australia)
Cricketer of the Year   1978   *95*
Photographs   1976   *376*
     1978   *88*
     1980   *379*
MacFarlan, Capt. W. (Loretto; Sandhurst)
Obituary   1902   *lxxiii*
MacFarlane, Capt. R. (Merchiston Castle)
Obituary   1918   *195*
McFarlane, T. A. (Otago)
Obituary   1968   *1004*
McGahey, C. P. (Essex; England)
Obituary   1936/I   *280*
Portrait and Biography   1902   *lxxix*

McGilvray, A. (Broadcaster; Writer)
'The A.B.C. Cricket Book – The Australian Tour of England 1968'
Book Review   1969   *1040*
'The A.B.C. Cricket Book – The Australian Tour of England 1972'
Book Review   1973   *1060*
'The A.B.C. Cricket Book – The Australian Tour of England 1977'
Book Review   1978   *1127*
'The Australian Tour of U.K. 1981'
Book Review   1982   *1272*
'New Zealand and India in Australia 1980-81'
Book Review   1982   *1272*
McGirr, H. M. (Wellington; New Zealand)
Obituary   1965   *969*
McGiverin, H. B. (Canada)
Obituary   1932/I   *249*
McGlew, D. J. (Natal; South Africa)
'Cricket Crisis' Book Review   1966   *1016*
'Cricket for South Africa' Book Review   1962   *1040*
Cricketer of the Year   1956   *62*
Photograph   1956   *54*
McGowan, J. S. T. (New South Wales Cricket Association)
Obituary   1923/I   *302*
MacGregor, G. (Uppingham; Cambridge University; Middlesex; England)
Obituary   1920/I   *180*
Portrait and Biography   1891   *xxxv*
Tribute by D. L. A. Jephson   1920/I   *247*
Views on High Scoring and L.B.W. Rule   1899   *lxxiv*
Views on Throwing   1895   *lvii*
McGregor, W. (Australian Team in New Zealand 1913-14)
Obituary   1982   *1205*
Machin, R. S. (Lancing; Cambridge University; Surrey)
Obituary   1969   *983*
Machin, W. V. (Gentlemen of Nottinghamshire)
Obituary   1916   *183*
McIlwraith, J. (Victoria; Australia)
Obituary   1940   *842*
McIntyre, A. J. (Surrey; England)
Benefit Match   1956   *552*
Career Figures   1959   *491*
Cricketer of the Year   1958   *61*
Photographs   1956   *544*
     1958   *53*
M'Intyre, W. (Nottinghamshire; Lancashire)
Benefit Match   1882   *127*
Obituary   1893   *xxxv*

McIver, C. D. (Forest School; Oxford University; Essex)
Obituary	1955	*934*
Schools Note	1902	*ci,civ*
1003 runs Schools Averages	1902	*450*

Mack, Rev. E. S. P. (Norfolk; Suffolk)
Obituary	1946	*448*

Mackarness, Rev. C. C. (Winchester)
Obituary	1919	*209*

Mackarness, Judge F. C. (Marlborough)
Obituary	1922/I	*272*

MacKay, 2nd Lieut. C. L. (Clifton; Gloucestershire)
Obituary	1916	*183*

Mackay, J. G. (Merchiston Castle; Toronto)
Obituary	1912/I	*172*

Mackay, J. R. M. (New South Wales)
Obituary	1954	*927*

Mackay, K. D. (Queensland; Australia)
Obituary	1983	*1250*
'Quest for the Ashes' Book Review	1967	*1016*
'Slasher Opens Up' Book Review	1965	*1020*

Mackay, Major M. (Bendigo C.C.)
Obituary	1917	*199*

Mackay, W. G. (Northumberland)
Obituary	1963	*1035*

Mackendrick, Lieut. G. K. (Trinity College School, Port Hope)
Obituary	1918	*215*

Mackenzie, A. O. M. (Loretto)
Obituary	1950	*911*

Mackenzie, A. W. (Canada)
Obituary	1908/I	*144*

Mackenzie, Lieut. B. M. S. (Haileybury)
Obituary	1919	*182*

Mackenzie, Sir C. (Writer)
Photograph	1973	*104*
'Shillings For W.G. – Looking Back Eighty Years'	1973	*103*

Mackenzie, D. (Western Australia)
Obituary	1980	*1151*

Mackenzie, Col. F. F. (Wellington)
Obituary	1935/I	268

Mackenzie, G. D. (Western Australia; Leicestershire; Australia)
Cricketer of the Year	1965	*91*
Photographs	1965	*77*
	1974	*467*

Mackenzie, Lieut. K. F. (Trinity College, Oxford)
Obituary	1918	*215*
Obituary	1893	*xxxv*

Mackenzie, R. T. H. (Cheltenham; Cambridge University)
Obituary   1935/I   *268*
McKegg, T. (Cumberland)
Obituary   1960   *954*
Mackeson, G. L. (President Kent)
Obituary   1951   *926*
McKibbin, T. R. (New South Wales; Australia)
Obituary   1941   *399*
Mackie, E. D. (Harrow)
Obituary   1928/I   *292*
Mackie, Rev. O. G. (Haileybury)
Obituary   1928/I   *293*
McKinna, G. H. (Manchester Grammar School)
Schools Note   1950   *708*
81 wkts Schools Averages   1950   *732*
Mackinnon, A. (Old Stagers)
Obituary   1921/I   *230*
Mackinnon, A. H. (Eastern Province; Transvaal; South Africa)
Obituary   1984   *1204*
Mackinnon, A. H. (Cameron Highlanders)
Obituary   1920/I   *155*
Mackinnon, D. (Buckinghamshire)
Obituary   1961   *950*
Mackinnon, F. A. (Harrow; Cambridge University; Kent; England)
Obituary   1948   *784*
Mackley, A. (Umpire)
Obituary   1983   *1250*
Macklin, 2nd Lieut. D. H. (King's, Rochester)
Obituary   1919   *182*
Mackrory, H. A. (Natal)
Obituary   1948   *786*
McLachlan, A. (Stockport C.C.)
Obituary   1918   *231*
M'Lachlan, N. (Loretto; Oxford University)
Obituary   1929/I   *252*
Maclagan, W. E. (Edinburgh Academy)
Obituary   1927   *283*
MacLaren, A. C. (Harrow; Lancashire; England)
'Archie – A Biography of A. C. MacLaren'
M. Down Book Review   1982   *1268*
In First Class Cricket   1896   *lxx*
In First Class Cricket   1912/I   *156*
Obituary   1945   *336*
'On the Preparation of Wickets'   1905   *lxxviii*
Portrait and Biography   1895   *xliv*
Schools Notes   1888   *274*
       1891   *299*

Team in Australia 1901-02	1903	*479*
McLaren, Capt. F. A. (Hampshire; Army)		
Obituary	1953	*994*
Maclaren, G. (Harrow; Lancashire)		
Obituary	1967	*971*
Maclaren, J. (Father of A. C.; Treasurer Lancashire)		
Obituary	1901	*lix*
Maclaren, Dr. J. A. (Harrow; Lancashire)		
Obituary	1953	*944*
McLaren, J. W. (Queensland; Australia)		
Obituary	1923/I	*310*
McLaren, Lieut. W. (Edinburgh Academy)		
Obituary	1918	*195*
Maclaurin, D. (Blair Lodge School; Peebleshire)		
Obituary	1916	*184*
75 wkts Schools Averages	1895	*321*
Maclean, Capt. A. P. (Upper Canada College)		
Obituary	1919	*182*
McLean, R. A. (Natal; South Africa)		
Cricketer of the Year	1961	*97*
Photograph	1961	*92*
'Pitch and Toss' Book Review	1958	*1013*
'Sackcloth without Ashes' Book Review	1959	*987*
Maclear, Capt. B. (Bedford Grammar School)		
Obituary	1916	*184*
Maclellan, Lieut. G. D. (Merchiston Castle)		
Obituary	1918	*195*
Macleod, A. (Felsted; Hampshire)		
Obituary	1984	*1204*
McLeod, C. E. (Victoria; Australia)		
Obituary	1919	*209*
McLeod, D. (Victoria)		
Obituary	1903	*lxxxii*
MacLeod, K. G. (Fettes; Cambridge University; Lancashire)		
Obituary	1968	*1004*
McLeod, L. M. (Fettes)		
Obituary	1908/I	*145*
MacLeod, M. F. (Tasmanian Cricket Association)		
Obituary	1908/I	*156*
M'Leod, N. (Australian Supporter)		
Obituary	1913/I	*203*
Mcleod, R. W. (Victoria; South Australia; Australia)		
Obituary	1908/I	*145*
MacLeod, W. M. (Fettes)		
Obituary	1933/I	*263*

McMahon, 2nd Lieut. C. (Military Cricket)
Obituary   1917   *201*

McMahon, J. W. (Surrey; Somerset)
Photograph   1957   *513*

McMahon, M. J. (Australian Sports Dealer)
Obituary   1909/I   *142*

McMaster, J. E. P. (England)
Obituary   1930/I   *258*

McMichael, S. (Victoria)
Obituary   1924/I   *265*

Macmillan, E. G. (Chairman Australian Cricket Board of Control)
Obituary   1971   *1028*

Mcmillan, 2nd Lieut. N. W. (Auckland)
Obituary   1943   *366*

Mcmillan, Q. (Transvaal; South Africa)
Obituary   1949   *866*

McMurray, T. (Surrey)
Obituary   1965   *969*

MacNab, Brig-Gen. C. L. (Military Cricket)
Obituary   1919   *182*

M'Nair, R. (Scotland)
Obituary   1905   *xcix*

Macnamara, Major G. (Army)
Obituary   1918   *195*

McNeilage, Pte. J. (Lynn Valley C.C., Vancouver)
Obituary   1918   *196*

McNeile, A. J. (Harrow)
Obituary   1930/I   *258*

McNeill, Rt. Hon. R. J. (Baron Cushenden; Harrow)
Obituary   1936/I   *292*

Macnutt, H. (U.S.A.)
Obituary   1928/I   *303*

Macpherson, R. (Fifeshire; American Club Cricket)
Obituary   1942   *360*

McRae, Temp. Surg. Lieut. F. M. (Somerset)
Obituary   1945   *324*

McReynolds, Lieut. QM. J. B. (Scarborough C.C.)
Obituary   1917   *201*

M'Shane, P. G. (Victoria; Australia)
Obituary   1905   *cv*

McVeagh, G. (Ireland)
Obituary   1969   *983*

McVicker, N. M. (Warwickshire; Leicestershire)
Photograph   1970   *576*

Macvictar, Lieut. J. E. C. (Aldenham)
Obituary   1919   *182*

McVittie, C. A. B. (Bedford School; Cambridge University; Kent)
Obituary 1974 *1076*
McWhinney, Gnr. S. M. (Upper Canada College)
Obituary 1917 *201*
McWilliam, Lieut. H. (Merchiston Castle)
Obituary 1917 *201*
Madden, D. A. (Australian Cricket Council)
Obituary 1924/I *265*
Madden-Gaskell, Major J. C. P. (Glamorgan; Somerset)
Obituary 1976 *1100*
Maddison, Rev. C. W. (Durham School)
Obituary 1921/I *230*
Maddock, A. L. (Journalist)
Obituary 1894 *xxxviii*
Maddocks, Lieut. J. A. (University College School)
Obituary 1917 *200*
Madras – in Ceylon 1966 1967 *893*
 1970 1971 *974*
 'Incident at' 1977 *995*
 Photograph of Ground 1982 *116*
Magee, H. (Philadelphia)
Obituary 1913/I *191*
Magill, Lieut. M. D. P. (Eton)
Obituary 1941 *388*
Magnay, Capt. J. C. F. (Harrow House Matches)
Obituary 1918 *195*
Magnay, Lt-Col. P. M. (Harrow)
Obituary 1918 *195*
Magniac, Lt-Col. E. (Clifton; North West India)
Obituary 1918 *196*
Magniac, Lt-Col. M. (Clifton; Army)
Obituary 1918 *196*
Mahaffy, Dr. Sir J. P. (Dublin University; Gentlemen of Ireland)
Obituary 1920/I *182*
Maiden Over' N. Joy Book Review 1951 *999*
Maidstone The Mote
 Plan of County Ground 1952 *383*
 ad passim
Mailer, Dr. R. (Victorian Cricket Association)
Obituary 1945 *347*
Mailey, A. A. (New South Wales; Australia)
Obituary 1968 *1004*
 'Ten for 66 and all that' Book Review 1959 *982*
 Testimonial Match 1957 *869*
Maitland, W. J. (Edinburgh Academy)
Obituary 1920/I *182*

Majendie, Rev. H. W. (Winchester; Wiltshire; Devon)
Obituary 1925 I 289
Majid Jahangir Khan (Punjab; Lahore; Cambridge University; Glamorgan; Queensland; Pakistan)
Cricketer of the Year 1970 67
Note on 1973 90
Photographs 1969 383
1970 58
1973 387
Makant, Capt. A. V. (Harrow)
Obituary 1916 184
Makant, J. W. (Repton)
Obituary 1925/I 289
Makant, Capt. R. K. (Harrow)
Obituary 1923/I 303
Makepeace, H. (Lancashire; England)
Benefit Match 1923/II 138
Obituary 1953 994
Makinson, J. (Owen's College; Cambridge University; Lancashire)
Obituary 1915/I 232
Malaysia in Ceylon 1971-72 1973 957
Malcolmson, Lieut. Adjt. H. (Pembroke College, Cambridge)
Obituary 1917 200
Malden, E. (Haileybury; Hertfordshire; Kent)
Obituary 1949 872
Malet, Rev. C. D. E. (Winchester)
Obituary 1931/I 260
Mallam, Capt. C. A. (Epsom College)
Obituary 1919 182
Mallam, C. G. C. (Uppingham; Rutland; Devon)
Obituary 1952 966
Mallam, T. W. (Cheltenham)
Obituary 1925/I 273
Mallender, N. A. (Northamptonshire)
Photograph 1982 510
Mallet, A. A. (South Australia; Australia)
'Spin Out' Book Review 1978 1124
Mallett, R. H. (Durham Cricket Administrator)
Obituary 1940 842
Mallinckrodt, K. W. (U.S.A.)
Obituary 1912 I 172
Malone, Lieut. M. E. (St. Andrews College, Toronto)
Obituary 1917 200
Malpass, J. (Durham Club Cricket)
Obituary 1917 256

Malthouse, S. (Derbyshire)
Obituary   1933   I   *263*

Malthouse, W. N. (Derbyshire)
Obituary   1962   *988*

Manfield, W. H. (Dulwich; Dorset)
Obituary   1939   *921*

Manger, 2nd Lieut. J. K. (Wellington; Dorset)
Obituary   1918   *196*

Mangin, Pte. H. R. F. (Osborne C.C., Montreal)
Obituary   1918   *215*

Mangold, C. A. (Eastern Province)
Obituary   1955   *934*

Manjrekar, V. L. (Bombay; Bengal; Andhra; Uttar Pradesh; Rajasthan; Maharashba; India)
Obituary   1984   *1204*

Mankad, M. H. (Vinoo; Western India; Nawanagar; Maharashtra; Gujerat; Bengal; Bombay; Rajasthan; India)
Career Figures   1979   *1082*
Cricketer of the Year   1947   *48*
'Vinoo Mankad' S. Vaidya Book Review   1971   *1078*
Obituary   1979   *1081*
Photograph   1947   *42*

Manley, H. (U.S.A. Club Cricket)
Obituary   1925/I   *273*

Manley, Lieut. J. F. (Ridley C.C., Vancouver)
Obituary   1918   *196*

Mann, Lieut. C. J. (Malvern)
Obituary   1919   *183*

Mann, E. J. (Marlborough; Cambridge University; Norfolk)
Obituary   1967   *975*

Mann, E. W. (Harrow; Cambridge University; Kent)
Obituary   1955   *934*

Mann, Capt. E. W. E. (Harrow)
Obituary   1944   *309*

Mann, F. G. (Eton; Cambridge University; Middlesex; England)
Schools Notes   1935/I   *296,300*
      1936/I   *313*
      1937/I   *304*
           308

Mann, F. T. (Malvern; Cambridge University; Middlesex; England)
Obituary   1965   *969*
Schools Notes   1905   *cxxxiii*
      1907   *cxlii*
      1908   *121*

Mann, N. B. F. (Natal; Eastern Province; South Africa)
Obituary   1953   *945*

Manners, Hon. J. N. (Eton)
Obituary — 1915/I — *233*

Manning, Cardinal H. E. (Harrow)
Obituary — 1893 — *xxxiii*

Manning, J. L. (Journalist)
Obituary — 1975 — *1081*

Manning, J. S. (South Australia; Northamptonshire)
Photograph — 1957 — *477*

Manning, T. E. S. (Wellingborough; Northamptonshire)
Obituary — 1976 — *1100*

Manning, W. J. M. (Cambridgeshire)
Obituary — 1955 — *934*

Mansell, V. M. (Journalist)
Obituary — 1916 — *184*

Mansfield, E. D. (Marlborough; Dorset)
Obituary — 1925/I — *273*

Mansfield, Hon. J. W. (Winchester; Cambridge University; Norfolk)
Obituary — 1933/I — *254*

Mantle, T. A. (Middlesex)
Obituary — 1885 — *8*

Maqsood, M. H. (Writer)
with Marchant M. I.
'Pakistan v England' Book Review — 1956 — *1024*

Maralanda, A. P. (Ceylon Schoolboys)
Obituary — 1967 — *972*

Marathon Match at Cambridge — 1974 — *791*

Marchant, F. (Eton; Cambridge University; Kent)
Obituary — 1947 — *692*

Marder, J. I. (President U.S.A. Cricket Association)
'Buying Back One's Past' — 1975 — *143*
Obituary — 1977 — *1046*

Marindin, Col. Sir F. A. (Royal Engineers)
Obituary — 1901 — *lix*

Marjoribanks, 2nd Lieut. M. E. (Glenalmond)
Obituary — 1919 — *199*

Marks, G. (Whitgift; Middlesex)
Obituary — 1939 — *913*

Marks, J. (New South Wales Supporter)
Obituary — 1908/I — *144*

Marks, Sgt. R. (Winnipeg C.C.)
Obituary — 1916 — *184*

Marks, V. J. (Blundells; Oxford University; Somerset; England)
Photograph — 1980 — *537*
Schools Note — 1974 — *828*

Marks, W. W. (Secretary Bedfordshire C.C.C.)
Obituary — 1926/I — *278*

Marlar, R. G. (Harrow; Cambridge University; Sussex)

'Ken Barrington: An Appreciation'	1982	*93*
'Decision Against England' Book Review	1984	*1262*
Photograph	1956	*568*
'The Universities in the Wisden Century'	1963	*697*

Marlborough v Cheltenham Centenary Match 1957 *790*

Marlow, 2nd Lieut. C. D. (King's Hospital, Dublin)

Obituary 1918 *196*

Marlow, F. W. (Staffordshire; Sussex)

Obituary 1953 *945*

Marlow, G. A. (Lincolnshire)

Obituary 1980 *1160*

Marlow, W. H. (Leicestershire)

Obituary 1977 *1052*

Marner, P. T. (Lancashire; Leicestershire)

Photographs	1959	*419*
	1961	*445*
	1964	*446*
	1967	*475*

Marques, C. L. (Hertfordshire)

Views on Laws 1957 *84*

Marr, A. P. (New South Wales; Australia)

Obituary 1941 *399*

Marriott, C. (Winchester; Oxford University; Leicestershire)

Obituary 1919 *209*

Marriott, Sir C. H. (Uppingham)

Obituary 1911/I *149*

Marriott, C. S. (St.Columba's; Cambridge University; Lancashire; Kent; England)

'The Complete Leg Break Bowler' Book Review	1969	*1028*
Obituary	1967	*972*

Marriott, 2nd Lieut. F. E. (Brasenose College, Oxford)

Obituary 1916 *185*

Marriott, Rev. G. S. (Winchester; Oxford University; Leicestershire)

Obituary 1906 *xciii*

Marriot, 2nd Lieut. G. V. (University College School)

Obituary 1919 *183*

Marriott, H. H. (Malvern; Cambridge University; Leicestershire)

Obituary 1950 *911*

Marsden, L/Cpl. A. (Derbyshire)

Obituary 1917 *200*

Marsden, Capt. E. (Gloucestershire)

Obituary 1916 *185*

Marsden, E. L. (Middlesex)

Obituary 1947 *693*

Marsden, Capt. J. A. (Royal High School, Edinburgh)
    Obituary   1919   *183*
Marsden-Smedley, 2nd Lieut. G. F. (Harrow)
    Obituary   1917   *200*
Marsh, E. C. (Malvern; Somerset; Devon)
    Obituary   1927/I   *283*
Marsh, J. (New South Wales)
    Obituary   1917   *256*
Marsh, J. F. (Amersham Hall; Cambridge University; Oxfordshire)
    Obituary   1928/I   *293*
Marsh, 2nd Lieut. N. C. (Birkenhead School)
    Obituary   1916   *185*
Marsh, R. W. (Western Australia; Australia)
    Action Photograph   1976   *39*
    Cricketer of the Year   1982   *81*
    'The Gloves of Irony' Book Review   1983   *1310*
    Photograph   1982   *73*
    'You'll Keep' Book Review   1977   *1098*
Marsh, Rev. T. H. (Bishop's Stortford College; Norfolk)
    Obituary   1942   *360*
Marsh, W. H. (Hertfordshire)
    Obituary   1969   *983*
Marshal, A. (Queensland; London County; Surrey)
    Obituary   1916   *185*
    Portrait and Biography   1909/I   *158*
Marshall, A. G. (Taunton; Someset)
    Obituary   1974   *1076*
Marshall, C. (Rugby; Cambridge University; Middlesex)
    Obituary   1905   *xcvii*
Marshall, C. E. D. (Dulwich)
    Obituary   1934/I   *270*
Marshall, E. A. (Nottinghamshire)
    Obituary   1971   *1028*
Marshall, Lt-Gen. Sir F. (IZingari)
    Obituary   1901   *l*
Marshall, 2nd Lieut. H. G. H. (Durham School)
    Obituary   1919   *18*
Marshall, H. M. (Westminster; Cambridge University)
    Obituary   1914/I   *18*
Marshall, H. P. (Broadcaster)
    Obituary   1974   *107*
Marshall, J. (Journalist; Writer)
    'The Duke Who Was Cricket' Book Review   1962   *104*
    'Headingley' Book Review   1971   *107*
    'Lord's' Book Review   1970   *106*
    'Old Trafford' Book Review   1972   *109*

'Sussex Cricket' Book Review	1960	*996*
Marshall, J. (Derbyshire)		
Obituary	1914/I	*190*
Marshall, J. C. (Rugby; Oxford University)		
Tribute to W. H. Ashdown	1980	*1145*
Marshall, J. F. (Rugby)		
Obituary	1951	*929*
Marshall, Rev. J. M. (New Zealand Club Cricket)		
	1905	*cv*
Marshall, Rev. Canon J. W. (King Edward's, Birmingham; Cambridge University)		
Obituary	1916	*186*
Marshall, K. W. (Edinburgh Academy; Scotland)		
1000 runs Schools Note	1931/I	*295*
Marshall, L. P. (Taunton; Somerset)		
Obituary	1979	*1083*
Marshall, M. D. (Barbados; Hampshire; West Indies)		
Cricketer of the Year	1983	*73*
Photographs	1982	*430*
	1983	*Plate*
Marshall, M. W. (Wellington, New Zealand)		
Obituary	1931/I	*260*
Marshall, R. E. (Barbados; Hampshire;.West Indies)		
Cricketer of the Year	1959	*49*
'Roy Marshall' J. Arlott Book Review	1962	*1050*
Note on	1962	*114*
Photographs	1956	*383*
	1958	*383*
	1959	*48*
	1961	*410*
	1964	*411*
	1966	*415*
	1971	*385*
'Test Outcast' Book Review	1971	*1079*
Marshall, R. M. (Giggleswick)		
Obituary	1946	*433*
Marshall, W. (Nottinghamshire; Groundsman Trent Bridge)		
Obituary	1944	*318*
Marshall, Lieut. W. (Durham Club Cricketer)		
Obituary	1916	*187*
Marshall, Lt-Col. W. R. (Ontario; Canada)		
Obituary	1917	*200*
Marshall, Lieut. W. S. (Canada)		
Obituary	1917	*200*
Marsham, Rev. C. D. B. (Oxford University; Oxfordshire)		
Obituary	1916	*187*

Marsham, C. H. B. (Eton; Oxford University; Kent)
Obituary 1929/I *252*
Marsham, C. J. B. (Oxford University)
Obituary 1902 *lxviii*
Marsham, G. (Eton; Kent)
Obituary 1928/I *293*
'A Short History of Kent Cricket for the Past Thirty Years
and More' 1907 *lxxxv*
Views on 'The Follow On' 1894 *lii*
Views on Throwing 1895 *lviii*
Marsham, Rev. Hon. J. (Kent)
Obituary 1927/I *283*
Marsham, R. H. B. (Oxford University; Oxfordshire; Buckinghamshire)
Obituary 1914/I *190*
Marson, 2nd Lieut. E. N. (Aston School)
Obituary 1916 *188*
Martin, A. W. (Groundsman Surrey)
Obituary 1953 *946*
Martin, Rev. C. (Eton)
Obituary 1911/I *149*
Martin, Capt. C. H. (Blundells)
Obituary 1917 *201*
Martin, E. (Middlesex)
Obituary 1925/I *273*
Martin, E. A. (Toronto C.C.)
Obituary 1923/I *316*
Martin, Comdr. E. G. (Eton, Oxford University; Worcestershire)
Obituary 1946 *442*
Martin, E. J. (Nottinghamshire)
Photograph 1955 *473*
Martin, F. (Kent; England)
Benefit Matches 1901 *63*
1909/II *7.*
Obituary 1922/I *26.*
Portrait and Biography 1892 *xxxv*
Martin, F. C. (Western Province)
Obituary 1936/I *29.*
Martin, 2nd Lieut. F. H. (Clifton)
Obituary 1918 *196*
Martin, F. R. (Jamaica; West Indies)
Obituary 1968 *100*
Martin, G. H. (Norfolk)
Obituary 1965 *97*
Martin, G. N. (Incogniti)
Obituary 1906 *xci.*

Martin, G. W. (Tasmania)
Obituary 1969 *984*
Martin, H. (Manhattan C.C.)
Obituary 1913/I *191*
Martin, M. T. (Rugby; Cambridge University; Middlesex; Warwickshire)
Obituary 1919/I *142*
Martin, Rev. R. (Marlborough)
Obituary 1928/I *294*
Martin, Sir R. B. 1st Bart. (West Kent C.C.)
Obituary 1917 *256*
Martin, T. R. (Groundsman Oval)
Obituary 1933/I *254*
Martin, W. A. (Coach Eton)
Obituary 1955 *934*
Martin-Jenkins, C. (Marlborough; Surrey; Broadcaster; Writer)
'Cricket Contest: The Post Packer Tests'
Book Review 1981 *1198*
'In Defence of the Ashes' Book Review 1980 *1203*
'The Jubilee Tests and the Packer Revolution'
Book Review 1978 *1124*
'M.C.C. in India 1976-77' Book Review 1978 *1122*
'Testing Time: M.C.C. in West Indies 1973-74'
Book Review 1975 *1120*
Martindale, E. A. (Barbados; West Indies)
Obituary 1973 *1012*
Martineau, C. (Uppingham)
Obituary 1936/I *282*
Martineau, G. D. (Journalist)
Obituary 1977 *1046*
Martineau, H. M. (Eton; Cricket Patron)
Obituary 1977 *1046*
Team in Egypt 1930 1931/II *710*
1931 1932/II *702*
1932 1933/II *694*
1933 1934/II *696*
1934 1935/II *689*
1936 1937/II *694*
Martineau, L. (Uppingham; Cambridge University)
Obituary 1907 *cxiii*
Martineau, Sir P. H. (Harrow)
Obituary 1945 *338*
Martingell, W. (Kent; Surrey)
Obituary 1898 *xlv*
Martyn, H. (Exeter School; Oxford University; Somerset; Devon; Cornwall)
Obituary 1929/I *253*

Marylebone Cricket Club (M.C.C.)

Tom Brown Centenary Match Photograph	1942		25
Centenary Week	1888		218
England Honorary Cricket Members	1965		345
	1982		359
	1984		323
Honorary Life Members	1982		359
Honorary Life Members Overseas	1961		553
	1969		333
150th Anniversary Celebrations	1938		261
'Lord's and the M.C.C.: Thirty Years of History'			
Sir F. E. Lacey	1931		275
M.C.C. (Cricket) Council Note on	1969		94
'M.C.C. Examine Amateur Status'	1958		111
M.C.C. or England Note on	1972		85
'M.C.C. and South Africa' M. Engel	1984		65
M.C.C. Under Fire Note on	1979		79
Paid Players admitted by M.C.C. Note on	1969		619
'Parliament of Cricket 1787-1937'	1938		242
Professionals Join M.C.C. Note on	1950		260
Secretaries of M.C.C. List of	1963		143

M.C.C. Touring Teams (Excludes those of Test Match Status)

in Argentina	1912	1913/II	575
in Bangladesh	1978-79	1980	1094
	1980-81	1982	968
in Bermuda	1974	1975	929
in British Honduras	1959-60	1961	831
in Canada	1937	1938	838
	1951	1952	898
	1959	1960	870
and U.S.A.	1967	1968	900
in Central Africa	1964-65	1966	895
in Channel Islands	1924	1925/II	576
	1925	1926/II	576
	1926	1927/II	637
	1927	1928/II	629
	1928	1929/II	636
	1929	1930/II	651
	1930	1931/II	640
	1931	1932/II	638
	1932	1933/II	637
	1933	1934/II	624
	1934	1935/II	638
	1935	1936/II	613
	1936	1937/II	611
	1937	1938	764

		1938	1939	*771*
		1939	1940	*712*
in Denmark		1922	1923/II	*554*
and Holland		1925	1926/II	*578*
		1983	1984	*500*
in East Africa		1957-58	1959	*819*
		1963-64	1965	*852*
'M.C.C. in Uganda' Book Review			1964	*1006*
		1973-74	1975	*958*
and Far East		1981-82	1983	*1187*
in Egypt		1909	1910/II	*507*
in Far East and Sri Lanka		1969-70	1971	*920*
in Far East and East Africa		1981-82	1983	*1187*
in Holland		1933	1934/II	*626*
in Hong Kong		1965-66	1967	*847*
		1974-75	1976	*957*
in India		1926-27	1928/II	*631*
in New Zealand		1906-07	1908/II	*503*
and Australia		1922-23	1924/II	*618*
		1929-30	1931/II	*642*
		1935-36	1937/II	*614*
in Pakistan ('A' Team)		1955-56	1957	*791*
'Pakistan Cricket on the March' Q. Butt				
Book Review			1958	*1011*
in Pakistan (Under 25) Team		1966-67	1968	*889*
in South Africa (Schools Team)		1965-66	1967	*902*
in Sri Lanka (Ceylon)		1951-52	1953	*773*
		1954-55	1956	*822*
		1961-62	1963	*867*
		1968-69	1970	*913*
		1969-70	1971	*920*
		1976-77	1978	*917*
in South America		1926-27	1928/II	*661*
		1958-59	1960	*867*
		1964-65	1966	*845*
in U.S.A. and Canada		1905	1906	*505*
		1907	1908/II	*496*
		1967	1968	*900*
and Far East		1981	1983	*1187*
in West Indies		1911	1912/II	*498*
		1912-13	1914/II	*515*
		1925-26	1927/II	*641*
Masefield, R. B. (Cambridge University)				
Obituary			1916	*188*
Mashonaland Country Districts in England 1964			1965	*799*
Book Review			1966	*1016*

Mason, F. R. (North Island, New Zealand)
  Obituary   1937/I   *275*

Mason, J. E. (Tonbridge; Kent)
  Obituary   1939   *913*

Mason, J. R. (Winchester; Kent; England)
  'In the Cricket Field'   1913/I   *169*
  Obituary   1959   *935*
  Portrait and Biography   1898   *xlix*
  Schools Notes   1891   *301*
                                            1893   *300*
                                            1894   *lv,lvi,lxii*

Mason, M. (Nottinghamshire Committee)
  Obituary   1918   *231*

Mason, R. (Writer)
  'Warwick Armstrong's Australians'
  Book Review   1972   *1094*
  'Walter Hammond' Book Review   1963   *1110*
  'Jack Hobbs' Book Review   1961   *999*
  'Plum Warner's Last Season' Book Review 1971   *1070*

Massey, W. M. (Stirlingshire; Quebec C.C.)
  Obituary   1918   *232*

Massie, H. H. (New South Wales; Australia)
  Obituary   1939   *913*

Massie, R. A. L. (Western Australia; Australia)
  Cricketer of the Year   1973   *86*
  Photograph   1973   *70*

Massie, R. J. A. (New South Wales)
  Obituary   1967   *972*

Master, H. C. (Norfolk)
  Obituary   1944   *318*

Masterman, Capt. H. W. (3rd Welsh Regiment)
  Obituary   1902   *lxxiii*

Masterman, Sir J. C. (Free Foresters; Oxfordshire)
  Obituary   1978   *1074*

Match Results in County Championship 1873-1939   1940   *116*
  Correction   1941   *61*

Mather, Lieut. A. N. (Canford School; Oxford University)
  Obituary   1945   *324*

Mather-Jackson, Sir A. H. Bart. (Harrow; Derbyshire)
  Obituary   1984   *1204*

Matheson, 2nd Lieut. C. B. (Glenalmond)
  Obituary   1918   *196*

Matheson, 2nd Lieut. C. B. (Glenalmond)
  Obituary   1918   *196*

Mathews, E. (Harrow; Oxford University)
  Obituary   1933/I   *263*

Mathews, J. K. (Felsted; Sussex)
  Obituary   1963   *1035*
Mathews, L. H. S. (St.Paul's)
  Obituary   1947   *693*
Maton, L. J. (Rugby; Wiltshire)
  Obituary   1934/I   *270*
Matson, H. (Aberdeenshire)
  Obituary   1957   *946*
Matthews, A. D. (St.David's Lampeter; Glamorgan; Northamptonshire; England)
  Obituary   1978   *1075*
Matthews, E. S. (Harrow)
  Obituary   1916   *189*
Matthews, F. C. (Nottinghamshire)
  Obituary   1962   *988*
Matthews, Major L. W. (Eton)
  Obituary   1936/I   *293*
Matthews, Sub-Lieut. M. H. (Westminster; Oxford University)
  Obituary   1941   *388*
Matthews, Hon. R. C. (Canadian Cricket Association)
  Obituary   1953   *946*
Matthews, T. G. (Gloucestershire)
  Obituary   1933/I   *255*
Matthews, T. J. (Victoria; Australia)
  Obituary   1945   *347*
Matthews, T. J. (Secretary Lancashire; Journalist)
  Obituary   1924/I   *265*
Matting is Better for Batting Note on   1982   *90*
Maturin, Dr. H. (Middlesex; Hampshire)
  Obituary   1921/I   *230*
Maude, D. (Writer)
  'A Century of Yorkshire County Cricket at Park Avenue, Bradford'
    Book Review   1982   *1258*
Maude, Lt-Gen. Sir F. S. (Military Cricket)
  Obituary   1918   *196*
Maude, F. W. (M.C.C.)
  Obituary   1924/I   *266*
Maude, J. (Eton; Oxford University)
  Obituary   1935/I   *268*
Maudsley, Professor R. H. (Malvern; Oxford University; Warwickshire)
  Obituary   1982   *1205*
Maul, H. C. (Warwickshire)
  Obituary   1941   *400*
Maul, Rev. J. B. (Uppingham; Cambridge University)
  Obituary   1933/I   *263*
Maul, Capt. S. D. (Uppingham; Sandhurst; Buckinghamshire)
  Obituary   1911/I   *150*

Maule, Rev. Dr. W. (Gentlemen of Kent)
  Obituary   1914/I   *190*
Maunes, C. T. (Perthshire; Scotland)
  Obituary   1939   *921*
Maurice, Col. D. B. (Uppingham, Berkshire)
  Obituary   1927/I   *295*
Maw, P. T. (Harrow; Herefordshire)
  Obituary   1941   *400*
Maxwell, C. R .(Brighton College; Nottinghamshire; Middlesex; Worcestershire)
  Obituary   1974   *1076*
  Schools Note   1932/II   *276,278*
                                                           280,293
  1037 runs Schools Averages   1932/I   *608*
Maxwell, Pte. J. H. (Wadham College, Oxford)
  Obituary   1918   *215*
May Another Dismal one Note on   1970   *74*
  Rain Ruined Note on   1980   *84*
  Wettest since 1773 Note on   1968   *91*
May, F. B. (Clifton)
  Obituary   1908/I   *144*
May, 2nd Lieut. H. G. (Sherborne)
  Obituary   1916   *189*
May, Lt-Col. J. (President Basingstoke C.C.)
  Obituary   1921/I   *230*
May, P. B. H. (Charterhouse; Cambridge University; Royal Navy; Surrey; England)
  Action Photographs   1958   *47*
                                                 1959   *37*
  Career Statistics   1971   *105*
  Cricketer of the Year   1952   *76a*
  'From Dr Grace to Peter May'
  H. Strudwick   1959   *61*
  England Maintain Mastery under May Note on   1957   *68*
  Gives up Captaincy Note on   1962   *113*
  May and Cowdrey Note on   1955   *81*
  May's Distinction Note on   1958   *72*
  'Peter May' R. Rodrigo Book Review   1961   *998*
  'Peter May – The Complete Master'
  J. Woodcock   1971   *101*
  Photographs   1952   *76*
                                               1954   *537*
                                             1955   *57*
                                             1956   *544*
                                           1971   *102*

Schools Notes	1945	*245*
	1946	*288, 291, 296*
	1947	*560, 566*
	1948	*645, 651*
	1956	*747*
Tributes to: G. Geary	1982	*1201*
Sir Frank Worrell	1968	*122*

May, P. R. (Cambridge University; London County; Surrey; Ceylon)
Obituary   1966   *969*

Maybin, Lieut. J. J. (Ayr C.C.)
Obituary   1917   *201*

Mayer, J. H. (Warwickshire)
Obituary   1982   *1205*

Mayes, Dr. A. D. A. (Queensland)
Obituary   1984   *1205*

Mayhew, Major T. G. (Uppingham; Kent)
Obituary   1966   *969*

Maylor, T. (Canadian Club Cricketer)
Obituary   1934/I   *270*

Maynard, Lieut. A. F. (Durham School; Durham)
Obituary   1917   *201*

Maynard, C. W. (Warwickshire; Lancashire)
Photograph   1980   *588*

Maynard, E. A. J. (Harrow; Derbyshire)
Obituary   1932/I   *249*

Mayne, E. R. (Victoria; South Australia; Australia)
Obituary   1963   *1038*

Mayne, H. B. (Westminster; Oxford University)
Obituary   1893   *xxxiii*

Mayo, H. E. (Surrey)
Obituary   1892   *xxxiv*

Mead, 2nd Lieut. C. (Charterhouse)
Obituary   1916   *189*

Mead, C. P. (Hampshire; Suffolk; England)
Benefit Matches   1921/II   *225*
                    1931/II   *371*
Hundredth Hundred   1928/II   *369*
Obituary   1959   *936*
Portrait and Biography   1912/I   *190*

Mead, E. A. (Nottinghamshire)
Benefit Match   1954   *507*

Mead, H. (Essex)
Obituary   1922/I   *262*

Mead, 2nd Lieut. R. E. C. (King's Canterbury)
Obituary   1918   *196*

Mead, W. (Essex; London County; England)
Benefit Match	1901	*194*
Obituary	1955	*935*
Portrait and Biography	1904	*lxxv*

Mead-Briggs, R. (Warwickshire)
Obituary	1957	*947*

Meade, S. (Philadelphia)
Obituary	1912/I	*173*

Meakin, B. (Staffordshire; Clifton; Gloucestershire)
Obituary	1965	*970*

Mears, Pte. A. (Brantford C.C., Ontario)
Obituary	1918	*196*

Meckiff, I. (Victoria; Australia)
'Thrown out' Book Review	1962	*1041*

Medlicott, W. S. (Harrow; Oxford University; Wiltshire)
Obituary	1971	*1028*

Medworth, C. O. (Writer)
'Noursemen in England' Book Review	1953	*996*

Meek, H. E. (Harrow)
Obituary	1921/I	*231*

Meeking, H. F. (Eton)
Obituary	1910/I	*141*

Meff, Lieut. W. B. (Aberdeenshire)
Obituary	1917	*201*

Meher-Homji, K. R. (Parsis; Bombay; Western India; India)
Obituary	1983	*1251*

Mehra, R. (Northern India; Delhi)
Obituary	1984	*1205*

Mehta, D. S. (Parsis)
Obituary	1929/I	*254*

Melbourne Cricket Club
Centenary	1955	*85*
Centenary Match	1940	*760*
and Women	1984	*1149*

Melbourne University Owls
in South East Asia 1967-68	1969	*927*

Melford, M. (Journalist; Writer)
'Botham Rekindles the Ashes' Book Review	1982	*1266*
'The D'Oliveira Case'	1969	*74*
'India 1932-1982'	1982	*117*
'Ups and Downs of the Springboks'	1970	*147*

Melle, Dr. B. G. Von. B. (Western Province; Transvaal; Oxford University; Hampshire)
Obituary	1967	*972*

Mellor, Judge. F. H. (Cheltenham; Cambridge University; Kent)
Obituary	1926/I	*279*

Melluish, G. C. (Essex; Northamptonshire)
Obituary 1978 *1075*
Melly, A. G. (Liverpool Club Cricket)
Obituary 1917 *256*
Melly, Lieut. R. E. (Coventry Club Cricket)
Obituary 1917 *202*
Melville, A. (Natal; Oxford University; Transvaal; Sussex; South Africa)
Cricketer of the Year 1948 *57*
Obituary 1984 *1205*
Photograph 1948 *40*
Tribute to: W. R. Hammond 1966 *118*
Melville, P. (Lancashire League)
Obituary 1980 *1160*
Melville, R. L. (Merion C.C., Philadelphia)
Obituary 1920/I *155*
Mence, M. D. (Bradfield; Warwickshire; Gloucestershire)
Schools Note 1963 *802*
84 wkts Schools Averages 1963 *813*
Menzies, Dr. H. (Middlesex)
Obituary 1937/I *288*
Menzies, Rt. Hon. Sir R. (President Kent; Prime Minister Australia)
'Cricket: An Enduring Art' 1963 *67*
Obituary 1979 *1083*
Photograph 1963 *66*
Tribute to: S. McCabe 1969 *983*
Mercer, J. (Sussex; Glamorgan; Northamptonshire)
Benefit Match 1937/II *414*
Portrait and Biography 1927/I *308*
Mercer, J. (Uxbridge C.C.)
Obituary 1928/I *294*
Merchant, M. I. (Writer)
with Maqsood, M. H. 'Pakistan v England'
Book Review 1956 *1024*
Merchant, V. M. (Hindus; Bombay; India)
'Duleep: The Man and His Game' Book Review 1964 *1003*
'India be Bold' 1959 *82*
Note on 1944 *58*
Portrait and Biography 1937/I *294*
'Twenty Years of Indian Test Cricket' 1952 *110*
Views on Growing Pains of Cricket 1956 *85*
Merewether, Capt. C. K. (Oriel College, Oxford)
Obituary 1918 *197*
Merewether, Capt. J. A. (Beaumont College)
Obituary 1917 *202*
Merewether, Rev. W. A. S. (Winchester)
Obituary 1929/I *254*

Merrett, Sir H. (President Glamorgan)
  Obituary   1960   *954*

Merrick, H. J. (Gloucestershire)
  Obituary   1962   *988*

Merriman, W. R. (Winchester)
  Obituary   1925/I   *274*

Merritt, W. E. (Canterbury; Northamptonshire; New Zealand)
  Obituary   1978   *1075*

Merry, C. A. (Trinidad; West Indies)
  Obituary   1965   *970*

Merry, Deputy Flight Comdr. D. (Trinidad)
  Obituary   1945   *324*

Mesham, Col. A. (Marlborough)
  Obituary   1919   *209*

Meston, S. P. (Gloucestershire; Essex)
  Obituary   1961   *950*

Metal Pitch Note on   1972   *464*

Metcalfe, E. J. (Eton; Hertfordshire; Queensland)
  Obituary   1952   *959*

Metcalfe, Capt. J. C. (Batley C.C.)
  Obituary   1919   *183*

Methods of Reckoning in
County Championship Matches   1940   *116*

Methuen, Lord (Eton)
  Obituary   1975   *1081*

Meyer, B. J. (Gloucestershire)
  Benefit Match   1972   *425*
  Photographs: 1962   *409*
                                           1969   *404*

Meyer, 2nd Lieut. C. C. W. (Beaumont College)
  Obituary   1917   *202*

Meyer, W. E. (Gloucestershire)
  Obituary   1955   *938*

Meyers, H. A. (New York Club Cricketer)
  Obituary   1926/I   *279*

Meynell, L. (Writer)
  'Plum Warner' Book Review   1952   *1018*

Meyrick-Jones, Rev. F. (Marlborough; Cambridge University; Hampshire; Kent; Norfolk)
  Obituary   1951   *926*

Mian, Mohammed Saeed (Northern India; Punjab; Pakistan's First International Captain)
  Obituary   1980   *1151*

Michell, W. G. (Wellington; Warwickshire)
  Obituary   1927/I   *295*

Micklem, L. (Eton)
Obituary   1920/I   *182*
Micklem, L. O. (Winchester)
Obituary   1953   *946*
Middlebrook, W. (Yorkshire)
Obituary   1920/I   *182*
Middlesex County Cricket Club
'A Middlesex Century' I. A. R. Peebles   1965   *128*
County Badge   1950   *426*
    ad passim
'Middlesex' T. C. F. Prittie Book Review   1953   *1000*
'Middlesex' E. M. Wellings Book Review   1973   *1052*
'Middlesex Cricketers' Association of Cricket Statisticians
Book Review   1977   *1088*
'Middlesex County Cricket Club 1921-1947'
N. Haig and H. R. Murrell Book Review   1951   *989*
Middlesex in Zimbabwe 1980-81   1982   *1140*
Middlesex Test Players for England, List   1965   *134*
Middlesex Win Championship Note on   1981   *95*
Team Portraits
Champion County   1947   1948   *34*
Joint Champions   1949   1950   *68*
    1974   1975   *490*
    1975   1976   *493*
    1976   1977   *493*
Gillette Cup Goes to Middlesex   1977   1978   *87*
    1977   1978   *477*
    1978   1979   *469*
    1979   1980   *493*
    1980   1981   *492*
    1981   1982   *497*
    1982   1983   *508*
    1983   1984   *470*
Middleton, H. W. (Junior) (Philadelphia)
Obituary   1920/I   *183*
Middleton, J. (Western Province; South Africa)
Obituary   1915/I   *249*
Middleton, R. F. (Chairman Australian Board of Control)
Obituary   1976   *1100*
Midgley, C. A. (Yorkshire)
Obituary   1943   *381*
Midlands Cricket Association
Views on Laws   1957   *86*
Midlands Knock-out Competition   1963   *693*
Middleton, Earl of (President Surrey)
Obituary   1943   *381*

Midwinter, E. (Writer)
  'W. G. Grace – His Life and Times'
  Book Review   1982   *1268*
Midwinter, W. E. (Victoria; Gloucestershire; England; Australia)
  'The Midwinter File' G. Parker   1971   *142*
Miéville, G. F. (Haberdasher's School)
  Obituary   1917   *201*
Mignon, E. (Middlesex)
  Obituary   1926/I   *279*
Mignon, W. (Grenada)
  Obituary   1966   *970*
Mihell, A. (Umpire)
  Obituary   1916   *189*
Milburn, C. (Northamptonshire; Durham; Western Australia; England)
  Benefit Match   1972   *524*
  Cricketer of the Year   1967   *78*
  'Largely Cricket' Book Review   1969   *1032*
  Note on   1960   *126*
  Photographs   1967   *68*
                 1868   *516*
Mildmay, Major Sir H. P. St.J. 6th Bart. (Hampshire)
  Obituary   1917   *256*
Miles, A. C. (Eton)
  Obituary   1920/I   *183*
Miles, 2nd Lieut. A. O. (Lancing)
  Obituary   1917   *202*
Miles, Col. C. N. (Eton)
  Obituary   1919   *210*
Miles, E. (Marlborough)
  Obituary   1950   *916*
Miles, E. V. (Border)
  Obituary   1983   *125*
Miles, 2nd Lieut. H. R. (Shrewsbury)
  Obituary   1917   *202*
Miles, Sir J. C. (Shrewsbury)
  Obituary   1964   *956*
Miles, Rev. P. E. (Harrow)
  Obituary   1911/I   *16.*
Miles, Major P. W. H. (Marlborough; Nottinghamshire)
  Obituary   1934/I   *27*
Miles, R. F. (Marlborough; Oxford University; Gloucestershire)
  Obituary   1931/I   *26*
Miles, W. H. (Oxbridge C.C.; Hampton Wick C.C.)
  Obituary   1896   *x*
Miles, W. S. (Harrow)
  Obituary   1973   *101*

Millar, C. C. H. (Weedkiller to Lord's)
Obituary   1943   *381*

Millar, Capt. S. G. (Loretto; West of Scotland)
Obituary   1917   *202*
Schools Note   1906   *cxxx*
78 wkts Schools Averages   1906   *479*

Millar-Hallett, 2nd Lieut. (Rugby)
Obituary   1917   *202*

Miller, A. M. (Eton; Wiltshire; England)
Obituary   1960   *954*

Miller, Lieut. A. W. B. (Fettes)
Obituary   1918   *197*

Miller, Rev. E. (Winchester)
Obituary   1902   *lxix*

Miller, G. (Chesterfield Grammar School; Derbyshire; England)
Photographs   1977   *361*
    1980   *365*
Schools Note   1973   *825*

Miller, J. H. (West of Scotland)
Obituary   1927/I   *284*

Miller, K. R. (Victoria; New South Wales; Nottinghamshire; Australia)
Awarded M.B.E.   1956   *75*
with R. S. Whitington 'Bumper' Book Review   1954   *976*
'Cricket from the Grandstand' Book Review   1960   *1001*
with R. S. Whitington 'Cricket Caravan'
Book Review   1952   *1012*
Cricketer of the Year   1954   *67*
with R. S. Whitington 'Fours Galore'
Book Review   1970   *1070*
with R. S. Whitington 'Gods or Flanelled Fools'
Book Review   1955   *994*
'Keith Miller: A Cricketing Biography'
M. Bose Book Review   1981   *1203*
'Keith Miller – The Golden Nuggett'
R. S. Whitington Book Review   1983   *1310*
Note on Big hitting   1946   *63*
Photograph   1954   *60*

Miller, N. (Dulwich; Surrey)
Obituary   1968   *1005*

Miller-Hallett, A. (President Sussex)
Obituary   1954   *928*

Milles-Lade, Hon. H. A. (Kent)
Obituary   1938   *941*

Milligan, F. W. (Yorkshire; England)
Obituary   1901   *lx*

Milligan, Capt. J. R. (Edinburgh Academy)
   Obituary   1920/I   15

Millman, G. (Bedfordshire; Nottinghamshire; England)
   Photographs   1958   50
                                            1964   51

Mills, Cpl. A. E. (Auckland Club Cricket)
   Obituary   1917   20

Mills, E. (Nottinghamshire; Surrey)
   Obituary   1900   xlv

Mills, G. (Auckland)
   Obituary   1943   38

Mills, Capt. G. D. (Haileybury; Sandhurst)
   Obituary   1918   19

Mills, G. T. (Worcestershire)
   Obituary   1984   120

Mills, I. (Auckland)
   Obituary   1958   96

Mills, J. (Gloucestershire)
   Obituary   1936/I   28

Mills, J. (Nottinghamshire)
   Obituary   1933/I   25

Mills, J. E. (Auckland; New Zealand)
   Obituary   1973   10

Mills, P. T. (Gloucestershire)
   Benefit Match   1925/II   20
   Obituary   1951   92

Mills, W. G. (Lancashire)
   Obituary   1903   lx

Miln, Capt. G. G. (King's School, Chester)
   Obituary   1919   18

Miln, W. W. (King's School, Chester)
   Obituary   1919   2

Milne, Capt. J. G. (West of Scotland)
   Obituary   1919   1

Milne, R. O. (Gentlemen of Warwickshire; Lancashire)
   Obituary   1928/I   2

Milne, W. (Northumberland)
   Obituary   1952   9

Milner, E. C. (Secretary East Molesey C.C.)
   Obituary   1912/I   1

Milner, G. T. (Northumberland Supporter)
   Obituary   1918   2

Milner, J. (Essex)
   Photograph   1962   3

Milton, C. A. (Gloucestershire; England)
   Action Photograph   1959

Benefit Match	1962	*417*
Cricketer of the Year	1959	*55*
Photographs	1953	*355*
	1955	*347*
	1959	*46*
	1968	*413*

Milton, Sir W. H. (Marlborough; Western Province; South Africa)
Obituary	1931/I	*261*

Minor Counties in East Africa 1982
	1983	*851*

Minshull, Capt. J. L. (Christ's College, Finchley)
Obituary	1918	*197*

Mirehouse, G. T. (Harrow; Cambridge University; Somerset; Devon)
Obituary	1924/I	*266*

Mirehouse, Rev. J. (M.C.C.)
Obituary	1912/I	*173*

Mirehouse, W. E. (Harrow; Cambridge University; Gloucestershire)
Obituary	1926/I	*279*

Mischler, N. M. (St.Paul's; Cambridge University)
Schools Note	1939	*680*
1218 runs Schools Averages	1939	*762*

Miskin, Major M. J. (King's, Rochester)
Obituary	1919	*199*

Missen, E. S. (Essex)
Obituary	1928/I	*294*

Mistri, Col. K. M. (Parsees)
Obituary	1961	*953*

Mitchell, A. (Yorkshire; England)
Benefit Match	1938	*581*
Obituary	1977	*1046*

Mitchell, A. (Writer)
'84 Not Out. The Story of Sir Arthur Sims, Kt'
Book Review	1963	*1112*

Mitchell, A. W. (Writer)
'Cricket Companions' Book Review	1951	*994*

Mitchell, B. (Transvaal; South Africa)
Action Photograph	1948	*37*
Portrait and Biography	1936/I	*296*

Mitchell, C. (Felsted; Kent)
Obituary	1938	*941*

Mitchell, C. S. (Philadelphia)
Obituary	1917	*256*

Mitchell, F. (St.Peters York; Cambridge University; Yorkshire; Transvaal; London County; England; South Africa)
Obituary	1936/I	*282*
Portrait and Biography	1902	*lxxvii*
Team in U.S.A. and Canada 1895	*1896*	*402*

Mitchell, Sir F. H. (Eton)
 Obituary   1952   959

Mitchell, Rev. H. (Uppingham)
 Obituary   1934/I   271

Mitchell, H. (Sussex)
 Obituary   1952   959

Mitchell, H. E. (West Bromwich Dartmouth C.C.)
 Obituary   1962   988

Mitchell, Capt. J. B. (Highfield School, Ontario)
 Obituary   1920/I   155

Mitchell, Capt. J. M. (Blair Lodge; Royal High School Edinburgh)
 Obituary   1916   189

Mitchell, Lt-Col. J. T. R. (Edinburgh Academy)
 Obituary   1919   18.

Mitchell, R. (Victoria)
 Obituary   1927/I   28

Mitchell, Pte, R. A. (Trinity College School, Port Hope)
 Obituary   1918   21

Mitchell, R. A. H. (Eton; Oxford University; Leicestershire; Warwickshire; Buckinghamshire)
 'R. A. H. Mitchell and Eton Cricket'   1899   x
 Appreciation of by Lord Harris and
 R. D. Walker   1906   lxxv
 Obituary   1906   xc
 Views on High Scoring and L.B.W. Rule   1899   b
 Views on 'The Follow On'   1894   xlv
 Views on Throwing   1895   l
 Views on the Reforms of 1889   1890   xxx
 Views on Some Questions of the Day   1890   x

Mitchell, R. H. (Eton)
 Obituary   1950   9

Mitchell, Lieut. R. W. (Eton)
 Obituary   1918   1.

Mitchell, W. (Lancashire League Cricket)
 Obituary   1939   9.

Mitchell-Innes, N. S. (Sedbergh; Oxford University; Somerset; Scotland; England)
 Schools Notes   1933/I   2
      1934/I   3

Mobbs, Sir A. N. (Bedford, Modern School)
 Obituary   1960   9.

Mobberley, Lieut. L. W. (Hampstead Nomads C.C.)
 Obituary   1917   2

Moberly, Rev. H. E. (Winchester; Oxford University)
 Obituary   1908/I   1

Moberly, Lieut. H. S. (Bedford Grammar)
Obituary   1916   *189*

Moberly, J. C. (Winchester; Hampshire)
Obituary   1929/I   *255*

Moberly, W. O. (Rugby; Oxford University; Gloucestershire)
Obituary   1915/I   *235*

Mockler-Ferryman, Lieut. H. (Wellington; Berkshire)
Obituary   1915/I   *235*

'Modern Batting' Lord Harris   1910/I   *113*

'Modern Batting' C. Toppin   1922/I   *242*

'Modern Batting and the Law of Leg-Before-Wicket'
Hon. R. H. Lyttelton   1921/I   *216*

'Modern County Cricket'
Colonel R. S. Rait Kerr   1952   *84*

Modi, R. S. (Bombay; Parsis; India)
'Cricket Forever' Book Review   1965   *1020*

Mody, D. E. (Parsis)
Obituary   1914/I   *191*

Moeran, E. H. (Marlborough; Dublin; America)
Obituary   1906   *cii*

Moffat, D. (Middlesex)
Obituary   1923/I   *303*

Moffatt, N. J. D. (Middlesex)
Obituary   1973   *1012*

Moggridge, Lieut. C. F. B. (Blundells)
Obituary   1919   *183*

Mohammad Brothers 'The Greatly Praised – Hanif and his Brothers'
B. Easterbrook   1976   *127*

Mohanty, B. C. (President Elect Indian Cricket Board)
Obituary   1981   *1146*

Mohottallage, D. B. (Ceylon)
Obituary   1976   *1104*

Moir, Lieut. A. G. (Fettes; Clackmannonshire)
Obituary   1916   *189*

Moir, H. G. (Marlborough)
Obituary   1930/I   *258*

Mold, A. W. (Lancashire; Northamptonshire; England)
Obituary   1922/I   *262*
Portrait and Biography   1892   *xli*

Molineux, Capt. G. K. (Winchester)
Obituary   1916   *190*

Moloney, Lieut. D. A. R. (Manawatu; Wellington; Otago; Canterbury; New Zealand)
Obituary   1945   *326*

Moltram, Capt. F. (Liverpool Institute XI)
Obituary   1918   *197*

Molyneux, J. G. (Penrith C.C)
Obituary 1976 *1100*

Monaghan, H. W. (Wellington; Canterbury)
Obituary 1960 *958*

Monckton, 1st Viscount of Brenchley (Harrow)
Obituary 1966 *970*

Moncrieff, Rev. Rt. Hon. R. C. (Harrow)
Obituary 1914/I *191*

Moncrieffe, H. J. 2nd Baron (Harrow)
Obituary 1910/I *141*

Moncrieffe, R. (Harrow)
Obituary 1910/I *142*

Money, Rev. W. B. (Harrow; Cambridge University; Surrey)
Obituary 1925/I *274*

Monkland, F. G. (Repton; Gloucestershire)
Obituary 1916 *190*

Monks, C. I. (Gloucestershire)
Obituary 1976 *1105*

Monnington, Canon T. P. (Marlborough)
Obituary 1938 *941*

Monro, R. W. (Harrow; Oxford University)
Obituary 1909/I *143*

Monson, Lord See under Oxenbridge, Lord

Montagnow, Lieut. B. (Highfield School, Ontario)
Obituary 1919 *200*

Monteath, 2nd Lieut. A. P. (Otago)
Obituary 1943 *366*

Monteath, Lt-Col. D. I. (Clifton)
Obituary 1946 *435*

Mongomerie, C. T. M. (IZingari)
Obituary 1902 *lxix*

Montgomery, 2nd Lieut. A. G. (St.Edmund's, Canterbury)
Obituary 1919 *18*

Montgomery, Rt. Rev. H. H. (Harrow)
Obituary 1933/I *25*

Montgomery, W. (Cricket Coach Oundle)
Obituary 1953 *946*

Montgomery, W. H. (Canada)
Obituary 1911/I *16*

Montgomery, W. W. (Merion C.C. Philadelphia)
Obituary 1922/I *26*

Montgomery of Alamein, Field Marshall Lord (St.Paul's)
Obituary 1977 *104*

Moody, 2nd Lieut. C. A. (King William's College, Isle of Man)
Obituary 1918 *19*

Moody, C. P. (Journalist)
Obituary	1939	*921*

Moody, Capt. R. H. M. (M.C.C.)
Obituary	1916	*219*

Moon, A. W. (Westminster)
Obituary	1922/I	*264*

Moon, 2nd Lieut. L. J. (Westminster; Cambridge University; Middlesex; England)
Obituary	1917	*203*

Moon, W. R. (Westminster; Middlesex)
Obituary	1944	*318*

Moor, Preb. G. H. (Radley; Gentlemen of Sussex)
Obituary	1917	*256*

Moore, C. R. (Radley)
Obituary	1922/I	*272*

Moore, D. (Broadcaster; Writer)
'Kent's Triumphant Revival'	1974	*74*

Moore, D. N. (Shrewsbury; Oxford University; Gloucestershire)
Appreciation of T. W. Goddard	1952	*123*
Schools Note	1930/I	*283-5,293*
1038 runs Schools Averages	1930/II	*644*

Moore, F. (Nottinghamshire)
Obituary	1901	*lix*

Moore, G. (New South Wales)
Obituary	1917	*257*

Moore, Lieut. H. E. (Trinity College School, Port Hope)
Obituary	1917	*203*

Moore, H. I. (Nottinghamshire; Lincolnshire)
Photograph	1967	*528*

Moore, J. (Hampshire)
Obituary	1981	*1146*

Moore, Lieut. M. E. J. (Glenalmond)
Obituary	1919	*183*

Moore, T. (Cheltenham)
Obituary	1926/I	*280*

Moore, W. (New South Wales; Western Australia)
Obituary	1957	*947*

Moore-Gwyn, J. E. (Winchester)
Obituary	1923/I	*303*

Moorhead, Col. A. H. (George Heriot's)
Obituary	1917	*203*

Moorhouse, G. (Journalist)
'Lord's' Book Review	1984	*1256*

Moorhouse, Lt.-Col. Sir H. C. (Brighton College)
Obituary	1936/I	*293*

Moorhouse, R. (Yorkshire)
Obituary	1922/I	*264*

Morant, E. J. H. E. (Brockenhurst Park Private Ground)
Obituary   1911/I   *150*

Morcom, Dr. A. F. (Repton; Cambridge University; Bedfordshire)
Obituary   1953   *946*

Mordaunt, E. C. (Wellington; Hampshire; Middlesex; Kent)
Obituary   1939   *914*

Mordaunt, G. J. (Wellington; Oxford University; Kent)
Obituary   1960   *954*

Mordaunt, Sir. H. J. 12th Bart. (Eton; Cambridge University; Hampshire; Middlesex)
Obituary   1940   *843*

Mordaunt, J. M. (Eton; Warwickshire)
Obituary   1925/I   *289*

Mordaunt, Canon O. (Eton; Warwickshire)
Obituary   1924/I   *266*

'More Jottings' R. Thoms   1890   *xlvii*

More, R. E. (Westminster; Oxford University; Middlesex)
Obituary   1937/I   *275*

Morgan, Lieut. A. J. (Dollar Academy)
Obituary   1919   *18*

Morgan, C. (Surrey)
Obituary   1905   *xcix*

Morgan, D. C. (Berkhamsted School; Derbyshire)
Photographs   1953   *29*
    1958   *30*
    1963   *37*
    1965   *34*
    1967   *35*

Morgan, E. N. (Christ's College, Brecon; Glamorgan)
Obituary   1977   *105*

Morgan, F. E. (Cambridgeshire)
Obituary   1916   *19*

Morgan, G. (Ireland)
Obituary   1981   *114*

Morgan, Capt. G. (Christchurch College, Oxford)
Obituary   1916   *19*

Morgan, G. T. (Belmont C.C., Philadelphia)
Obituary   1926/I   *28*

Morgan, J. H. (Journalist; Writer)
'Glamorgan' Book Review   1953   *99*
'Glamorgan's March of Progress'   1949   *10*
'Glamorgan – A Peep into the Past'   1970   *8*
Obituary   1979   *108*

Morgan, J. T. (Charterhouse; Cambridge University; Glamorgan)
Obituary   1977   *104*

Morgan, Capt. R. C. (Winchester)
Obituary   1920/I   *15*

Morgan, S. (Warwickshire)
  Obituary 1914/I *191*
Morgan, S. (Ireland)
  Obituary 1982 *1206*
Morgan, 2nd Lieut. S. B. (Clifton)
  Obituary 1916 *190*
Morgan, W. (Lansdown C.C.; Glamorgan)
  Obituary 1915/I *235*
Morgan, Lieut. W. C. (King Edward VII Grammar School, King's Lynn; King's Lynn C.C.)
  Obituary 1917 *204*
Morgan-Owen, H. (Shrewsbury; Oxford University)
  Obituary 1954 *928*
Morgan-Owen, J. G. (Bromsgrove School)
  Obituary 1917 *204*
Morice, F. H. (New Zealand Club Cricket)
  Obituary 1913/I *191*
Morice, Lieut. N. A. (Malvern)
  Obituary 1917 *204*
Morice, W. N. (U.S.A.)
  Obituary 1935/I *269*
Morkel, D. P. B. (Western Province; South Africa)
  Obituary 1981 *1146*
Morley, F. (Nottinghamshire; England)
  Benefit Match for Family of 1886 *169*
  Obituary 1885 *8*
Morley, H. A. (Derbyshire)
  Obituary 1955 *938*
Morley, T. (Nottinghamshire; Norfolk)
  Obituary 1920/I *183*
Morrah, P. (Writer)
  'Alfred Mynn and the Cricketers of his Time'
  Book Review 1964 *996*
Morres, E. R. (Winchester; Oxford University)
  Obituary 1955 *935*
Morres, H. F. M. (Oxford University; Buckinghamshire; Dorset)
  Obituary 1936/I *293*
Morris, A. R. (New South Wales; Australia)
  Cricketer of the Year 1949 *93*
  with P. Landsberg 'Operation Ashes'
  Book Review 1957 *997*
  Photograph 1949 *72*
  Retirement 1956 *902*
Morris, C. C. (Philadelphia; U.S.A.)
  Obituary 1972 *1053*

Morris, F. G. (English Schools Cricket Association)
Obituary 1969 *984*

Morris, H. (Blundells; Glamorgan)
Schools Note 1983 *899*
1032 runs Schools Averages 1983 *910*

Morris, Col. J. (New South Wales)
Obituary 1923/I *310*

Morris, Lieut. L. S. (Royal Navy)
Obituary 1943 *369*

Morris, P. (Glamorgan)
Obituary 1976 *1100*

Morris, P. (Writer)
with M. Cumming 'Meet the Test Stars'
Book Review 1962 *1036*

Morris, P. E. (Essex)
Obituary 1946 *442*

Morris, T. H. (Merion C.C., Philadelphia)
Obituary 1914/I *191*

Morrison, C. (1906 West Indies in England; Jamaica)
Obituary 1949 *866*

Morrison, G. N. (Canada)
Obituary 1921/I *231*

Morrison, Lieut. J. B. (Carlton C.C., Edinburgh)
Obituary 1919 *183*

Morrison, J. S. F. (Charterhouse; Cambridge University; Somerset)
Obituary 1962 *988*

Morrison, P. H. (Loretto)
Obituary 1937/I *276*

Morron, G. A. (Ireland)
Obituary 1915/I *235*

Morse, Lieut. E. H. T. (Edmonton C.C., Alberta)
Obituary 1918 197

Morse, S. (Marlborough)
Obituary 1930/I *259*

Morse, S. A. (Charterhouse; Norfolk)
Obituary 1970 *1023*

Mortesen, O. (Derbyshire)
Note on 1984 *49*

Mortimer, Lieut. E. (Northumberland)
Obituary 1916 *191*

Mortimer, J. (Aberdeenshire; Scotland)
Obituary 1969 *990*

Mortimer, Lt-Col. J. (Driffield Town C.C.)
Obituary 1917 *204*

Mortimer, L. (Clifton)
Obituary 1945 *338*

Mortimer, S. Sgt. O. (Secretary Suffolk)
  Obituary   1918   *197*

Mortimer, Sir R. G. E. (Lancashire; Harrow)
  Obituary   1956   *975*

Mortimer, W. (Marlborough)
  Obituary   1917   *257*

Mortimer, W. B. (Royal Lancaster Grammar School)
  Obituary   1916   *151*

Mortimore, J. B. (Gloucestershire; England)
  Benefit Match   1966   *410*
  Photographs   1959   *360*
                           1962   *409*
                           1964   *394*
                           1965   *400*
                           1968   *413*

Mortis, 2nd Lieut. E. J. (Queen Elizabeth College, Guernsey)
  Obituary   1919   *184*

Mortlock, W. (Surrey; United England XI)
  Benefit Match   1871   *87*
  Biography   1870   *86*
  Obituary   1885   *8*

Morton, A. (Derbyshire)
  Benefit Match   1925/II   *404*
  Obituary   1936/I   *285*

Morton, A. H. A. (Eton)
  Obituary   1914/I   *191*

Morton, C. H. (Rossall; Norfolk)
  Obituary   1946   *442*

Morton, F. L. (South Australia; Victoria)
  Obituary   1972   *1054*

Morton, P. H. (Rossall; Cambridge University; Surrey; Norfolk)
  Obituary   1926/I   *280*

Morton, Dr. R. L. (President Victorian Cricket Association)
  Obituary   1948   *786*

Moseley, E. A. (Glamorgan; Barbados)
  Photograph   1982   *401*

Moseley, H. R. (Somerset; Barbados)
  Benefit Match   1980   *790*
  Photograph   1974   *525*

Moses, H. (New South Wales; Australia)
  Obituary   1939   *914*

Moss, A. E. (Middlesex; England)
  Benefit Match   1963   *529*
  Photograph   1953   *452*
                           1959   *454*

Moss, Sqn. Ldr. E. H. (Malvern; Oxford University)
Obituary 1946 *435*
Moss, J. (Nottinghamshire; Umpire)
Obituary 1951 *926*
Moss, S. (Bacup C.C.)
Obituary 1924/I *266*
Mott, C. C. (Rugby; Warwickshire; Staffordshire; Derbyshire)
Obituary 1931/I *262*
Mott, 2nd Lieut. F. S. (Cranleigh School)
Obituary 1917 *204*
Motz, R. C. (Canterbury; New Zealand)
Cricketer of the Year 1966 *73*
Photograph 1966 *63*
Moulder, J. W. H. (Surrey; London County; Transvaal)
Obituary 1935/I *277*
Moule, Capt. F. G. (St.Kilda C.C.)
Obituary 1919 *200*
Moule, W. H. (Victoria; Australia)
Obituary 1940 *843*
Moult, T. (Poet; Journalist)
Obituary 1975 *1081*
Mounsey, J. T. (Yorkshire)
Obituary 1950 *911*
Mounteney, A. (Leicestershire)
Obituary 1934/I *271*
Moxley, J. (Journalist)
Obituary 1981 *1146*
Moyes, Lieut. A. B. (Stirling High School)
Obituary 1919 *184*
Moyes, A. G. (South Australia; Broadcaster; Journalist)
'Australian Survey:
Bradman – Past, Present and Future' 1945 *50*
'Benaud' Book Review 1963 *1110*
'Benaud and Co: The Story of the Tests
1958-59' Book Review 1960 *999*
'The Fight for the Ashes 1950-51'
Book Review 1952 *1013*
'The Fight for the Ashes 1954-55'
Book Review 1956 *1026*
Obituary 1964 *950*
'The South Africans in Australia'
Book Review 1954 *981*
'With the M.C.C. in Australia 1962-63'
Book Review 1964 *999*
'With the West Indies in Australia 1951-52'

Book Review	1953	*997*
'With the West Indies in Australia 1960-61'		
Book Review	1962	*1037*
Moyle, Dr. J. B. (Winchester; Devon)		
Obituary	1931/I	*262*
Mubarak, Ali (Nairobi C.C.)		
Obituary	1974	*1076*
Mufasir-Ul-Haq (Karachi; P.W.D.; National Bank; Pakistan)		
Obituary	1984	*1206*
Mugliston, F. H. (Rossall; Cambridge University; Lancashire)		
Obituary	1933/I	*256*
Muir, Lieut. A. R. (Sydney University)		
Obituary	1919	*200*
Muir, 2nd Lieut. B. (Malvern)		
Obituary	1916	*191*
Muir, G. H. (Secretary Hampshire)		
Obituary	1940	*843*
Mulholland, Capt. Hon. A. E. S. (Eton; Army)		
Obituary	1915/I	*236*
Mulholland, Sir H. G. H. Bart. (Eton; Cambridge University)		
Obituary	1972	*1054*
Mullagh, J. (Victoria)		
Obituary	1892	*xxxiv*
Mulvaney, D. J. (Writer)		
'Cricket Walkabout – The Australian Aboriginal Cricketers on		
Tour 1867-68' Book Review	1969	*1023*
Muncer, B. L. (Middlesex; Glamorgan)		
Benefit Matches	1955	*336*
	1972	*349*
Obituary	1983	*1251*
Photographs	1950	*322*
	1953	*335*
Munday, Lieut. L. C. (Military Cricket)		
Obituary	1917	*225*
Munds, E. (Groundsman Hythe C.C.)		
Obituary	1930/I	*259*
Munds, R. (Kent)		
Obituary	1963	*1035*
Munn, D. L. (Secretary South Australian Cricket Association)		
Obituary	1980	*1160*
Munnion, H. (Sussex)		
Obituary	1905	*c*
Munro, D. A. (President Metropolitan District League of New York)		
Obituary	1911/I	*150*
Munro, R. M. C. (Harrow)		
Obituary	1947	*693*

Munt, Col. H. R. (Westminster)
  Obituary   1966   970
Murch, W. (Gloucestershire; London County; Wiltshire)
  Obituary   1929/I   255
Murdin, J. V. (Northamptonshire)
  Obituary   1972   1054
Murdoch, A. M. (North Sydney C.C.)
  Obituary   1920/I   194
Murdoch, G. C. (Alberta C.C.; Balmain C.C., Australia)
  Obituary   1907   cxiv
Murdoch, J. A. (Assistant Secretary Middlesex)
  Benefit Match   1908/II   136
  Obituary   1908/I   145
  Testimonial Match   1887   61
Murdoch, P. M. (Blair Lodge School)
  80 wkts Schools Averages   1899   353
Murdoch, W. L. (Sussex; New South Wales; London County; Australia; England)
  Obituary   1912/I   173
  Views on Throwing   1895   liv
Murdoch-Cozens, Lt.-Col. A. J. (Brighton College; Sussex)
  Obituary   1971   1028
  Schools Note   1913/I   220
  82 wkts Schools Averages   1913/II   494
Murdock, Major E. G. (Somerset; Gloucestershire)
  Obituary   1927/I   284
Murly-Gotto, 2nd Lieut. J. (Haileybury)
  Obituary   1917   204
Murphy, D. J. (Ireland)
  Obituary   1984   1206
Murphy, J. P. (Member Surrey)
  Obituary   1908/I   146
Murphy, V. V. (British Columbia)
  Obituary   1914/I   191
Murray, Dr. A. (President Missouri Cricket Association)
  Obituary   1938   941
Murray, A. L. (Warwickshire)
  Obituary   1982   1206
Murray, Lieut. G. R. (Cheltenham)
  Obituary   1917   204
Murray, J. (Eton)
  Obituary   1938   941
Murray, Hon. J. (Patron Victoria)
  Obituary   1917   257
Murray, Lieut. J. C. (Edinburgh Academy; Scotland)
  Obituary   1918   197

Murray, J. T. (Middlesex; England)

Benefit Matches	1967	*500*
	1976	*325*
Career Figures	1976	*124*
Celebration	1967	*92*
Cricketer of the Year	1967	*84*
'John Murray M.B.E. Champion Keeper'		
J. M. Brearley	1976	*120*
Note on	1962	*113*
Photographs	1958	*463*
	1961	*482*
	1965	*488*
	1967	*71*
	1976	*121*

Murray, Capt. P. H. (Malvern)

Obituary	1917	*225*

Murray, R. M. (Wellington, New Zealand)

Obituary	1952	*959*

Murray, W. (Treasurer Perthshire C.C.C.)

Obituaries	1963	*1034*
	1964	*954*

Murray-Wood, W. (Mill Hill; Oxford University; Kent)

Obituary	1969	*984*

Murrell, H. R. (Kent; Middlesex)

Benefit Match	1923/II	*179*
with N. Haig 'Middlesex County Cricket Club 1921-1947'		
Book Review	1951	*989*
Obituary	1953	*946*

Murrell, W. C. (Pioneer of South African Cricket)

Obituary	1910/I	*142*

Murrin, J. B. (Groundsman Kent)

Obituary	1947	*693*

Mursell, Rev. A. (Member Surrey)

Obituary	1915/I	*236*

Musgrove, H. (Victoria; Australia)

Obituary	1932/I	*249*

Mushtaq, Ali (Holkar; India)

'Cricket Delightful' Book Review	1968	*1052*

Mushtaq, Mohammad (Pakistan International Airways; Karachi; Shropshire; Northamptonshire; Pakistan)

Benefit Match	1977	*747*
Cricketer of the Year	1963	*165*
Photographs	1963	*157*
	1969	*516*
	1972	*514*

Musson, F. W. (Tonbridge; Lancashire)
Obituary 1963 *1035*
Musson, Wing Comdr. R. G. (Tonbridge; R.A.F.)
Obituary 1944 *307*
Mycroft, T. (Derbyshire)
Benefit Match 1896 *104*
Obituary 1912/I *175*
Mycroft, W. (Derbyshire)
Benefit Match 1884 *251*
Obituary 1895 *xxxix*
Myers, Pte. A. (St.Judes C.C., Winnipeg)
Obituary 1918 *215*
Myers, L/Cpl. E. B. (Surrey)
Obituary 1917 *204*
Myers, Pte. F. W. (Secretary Yorkshire Society C.C., Toronto)
Obituary 1918 *197*
Myers, H. (Yorkshire)
Obituary 1945 *338*
Myers, M. (Yorkshire)
Obituary 1920/I *183*
Mynn, A. (Kent; All England XI; Sussex)
'Alfred Mynn and the Cricketers of His Time'
P. Morrah Book Review 1964 *996*
'My Happy Life in Cricket' F. E. Woolley 1939 *53*
Mylne, Capt. E. G. (Keeble College, Oxford)
Obituary 1917 *225*
'My Years at Cambridge' G. H. Longman 1929/I *263*
Nagel, L. E. (Victoria; Australia)
Obituary 1972 *1054*
Naoomal, J. (Sind; India)
Obituary 1981 *1146*
Napier, Rev. C. W. A. (Harrow; Oxford University)
Obituary 1910/I *151*
Napier, Lieut. G. G. (Marlborough; Cambridge University; Middlesex)
Obituary 1916 *191*
Napier, Rev. J. R. (Marlborough; Cambridge University; Lancashire)
Obituary 1940 *843*
Napper, E. (Sussex)
Obituary 1896 *xxxix*
Napper, E. (Surrey)
Obituary 1910/I *142*
Napper, W. (Sussex)
Obituary 1898 *xlv*
Narayan Singh, Prince K. H. (Somerset)
Obituary 1921/I *231*

Nash, A. J. (Glamorgan)
Obituary 1957 *947*
Nash, E. H. (Rugby)
Obituary 1933/I *256*
Nash, G. (Lancashire; Buckinghamshire)
Obituary 1904 *lxxxv*
Nash, J. H. (Secretary Yorkshire)
Obituary 1978 *1075*
Nash, L. C. F. (Harrow)
Obituary 1952 *959*
Nash, M. A. (Glamorgan; Shropshire)
Benefit Match 1979 *709*
Photographs 1970 *389*
1975 *395*
Nash, P. G. E. (St.Paul's, Berkshire)
Obituary 1983 *1251*
Nash, Rev. W. W. H. (King's Bruton; Gloucestershire)
Obituary 1972 *1054*
Nason, Capt. J. W. W. (Cambridge University; Sussex; Gloucestershire)
Obituary 1917 *204*
National Cash Register Test Award 1969 *655*
National Club Cricket Association
Views on the Laws 1957 *86*
National Cricket Association
Formation 1966 *325*
Note on 1968 *90*
National Defence (India) Fund Matches 1973 *952*
Naumann, Major F. C. G. (Malvern; Oxford University; Surrey)
Obituary 1948 *786*
Naumann, J. H. (Malvern; Cambridge University; Sussex)
Obituary 1966 *975*
Navaranta, B. (Ceylon)
Obituary 1980 *1151*
Naylor, Lieut. R. E. (Eton; Montgomeryshire)
Obituary 1916 *192*
Naylor, Major U. S. (Indian Regimental Cricket)
Obituary 1917 *205*
Nayudu, Col. C. K. (Hindus; Vizianagran; Madras; Central Provinces; Holkar;
United Provinces; India)
Memorial Fund Match 1969 *916*
Obituary 1968 *1005*
Portrait and Biography 1933/I *267*
Neale, Lieut. A. H. (St.Columba's, Dublin)
Obituary 1917 *205*
Neale, Lt-Col. G. H. (Lancing; Peshawar)
Obituary 1916 *192*

395

Neale, P. A. (Worcestershire ; Lincolnshire)
  Photograph 1980 *603*
Neale, W. L. (Gloucestershire)
  Benefit Match 1947 *287*
  Obituary 1956 *975*
Neame, Major A. (Harrow)
  Obituary 1917 *205*
Neame, Major G. (Cheltenham)
  Obituary 1919 *184*
Neame, Capt. G. T. (Cheltenham)
  Obituary 1917 *205*
Neame, L. B. (Haileybury; Kent)
  Obituary 1971 *1028*
Neame, L. H. (Crystal Palace C.C.)
  Obituary 1925/I *275*
Near to Death Photograph 1983 *Plate*
Neate, H. R. (Bedfordshire)
  Obituary 1967 *973*
Neath Plan of County Ground 1971 *353*
Need, P. (Pavilion Attendant at Lord's)
  Benefit Match 1901 *303*
  Obituary 1925/I *275*
Needham, Sir C. (President Lancashire)
  Obituary 1945 *338*
Needham, E. (Derbyshire)
  Obituary 1937/I *276*
Needham, P. R. (Emanuel School)
  Schools Note 1970 *816*
  80 wkts Schools Averages 1970 *830*
Neill, R. (Auckland)
  Obituary 1931/I *262*
Neilson, Capt. D. F. (St.Bees)
  Obituary 1919 *184*
Neilson, H. F. (Loretto)
  78 wkts Schools Averages 1949 *72*
Neilson, R. T. (Merchiston Castle)
  Obituary 1946 *442*
Nelson, G. H. (Radley; Hertfordshire)
  Obituary 1927/I *284*
Nelson, G. M. B. (Rugby; Warwickshire)
  Obituary 1970 *102*
Nelson, 2nd Lieut. R. P. (St George's Harpenden; Cambridge University;
Middlesex; Northamptonshire)
  Obituary 1941 *38*
  'R. P. Nelson Memoir' R. Nelson and H. Strickland
  Book Review 1957 *100*

Nelson, R. (Son of R. P. Nelson)
with H. Strickland 'R. P. Nelson Memoir'
Book Review | 1957 | *1000*

Nelson, Capt. T. A. (Edinburgh Academy)
Obituary | 1918 | *198*

Nepean, Rev. C. E. B. (Charterhouse; Oxford University; Middlesex; Kent)
Obituary | 1904 | *lxxx*

Nepean, Sir C. E. M. Y. (Winchester)
Obituary | 1954 | *928*

Nepean, E. A. (Sherborne; Oxford University; Middlesex)
Obituary | 1907 | *cxiv*

Nesbitt, A. S. (Bradfield; Worcestershire)
Obituary | 1915/I | *236*

~ser, Justice. V. H. (Oxford University; Transvaal)
Obituary | 1957 | *947*
Obituary Addition | 1958 | *967*

Nethersole, N. V. (Oxfordshire; Jamaica)
Obituary | 1960 | *954*

Neve, J. T. (Cheltenham)
Obituary | 1977 | *1048*

Nevile, Capt. B. P. (Lincolnshire; Worcestershire)
Obituary | 1917 | *205*

Nevill, Capt. W. P. (Dover College)
Obituary | 1917 | *205*

Neville, Lieut. H. G. (Lincolnshire)
Obituary | 1916 | *192*

Neville, Rev. L. See under Braybrooke, 6th Lord

Neville, P. (Ireland)
Obituary | 1979 | *1092*

New, 2nd Lieut. B. B. (Bournemouth School)
Obituary | 1918 | *198*

Newbery, Pte. E. J. (U.S.A. Club Cricket)
Obituary | 1919 | *184*

Newbury, A. L. (Sussex)
Obituary | 1977 | *1048*

Newcombe, Lieut. C. N. (Derbyshire)
Obituary | 1916 | *193*

Newcombe, H. C. E. (New South Wales)
Obituary | 1909/I | *143*

Newell, A. L. (New South Wales)
Obituary | 1909/I | *143*

Newett, F. B. (Rossall; North of Ireland C.C.)
Obituary | 1914/I | *199*

Newhall, C. A. (Gentlemen of Philadelphia)
Obituary | 1928/I | *294*

Newhall, D. S. (Philadelphia; U.S.A.)
Obituary 1914/I *191*
Newhall, G. M. (Young America C.C., U.S.A.)
Obituary 1922/I *265*
Newhall, H. L. (Young America C.C., U.S.A.)
Obituary 1919 *210*
Newhall, R. S. (Gentlemen of Philadelphia)
Obituary 1911/I *150*
Newham, W. (Ardingly; Sussex; England)
Obituary 1945 *338*
Views on 'The Follow On' 1894 *l*
Newland, P. M. (South Australia)
Obituary 1917 *257*
Newman, Lt-Col. A. C. (Member Kent; Essex)
Obituary 1973 *1012*
Newman, D. L. (Middlesex)
Obituary 1960 *954*
Newman, F. C. W. (Bedford Modern; Bedfordshire; Surrey)
Obituary 1967 *973*
Newman, G. C. (Eton; Oxford University; Middlesex)
Obituary 1983 *125*
Newman, J. A. (Hampshire; Canterbury)
Benefit Match 1925/II *315*
Obituary 1974 *107*
Obituary Correction 1975 *108*
Newman, L. W. (Alexandra Park C.C.)
Obituary 1965 *97*
Newman, P. G. (Derbyshire)
Photograph 1982 *37*
Newman, W. (Berkhampsted C.C.)
Obituary 1895 *xxxvi*
Newman, W. (Montpelier C.C.)
Obituary 1920/I *18*
Newnham, Lt-Col. A. T. H. (Malvern; Gloucestershire)
Obituary 1942 *36*
Newnham, L. (Writer)
'Essex County Cricket Club 1876-1975'
Book Review 1978 *11*
Newnham-Davies, Lt-Col. N. (Old Stagers)
Obituary 1918 *2*
Newsome, Lieut. R. H. A. (Merchant Taylors)
Obituary 1919 *18*
New South Wales
in Ceylon 1914 1915/II *5*
in New Zealand 1924 1925/II *5*

Newstead, Major G. P. (Rugby)
Obituary   1916   *193*
Newstead, J. T. (Yorkshire)
Portrait and Biography   1909/I   *163*
No Obituary Recorded
Newsum, A. G. C. (American Club Cricket)
Obituary   1917   *258*
Newsum, Lt-Col. H. N. (Lincolnshire)
Obituary   1969   *984*
Newton, Col. A. C. (Tasmania)
Obituary   1980   *1151*
Newton, A. E. (Eton; Somerset; Oxford University)
Obituary   1953   *947*
Newton, A. J. E. (Cheltenham)
Obituary   1931/I   *262*
Newton, E. J. (Hampshire)
Obituary   1907   *cxiv*
Newton, F. A. (Derbyshire)
Obituary   1925/I   *275*
Newton, S. C. (Victoria College; Jersey; Cambridge University; Somerset;
Middlesex)
Obituary   1917   *258*
Newton, Lieut. W. T. (Uppingham)
Obituary   1917   *206*
Newton-Thompson, J. O. (Oxford University)
Obituary   1975   *1081*
New York Veterans in Bermuda 1913   1914/II   *514*
New Zealand
in Australia   1913-14   1915/II   *511*
                             1937   1939   *814*
                             1961   1963   *948*
                             1967-68   1969   *859*
                             1969-70   1971   *916*
                             1973-74   1975   *930*
                             1980-81   1982   *969*
'New Zealand in Australia and India'
Ed. by A. McGilvray Book Review   1982   *1272*
                             1982-83   1984   *938*
in Bermuda   1965   1966   *296*
in England   1927   1928/II   *450*
                             1931   1932/II   *1*
                             1937   1938   *192*
Team Portrait   1937   1938   *33*
                             1949   1950   *207*
Team Portrait   1949   1950   *67*

'Cricket Companions' A. W. Mitchell			
Book Review		1951	*994*
'Gone with the Cricketers' J. Arlott			
Book Review		1951	*1001*
	1958	1959	*225*
Note on		1958	*74*
Team Portrait	1958	1959	*40*
'Cricket Journal' J. Arlott Book Review		1959	*998*
'Cricketers from New Zealand' G. Ross			
Book Review		1959	*991*
	1965	1966	*270*
Team Portrait	1965	1966	*54*
'Red Leather and Silver Fern' R. T. Brittenden			
Book Review		1966	*1014*
'The 1965 Tourists' G. Ross Book Review		1966	*1022*
'Rothmans Test Cricket Almanack'			
Book Review		1966	*1024*
	1969	1970	316
Note on		1969	*96*
Team Portrait	1969	1970	*53*
'Rothmans Cricket Almanack' Book Review		1970	*1074*
'Scoreboard 69' R. T. Brittenden			
Book Review		1971	*1081*
	1973	1974	*298*
Team Portrait	1973	1974	*44*
World Cup Tournament	1975	1976	*300*
Team Portrait	1975	1976	*301*
	1978	1979	*307*
Team Portrait	1978	1979	*60*
World Cup Tournament	1979	1980	*297*
World Cup Tournament	1983	1984	*293*
	1983	1984	*271*
Team Portrait	1983	1984	*273*
'Coney makes winning hit at Headingley'			
Photograph		1984	*Plate*
'New Zealand Team Celebrates'			
Photograph		1984	*Plate*
'New Zealand's Historic Victory Note on		1984	*49*
'Kiwis and Indians' P. Eagar and A. Ross			
Book Review		1984	*1262*
in Holland	1965	1966	*296*
in India			
and Pakistan	1955-56	1957	*813*
and Pakistan	1964-65	1966	*896*

'Red Leather and Silver Fern'
R. T. Brittenden Book Review   1966   *1014*
and Pakistan   1969-70   1971   *850*
'Scoreboard 69' R. T. Brittenden
Book Review   1971   *1081*
and Pakistan   1976-77   1978   *930*
in Pakistan
and India   1955-56   1957   *813*
'Pakistan Cricket on the March' Q. Butt
Book Review   1958   *1011*
and India   1964-65   1966   *896*
'Red Leather and Silver Fern'
R. T. Brittenden Book Review   1966   *1014*
and India   1969-70   1971   *850*
'Scoreboard 69' R. T. Brittenden
Book Review   1971   *1081*
'Sporting Wickets' Q. Butt Book Review   1971   *1080*
and India   1976-77   1978   *930*
in South Africa   1953-54   1955   *786*
     1961-62   1963   *899*
'J. Reid's Kiwis' R. S. Whitington
Book Review   1963   *1108*
in U.S.A.   1965   1966   *297*
in West Indies   1971-72   1973   *879*
New Zealand Women in England 1954   1955   *978*
     1966   1967   *909*
Chronological List of Articles, Notes etc.
'Growth of New Zealand Cricket'
A. H. H. Gilligan   1949   *125*
New Zealand Flourished   Note on   1950   *111*
World's Smallest Test Score   1956   *111*
Auckland Scoreboard Photograph   1956   *49*
'The Story of New Zealand Cricket'
C. Bray   1958   *98*
Notable Bowling in Note on   1974   *72*
Nice, E. H. L. (Surrey)
Obituary   1947   *693*
Nichol, Pte. G. (Five Cs C.C., British Columbia)
Obituary   1918   *215*
Nichol, M. (Durham; Surrey; Worcestershire)
Obituary   1935/I   *269*
Nicholas, F. W. H. (Forest School; Essex; Bedfordshire)
Obituary   1973   *1014*
Nicholls, B. E. (Winchester; Oxford University; Sussex)
Obituary   1946   *442*

Nicholls, C. H. (Winchester)
Obituary 1939 *914*
Nicholls, D. (Kent)
Photograph 1970 *436*
Nicholls, R. B. (Gloucestershire)
Benefit Match 1967 *416*
Photographs 1958 *363*
1961 *392*
1963 *428*
1965 *400*
1971 *368*
Nicholls, R. O. (Point St. Charles C.C.)
Obituary 1920/I *156*
Nicholls, R. W. (Rugby; Middlesex)
Obituary 1949 *866*
Nicholls, S. (Wellington)
Obituary 1930/I *259*
Nichols, G. B. (Gloucestershire; Somerset; Devon)
Benefit Match 1896 *152*
Obituary 1912/I *175*
Nichols, M. S. (Essex; England)
Benefit Match 1937/II *280*
Obituary 1962 *989*
Portrait and Biography 1934/I *288*
Nicholson, A. G. (Yorkshire)
Photographs 1965 *528*
1968 *637*
Nicholson, Lieut. A. S. (Edinburgh Garrison)
Obituary 1920/I *156*
Nicholson, Major E. F. D. (Sandhurst)
Obituary 1918 *198*
Nicholson, F. (Griqualand West; South Africa)
Obituary 1983 *1252*
Nicholson, S. R. (Wiltshire)
Obituary 1922/I *265*
Nicholson, Lieut. T. E. (Berwick C.C.)
Obituary 1917 *206*
Nicholson, T. R. (New York Club Cricket)
Obituary 1912/I *176*
Nicholson, W. (Yorkshire)
Obituary 1915/I *236*
Nicholson, W. (Harrow; M.C.C.)
Obituary 1910/I *142*
Nicholson, W. (Maidenhead C.C.)
Obituary 1917 *258*

402

Nicol, Lieut. H. L. (St. Andrews College, Toronto)
Obituary   1919   *184*

Nicolson, J. F. W. (Oxford University; Natal; South Africa)
Obituary   1936/I   *285*

Nickalls, Lt-Col. C. P. (Rugby)
Obituary   1926/I   *281*

Niemeyer, W. E. (Transvaal)
Obituary   1938   *949*

Night Experiment Note on   1981   *95*

Nightingale, F. (Reigate Priory C.C.)
Obituary   1914/I   *192*

Nightingale, 2nd Lieut. F. L. (Dulwich; Surrey Clubs)
Obituary   1917   *225*

Nightingale, J. (Secretary Reigate Priory C.C.)
Obituary   1918   *232*

Nightwatchman Fails Photograph   1966   *58*

Nineties Note on   1967   *93*

Nisbet, Capt. F. S. (Manchester Regiment)
Obituary   1915/I   *236*

Nissar, M. (Southern Punjab; India)
Obituary   1964   *951*

Nitschke, H. C. (South Australia; Australia)
Obituary   1983   *1252*

Nixon, A. C. (Charterhouse)
Obituary   1902   *lxxiii*

Nixon, J. (Queens Park C.C., Durban)
Obituary   1909/I   *143*

Nixon, T. (Nottinghamshire)
Obituary   1878   *202*

Nixon, 2nd Lieut. W. H. (Fenton C.C.)
Obituary   1918   *198*

Noakes, J. N. (Beckenham C.C.)
Obituary   1919   *210*

Noakes, W. F. (Metropolitan Cricket)
Obituary   1920/I   *194*

No Ball Note on   1948   *89*

Noble, Sir J. H. B. (Cricket Enthusiast)
Obituary   1938   *941*

Noble, M. A. (New South Wales; Australia)
Memoir of (H. Preston)   1941   *28*
Photograph   1941   *29*
Portrait and Biography   1900   *lx*
Testimonial Match   1909/II   *526*

Noble, W. W. (U.S.A.)
Obituary   1919   *213*

Noel, E. B. (Winchester)
Obituary   1929/I   255
Noel, J. (South Australia)
Obituary   1939   914
Noonan, D. J. (New South Wales)
Obituary   1930/I   259
Norden, R. W. (Transvaal)
Obituary   1953   947
Norfolk County Cricket Club
Views on Laws   1957   84
Norfolk, 15th Duke of (President Sussex)
Obituary   1918   232
Norfolk, 16th Duke of (President Sussex; President M.C.C.)
Obituary   1976   1100
Photograph   1963   149
Team in Jamaica   1957   1958   853
Team in West Indies   1970   1971   922
Norman, E. (Eton)
Obituary   1924/I   267
Norman, F. H. (Eton; Cambridge University; Kent)
Obituary   1917   258
Norman, Sub-Lieut. J. (St. Paul's)
Obituary   1916   193
Norman, Dr. J. E. (Secretary Hertfordshire C.C.C.)
Obituary   1942   360
Views on Second Class Counties and
L.B.W. Rule   1903   lxvii
Norman, M. E. J. C. (Northamptonshire; Leicestershire)
Photographs   1960   499
                                                        1962   522
Norman, P. (Eton)
Obituary   1932/I   249
Norman, R. C. (Eton)
Obituary   1965   973
Normington, J. (Bingley C.C.)
Obituary   1924/I   275
Nornable, C. E. (Derbyshire)
Obituary   1971   1028
Norris, E. (All Philadelphia)
Obituary   1942   360
Norris, E. S. (Rossall)
Obituary   1924/I   267
Norris, O. T. (Charterhouse; Oxford University)
Obituary   1973   1077
Norsworthy, G. (Winchester)
Obituary   1922/I   265

North, T. H. (Canterbury)
Obituary   1943   *381*
Northampton Plan of County Ground   1950   *444*
         ad passim

Northamptonshire County Cricket Club
County Badge   1950   *443*
         ad passim
'Northamptonshire Cricket' J. D. Coldham
Book Review   1960   *995*
'A Northamptonshire Cricket Song' in Northamptonshire
Past and Present J. D. Coldham
Book Review   1976   *1140*
'Ups and Downs of Northamptonshire'
J. D. Coldham   1958   *103*
Team Portraits   1944   1945   *39*
         1974   1975   *505*
         1975   1976   *509*
         1976   1977   *509*
         1977   1978   *493*
         1978   1979   *484*
         1979   1980   *507*
         1980   1981   *507*
         1981   1982   *512*
         1982   1983   *525*
         1983   1984   *486*

Northcote, Dr. P. (Middlesex; Kent)
Obituary   1936/I   *293*
Northern Cricket XI
Team Portrait   1943   1944   *37*
Northern Districts, New Zealand
'Innings Established' (History of Northern Districts)
Book Review   1983   *1303*
North of England XI
Team Portrait   1944   1945   *38*
Northey, Lieut. A. (Gentlemen of Yorkshire)
Obituary   1916   *219*
Northey, Rev. A. E. (Harrow; Cambridge University)
Obituary   1912/I   *176*
Northey, Rev. E. W. (Surrey Committee)
Obituary   1915/I   *237*
Northey, Lt-Col. G. (President Lansdown C.C.)
Obituary   1907   *cxiv*
Northway, R. P. (Northamptonshire; Somerset)
Obituary   1937/I   *276*
Norton, Dr. S. (Kent)
Obituary   1907   *cxv*

Norton, W. S. (Kent)
Obituary   1917   *259*
Norwood, Sir C. (Merchant Taylors)
Obituary   1957   *947*
Nosworthy, Lieut. A. J. (Ridley College, Ontario)
Obituary   1919   *200*
Notable First Ball Duke of Edinburgh
Photograph   1950   *65*
Notcutt, S. A. (Suffolk)
Obituary   1924/I   *267*
'Notes' R. C. Robertson-Glasgow   1942   *58*
'Notes on the 1939 Season'
R. C. Robertson-Glasgow   1940   *49*
'Notes on the 1940 Season'
R. C. Robertson-Glasgow   1941   *55*
'Notes on Season 1942'
R. C. Robertson-Glasgow   1943   *48*
Nothling, Dr. O. E. (New South Wales; Australia)
Obituary   1966   *970*
Nottinghamshire County Cricket Club
'Centenary of Trent Bridge' A. W. Shelton   1938   *461*
Championship Returns to Trent Bridge Note on   1982   *89*
'A Complete Register of Cricketers to Represent Nottingham Old Club and Nottinghamshire County Cricket Club from 1821-1965'
P. Whynne-Thomas Book Review   1967   *1011*
County Badge   1950   *460*
    ad passim
'Milestones of Nottinghamshire Cricket'
P. Whynne-Thomas Book Review   1982   *1255*
'Nottinghamshire Cricketers 1821-1914'
P. Whynne-Thomas Book Review   1972   *1091*
'Nottinghamshire's Notable Part in the Growth of Cricket'
R. T. Simpson   1967   *134*
Team Portraits   1974   1975   *520*
    1975   1976   *524*
    1976   1977   *524*
    1977   1978   *509*
    1978   1979   *500*
    1979   1980   *523*
    1980   1981   *522*
    1981   1982   *527*
    1982   1983   *543*
    1983   1984   *503*
Noughts 'The Dreaded Cypher'
B. Easterbrook   1971   *152*

Nourse, A. D. (Natal; South Africa)

Career Figures	1982	*1207*
'Cricket in the Blood' Book Review	1951	*994*
'Cricketer of the Year'	1948	*59*
Note on	1944	*58*
'Noursemen in England' Book Review	1953	*996*
Obituary	1982	*1206*
Photograph	1948	*43*

Nourse, A. W. (Natal; Transvaal; Western Province; South Africa)

Obituary	1949	*866*

Novelli, L. W. (Rugby)

Obituary	1915/I	*237*

Noverre, Major A. K. (Military Cricket)

Obituary	1919	*184*

Nugawela, Major E. A. (Royal College XI, Colombo)

Obituary	1974	*1084*

Nugent, Lt-Col. Lord (Eton; President M.C.C.)

Obituary	1974	*1077*

Nunes, R. K. (Dulwich; Jamaica; West Indies)

Obituary	1959	*937*
Schools Note	1913/I	*219*

Nunn, Major J. H. (Phoenix C.C., Ireland)

Obituary	1918	*198*

Nupen, E. P. (Transvaal; South Africa)

Obituary	1978	*1076*

Nurse, S. M. (Barbados; West Indies)

Cricketer of the Year	1967	*81*
Photograph	1967	*69*

Nuttall, R. H. (Hastings Club Cricketer)

Obituary	1907	*cxv*

Nuttall, W. (Lancashire League)

Obituary	1920/I	*183*

Nutter, A. E. (Lancashire; Northamptonshire)

Photograph	1952	*452*

Nutter, E. (Lancashire)

Obituary	1904	*lxxxv*

Nyren, J. (Hampshire)

'The Young Cricketers Tutor' Book Review	1975	*1128*

Oakeley, Sir C. W. A. 4th Bart. (President Kent)

Obituary	1916	*193*

Oakes, A. (Groundsman Horsham)

Obituary	1966	*970*

Oakley, C. L. (Bedford School)

Schools Note	1939	*680,685*
1018 runs Schools Averages	1939	*739*

Oakley, J. B. (Surrey Committee)
Obituary 1911/I *151*
Oakman, A. S. M. (Sussex; England)
'How I became a Cricketer' Book Review 1961 *998*
Photographs 1957 *556*
1962 *601*
Oates, A. W. (Nottinghamshire)
Obituary 1969 *984*
Oates, F. H. (Harrow)
Obituary 1924/I *267*
Oates, Lt-Col, J. S. C. (Harrow)
Obituary 1979 *1083*
Oates, Capt. L. E. G. (Scott's Expedition)
Obituary 1914/I *199*
Oates, T. W. (Nottinghamshire)
Benefit Match 1924/II *75*
Obituary 1950 *911*
Oates, W. (Yorkshire)
Obituary 1941 *400*
Oates, Lt-Col. W. C. (Harrow; Nottinghamshire)
Obituary 1943 *381*
Oates, Capt. W. H. C. (Harrow; Secretary Nottinghamshire)
Obituary 1896 *xxxix*
Views on Some Questions of the Day 1890 *xliv*
Oatley, J. N. (New South Wales)
Obituary 1927/I *296*
O'Beirne, Lieut. A. J. L. (Radley)
Obituary 1918 *198*
Obeysekera, F. A. (Royal School, Ceylon)
Obituary 1963 *1035*
O'Brien, 2nd Lieut. L. J. F. (Stonyhurst College; Paddington C.C.)
Obituary 1918 *198*
O'Brien, R. (Queensland)
Obituary 1923/I *303*
O'Brien, R. (Wellington; Cambridge University; Ireland)
Obituary 1960 *954*
O'Brien, Lieut. R. E. (Bradfield; Sandhurst)
Obituary 1920/I *156*
O'Brien, Sir T. C. 3rd Bart. (Downside; Oxford University; Middlesex; England)
Obituary 1949 *867*
O'Brien, Lieut. T. J. A. (Beaumont College)
Obituary 1917 *206*
Observe the Laws
Note on 1945 *63*

O'Callaghan, 2nd Lieut. D. Mck. M. (Cheltenham)

Obituary	1916	*194*

Ochse, A. L. (Eastern Province; South Africa)

Obituary	1950	*912*

O'Connor, J. (Essex; Buckinghamshire; England)

Benefit Match	1934/II	*186*
Career Figures	1978	*1077*
Obituary	1978	*1076*

O'Connor, J. D. A. (New South Wales; South Australia; Australia)

Obituary	1942	*360*

Odd, M. (Cricket Bat Maker)

Obituary	1952	*959*

Oddie, Lieut. F. A. J. (Secretary Sussex)

Obituary	1917	*206*

Oddy, L/Cpl. G. (New Westminster C.C., British Columbia)

Obituary	1920/I	*156*

Odell, 2nd Lieut. W. W. (Leicestershire; London County)

Obituary	1918	*198*

Odhams, P/O. B. E. L. (King's College, Wimbledon)

Obituary	1943	*369*

O'Dowd, A. C. (West Indies Board of Control)

Obituary	1946	*442*

O'Flaherty, Capt. D. H. (North of Ireland C.C.)

Obituary	1917	*206*

Ogden, Dr. E. J. (President Chicago C.C.)

Obituary	1911/I	*151*

Ogden, Dr. E. R. (Chicago C.C.; Canada)

Obituary	1914/I	*192*

Ogden, L. (Charterhouse; Canadian Club Cricket)

Obituary	1916	*194*

O'Gorman, J. G. (Surrey)

Obituary	1975	*1081*

O'Hanlon; W. J. (New South Wales)

Obituary	1941	*400*

Ohlson, F. H. (Auckland)

Obituary	1943	*381*

O'Keefe, F. A. (New South Wales; Victoria)

Obituary	1925/I	*275*

Old, C. M. (Yorkshire; Warwickshire; Northern Transvaal; England)

Cricketer of the Year	1979	*72*
Photographs	1970	*610*
	1973	*588*
	1979	*66*
	1981	*612*

Oldaker, F. A. (Epsom C.C.)

Obituary	1908/I	*146*

Old England XI Team Portrait   1946   1947   37

'Oldest Living Cricketer' H. Jenner-Fust   1898   lix

Oldest Test Player Note on   1948   88

Oldfield, N. (Lancashire; Northamptonshire; England)
  Photograph   1950   443

Oldfield, W. A. (New South Wales; Australia)
  Career Figures   1977   137
  'W. A. Oldfield – The Star Keeper' Obituary Tribute
  R. Ryder   1977   134
  Oldfield – Kippax Testimonial   1950   844
  Photograph   1977   135
  Portrait and Biography   1927/I   306
  Tribute to: W. Hammond   1966   118

Oldham, S. (Yorkshire; Derbyshire)
  Career Figures   1984   1250

Oldham, S. T. (Baltimore C.C.)
  Obituary   1917   267

Oldridge, 2nd Lieut. P. H. (Liverpool Collegiate School)
  Obituary   1919   184

Oldroyd, E. (Yorkshire)
  Benefit Match   1928/II   103
  Obituary   1966   976

Old Trafford
  Barnes injured at Photograph   1949   69
  Centenary   1957   117
  Centenary Match   1958   430
  England Team at Photograph   1950   1951   59
                                1959   1960   91
  Laker's Record at Photographs   1957   49,51
  Old Trafford of the Future Artist's Impression
  Photograph   1946   33
  'Old Trafford Humiliated' Sir N. Cardus   1975   102
  'Old Trafford' J. Marshall
  Book Review   1972   1094
  'One Hundred Years of Old Trafford' Lancashire C.C.C.
  Book Review   1958   1010
  Plan of Ground   1950   39
                         ad passim
  Youths Defy Weather at Photograph   1955   6
  33,000 at Note on   1971   8

Oliff, C. (Auckland)
  Obituary   1962   98

Oliphant, J. S. (Wimbledon C.C.)
  Obituary   1926/I   28

Oliphant, P. J. (Edinburgh Academy; Scotland)
  Obituary   1980   115

Oliver, C. J. (Canterbury)
  Obituary   1978   *1079*
Oliver, C. N. J. (New South Wales)
  Obituary   1921/I   *231*
Oliver, Lt-Col. Sir F. (President Leicester C.C.C.)
  Obituary   1940   *843*
Oliver, F. G. (Cheltenham)
  Obituary   1928/I   *294*
Oliver, L. (Derbyshire)
  Obituary   1951   *930*
Oliver, P. R. (Warwickshire)
  Career Figures   1984   *1250*
  Photograph   1982   *588*
Oliver, Capt. R. H. (Wiltshire)
  Obituary   1916   *219*
Olivier, E. (Repton; Cambridge University; Hampshire)
  Obituary   1926/I   *281*
Olivier, Capt. S. R. (Hampshire)
  Obituary   1934/I   *280*
Olliff, J. S. (St.Paul's)
  Obituary   1952   *959*
Olliver, Brig. C. O. (Winchester)
  Obituary   1973   *1012*
Ollivier, Major G. L. (Sherborne)
  Obituary   1919   *184*
Ollivierre, C. A. (Derbyshire)
  Obituary   1950   *912*
Ollivierre, H. (St.Vincent)
  Obituary   1908/I   *146*
Ollivierre, R. C. (St.Vincent)
  Obituary   1938   *941*
O'Maille, C. (Ireland)
  Obituary   1978   *1079*
One Day Championship Plan Rejected   1967   *87*
One Day Cricket Notes on   1965   *104*
                                                          1970   *74*
One Day Match Controversy   1951   *120*
O'Neil, A. (Brechin C.C.)
  Obituary   1943   *382*
O'Neill, N. C. (New South Wales; Australia)
  Cricketer of the Year   1962   *107*
  'Ins and Outs' Book Review   1965   *1020*
  Photograph   1962   *92*
O'Neill, W. P. (Philadelphia; U.S.A.)
  Obituary   1967   *973*
Ongley, A. M. (Hawke's Bay; Westland; Manawatu)
  Obituary   1976   *1105*

Onslow, 4th Earl of See under Hillier, Rt. Hon. W.
Onslow, D. R. (Brighton College; Cambridge University; Sussex)
  Obituary   1909/I   14
'On the Preparation of Wickets'
  A. C. MacLaren   1905   *lxxv*
Ontong, R. C. (Border; Transvaal; Glamorgan; Northern Transvaal; Boland)
  Photograph   1980   39
Opening Partnership World Record   1978   102
Openshaw, W. E. (Harrow; Lancashire)
  Obituary   1916   19
Opportunities, Missed Note   1965   10
Orchard, D. A. (Canterbury)
  Obituary   1949   8
Ord, J. S. (Warwickshire)
  Benefit Match   1951   5
O'Reilly, D. (Sydney Club Cricket)
  Obituary   1925/I   2
O'Reilly, T. J. (New York Club Cricket)
  Obituary   1911/I   1
O'Reilly, W. J. (New South Wales; Australia)
  'Clarrie Grimmett'   1981   1
  'Cricket Task Force' Book Review   1952   10
  Photograph with C. Grimmett   1981   1
  Portrait and Biography   1935/I   2
  Testimonial Match   1958   8
  'Time of the Tiger – The Bill O'Reilly Story'
  R. S. Whitington Book Review   1971   10
  Tribute to W. R. Hammond   1966   1
Orford, L. A. (Uppingham; Cambridge University)
  Obituary   1949   8
'Origin of the Ashes'   1945
      ad passim
Orlebar, Rev. A. (Rugby; Bedfordshire)
  Obituary   1913/I   1
Omerod, Major C. B. Sir (St. Paul's; Army; Oxfordshire)
  Obituary   1984   12
Ormond, 2nd Lieut. A. (Wanganui School, New Zealand)
  Obituary   1917   2
Ormrod, J. A. (Worcestershire; Lancashire)
  Benefit Match   1978   5
  Photographs   1967   6
      1968   6
      1974   5
      1978   5
Ormsby, G. (New York)
  Obituary   1969   9

rmsby, R. H. (Durham School; New York Veterans Cricket Association)
  Obituary 1922/I *265*

rmsby, Brig.-Gen. V. A. (Winchester; Sandhurst)
  Obituary 1918 *199*

rnsby, J. A. (Doncaster Grammar School)
  Obituary 1916 *194*

r, Capt. A. R. (Loretto; Stirling County)
  Obituary 1916 *195*

r, H. R. (Bedford School; Bedfordshire; Western Australia)
  Obituary 1941 *400*

r, J. H. (Loretto; Scotland)
  86 wkts Schools Averages 1897 *365*

born, F. (Leicestershire)
  Obituary 1956 *978*

borne, Lieut. B. (Harrow)
  Obituary 1916 *219*

borne, G. (Middlesex)
  Obituary 1914/I *192*

borne, 2nd Lieut. W. E. (Mercer's School)
  Obituary 1917 *206*

croft, P. W. (Nottinghamshire)
  Obituary 1934/I *271*

croft, W. (Nottinghamshire; All England XI)
  Benefit Match 1883 *275*
  Obituary 1906 *xciv*

tler, H. (Yorkshire)
  Obituary 1912/I *184*

wald, J. (Eton)
  Obituary 1918 *232*
  'Tempora! O'Mores! Photograph 1983 *Plate*

her Long Partnerships 1932/I *152*

away, C. J. (Middlesex)
  Obituary 1879 *120*

away, Sgt. D. A. (Surrey Colts)
  Obituary 1946 *433*

chterlong, Major J. P. H. (Woolwich R.M.C.)
  Obituary 1918 *199*
  ur Young Cricketers' Sir P. Warner 1911/I *144*

terbridge, A. A. (Administrator U.S.A. Cricket)
  Obituary 1918 *232*

terbridge, A. E. (Staten Island C.C.)
  Obituary 1922/I *265*

t of Bounds' Photograph 1983 *Plate*

tschoorn, L. (Worcestershire)
  Benefit Match 1960 *627*

Oval

Bradman's Last Test Appearance Photograph		1949	
Desolate Test Scene Photograph		1969	
England Team at Photographs	1946	1947	
	1949	1950	
	1951	1952	
	1952	1953	
	1953	1954	
	1956	1957	
	1966	1967	
	1968	1969	
	1972	1973	
	1977	1978	
	1983	1984	*Pl*
Exciting Moment at Photograph		1953	
George VI, King at Photograph		1947	
Hero Worship at Photograph		1971	
Last Wicket Records at Photograph		1947	
Len Hutton on Balcony Photograph		1954	
Moment of Triumph Photograph		1969	
New Oval Proposed Note on		1967	
Oval in 1945 Photograph		1946	
Plan of Ground		1950	
		ad passim	
Presentation to J. C. Laker Photograph		1957	
Prison Cage Photograph		1946	
Scoreboard Photograph		1939	
'The Story of the Oval' L. Palgrave			
Book Review		1950	
Tense Moment in 1953		1954	
War Damage at: Note on		1944	
'P. F. Warner at'		1917	
Over, Notes on Problems, Restrictions etc.		1943	
		1944	
		1947	
		1967	
		1973	
		1980	
		1981	94
		1982	
Over, J. (Oval Groundsman)			
Obituary		1940	
Over, W. (Victoria)			
Obituary		1912/I	

Overseas Players Notes on Problems, Talents etc.		1969	*90*
		1972	*90*
		1980	*85,86*
		1981	*96*
		1983	*83*
'Over Fifty in the County Championships' Statistics			
E. L. Peake		1972	*361*
Overton, W. (Wiltshire)			
Obituary		1950	*912*
Owen, Lieut. G. C. (Leigh C.C.)			
Obituary		1919	*184*
Owen, Col. G. P. (Marlborough)			
Obituary		1934/I	*271*
Owen, H. G. P. (Trent College; Cambridge University; Essex)			
Obituary		1913/I	*192*
Owen, Lieut. I. E. (Mill Hill)			
Obituary		1919	*184*
Owen, Rev. J. R. B. (Trent College)			
Obituary		1922/I	*265*
Owen, Rev. L. E. (Winchester)			
Obituary		1910/I	*144*
Owen, Rev. P. H. (Winchester)			
Obituary		1909/I	*144*
Owen, Canon R. (Repton; Staffordshire; Derbyshire)			
Obituary		1905	*c*
Owen-Smith, H. G. O. (Western Province; Oxford University; Middlesex; South Africa)			
Portrait and Biography		1930/I	*279*
Oxenbridge, Lord (President Surrey)			
Obituary		1899	*xliv*
Oxenham, R. K. (Queensland; Australia)			
Obituary		1940	*844*
'Oxford Cricket, Recollections of'			
H. D. Leveson Gower		1937/I	*249*
'Oxford Memories' Lord Harris		1928/I	*305*
Oxford – The Parks Note		1969	*145*
Oxford University v Cambridge University			
Centenary Dinner		1928/I	*350*
Oxford University Past and Present v Cambridge University Past and Present			
		1970	*752*
Oxford University C.C.			
Team Portraits	1981	1982	*635*
	1982	1983	*656*
	1983	1984	*619*

Oxford University Authentics
in India 1902-03   1904   *467*

Oxlade, R. A. (Australian Board of Control)
Obituary   1956   *975*

Oyston, C. (Yorkshire)
Obituary   1943   *382*

Pabst, Dr. J. C. (Auckland)
Obituary   1925/I   *276*

Pacey, J. (Philadelphia C.C.)
Obituary   1927/I   *284*

Packe, Major C. W. C. (Army; Leicestershire)
Obituary   1945   *324*

Packe, Lt-Col. E. C. (Vice President Leicestershire)
Obituary   1962   *989*

Packe, M. St.J. (Wellington; Cambridge University; Leicestershire)
Obituary   1980   *1160*

Packer, K. (Australian Cricket Circus)
'The Packer Affair' H. Blofeld
Book Review   1979   *1136*
'The Packer Case' G. Ross   1978   *123*
      1979   *88*
      1980   *121*

Packer, S. C. (Secretary Leicestershire)
Obituary   1962   *989*

Packham, H. A. (Rossall; Surrey)
Obituary   1981   *1146*

Padgett, D. E. V. (Yorkshire; England)
Benefit Match   1970   *619*
Photographs   1960   *632*
      1968   *632*

Padley, G. (Secretary Yorkshire)
Obituary   1912/I   *176*

Pad Play Notes on   1947   *6*
      1958   *7*
      1959   *7*
      1963   *14*

Padwick, E. W. (Writer)
'Bibliography of Cricket' Book Review   1978   *111*

Padwick, T. (Cricket Book Collector)
Obituary   1899   *xl*

Page, Sir A. L. (Harrow)
Obituary   1959   *93*

Page, C. (Northumberland)
Obituary   1912/I   *17*

Page, C. C. (Malvern; Cambridge University; Middlesex)
Obituary   1922/I   *26*

Page, D. A. C. (Cheltenham; Gloucestershire)
Obituary — 1937/I — *276*

Page, H. (Buckinghamshire)
Obituary — 1946 — *443*

Page, H. V. (Cheltenham; Oxford University; Gloucestershire)
Obituary — 1928/I — *295*

Page, J. C. T. (Kent)
Photograph — 1959 — *401*

Page, Capt. J. K. (Wolverhampton C.C.)
Obituary — 1919 — *184*

Page, M. (Writer)
'Bradman: The Illustrated Biography'
Book Review — 1984 — *1264*

Page, M. H. (Derbyshire)
Photographs — 1969 — *347*
— 1974 — *368*

Page, 2nd Lieut. R. C. (Bradfield College; Staffordshire)
Obituary — 1919 — *185*

Page, T. (Club Cricket Windsor District)
Obituary — 1909/I — *144*

Page, W. (Derbyshire)
Obituary — 1905 — *c*

Pagenstecher, Dr. G. (Essex Committee)
Obituary — 1917 — *259*

Paget, Lt-Col. A. E. S. L. (Military Cricket)
Obituary — 1918 — *199*

Paget, Capt. S. J. (Winchester)
Obituary — 1919 — *185*

Paget-Cooke, Sir H. (Cheltenham)
Obituary — 1924/I — *267*

Paice, L. J. (Club Cricket)
Obituary — 1900 — *xlviii*

Paine, Lt-Col. A. I. (Harrow)
Obituary — 1950 — *912*

Paine, G. A. E. (Middlesex; Warwickshire; England)
Benefit Match — 1939 — *551*
Career Figures — 1979 — *1084*
Obituary — 1979 — *1084*
Portrait and Biography — 1935/I — *286*

Paine, W. A. (Jamaica Cricket Council)
Obituary — 1908/I — *146*

Painter, J. (Gloucestershire)
Benefit Match — 1895 — *161*
Obituary — 1901 — *lxii*

Paintings at Lord's
Doubts Note on — 1984 — *51*

417

Pairandeau, L. E. (New York Club Cricketer)

Obituary		1921/I	*231*

Paish, A. (Gloucestershire)

Obituary		1950	*916*

Pakistan

in Australia	1964-65	1966	*832*
	1972-73	1974	*912*
	1976-77	1978	*920*
	1978-79	1980	*1020*
	1981-82	1983	*975*
in England	1954	1955	*215*
Team Portrait	1954	1955	*61*
Well Done!		1955	*82*
'Pakistan on the Cricket Map' Q. Butt			
Book Review		1956	*1023*
'Pakistan v England' M. H. Maqsood and M. I. Merchant			
Book Review		1956	*1024*
'Shabash! Pakistan' F. S. Hussain			
Book Review		1956	*1023*
'Test Status on Trial' A. H. Kardar			
Book Review		1956	*1023*
	1962	1963	*300*
Team Portrait	1962	1963	*153*
Note on		1961	*116*
'Cricketers from Pakistan' G. Ross			
Book Review		1963	*1112*
'Cricketers from Pakistan' Book Review		1963	*1113*
'Rothmans Pakistan Cricket Almanack' G. Ross			
Book Review		1963	*1113*
Pakistan England Tour 1962			
Book Review		1963	*1113*
	1967	1968	*307*
Team Portrait	1967	1968	*65*
'The Oval Memories' Q. Butt Book Review		1969	*1032*
	1971	1972	*295*
Team Portrait	1971	1972	*64*
	1974	1975	*327*
Team Portrait	1974	1975	*73*
World Cup Tournament	1975	1976	*300*
Team Portrait	1975	1976	*302*
	1978	1979	*288*
Team Portrait	1978	1979	*59*
World Cup Tournament	1979	1980	*297*
	1982	1983	*321*
Team Portrait	1982	1983	*322*
'Summer of the All-Rounder' P. Eagar and A. Ross			
Book Review		1983	*1300*

World Cup Tournament	1983	1984	*293*
in India	1952-53	1953	*872*
'Inaugural Test Matches' A. H. Kardar			
Book Review		1955	*990*
	1960-61	1962	*854*
	1979-80	1981	*994*
'Glorious Battle' S. Talati Book Review		1983	*1307*
'Pakistan in India 1979-80' C. K. Haridass			
Book Review		1981	*1206*
in New Zealand	1964-65	1966	*832*
	1972-73	1974	*929*
	1978-79	1980	*1006*
in Sri Lanka	1964	1965	*903*
	1976	1977	*929*
in West Indies	1957-58	1959	*803*
'Green Shadows' A. H. Kardar Book Review		1960	*997*
'Cricket Wanderers: Pakistan v West Indies 1958'			
Q. Butt Book Review		1960	*998*
	1976-77	1978	*955*
Chronological List of Articles, Notes etc.			
Test Status Given		1953	*987*
'Growth of Pakistan Cricket' A. H. Kardar		1954	*97*
'The Rise of Cricket in Pakistan'			
G. M. Khan		1967	*153*
'Dates in Pakistan Cricket History'			
R. Bowen		1967	*157*
Pakistans Good Show Note		1972	*86*
Pakistan Protests		1984	*1139*
Pakistan U19 in England	1974	1975	*1026*
in Sri Lanka	1975	1976	*1045*
U25 in Sri Lanka	1973	1975	*970*
Pakistan Eaglets in England	1963	1964	*684*
Palairet, H. H. (Exeter College; Oxford University)			
Obituary		1924/I	*267*
Palairet, L. C. H. (Repton; Oxford University; Somerset; England)			
Obituary		1934/I	*271*
Portrait and Biography		1893	*xli*
Schools Note		1890	*230*
Views on Throwing		1895	*lviii*
Palairet, R. C. N. (Repton; Oxford University; Somerset)			
Obituary		1956	*975*
Palgrave, L. (Writer)			
'The Story of the Oval' Book Review		1950	*973*
Palia, P. E. (United Provinces; Mysore; India)			
Obituary		1982	*1207*

Pallett, H. J. (Warwickshire)

Benefit Match	1898	*129*
Obituary	1918	*232*

Palmer, C. H. (Worcestershire; Leicestershire; England; President M.C.C.)

Career Figures	1958	*97*
Note on	1946	*200*
Photographs	1951	*415*
	1952	*417*
	1953	*433*
	1955	*419*
	1957	*440*

Palmer, Lt.-Col. C. H. (Radley; Hampshire; Worcestershire)

Obituary	1916	*195*

Palmer, G. E. (Victoria; Australia)

Obituary	1911/I	*151*

Palmer, H. (Umpire)

Obituary	1960	*955*

Palmer, Rev. Canon H. (Marlborough)

Obituary	1932/I	*249*

Palmer, H. J. (Essex)

Obituary	1968	*1005*

Palmer, K. E. (Somerset; England)

Photographs	1962	*560*
	1964	*530*

Palmer, R. (Kent)

Obituary	1940	*844*

Palmer, Lieut. R. (Winnipeg C.C.)

Obituary	1917	*206*

Palmer, R. C. (Winchester)

Obituary	1924/I	*268*

Palmer, R. H. R. (Eton; Berkshire)

Obituary	1971	*1028*

Palmer, Lieut. R. J. A. (Weymouth College)

Obituary	1917	*206*

Panter, G. (Leicestershire; Umpire)

Obituary	1897	*xxxix*

Papenfus, Air Sgt. C. F. B. (Orange Free State)

Obituary	1943	*369*

Papillon, G. K. (Northumberland)

Obituary	1943	*382*
Correction	1944	*328*

Paramore, Lieut. R. E. P. (Exeter School)

Obituary	1917	*206*

Pardon, C. F. (Editor of Wisden 1887-1890)

Obituary	1891	*xi*

Pardon, E. S. (Journalist; Wisden Staff)
Obituary 1899 *xlvii*
Pardon, S. H. (Editor of Wisden 1891-1925)
Photograph 1963 *77*
Special Memoir of (Obituary) 1926/I *28*
Tributes to 1926/I *30*
Parfitt, His Hon. Judge J. J. (Surrey; Somerset; Warwickshire)
Obituary 1927/I *285*
Parfitt, P. H. (Middlesex; England)
Cricketer of the Year 1963 *168*
Photographs 1962 *504*
1963 *159*
1970 *481*
Parish, R. J. (Australian Cricket Administrator)
'Australia – A New Era' 1984 *69*
Park, A. H. (New South Wales)
Obituary 1925/I *276*
Park, Lieut. F. A. K. (Manchester Grammar School)
Obituary 1919 *185*
Park, Capt. J. W. H. (St.John's School, Leatherhead)
Obituary 1918 *199*
Park, L. J. (Warwick C.C., Sydney)
Obituary 1907 *cxv*
Park, Dr. R. L. (Victoria; Australia)
Obituary 1949 *873*
Obituary 1950 *916*
Parke, A. W. (Winchester)
Obituary 1922/I *266*
Parke, E. A. (Kent)
Obituary 1924/I *268*
Parke, Lieut. J. A. (Winchester)
Obituary 1916 *195*
Parke, Lieut. W. E. (Winchester; Dorset)
Obituary 1915/I *237*
Parker, C. W. L. (Gloucestershire; England)
Benefit Match 1923/II *259*
Obituary 1960 *955*
Portrait and Biography 1923/I *315*
Parker, Gunner E. F. (Western Australia)
Obituary 1919 *185*
Parker, G. (Crypt School; Gloucestershire; Cambridge University; Gloucestershire)
'Gloucestershire Road' Book Review 1984 *1258*
'The Midwinter File' 1971 *142*
Parker, Pte. G. (St.John's C.C., Calgary, Canada)
Obituary 1918 *216*

Parker, I. T. (Scotland)
    Obituary   1962   *989*
Parker, J. (Batley C.C.)
    Obituary   1920/I   *183*
Parker, J. F. (Surrey)
    Benefit Match   1952   *523*
    Obituary   1984   *1206*
Parker, J. M. (Worcestershire; Northern Districts; New Zealand)
    Photograph   1973   *573*
Parker, Major. L. (Marlborough)
    Obituary   1918   *199*
Parker, P. W. G. (Collyers School; Cambridge University; Natal; Sussex; England)
    Photograph   1979   *547*
    Schools Notes   1974   *828*
                                       1976   *862*
Parker, Capt. W. M. (Winchester; Army; Sandhurst)
    Obituary   1916   *195*
Parkes, Capt. H. R. (Uppingham; London County)
    Obituary   1921/I   *232*
Parkhouse, W. G. A. (Wycliffe College; Glamorgan; England)
    Benefit Match   1958   *352*
    Note on   1945   *153*
    Photographs   1950   *322*
                                       1951   *324*
                                       1956   *343*
                                       1958   *345*
                                       1960   *376*
                                       1961   *372*
Parkin, C. H. (Yorkshire; Lancashire; England)
    Benefit Match   1926/II   *107*
    Obituary   1944   *318*
    Portrait and Biography   1924/I   *281*
Parkin, D. C. (Eastern Province; Transvaal; Griqualand West; South Africa)
    Obituary   1939   *921*
Parkin, I. U. (Oxford University Authentics)
    Obituary   1949   *868*
Parkinson, K. W. (President Yorkshire)
    Obituary   1982   *1207*
Parkinson, Sir L. (Blackpool C.C.)
    Obituary   1937/I   *277*
Parkinson, L. W. (Lancashire)
    Obituary   1971   *1034*
Parkinson, M. (Broadcaster; Journalist)
    'Cricket Mad' Book Review   1970   *1064*

Parks, H. W. (Sussex)
Benefit Match	1949	*518*

Parks, J. H. (Canterbury; Sussex; England)
Benefit Match	1940	*479*
Obituary	1981	*1146*
Portrait and Biography	1938	*38*

Parks, J. M. (Sussex; Somerset; England)
Cricketer of the Year	1968	*83*
Photographs	1953	*549*
	1955	*530*
	1958	*566*
	1960	*574*
	1968	*66*
'Runs in the Sun' Book Review	1962	*1042*
'Time to Hit Out' Book Review	1968	*1052*

Parkyns, Sir T. M. F. 7th Bart. (Eton; Suffolk)
Obituary	1927/I	*285*

'Parliament of Cricket: M.C.C. 1787-1937'
	1938	*242*

Parnaby, Brig. A. H. (Durham; Army)
Obituary	1975	*1082*

Parnham, C. (Nottinghamshire Club Cricketer)
Obituary	1923/I	*303*

Parnham, J. (Leicestershire)
Obituary	1909/I	*144*

Parr, G. (Nottinghamshire; All England XI)
Benefit Match	1879	*152*
Biography	1878	*202*
Obituary	1892	*xxxiii*

Parr, H. B. (Cheltenham; Lancashire)
Obituary	1931/I	*262*

Parr-Dudley, 2nd Lieut. J. H. (Cranbrook School)
Obituary	1917	*206*

Parr-Dudley, 2nd Lieut. W. (Cranbrook School)
Obituary	1919	*185*

Parratt, J. (Yorkshire)
Obituary	1906	*xcvi*

Parrington, W. F. (Rossall; Durham; Derbyshire)
Obituary	1983	*1252*

Parris, F. (Sussex)
Obituary	1942	*361*

Parry, A. H. (Northamptonshire Committee)
Obituary	1962	*989*

Parry, E. H. (Charterhouse)
Obituary	1933/I	*263*

Parry, J. T. (Buckinghamshire)
Obituary	1908/I	*146*

Parry-Okeden, W. E. (East Melbourne C.C.)
  Obituary   1927/I   *285*
Parsees in England   1886   1887   *285*
                                  1888   1889   *332*
Parsons, A. E. W. (Sussex; Auckland)
  Photograph   1976   *569*
Parsons, Capt. E. K. (Repton)
  Obituary   1917   *207*
Parsons, G. J. (Leicestershire)
  Photograph   1982   *477*
Parsons, H. F. (Victoria)
  Obituary   1939   *921*
Parsons, Rev. Canon J. H. (Warwickshire)
  Benefit Match   1927/II   *343*
  'Cricket Militant – The Life of Jack Parsons'
  G. Howat Book Review   1981   *1203*
  Obituary   1982   *1207*
Parsons, R. (F. Ayres and Company)
  Obituary   1894   *xxxvii*
Parton, C. J. (Rugby; Oxford University)
  Obituary   1954   *928*
Partridge, Brig. H. C. (Sherborne; Dorset)
  Obituary   1946   *433*
Partridge, Capt. H. R. (Leys School)
  Obituary   1919   *185*
Partridge, N. E. (Malvern, Cambridge University; Warwickshire)
  Obituary   1983   *1252*
  Photograph   1919   *150*
  Public School Cricketer of the Year   1919   *154*
Partridge, S. M. (King Edward's School, Birmingham)
  Schools Notes   1977   *817*
  1054 runs Schools Averages   1977   *840*
Passingham, Capt. E. G. (Eastbourne College)
  Obituary   1919   *200*
Pataudi Ifikhar Ali, Nawab of (Oxford University; Worcestershire; England; India; Southern Punjab)
  Obituary   1953²   *947*
  Portrait and Biography   1932/I   *269*
Pataudi, Mansur Ali Khan, Nawab of (Junior) (Winchester; Oxford University; Sussex; Hyderabad; India)
  Cricketer of the Year   1968   *71*
  Photograph   1968   *70*
  Schools Notes   1957   *736*
                                        1958   *750*
                                        1959   *722*
                                        1960   *743,745*

1068 runs Schools Averages	1960	*797*
'Tiger's Tale' Book Review	1970	*1068*

Patefield, T. W. (Bradford C.C.)
Obituary 1955 *935*

Patel, D. N. (Worcestershire)
Photograph 1982 *603*

Patel, J. M. F. (Indian Cricket Writer)
Obituary 1919 *210*

Paterson, Lt.-Col. A. S. (Somerset)
Obituary 1939 *921*

Paterson, Lieut. R. D. (Rock Ferry C.C.)
Obituary 1917 *207*

Paterson, R. F. T. (Brighton College; Essex)
Obituary 1981 *1147*

Paterson, Major W. H. (Farnham Grammar School)
Obituary 1916 *196*

Paterson, Capt. W. P. (Edinburgh Academy)
Obituary 1917 *207*

Patey, Capt. E. (Norwich Grammar School)
Obituary 1918 *199*

Patiala, The Maharajah of (Patron Indian Cricket)
Obituary 1901 *lxii*

Patiala, The Maharajah of (Patron Indian Cricket)
Obituary 1939 *914*

Patiala, The Maharajah of Lt.-Gen. (Y. Singh; Southern Punjab; Patiala; India)
Obituary 1975 *1082*

Paton, Sqn.Ldr. G. W. (Uppingham)
Obituary 1946 *435*

Paton, 2nd Lieut. J. L. (Perthshire)
Obituary 1916 *196*

Paton, 2nd Lieut. L. (Dulwich)
Obituary 1918 *199*

Paton-Williams, Canon F. (President Lancashire)
Obituary 1975 *1082*

Patrick, C. W. (New South Wales)
Obituary 1921 *244*

Patrick, J. C. (Winchester)
Obituary 1975 *1082*

Patrick, W. R. (Canterbury; Otago)
Obituary 1949 *873*

Patterson, C. S. (Philadelphia Club Cricket)
Obituary 1925/I *276*

Patterson, G. S. (Gentlemen of Philadelphia; Haverford College; Pennsylvania University)
Obituary 1944 *319*

Patterson, Rev. J. I. (Oxford University; Kent)
Obituary 1944 *319*
Patterson, W. H. (Harrow; Oxford University; Kent)
Obituary 1947 *693*
Views on Reforms of 1889 1890 *xxxvii*
Views on Some Questions of the Day 1890 *xlv*
Views on Throwing 1895 *lvii*
Patterson, W. S. (Uppingham; Cambridge University; Lancashire)
Obituary 1940 *844*
Patteson, T. C. (Canada)
Obituary 1908/I *146*
Pattisson J. L. (Secretary Civil Service C.C.)
Obituary 1916 *196*
Pattisson, W. B. (Tonbridge; Kent)
Obituary 1914/I *192*
Paul, A. G. (Lancashire)
Obituary 1948 *786*
Paul, 2nd Lieut. E. K. M. (Marlborough)
Obituary 1919 *185*
Paul, J. S. M. (Marlborough)
Obituary 1933/I *256*
Paull, R. K. (Millfield School; Cambridge University; Somerset)
Schools Note 1964 *743*
1009 runs Schools Averages 1964 *774*
Pawle, Capt. B. (Haileybury)
Obituary 1916 *196*
Pawley, T. E. (Kent)
Obituary 1924/I *268*
Pawling, S. S. (Treasurer Middlesex)
Obituary 1923/I *303*
Pawson, A. C. (Winchester; Oxford University)
Obituary 1970 *1023*
Pawson, H. A. (Winchester; Oxford University; Kent)
'Runs and Catches' Book Review 1981 *1206*
Paxton, 2nd Lieut. A. F. C. (Epsom College)
Obituary 1917 *207*
Payne, A. (Leicestershire)
Obituary 1909/I *145*
Payne, A. C. (Northamptonshire)
Obituary 1974 *1077*
Payne, A. U. (St. Edmund's School, Canterbury; Cambridge University;
Buckinghamshire)
Obituary 1978 *1079*
Payne, C. (Sussex; Kent)
Obituary 1910/I *144*

Payne, C. A. L. (Charterhouse; Middlesex; Oxford University)
Obituary 1978 *1085*

Payne, I. R. (Emanuel School; Surrey)
1144 runs, 79 wkts, Schools Averages 1977 *833*

Payne, J. (New South Wales; Umpire)
Obituary 1929/I *256*

Payne, J. (Bedfordshire)
Obituary 1976 *1101*

Payne, J. H. (Lancashire)
Obituary 1943 *382*

Payne, M. W. (Wellington; Cambridge University; Middlesex)
Obituary 1965 *973*

Payne, R. (Sussex)
Obituary 1907 *cxv*

Payne, W. (Sussex)
Obituary 1910/I *145*

Paynter, E. (Lancashire; England)
Career Figures 1980 *1153*
'Cricket all the Way' Book Review 1963 *1111*
Obituary 1980 *1152*
Photograph 1946 *40*
Portrait and Biography 1938 *39*
Tribute to: R. C. Robertson-Glasgow 1946 *41*

Payton, J. I. (Warwickshire Patron)
Obituary 1917 *260*

Payton, W. R. D. (Nottinghamshire)
Benefit Match 1931/II *183*
Obituary 1944 *319*

Peacey, Rev. Canon J. R. (St.Edmund's School, Canterbury; Sussex)
Obituary 1972 *1054*

Peach, C. W. (Kent)
Obituary 1981 *1148*

Peach, F. G. (Derbyshire)
Obituary 1966 *970*
'Scraps from a Cricketer's Memory'
Book Review 1981 *1206*

Peach, H. A. (Surrey)
Benefit Match 1930/II *323*
Obituary 1962 *989*

Peachey, C. B. (Esher C.C.)
Obituary 1912/I *176*

Peacock, H. St.G. (Eton)
Obituary 1954 *928*

Peacocke, Rt-Rev. Dr. J. (Vice-President North West Cricket Union)
Obituary 1963 *1035*

427

Peake, Rev. E. (Marlborough; Oxford University; Gloucestershire; Berkshire)
Obituary   1946   443

Peake, E. L. (Writer)
'Over Fifty in the County Championship'
Statistics   1972   361

Peake, J. F. (Secretary New Zealand Cricket Council)
Obituary   1929/I   256

Pearce, Lieut. G. M. (Highfield School, Ontario)
Obituary   1920/I   156

Pearce, H. G. (Gentlemen of Philadelphia)
Obituary   1937/I   277

Pearce, P. (Ground Superintendent Lord's)
Obituary   1912/I   176

Pearce, T. A. (Charterhouse; Kent)
Obituary   1983   1253

Pearce, T. N. (Christ's Hospital; Essex)
Views on L.B.W. Experiment   1936/I   344

Pearce, Sir W. (Kent; Essex)
Obituary   1933/I   257

Peare, W. G. (Warwickshire)
Obituary   1981   1147

Pearse, A. A. (Somerset)
Obituary   1983   125

Pearse, Capt. B. (King's College, Taunton)
Obituary   1945   32

Pearse, C. O. C. (Natal; South Africa)
Obituary   1954   92

Pearson, A. (Loretto; Rugby; Oxford University; Scotland)
Obituary   1933/I   264

Pearson, Rev. A. C. (Winchester)
Obituary   1917   266

Pearson, 2nd Lieut. A. J. W. (St.Paul's)
Obituary   1917   207

Pearson, C. H. (St.Paul's)
Obituary   1981   1148

Pearson, Lieut. C. H. (Denstone College; Wolverhampton C.C.)
Obituary   1917   20

Pearson, F. (Worcestershire)
Obituary   1964   95

Pearson, H. E. (Yorkshire)
Obituary   1904   lxxxi

Pearson, Pte. J. (Watson's College)
Obituary   1916   19

Pearson, Sir R. B. (Loretto; Oxford University)
Obituary   1955   93

428

earson, R. L. (Haverford College, U.S.A.)
Obituary 1921/I 232
earson-Gregory, T. S. (Rugby; Leicestershire)
Obituary 1936/I 285
eat, C. U. (Sedbergh; Oxford University)
Obituary 1980 1155
eate, E. (Yorkshire; England)
Obituary 1901 lx
eate, E. (Yorkshire League Cricket)
Obituary 1975 1082
echell, Capt. C. A. K. (Eton)
Obituary 1900 lv
eck, I. G. (Bedford School; Cambridge University; Northamptonshire)
Schools Note 1977 810
1181 runs Schools Averages 1977 821
edcock, C. A. (Harrow)
Obituary 1903 lxxxii
edder, F. (Tasmania)
Obituary 1927/I 285
edder, Major G. R. (Repton; Norfolk)
Obituary 1965 970
eden, D. M. (Scotland)
Obituary 1980 1160
eden, Mrs, M. (Australian Women)
Obituary 1983 1253
edley, G. (Staffordshire)
Obituary 1968 1005
eebles, H. M. (Harrow)
Obituary 1945 339
eebles, I. A. R. (Glasgow Academy; Oxford University; Middlesex; Scotland; ngland)
'G. O. Allen – Mr Cricket' 1977 122
'Batters Castle' Book Review 1959 986
'Bowlers Turn' Book Review 1961 993
'Denis Compton' Book Review 1972 1100
'The Fight for the Ashes 1958-59'
Book Review 1960 1000
'Patsy Hendren' Book Review 1970 1067
'Ian Peebles on the Ashes' Book Review 1956 1026
with D. Raitt-Kerr 'Lord's 1946-1970'
Book Review 1972 1094
'A Middlesex Century' 1965 128
Obituary 1981 1147
Portrait and Biography 1931/I 287
'Spinners Yarn' Book Review 1978 1124
'Straight from the Shoulder' Book Review 1969 1026

429

    Tribute to R. W. V. Robins   1969   980

    'Two Eras of Australian Pace'   1956   109

    Views on Growing Pains of Cricket   1956   8.

    'Woolley – The Pride of Kent' Book Review   1970   1070

Peel, 2nd Lieut. A. E. (Bedford School)

    Obituary   1919   185

Peel, B. L. (Bedfordshire)

    Obituary   1946   443

Peel, 2nd Lieut. C. N. (Public School C.C., Vancouver)

    Obituary   1918   214

Peel, R. (Yorkshire; England)

    Benefit Match   1895   39

    In the Cricket Field   1895   lxix

    Obituary   1942   364

    Portrait and Biography   1889   xxx

    Views on the Reforms of 1889   1890   xxxvii

    Views on Some Questions of the Day   1890   xl

Peel, Sir R. Bart. (Harrow)

    Obituary   1935/I   276

Peel, R. T. (Oxford University Trials)

    Obituary   1946   43

Peerless, Lieut. A. N. (Winnipeg C.C.)

    Obituary   1917   20

Pegler, S. J. (Transvaal; South Africa)

    Obituary   1973   101.

Peglotte, A. S. (Ceylon Club Cricket)

    Obituary   1913/I   19

Peirce, E. T. (Scotland)

    Obituary   1905

Peirce, Lt-Col. H. E. (Addiscombe C.C.)

    Obituary   1980   115

Peiris, D. L. (Sri Lanka)

    Obituary   1977   105

Pelham, A. G. (Eton; Cambridge University; Somerset; Sussex)

    Obituary   1970   102

Pelham, Hon. A. L. (Royal Agricultural College, Cirencester; Monmouthshire)

    Obituary   1930/I   25

Pelham, Hon. F. G. See under Chichester, Earl of

Pelham, J. B. See under Chichester, 8th Earl of

Pelham, Rev. Canon S. (Harrow; Oxford University; Norfolk)

    Obituary   1927/I   28

Pelham, Hon. T. H. W. (Eton)

    Obituary   1917   26

Pell, O. C. (Rugby; Cambridge University)

    Obituary   1892   xxx

Pellew, C. E. (South Australia; Australian Imperial Forces; Australia)
    Obituary   1982   *1208*

Pember, Dr. F. W. (Harrow)
    Obituary   1955   *935*

Pemberton, C. (Ireland)
    Obituary   1980   *1160*

Pemberton, R. H. (Eton)
    Obituary   1932/I   *250*

Pembroke, 14th Earl of (President MCC)
    Obituary   1914/I   *193*

Pendrigh, 2nd Lieut. A. C. (Whitgift Grammar School)
    Obituary   1918   *199*

Penguins (Port Elizabeth, South Africa)
    in England   1970   1971   *847*
                      1976   1977   *972*

Penn, Capt. E. F. (Eton; Cambridge University; Norfolk)
    Obituary   1916   *197*

Penn, F. (Kent; England)
    Obituary   1917   *260*

Penn, F. (Junior) (Kent)
    Obituary   1962   *990*

Pennefather, G. E. M. (Harrow)
    Obituary   1976   *1101*

Pennell, V. C. (Lincolnshire)
    Obituary   1977   *1048*

Pennington, Lieut. H. C. (Christ's Hospital)
    Obituary   1918   *199*

Pennysylvania University in England 1907   1908/II   *475*

Penny, Dr. J. A. C. (Ireland)
    Obituary   1917   *261*

Pennycuick, Col. J. (Indian Club Cricket)
    Obituary   1912/I   *177*

Penruddocke, Capt. C. P. (Bradfield)
    Obituary   1918   *216*

Pentecost, J. (Kent)
    Benefit Match   1893   *136*
    Obituary   1903   *lxxiii*

Pentelow, J. N. (Journalist)
    Obituary   1932/I   *250*
    'J. N. Pentelow: A Biographical Study'
    I. Rosenwater Book Review   1970   *1068*

Pepall, G. (Gloucestershire)
    Obituary   1954   *928*

Pepper, C. G. (New South Wales; Australian Services; Umpire)
    Big Hitting Note   1946   *63*

Pepper, C. H. (New York Enthusiast)
Obituary 1919 *210*
Pepys, Capt. A. (Eton)
Obituary 1921/I *232*
Pepys, 2nd Lieut. F. (Charterhouse)
Obituary 1916 *220*
Pepys, Rev. J. A. (Eton; Oxford University; Kent)
Obituary 1925/I *276*
Pepys, Capt. R. W. (Gentlemen of Worcestershire)
Obituary 1916 *220*
Perceival, Rev. Preb. L. J. (Clifton; Herefordshire)
Obituary 1942 *362*
Percentage of Hundreds Records Section
Perch, J. (Groundsman Granville Lee C.C.)
Obituary 1920/I *183*
Percival, J. D. (Radley; Westminster; Oxford University; Gloucestershire)
Obituary 1984 *1207*
Percival, R. (Amateur Player)
Throwing the Cricket Ball 1972 *113*
1977 *107*
Percy, R. H. G. (Griqualand West)
Obituary 1949 *868*
Pereira, Rev. E. (Oratory School Brompton; Warwickshire)
Obituary 1940 *845*
Perera, B. S. (Sri Lankan Club Cricket)
Obituary 1976 *1105*
Perera, C. (Singalese Sports Club)
Obituary 1914/I *193*
Perera, C. E. (Ceylon)
Obituary 1908/I *147*
Perera, G. C. (Royal College, Ceylon)
Obituary 1974 *1084*
Perkins, Col. A. F. Q. (Wellington)
Obituary 1941 *390*
Perkins, H. (Bury St.Edmunds School; Cambridge University; Cambridgeshire; Hertfordshire; Secretary M.C.C.)
Obituary 1917 *261*
Perkins, Pte. H. E. (Canadian Pacific C.C., Winnipeg)
Obituary 1917 *225*
Perkins, H. P. (U.S.A. Supporter)
Obituary 1910/I *151*
Perkins, Pte. L. N. (Canadian Pacific C.C., Winnipeg)
Obituary 1917 *225*
Perkins, T. T. N. (St. John's, Leatherhead; Cambridge University; Kent; Herttordshire; Wiltshire)
Obituary 1947 *694*

Perks, R. T. D. (Worcestershire; Hertfordshire; Monmouthshire; England)
Benefit Match	1948	*538*
Obituary	1978	*1080*
Photographs	1950	*551*
	1952	*566*
	1955	*569*
Retirement Note	1956	*611*

Perks, 2nd Lieut. W. L. (Stourbridge C.C.)
Obituary	1917	*207*

Perrin, F. (Club Cricketer)
Obituary	1910/I	*145*

Perrin, P. A. (Essex)
Obituary	1946	*443*
Portrait and Biography	1905	*cx*

Perrott, W. I. (Secretary Western Province Cricket Union)
Obituary	1923/I	*303*

Perryman, S. P. (Warwickshire; Worcestershire)
Career Figures	1984	*1250*
Photographs	1976	*585*
	1979	*563*

Persee, 2nd Lieut. R. A. (Winchester)
Obituary	1916	*197*

Pershke, Flt-Lieut. W. J. (Uppingham; Oxford University)
Obituary	1945	*324*

Personal Achievements Note on
	1950	*114*

Personalities and Variety lack of
Note on	1967	*88*

Persse, Major H. W. (Hampshire)
Obituary	1919	*185*

Perth – Alderman Carried off Injured
Photograph	1984	*Plate*

Peru
in Argentina 1968	1969	*928*

Peters, E. A. (South Australia)
Obituary	1904	*lxxxv*

Pettifer, H. (Cricket Bat Maker)
Obituary	1912/I	*177*

Pettiford, J. (New South Wales; Kent)
Benefit Match	1960	*443*
Obituary	1965	*970*
Photograph	1955	*385*

Prevensey, Viscount (See under **Sheffield, 3rd Earl of**)

Pfeiffer, Capt. C. W. K. (Essex; Devon)
Obituary	1952	*959*

Phadre, Prof. N. S. (Writer)
'India v M.C.C. Tests 1951-52'
Book Review 1953 *998*
Phair, Rev. Canon E. E. M. (St.Johns C.C., Winnipeg)
Obituary 1916 *197*
Phebey, A. H. (Kent)
Benefit Match 1961 *440*
Photograph 1957 *403*
Phelan, P. J. (Essex)
Photograph 1965 *366*
Philadelphia in England 1884 1885 *33*
1889 1890 *251*
1897 1898 *302*
1903 1904 *321*
1908 1909/II *350*
Philadelphia Pilgrims in England 1921 1922/II *583*
'Philatelic Cricket' M. Williams 1984 *72*
Philbrick, Comdr. H. F. (Bombay Gymkhana)
Obituary 1909/I *145*
Philcox, E. A. (Harrow)
Obituary 1896 *xli*
Philipson, H. (Eton; Oxford University; Middlesex; Northumberland; England)
Obituary 1936/I *286*
Philler, G. S. (Merion C.C., U.S.A.)
Obituary 1915/I *237*
Phillip, F. (St.Lucia)
'Francis "Mindoo" Phillip: A Portrait from Memory'
S. French Book Review 1982 *1270*
Phillip, N. Essex; (Windward Islands; Combined Islands; West Indies)
Photograph 1979 *359*
Phillipps, J. H. (Manager New Zealand Touring Teams)
Obituary 1978 *1080*
Phillipps, Rev. T. D. (Canada)
Obituary 1916 *198*
Phillips, A. H. (Oxfordshire)
Obituary 1976 *1101*
Phillips, C. B. (Winchester)
Obituary 1932/I *250*
Phillips, C. S. (New York Club Cricket)
Obituary 1912/I *184*
Phillips, Lieut. E. S. (Marlborough; Cambridge University; Monmouthshire)
Obituary 1916 *198*
Phillips, F. (Kent)
Obituary 1973 *1013*
Phillips, F. A. (Rossall; Oxford University; Essex; Somerset)
Obituary 1956 *975*

Phillips, G. C. (Marlborough)
Obituary 1939 *914*

Phillips, H. (Sussex)
Benefit Match 1887 *210*
Obituary 1920/I *183*

Phillips, Lieut. H. H. (Hertford Grammar School)
Obituary 1916 *198*

Phillips, J. (Sussex)
Obituary 1906 *xcvi*

Phillips, J. (Canterbury; Victoria; Umpire)
Benefit Match 1900 *301*
Obituary 1931/I *263*

Phillips, J. B. (Oratory School)
75 wkts Schools Averages 1952 *739*

Phillips, J. S. (Shropshire)
Obituary 1910/I *145*

Phillips, Capt. L. (Monmouthshire)
Obituary 1916 *199*

Phillips, L. J. (Essex)
Obituary 1980 *1155*

Phillips, Major P. A. (Canford School)
Obituary 1945 *325*

Phillpotts, W. F. (Winchester)
Obituary 1910/I *145*

Philpott, F. G. (Marlborough)
Obituary 1930/I *259*

Phipps, W. W. (Eton)
Obituary 1912/I *178*

Physical Fitness, Importance of
Note on 1954 *83*

Pickard, Rev. H. A. (Rugby)
Obituary 1906 *xcvi*

Pickering, E. H. U. (Journalsit)
Obituary 1910/I *151*

Pickering, W. P. (Eton; Cambridge University; Surrey; Canada; IZingari)
Obituary 1906 *xcvi*

Pickett, H. (Essex)
Benefit Match 1898 *57*
Obituary 1908/I *147*

Pidcock, R. G. (Winchester)
Obituary 1953 *948*

Pienaar, A. J. (South African Cricket Association)
Obituary 1954 *928*

Pierce, M. (New South Wales; Queensland)
Obituary 1914/I *193*

Pigg, 2nd Lieut. B. W. (Tonbridge; Cambridge University; Cambridgeshire)
Obituary 1918 *216*
Pigg, C. (Abingdon House; Cambridge University; Hertfordshire;
Northamptonshire; Cambridgeshire)
Obituary 1930/I *259*
Views on the Reforms of 1889 1890 *xxxviii*
Pigg, H. (Abingdon House; Cambridge University; Hertfordshire;
Northamptonshire)
Obituary 1914/I *193*
Piggot, J. I. (Cheltenham,; Surrey)
Obituary 1966 *970*
Piggot, P. (Journalist)
Obituary 1960 *955*
Pigot, D. R. (Ireland)
Obituary 1968 *1009*
Pigot, J. P. M. (Dublin University)
Obituary 1981 *1148*
Pigott, A. C. S. (Harrow; Sussex; Wellington; England)
Photograph 1980 *572*
Pike, A. (Nottinghamshire)
Obituary 1908/I *147*
Pilch, G. E. (Norfolk)
Obituary 1981 *1148*
Pilkington, C. C. (Eton; Oxford University)
Obituary 1951 *926*
Pilkington, Col. F. C. (Eton)
Obituary 1948 *786*
Pilkington, H. C. (Eton; Oxford University; Middlesex)
Obituary 1943 *382*
Pilkington, T. A. (Eton; M.C.C.)
Obituary 1982 *1208*
1983 *1253*
Pilkington, Cpl. W. F. L. (Victoria C.C., British Columbia)
Obituary 1917 *225*
Pillans, A. A. (Hampshire)
Obituary 1902 *lxx*
Pilling, H. (Lancashire)
Photographs 1966 *449*
1968 *465*
1973 *446*
1977 *459*
Pilling, R. (Lancashire; England)
Benefit Match 1890 *274*
Obituary 1892 *xxxii*
Portrait and Biography 1891 *xxxiii*

Pilling, W. (Lancashire)
   Obituary   1925/I   *277*
Pillow, L/Cpl. G. T. (Toronto Club Cricket)
   Obituary   1918   *216*
Pinch, F. B. (Glamorgan)
   Obituary   1962   *990*
Pinder, G. (Yorkshire)
   Benefit Match   1881   *198*
   Obituary   1904   *lxxvii*
Pinkham, Capt. E. F. (Trinity College School, Port Hope)
   Obituary   1917   *207*
Pinney, Major B. (Winchester)
   Obituary   1942   *350*
Pinney, Lt-Col. G. A. (President Dorset C.C.C.)
   Obituary   1969   *984*
Pinney, Rev. J. C. (Eton)
   Obituary   1913/I   *203*
Piper, W. J. (Journalist; Scorer Devon)
   Obituary   1941   *401*
Pitches
   Notes on   1944   *65*
                                      1947   *70*
                                      1950   *112*
                                      1958   *77*
                                      1959   *74,79*
                                      1966   *77*
                                      1970   *77*
Pitou, J. H. (Transvaal; Natal)
   Obituary   1943   *382*
Pitt, T. A. (Northamptonshire)
   Obituary   1958   *962*
Pitts, S. J. (President South African Cricket Association)
   Obituary   1961   *950*
Pix, T. S. (Harrow)
   Obituary   1901   *lxii*
Place, W. (Lancashire; England)
   Benefit Match   1953   *426*
   Photograph   1953   *414*
Plan for Knock-out Competition   1946   *126*
'Planning for Post War Cricket' N. Preston
   Note on   1945   *81*
Platt, J. W. (Surrey)
   Obituary   1956   *976*
Platt, S. R. (Vice-President Lancashire)
   Obituary   1903   *lxxviii*

Platt, Rev. T. D. (Harrow)
Obituary 1904 *lxxxvi*
Platten, G. (Norfolk)
Obituary 1918 *233*
Platten, Rev. T. E. (Marlborough)
Obituary 1924/I *268*
Platts, J. (Derbyshire; Umpire)
Benefit Match 1886 *327*
Obituary 1899 *xlviii*
Platts, Lieut. R. H. (Oundle)
Obituary 1919 *186*
Player, A. S. (Auckland)
Obituary 1964 *954*
Player, J. A. (President Nottinghamshire)
Obituary 1960 *955*
'Play Back'
D. L. A. Jephson 1904 *lxviii*
Plender, Rt. Hon. Bart. (President Kent)
Obituary 1947 *694*
Plenty, C. M. (Writer)
'The Book of Gloucestershire County Cricket
Records from 1919 to 1960' Book Review 1962 *1034*
Plowden, Sir H. M. (Harrow, Hampshire; Cambridge University)
Obituary 1921/I *232*
'Personal Recollections of John Wisden' 1913/I *126*
Plowen, W. F. (Stonyhurst College)
Obituary 1915/I *237*
Plumb, T. (Buckinghamshire; Northamptonshire)
Obituary 1906 *xcvii*
Plumer, C. G. (M. C. C.)
Obituary 1915/I *237*
Plummer, Capt. L. D. (St.Bees School; Northumberland)
Obituary 1917 *208*
Plunket, 5th Baron (Donator of the Plunket Shield)
Obituary 1921/I *233*
Pochin, E. C. (Repton)
Obituary 1918 *233*
Pocock, N. E. J. (Shrewsbury; Hampshire)
Photograph 1981 *431*
Pocock, P. I. (Surrey; Northern Transvaal; England)
Benefit Match 1978 *766*
Photographs 1968 *566*
1969 *568*
1973 *530*
Pode, J. D. (Winchester)
Obituary 1922/I *267*

438

Podmore, A. (Writer)
Obituary 1938 *942*
Podmore, G. (Club Cricket)
Obituary 1934/I *272*
Pogson, H. (Bombay Club Cricket)
Obituary 1907 *cxv*
Pogson, R. (Journalist; Author 'Index to Wisden 1864-1943')
'Lancashire' Book Review 1953 *1000*
Obituary 1968 *1005*
Poidevin, Dr. L. O. S. (New South Wales; London County; Lancashire)
Obituary 1932/I *250*
Poile, Pte. G. (Canadian Club Cricket)
Obituary 1917 *208*
Polack, 2nd Lieut. B. J. (Clifton)
Obituary 1917 *208*
Polhill-Turner, Rev. A. T. Obituary (Eton)
Obituary 1937/I *288*
Polhill-Turner, C. H. (Eton)
Obituary 1939 *914*
Politics Notes on 1982 *87*
1983 *76*
'Politics, The Escalating Effects of on Cricket'
W. A. Hadlee 1982 *106*
Pollard, D. (Yorkshire)
Obituary 1910/I *145*
Pollard, J. (Lancashire League Cricket)
Obituary 1952 *960*
Pollard, M. (Women's Cricket Association)
Obituary 1983 *1253*
Pollard, R. (Lancashire; England)
Benefit Match 1950 *406*
Pollard, Lieut. R. T. (St. Paul's)
Obituary 1916 *199*
Pollock, P. M. (Eastern Province; South Africa)
with R. G. Pollock 'Bouncers and Boundaries'
Book Review 1971 *1079*
Cricketer of the Year 1966 *69*
Photograph 1966 *61*
Pollock, R. G. (Eastern Province; Transvaal; South Africa)
with P. M. Pollock 'Bouncers and Boundaries'
Book Review 1971 *1079*
Cricketer of the Year 1966 *67*
'Down the Wicket' Book Review 1969 *1032*
Photographs 1966 *60*
1971 *68*

Pollock, W. (Ireland)
Obituary 1974 *1085*
Pollock, Sqn. Ldr. W. (Cricket Journalist)
Obituary 1945 *325*
Ponsford, W. H. (Victoria; Australia)
Portrait and Biography 1935/I *279*
Testimonial Match 1941 *64*
Ponsonby, Col. Sir C. (IZingari)
Obituary 1977 *1048*
Ponsonby, C. B. (Worcestershire)
Obituary 1946 *444*
Ponsonby, Hon. F. See under Bessborough, Earl of
Ponsonby, Hon, F. J. W. (Eton)
Obituary 1934/I *273*
Ponsonby-Fane, J. H. (Harrow)
Obituary 1917 *262*
Ponsonby-Fane, Sir S. (Surrey; Middlesex; President Somerset; Treasurer M.C.C.)
Personal Recollections of John Wisden 1913/I *12.*
Special Memoir of (Obituary) 1916 *138*
Pont, K. R. (Essex)
Photograph 1978 *371*
Pontifex, Sir C. (King's College School; Cambridge University)
Obituary 1913/I *19.*
Pontifex, D. D. (Surrey; Somerset)
Obituary 1935/I *27c*
Pool, C. J. T. (Northamptonshire)
Obituary 1955 *935*
Pool, A. B. (Bedfordshire)
Obituary 1981 *1148*
Poole, Capt. A. G. (Bristol Grammar School)
Obituary 1919 *186*
Poole, A. W. H. (Bedfordshire)
Obituary 1959 *937*
Poole, C. J. (Nottinghamshire; England)
Benefit Match 1961 *52.*
Photographs 1952 *47c*
1955 *47.*
1958 *502*
Poole, J. L. (U.S.A.)
Obituary 1937/I *278*
Poole, 2nd Lieut. J. S. (Rugby)
Obituary 1916 *19c*
Pooley, Hon. C. E. (Victoria C.C., British Columbia)
Obituary 1913/I *19.*

Pooley, E. (Surrey)
  Benefit Match   1884   *153*
  Biography   1883   *132*
  Obituary   1908/I   *147*

Poore, Major R. A. (Sherborne)
  Obituary   1918   *199*

Poore, Brig.-Gen. R. M. (Natal; Hampshire; South Africa)
  Obituary   1939   *914*
  Portrait and Biography   1900   *lxi*

Pope, C. A. (Wellington)
  Obituary   1907   *cxv*

Pope, C. G. (Harrow; Cambridge University; Bedfordshire)
  Obituary   1960   *956*

Pope, D. F. (Gloucestershire; Essex)
  Obituary   1935/I   *270*

Pope, F. (Groundsman Edgbaston)
  Obituary   1962   *990*

Pope, Dr. R. J. (New South Wales; Scotland; Australia)
  Obituary   1953   *948*

Pope, Lieut. R. T. B. (Bradfield)
  Obituary   1916   *199*

Popham, R. F. (Repton; Norfolk)
  Obituary   1976   *1101*

Popplewell, N. M. F. (Radley; Cambridge University; Somerset; Buckinghamshire)
  Photograph   1981   *535*

Porch, R. B. (Malvern; Oxford University; Somerset)
  Obituary   1964   *953*

Portal, Viscount C. F. A. Marshall of the R.A.F. (Winchester; President M.C.C)
  Obituary   1972   *1054*

Portal, Sir G. H. (Eton)
  Obituary   1895   *xxxvii*

Porter, A. A. (Ridley College, Ontario)
  Obituary   1919   *213*

Porter, Rev. A. L. (Somerset; Hampshire)
  Obituary   1939   *921*

Porter, A. M. (Harrow)
  Obituary   1901   *lxii*

Porter, C. (Writer)
  'The White Horse and the Kangaroo'
  Book Review   1982   *1258*

Porter, G. (Derbyshire; Umpire)
  Obituary   1909/I   *145*

Porter, Rev. J. (Treasurer Cambridge University C.C.)
  Obituary   1901   *lxii*

Porter, Pte. T. C. (Lancashire)
Obituary   1916   *199*
Portman, F. J. (Radley; Berkshire; Somerset)
Obituary   1907   *cxvii*
Portsmouth United Services Ground
Plan of County Ground   1953   *376*
     ad passim
Port of Spain, Trinidad Riot
Photograph   1961   *90*
Portus, J. (New South Wales Cricket Association)
Obituary   1925/I   *277*
Positive Cricket Note on   1966   *75*
Posno, B. M. (Orleans C.C.)
Obituary   1902   *lxx*
Post, J. M. (Eton)
Obituary   1936/I   *293*
Posthuma, C. J. (London County; Holland)
Obituary   1940   *845*
Postill, R. (Hertfordshire)
Obituary   1982   *1209*
Postles, A. J. (Auckland)
Obituary   1977   *1048*
Pot Holes Note on   1983   *572*
Potter, J. (Northamptonshire; Kent; Surrey; Wiltshire)
Obituary   1907   *cxv*
Potter, T. O. (Lancashire)
Obituary   1911/I   *163*
Pottinger, G. (Journalist)
Obituary   1979   *1085*
Pougher, A. D. (Leicestershire; England)
Benefit Matches   1901   *245*
     1911/II   *52*
Obituary   1927/I   *285*
Poulier, H. E. (Ceylon)
Obituary   1980   *1155*
Poulton, R. M. (Secretary Nottinghamshire)
Obituary   1981   *1148*
Poulton-Palmer, R. W. (Rugby)
Obituary   1916   *200*
Powell, A. (Journalist)
with S. C. Caple 'The Graces (E.M., W.G., G.F.)'
Book Review   1976   *1150*
Obituary   1964   *951*
Powell, A. G. (Charterhouse; Cambridge University; Essex; Suffolk)
Obituary   1983   *1253*

well, A. J. (Worcestershire)
Obituary | 1980 | *1155*

well, A. P. (Mill Hill School; Middlesex)
1065 runs Schools Averages | 1928/II | *615*

well, E. O. (Surrey; Hampshire)
Obituary | 1929/I | *256*

well, Major G. F. W. (Harrow House Matches)
Obituary | 1918 | *199*

well, 2nd Lieut. L. M. (Loretto; Kent)
Obituary | 1916 | *200*

well, M. (Harrow)
Obituary | 1930/I | *260*

well, Lieut. R. H. (Haileybury; Journalist)
Obituary | 1920/I | *156*

well, W. (Kent)
Obituary | 1955 | *935*

wnall, Lieut. L. H. Y. (Clifton)
Obituary | 1916 | *200*

wys, W. N. (Cambridge University; Derbyshire)
Obituary | 1893 | *xxxiii*

wys-Keck, Capt. H. J. (Worcestershire)
Obituary | 1983 | *949*

ynton, Dr. F. J. (Marlborough; Somerset)
Obituary | 1944 | *320*

yntz, E. S. M. (Haileybury; Somerset)
Obituary | 1935/I | *271*

yntz, Col. H. S. (Somerset)
Obituary | 1956 | *976*

agg, S. (West Indies Young Cricketers)
Obituary | 1984 | *1207*

att, Brig – Gen. E. St.G. (Army)
Obituary | 1919 | *186*

att, Lieut. J. S. (Blundells)
Obituary | 1918 | *200*

att, R. (Derbyshire)
Obituary | 1984 | *1207*

att, R. C. E. (Surrey)
Obituary | 1978 | *1080*

att, W. E. (Leicestershire)
Obituary | 1976 | *1105*

att–Barlow, Commdr. B. A. (M.C.C.)
Obituary | 1915/I | *237*

eece, C. R. (Known as C.A.)(Worcestershire)
Obituary | 1967 | *973*
Correction | 1977 | *1048*

Preece, H. C. (Cheshire; Essex)
    Obituary   1938   9

Preeston, 2nd Lieut. P. S. (Felsted)
    Obituary   1919   1

Prentice, F. T. (Leicestershire)
    Obituary   1980   11

Prentice, L. R. V. (Middlesex)
    Obituary   1929/I   2

Prescott-Westcar, C. W. (Kent Supporter)
    Obituary   1911/I   1

Presentation to F. E. Lacey   1924/II   6

Pressbox, Hints from the   1893   x

Pressdee, J. S. (Glamorgan; North East Transvaal)
    Benefit Match   1965   3
    Photographs   1959   3
                                    1965   3

Prest, E. P. (Eton; Cambridge University)
    Obituary   1904   *lxxx*

Prest, H. E. W. (Malvern; Cambridge University; Kent)
    Obituary   1955   9
                                    1956   9

Prest, S. B. (Marlborough; Cambridgeshire)
    Obituary   1934/I   2

Preston, B. (Winchester; Cambridge University; Suffolk)
    Obituary   1915/I   2

Preston, H. (Editor of Wisden 1944-1951)
    'Appreciation of Lord Hawke'   1939
    'County Championship Reviewed'   1942
    'Andrew Ducat'   1943
    'W. G. Grace Centenary'   1949
    'Sir Stanley Jackson'   1948
    'M. A. Noble'   1941
    Photographs   1961
                                    1981
    'Hubert Preston' (Obituary) N. Cardus   1961
    Tribute to C. B. Fry   1957

Preston, H. J. (Kent; Scotland)
    Obituary   1965   9

Preston, J. (Warwickshire Club Cricketer)
    Obituary   1904   *lx*

Preston, J. (Warwickshire)
    Obituary   1914/I

Preston, K. C. (Essex)
    Benefit Match   1960
    Photographs   1956
                                    1959

reston, N. (Editor of Wisden 1951-1980)

'Judge hits Cricket Ban for Six'	1978	*128*
Photographs	1979	*83*
	1981	*101*
'Planning Post War Cricket'	1943	*62*
'Norman Preston M.B.E.' J. Woodcock	1981	*100*
'A Wisden Occasion – Awarded M.B.E.'	1979	*83*
'A Wisden Occasion –		
Twenty First Anniversary Dinner'	1972	*160*
'Frank Woolley'	1979	*104*

eston, P. R. (Wellington, New Zealand)

Obituary	1961	*950*

eston-Thomas, H. (Incogniti)

Obituary	1911/I	*163*

etty, Dr. H. C. (Surrey; Northamptonshire)

Obituary	1953	*949*

ice, Ab/Seaman. D. (Western Province)

Obituary	1943	*366*

ice, Lieut. H. B. (Quebec C.C.)

Obituary	1916	*200*

ice, H. L. (Bishop's Stortford College; Oxford University)

Obituary	1944	*320*

ice, H. W. (Highgate School)

Obituary	1922/I	*267*

ice, J. S. E. (Middlesex; England)

Photographs	1964	*480*
	1967	*493*
	1972	*498*

ice, 2nd Lieut. S. J. (Bishop's Stortford College)

Obituary	1917	*208*

ice, V. R. (Bishop's Stortford College; Oxford University; Surrey)

Obituary	1974	*1077*

ice, W. (Nottinghamshire; Umpire)

Benefit Match	1888	*215*
Obituary	1895	*xli*

ice, W. F. F. (Middlesex; England)

Benefit Match	1939	*444*
Obituary	1970	*1024*

ice-Jenkin, 2nd Lieut. R. D. (Blundells)

Obituary	1916	*220*

ice-Williams, D. (University College School)

'7 wkts Schools Averages	1900	*448*

chard, Major H. V. H. (Fettes; Hampshire)

Obituary	1923/I	*304*

de, T. (Yorkshire)

Obituary	1920/I	*184*

Prideaux, R. M. (Tonbridge; Cambridge University; Kent; Sussex; Orange Fre
State; Northamptonshire; England)

Photographs	1965	5(
	1967	5.
	1971	4(
	1973	5.
Schools Notes	1956	7.
	1957	7.
	1958	7.

Prideaux, Sir W. S. (Eton)

Obituary	1929/I	2

Pridgeon, A. P. (Worcestershire)

Photograph	1979	5

Pridham, Major C. H. B. (Somerset Stragglers)

Obituary	1953	9

Pridmore, Major R. G. (Hertfordshire; Warwickshire)

Obituary	1919	1

Priestley, Sir A. (Patron of Team in West Indies 1896-97)

Obituary	1934/I	2
Team in West Indies 1896-97	1898	3

Priestley, Capt. A. B. (Army)

Obituary	1915/I	2

Priestley, L/Cpl. D. L. (Tewkesbury Grammar School; Gloucestershire)

Obituary	1918	2

Priestley, H. W. (Uppingham; Cambridge University; Buckinghamshire)

Obituary	1934/I	

Prime Ministers, At Cricket Note on

	1965	

Pringle, D. (Kenya; East Africa)

Obituary	1976	1.

Pringle, D. R. (Felsted; Cambridge University; Essex; England)

Schools Notes	1976	8
	1977	
	1978	
	1979	

Pringle, Lieut. R. S. (Winchester)

Obituary	1915/I	

Prior, C. B. L. (Norfolk)

Obituary	1965	

Prichard, D. E. (South Australia)

Obituary	1984	1

Pritchard, T. L. (Wellington; Warwickshire; Kent)

Benefit Match	1953	

Pritchett, G. E. B. (Hertfordshire)

Obituary	1921/I	

Prittie, Hon. T. C. (Writer)

'Cricket in Israel'	1975	*157*
'Middlesex' Book Review	1953	*1000*

Prizeman, J. G. (Secretary Central Lancashire League)

Obituary	1916	*200*

Problems of Cricket Note on	1957	*70*

Probyn, P. C. (Westminster)

Obituary	1905	*cv*

Procter, M. J. (Natal; Western Province; Rhodesia; Gloucestershire; South Africa)

Career Figures	1982	*102*
'Cricket Bucanneer' Book Review	1977	*1098*
Cricketer of the Year	1970	*63*
Photographs	1969	*404*
	1970	*57*
	1973	*402*
	1975	*411*
	1980	*410*
	1982	*98,101*
'Mike Procter and Cricket' Book Review	1982	*1270*
'Mike Procter – A Great All-Rounder'		
A. Gibson	1982	*99*
Mike Procter's Great Season – Note	1980	*86*
Schools Note	1964	*795*

Proctor, Sir P. D. (Harrow)

Obituary	1984	*1207*

Prodger, J. M. (Kent)

Photograph	1959	*401*

Promnitz, H. L. E. (Border; Griqualand West; Orange Free State; South Africa)

Obituary	1984	*1207*

Prosser, G. (Warwickshire Groundsman)

Award	1973	*296*

Prothero, Lt-Col. A. G. (Westminster; Monmouthshire)

Obituary	1930/I	*260*

Prothero, R. E. Lord Ernle (Marlborough; Hampshire)

Obituary	1938	*942*

Protheroe-Smith, Lt-Col. Sir H. B. (President Cornwall)

Obituary	1962	*990*

Proud, E. B. (Durham)

Obituary	1968	*1005*

Proud, R. B. (Winchester; Oxford University; Hampshire)

Obituary	1962	*990*

Prudential World Cup 1975	1976	*300*

'Prudential Cup Review – International Championship Cricket'

Ed. G. Ross Book Review	1976	*1145*
Prudential World Cup 1979	1980	*297*

Prudential World Cup 1983   1984   *293*
'Cricket World Cup' D. Hodgson
Book Review   1984   *1262*
Pryce-Jenkin, F. J. (Winchester)
Obituary   1971   *1028*
Pryce-Jones, Lieut. R. E. (Calgary C.C., Canada)
Obituary   1918   *216*
'Public School in the Wisden Century'
D. Eagar   1963   *787*
Public Schools XI at Lord's 1942
Team Portrait   1943   *27*
Public Schools Team (British) in U.S.A.
and Canada 1939   1940   *610*
Public Schools – Writers on
    C. B. Fry   1894
    W. J. Ford   1896-1904
    W. J. Seton   1905-1906
    S. H. Pardon   1907
    C. Toppin   1908-1911
    F. B. Wilson   1912
    E. B. Noel   1913-1921
    F. B. Wilson and E. B. Noel   1922
    H. S. Altham   1923-1928
    A. Podmore   1929-1937
    A. Podmore and H. Winterbotham   1938
    H. Winterbotham   1939
    C. Burton   1940
    H. Whitaker   1941
    G. H. M. Cartwright   1942-1944
    E. M. Wellings   1945-1972
    R. Alston   1973
Public Will Decide Note on   1978   *102*
Puckle, Sir F. H. (Uppingham)
Obituary   1967   *973*
Puddefoot, S. E. (Essex)
Obituary   1973   *1013*
Pugh, J. G. (Rugby; Warwickshire)
Obituary   1965   *971*
Schools Note   1922   *281,294*
1034 runs Schools Averages   1922/II   *559*
Pullan, C. D. A. (Malvern; Worcestershire)
Obituary   1971   *1028*
Pullan, D. A. (Nottinghamshire)
Photograph   1972   *529*

Pullar, G. (Lancashire; Gloucestershire; England)

Benefit Match	1968	*469*
Cricketer of the Year	1960	*110*
Note on	1969	*478*
Photograph	1960	*88*

Pulle, J. (Sri Lanka)

Obituary	1983	*1254*

Pullen, W. W. F. (Gloucestershire; Somerset; Glamorgan)

Obituary	1938	*942*

Pullin, A. W. ('Old Ebor'; Journalist)

Obituary	1935/I	*271*

Pullin, C. K. (Umpire)

Benefit Match	1882	*149*
Obituary	1895	*xxxviii*
Views on the Reforms of 1889	1890	*xxxvii*
Views on Some Questions of the Day	1890	*xlii*

Pulman, Rev. W. W. (Marlborough; Oxford University)

Obituary	1937/I	*278*

Punchard, Lieut. J. S. (Sedbergh)

Obituary	1920/I	*156*

Punchard, T. W. (Sedbergh; Westmoreland)

Obituary	1924/I	*275*

Purdie, Pte. J. (Lynn Valley C.C., Vancouver)

Obituary	1918	*216*

Puttock, E. C. (Sussex)

Obituary	1970	*1024*

Pycroft, Rev. J. (Oxford University; Journalist)

Obituary	1896	*xxxix*

Pye-Smith, Dr. E. J. (Cheltenham; Cambridge University; Yorkshire)

Obituary	1984	*1207*

Quaife, F. C. (Sussex)

Obituary	1969	*985*

Quaife, W. (Sussex; Warwickshire; Suffolk)

Obituary	1944	*321*

Quaife, W. G. (Warwickshire; Griqualand West; Sussex; England)

Benefit Match	1928/II	*272*
Farewell Match	1929/II	*334*
Obituary	1952	*960*
Portrait and Biography	1902	*lxxxiv*

Qualification – Too Easy Note on 1951 *118*

Queensland Centenary Match 1961 *875*

Queensland Cricket and Cricketers 1861-1981'

W. Torrens Book Review	1983	*1298*

Quentin, Rev. G. A. F. (Shrewsbury; Gloucestershire)

Obituary	1929/I	*257*

Quest, C. (Northamptonshire Club Cricket)
Obituary	1914/I	19:

Question to Counties Note on   1952   9:

Quibell, S. (Leys School)
Schools Note	1908/I	12(
81 wkts Schools Averages	1908/II	46:

Quick, A. (Journalist)
Obituary	1970	1024

Quill, Lt-Col. J. J. (Devon)
Obituary	1927/I	287

Quin, A. L. (Adelaide)
Obituary	1908/I	14:

Quin, N. A. (Griqualand West; South Africa)
Obituary	1935/I	27.

Quinton, Brig-Gen. F. W. D. (Marlborough; Devon; Hampshire)
Obituary	1927/I	287

Quinton, J. M. Q. (Hampshire)
Obituary	1923/I	30

Rabjohns, D. (Worcestershire Scorer)
Obituary	1959	93:

Radcliffe, Sir J. R. Bart. (Yorkshire)
Obituary	1970	102

Radcliffe, G. (Cheshire; Lancashire)
Obituary	1952	96(

Radcliffe, O. G. (Somerset; Gloucestershire; Wiltshire)
Obituary	1941	40.

Radley, C. T. (Middlesex; England)
Cricketer of the Year	1979	7.
Photographs	1969	49:
	1972	49(
	1975	48:
	1979	6:
	1980	49(

Rae, E. (Founder of Cricket in Russian Lapland)
Obituary	1924/I	268

Rae, E. A. (Jamaica)
Obituary	1970	102

Rae, Major J. E. P. (St.Bees School)
Obituary	1918	20(

Raiji, V. (Writer)
'L. P. Jai – Memories of a Great Batsman' Book Review	1977	109(
'Ranji – the Legend and the Man' Book Review	1964	100(
'Victor Trumper' Book Review	1965	102.

Raikes, E. B. (Haileybury; Norfolk)
Obituary   1933/I   *264*

Raikes, Rev. G. B. (Shrewsbury; Oxford University; Hampshire; Norfolk)
Obituary   1967   *974*

Raikes, Lt-Col. K. C. (Shrewsbury; Monmouthshire)
Obituary   1973   *1078*

Raikes, Rev. W. A. (Wellington)
Obituary   1929/I   *257*

Rail, Lieut. R. A. (Western Province)
Obituary   1918   *200*

Rain and More Rain
Note on   1981   *92*

Rainsford, Rev. W. S. (New York Club Cricket)
Obituary   1935/I   *277*

Raitt Kerr D. (Writer)
with I. A. R. Peebles 'Lord's 1946-1970'
Book Review   1972   *1094*

Raitt Kerr, Col R. S. (Rugby; Secretary M.C.C.)
'Modern County Cricket'   1952   *84*
Obituary   1962   *990*

Raitt, Lt-Col. F. J. (Hampshire)
Obituary   1945   *339*

Rajan, S. (Writer)
'India v West Indies' Book Review   1972   *1100*

Ralli, E. P. C. (Eton)
Obituary   1936/I   *287*

Ralph, L. H. R. (Essex)
Photograph   1958   *325*

Ralston, Lt-Col. F. W. (Philadelphia; U.S.A.)
Obituary   1921/I   *234*

Ramadhin, S. (Trinidad; Lancashire; Lincolnshire; West Indies)
Cricketer of the Year   1951   *71*
Photograph   1951   *65*

Ramier, Capt. L. S. (Madras Medical College)
Obituary   1919   *186*

Ramsay, Lieut. J. M. (Harrow)
Obituary   1918   *200*

Ramsay, M. F. (Harrow)
Obituary   1949   *873*

Ramsay, 2nd Lieut. N. (Harrow)
Obituary   1917   *208*

Ramsbotham, Col. W. H. (Uppingham; Cambridge University; Sussex)
Obituary   1980   *1161*

Ramsbottom, 2nd Lieut. R. (Bury C.C.)
Obituary   1917   *208*

Ramshaw, T. (Durham)
Obituary   1921/I   *234*

Randall, D. W. (Nottinghamshire; England)
Action Photograph	1980	*64*
Cricketer of the Year	1980	*73*
Photographs	1974	*510*
	1979	*498*
	1980	*66*

Randall, Capt. G. P. (Merchant Taylors)
Obituary	1919	*186*

Randall, Rt. Rev. J. L. (Winchester)
Obituary	1923/I	*304*

Randall, W. R. (Winchester; Glamorgan)
Obituary	1931/I	*264*

Randell, A. C. (Western Australia)
Obituary	1960	*958*

Randell, R. H. (Border)
Obituary	1980	*1161*

Randolph, Rev. C. (Eton; Oxford University)
Obituary	1913/I	*193*

Randolph, C. F. (Winchester)
Obituary	1913/I	*193*

Random Thoughts Note on
	1983	*84*

Randon, C. (Leicestershire)
Obituary	1911/I	*152*

Ranji, L. (Hindus)
Obituary	1950	*916*

Ranjitsinhji, K. S. (Afterwards **H. H. the Jam Saheb of Nawanagar**; Cambridge University; Cambridgeshire; Sussex; London County; England)
In Eleven-a-Side Matches	1901/I	*xcviii*
In First Class Cricket	1909/I	*165*
Portrait and Biography	1897	*xlviii*
'Ranjitsinhji' Sir S. Jackson	1934/I	*251*
'Ranji – A Centenary Album' Book Review	1973	*1058*
'Ranji – The Legend and the Man V. Raiji Book Review	1964	*1004*
'Ranji – The Prince of Cricketers' A. Ross Book Review	1984	*1268*
Scores in First Class Matches 1896	1897	*liii*
Special Obituary Memoir of S. J. Southerton	1934/I	*253*
Team in U.S.A. and Canada 1899	1900	*479*

Ranken, R. B. (Oxford University)
Obituary	1904	*lxxxvi*

Ransford, H. F. (Melbourne C.C.)
Obituary	1948	*786*

Ransford, V. S. (Victoria; Australia)
Obituary	1959	*937*
Portrait and Biography	1910/I	*158*

Raper, R. W. (M.C.C.)
Obituary 1916 *201*

Raphael, A. L. (Harrow)
Obituary 1974 *1078*

Raphael, E. G. (Harrow)
Obituary 1946 *444*

Raphael, F. C. (New Zealand Administrator)
Obituary 1941 *401*

Raphael, Lieut. J. E. (Merchant Taylors; Oxford University; Surrey)
Obituary 1918 *200*
Schools Note 1902 *ci,civ*
1397 runs, 76 wkts Schools Averages 1902 *455*

Raphael, R. H. (Wellington)
Obituary 1911/I *153*

Rashleigh, J. (Harrow; Oxford University)
Obituary 1906 *xcviii*

Rashleigh, Canon W. (Tonbridge; Oxford University; Kent)
Obituary 1938 *942*

Ratcliffe, A. (Rydal; Cambridge University; Surrey; Denbighshire; Buckinghamshire)
Obituary 1968 *1005*

Ratcliffe, G. (Derbyshire)
Obituary 1929/I *257*

Ratcliffe, R. M. (Lancashire)
Photograph 1979 *437*

Ratnam, K. V. G. (Writer)
with K. I. Dutt 'Vizzy Commemoration Souvenir Book Review 1967 *1020*

Rattigan, Capt. C. S. (Harrow; Cambridge University)
Obituary 1917 *208*

Rattigan, Sir T. M. (Harrow; Playwright)
Obituary 1978 *1080*

Rattigan, W. F. A. (Harrow; Oxford University)
Obituary 1953 *949*

Raven, E. E. (Uppingham)
Obituary 1952 *966*

Raven, R. O. (Wellingborough Grammar School; Northamptonshire)
Obituary 1937/I *278*

Raw, 2nd Lieut. R. (Clifton)
Obituary 1916 *200*

Rawes, Lieut. D. (Dover College)
Obituary 1916 *201*

Rawle, Lieut. C. W. F. (Toronto Club Cricket)
Obituary 1918 *216*

Rawlence, Col. J. R. (Wellington; Hampshire; Army)
Obituary 1984 *1207*

Rawlin, E. R. (Yorkshire)
  Obituary   1944   *321*

Rawlin, J. T. (Yorkshire; Middlesex)
  Benefit Matches   1897   *50*
                              1912/II   *47*
  Obituary   1925/I   *277*

Rawlinson, Gen. 1st Lord (Military Cricket)
  Obituary   1926/I   *282*

Rawlinson, E. B. (Yorkshire)
  Obituary   1893   *xxxiv*

Rawlinson, Canon G. (Oxford University)
  Obituary   1903   *lxxix*

Rawlinson, T. (Colts of England)
  Obituary   1904   *lxxvii*

Rawnsley, Canon H. D. (Uppingham)
  Obituary   1921/I   *234*

Rawnsley, W. F. (Uppingham)
  Obituary   1928/I   *295*

Rawson, Capt. A. (Royal High School, Edinburgh)
  Obituary   1919   *186*

Rawson, Admiral Sir H. H. (Patron New South Wales Cricket Association)
  Obituary   1911/I   *153*

Rawson, Col. H. R. (Kent)
  Obituary   1925/I   *277*

Rawson, Col. R. H. (Eton)
  Obituary   1919   *210*

Rawson, W. S. (Westminster)
  Obituary   1933/I   *257*

Raynbird, H. E. (Hackwood Park C.C.)
  Obituary   1916   *220*

Rayner, E. (West Australian Club Cricketer)
  Obituary   1911/I   *153*

Rayner, 2nd Lieut. J. (St Paul's)
  Obituary   1917   *208*

Raynor, K. (Ipswich School; Suffolk; Leicestershire)
  Obituary   1974   *1078*

Raynor, S. (Derbyshire; Worcestershire)
  Obituary   1908/I   *149*

Read, E. G. (St. Edmund's, Oxford; Hampshire; Sussex)
  Obituary   1922/I   *267*

Read, H. M. (Ireland)
  Obituary   1974   *1085*

Read, J. M. (Surrey; England)
  Benefit Match   1894   *208*
  Obituary   1930/I   *260*
  Portrait and Biography 1890   *xxix*

Views on the 'Follow on'	1894	*liii*
Read, R. J. (Canterbury)		
Obituary	1976	*1105*
Read, W. W. (Surrey; England)		
Obituary	1908/I	*149*
Portrait and Biography	1893	*xl*
Special Memoir of	1907	*clxxiv*
Team in South Africa 1891-92	1893	*352*
Testimonial Match	1896	*13*
Reaney, L. (Umpire)		
Obituary	1893	*xxxv*
Reaney, T. R. (Belmont C.C., Philadelphia)		
Obituary	1908/I	*151*
Reay, G. M. (Surrey)		
Obituary	1968	*1006*
Reay, Rev. Canon T. O. (Eton)		
Obituary	1915/I	*238*
Reay, L/Cpl. W. F. (Surrey Club Cricket)		
Obituary	1917	*226*
'Recollections of Oxford Cricket'		
H. D. Leveson Gower	1937/I	*249*
'Recollections of F. R. Spofforth' Lord Harris, Earl Darnley,		
C. I. Thornton	1927/I	*299*
Records Usually See Records Section of the current Wisden		
Records Notes on	1949	*117*
	1978	*106*
Reddick, T. B. (Middlesex; Nottinghamshire; Western Province)		
Obituary	1983	*1254*
Reddy, S. J. (South African Cricket Board of Control)		
Obituary	1979	*1085*
Redfearn, J. (Victoria)		
Obituary	1917	*262*
Redgate, O. (Nottinghamshire)		
Obituary	1914/I	*193*
Redman, J. (Somerset; Wiltshire)		
Obituary	1982	*1209*
Redpath, D. (New Zealand Club Cricket)		
Obituary	1926/I	*288*
Redpath, I. (Victoria; Australia)		
'Always Ready' Book Review	1978	*1126*
Redwood, Major A. C. (U.S.A. Club Cricketer)		
Obituary	1924/I	*275*
Reed, B. L. (Hampshire)		
Photograph	1968	*430*
Reed, Capt. D. B. (University College School)		
Obituary	1917	*209*

Reed, Rev. F. (Somerset)
   Obituary   1913/I   *193*
Reed, Corpl. S. (Devon)
   Obituary   1917   *209*
Reedman, J. C. (South Australia; Australia)
   Obituary   1925/I   *278*
Rees, E. L. (Glamorgan)
   Obituary   1912/I   *178*
Rees., R. B. (South Australia)
   Obituary   1967   *974*
Rees, W. L. (Victoria; Auckland)
   Obituary   1913/I   *194*
Reese, D. (Canterbury; Essex; London County)
   Obituary   1954   *929*
Reese, T. W. (Canterbury)
   Obituary   1950   *912*
Reeves, Capt. G. B. (Bedford Grammar School)
   Obituary   1918   *202*
Reeves, W. (Essex; Umpire)
   Benefit Match   1922/II   *365*
   Obituary   1945   *339*
'Reflections' E. P. Hendren   1938   *47*
'Reforms of 1889'   1890   *xxxvi*
Rehman, R. (Leicestershire)
   Obituary   1967   *974*
Reid, A. (Western Province)
   Obituary   1949   *868*
Reid, A. B. J. (Western Province)
   Obituary   1978   *1080*
Reid, C. F. (Harrow)
   Obituary   1899   *xlviii*
Reid, Lieut. G. (Coquitlam C.C., Vancouver)
   Obituary   1918   *202*
Reid, Rt. Hon. Sir G. H. (President New South Wales Cricket Association)
   Obituary   1919   *210*
Reid, Lieut. G. M. (Charterhouse)
   Obituary   1919   *186*
Reid, Capt. G. P. S. (Borlase School, Marlow)
   Obituary   1918   *202*
Reid, Capt. J. G. (Cheltenham)
   Obituary   1917   *209*
Reid, J. J. (Gentlemen of the South)
   Obituary   1921/II   *347*
Reid, J. R. (Wellington; Otago; New Zealand)
   Cricketer of the Year   1959   *53*
   'A Million Miles of Cricket' Book Review   1968   *1052*

Photographs	1959	*37,44*
Record: Note on	1963	*976*
'Sword of Willow' Book Review	1963	*1111*
Reid, 2nd Lieut. J. S. (Sedbergh School)		
Obituary	1918	*202*
Reid, N. (Western Province; South Africa)		
Obituary	1948	*786*
Reid, O. A. (Radley)		
Obituary	1922/I	*272*
Reid, R. T. See under Loreburn, Lord		
Reid, W. (Writer)		
'Grange Club Centenary'	1933/II	*639*
Reid, W. H. (Uddington, C.C.)		
Obituary	1950	*912*
Reidy, B. W. (Lancashire; Cumberland)		
Photograph	1980	*458*
Relf, A. E. (Sussex; Auckland; Norfolk; England)		
Benefit Match	1922/II	*269*
Obituary	1938	*943*
Portrait and Biography	1914/I	*234*
Relf, J. (Father of A.E., R.R.; Club Cricketer)		
Obituary	1922/I	*267*
Relf, R. R. (Berkshire; Sussex)		
Benefit Match	1925/II	*283*
Obituary	1966	*970*
Remarkable Catch, A (T. G. Evans)		
Photograph	1950	*70*
Remnant, E. R. (Hampshire)		
Obituary	1970	*1024*
Remnant, G. H. (Kent)		
Obituary	1942	*362*
Remnant, Lt-Col. Hon. P. F. (Eton; Berkshire)		
Obituary	1969	*985*
Remnant, 2nd Baron R. J. F. Remnant (Eton; Berkshire)		
Obituary	1968	*1006*
Rendel, A. E. (President New York C.C.)		
Obituary	1928	*295*
Renny-Tailyour, Col. H. W. (Cheltenham; Kent; Aberdeenshire)		
Obituary	1921/I	*234*
Renton, Lieut. H. N. L. (Harrow)		
Obituary	1916	*201*
Rest of the World in England 1970	1971	*291*
Team Portrait	1971	*67*
Reunert, J. (Harrow; Cambridge University)		
Obituary	1947	*694*

Revill, A. C. (Derbyshire; Leicestershire)
Photographs	1951	*288*
	1959	*437*

Revill, T. F. (Derbyshire)
Obituary	1980	*1155*

Reynolds, B. L. (Northamptonshire)
Photograph	1964	*496*

Reynolds, Rev. E. M. (Liverpool College; Cambridge University)
Obituary	1909/I	*145*

Reynolds, H. (Nottinghamshire)
Obituary	1895	*xxxviii*

Reynolds, H. (Madras)
Obituary	1906	*xcviii*

Rheinberg, N. (Women's Cricket)
'Enid Bakewell – Champion Woman Cricketer'	1970	*119*

Rhodes, A. C. (Yorkshire)
Obituary	1958	*962*

Rhodes, A. E. G. (Derbyshire; Umpire)
Obituary	1984	*1207*
Photograph	1951	*288*

Rhodes, Col. F. W. (Eton)
Obituary	1906	*xcviii*

Rhodes, Brig-Gen. Sir G. D. (Kenya)
Obituary	1972	*1055*

Rhodes, H. J. (Derbyshire; England)
Note on	1966	*80*
Photographs	1959	*306*
	1961	*337*
	1964	*343*
	1966	*348*
'Harold Rhodes Testimonial' Book Review	1969	*1040*

Rhodes, P. E. F. (Worksop College)
Schools Note	1938	*696*
77 wkts Schools Averages	1938	*769*

Rhodes, W. (Yorkshire)
Obituary	1942	*362*

Rhodes, W. R. (Yorkshire; England)
Benefit Match	1912/II	*136*
Career Figures	1974	*96*
'Hirst and Rhodes' A. A. Thomson		
Book Review	1960	*1003*
'The Memorial Service for Wilfred Rhodes'		
Book Review	1974	*1125*
Obituary	1974	*1078*
Painting (Photograph of)	1974	*93*
Portrait and Biography	1899	*lxiii*

'Wilfred Rhodes'	1931/I	*331*
'Wilfred Rhodes – Yorkshire Personified'		
Sir N. Cardus	1974	*92*
'Wilfred Rhodes' S. Rogerson Book Review	1961	*999*
Wilfred Rhodes Trophy	1956	*75*
Tributes to: S. F. Barnes	1968	*114*
Sir J. Hobbs	1964	*104*
Sir S. Jackson	1948	*80*
H. Strudwick	1971	*1032*
Rhodesian Schools in England 1962	1963	*865*
Rhys, H. R. J. (Shrewsbury; Glamorgan)		
Obituary	1971	*1028*
Ricardo, A. (IZingari)		
Obituary	1910/I	*151*
Ricardo, Col. F. C. (Grenadier Guards)		
Obituary	1925/I	*278*
Rice, C. E. B. (Nottinghamshire; Transvaal)		
Cricketer of the Year	1981	*85*
Photographs	1976	*521*
	1979	*498*
	1981	*77*
Rice, R. W. (Gloucestershire; Oxford University; Bedfordshire)		
Obituary	1939	*915*
Rice, Father. W. I. (Warwickshire)		
Obituary	1956	*976*
Rich, A. (Cambridgeshire)		
Obituary	1958	*962*
Richard, R. M. (Merchiston Castle)		
Schools Note	1973	*829*
79 wkts Schools Averages	1973	*857*
Richards, Lt.-Col. A. C. (Eton; Hampshire)		
Obituary	1931/I	*264*
Richards, B. A. (Natal; Gloucestershire; Hampshire; South Australia; South Africa)		
Benefit Match	1978	*724*
Cricketer of the Year	1969	*65*
Hits 325 Runs in a Day	1971	*399*
Photographs	1969	*58*
	1972	*431*
	1974	*423*
	1977	*426*
'Barry Richards on Cricket – Attack to Win'		
Book Review	1974	*1126*
Schools Note	1964	*795*
Richards, C. H. (Editor; Publisher)		
Obituary	1910/I	*145*

459

Richards, C. J. (Surrey)
Photograph   1978   53

Richards, C. J. R. (Lancing; Hampshire)
Obituary   1935/I   27

Richards, G. (Glamorgan)
Photograph   1977   39

Richards, H. E. (Journalist)
Obituary   1980   115

Richards, Rt. Rev. Dr. I. (Auckland)
Obituary   1937/I   27

Richards, I. V. A. (Leeward Islands; Somerset; Queensland; West Indies)
Cricketer of the Year   1977   9
Photographs   1975   53
                                      1977   9
                                      1982   54

Richards, W. (Warwickshire; Umpire)
Obituary   1918   23

Richardson, A. (U.S.A. Club Cricketer)
Obituary   1921/I   23

Richardson, A. G. (King's Canterbury; Somerset; Gloucestershire; Bedfordshire; Orange Free State)
Obituary   1936/I   29

Richardson, A. J. (South Australia; Australia)
Benefit Match   1950   83
Obituary   1974   107

Richardson, A. W. (Winchester; Derbyshire)
Obituary   1984   120

Richardson, C. A. (Wellington, New Zealand)
Obituary   1950   91

Richardson, D. W. (Worcestershire; England)
Benefit Match   1968   62
Photographs   1958   61
                                      1961   61
                                      1963   65

Richardson, Ven. Archdeacon E. S. (Rossall)
Obituary   1923/I   31

Richardson, F. S. (Repton)
Obituary   1935/I   27

Richardson, H. (Nottinghamshire)
Obituary   1941   46

Richardson, H. A. (Tonbridge; Cambridge University; Kent)
Obituary   1922/I   26

Richardson, J. M. (Harrow; Cambridge University)
Obituary   1913/I   1

Richardson, 2nd Lieut. J. S. (Charterhouse)
Obituary   1918   20

Richardson, L. (Orange Free State)
Obituary 1937/I *288*

Richardson, L. W. (Tasmania)
Obituary 1984 *1208*

Richardson, P. E. (Worcestershire; Kent; England)
Cricketer of the Year 1957 *57*
Photographs 1954 *600*
1957 *56*
1962 *448*

Richardson, R. T. (Marlborough)
Obituary 1931/I *264*

Richardson, S. (Derbyshire)
Obituary 1939 *916*

Richardson, T. (Surrey; Somerset; London County; England)
Benefit Match 1900 *20*
Bowling in First Class Cricket 1898 *lxxxix*
'Giant of the Wisden Century'
N. Cardus 1963 *99*
Obituary 1913/I *195*
Photograph 1963 *100*
Portrait and Biography 1897 *xlvii*

Richardson, T. H. (Staffordshire; Derbyshire)
Obituary 1925/I *290*

Richardson, V. Y. (South Australia; Australia)
Obituary 1970 *1025*
'The Vic Richardson Story' Book Review 1968 *1052*
Testimonial Matches 1935/II *680*
1939 *810*

Richardson, W. A. (New South Wales)
Obituary 1931/I *264*

Richardson, W. E. (Liverpool College; Worcestershire)
Obituary 1972 *1055*

Riches, N. V. H. (Glamorgan; Wales)
Career Figures 1976 *1102*
Obituary 1976 *1101*

Richmond, 2nd Duke of (Patron of Cricket)
'The Duke who was Cricket' J. Marshall
Book Review 1962 *1040*

Richmond, T. L. (Nottinghamshire; England)
Benefit Match 1928/II *81*
Obituary 1958 *962*

Rickett, Capt. R. A. (University College of Nottingham)
Obituary 1917 *209*

Ricketts, G. W. (Winchester; Oxford University; Surrey)
Obituary 1928/I *295*

Ricketts, J. (Lancashire)
    Obituary 1895 x

Ricketts, Lieut. N. H. (Toronto C.C.)
    Obituary 1918 21

Riddell, V. H. (Clifton; Cambridge University)
    Obituary 1977 104

Ridding, Rev. C. H. (Winchester; Oxford University; Hampshire; Oxfordshire)
    Obituary 1906 xcvi

Ridding, Rt. Rev. G. (President Nottinghamshire)
    Obituary 1905

Ridding, Rev. W. (Winchester; Oxford University)
    Obituary 1901 lx

Ridgebacks – Rhodesia – Banned 1977 80

Ridgway, C. R. (Staffordshire; South African Cricket Association)
    Obituary 1947 69

Ridgway, F. (Kent; England)
    Benefit Match 1959 41
    Photographs 1952 38
     1954 40
     1957 40

Ridley, A. W. (Eton; Oxford University; Middlesex; Hampshire)
    Obituary 1917 20

Ridley, G. V. N. (Essex)
    Obituary 1955 93

Ridley, J. N. (Oxford University Authentics)
    Obituary 1904 lxx

Riekey, Pte. D. T. (U.S.A. Club Cricket)
    Obituary 1918 20

Righton, E. G. (Worcestershire)
    Obituary 1965 9

Riley, A. (Umpire)
    'Umpires Associations' 1963 7

Riley, E. (New York Veterans Cricket Association)
    Obituary 1911/I 1

Riley, H. (Yorkshire)
    Obituary 1923/I 3

Riley, M. (Yorkshire)
    Obituary 1900

Riley, R. (Stonyhurst College)
    103 wkts Schools Averages 1914/II 4

Riley, Capt. S. J. (Evesham Grammar School)
    Obituary 1917 2

Riley, Gun. W. (Nottinghamshire)
    Obituary 1918 2

Riley, W. N. (Worcester Grammar School; Cambridge University; Leicestershire)
    Obituary 1956 9

Rimington, G. A. (Cumberland)
   Obituary   1933/I   *264*

Ringrose, W. (Liverpool C.C.; Yorkshire; Scorer Yorkshire)
   Obituary   1944   *321*

Rippon, A. D. E. (Somerset)
   Obituary   1964   *951*

Rippon, A. E. S. (Somerset)
   Obituary   1967   *974*

Rippon, 2nd Lieut. N. (Giggleswick School)
   Obituary   1916   *202*

Rising Passions Photograph   1983   *Plate*

Ritchie, Lt-Col. D. M. (Loretto; Lancashire)
   Obituary   1975   *1082*
   Schools Note   1911/I   *134*
   75 wkts Schools Averages   1911/II   *446*

Ritchie, Capt. J. A. (Scotland)
   Obituary   1943   *382*

Ritson, Capt. F. (Sedbergh School)
   Obituary   1918   *202*

Rivett-Carnac, Rev. Sir G. 6th Bart. (Harrow)
   Obituary   1933/I   *257*

Rix, Capt. L. G. (University College, Hampstead)
   Obituary   1918   *202*

Rixon, Lt-Col. T. M. (Merchant Taylors)
   Obituary   1918   *203*

Roach, Fl. Sgt. W. A. (Western Australia)
   Obituary   1946   *435*

Robarts, 2nd Lieut. F. W. (Metropolitan Club Cricket)
   Obituary   1916   *202*

Robbins, V. C. (Natal)
   Obituary   1948   *786*

Roberts, Sir A. F. (Merchiston Castle)
   Obituary   1962   *990*

Roberts, A. M. E. (Leeward Islands; Combined Islands; Hampshire; Leicestershire; New South Wales; West Indies)
   Cricketer of the Year   1975   *90*
   Photograph   1975   *81*

Roberts, A. W. (Canterbury; Otago; New Zealand)
   Obituary   1979   *1085*

Roberts, Capt. C. L. N. (St.John's School, Leatherhead)
   Obituary   1918   *203*

Roberts, C. P. (Lincolnshire; Worcestershire)
   Obituary   1978   *1080*

Roberts, D. (St.Bees School; Surrey)
   Obituary   1969   *985*

Roberts, D. A. (Haverford College)
Obituary   1913/I   *198*
Roberts, E. L. (Journalist; Statistician)
Obituary   1955   *936*
Test Captains 1876-1939   1942   *86*
'Yorkshire's Twenty Two Championships 1893-1946'
Book Review   1950   *974*
Roberts, Capt. F. B. (Rossall; Cambridge University; Gloucestershire; Oxfordshire)
Obituary   1917   *209*
Roberts, F. G. (Gloucestershire; Umpire)
Benefit Match   1898   *94*
Obituary   1937/I   *278*
Roberts, Field Marshall Earl (M.C.C.)
Obituary   1915/I   *238*
Roberts, H. E. (Sussex)
Obituary   1964   *951*
Roberts, I. J. (Trinity School, Croydon)
Schools Note   1980   *868*
79 wkts Schools Averages   1980   *925*
Roberts, J. E. (New York Club Cricketer)
Obituary   1914/I   *194*
Roberts, J. H. (Uppingham; Middlesex; Buckinghamshire)
Obituary   1912/I   *178*
Roberts, L. D. (Writer)
'With the West Indies in Australia'
Book Review   1962   *1038*
Roberts, 2nd Lieut. M. G. (King's School, Worcester)
Obituary   1918   *203*
Roberts, R. (Bacup C.C.)
Obituary   1925/I   *278*
Roberts, R. A. (Journalist; Writer)
'The Fight for the Ashes 1961' Book Review   1962   *1040*
Obituary   1966   *971*
'Ron Roberts' Book Review   1967   *1019*
'Sixty Years of Somerset Cricket' Book Review   1953   *999*
Roberts, T. (Burnley C.C.)
Obituary   1919   *210*
Roberts, T. W. (Ceylon)
Obituary   1977   *1048*
Roberts, 2nd Lieut. W. A. (St. Paul's)
Obituary   1918   *203*
Roberts, W. B. (Lancashire)
Obituary   1952   *960*
Photograph   1950   *393*

464

Robertson, A. (President Irish Cricket Union)
Obituary	1979	*1092*

Robertson, Lt-Col. F. M. B. (Eton)
Obituary	1927/I	*287*

Robertson, G. P. (Oxford University; Victoria)
Obituary	1896	*xxxviii*

Robertson, J. D. (Middlesex; England)
Benefit Matches	1952	*438*
	1960	*496*
Cricketer of the Year	1948	*63*
Photographs	1948	*44*
	1951	*434*
	1952	*434*
	1956	*465*
	1958	*463*

Robertson, Lieut. J. M. (Aberdeenshire; Scotland)
Obituary	1943	*366*

Robertson, W. (Canterbury; Scotland)
Obituary	1913/I	*198*

Robertson, W. P. (Harrow; Cambridge University; Middlesex)
Obituary	1951	*927*

Robertson, W. R. (Victoria; Australia)
Obituary	1939	*916*

Robertson-Durham, J. A. (Edinburgh Academy)
Obituary	1952	*961*

Robertson-Glasgow, R. C. (Charterhouse; Oxford University; Somerset)
'A. V. Bedser – A Giant among Bowlers'	1953	*95*
'Compton and Edrich'	1948	*45*
'Crusoe on Cricket' Book Review	1967	*1014*
'M. P. Donnelly'	1950	*107*
W. R. Hammond in First Class Cricket	1942	*33*
'The Joy of Cricket'	1963	*173*
'M. Leyland'	1943	*31*
'Notes'	1942	*58*
'Notes on 1939 Season'	1940	*49*
'Notes on 1940 Season'	1941	*55*
'Notes on Season 1942'	1943	*48*
Obituary	1966	*971*
'Edmund Paynter'	1946	*41*
'South Africa and England'	1947	*55*
'Story of the Test Matches' Book Review	1952	*1014*
'Then and Now'	1951	*87*
Tribute to H. Sutcliffe	1979	*99*
'Hedley Verity Memorial'	1944	*41*
'Views and Values'	1945	*46*

Robertson-Walker, J. (Edingburgh Academy; Middlesex; Scotland)
Obituary   1928/I   *296*
Robins, D. H. (Patron of Cricket)
U23 Team in Australia and New Zealand 1979-80   1981   *1014*
  Team in Far East   1977   1979   *1038*
  Team in South Africa   1973   1975   *960*
                                           1975   1976   *991*
                                           1976   1977   *961*
Robins, R. W. V. (Highgate School; Cambridge University; Middlesex; England)
Obituary   1969   *985*
Portrait and Biography   1930/I   *280*
Schools Notes   1925/I   *298,321,322*
                                                  1926/I   *301,324*
Selectors Photograph   1963   *150*
Tributes to: A. P. Freeman   1966   *965*
        W. Woodfull   1966   *974*
Views on Growing Pains of Cricket   1956   *84*
Views on L.B.W. Experiment   1936/I   *343*
Robinson, A. (Gloucestershire Committee)
Obituary   1914/I   *194*
Robinson, A. (Northamptonshire)
Obituary   1946   *444*
Robinson, Rev. A. E. (Repton)
Obituary   1928/I   *296*
Robinson, A. L. (Yorkshire)
Photograph   1978   *602*
Robinson, Canon C. D. (Cambridge University; Natal; Buckinghamshire)
Obituary   1949   *868*
Robinson, Lt-Col. C. L. (Durham School)
Obituary   1916   *202*
Robinson, C. W. (Wellington)
Obituary   1949   *873*
Robinson, Lt-Col. D. C. (Marlborough; Essex; Gloucestershire)
Obituary   1964   *951*
Robinson, E. (Yorkshire)
Obituary   1943   *382*
Robinson, Emmott (Yorkshire; Umpire)
Benefit Match   1931/II   *160*
Obituary   1970   *1025*
Photograph   1970   *83*
'Emmott Robinson' Sir N. Cardus   1970   *82*
Robinson, Capt. E. A. (Robinson's XI)
Obituary   1917   *210*
Robinson, E. P. (Yorkshire; Somerset)
Photograph   1952   *487*

Robinson, Sir F. G. (Clifton; Gloucestershire)
Obituary 1968 *1006*
Robinson, Capt. F. W. (Trinity College School, Port Hope)
Obituary 1917 *226*
Robinson, G. (Uppingham)
Obituary 1962 *990*
Robinson, G. E. (Oxford University)
Obituary 1949 *873*
Robinson, J. J. (Cambridge University)
Obituary 1960 *956*
Robinson, J. S. (Nottinghamshire)
Obituary 1899 *xliv*
Robinson, Capt. Adjt. J. Y. (Radley)
Obituary 1917 *210*
Robinson, Capt. L. C. D. (Bedford School; Bedfordshire)
Obituary 1936/I *287*
Robinson, L. G. (Patron of Cricket)
Obituary 1923/I *304*
Robinson, L. M. (Marlborough)
Obituary 1958 *963*
Robinson, Major N. S. (Leys School; Bedford Grammar School)
Obituary 1919 *186*
Robinson, Lt-Col. P. G. (Clifton; Gloucestershire)
Obituary 1952 *961*
Robinson, P. J. (Worcestershire; Somerset)
Benefit Match 1975 *724*
Photographs 1968 *549*
1971 *498*
Robinson, R. (Journalist)
Obituary 1983 *1254*
Robinson, Lieut. R. (Wellingborough Grammar School)
Obituary 1919 *186*
Robinson, 2nd Lieut. R. H. (Essex)
Obituary 1919 *200*
Robinson, R. L. Sir (Oxford University)
Obituary 1953 *949*
Robinson, R. T. (Nottinghamshire; England)
Photograph 1982 *525*
Robinson, T. (Somerset)
Obituary 1960 *956*
Robinson, Comdr. V. J. (Gloucestershire)
Obituary 1980 *1155*
Robinson, W. (Auckland)
Obituary 1929/I *257*
Robinson, Rt. Rev. Monsignor W. C. (Winchester)
Obituary 1915/I *238*

Robison, W. C. (New South Wales)
Obituary 1917 *263*
Robson, C. (Middlesex; Hampshire)
Obituary 1944 *321*
Robson, E. (Cheshire; Somerset)
Benefit Match for the family of 1925/II *248*
Obituary 1925/I *278*
Robson, Lt-Col. Frank W. (Yorkshire Gentlemen)
Obituary 1919 *187*
Robson, Lt-Col. Frederich W. (Pocklington Grammar School; Yorkshire
Gentlemen)
Obituary 1919 *187*
Robson, H. (Northumberland; Durham)
Obituary 1969 *986*
Rochdale, Baron (Kemp G.) (Shrewsbury; Cambridge University; Lancashire)
Obituary 1946 *444*
Rock, D. J. (Hampshire)
Photograph 1978 *413*
Rock, Dr. H. O. (New South Wales)
Obituary 1979 *1086*
Rocyn-Jones, Major A. H. (Monmouthshire)
Obituary 1946 *433*
Roderick, Capt. H. B. (Rugby)
Obituary 1918 *203*
Rodger, Sir J. P. (Eton; Kent)
Obituary 1911/I *153*
Rodrigo, R. (Writer)
'Peter May' Book Review 1961 *998*
Rodriquez, C. E. ('Emeriti' Cricketer)
Obituary 1914/I *199*
Rodwell, J. (Leicestershire)
Obituary 1912/I *178*
Roe, 2nd Lieut. A. J. H. (Merchant Taylors)
Obituary 1916 *202*
Roe, W. N. (Clergy Orphan School, Canterbury; Cambridge University;
Somerset)
Obituary 1938 *943*
Roe, W. N. (Eton; Buckinghamshire)
Obituary 1979 *1086*
Roebuck, P. M. (Millfield School; Somerset; Cambridge University)
Photograph 1978 *522*
'Slices of Cricket' Book Review 1983 *1306*
Roebuck, T. G. (Claremont C.C., Jersey City, U.S.A.)
Obituary 1923/I *305*
Roffey, Sir G. W. (Harrow)
Obituary 1941 *401*

Rogers, Rev. E. H. (President Thames Ditton C.C.)
  Obituary   1911/I   *153*
Rogers, 2nd Lieut. E. H. (Shrewsbury; Gentlemen of Worcestershire)
  Obituary   1917   *210*
Rogers, Lt-Col. F. G. (Gloucestershire)
  Obituary   1968   *1006*
Rogers, H. M. (Harrow)
  Obituary   1916   *202*
Rogers, J. H. (Birkenhead School; Cheshire)
  Schools Notes 1000 runs   1930   *283*
                                               1955   *698*
Rogers, Capt. L. N. (Marlborough)
  Obituary   1918   *203*
Rogers, N. H. (Hampshire)
  Photographs   1951   *360*
                                               1952   *363*
                                               1955   *366*
  Retirement   1956   *567*
Rogers, Lieut. P. A. M. (Bradfield)
  Obituary   1918   *203*
Rogers, 2nd Lieut. R. (Malvern)
  Obituary   1917   *210*
Rogers, S. S. (Highgate School; Somerset)
  Obituary   1970   *1026*
Rogers, Major W. F. (United Services)
  Obituary   1918   *203*
Rogers, Col. W. L. (Rugby)
  Obituary   1949   *868*
Rogerson, S. (Writer)
  'Wilfred Rhodes' Book Review   1961   *999*
Rokeby, R. T. (Charterhouse; American Club Cricket)
  Obituary   1925/I   *279*
Roll, H. (Warwickshire)
  Obituary   1968   *1006*
Rolle, Hon. M. G. K. (Eton; Devon)
  Obituary   1908/I   *152*
Roller, C. T. (Westminster; Essex)
  Obituary   1915/I   *249*
Roller – Heavy Note on   1964   *92*
Roller, W. E. (Surrey; Westminster)
  Obituary   1950   *912*
Romans, G. (Gloucestershire)
  Obituary   1947   *694*
Rome – Cricket in Note on   1967   *94*
Rome, D. A. M. (Harrow; Middlesex)
  Obituary   1971   *1028*

Romer, Lt-Col. M. N. (Free Foresters)
Obituary 1978 *1081*
Romford – Gidea Park
Plan of County Ground 1956 *324*
1959 *324*
1963 *393*
Romney, F. W. (Malvern; Worcestershire)
Obituary 1965 *973*
Ronald, Capt. J. Mc B. (Old Stagers)
Obituary 1916 *202*
Roope, G. R. J. (Bradfield; Surrey; Berkshire; Griqualand West; England)
Benefit Match 1981 *781*
Photographs 1970 *542*
1978 *537*
Schools Notes 1963 *805*
1964 *739,741,742*
1965 *744*
Root, C. F. (Derbyshire; Worcestershire; England)
Benefit Match 1929/II *456*
Obituary 1955 *936*
Roper, E. (Clifton; Lancashire; Yorkshire)
Obituary 1922/I *267*
Rorie, Capt/Adjt. T. H. B. (Forfarshire)
Obituary 1917 *210*
Rorke, G. (New South Wales; Australia)
'The Drag' Photograph 1960 *96*
Rose, B. C. (Somerset; England)
Cricketer of the Year 1980 *77*
Photographs 1976 *537*
1979 *514*
1980 *69*
Rose, W. M. (Lob Bowler M.C.C.)
Obituary 1922/I *272*
Rosebery, 5th Earl of (Vice-President Surrey)
Obituary 1930/I *261*
Rosebery, 6th Earl of (Eton; Buckinghamshire; Middlesex; Surrey)
Obituary 1975 *1082*
Rosenwater, I. (Journalist; Writer; Broadcaster)
'F. S. Ashley-Cooper: The Herodotus of Cricket'
Book Review 1965 *1014*
'Bermuda Cricket' Book Review 1962 *1048*
'Sir Donald Bradman: A Biography'
Book Review 1979 *1127*
'Sir David Donald Bradman – Selector' 1972 *108*
'Alfred James Gaston: A Study in Enthusiasm'
Book Review 1976 *1143*

'A History of Wicket Covering in England'	1970	*131*
'Arthur Langford: A Memoir' Book Review	1978	*1124*
'J. N. Pentelow – A Biographical Enquiry'		
Book Review	1970	*1068*
'South African Tour Dispute'	1970	*128*
'West Indies Cricket Tour 1963' Book Review	1964	*1006*
Rose-Price, M. P. (Tonbridge)		
Schools Note	1940	*607,608,664*
78 wkts Schools Averages	1940	*705*
Roseveare, Lieut. F. B. (Sedbergh)		
Obituary	1918	*203*
Roslyn, H. E. (Journalist)		
Obituary	1948	*787*
Ross, A. (Journalist; Writer)		
'Australia 55' Book Review	1956	*1027*
'Australia 63' Book Review	1964	*1000*
'Cape Summer and the Australians'		
Book Review	1958	*1012*
with P. Eagar ' Kiwis and Indians'		
Book Review	1984	*1262*
'Ranji – Prince of Cricketers' Book Review	1984	*1268*
with P. Eagar 'Summer of the All-Rounder'		
Book Review	1983	*1306*
with P. Eagar 'A Summer to Remember'		
Book Review	1982	*1266*
with P. Eagar 'Summer of Speed' Book Review	1984	*1261*
'Through the Caribbean' Book Review	1961	*993*
'The West Indies at Lord's' Book Review	1964	*1000*
Ross, Major A. J. R. (Military Cricket)		
Obituary	1918	*203*
Ross, G. (Writer; Journalist)		
'The 1964 Australians' Book Review	1965	*1024*
'Cricketers from Australia' Book Review	1957	*999*
'Cricketers from Australia' Book Review	1962	*1036*
'Cricketers from India' Book Review	1960	*997*
'Cricketers from New Zealand' Book Review	1959	*991*
'Cricketers from Pakistan' Book Review	1963	*1112*
'Cricketers from South Africa' Book Review	1961	*992*
'Cricketers from West Indies' Book Review	1958	*1014*
'Cricketers from West Indies' Book Review	1964	*1006*
'Cricketers from West Indies' Book Review	1967	*1021*
'Cricket's Strongest Wind of Change'	1974	*140*
'Gillette Cup Spans the World'	1977	*156*
'The Greatest Centenary of them All'	1976	*96*
'The Packer Case'	1978	*123*
'The Packer Case' continued	1979	*88*

'The Packer Case' continued	1980	*121*
Photograph	1979	*83*
Prudential Cup Review – International Championship Cricket		
Book Review	1976	*300*
'Rothmans Pakistan Test Almanack'		
Book Review	1963	*1113*
'Rothmans Test Cricket Almanack'		
Book Review	1964	*1006*
'Surrey' Book Review	1972	*1096*
'The Surrey Story' Book Review	1958	*1010*
'The 1965 Tourists' Book Review	1966	*1022*
'200 Years of the Laws'	1975	*128*

Ross, H. (Somerset)
Obituary	1939	*916*

Ross, Lt.-Col. H. A. (Loretto)
Obituary	1919	*187*

Ross, Major J. A. (Trinity College, Port Hope)
Obituary	1920/I	*157*

Ross, N. D. C. (Uppingham; Cambridge University)
Obituary	1935/I	*277*

Ross, T. D. (Lincolnshire)
Obituary	1981	*1148*

Ross, Lieut. W. S. (Brighton College)
Obituary	1918	*203*

Ross-Slater, A. (Worcestershire Scorer)
Obituary	1982	*1209*

Rosser, J. (Victoria; Queensland)
Obituary	1927/I	*287*

Rosslyn, Lord (Eton; Northamptonshire)
Obituary	1940	*845*

Rostron, L. W. S. (Winchester)
Obituary	1917	*263*

Rotherham, G. A. (Rugby; Cambridge University; Warwickshire; Wellington, New Zealand)
Photograph	1918	*150*
Public School Bowler of the Year	1918	*152*

Rotherham, H. (Uppingham; Warwickshire)
Obituary	1940	*845*

Rothery, J. W. (Yorkshire)
Obituary	1920/I	*15*

Roughton, Pte. C. G. (St. Johns C.C., Calgary)
Obituary	1917	*226*

Rought-Rought, D. C. (Norfolk; Cambridge University)
Obituary	1971	*1029*

Rought-Rought, R. C. (Norfolk; Cambridge University)
Obituary	1980	*1156*

Round, F. R. (Balliol College, Oxford)
  Obituary   1921/I   *235*
Round, Rt. Hon. J. (Eton; Essex)
  Obituary   1917   *264*
Round, Capt. J. M. (Haileybury)
  Obituary   1918   *216*
Round, Capt. W. H. (St.John's School, Leatherhead)
  Obituary   1917   *210*
Roupell, J. H. T. (Uppingham)
  Obituary   1921/I   *135*
Rouse, S. J. (Warwickshire)
  Photograph   1978   *570*
Routledge, L. A. (Harrow)
  Obituary   1936/I   *287*
Rowan, E. A. B. (Transvaal; South Africa)
  Cricketer of the Year   1952   *79*
  Note on   1944   *58*
  Photograph   1952   *72*
Rowan, L. (Umpire)
  'The Umpire's Story' Book Review   1974   *1125*
Rowbotham, D. (Journalist)
  Obituary   1969   *986*
Rowbotham, J. (Yorkshire)
  Benefit Match   1874   *143*
  Biography   1873   *172*
  Obituary   1901   *lxvi*
Rowe, C. J. C. (King's Canterbury; Kent; Glamorgan)
  Photograph   1977   *443*
Rowe, D. (Marlborough)
  Obituary   1935/I   *272*
Rowe, E. F. (Felsted; Essex)
  Obituary   1919   *210*
Rowe, F. C. C. (Harrow; Cambridge University)
  Obituary   1898   *lxiii*
Rowe, F. E. (Marlborough; Essex; Berkshire)
  Obituary   1929/I   *257*
Rowe, L. G. (Jamaica; Derbyshire; West Indies)
  Photograph   1975   *365*
Rowell, W. I. (Marlborough; Cambridge University)
  Obituary   1917   *264*
Rowland, H. W. (Baltimore Sons C.C., St.George)
  Obituary   1913/I   *198*
Rowlands, W. H. (Bootham School; Gloucestershire)
  Obituary   1949   *868*
Rowley, A. B. (Rossall; Lancashire)
  Obituary   1912/I   *178*

Rowley, Edmund B. (Rossall; Lancashire)
Obituary 1906 *xcix*
Rowley, Ernest B. (Lancashire)
Obituary 1963 *1035*
Rowley, J. (Lancashire)
Obituary 1909/I *145*
Rowley, Joseph (Albert C.C., Sydney)
Obituary 1917 *264*
Rowley, 2nd Lieut. W. A. (St.John's School, Leatherhead)
Obituary 1918 *204*
Rowntree, R. W. (Auckland)
Obituary 1970 *1028*
Rowstron, F/O. G. (Eton)
Obituary 1942 *351*
Royal Air Force 1941 Team Portrait 1942 *29*
1942 Team Portrait 1943 *26*
Royal Australian Air Force 1944
Team Portrait 1945 *34*
Royal Interest Note on 1954 *86*
Royal Navy 1944 Team Portrait 1945 *36*
Royds, Rev. C. T. (Rugby)
Obituary 1901 *lxii*
Royle, G. M. (Nottinghamshire)
Obituary 1911/I *15.*
Royle, J. S. (Harrow)
Obituary 1937/I *276*
Royle, Dr. P. (Lancashire Supporter)
Obituary 1892 *xxxiv*
Royle, Rev. V. P. F. A. (Rossall; Oxford University; Lancashire; England)
Obituary 1930/I *26.*
Rubie, Lt-Col. C. B. (Sussex)
Obituary 1940 *84.*
Rucker, C. E. S. (Charterhouse; Oxford University; Kent)
Obituary 1966 *97.*
Rucker, Capt. P. W. (Charterhouse; Oxford University)
Obituary 1941 *39*
Rucker, Lieut. R. S. (Charterhouse)
Obituary 1919 *18*
Rudd, C. D. (South African Supporter)
Obituary 1917 *26*
Rudd, C. J. L. (Harrow)
Obituary 1951 *92*
Rudd, G. E. (Leicestershire)
Obituary 1922/I *26*
Rudston, H. (Yorkshire)
Obituary 1964 *95*

gby School Tom Brown Centenary Match	1942	22
Photograph of Centenary Match	1942	26
ggles-Brise, Sir E. Bart. (Eton)		
Obituary	1936/I	288
ggles-Brise, Major Gen. Sir H. G. (Winchester; Oxford University; Essex)		
Obituary	1928/I	296
ndall, G. W. (Clifton; Wiltshire)		
Obituary	1927/I	287
ndell, J. U. (South Australia)		
Obituary	1923/I	305
ndle, 2nd Lieut. C. N. (Victoria College, Jersey)		
Obituary	1916	203
nting, W. J. (Secretary South Melbourne C.C.)		
Obituary	1913/I	198
sh, H. R. (Chairman Australian Board of Control)		
Obituary	1929/I	257
sh, J. H. (Sydney Club Cricket)		
Obituary	1923/I	311
sh, M. (President Radnor C.C.)		
Obituary	1910/I	152
shbrooke, Vice Admiral E. G. N. (Secretary M.C.C. Youth Cricket sociation)		
Obituary	1973	1013
shby, T. (Surrey)		
Obituary	1963	1036
shton, F. (Lancashire)		
Obituary	1977	1052
hton, H. (New York Club Cricketer)		
Obituary	1934/I	273
ton, Rev. J. (Umpire Chicago Club Cricket)		
Obituary	1918	233
hton, J. L. (Rugby)		
Obituary	1937/I	279
sel, J. S. (North of Ireland; Northumberland)		
Obituary	1903	lxxviii
sell, A. C. (C.A.G.)(Essex; England)		
Obituary	1962	990
ortrait and Biography	1923/I	313
sell, A. I. (Hampshire)		
Obituary	1962	991
sell, Lord C. (M.C.C.)		
bituary	1895	xl
sell, C. R. (Devon)		
bituary	1975	1082
sell, Capt. J. (Glasgow Academy)		
bituary	1918	204

Russell, 2nd Lieut. J. E. (Dulwich)
    Obituary   1918
Russell, Major L. G. (Hampshire)
    Obituary   1947
Russell, S. E. (Middlesex; Gloucestershire)
    Photograph   1966
Russell, T. M. (Essex)
    Obituary   1928/I
Russell, W. (Glamorgan)
    Obituary   1909/I
Russell, W. (U.S.A. Club Cricketer)
    Obituary   1919
Russell, Sir W. 3rd Bart (Fettes)
    Obituary   1916
Russell, W. E. (Middlesex; England)
    Benefit Match   1970
    Photographs   1961
                                      1963
                                      1965
                                      1971
Russian Story Note on   1951
Rutherford, A. P. (Repton; Hampshire)
    Obituary   1981
Rutherford, J. S. (Hampshire)
    Obituary   1944
Rutland County Cricket Club
    Formation   1968
Rutland, 8th Duke of (President M.C.C.)
    Obituary   1926/I
Rutley, H. (Toronto Club Cricketer)
    Obituary   1924/I
Rutnagar, D. (Writer; Journalist)
    'Indian Cricket – Its Problems and Players'   1967
Rutter, A. (Rugby)
    Obituary   1909/I
Rutter, E. (Rugby; Middlesex)
    Obituary   1927/I
Rutter, R. H. (Tonbridge; Buckinghamshire)
    Obituary   1975
Rutty, A. W. F. (Sherborne; Surrey)
    Obituary   1933/I
Rutty, W. H. (Manhattan C.C.)
    Obituary   1919
Ryan, F. (Bedford Grammar; Hampshire; Glamorgan)
    Obituary   1955

an, Capt. J. H. A. (Sandhurst; Northamptonshire)

Obituary	1916	*203*

an, Capt. J. S. (Merchant Taylors)

Obituary	1917	*211*

an, M. (Victorian Club Cricketer)

Obituary	1912/I	*184*

an, Dr. W. H. (County Limerick)

Obituary	1928/I	*297*

der, J. (Victoria; Australia)

Obituary	1978	*1081*
Testimonial Match	1932/II	*688*

der, R. (Writer)

F. R. Foster – A Prince of the Golden Age'	1976	*134*
And Gilligan Led them Out'	1970	*124*
The Glorious Uncertainty'	1974	*117*
The Great Wicket-Keepers'	1972	*137*
Gilbert Jessop – the most Exciting Cricketer of All'	1975	*137*
W. A. Oldfield – The Star Keeper'	1977	*134*
The Pleasures of Reading Wisden'	1965	*95*
E. J. (Tiger) Smith'	1980	*96*
Warwickshire – The Unpredictable'	1968	*124*
The Warwickshire Way'	1973	*127*

der, R. C. (Secretary Worcestershire)

Obituary	1974	*1078*

der, R. V. (Secretary Warwickshire)

Obituary	1950	*913*
Retirement Note on	1945	*194*
Trials of a County Secretary'	1936/I	*257*

er-Richardson, W. (Manchester Grammar School; Free Foresters)

Obituary	1921/I	*235*

, G. T. (Norfolk)

Obituary	1944	*321*

ance, H. (Secretary Lancashire)

Obituary	1933/I	*257*

, Rev. J. C. (Eton; Oxford University)

Obituary	1901	*lxiii*

tt, A. (Leicestershire)

Benefit Match	1892	*171*
Obituary	1916	*220*

ie, C. C. (Sydney C.C.)

Obituary	1922/I	*268*

s, E. T. (Journalist)

Obituary	1911/I	*154*

s, Lieut. R. T. S. (Public Schools C.C., Vancouver)

Obituary	1917	*211*

Sadiq Mohammad (Gloucestershire; Tasmania; Essex; Karachi; Pakistan
International Airways; United Banks; Pakistan)
<table>
<tr><td>Action Photograph</td><td>1975</td></tr>
<tr><td>Photographs</td><td>1974</td></tr>
<tr><td></td><td>1977</td></tr>
<tr><td></td><td>1980</td></tr>
</table>

Sadler, J. (West Surrey Club Cricketer)
<table>
<tr><td>Obituary</td><td>1925/I</td></tr>
</table>

Sadler, T. (Surrey Club Cricketer)
<table>
<tr><td>Obituary</td><td>1916</td></tr>
</table>

Sainsbury, E. (Sherborne; Somerset; Gloucestershire)
<table>
<tr><td>Obituary</td><td>1933/I</td></tr>
</table>

Sainsbury, F. J. (Essex; Somerset)
<table>
<tr><td>Obituary</td><td>1920/I</td></tr>
</table>

Sainsbury, P. J. (Hampshire)
<table>
<tr><td>Cricketer of the Year</td><td>1974</td></tr>
<tr><td>Hampshire without Sainsbury Note on</td><td>1977</td></tr>
<tr><td>Photographs</td><td>1958</td></tr>
<tr><td></td><td>1965</td></tr>
<tr><td></td><td>1969</td></tr>
<tr><td></td><td>1974</td></tr>
<tr><td>'P. Sainsbury – An Appreciation' J. Arlott</td><td></td></tr>
<tr><td>Book Review</td><td>1966</td></tr>
</table>

St.Helier, Rt. Hon. Lord (Cricket Festival Patron)
<table>
<tr><td>Obituary</td><td>1906</td></tr>
</table>

St.Hill, A. B. (West Indies Supporter)
<table>
<tr><td>Obituary</td><td>1912/I</td></tr>
</table>

St.Hill, E. L. (Trinidad; West Indies)
<table>
<tr><td>Obituary</td><td>1958</td></tr>
</table>

Saker, K. (Malaysia)
<table>
<tr><td>All 10 Wickets Note on</td><td>1984</td></tr>
</table>

Salaries of Cricketers Notes on
<table>
<tr><td></td><td>1981</td></tr>
<tr><td></td><td>1983</td></tr>
</table>

Sale, Lieut. A. G. (Repton)
<table>
<tr><td>Obituary</td><td>1917</td></tr>
</table>

Sale, E. V. (Auckland)
<table>
<tr><td>Obituary</td><td>1920/I</td></tr>
</table>

Sale, P/O. J. R. (Marlborough)
<table>
<tr><td>Obituary</td><td>1942</td></tr>
</table>

Sale, R. (Repton; Oxford University; Derbyshire)
<table>
<tr><td>Obituary</td><td>1971</td></tr>
</table>

Sale, Lieut. R. L. (Clifton)
<table>
<tr><td>Obituary</td><td>1919</td></tr>
</table>

Sale, W. W. (Marlborough)
<table>
<tr><td>Obituary</td><td>1930/I</td></tr>
</table>

Sales, Lieut. G. E. (Kentish Association C.C., Winnipeg)
Obituary 1920/I *157*

Salmon, Sir E. C. H. (Malvern; Buckinghamshire)
Obituary 1947 *694*

Salmon, G. H. (Leicestershire)
Obituary 1979 *1086*

Salmon, H. (West Hartlepool C.C.)
Obituary 1945 *340*

Salmon, L. R. W. (All Hallows School)
100 wkts Schools Averages 1928/II *596*

Salt, Capt. W. P. (Shrewsbury)
Obituary 1917 *211*

Salter, G. F. (Sussex)
Obituary 1912/I *179*

Salter, M. G. (Cheltenham; Oxford University; Gloucestershire)
Obituary 1974 *1078*

Samms, W. J. (Kent)
Obituary 1966 *972*

Sampher, Pte (Canada; New Westminster C.C., British Columbia)
Obituary 1920/I *157*

Sample, C. H. (Edinburgh Academy; Northumberland)
Obituary 1939 *916*

Sampson, R. K. (Sussex)
Obituary 1928/I *297*

Samson, Capt. A. L. (Merton College, Oxford)
Obituary 1918 *217*

Samson, Lieut. O. M. (Cheltenham; Oxford University; Somerset)
Obituary 1919 *187*

Samson, Rev. R. G. (Oakham)
Obituary 1947 *694*

Samuda, Major C. M. A. (Military Cricket)
Obituary 1918 *204*

Samuel, Lieut. W. G. (Ipswich Grammar School)
Obituary 1919 *187*

Sandell, W. H. (Whitgift Grammar School)
Schools Note 1899 *lxxxvi*
75 wkts Schools Averages 1899 *371*

Sandeman, Capt. G. A. C. (Eton; Hampshire)
Obituary 1916 *203*

Sanders, E. J. (Secretary Devon)
Obituary 1905 *c*
Team in U.S.A. and Canada 1885 1886 *350*
1886 1887 *289*

Sanders, Capt. G. (Felsted)
Obituary 1922/I *269*

Sanders, W. (Warwickshire)
  Obituary   1966   972

Sanderson, 2nd Lieut. F. B. (Grange C.C.)
  Obituary   1917   211

Sanderson, G. B. (Malvern, Worcestershire; Warwickshire)
  Obituary   1966   976

Sanderson, Lieut. H. S. (Charterhouse)
  Obituary   1916   204

Sanderson, J. T. (Harrow)
  Obituary   1939   910

Sanderson, Sir L. (Harrow)
  Obituary   1945   346

Sandford, Ven. E. G. (Rugby; Oxford University)
  Obituary   1911/I   15

Sandford, J. R. P. (Marlborough)
  Obituary   1917   26

Sandford, T. C. G. (Marlborough; Oxford University)
  Obituary   1943   38

Sandford, T. F. (Marlborough)
  Obituary   1964   95

Sandham, A. (Surrey; England)
  Benefit Matches   1928/II   17
                                                        1936/II   32
  Career Figures   1972   12
  Hundredth Hundred   1936/II   42
  'A Lifetime with Surrey – Stealing Singles with
  Jack Hobbs'   1972   11
  Obituary   1983   125
  Photograph   1972   11
  Portrait and Biography   1923/I   31
  Tribute to Sir J. Hobbs   1964   16

Sandman, D. Mck. (Canterbury; New Zealand)
  Obituary   1974   107

Sands, J. (Sussex)
  Obituary   1904   lxxxv

Sandwith, Rev. W. F. G. (Westminster; Radnorshire; Norfolk)
  Obituary   1950   91

Sankey, A. (Leicestershire)
  Obituary   1923/I   36

Sankey, C. (Leicestershire; Suffolk)
  Obituary   1928/I   2

Sankey, T. (Shropshire; Oxfordshire; Buckinghamshire; Berkshire)
  Obituary   1911/I   1

Santall, F. R. (Warwickshire)
  Benefit Match   1936/II   2
  Obituary   1951   9

Santall, S. (Northamptonshire; Warwickshire)
Benefit Match	1909/II	*214*
Obituary	1958	*963*

Saravanamuttu, M. (Indian Gymkhana; Ceylon)
Obituary	1971	*1029*

Saravanamuttu, P. (Ceylon)
Obituary	1951	*927*

Saravanamuttu, Lieut. Col. S. (Cambridge University; Ceylon)
Obituary	1958	*963*

Sarbadhikary, B. (Writer)
'My World of Cricket' Book Review	1965	*1021*

Sarel, Major W. G. M. (Surrey; Kent; Sussex; Northumberland; Trinidad)
Obituary	1951	*927*

Sarfraz Nawaz (Northamptonshire; Lahore; United Banks; Pakistan)
Photograph	1976	*506*

Sarwate, C. T. (Central Provinces and Berar; Maharashtra; Bombay; Holkar; India)
'Last Wicket Record at the Oval' Photograph	1947	*38*

Sathasivam, M. (Ceylon; Singapore; Malaya)
Obituary	1978	*1081*

Saunders, D. W. (Canada)
Obituary	1931/I	*265*

Saunders, J. V. (Victoria; Wellington; Australia)
Obituary	1928/I	*297*

Saunders, Capt. N. M. (Lancing)
Obituary	1920/I	*157*

Saunders, S. R. (Canada)
Obituary	1951	*927*

Saunders, Lieut. T. B. (Trinity College, Port Hope)
Obituary	1917	*211*

Savage, J. S. (Leicestershire; Lancashire)
Photographs	1959	*437*
	1961	*465*
	1964	*464*
	1968	*465*

Savigny, J. H. (Tasmania)
Obituary	1924/I	*269*

Savigny, W. H. (Tasmania)
Obituary	1924/I	*276*

Savile, G. (Rossall; Cambridge University; Yorkshire)
Obituary	1905	*ci*

Saville, Capt. C. A. (Middlesex)
Obituary	1919	*200*

Saville, G. J. (Essex)
Photograph	1971	*335*

Saville, Capt. S. E. B. (Bedford Grammar School)
Obituary   1917   *211*
Saville, S. H. (Marlborough; Cambridge University; Middlesex)
Obituary   1967   *974*
Savory, 2nd Lieut. E. H. (Lancing)
Obituary   1919   *200*
Sawyer, C. M. (Lancashire)
Obituary   1922/I   *269*
Saxton, G. S. (Clifton)
Obituary   1918   *241*
Sayagee, D. (Holkar)
Obituary   1959   *937*
Sayer, A. L. (East Sussex C.C.)
Obituary   1912/I   *179*
Sayer, Lieut. C. O. (Queens College, Oxford)
Obituary   1918   *217*
Sayer, D. M. (Maidstone Grammar School; Oxford University; Kent)
Benefit Match   1972   *459*
Sayles, G. (Berkshire)
Obituary   1972   *1055*
Sayres, H. (Merion C.C., Philadelphia)
Obituary   1919   *211*
Scales, H. S. (Statistican)
Obituary   1975   *1083*
Scanlon, E. (New South Wales)
Obituary   1917   *265*
Scarborough
'Over 100 Years of Scarborough Festival'
J. M. Kilburn   1977   *151*
Plan of County Ground   1950   *630*
    ad passim
Scattergood, A. C. (Haverford College)
Obituary   1919   *213*
Schiff, 2nd Lieut. A. S. B. (Brighton College)
Obituary   1918   *204*
Schilizzi, S. (President Northamptonshire)
Obituary   1962   *991*
Schleswig-Holstein, H. H. Duke of (Charterhouse)
Obituary   1932/I   *251*
Schneider, K. J. (Victoria)
Obituary   1929/I   *257*
Schneider, 2nd Lieut. S. S. (Mid Sussex Club Cricketer)
Obituary   1917   *211*
Schofield, L/Cpl. A. (Wanderers C.C., Winnipeg)
Obituary   1918   *204*

Scholes, 2nd Lieut. W. P. (Wyggeston Grammar School)
Obituary   1916   *204*
Scholey, Lieut. C. H. N. (Clare College, Cambridge)
Obituary   1916   *204*
Scholtz, Capt. J. (Hamilton C.C., Bermuda)
Obituary   1912/I   *179*
'Schoolboys' Bowling' F. R. Spofforth   1904   *lxvi*
Schultz, S. S. (Later **Storey**)(Uppingham; Cambridge University; Lancashire; England)
Obituary   1938   *944*
Schute, Lieut. J. H. (Ireland)
Obituary   1916   *204*
Schwartz, Major R. O. (St.Paul's; Middlesex; Oxfordsshire; Transvaal; South Africa)
Obituary   1919   *187*
Portrait and Biography   1908/I   *164*
Sclater, Lieut. A. N. (Ridley College, Ontario)
Obituary   1920/I   *157*
Scobell, Col. B. (Cricket Fanatic)
Obituary   1914   *194*
Scobell, G. B. (Lansdown C.C.; Exeter College, Oxford)
Obituary   1921/I   *235*
Scobie, Capt. I. M. (Sandhurst)
Obituary   1917   *211*
Scorer, R. I. (Warwickshire)
Obituary   1977   *1049*
Scorers of 2000 Runs Plus Note on   1960   *121*
Scott, A. (South Australia)
Obituary   1908/I   *152*
Scott, Lieut. A. E. M. (Eastbourne College)
Obituary   1917   *211*
Scott, A. P. (Marlborough)
Obituary   1934/I   *273*
Scott, Ven. A. T. (Brighton College; Cambridge University; Cambridgeshire; Norfolk)
Obituary   1926/I   *282*
Scott, Capt. A. W. H. (Malvern)
Obituary   1916   *204*
Scott, Rt. Rev. C. P. (Charterhouse)
Obituary   1928/I   *298*
Scott, D. (Journalist; Writer)
Obituary   1923/I   *305*
Scott, E. K. (Clifton; Oxford University; Gloucestershire)
Schools Note   1938   *675,681*
79 wkts Schools Averages   1938   *736*

Scott, Dr. E. J. L. (Lincoln College, Oxford)
   Obituary   1919   *211*
Scott, Hon. Sir E. S. (Winchester)
   Obituary   1954   *929*
Scott, Lord Lt-Col. G. M. D. (Eton)
   Obituary   1953   *949*
Scott, Lord G. W. (Eton; Oxford University; Middlesex)
   Obituary   1948   *787*
Scott, H. (Umpire)
   Obituary   1957   *947*
Scott, Dr. H. J. H. (Victoria; Australia)
   Obituary   1911/I   *155*
Scott, Rev. H. Von. E. (Cambridge University Seniors)
   Obituary   1927/I   *288*
Scott, Sir J. (Oxford University)
   Obituary   1905   *ci*
Scott, Dr. J. A. (Belmont C.C., Philadelphia; Philadelphia)
   Obituary   1910/I   *147*
Scott, J. F. (New South Wales Club Cricketer)
   Obituary   1910/I   *152*
Scott, J. G. (Aberdeenshire)
   Obituary   1939   *316*
Scott, 2nd Lieut. J. G. A. (Northampton Saturday C.C.)
   Obituary   1917   *212*
Scott, J. G. C. (Marlborough; Cambridge University; Sussex)
   Obituary   1947   *695*
Scott, Major K. B. (Winchester; Oxford University; Sussex)
   Obituary   1944   *307*
Scott, M. E. (Northamptonshire; Durham)
   Photograph   1965   *504*
Scott, M. S. (Worcestershire)
   Photograph   1982   *603*
Scott, Hon. O. (Gloucestershire)
   Obituary   1949   *869*
Scott, O. C. (Jamaica; West Indies)
   Obituary   1962   *991*
Scott, R. (Scotland)
   Obituary   1918   *234*
Scott, R. S. G. (Winchester; Oxford University; Sussex)
   Obituary   1958   *963*
Scott, S. W. (Brentwood; Middlesex; Herefordshire)
   Obituary   1934/I   *274*
   Portrait and Biography   1893   *xxxviii*
Scott, T. G. (Bradfield)
   Obituary   1934/I   *274*

Scott, V. J. (Auckland; New Zealand)
Obituary   1981   *1149*
Scott, W. (Belmont C.C., Philadelphia)
Obituary   1908/I   *152*
Scott, W. G. (Aberdeenshire; Canada)
Obituary   1972   *1055*
Scott, Dr. W. J. (Middlesex)
Obituary   1921/I   *235*
Scott, W. M. (Craigmount School)
Obituary   1945   *340*
Scott-Chad, Lt-Col. G. N. (Eton; Norfolk)
Obituary   1951   *927*
Scottish Enthusiasm Note on   1953   *671*
Scotton, W. H. (Nottinghamshire; England)
Obituary   1894   *xxxv*
Scovell, B. (Journalist; Writer)
'Ken Barrington – A Tribute' Book Review   1983   *1308*
'Everything that's Cricket' Book Review   1967   *1016*
Scrymgeour, Pte. J. S. (Perthshire)
Obituary   1917   *212*
Scully, J. S. (Pennsylvania; Philadelphia)
Obituary   1906   *xcix*
Seabrook, F. J. (Haileybury; Cambridge University; Gloucestershire)
Obituary   1980   *1156*
Seagram, P. F. (Toronto)
Obituary   1942   *351*
Seal, F. (Albion C.C., Toronto)
Obituary   1920/I   *194*
Seal, W. B. (U.S.A. Club Cricketer)
Obituary   1939   *916*
Sealy, J. E. D. (Barbados; Trinidad; West Indies)
Obituary   1983   *1255*
Record by   1941   *64*
Searle, J. (New South Wales)
Obituary   1938   *949*
Seccull, A. W. (Transvaal; South Africa)
Obituary   1946   *444*
Second Class Championship Records   1940   *117*
**Second Class Counties and
Leg Before Wicket, The'**   1903   *lxii*
Secretan, H. H. (Canterbury)
Obituary   1912/I   *179*
Seddon, D. C. (New South Wales)
Obituary   1979   *1086*
Seddon, Lt-Col. E. M. (Military Cricket)
Obituary   1918   *204*

'Seeing Cricket After Four Years'

E. M. Wellings	1945	*54*
Sefton, Earl of (Trustee M.C.C.)		
Obituary	1898	*xlv*
Seitz, J. A. (Oxford University; Victoria)		
Obituary	1973	*1015*
Selby, J. (Nottinghamshire; England)		
Benefit Match	1888	*60*
Obituary	1895	*xxxvii*
Selby, W. (Nottinghamshire)		
Obituary	1893	*xxxiii*
Selection Committee for Tests at Home		
List of	1962	*124*
Selectors Notes on	1949	*118*
	1951	*116*
	1959	*73*
	1969	*160*
	1977	*111*
Selectors England Photographs	1963	*150*
	1984	*Plate*
Selincourt, H. De (Cricket Writer)		
Obituary	1952	*961*
Sellar, Lt-Col. T. B. (Military Cricket)		
Obituary	1925/I	*280*
Sellars, Capt. E. F. (Loretto)		
Obituary	1920/I	*157*
Sellars, T. (Grange C.C.)		
Obituary	1916	*205*
Sellers, A. (Yorkshire)		
Obituary	1942	*363*
Sellers, A. B. (St.Peter's York; Yorkshire)		
Appreciation of H. Verity	1944	*51*
Obituary	1982	*1209*
Portrait and Biography	1940	*39*
'Rebuilding Yorkshire Cricket'	1948	*71*
Tributes to: A. Mitchell	1977	*1047*
H. Sutcliffe	1979	*98*
Views on L.B.W. Experiement	1936/I	*343*
Selvey, M. W. W. (Battersea Grammar School; Cambridge University; Glamorgan; Surrey; Middlesex; Orange Free State; England)		
Photographs	1973	*474*
	1977	*490*
	1980	*490*
Sen, P. (Bengal; India)		
Obituary	1971	*1029*

Senanayake, D. S. (St. Thomas's, Ceylon)
Obituary — 1974 — *1079*

Seneviratne, A. (Wesley College, Colombo)
Obituary — 1970 — *1026*

Senkler, J. H. (Canada)
Obituary — 1927/I — *289*

Serjeant, Sir D. M. (Victoria)
Obituary — 1930/I — *262*

Sesha Chari, Kilvidi (All India)
Obituary — 1918 — *234*

Seton, Capt. W. J. (Incogniti; Journalist)
Obituary — 1913/I — *198*

Seton-Karr, W. S. (Rugby)
Obituary — 1912/I — *184*

Settle, Lt-Col. R. H. N. (Military Cricket)
Obituary — 1919 — *188*
'Settlement of the Bowling Controversy,' The — 1935/I — *325*

Severn A. (Derbyshire)
Obituary — 1951 — *929*

Severn, A. R. (Westminster)
Obituary — 1930/I — *263*

Severn, Dr. C. B. (Hollywood C.C.)
Obituary — 1983 — *1256*

Severn, E. C. W. (Eton)
Obituary — 1937/I — *289*

Sewell, Rev. A. (Radley)
Obituary — 1949 — *873*

Sewell, C. O. H. (Natal; Gloucestershire)
Obituary — 1952 — *961*

Sewell, D. C. C. (Wellingborough)
Obituary — 1915/I — *239*

Sewell, E. H. D. (Bedford Grammar School; Bedfordshire; Essex; Journalist)
Obituary — 1948 — *787*

Sewell, F. A. S. (Weymouth College; Cambridge University; Dorset;
Bedfordshire)
Obituary — 1965 — *971*

Sewell, Major H. W. (Sedbergh)
Obituary — 1927/I — *296*

Sewell, J. J. (Marlborough; Middlesex)
Obituary — 1898 — *xlv*

Sewell, R. P. (Essex)
Obituary — 1902 — *lxx*

Sewell, W. A. (President Natal Cricket Association)
Obituary — 1932/I — *251*

Seymour, Archdeacon A. E. (Charterhouse)
Obituary — 1910/I — *152*

Seymour, C. R. (Harrow; Hampshire)
Obituary ..... 1936/I *293*
Seymour, E. N. (Ireland)
Obituary ..... 1981 ..... *1149*
Seymour, J. (Sussex; Northamptonshire)
Obituary ..... 1969 ..... *990*
Seymour, J. (Kent; London County)
Benefit Match ..... 1921/I *129*
Obituary ..... 1931/I *265*
Shackleton, D. (Hampshire; Dorset; England)
Benefit Matches ..... 1959 ..... *393*
..... 1968 ..... *442*
Cricketer of the Year ..... 1959 ..... *51*
Photographs ..... 1950 ..... *357*
..... 1952 ..... *363*
..... 1953 ..... *375*
..... 1954 ..... *382*
..... 1956 ..... *383*
..... 1957 ..... *384*
..... 1959 ..... *47*
..... 1962 ..... *426*
Retirement Note on ..... 1969 ..... *94*
Shackleton, J. H. (Gloucestershire)
Photograph ..... 1978 ..... *399*
Shacklock, F. (Nottinghamshire; Derbyshire)
Obituary ..... 1938 ..... *944*
Shackerley, Sir G. H. (Harrow)
Obituary ..... 1946 ..... *445*
Shakespear, Major G. F. C. (Wellington)
Obituary ..... 1920/I *157*
Shakespeare, Wing-Comdr. W. H. N. (Worcestershire)
Obituary ..... 1977 ..... *1049*
Shalders, W. A. (Griqualand West; Transvaal; South Africa)
Obituary ..... 1918 ..... *234*
Shand, F. L. (Harrow; Stirlingshire; Kincardineshire)
Obituary ..... 1922/I *269*
Shanley, Lt-Col C. N. (Assistant Manager Canadian Tour to England 1887)
Obituary ..... 1920/I *157*
Shanmuganathan, T. (Sri Lanka)
Obituary ..... 1984 ..... *1208*
Shapcott, Air-Commodore M. S. (Alleyus; Surrey)
Obituary ..... 1978 ..... *1081*
Shardlow, B. (Staffordshire)
Obituary ..... 1977 ..... *1049*

Sharp, A. T. (Leicestershire)
Obituary   1974   *1079*

Sharp, G. (Northamptonshire)
Photographs   1975   *502*
    1978   *490*

Sharp, H. P. H. (Middlesex)
Benefit Matches   1956   *471,482*
    1972   *349*
Retirement Note on   1956   *567*

Sharp, J. (Lancashire; England)
Benefit Match   1911/II   *79*
Obituary   1939   *917*

Sharp, Gen. Sir J. A. T. (Repton; Cambridge University; Leicestershire)
Obituary   1978   *1082*

Sharp, Major J. S. (Trinity Hall, Cambridge)
Obituary   1918   *204*

Sharp, K. (Yorkshire; Griqualand West)
Photograph   1979   *595*

Sharp, N. (Warwickshire)
Obituary   1979   *1092*

Sharp, Lieut. S. O. (Bedford Grammar School; Rotherham Town C.C.)
Obituary   1917   *212*

Sharp, W. R. (Clifton; Scotland)
Obituary   1926/I   *283*

Sharp Practice Note on   1982   *89*

Sharpe, Rev. C. M. (Cambridge University; Yorkshire; Hertfordshire)
Obituary   1936/I   *288*

Sharpe, J. W. (Northamptonshire; Surrey; England)
Obituary   1937/I   *279*
Portrait and Biography   1892   *xxxix*

Sharpe, P. J. (Worksop College; Yorkshire; Derbyshire; England)
Action Photograph   1970   *55*
Benefit Match   1972   *641*
Cricketer of the Year   1963   *163*
Photographs   1963   *156*
    1967   *634*
Schools Note   1956   *742*
1251 runs Schools Averages   1956   *803*
'The Phil Sharpe Benefit' Book Review   1972   *1102*
Sharpe moves to Bradford League Note   1977   *115*

Sharpe, S. (Nottinghamshire)
Obituary   1925/I   *280*

Shaw, A. (Nottinghamshire; Sussex; England)
Benefit Matches   1880   *54*
    1893   *252*
Biography   1879   *161*

Obituary		1908/I	*130*
Presentation to		1876	*46,163*
Team in Australia	1881-82	1883	*217*
	1884-85	1886	*17*
and Shrewsbury A)	1886-87	1888	*322*

Shaw, A. (Golcar C.C.)
Obituary   1917   *265*

Shaw, B. H. G. (Marlborough; Sandhurst)
Obituary   1915/I   *239*

Shaw, D. B. (Marlborough)
Obituary   1927/I   *296*

Shaw, Gunner D. G. (Journalist)
Obituary   1944   *308*

Shaw, Lieut. E. A. (Marlborough; Oxford University; Buckinghamshire)
Obituary   1917   *212*

Shaw, Rt. Rev. E. D. (Forest School; Oxford University; Essex; Middlesex; Hertfordshire; Buckinghamshire)
Obituary   1938   *945*

Shaw, H. C. (Scotland)
Obituary   1972   *1057*

Shaw, J. (Yorkshire)
Obituary   1922/I   *269*

Shaw, J. C. (Nottinghamshire)
Benefit Match   1885   *151*

Shaw, Adj. Lt-Col. R. E. F. (Forest School)
Obituary   1919   *188*

Shaw, S. (Vice President Yorkshire)
Obituary   1931/I   *266*

Shaw, V. K. (afterwards **Shaw-Mackenzie**) (Haileybury; Cambridge University; Kent)
Obituary   1907   *cxvii*

Shaw, 2nd Lieut. W. R. (Borlase School)
Obituary   1919   *189*

Shawcroft, J. (Writer)
'History of Derbyshire County Cricket Club 1810-1970'
Book Review   1973   *1050*

Sheehy, T. (Tasmania)
Obituary   1914/I   *194*

Sheen, S. (Writer)
'The Geoffrey Boycott File' Book Review   1983   *1308*

Sheepshanks, E. R. (Eton; Yorkshire)
Obituary   1938   *945*

Sheet, Lieut. J. R. (St. George's College, Guildford)
Obituary   1919   *189*

Sheffield, 3rd Earl of (President Sussex)
Obituary   1910/I   *146*

Team in Australia 1891-92   1893   *329*

Sheffield, E. J. (Surrey; Kent)
Obituary   1972   *1055*

Sheffield Bramall Lane
'Farewell Bramall Lane – K. Farnsworth'   1974   *135*
Photograph   1974   *136*
Plan of County Ground   1950   *573*
                                                   ad passim

Sheldon, Capt. A. B. (Haileybury)
Obituary   1945   *325*

Shelley, Sir J. 10th Bart. (Devon)
Obituary   1977   *1049*

Shelmerdine, D. O. (Cheltenham; Cambridge University; Lancashire)
Obituary   1968   *1006*

Shelton, A. W. (President Nottinghamshire)
'Centenary of Trent Bridge'   1938   *461*
Obituary   1939   *917*

Shenton, J. C. L. (Middlesex)
Obituary   1902   *lxxiv*

Shepard, Major W. J. H. (Haileybury)
Obituary   1945   *325*

Shepherd, D. J. (Glamorgan)
Benefit Match   1961   *380*
Cricketer of the Year   1970   *70*
Photographs   1953   *335*
                                                   1957   *344*
                                                   1959   *341*
                                                   1963   *409*
                                                   1965   *383*
                                                   1968   *397*
                                                   1970   *59*
'Don Shepherd Testimonial Brochure'
Book Review   1969   *1040*

Shepherd, D. R. (Gloucestershire)
Photograph   1972   *415*

Shepherd, Rev. J. M. (Rossall)
Obituary   1930/I   *263*

Shepherd, J. N. (Kent; Gloucestershire; Rhodesia; Barbados; West Indies)
Benefit Match   1980   *756*
Cricketer of the Year   1979   *75*
Photographs   1969   *442*
                                                   1974   *437*
                                                   1979   *67*

Shepherd, J. S. F. (Otago)
Obituary   1972   *1057*

Shepherd, T. F. (Surrey)
Benefit Match   1932/II   26
Obituary   1958   96
Shepherd, W. (Surrey)
Obituary   1920/I   18
Shepherd, Major W. H. (Vice Pesident Yorkshire)
Obituary   1914/I   19
Shepley-Smith, A. M. (Westminster)
Obituary   1962   99
Sheppard, Rt. Rev. D. S. (Sherborne; Cambridge University; Sussex; England)
Cricketer of the Year   1953   6
Note on   1962   1
'Parson's Pitch' Book Review   1965   102
Photographs   1950   5
     1952   52
     1953   6
     1954   5
Schools Notes   1947   57
     1948   645.66
Sheppard, H. H. (Scotland)
Obituary   1980   116
Sheppard, R. A. (Whitgift; Surrey)
Obituary   1954   9
Shepstone, G. H. (Repton; Transvaal; South Africa)
Obituary   1943   38
Sheridan, E. O. (New South Wales)
Obituary   1925/I   29
Sheridan, P. (Secretary Sydney Cricket Ground)
Obituary   1911/I   1
Sheridan, R. O. (Philadelphia C.C.)
Obituary   1913/I   1
Sherman, T. (Surrey)
Obituary   1912/I   1
Sherrin, T. (Australian Cricket Ball Maker)
Obituary   1914/I   1
Sherwell, N. B. (Tonbridge; Cambridge University; Middlesex)
Obituary   1961   9
Sherwell, P. W. (Cornwall; Transvaal; South Africa)
Fastest Hundred in Test Cricket Note on   1983   1
Obituary   1949   8
Sherwell, 2nd Lieut. R. (Tonbridge)
Obituary   1917   2
Sherwin, M. (Nottinghamshire; England)
Benefit Matches   1895
     1897
Obituary   1911/I   1

Portrait and Biography	1891	*xxxiii*
herwin, W. H. (Cricket Outfitter)		
Obituary	1953	*949*
ields, Major J. (Leicestershire)		
Obituary	1961	*951*
ilton, J. E. (Warwickshire)		
Obituary	1900	*liii*
immim, W. (Canadian Supporter)		
Obituary	1912/I	*184*
inde, S. G. (Baroda; Bombay; India)		
Obituary	1956	*977*
ine, E. B. (Kent; Cambridge University)		
Obituary	1953	*949*
ine, Lieut. J. D. (Downside)		
Obituary	1916	*221*
ipman, A. W. (Leicestershire)		
Benefit Match	1935/II	*363*
Obituary	1981	*1149*
ipman, W. (Leicestershire)		
Obituary	1944	*322*
ipton, W. L. (Repton; Derbyshire)		
Obituary	1942	*363*
irley, Lt.-Col. W. (Writer)		
Obituary	1931/I	*266*
irley, W. R.De La Cour (Eton; Cambridge University; Hampshire)		
Obituary	1971	*1029*
ooter, T. (Nottinghamshire)		
Obituary	1920/I	*185*
ore, G. R. E. (British Columbia)		
Obituary	1927/I	*289*
orlt, Lieut. W. E. (Charterhouse)		
Obituary	1918	*204*
orrocks, Sgt. E. (Somerset)		
Obituary	1917	*213*
hort History of Kent Cricket for the Past 30 Years and More'		
G. Marsham	1907	*lxxxv*
ortland, N. A. (Stoke School; Coventry; Warwickshire)		
Obituary	1974	*1079*
otton, W. (Yorkshire)		
Obituary	1910/I	*146*
oubridge, T. (Sussex)		
Obituary	1939	*921*
owering, R. V. (President Somerset)		
Obituary	1981	*1149*
rapnel, Capt. V. G. F. (Wilson's Grammar School)		
Obituary	1919	*189*

493

Shrewsbury, A. (Nottinghamshire; England)
Benefit Match	1894	1!
in First Class Cricket	1904	xcv
Obituary	1904	lx
Portrait and Biography	1890	xx
Team in Australia	1887-88	1889	3
and A. Shaw)	1886-87	1888	3.

Shrewsbury, A. (Junior) (Nottinghamshire)
Obituary	1918	2

Shrewsbury, W. (Nottinghamshire)
Obituary	1932/I	2.

Shuker, A. (Derbyshire)
Obituary	1910/I	1

Shuldham, W. F. Q. (Marlborough; Somerset)
Obituary	1972	10:

Shuter, J. (Kent; Surrey; England)
Captaincy note	1948	‹
Obituary	1921/I	2.
Views on High Scoring and L.B.W. Rule	1899	lxx
Views on 'The Follow On'	1894	xlv

Shuter, L. A. (Surrey)
Obituary	1929/I	2

Shuttleworth, K. (Lancashire; Leicestershire; England)
Photograph	1969	4

Shuttleworth, Lieut. K. C. (Forest School)
Obituary	1918	2

Sibbles, F. M. (Lancashire)
Benefit Match	1938	4
Obituary	1974	1C

Sickler, G. (Umpire)
Obituary	1965	9

Sidebotham, Lieut. J. F. (Shrewsbury)
Obituary	1917	2

'Sidelights on the Tests'
V. G. J. Jenkins	1948	

Sides, F. W. (Victoria; Queensland)
Obituary	1945	3

Sidley, 2nd Lieut. J. W. (Haileybury, Throwing the Cricket Ball Champion)
Obituary	1917	2

Sidney, T. S. (Writer)
Obituary	1918	2

Sidwell, T. E. (Leicestershire)
Benefit Match	1927/II	
Obituary	1959	3

Siedle, I. J. (Natal; South Africa)
Obituary	1983	1:

Siegle, C. R. A. (Dulwich)
Obituary   1909/I   *146*

Sievers, M. W. (Victoria; Australia)
Obituary   1969   *986*

Sievwright, R. W. (Aberdeenshire; Scotland)
Obituary   1948   *787*

Silcock, F. (Essex; United South of England XI)
Obituary   1898   *xliv*

Silcock, J. (Bishop's Stortford C.C.)
Obituary   1917   *265*

Sillitoe, Lt-Col. W. H. (Secretary Surrey)
Obituary   1981   *1149*

Sills, 2nd Lieut. C. C. (Oakham; Sandhurst)
Obituary   1915/I   *239*

Sim, A. C. (Marlborough)
Obituary   1919   *211*

Sime, His Hon. W. A. (Bedford School; Oxford University; Bedfordshire; Nottinghamshire)
Obituary   1984   *1208*

Simmons, G. T. W. (Journalist)
Obituary   1955   *936*

Simmons, J. (Lancashire; Tasmania)
Photographs   1972   *465*
    1977   *459*

Simms, H. L. (Sussex; Warwickshire)
Obituary   1943   *383*

Simonds, Col. J. (Treasurer Berkshire)
Obituary   1906   *xcix*

Simpkins, Capt. H. H. (King Edward's, Bath)
Obituary   1919   *189*

Simpson, 2nd Lieut. A. B. T. (Bedford Grammar School)
Obituary   1918   *217*

Simpson, E. P. (Wellington)
Obituary   1926/I   *283*

Simpson, E. T. B. (Oxford University; Yorkshire)
Obituary   1945   *340*

Simpson, G. A. (Kent)
Obituary   1958   *964*

Simpson, Capt. G. B. (Harrogate C.C.)
Obituary   1916   *205*

Simpson, Capt. H. B. (Wellingborough; Northamptonshire)
Obituary   1925/I   *280*

Simpson, R. B. (New South Wales; Western Australia; Australia)
Action Photograph   1965   *74*
Australians Debt to Note on   1965   *101*
'The Australians in England 1968'
Book Review   1969   *1033*

'Captain's Story' Book Review	1967	*1020*
Cricketer of the Year	1965	*81*
Photograph	1965	*80*
Tribute to A. T. W. Grout	1969	*981*
Simpson, R. T. (Nottingham High School; Nottinghamshire; Sind; England)		
Cricketer of the Year	1950	*83*
Notes on	1944	*173*
	1945	*64,181*
		199
'Nottinghamshire's Notable Part in the		
Growth of Cricket'	1967	*134*
Photographs	1950	*75*
	1951	*469*
	1952	*470*
	1953	*490*
	1954	*497*
	1960	*517*
Record of Service	1961	*652*
Simpson, W. F. (Middlesex)		
Obituary	1968	*1006*
Simpson-Hayward, G. H. T. (Malvern; Cambridge University; Worcestershire; England)		
Obituary	1937/I	*280*
Schools Note	1894	*lx*
Sims, Sir A. C. (New Zealand Representative to I.C.C.)		
Obituary	1970	*1026*
'84 Not out' A. Mitchell Book Review	1963	*1112*
Sims, J. M. (Middlesex; England)		
Benefit Matches	1947	*356*
	1951	*448*
Obituary	1974	*1079*
Simson, R. F. (Edinburgh Academy)		
Obituary	1915/I	*239*
Sinclair, Lieut. A. M. (Winchester)		
Obituary	1945	*325*
Sinclair, J. H. (London County ; Transvaal; South Africa)		
Fastest Hundred in Test Cricket Note on	1983	*107*
Obituary	1914/I	*194*
Sinclair, S. G. (Liverpool C.C.)		
Obituary	1914/I	*195*
Sincock, H. (South Australia)		
Obituary	1983	*1256*
Sinfield, R. A. (Gloucestershire; Hertfordshire; England)		
Benefit Match	1939	*362*
Singh, Lt.-Col. K. S. (Rugby; Cambridge University; Kent)		
Obituary	1981	*1149*
Single Wicket Competition 1964 Onwards		

Sinkins, Col. W. S. (Vice President Hampshire)
Obituary 1918 *234*
Six-A-Side Indoor Cricket Note on 1976 *66*
'Sixties, Cricket in the, and at the Present Day'
A. Lubbock 1909/I *109*
Skeet, C. H. L. (St.Paul's; Oxford University; Middlesex)
Obituary 1979 *1086*
Skelding, A. (Leicestershire; Umpire)
Benefit Match 1928/II *188*
Obituary 1961 *951*
Skimming, E. H. B. (Marlborough)
Obituary 1958 *964*
Skinner, A. F. (Leys; Suffolk; Cambridge University; Derby; Northamptonshire)
Obituary 1983 *1256*
Skinner, C. M. (Northumberland)
Obituary 1919 *211*
Skinner, H. (President South Melbourne C.C.)
Obituary 1913/I *198*
Skoltowe, 2nd Lieut. C. M. (Forest School)
Obituary 1918 *217*
Skoulding, 2nd Lieut. A. C. (Melton C.C.)
Obituary 1918 *204*
Skrimshire, Dr. J. F. (President Norfolk)
Obituary 1920/I *185*
Slack, J. (Queensland)
Obituary 1904 *lxxxv*
Slack, W. N. (Windward Islands; Middlesex)
Photograph 1982 *495*
Slade, D. N. F. (Worcestershire)
Photographs 1959 *591*
1961 *612*
1970 *594*
Slade, F. A. (Ardingly; Manhattan C.C.)
Obituary 1914/I *195*
Slatem, J. J. (Transvaal)
Obituary 1943 *387*
Slater, A. G. (Derbyshire)
Obituary 1950 *913*
Slater, Henry (Derbyshire)
Obituary 1917 *265*
Slater, Herbert (Derbyshire)
Obituary 1959 *937*
Slater, Air Marshall Sir L. H. (R.A.F.)
Obituary 1962 *992*

Slater, R. A. (Oratory School)

Schools Notes	1941	*223*
	1942	*245*
77 wkts Schools Averages	1941	*262*
80 wkts Schools Averages	1942	*310*

Slater, W. D. (Yeadon C.C.)

Obituary	1931/I	*266*

Slatter, S. (Steevie at Lord's)

Obituary	1872	*71*

Slatter, S. C. (Cross Arrows C.C.)

Obituary	1914/I	*195*

Slatter, W. H. (Clerk of Works at Lord's)

Obituary	1930/I	*263*

Slight, J. (Victoria; Australia)

Obituary	1931/I	*266*

Slingsby, J. W. (Abingdon School)

Schools Note	1979	*836*
1003 runs Schools Averages	1979	*839*

Sloan, Major F. A. (Hon. Sec. Army Cricket Association)

Obituary	1952	*961*

Sloane-Stanley, Capt. H. H. (Haileybury)

Obituary	1919	*189*

Slocock, 2nd Lieut. L. A. N. (Marlborough)

Obituary	1918	*217*

Slocombe, P. A. (Millfield School; Somerset)

Photograph	1976	*537*

Slossom, Capt. J. S. (Staten Island C.C.)

Obituary	1920/I	*158*

Slough v London Counties 1940

Team Portraits	1941	*27*

Slow Scoring Note on

	1954	*83*

Smailes, T. F. (Yorkshire; England)

Benefit Match	1949	*570*
Obituary	1971	*1029*

Smales, K. (Nottinghamshire; Yorkshire)

Photograph	1957	*496*

Small, J. A. (Trinidad; West Indies)

Obituary	1959	*937*

Smart, C. C. (Glamorgan; Warwickshire)

Obituary	1976	*1102*

Smart, J. A. (Warwickshire; Umpire)

Obituary	1980	*1156*

Smedley, M. J. (Nottinghamshire)

Benefit Match	1976	*733*

Photographs	1966	*517*
	1968	*533*
	1973	*502*
	1975	*517*
Smeeth, 2nd Lieut. W. S. (Loretto)		
Obituary	1918	*204*
Smethurst, 2nd Lieut. J. (Oxton C.C.)		
Obituary	1917	*213*
Smith, A. (Lancashire; Derbyshire)		
Obituary	1910/I	*152*
Smith, A. (Sussex)		
Obituary	1924/I	*269*
Smith, A. C. (King Edward's, Birmingham; Oxford University; Warwickshire; England)		
Photographs	1963	*631*
	1966	*587*
	1968	*602*
	1969	*57*
	1970	*576*
Smith, A. E. (South Australia)		
Obituary	1984	*1209*
Smith, A. F. (Yorkshire; Umpire)		
Obituary	1916	*205*
Smith, A. F. (Wellington; Cambridge University; Middlesex)		
Obituary	1937/I	*281*
Smith, Sir A. L. (President M.C.C.)		
Obituary	1902	*lxx*
Smith, A. R. (Lucas C.C., Jamaica)		
Obituary	1908/I	*152*
Smith, A. R. (Loretto)		
Obituary	1927/I	*289*
Smith, B. C. (Northamptonshire; Umpire)		
Obituary	1943	*383*
Smith, C. (Lancashire; Yorkshire)		
Benefit Match	1904	*75*
Obituary	1926/I	*283*
Smith, C. (Sussex)		
Obituary	1910/I	*147*
Smith, Sir C. A. (Charterhouse; Cambridge University; Sussex; Transvaal; Hollywood C.C.; England)		
Obituary	1949	*870*
'Sir Aubrey' D. Rayvern Allen Book Review	1983	*1310*
Smith, C. E. (Rossall)		
Obituary	1918	*234*
Smith, C. I. J. (Wiltshire; Middlesex; England)		
Obituary	1980	*1156*

Portrait and Biography	1935/I	*288*
Smith, C. J. (Cambridgeshire)		
Obituary	1960	*956*
Smith, C. J. (Harrow; Middlesex)		
Obituary	1931/I	*267*
Smith, C. J. E. (Transvaal; South Africa)		
Obituary	1948	*788*
Smith, C. L. (Glamorgan; Natal; Hampshire; England)		
Cricketer of the Year	1984	*63*
Photographs	1981	*431*
	1984	*Plate*
Smith, C. L. A. (Sussex)		
Obituary	1950	*914*
Smith, C. M. (Eton)		
Obituary	1928/I	*299*
Smith, C. R. (Secretary New Zealand Cricket Council)		
Obituary	1921/I	*237*
Smith, D. (Derbyshire; England)		
Career Figures	1980	*1157*
Obituary	1980	*1156*
Portrait and Biography	1936/I	*299*
Smith, D. (Somerset; Worcestershire; Glamorgan)		
Obituary	1950	*914*
Smith, Capt. D. G. (Sherborne)		
Obituary	1917	*213*
Smith, D. H. K. (Derbyshire; Orange Free State)		
Photograph	1970	*358*
Smith, D. M. (Surrey; Worcestershire)		
Photograph	1980	*555*
Smith, D. R. (Gloucestershire; England)		
Benefit Match	1969	*418*
Photographs	1958	*363*
	1961	*392*
	1966	*398*
Smith, D. V. (Sussex; England)		
Career Record	1963	*1042*
Photographs	1956	*568*
	1957	*556*
Smith, E. (Derbyshire)		
Photographs	1963	*375*
	1969	*349*
Smith, E. (Clifton; Oxford University; Yorkshire)		
Obituary	1946	*445*
Views on Throwing	1895	*lv*
Smith, E. (Yorkshire)		
Obituary	1973	*1013*

Smith, E. F. (President Club Cricket Conference; Buckinghamshire)
  Obituary 1983 *1257*
Smith, E. J. ('Tiger') (Warwickshire; England)
  Benefit Match 1923/II *274*
  Career Figures 1980 *101*
  Photographs 1980 *97*
                     100

  'E. J. (Tiger) Smith'
  Obituary R. Ryder 1980 *96*
  'Tiger Smith of Warwickshire and England'
  Book Review 1982 *1270*
Smith, Sir E. T. (President South Australian Cricket Association)
  Obituary 1921/I *244*
Smith, F. (Yorkshire)
  Obituary 1906 *c*
Smith, F. E. (London County; Surrey)
  Obituary 1944 *322*
Smith, F. E. (Waitaki)
  Obituary 1943 *367*
Smith, F. G. (President Melbourne C.C.)
  Obituary 1901 *lxiii*
Smith, Rev. G. H. (Staffordshire; Northamptonshire)
  Obituary 1928/I *299*
Smith, G. J. (Essex)
  Photograph 1962 *372*
Smith, Canon Rev. G. M. (Tonbridge)
  Obituary 1918 *234*
Smith, G. O. (Charterhouse; Oxford University; Surrey; Hertfordshire)
  Obituary 1944 *322*
Smith, H. (Gloucestershire; England)
  Benefit Match 1929/II *206*
  Obituary 1938 *945*
Smith, H. A. (Leicestershire)
  Benefit Match 1940 *374*
  Obituary 1950 *916*
Smith, H. C. (Tasmania)
  Obituaries 1978 *1082*
              1979 *1087*
Smith, I. S. (Winchester)
  Obituary 1973 *1013*
Smith, J. (Yorkshire; Worcestershire)
  Obituary 1910/I *147*
Smith, J. (Derbyshire)
  Obituary 1899 *l*
Smith, J. H. (Repton)
  Obituary 1924/I *269*

Smith, J. J. (Scorer Gloucestershire)

Obituary	1900	*liii*

Smith, K. D. (Warwickshire)

Photograph	1977	*588*

Smith, L. (Writer)

'The Throwing Controversy'	1961	*111*

Smith, L. A. (Middlesex; Northamptonshire)

Obituary	1980	*1161*

Smith, L. D. (Otago; South Island)

Obituary	1980	*1161*

Smith, M. J. (Middlesex)

Photographs	1968	*500*
	1970	*481*
	1973	*474*
	1975	*487*

Smith, M. J. K. (Stamford School; Oxford University; Leicestershire; Warwickshire; England)

Captaincy – Takes Over Note on	1965	*103*
Career Figures	1976	*114*
Cricketer of the Year	1960	*107*
Photographs	1958	*587*
	1960	*85*
	1962	*622*
	1964	*585*
	1971	*546*
Retirement Note	1968	*94*
Schools Notes	1949	*688*
	1951	*722*
	1952	*696*
'M. J. K. Smith Lays Down his Bat' J. Woodcock	1976	*111*
'M. J. K. Smith Leaves the Field Photograph	1976	*113*
3245 Runs in Season	1960	*251*

Smith, M. W. (Tonbridge; Kent)

Obituary	1976	*1103*

Smith, N. (Essex; Yorkshire)

Photographs	1977	*379*
	1980	*379*

Smith, O. G. ('Collie') (Jamaica; West Indies)

Cricketer of the Year	1958	*60*
Obituary	1960	*956*
Photograph	1958	*55*

Smith, P. (Writer)

'England v West Indies' Book Review	1982	*1266*

Smith, R. (Essex)

Benefit Match	1952	*323*
Photographs	1951	*305*
	1953	*316*
	1954	*323*

Smith, Lieut. R. E. (Edinburgh Academy)

Obituary	1919	*189*

Smith R. P. (Also known as **Stevens**) (Derbyshire)

Obituary	1900	*li*

Smith, S. (South Australian Board of Control; Manager Australians in England 1921, 1926)

Obituary	1973	*1013*

'Rothmans Test Cricket Almanacks

Book Reviews	1962	*1036*
	1963	*1114*
	1964	*1006*

Smith, S. G. (Trinidad; Auckland; Northamptonshire; West Indies)

Obituary	1964	*952*
Portrait and Biography	1915/I	*204*

Smith, Capt. S. P. (Walsall C.C.)

Obituary	1918	*204*

Smith, T. (Secretary Umpire's Association)

Retirement Note	1979	*82*
'Umpiring'	1960	*103*

Smith, T. (Massachusetts State League Cricket; U.S.A.)

Obituary	1920/I	*185*

Smith, T. (Nottinghamshire Colts)

Obituary	1915/I	*239*

Smith, T. P. B. (Essex; England)

Benefit Match	1948	*295*
Cricketer of the Year	1947	*50*
Obituary	1968	*1007*
Photograph	1947	*43*

Smith, W. (London County; Oxfordshire)

Obituary	1943	*383*

Smith, Alderman W. (Sussex Committee)

Obituary	1911/I	*157*

Smith, W. A. (Surrey)

Photograph	1968	*566*

Smith, W. B. (British Guiana Club Cricketer)

Obituary	1921/I	*237*

Smith, W. C. (Surrey)

Benefit Match	1913/II	*211*
Obituary	1947	*695*
Portrait and Biography	1911/I	*169*

Smith, W. G. (Whitgift Grammar School)

Schools Note	1899	*lxxxvi*

91 wkts Schools Averages	1899	*371*
Smith, 2nd Lieut. W. R. S. (Shrewsbury)		
Obituary	1919	*200*
Smith, 2nd Lieut. W. W. (Rugby)		
Obituary	1917	*213*
Smith-Masters, Capt. B. S. (Military Cricket)		
Obituary	1917	*213*
Smith-Masters, W. A. (Kent)		
Obituary	1938	*945*
Smithers, E. A. (Treasurer Sussex)		
Obituary	1915/I	*239*
Smithson, F. (Manager American Cricket Grounds)		
Obituary	1909/I	*146*
Smithson, G. A. (Hertfordshire; Leicestershire; Yorkshire; England)		
Obituary	1971	*103(*
Photograph	1948	*3{*
Smithson, S. (Yorkshire Club Cricketer)		
Obituary	1913/I	*203*
Smoker, G. (Hampshire; Cheshire)		
Obituary	1971	*103*
Smyth, Capt. A. B. (Aldershot Command)		
Obituary	1916	*22*
Smythe, G. E. (Charterhouse)		
Obituary	1902	*lxxiv*
Snaith, J. C. (Nottinghamshire)		
Obituary	1937/I	*281*
Snake on Pitch	1968	*347*
Snedden, A. N. C. (Auckland)		
Obituary	1970	*1028*
Snell, A. P. (Haileybury; Essex)		
Obituary	1938	*945*
Snell, Lieut. C. (Mill Hill School)		
Obituary	1917	*213*
Snell, C. A. (Oundle)		
Obituary	1923/I	*305*
Snell, E. (Winchester; Sussex)		
Obituary	1974	*1080*
Snell, H. S. (Wiltshire)		
Obituary	1943	*383*
Snell, 2nd Lieut. P. S. (Campbell College, Belfast)		
Obituary	1916	*205*
Snooke, S. D. (Western Province; South Africa)		
Obituary	1961	*953*
Snow Prevents Play at Buxton Photograph	1976	*4(*

```
1968
1973
1964
1969                            1054                1950        973
1971                              95                1978       1118
1972                              72                1978        151
1968                             534
968                               68                1918        204
977                              529
                                  88  Warwickshire; England)   1981       1149
         7                        87                1973         73
                                1100                1977       1100
                                                    1966        569
            106                                     1973         72
            133
                                                    1974        123
      61    ricket Association)
     108    ds'                                   1932/I        251
    1082    a; Jamaica)
     145    ; Kent)                                 1965        971

     398    ng's School, Peterborough; Northamptonshire)
                                                    1982       1209
     992
     274    H. J. (Rugby; Oxford University)
                                                    1918        205
            (Merchant Taylors, Crosby; Cambridge University)
            Note                                    1972        839
      42    ns Schools Averages                     1972        867
        , Major A. (Umpire)
        ituary                                      1916        205
```

mes, W. A. (Brighton College; Sussex)
  Obituary   1917   265

oar, T. (Camarthenshire; Hampshire)
  Benefit Match   1901   261

obers, Sir G. St.A. (Barbados; Nottinghamshire; South Australia; West Indies)

Action Photograph	1967	127,129,131
Benefit Match	1973	694
Big Prize Note on	1968	88
Café Royal Centenary Trophy	1969	655
Career Figures in Test Cricket	1975	110
'Cricket Crusader' Book Review	1967	1020
Cricketer of the Year	1964	73
with J.S. Barker 'Cricket in the Sun'		
Book Review	1968	1046
Double Wicket Trophy Triumph	1970	946
Highest Test Score	1959	80

'King Cricket' Book Review
Note on
Photographs

Sheffield Shield Feats
Signs for Nottinghamshire
'Sir Gary' T. Bailey Book Review 1
'Sir Garfield Sobers – Cricket's Most Versatile Performer'
J. Arlott 197
Sobers in Test Cricket – Statistics 196
With the Wisden Trophy
   Photographs 1967
                    1975
Solan, J. M. (Journalist)
   Obituary 1978
   'Through the Crystal Ball' 1963
Solanky, J. W. (Devon; Glamorgan; East Africa)
   Photograph 1974
Solbé, E. P. (Tonbridge; Kent)
   Obituary 1962
Solbé, F. de L. (Dulwich; Blair Lodge School; Kent)
   Obituary 1934/I
'Some Current Topics, Special Articles on' 1897
'Some Dates in the History of Cricket'
   H. S. Altham 1941
                  ad passim
'Some Questions of the Day' 1890
Somers-Cocks, A. (Barbados)
   Obituary 1924/I 26
Somers-Cox, Capt. R. (Agricultural College, Aspatria)
   Obituary 1919 189
Somerset, A. W. F. (Wellington; Somerset)
   Obituary 1938 945
Somerset County Cricket Club
   in Bermuda 1974 1975 929
   County Badge 1950 476
                  ad passim
   'Sixty Years of Somerset Cricket' R. Roberts
   Book Review 1953 999
   'Somersetshire Cricketers 1875-1974'
   Association of Cricket Statisticans
   Book Review 1976 1140
   Somerset Share: Note on 1980 87

Somerset's Test Match Contribution

Photograph		1981	72
'The Story of Somerset' E. Hill		1959	99
Team Portraits	1974	1975	536
	1975	1976	540
	1976	1977	540
	1977	1978	524
	1978	1979	516
	1979	1980	539
	1980	1981	537
	1981	1982	543
	1982	1983	559
	1983	1984	509
Triumphant at Last Note on		1980	83

Somerset, Lieut. F. A. (Southgate C.C.; Littlehampton C.C.)

Obituary	1917	214

Somervell, R. C. (Auckland)

Obituary	1968	1007

Sommers, Lt-Col. Lord (Charterhouse; Worcestershire; President M.C.C.)

Obituary	1945	340

Sondes, 2nd Earl – Lord Throwley (Eton; Kent)

Obituary	1908/I	152

Sorrie, J. W. (Scotland)

Obituary	1956	977

Sothern-Estcourt, Fl/Sgt. E. G. A. (Harrow)

Obituary	1945	326

Souter, Capt. I. M. (Haileybury)

Obituary	1943	367

Souter, V. J. (Victoria)

Obituary	1916	206

South Africa

in Australia	1910-11	1912/II	500
and New Zealand	1931-32	1933/II	642
and New Zealand	1952-53	1954	790
'Bumper' K. R. Miller and R. S. Whitington			
Book Review		1954	976
'Caught by the Springboks' J. Cheetham			
Book Review		1955	990
'The South Africans in Australia 1952-53'			
A. G. Moyes Book Review		1954	981
and New Zealand	1963-64	1965	818
'Bradman, Benaud and Goddard's Cinderellas'			
R. S. Whitington Book Review		1965	1018

in England	1894	1895	*335*
	1901	1902	*466*
	1904	1905	*328*
	1907	1908/II	*1*
	1912	1913/II	*63*
	1924	1925/II	*1*
'And Gilligan Led them Out' R. Ryder		1970	*124*
	1929	1930/II	*1*
	1935	1936/II	*1*
	1947	1948	*182*
Team Portrait	1947	1948	*36*
	1951	1952	*209*
Team Portrait	1951	1952	*67*
1951 Action Photograph		1952	*70*
'Noursemen in England' C. O. Medworth Book Review		1953	*996*
	1955	1956	*220*
Team Portrait	1955	1956	*47*
Action Photograph	1955	1956	*50*
'South Africa offers Serious Challenge' Sir N. Cardus		1955	*88*
'Behind the South African Tests' N. Cutter Book Review		1956	*1028*
'England v South Africa' B. Harris Book Review		1956	*1028*
'I Declare' J. Cheetham Book Review		1957	*995*
	1960	1961	*264*
Team Portrait	1960	1961	*86*
Welcome – Note on	1960	1960	*124*
'Cricketers from South Africa' G. Ross Book Review		1961	*992*
'Cricket Overthrown' C. Fortune Book Review		1961	*994*
'Cricket on Trial' J. Arlott Book Review		1961	*1006*
'Perchance to Bowl' J. Waite Book Review		1962	*1042*
	1965	1966	*298*
Team Portrait	1965	1966	*55*
Team Chosen	1970	1971	*41*
'South African Tour Dispute 1970' I. Rosenwater		1971	*128*
'The Cricket Conspiracy' D. Humphrey Book Review		1976	*1138*
in New Zealand			
and Australia	1931-32	1933/II	*642*
and Australia	1952-53	1954	*790*
and Australia	1963-64	1965	*818*
'Bradman, Benaud and Goddard's Cinderellas'			

R. S. Whitington Book Review		1965	*1018*
South African Fezela in England	1961	1962	*727*
Non-White Team in East Africa	1958	1960	*895*
Schools in England	1963	1964	*795*
	1967	1968	*822*
Universities in England	1967	1968	*711*

Chronological List of Articles and Notes:

'South African Bowling' R. E. Foster		1908/I	*106*
England v South Africa:			
A Survey of 34 matches F. Ashley-Cooper		1924/I	*219*
'South Africa and England'			
R. C. Robertson-Glasgow		1947	*55*
'Ups and Downs on the Veld' (with statistics of England v South Africa)			
L. Duffus		1951	*104*
'South Africa Offers Serious Challenge'			
Sir N. Cardus		1955	*88*
South African Status Note on		1962	*117*
South Africa's Responsibility Note on		1970	*78*
'And Gilligan led them out' R. Ryder		1970	*124*
'Ups and Downs of the Springboks'			
M. Melford		1970	*147*
'Notable Dates in South African Cricket History'			
R. Bowen		1970	*153*
'South African Tour Dispute'			
I. Rosenwater		1971	*128*
Dark Coloured players in Note on		1974	*72*
Move for Normal Cricket Note on		1976	*66*
South African Dilemma Note on		1983	*79*
Views of Prime Minister on South African Tour			
Note on		1983	*80*
'South Africa: Progress Towards Non-Racial Cricket'			
G. Johnson		1983	*104*
South African Repercussions Note on		1984	*51*
M.C.C. and South Africa' M. Engel		1984	*65*
South African Tour Petition Photograph		1984	*66*

outhall, E. (Buckinghamshire)

Obituary		1924/I	*276*

outham, Major G. H. (Upper Canada College; Toronto Zingari)

Obituary		1917	*214*

outh America

in England	1932	1933/II	*508*

See also under Individual Countries

outhampton Plan of County Ground

		1950	*358*
		ad passim	

509

Southend Southchurch Park
  Plan of County Ground   1950   307
                                     ad passim

Southern, Lieut. G. C. (Clifton)
  Obituary   1916   206
Southern, Comdr. J. D. (Malvern; Derbyshire)
  Obituary   1973   1013
Southern, J. W. (Hampshire)
  Career Figures   1984   1250
  Photograph   1977   426
Southerton, J. (Surrey; Hampshire; Sussex; England)
  Biography   1878   153
Southerton, S. J. (Editor Wisden 1934-35)
  On Bowling Controversy   1934/I   332
  Special Memoir of (Obituary)   1936/I   27
  Tributes to   1936/I   29
Southerton, W. (Surrey Colts)
  Obituary   1920/I   185
Southwark, 1st Lord (Vice President Surrey)
  Obituary   1930/I   26
Southwell, Capt. F. E. G. (Bedford County School)
  Obituary   1918   20
Sowden, A. (Yorkshire)
  Obituary   1922/I   26
Sowter, U. (Derbyshire)
  Obituary   1911/I   15
Soyza, D. S. (Umpire in Ceylon)
  Obituary   1964   95
Spalding, A. F. M. (Old Stagers)
  Obituary   1912/I   18
Spalding, A. G. (Chicago C.C.)
  Obituary   1916   20
Sparkes, J. B. (Sunderland C.C.)
  Obituary   1933/I   26
Sparks, C. J. (President Cheshire C.C.C.)
  Obituary   1971   1034
Sparrow, H. (Warwickshire; Worcestershire)
  Obituary   1920/I   18
Spearing, S. M. H. (Cheshire; British Empire XI)
  Obituary   1945   32
Specialists Too Many Note on   1952   1
Spedding, Lieut. E. C. (Otago High School)
  Obituary   1917   24
Speed, Major F. E. (Rugby; Herefordshire)
  Obituary   1929/I   25

Spence, Major F. R. (Ridley College, Ontario)
    Obituary   1919   *200*
Spencer, C. T. (Leicestershire)
    Photographs   1960   *464*
                                      1965   *472*
Spencer, 5th Earl of – J. P. Spencer (President Northamptonshire and M.C.C.)
    Obituary   1911/I   *157*
Spencer, G. A. (President Nottinghamshire)
    Obituary   1958   *964*
Spencer, J. (Brighton and Hove Grammar School; Cambridge University; Wiltshire; Sussex)
    Photographs   1974   *553*
                                      1978   *554*
Spencer, R. (Harrow; Cambridge University; Northumberland)
    Obituary   1927/I   *289*
Spencer, R. S. (Hertfordshire)
    Obituary   1906   *c*
Spencer, S. B. (Parsees)
    Obituary   1907   *cxv*
Spencer-Parker, R. (Stragglers of Rhodesia)
    Obituary   1982   *1210*
Spencer-Smith, Rev. C. S. (Eton)
    Obituary   1912/I   *180*
Spencer-Smith, Capt. G. J. (Eton)
    Obituary   1929/I   *258*
Spencer-Smith, Rev. O. (Eton; Oxford University; Hampshire)
    Obituary   1921/I   *237*
Spens, Major-Gen. J. (Haileybury; Hampshire)
    Obituary   1935/I   *272*
Spens, Major L. T. (Rugby; Sandhurst)
    Obituary   1922/I   *269*
Spicer, N. (Leys School; Cambridge University)
    Obituary   1937/I   *281*
Spicer, P. A. (Essex)
    Obituary   1970   *1026*
Spiers, F. W. (Restauranteer)
    Obituary   1912/I   *180*
Spiller, W. J. (Glamorgan)
    Obituary   1971   *1030*
Spillman, G. (Middlesex)
    Obituary   1912/I   *180*
'Spin Bowling' A. P. E. Freeman   1938   *41*
Spink, Lieut. E. M. (St.Bees)
    Obituary   1919   *189*
Spinners, Notes on   1975   *100*
                                      1983   *84*

Spirit of Cricket Note on   1972   84

Spiro, D. G. (Harrow; Cambridge University)
    Obituary   1936/I   288

Spofforth, F. R. (New South Wales; Victoria; Derbyshire; Australia)
    Obituary   1927/I   289
    'Schoolboys' Bowling'   1904   *lxvi*
    Recollections of (Harris; Darnley; Thornton)   1927/I   302
    Views on 'Throwing' and 'The Follow on'   1898   *lvii*

Spong, A. J. (Club Cricket Conference)
    Obituary   1961   951

Sponsorship Notes on   1972   84
    1973   89
    1981   92
    1982   89

Sponsorship Women Note on   1983   1194

Spooner, A. F. (Haileybury; Lancashire)
    Obituary   1966   972

Spooner, Brig-Gen. A. H. (Haileybury; Lancashire)
    Obituary   1946   445

Spooner, Sgt. J. (Galt C.C., Ontario)
    Obituary   1917   226

Spooner, R. H. (Marlborough; Lancashire; England)
    Obituary   1962   992
    Portrait and Biography   1905   *cix*
    Schools Notes   1898   *lxi*
    1899   *lxxxi*
    1900   *lxxviii,*
    lxxix,
    lxxxii

Spooner, R. T. (Durham; Warwickshire; England)
    Benefit Match   1958   603
    Photograph   1952   544

Spottiswoode, C. A. (Old Stagers)
    Obituary   1916   200

Spottiswoode, W. H. (Kent)
    Obituary   1916   200

Spragg, A. S. (North Brisbane C.C.)
    Obituary   1905   c

Spragge, Dr. E. W. (Toronto C.C.)
    Obituary   1921/I   24

Spring, Major T. C. (Devon; Somerset; Northumberland)
    Obituary   1927/I   29

Springall, J. D. (Nottinghamshire)
    Photograph   1961   51

'Springboks, Ups and Downs of ' M. Melford   1970   14

512

Sprot, E. M. (Harrow; Hampshire)
　Obituary 1946 *445*
Sprot, H. M. (Eton)
　Obituary 1973 *1014*
Spry, E. (Gloucestershire)
　Obituary 1959 *938*
Spry, J. (Groundsman Gloucestershire)
　Obituary 1926/I *283*
Spurway, Lieut. A. P. (Osbourne; Dartmouth Naval Colleges)
　Obituary 1916 *206*
Spurway, Rev. E. B. C. (Supporter Somerset)
　Obituary 1908/I *153*
Spurway, Rev. E. P. (Wellington C.C.; Somerset)
　Obituary 1915/I *239*
Spurway, Capt. R. P. (Somerset)
　Obituary 1899 *1*
Squire, A. P.
Squire, H. F. (Writers)
'Pre Victorian Sussex Cricket' Book Review 1952 *1016*
Squires, H. S. (Surrey)
　Benefit Match 1949 *505*
　Obituary 1951 *927*
Sri Lanka (Ceylon)
　in Australia and New Zealand 1982-83 1984 *942*
　in Bangladesh 1978 1979 *1036*
　in England (Cancelled) 1968 1969 *921*
　World Cup 1975 1976 *300*
　Team Portrait 1975 1976 *305*
　World Cup 1979 1980 *297*
　　　 1979 1980 *318*
　　　 1981 1982 *339*
　World Cup 1983 1984 *293*
　in India 1932-33 1934/II *695*
　　　 1964-65 1966 *852*
　　　 1975-76 1977 *928*
　　　 1982-83 1984 *918*
　U25 in India 1980-81 1982 *1139*
　in Pakistan 1966 1967 *895*
　　　 1974 1975 *972*
　U19 in Pakistan 1976 1977 *986*
　　　 1981-82 1983 *1015*
　in Singapore and Malaya 1958 1959 *863*
　Arora (Rebels) in South Africa 1982-83 1984 *1051*
　Schoolboys in Western Australia 1959 1961 *891*
　Ceylon take the I.C.C. Trophy: Photograph 1980 *61*
　Test Status Note on 1982 *88*
　World Cup Team Team Portrait 1975 1976 *305*

Stacey, F. H. (President Durban Cricket Association)
    Obituary   1962   *992*

Stackpole, K. R. (Victoria; Australia)
    Cricketer of the Year   1973   *79*
    Photograph   1973   *71*

Stafford, Capt. T. C. (Sutton C.C.)
    Obituary   1917   *214*

Staggerers of South Africa in England 1970   1971   *847*

Stainton, J. H. (Journalist)
    Obituary   1933/I   *258*

Stallybrass, Dr. W. T. S. (Hon. Treasurer Oxford University C.C.)
    Obituary   1949   *870*

Stamps Photograph of   1984   *73*

Stanborough, W. F. H. (Charterhouse; Cambridge University)
    Obituary   1952   *966*

Stanbrough, M. H. (Charterhouse)
    Obituary   1906   *cii*

Stancomb, Capt. A. J. G. (Wiltshire)
    Obituary   1939   *918*

Stancomb, F. W. (Harrow; Wiltshire)
    Obituary   1937/I   *28*

Standen, J. A. (Worcestershire)
    Photograph   1965   *60*

Standen, Lieut. L. J. D. (St.Edward's, Oxford)
    Obituary   1917   *214*

Stange, Capt. G. N. (King's College School)
    Obituary   1919   *188*

Stanger-Leathes, C. F. (Sherborne; Northumberland)
    Obituary   1967   *97*

Stanhope, Hon. H. E. (Harrow)
    Obituary   1895   *xli*

Stanley, E. J. (Committee Somerset)
    Obituary   1908/I   *15*

Stanley, H. T. (Somerset)
    Obituary   1901   *lxi*

Stanley, Lt-Col. K. B. (Hon. Secretary Free Foresters)
    'Centenary of Free Foresters'   1956   *12*
    Obituary   1969   *98*

Stanley-Clarke, Brig. A. C. L. (Winchester; Army)
    Obituary   1984   *120*

Stannard, G. (Sussex)
    Obituary   1973   *101*

Stanning, H. D. (Rugby)
    Obituary   1947   *69*

Stanning, J. (Rugby; Leyland C.C.)
    Obituary   1905   *c*

Stanning, J. (Junior) (Rugby; Cambridge University; Lancashire; Cheshire)
Obituary	1930/I	*263*

Stanton, H. V. L. (Journalist)
Obituary	1934/I	*274*

Stanton, J. L. (Marlborough; Gloucestershire)
Obituary	1974	*1080*

Stanyforth, Lt.-Col. R. T. (Eton; Yorkshire; England)
Obituary	1965	*971*

Staples, A. (Nottinghamshire)
Benefit Match	1938	*473*
Obituary	1966	*972*

Staples, S. J. (Nottinghamshire; England)
Benefit Match	1933/II	*175*
Obituary	1951	*928*
Portrait and Biography	1929/I	*272*

Stapleton, L. (Writer)
'A Sussex Cricket Odyssey' Book Review	1980	*1212*

'Stars of the Tests' E. M. Wellings | 1963 | *115*

Statham, J. B. (Lancashire; England)
Awarded C.B.E. Action Photograph	1966	*57*
Career Figures	1969	*118*
Cricketer of the Year	1955	*69*
'Cricket Merry Go-Round' Book Review	1957	*1000*
'Flying Bails' Book Review	1962	*1042*
Photographs	1952	*400*
	1955	*68*
	1956	*423*
	1958	*423*
	1962	*136*
	1967	*459*
	1969	*115*
'A Spell at the Top' Book Review	1970	*1068*
'J. B. Statham – Gentleman George'		
Sir N. Cardus	1969	*114*
'Statham and Trueman: An Appreciation'		
J. M. Kilburn	1962	*134*

Status of Matches in the U.K. | 1972 | *595*

Staunton, Rev. H. (Nottinghamshire)
Obituary	1919	*189*

Stead, B. (Nottinghamshire; Yorkshire; Northern Transvaal; Essex)
Benefit Match	1977	*750*
Photograph	1973	*502*
Obituary	1981	*1150*

Steadman, Rev. H. C. P. (Cambridge University; Bedfordshire; Leicestershire)
Obituary	1906	*ciii*

Steadman, R. K. (Trinity School, Croydon)
Schools Note	1980	*868*

1084 runs Schools Averages 1980 925

Stedman, F. (Surrey)
    Obituary 1919 *211*

Steel, A. G. (Marlborough; Cambridge University; President M.C.C.; Lancashire; England)
    'Cambridge Memories' 1891 *xxxvii*
    Obituary 1915/I *240*
    'Personal Recollections of W. G. Grace' 1896 *liii*
    Suggested Reforms 1900 *lxvii*
    Tribute by Hon. R. H. Lyttelton 1915/I *171*
    Views on the Reforms of 1889 1890 *xxxviii*
    Views on Some Questions of the Day 1890 *xli*

Steel, Lieut. A. I. (Eton; Middlesex; Calcutta C.C.)
    Obituary 1918 *205*

Steel, A. J. (Shrewbury)
    Obituary 1928/I *299*

Steel, D. Q. (Uppingham; Cambridge University; Lancashire)
    Obituary 1934/I *275*

Steel, E. E. (Marlborough; Lancashire)
    Obituary 1942 *363*

Steel, H. B. (Repton; Lancashire)
    Obituary 1912/I *181*

Steel, J. (Fettes; Cumberland)
    Obituary 1934/I *275*

Steele, D. A. (Hampshire)
    Obituary 1936/I *288*

Steele, D. S. (Northamptonshire; Derbyshire; Leicestershire; Staffordshire; England)
    'Come in Number 3' Book Review 1978 *1126*
    Cricketer of the Year 1976 *47*
    Photographs 1973 *488*
     1976 *46*
     1980 *365*
    To the Rescue Note on 1976 *61*

Steele, F. (Middlesex)
    Obituary 1916 *207*

Steele, J. F. (Leicestershire; Glamorgan; Natal)
    Photographs 1972 *481*
     1976 *473*
     1981 *475*

Stein, C. A. (Secretary Surrey)
    Obituary 1910/I *148*

Stein, Corp. C. D. P. (Lynn Valley C.C., British Columbia)
    Obituary 1918 *217*

Stenhouse, Major H. W. (Military Cricket)
    Obituary 1917 *214*

Stephen, J. C. (Harrow)
    Obituary   1925/I   *280*
Stephen, Sir M. H. (Treasurer New South Wales Cricket Association)
    Obituary   1921/I   *238*
Stephen, N. K. (Fettes; Cambridge University)
    Obituary   1949   *870*
Stephen, W. W. (Trustee Sydney Cricket Ground)
    Obituary   1905   *cv*
Stephens, B. J. B. (Winchester)
    Obituary   1951   *928*
Stephens, F. G. (Rossall; Warwickshire)
    Obituary   1971   *1030*
Stephens, R. T. (Queensland Cricket Association)
    Obituary   1953   *950*
Stephenson, Lieut. C. E. S. (New York Club Cricketer)
    Obituary   1918   *217*
Stephenson, Major D. C. (Suffolk Club Cricketer)
    Obituary   1919   *189*
Stephenson, E. (Yorkshire)
    Obituary   1900   *lv*
Stephenson, E. K. (Norfolk)
    Obituary   1970   *1026*
Stephenson, G. R. (Hampshire; Derbyshire)
    Photographs   1972   *431*
     1975   *426*
     1979   *405*
Stephenson, H. H. (Surrey; All England XI)
    Benefit Match   1872   *95*
    Biography   1871   *91*
    Obituary   1897   *xlii*
    Views on the Reforms of 1889   *1890*   *xxxviii*
    Views on Some Questions of the Day   1890   *xlii*
Stephenson, H. W. (Somerset)
    Benefit Match   1958   *540*
    Photographs   1954   *518*
     1955   *490*
     1960   *535*
     1963   *574*
Stephenson, J. S. (Shrewbury; Oxford University; Yorkshire)
    Obituary   1976   *1103*
Stephenson, Lieut.-Col. J. W. A. (Buckinghamshire; Essex; Worcestershire)
    Obituary   1983   *1257*
    Team v British Empire XI Team Portrait   1941   *26*
Stephenson, Rev. T. W. (Cumberland)
    Obituary   1937/I   *282*

Sterling, 2nd Lieut. J. L. (Sedbergh; Glasgow Academy)
Obituary 1916 *207*
Stevens, G. (Norfolk)
Obituary 1958 *965*
Stevens, G. A. (Norfolk)
Obituary 1964 *952*
Stevens, G. T. S. (University College School; Oxford University; Middlesex; England)
Obituary 1971 *1030*
Photograph 1918 *150*
Public School Bowler of the Year 1918 *152*
Schools Note 1917 *152*
 1918 *152*
 1919 *154*
 1920/I *259*
Stevens, Canon Rev. H. B. (Tonbridge)
Obituary 1925/I *280*
Stevens, J. E. (Sherborne; Wiltshire)
Obituary 1924/I *270*
Stevens, L. C. (President Eastbourne C.C.)
Memorial Match 1970 *768*
Obituary 1969 *987*
Stevens, Major N. W. (Norfolk)
Obituary 1920/I *186*
Stevenson, G. B. (Yorkshire; England)
Photograph 1978 *602*
Stevenson, H. J. (Edingburgh Academy)
Obituary 1946 *446*
Stevenson, K. (Hampshire; Derbyshire)
Photograph 1980 *426*
Stevenson, L. E. (St. Peter's, York)
Obituary 1932/I *251*
Stevenson, M. (Writer; Rydal; Cambridge University; Derbyshire)
'Yorkshire' Book Review 1973 *1052*
Stevenson, 2nd Lieut. P. W. J. (Christ's Hospital)
Obituary 1916 *207*
Stevenson, Capt. R. D. (Edinburgh Academy)
Obituary 1917 *214*
Stevenson-Moore, N. S. (Winchester)
Obituary 1945 *341*
Steventon, E. H. (North Staffordshire; Cheshire)
Obituary 1962 *992*
Stewart, Lt-Col. C. J. T. (Royal Military College; Ontario; Wanderers C.C.; Halifax)
Obituary 1920 *158*

Stewart, Dr. H. C. (Kent)
  Obituary   1943   *383*
Stewart, Lieut. J. A. L. (Winchester)
  Obituary   1916   *208*
Stewart, J. H. (Western Province)
  Obituary   1943   *384*
Stewart, J. M . (Junior) (Philadelphia)
  Obituary   1904   *lxxxiii*
Stewart, Major-Gen. Sir J. M. (Malvern)
  Obituary   1944   *323*
Stewart, M. J. (Alleyns School; Surrey; England)
  Benefit Match   1966   *561*
  Cricketer of the Year   1958   *65*
  Photographs   1957   *533*
                                          1958   *54*
                                          1961   *554*
                                          1963   *593*
                                          1966   *552*
                                          1981   *530*
  Schools Notes   1948   *649*
                                          1949   *673*
                                          1950   *699*
                                          1951   *706*
Stewart, Major R. B. (Wellington; Eastern Province; South Africa)
  Obituary   1914/I   *195*
Stewart, R. H. (See under Galloway 11th Earl)
Stewart, R. J. (President Manhattan C.C.)
  Obituary   1915/I   *240*
Stewart, W. J. (Warwickshire; Northamptonshire)
  Benefit Match   1968   *615*
  Photographs   1960   *594*
                                          1963   *631*
                                          1969   *603*
Stewart-Brown, H. (Harrow)
  Obituary   1949   *873*
Stewart-Mackenzie of Seaforth, Major Hon. F. (Committee Surrey)
  Obituary   1944   *308*
Stewart-Morgan, W. G. (Christ's College, Brecon; Glamorgan)
  Obituary   1974   *1080*
Steyn, Lieut. S. S. L. (Diocesan College, Rondesbosch, South Africa)
  Obituary   1918   *205*
Stiemens, A. W. (Framlingham College)
  82 wkts Schools Averages   1906   *476*
Stiles, F. W. T. (New Jersey Club Cricket)
  Obituary   1922/I   *269*

Still, R. S. (New South Wales; Tasmania)
    Obituary 1908/I *153*
Stinson, T. H. (Upper Canada College)
    Obituary 1920/I *158*
Stirling, Sir J. (Harrow)
    Obituary 1976 *1103*
Stirling, Lieut. R. K. (Exeter School)
    Obituary 1916 *208*
Stobart, St. C. K. M. (Winchester; Oxford University)
    Obituary 1909/I *146*
Stock, Capt/Adjt. A. B. (Eton)
    Obituary 1918 *217*
Stock, B. (Paris C.C, Ontario)
    Obituary 1919 *211*
Stock, W. B. (Paris C.C., Ontario)
    Obituary 1920/I *194*
Stockdale, 2nd Lieut. A. W. S. (Sunderland C.C.)
    Obituary 1916 *207*
Stockdale, Brig-Gen. H. E. (Wellington)
    Obituary 1955 *937*
Stockdale, Lieut. W. E. (Retford C.C.)
    Obituary 1916 *207*
Stocks, F. W. (Denstone; Oxford University; Leicestershire)
    Obituary 1930/I *264*
Stocks, F. W. (Nottinghamshire)
    Benefit Match 1957 *505*
    Career Figures 1958 *97*
Stocks, J. L. (Rugby)
    Obituary 1938 *946*
Stockton, A. F. (Treasurer Lancashire)
    Obituary 1938 *946*
Stockton, Sir E. (Treasurer Lancashire)
    Obituary 1940 *845*
Stockwin, A. (Groundsman Northamptonshire)
    Obituary 1923/I *305*
Stoddart, A. E. (Middlesex; England)
    In the Cricket Field 1916 *125*
    'My Dear Victorious Stod' D. Frith
    Book Review 1971 *1080*
    Portrait and Biography 1893 *xxxix*
    Special Memoir of (Obituary) 1916 *123*
    Team in Australia 1894-95 1896 *367*
    1897-98 1899 *382*
Stoddart, W. B. (Lancashire)
    Obituary 1936/I *289*

Stoever, D. P. (Gentlemen of Philadelphia)
Obituary   1932/I   *251*

Stogdon, Rev. E. (Harrow; Cambridge University)
Obituary   1952   *961*

Stogdon, J. H. (Harrow; Cambridge University; Middlesex)
Obituary   1945   *341*

Stokes, C. (Treasurer Yorkshire)
Obituary   1914/I   *196*

Stokes, F. (Rugby; Kent)
Obituary   1930/I   *264*

Stokes, G. (Kent)
Obituary   1923/I   *311*

Stokes, Dr. J. (Haverford University)
Obituary   1973   *1014*

Stokes, J. L. (Toronto Club Cricket)
Obituary   1926/I   *288*

Stokes, Dr. L. (Kent)
Obituary   1934/I   *275*

Stokes, Dr. S. E. (Haverford University)
Obituary   1973   *1014*

Stollmeyer, J. .B (Trinidad; West Indies)
'Everything Under the Sun' Book Review   1984   *1268*
Views on Growing Pains of Cricket   1955   *89*

Stone, Major C. C. (Uppingham; Leicestershire)
Obituary   1952   *961*

Stone, J. (Hampshire; Glamorgan; Umpire)
Benefit Match   1913/II   *193*
Obituary   1943   *384*

Stone, N. (Writer)
'The Rise of Worcestershire'   1963   *124*

Stone, Capt. N. H. (Malvern)
Obituary   1919   *190*

Stonehill, Rev. W. M. (Supporter New York Cricket)
Obituary   1909/I   *146*

Stonehouse, Rev. J. (Supporter Nottinghamshire)
Obituary   1893   *xxxiii*

Stoner, Pte. J. E. (Eastbourne Club Cricket)
Obituary   1917   *214*

Stones, C. E. (Westminster; Surrey)
Obituary   1955   *1083*

Stones, H. (Yorkshire Colts)
Obituary   1945   *341*

Stoney, 2nd Lieut. T. R. (Wellington)
Obituary   1919   *190*

Stopford, Major H. F. (Military Cricket)
Obituary   1917   *214*

Stops, J. F. (Wellingborough; Northamptonshire)
  Obituary   1945   *341*
Storer, H. (Derbyshire)
  Obituary   1909/I   *146*
Storer, H. (Junior) (Derbyshire)
  Obituary   1968   *1007*
Storer, W. (Derbyshire; England)
  Benefit Match   1903   *165*
  Obituary   1913/I   *198*
  Portrait and Biography   1899   *lvii*
Storey, J. (Balmain C.C., New South Wales)
  Obituary   1922/I   *270*
Storey, S. J. (Surrey; Sussex)
  Benefit Match   1974   *547*
  Photograph   1967   *563*
      1972   *562*
Storey, S. S. (See under Schultz, S. S.)
Stork, J. B. (Sedbergh; Northamptonshire)
  Obituary   1945   *341*
Stormonth-Darling, Lt.-Col. J. C. (Military Cricket)
  Obituary   1917   *215*
Story, Col. W. F. (Nottinghamshire)
  Obituary   1940   *845*
Stott, W. B. (Yorkshire)
  Photographs   1958   *630*
      1960   *632*
      1961   *632*
Stovold, A. W. (Gloucestershire; Orange Free State)
  Photograph   1978   *399*
Stow, Lt.-Col. M. B. (Repton)
  Obituary   1917   *215*
Stow, M. H. (Harrow; Cambridge University)
  Obituary   1912/I   *181*
Stow, V. A. S. (Oxford University)
  Obituary   1969   *987*
Stowell, Sgt. A. (Ardingly)
  Obituary   1917   *215*
Strachan, G. (Cheltenham, Gloucestershire; Middlesex; Surrey)
  Obituary   1903   *lxxii*
Straker, G. F. (Rugby)
  Obituary   1974   *1080*
Stranger, 2nd Lieut. G. J. (Borlase School)
  Obituary   1919   *190*
Stranger, Capt. H. E. K. (Borlase School)
  Obituary   1919   *190*

Stratford, A. H. (Malvern; Middlesex)
    Obituary   1915/I   *240*

Strathairn, Lieut. H. W. (Edinburgh Institution)
    Obituary   1918   *205*

Strathy, F/Lt. F. S. (Toronto C.C.)
    Obituary   1918   *205*

Strauss, Major S. F. F. (Griqualand West)
    Obituary   1947   *695*

Strawson, R. A. (Lincolnshire)
    Obituary   1917   *266*

Streatfeild, A. H. O. (Marlborough)
    Obituary   1935/I   *273*

Streatfeild, Rev. C. W. (Winchester)
    Obituary   1914/I   *196*

Streatfeild, E. C. (Charterhouse; Cambridge University; Surrey)
    Obituary   1933/I   *258*

Streatfeild, Rev. G. S. (Winchester)
    Obituary   1922/I   *270*

Streatfeild, Col. Sir H. (President Kent)
    Obituary   1939   *918*

Streatfeild-Moore, A. M. (Charterhouse; Kent)
    Obituary   1941   *401*

Street, A. E. (Surrey; Umpire)
    Obituary   1952   *962*

Street, E. C. (Kent)
    Obituary   1966   *972*

Street, Major E. R. (Guelph C.C., Canada)
    Obituary   1918   *217*

Street, Lieut. F. (Westminster; Essex)
    Obituary   1917   *215*

Street, F. E. (Uppingham; Kent)
    Obituary   1929/I   *259*

Street, G. (Surrey)
    Obituary   1876   *150*

Street, G. B. (Sussex; England)
    Obituary   1925/I   *280*

Street, J. (Surrey; Umpire)
    Benefit Match   1881   *139*
    Obituary   1907   *cxv*

Streeton, P. (Writer)
    'P. G. H. Fender: A Biography' Book Review   1982   *1267*

Stricker, L. A. (Transvaal; South Africa)
    Obituary   1961   *951*

Strickland, H. (Writer)
    with R. Nelson 'R. P. Nelson – Memoir'
    Book Review   1957   *1000*

Stringer, Lt-Col. F. W. (Army)
Obituary 1917 *215*
Stringer, P. M. (Yorkshire; Leicestershire)
Photograph 1971 *433*
Strong, C. I. (Harrow)
Obituary 1915/I *241*
Structure of the English Game Note on 1983 *81*
Strudwick, H. (Surrey; Scorer Surrey; England)
Benefit Matches 1912/II *100*
1925/II *146*
'Dr. Grace to Peter May' 1959 *61*
Obituary 1971 *1031*
Photograph 1971 *115*
Portrait and Biography 1912/I *192*
'Herbert Strudwick' Sir N. Cardus 1971 *114*
Tributes to: S. F. Barnes 1968 *114*
Sir J. Hobbs 1964 *103*
M. Tate 1957 *949*
Strutt, G. H. (Patron Derbyshire)
Obituary 1896 *xl*
Strutt, H. (See under Belper, 2nd Lord)
Stuart, Capt. C. E. (Bath College)
Obituary 1918 *205*
Stuart, Canon E. A. (Harrow)
Obituary 1918 *235*
Stuart, H. (Journalist)
Obituary 1915/I *241*
Stuart, 2nd Lieut. R. A. (George Watson's College)
Obituary 1916 *208*
Stuart, Capt. W. G. S. (George Watson's College; Scotland)
Obituary 1918 *205*
Stuart-French, Major P. W. G. (Sherborne; Cork)
Obituary 1955 *937*
Stubberfield, H. (Sussex; Umpire)
Obituary 1919 *211*
Stubbings, J. (Derbyshire)
Obituary 1913/I *199*
Studd, A. H. (Eton)
Obituary 1920/I *186*
Studd, C. T. (Eton; Cambridge University; Middlesex; England)
Obituary 1932/I *252*
'C. T. Studd: Cricketer and Missionary'
'World Wide Evangelization Crusade'
Book Review 1974 *1126*
Studd, Capt. E. B. T. (Harrow)
Obituary 1952 *962*

Studd, E. J. C. (Cheltenham)
  Obituary   1910/I   *148*
Studd, G. B. (Eton; Cambridge University; Middlesex; President M.C.C.; England)
  Obituary   1946   *446*
Studd, Brig-Gen. H. W. (Eton; Middlesex; Hampshire)
  Obituary   1948   *788*
Studd, Sir J. E. K. (Eton; Cambridge University; Middlesex)
  Obituary   1945   *341*
Studd, Sir K. 3rd Bart. (Winchester)
  Obituary   1978   *1082*
Studd, R. A. (Eton; Cambridge University; Hampshire)
  Obituary   1949   *870*
Stumping – Art of – Photograph   1952   *69*
Sturt, Rev. H. (Hertfordshire)
  Obituary   1952   *962*
Subba Row, R. (Whitgift; Cambridge University; Surrey; Northamptonshire; England)
  Cricketer of the Year   1961   *100*
  Photographs   1959   *472*
       1961   *93*
  Schools Notes   1949   *691*
       1950   *715*
       1951   *724*
Subbaroyan, Dr. P. (President Indian Cricket Board of Control)
  Obituary   1963   *1036*
Success of the L.B.W. Experiment   1936/I   *341*
  (Discussion)
Suffield, 5th Lord (President M.C.C.)
  Obituary   1915/I   *241*
Sugden, Rev. A. N. B. (Writer)
  'W. G. Grace' Book Review   1967   *1018*
Sugden, H. E. (Derbyshire)
  Obituary   1914/I   *196*
Sugg, F. H. (Yorkshire; Derbyshire; Lancashire; England)
  Benefit Match   1898   *11*
  Obituary   1934/I   *276*
  Portrait and Biography   1890   *xxxiii*
Sugg, W. (Derbyshire; Yorkshire)
  Benefit Match   1899   *156*
  Obituary   1934/I   *276*
Suggested Reforms
  Lord Harris and A. G. Steel   1900   *lxvii*
Sukuna-Ratu, Sir J. L. V. (Fiji Cricket Association)
  Obituary   1959   *938*

Sulin, T. R. (IZingari of Natal)
Obituary   1913/I   199
Sulley, J. (Nottinghamshire)
Obituary   1933/I   258
Sullivan, D. (Surrey; Glamorgan)
Obituary   1969   987
Sullivan, J. H. B. (Rossall; Yorkshire)
Obituary   1934/I   280
Sully, H. (Somerset; Northamptonshire)
Photograph   1968   516
Sumby, J. (Brantford C.C., Ontario)
Obituary   1920/I   158
Summer – Glorious 1955
Note on   1956   73
Summerhayes, Capt. J. A. (St.Lawrence College)
Obituary   1919   190
Summers, F. T. (Worcestershire)
Obituary   1968   1007
Summers, G. F. (Surrey)
Obituary   1984   1209
Summers, L. S. H. (Emanuel School; Surrey)
Obituary   1978   1082
101 wkts Schools Averages   1922/II   548
Sunday Cricket in Australia   1966   857
                First match at Lord's   1966   494
                Notes on   1957   72
                                            1966   82
'Sunday Cricket – Thrills of' J. C. Laker 1971   122
Supporters – Help Counties Photograph   1955   59
Surfleet, Dr. D. F. (University College School)
Schools Note   1931/I   294, 295
                                                          316
83 wkts Schools Averages   1931/II   635
Surguy, M. R. (Eltham College)
Schools Note   1983   900
1,159 runs Schools Averages   1983   917
Surrey County Cricket Club
Champions 1952 Note on   1953   78
'Champions Again' W. S. Surridge and
P. B. H. May Photograph   1955   5
County Badge   1950   494
                                            ad passim
W. G. Grace and the Surrey Club   1897   liv
Honorary Life Members List   1973   54
'Hundred Years of Surrey Cricket'
H. D. Leveson Gower   1946   5

'A Lifetime with Surrey' A. Sandham		1972	*114*
Message to and from the King (George VI)		1946	*252*
Revival Note on		1951	*123*
in Rhodesia 1959		1960	*898*
'The Story of the Oval' L. Palgrave			
Book Review		1950	*973*
'Surrey' G. Ross Book Review		1972	*1096*
Surrey Centenary Match v Old England XI			
Team Portrait		1947	*37*
'Surrey Cricketers 1839-1980' Association of Cricket Statisticians			
Book Review		1982	*1254*
'Surrey's Lively Close Fielding Photograph		1958	*51*
Surrey's Six Championships Note on		1958	*75*
'The Surrey Story' G. Ross Book Review		1958	*1010*
Team Portraits			
Joint Champions	1950	1951	*63*
County Champions	1952	1953	*56*
	1953	1954	*59*
	1954	1955	*58*
	1955	1956	*46*
County Champions for the fifth			
successive year	1956	1957	*48*
County Champions for the sixth			
successive year	1957	1958	*50*
County Champions for the seventh			
successive year	1958	1959	*42*
County Champions	1971	1972	*60*
Benson and Hedges Cup Winners	1974	1975	*552*
	1975	1976	*556*
	1976	1977	*557*
	1977	1978	*540*
	1978	1979	*533*
	1979	1980	*558*
	1980	1981	*552*
	1981	1982	*559*
	1982	1983	*575*
	1983	1984	*536*
Triple Champions Note on		1955	*83*
with Queen Elizabeth II Photograph		1956	*45*
Surridge, P. (Cricket Bat Manufacturer)			
Obituary		1952	*961*
Surridge, W. S. (Surrey)			
Championships Again Photograph with			
P. B. H. May		1955	*57*
Cricketer of the Year		1953	*74*
Photograph		1953	*63*

'Stuart Surridge – Surrey's Inspiration'			
D. R. Jardine		1957	*88*
Team in Bermuda	1961	1962	*927*
'Bermuda Cricketer' I. Rosenwater			
Book Review		1962	*1048*
Views on Growing Pains of Cricket		1956	*87*

Sussex County Cricket Club

'A Complete Record of Sussex Cricket 1728-1957'			
G. Washer Book Review		1959	*985*
County Badge		1950	*514*
		ad passim	
'Cricket and the Sussex County By-Election of 1741'			
T. J. Mc Cann Book Review		1978	*1118*
'Pre-Victorian Sussex Cricket' A. P. and			
H. F. Squire Book Review		1952	*1016*
'Sussex' Sir Home Gordon Book Review		1951	*990*
'Sussex Cricket' J. Marshall Book Review		1960	*996*
'A Sussex Cricket Odyssey' L. Stapleton			
Book Review		1980	*1212*
'Sussex County Cricket Club – Hove 1872-1972'			
The Club Book Review		1973	*1052*
Sussex Scoreboard Photograph		1947	*39*
'Sussex through the years' A. E. R. Gilligan		1954	*108*
Sussex Thrive under Long Note on		1979	*78*
Team Portraits	1974	1975	*568*
	1975	1976	*572*
	1976	1977	*574*
	1977	1978	*557*
	1978	1979	*549*
	1979	1980	*574*
	1980	1981	*568*
	1981	1982	*575*
	1982	1983	*592*
	1983	1984	*552*

Susskind, B. V. (Orange Free State)

Obituary		1955	*937*

Susskind, M. J. (University College School; Cambridge University; Middlesex; Transvaal; South Africa)

Obituary		1958	*965*
Schools Notes		1909/I	*116*
		1910/I	*117,128*

Sutcliffe, B. (Auckland; Otago; Northern Districts; New Zealand)

'Between Overs' Book Review		1964	*1004*
Cricketer of the Year		1950	*85*
Photograph		1950	*74*

'Bert Sutcliffe's Book for Boys'
| P. Booth Book Review | 1963 | *1112* |

Sutcliffe, H. (Yorkshire; England)
| Benefit Match | 1930/II | *157* |
| Career Figures | 1979 | *99* |

'Holmes and Sutcliffe: Run Stealers'
L. Duckworth Book Review	1971	*1076*
Hundredth Hundred	1933/II	*104*
In First Class Cricket	1941	*32*
Photographs	1941	*33*
	1972	*131*
	1979	*97*
Portrait and Biography	1920/I	*253*
Records by	1941	*65*

'Herbert Sutcliffe' (Obituary Memoir)
| J. M. Kilburn | 1979 | *96* |

Three Yorkshire Centurions – Hutton, Sutcliffe, Boycott
Photograph	1978	*142*
Tributes to G. Duckworth	1967	*966*
K. Duleepsinhji	1960	*951*
Sir J. Hobbs	1964	*103*
H. Strudwick	1971	*1032*
W. Woodfull	1966	*975*
Views on Growing Pains of Cricket	1956	*83*

Sutcliffe, W. H. H. (Rydal; Yorkshire)
| Career Figures | 1958 | *97* |
| Photograph | 1956 | *632* |

Sutherland, C. L. (Eton)
| Obituary | 1912/I | *182* |

Sutherland, D. (Victoria)
| Obituary | 1972 | *1055* |

Sutherland, Lt-Col. H. (Bedford School; Bedfordshire)
| Obituary | 1961 | *951* |

Sutherland, H. B. (Eton; Kent)
| Obituary | 1916 | *208* |

Sutthery, A. M. (Oundle; Cambridge University; Devon; Northamptonshire; Shropshire)
| Obituary | 1938 | *946* |

Suttle, K. G. (Sussex)
Photographs	1959	*552*
	1961	*571*
	1963	*612*
	1965	*572*

Sutton, H. N. (Vice President Derbyshire)
| Obituary | 1915/I | *242* |

Sutton, T. R. (Journalist)
   Obituary   1897   *xlii*

Swain, W. (Yorkshire)
   Obituary   1911/I   *157*

Swale, C. A. L. (Settle C.C.; Gentlemen of Yorkshire)
   Obituary   1915/I   *249*

Swalwell, Major R. S. (Dorset; Worcestershire)
   Obituary   1931/I   *267*

Swamy, V. N. (Services; India)
   Obituary   1984   *1209*

Swan, H. D. (President Essex)
   Obituary   1942   *363*

Swan, J. J. (Surrey)
   Obituary   1925/I   *281*

Swan, Capt. W. D. (Victoria College, Jersey)
   Obituary   1939   *918*

Swann, Capt. H. N. (Military Cricket)
   Obituary   1918   *206*

Swannell, E. (Groundsman Lord's)
   Testimonial Fund   1972   *348*

Swann-Mason, Rev. R. S. (Perse School)
   Obituary   1943   *384*

Swansea St Helens
   Plan of County Ground   1951   *325*
                         ad passim

Swanton, E. W. (Broadcaster; Journalist; Writer; Middlesex)
   Team's Commonwealth Tour   1964   1965   *857*
   Team in West Indies   1956   1957   *882*
                         1961   1962   *878*
   Tribute to J. H. W. Fingleton   1982   *1199*
   Articles in Chronological Order:
   'Cricket under the Japs'   1946   *48*
   'Radio Reflections'   1981   *114*
   Book Reviews in Chronological Order:
   'Denis Compton'   1950   *979*
   'Elusive Victory'   1952   *1013*
   'The Test Matches of 1953'   1954   *984*
   'West Indian Adventure'   1955   *991*
   'Victory in Australia'   1956   *1027*
   'The Test Matches of 1956'   1957   *997*
   'Report from South Africa'   1958   *1014*
   'West Indies Revisited'   1961   *994*
   'The Ashes in Suspense'   1964   *1000*
   'Sort of a Cricket Person'   1973   *1058*
   'Follow on'   1978   *1126*
   'As I said at the Time'   1984   *1258*

Swarbrook, F. W. (Derbyshire; Griqualand West; Orange Free State)
Photograph 1974 *368*

Swart, P. D. (Glamorgan; Rhodesia; Western Province; Boland)
Photograph 1979 *375*

Swayne, J. M. (Winchester; Wiltshire)
Obituary 1945 *342*

Sweet, Rev. C. F. L. (Winchester)
Obituary 1933/I *259*

Sweet-Escott, R. B. (Glamorgan)
Obituary 1908/I *153*

Sweet-Escott, W. S. (Glamorgan)
Obituary 1927/I *292*

Sweetland, E. H. (Middlesex)
Obituary 1979 *1087*

Sweetland, 2nd Lieut. R. G. (Westminster C.C., British Columbia)
Obituary 1920/I *158*

Sweetnam, J. (Bathurst C.C., New South Wales)
Obituary 1920/I *186*

Swetman, R. (Surrey; Nottinghamshire; Gloucestershire; England)
Photographs 1959 *531*
1967 *528*

Swift, B. T. (St. Peter's, Adelaide; Cambridge University)
Obituary 1959 *938*

Swift, J. (Australian Umpire)
Obituary 1911/I *157*

Swift, Rev. J. M. (Cheshire; Lancashire)
Obituary 1950 *914*

Swift, J. S. (Victoria)
Obituary 1927/I *292*

Swinburne, J. W. (Northamptonshire)
Photograph 1971 *465*

Swinfen, 1st Baron of Chertsey (Patron Worcestershire)
Obituary 1920/I *186*

Swinford, Capt. T. F. (Kent)
Obituary 1916 *208*

Swinstead, F. H. (Club Cricketer)
Obituary 1939 *921*

Swinstead, G. H. (Hampstead C.C.)
Obituary 1927/I *292*

Swinyard, T. (Canadian Club Cricket)
Obituary 1916 *208*

Swire, S. H. (Lancashire)
Obituary 1906 *civ*

Sydenham, D. A. D. (Surrey)
Photograph 1963 *593*

Sydney Cricket Ground
　Scoreboard Photograph 1939 *46*
　Tests Threat Note on 1978 *103*
Syed, H. S. (Muslims)
　Obituary 1958 *965*
Sykes, Lieut. F. W. (Giggleswick Grammar School)
　Obituary 1919 *190*
Sykes, Capt. O. J. (Madras Presidency)
　Obituary 1917 *215*
Sykes, Dr. R. P. (Formby C.C.)
　Obituary 1918 *235*
Symes, W. C. (St.John's, Leatherhead)
　Obituary 1962 *993*
Symes-Thompson, Rev. F. (Harrow)
　Obituary 1949 *870*
Symes-Thompson, H. (Winchester; Cambridge University)
　Obituary 1953 *950*
Symington, 2nd Lieut. G. C. (Ardingly)
　Obituary 1918 *206*
Symonds, H. G. (Glamorgan)
　Obituary 1946 *446*
Symons, Lieut. C. A. (King Edward's, Bath)
　Obituary 1916 *208*
Syree, Dr. A. H. (Kent)
　Obituary 1925/I *281*
Tabassum, Parvez (Nairobi)
　Obituary 1974 *1080*
Taberer, H. M. (Oxford University; Natal; Essex; Rhodesia; Transvaal)
　Obituary 1933/I *259*
Taberer, W. S. (Rhodesia)
　Obituary 1939 *918*
Tabor, A. (Harrow; Middlesex; Ceylon)
　Obituary 1927/I *296*
Tabor, A. S. (Eton; Cambridge University; Middlesex; Surrey)
　Obituary 1928/I *299*
Tabor, R. M. (Eton)
　Obituary 1926/I *283*
Tagart, Lt.-Col. E. O. (Clifton)
　Obituary 1931/I *267*
Tagart, N. D. (Clifton; Gloucestershire)
　Obituary 1914/I *196*
Tait, J. (Masseur Surrey)
　Obituary 1967 *974*
Tait, J. R. (Glamorgan)
　Obituary 1946 *446*

Tait, R. G. (Aberdeenshire; Forfarshire; Scotland)
Obituary 1974 *1080*
Talati, S. (Writer)
'Glorious Battle' Book Review 1983 *1307*
Talbot, Lt.-Col. A. C. (Eton)
Obituary 1922/I *272*
Talbot, B. (Winchester)
Obituary 1937/I *282*
Talbot, Rt. Hon. Sir G. J. (Winchester)
Obituary 1939 *918*
Talbot, J. E. (Eton)
Obituary 1938 *946*
Talbot, R. O. (Canterbury; Otago)
Obituary 1984 *1209*
Talent Notes on 1960 *123*
 1965 *104,106*
Tallon, D. (Queensland; Australia)
Cricketer of the Year 1949 *98*
Photograph 1949 *74*
Tamil Nadu in Sri Lanka 1974 1975 *971*
 1981 1982 *1139*
Tancred, A. B. (Griqualand West; South Africa)
Obituary 1913/I *203*
Tancred, L. J. (Transvaal; South Africa)
Obituary 1935/I *273*
Tancred, V. (Transvaal; South Africa)
Obituary 1905 *cii*
Tandy, Brig-Gen. E. N. (Wellington)
Obituary 1954 *929*
Tandy, J. H. (Transvaal)
Obituary 1955 *937*
Tanner, A. R. (Middlesex)
Obituary 1967 *975*
Tanner, Brig-Gen. J. A. (Woolwich R.M.A.)
Obituary 1918 *206*
Tapp, Capt. T. A. (Rugby)
Obituary 1918 *206*
Tapscott, G. L. (Griqual and West; South Africa)
Obituary 1943 *387*
Tapscott, L. E. (Griqual and West; South Africa)
Obituary 1935/I *273*
Tarbox, C. V. (Percy) (Worcestershire; Hertfordshire)
Obituary 1979 *1087*
Tarilton, P. H. (Jamaica)
Obituary 1954 *929*

Tarrant, F. A. (Middlesex; Victoria)

Benefit Match	1915/II	29
Obituary	1952	962
Portrait and Biography	1908/I	163

Tarrant, W. G. (Emanuel School; Spencer C.C.)

Obituary	1981	1150

Tate, E. (Hampshire; Devon)

Obituary	1954	929

Tate, F (Hampshire)

Obituary	1936/I	289

Tate, F. W. (Sussex; England)

Benefit Match	1902	83
Obituary	1944	323

Tate, M. W. (Sussex; England)

Benefit Match	1931/II	251
Obituary	1957	947
Portrait and Biography	1924/I	279
Record by	1941	65
'Maurice Tate' J. Arlott Book Review	1952	1022
'Maurice Tate' G. Brodribb Book Review	1977	1100

Tatham, C. R. (Islington Albion C.C.)

Obituary	1896	xlii

Tatham, Capt. G. B. (Trinity College, Cambridge)

Obituary	1919	190

Tatham, Rev. W. M. (Marlborough)

Obituary	1939	918

Tattersall, Lieut. H. V. (Manhattan C.C.)

Obituary	1917	215

Tattersall, R. (Lancashire; England)

Benefit Match	1961	459
Photographs	1951	396
	1953	414
	1954	421
	1955	403
	1957	422

Taunton Plan of County Ground

	1950	477
	ad passim	

Tavaré, C. J. (Sevenoaks; Oxford University; Kent; England)

Photograph	1978	428
Schools Note	1974	828
1036 runs Schools Averages	1974	871

Taverner, 2nd Lieut. A. F. (Oakham)

Obituary	1917	215

Tayfield, H. J. (Natal; Rhodesia; Transvaal; South Africa)

Cricketer of the Year	1956	64
Photograph	1956	55

Tayler, A. C. (Artist)
    Obituary   1927/I   *297*

Tayler, C. J. (Gloucestershire)
    Obituary   1960   *957*

Tayler, 2nd Lieut. A. C. (Haileybury)
    Obituary   1917   *216*

Tayler, A. D. (Cricketologist)
    Obituary   1924/I   *270*

Tayler, Brig-Gen. A. H. M. (Clifton)
    Obituary   1935/I   *273*

Tayler, 2nd Lieut. B. A. (Derbyshire Club Cricketer)
    Obituary   1919   *201*

Tayler, B. R. (Brentwood; Essex)
    Cricketer of the Year   1972   *76*
    Photographs   1957   *325*
                                              1960   *359*
                                              1966   *364*
                                              1972   *68*

Tayler, B. R. (Canterbury; Wellington, New Zealand)
    'Fastest Hundred in Test Cricket' Note on   1983   *109*

Tayler, C. (Journalist)
    Obituary   1978   *1082*

Tayler, C. F. (Assistant Secretary Norfolk)
    Obituary   1920/I   *186*

Tayler, C. H. (Westminster; Oxford University; Leicestershire; Buckinghamshire)
    Obituary   1967   *975*

Tayler, C. J. (Warwickshire; Staffordshire)
    Obituary   1961   *952*

Tayler, Dr. C. J. (Gloucestershire)
    Obituary   1953   *950*

Tayler, Sgt. C. W. (Secretary Derbyshire)
    Obituary   1917   *216*

Tayler, D. (Natal)
    Obituary   1928/I   *299*

Tayler, D. (Warwickshire)
    'Derief Taylor the National Coach'
    W. G. Wanklyn   1977   *154*

Tayler, D. D. (Warwickshire; Auckland, New Zealand)
    Obituary   1982   *1210*

Tayler, D. J. S. (Surrey; Somerset; Griqualand West)
    Benefit Match   1979   *758*
    Photographs   1971   *498*
                                          1978   *522*

Tayler, E. F. (Marlborough; Surrey)
    Obituary   1903   *lxxii*

Taylor, E. J. (Rugby; Gloucestershire)
Obituary — 1938 — *949*
Taylor, F. (Clifton; Gloucestershire)
Obituary — 1937 — *282*
Taylor, F. H. (Haverford College)
Obituary — 1935/I — *274*
Taylor, F. H. (Derbyshire)
Obituary — 1964 — *952*
Taylor, Col. F. P. S. (Marlborough)
Obituary — 1925/I — *281*
Taylor, 2nd Lieut. G. E. (Chigwell School)
Obituary — 1919 — *190*
Taylor, 2nd Lieut. G. F. W. (Malvern)
Obituary — 1918 — *206*
Taylor, G. M. (Lancashire Scorer)
Obituary — 1981 — *1150*
Taylor, Lieut. H. N. (Ridley College, Ontario)
Obituary — 1917 — *216*
Taylor, H. W. (Natal; Transvaal; South Africa)
Obituary — 1974 — *1081*
Portrait and Biography — 1925/I — *291*
Taylor, J. (Yorkshire)
Obituary — 1925/I — *282*
Taylor, J. E. (Supporter Oval)
Obituary — 1930/I — *264*
Taylor, J. M. (New South Wales; Australia)
Obituary — 1972 — *1055*
Testimonial Match — 1957 — *869*
Taylor, Dr. J. W. (North of Ireland)
Obituary — 1925/I — *282*
Taylor, K. (Auckland; Yorkshire; Norfolk; England)
Photograph — 1962 — *665*
'Ken Taylor Benefit' Book Review — 1969 — *1040*
Taylor, L. B. (Leicestershire; Natal)
Photographs — 1979 — *452*
— 1982 — *477*
Taylor, 2nd Lieut. L. F. (Staffordshire)
Obituary — 1918 — *206*
Taylor, M. (Hertfordshire)
Obituary — 1917 — *266*
Taylor, M (Ruthin School)
1003 runs, 110 wkts, Schools Notes — 1947 — *562*
Schools Notes — 1955 — *698*
Taylor, M. L. (Lancashire; Dorset)
Obituary — 1979 — *1088*

Taylor, M. N. S. (Nottinghamshire; Hampshire)

Photographs	1969	*534*
	1976	*425*

Taylor, 2nd Lieut. P. (East Stirlingshire)

Obituary	1917	*216*

Taylor, 2nd Lieut. R. F. (Malvern)

Obituary	1916	*208*

Taylor, Brig-Gen. R. H. B. (Cheltenham)

Obituary	1943	*384*

Taylor, R. W. (Derbyshire; England)

Cricketer of the Year	1977	*105*
Photographs	1967	*352*
	1972	*363*
	1976	*360*
	1977	*91*

Taylor, 2nd Lieut. R. W. (Newcastle Royal Grammar School)

Obituary	1917	*216*

Taylor, Brig-Gen. S. C. (Military Cricket)

Obituary	1919	*190*

Taylor, T. L. (Uppingham; Cambridge University; Yorkshire)

Obituary	1961	*952*
Portrait and Biography	1901	*lxxii*
Tribute to Sir S. Jackson	1948	*81*

Taylor, 2nd Lieut. T. R. (Castleton C.C.)

Obituary	1916	*209*

Taylor, W. H. (Lord's Hotel)

Obituary	1912/I	*182*

Taylor, Col. W. H. (Worcestershire)

Obituary	1960	*957*

Taylor, W. T. (Derbyshire; Writer)

'History of Derbyshire Cricket'	1953	*104*
Obituary	1977	*1049*

Teachers Trounced (W. Indies v England)

Note on	1951	*116*

Teape, C. A. (Eton; Oxford University; Middlesex)

Obituary	1926/I	*284*

Teape, 2nd Lieut. C. L. (St. John's, Leatherhead)

Obituary	1917	*216*

Tebbut, C. M. (Treasurer Essex)

Obituary	1899	*1*

Tebbutt, G. (Journalist)

Obituary	1974	*1081*

Tebbutt, H. C. (Leys School; Cambridgeshire)

Obituary	1933/I	*259*
Schools Notes	1905	*cxxi,cxxix*
1443 runs Schools Averages	1905	*449*

Tedder, Lord, Marshal of R.A.F. (President Surrey)
  Obituary   968   *1007*

Teele, R. (Sydney University)
  Obituary   1930/I   *268*

Teesdale, H. (Winchester; Oxford University; Surrey)
  Obituary   1972   *1056*

Teesdale, M. J. (Winchester)
  Obituary   1929/I   *259*

Television Payments Note on   1963   *924*

Tempest-Hicks, Capt. C. E. (Sandhurst)
  Obituary   1919   *190*

Temple, J. F. (Yorkshire)
  Obituary   1971   *1032*

Templer, Judge F.G. (Harrow)
  Obituary   1919   *212*

Tenby, 1st Viscount, Major G. Lloyd-George (Eastbourne College)
  Obituary   1968   *1008*

Tendall, R. E. F. (St. Peter's, York; Kent)
  Obituary   1973   *1014*

Tennant, H. N. (Merchiston Castle; Loretto; Lancashire)
  Obituary   1906   *cii*

Tennent, Major B. C. (Edinburgh University)
  Obituary   1919   *190*

Tennent, H. (West of Scotland C.C.)
  Obituary   1920/I   *180*

Tennyson, 3rd Lord H. L. (Eton; Hampshire; England)
  Obituary   1952   *96*
  Portrait and Biography   1914/I   *23*
  'Sticky Wickets' Book Review 1951   *99*
  Team in India 1937-38   1939   *77*
  Team in Jamaica 1927   1928/II   *67*
               1928   1929/II   *66*
               1932   1933/II   *69*
  Team in South Africa 1924-25 1926/II   *62*

Tennyson, Capt. Hon. A. A. (Trinity College, Cambridge)
  Obituary   1919   *190*

Terry, Rev. F. W. (Somerset; Canada)
  Obituary   1937/I   *28*

Terry, H. F. (Uppingham)
  Obituary   1933/I   *26*

Test Batsmen, Finding them Note on 1971   *9*

Test Centuries after the age of 39 List of 1969   *9*

Test Cricket Note on   1981   *9*

Test Hat-Tricks Table   1961   *67*

Test Match, First 1877 Scorecard 1976   *10*

Test Match Grounds Chronological Sequence 1981   *98*

Test Match Second 1877 Scorecard	1976	*106*
Test Match Status of Notes	1965	*106*
	1971	*92*
Test Matches Evolution of Note	1973	*94*
Length of Note	1950	*112*
'Test Players, How They are Raised'		
L. Hassett	1952	*107*
Test Selection Committees List of	1950	*954*
Test Stars Note on	1958	*74*
Test Totals–Smallest Photograph	1956	*49*
Tests – Duration of Note on	1960	*124*
Tests – Five Day Note on	1968	*92*
Tests – Money In Note on	1955	*85*
Tests – More of Note on	1982	*87*
Tests – Six Day Note on	1969	*89*
Tetley, Capt. J. C. D. (Charterhouse)		
Obituary	1918	*206*
Thackray, R. (Griqualand West)		
Obituary	1945	*342*
Thames Calamity Fund Match	1879	*141*
Tharp, A. K. (Haileybury; Suffolk; Cambridgeshire; Norfolk)		
Obituary	1929/I	*259*
Thatcher, Mrs. M (Prime Minister U.K.)		
Views on South African Tour	1983	*80*
Thain, C. (Surrey)		
Obituary	1970	*1026*
Thayer, H. C. (Gentlemen of Philadelphia; U.S.A.)		
Obituary	1937/I	*283*
Thayer, J.B. (Philadelphia)		
Obituary	1913/I	*199*
'Then and Now' R. C. Robertson–Glasgow	1951	*87*
Theobald, Canon Rev. C (Winchester)		
Obituary	1931/I	*267*
Theobald, Lt-Col. C. E. (Winchester)		
Obituary	1938	*949*
Theophilus, D. A. (Eastern Province)		
Obituary	1937/I	*283*
Thesiger, Hon. Sir E. P. (I Zingari)		
Obituary	1929/I	*259*
Thesiger, Hon. F. J. N. (see under Chelmsford, Lord)		
Thesiger, Capt. Hon. W. G. (Cheltenham)		
Obituary	1921/I	*238*
Thevenard, T. O. (Bedford School; Bedfordshire)		
Obituary	1945	*326*
Thewlis H. (Yorkshire)		
Obituary	1921/I	*238*

Thewlis, J. (Yorkshire)
Benefit Match	1876	*179*
Obituary	1901	*lxvi*

Thomas, A. E. (Northamptonshire)
Obituary	1966	*972*

Thomas, Capt. A. L. (St. Dunstan's)
Obituary	1919	*191*

Thomas, Capt. A. V. (Repton)
Obituary	1916	*209*

Thomas, Lieut. D. C. S. (King's, Worcester)
Obituary	1919	*191*

Thomas, F. E. (Clifton; Gloucestershire)
Obituary	1925/I	*282*

Thomas, F. Freeman (see under Willingdon, Marquess of)

Thomas, Capt. G. O. (North Wales Club Cricketer)
Obituary	1916	*209*

Thomas, H. F. B. (Secretary Lancashire Schools Cricket Association)
Obituary	1976	*1103*

Thomas, Lieut. H. W. (Monmouth Grammar School)
Obituary	1917	*216*

Thomas, P. (Writer)
'Yorkshire Cricketers 1839 - 1939'
Book Review	1974	*1118*

Thomas, P. (Troon)
Obituary	1975	*1083*

Thomas, P. F. (Cricket Writer)
Obituary	1933/I	*264*

Thomas, R. P. (Oxfordshire)
Obituary	1968	*1008*

Thomas, Lieut. T. S. (King's, Worcester)
Obituary	1919	*191*

Thomas, 2nd Lieut. W. N. (Shropshire)
Obituary	1917	*216*

Thompson, A. (Middlesex)
Benefit Matches	1956	*471,482*
Retirement Note	1956	*56*

Thompson, 2nd Lieut. A. H. (Charterhouse)
Obituary	1916	*209*

Thompson, C. (Sedbergh; Northumberland)
Obituary	1920/I	*180*

Thompson, 2nd Lieut. C. V. (Forest School)
Obituary	1918	*206*

Thompson, E. (Marlborough)
Obituary	1955	*937*

Thompson, F. A. (Nairn County)
Obituary	1952	*96*

540

Thompson, 2nd Lieut. G. E. (Harrow)
  Obituary   1917   *216*
Thompson, G. H. (Secretary Essex)
  Obituary   1930/I   *264*
Thompson, G. J. (Wellingborough; Northamptonshire; England)
  Memorial to   1944   *169*
  Obituary   1944   *324*
  Portrait and Biography   1906   *cxii*
Thompson, G. (Rossall)
  Obituary   1947   *695*
Thompson, H. (Leicestershire)
  Obituary   1942   *363*
Thompson, H. S. (Sydney Cricketer)
  Obituary   1908/I   *153*
Thompson, Lieut. J. (South Shields C.C.)
  Obituary   1918   *206*
Thompson. J. R. (Tonbridge; Cambridge University; Warwickshire)
  Views on Laws   1957   *83*
Thompson, L. (West of Scotland C.C.)
  Obituary   1905   *cii*
Thompson, N. (New South Wales; Australia)
  Obituary   1897   *xl*
Thompson, P. (Scorer Oxford University)
  Obituary   1974   *1081*
Thompson, R. G. (Warwickshire)
  Photograph   1960   *594*
Thompson R. H. (Harrow)
  Obituary   1949   *870*
Thompson, Pte. T. (Scorer Hertfordshire)
  Obituary   1918   *206*
Thompson, V. (Melbourne C.C.)
  Obituary   1902   *lxxiv*
Thompson, V. (Harrow; Northumberland)
  Obituary   1948   *788*
Thompson, Lt-Col. W. D. M. (Military Cricket)
  Obituary   1919   *191*
Thompson, W. E. (Derbyshire)
  Obituary   1955   *937*
Thoms, R. (Middlesex)
  Benefit Match   1879   *114*
  'A Few Jottings'   1889   *xxxv*
  'More Jottings'   1890   *xlviii*
  Obituary   1904   *lxxiii*
  Views on High Scoring and the L.B.W. Rule   1899   *lxxii*
  Views on "The Follow On"   1894   *l*
  Views on L.B.W. Rule   1888   *357*

Thomson, A. A. (Journalist; Writer)
'The Great Cricketer' (W. G. Grace)
Book Reviews 1958 *1015*
 1969 *1032*
'The Googly Summer' 1968 *102*
'Hirst and Rhodes' Book Review 1960 *1003*
'Hutton and Washbrook' Book Review 1964 *1001*
'My Favourite Summer' 1967 *118*
Obituary 1969 *987*
'When I was a Lad' Book Review 1965 *1022*
Thomson, Capt. A. G. (Edinburgh Academy)
Obituary 1919 *201*
Thomson, Dr. A. G. (Philadelphia; U.S.A.)
Obituary 1919 *214*
Thomson, Lieut./Adjt. A. L. St. C. (Bedford Grammar School)
Obituary 1918 *200*
Thomson, E. A. C. (Journalist; Secretary of Club Cricket Conference)
Obituary 1942 *363*
Thomson, Major E. P. (Fettes)
Obituary 1915/I *24*
Thomson, E. W. S. (Argentine Cricket Association)
Obituary 1956 *97*
Thomson, Lieut. H. R. (Highfields School, Ontario)
Obituary 1919 *20*
Thomson, J. R. (New South Wales; Queensland; Middlesex; Australia)
Lillee and Thomson—Attraction 1976 *6*
£40,000 Contract Note on 1976 *104*
Thomson, N. I. (Sussex, England)
Photographs 1954 *56*
 1955 *53*
 1958 *56*
 1959 *55*
 1960 *57*
 1965 *57*
Thomson, W. W. (Surrey Committee)
Obituary 1916 *20*
Thorn, H. W. (Essex)
Obituary 1984 *120*
Thorn, P. (Writer)
with V. Issacs 'Hampshire Cricketers 1800–1982'
Book Review 1984 *125*
'Worcestershire Cricketers'
Book Review 1975 *111*
Thornber, H (Cheshire)
Obituary 1914/I *19*
Views on the Reforms of 1889 1890 *xxxvi*

542

Thorne, Lieut. A. B. (Haileybury)
Obituary   1919   *191*

Thorne, Capt. C (Haileybury)
Obituary   1917   *216*

Thorne, Lt-Col. G. C. (Rugby; Norfolk; Army)
Obituary   1944   *308*

Thornley, Bill (Scorer Nottinghamshire)
Obituary   1984   *1209*

Thornton, A. J. (Devon; Hampshire; Sussex; Kent)
Obituary   1932/I   *253*

Thornton, C. I. (Eton; Cambridge University; Kent; Middlesex)
Memoir of (Lord Harris)   1930/I   *316*
Obituary   1930/I   *266*
Recollections of F. R. Spofforth   1927/I   *299*
Views on the Reforms of 1889   1890   *xxxix*
Views on Some Questions of the Day   1890   *xliv*

Thornton, E. A. (South Australian Clubs Cricketer)
Obituary   1910/I   *148*

Thornton, Dr. P. G. (Yorkshire; Middlesex; Transvaal; Scotland; Ceylon; South Africa)
Obituary   1940   *846*

Thornton, J. (Victoria)
Obituary   1921/I   *244*

Thornton, J. R. (Sussex)
Obituary   1917   *266*

Thornton, P. M. (Secretary Middlesex)
Obituary   1919   *212*

Thornton, R. T. (Devon; Dorset; Wiltshire; Kent)
Obituary   1929/I   *259*

Thornton, W. A. (Winchester; Oxford University; Devon)
Obituary   1916   *209*

Thorogood, F. (Journalist)
Obituary   1951   *928*

Thorpe, C. (Northamptonshire)
Obituary   1954   *929*

Thorpe, J. (Essex Club Cricketer; Hertfordshire)
Obituary   1950   *914*

Thoseby, W. (Devon)
Obituary   1960   *957*

Thresher, Rev. J. H. (Winchester)
Obituary   1915/I   *242*

Thring, Sir A. T. (Winchester)
Obituary   1933/I   *259*

Thring, J. G. (Uppingham)
Obituary   1921/I   *238*

543

Thring, L. C. R. (Marlborough; Wiltshire; Bedfordshire)
Obituary 1935/I 274
Throw, Definitions and Notes on 1959 74,75,76
1960 123
1968 93
'Throw and Drag' H. Gee 1960 97
'Throwing Controversy, The' L. Smith 1961 111
Throwing the Cricket Ball 1943 93
Throwing in First Class Cricket – Discussion 1895 lu
Throwing A History–'Straight from the Shoulder'
I. A. R. Peebles Book Review 1969 1026
Throwing–Notes by the Editor 1898 lvii
1899 xc
1952 98
1953 86
1961 124
1966 79
1967 114
Throwing–Photograph of G. Griffin 1961 89
'Throwing Report' 1967 114
Throwley, Viscount (see under Sondes, 2nd Earl)
Thuillier, Capt. G. F. (Dover College)
Obituary 1920/I 158
Thurgar, Capt. R. W. (Norfolk)
Obituary 1919 20
Thurgar, W. A. (Norfolk)
Obituary 1948 78
Thurlow, 2nd Lieut. A. G. (Felsted)
Obituary 1916 216
Thurlow, H. M. (Queensland; Australia)
Obituary 1977 105.
Thursby, W. P. (Eton)
Obituary 1978 108.
Thursfield, Sub-Lt. J. B. (Winchester)
Obituary 1947 69
Thurston, H. P. (Thornbury C.C.)
Obituary 1921/I 24
Thwaite Dr. H. (President Warwickshire)
Obituary 1958 96.
Thynne, Major-Gen. Sir R. T. (Radley)
Obituary 1928/I 30
Tied Matches in First Class Cricket Note on 1953 8
Tied Matches–Unequal Reward Note on 1951 12
Tied Test Match (Australia v West Indies 1960-61)
'The Greatest Test of All'
J. H. Fingleton Book Review 1962 103

'The Greatest Test Match' E. M. Wellings	1961	*105*
Note on	1961	*120*
Tilbury, Capt. A. (Kings County C.C., Brooklyn)		
Obituary	1918	*207*
Tilford Green Note on	1944	*61*
Tillard, C. (Repton; Cambridge University; Norfolk; Surrey)		
Obituary	1945	*342*
Tillard, Lt-Col. E. D. (Somerset)		
Obituary	1968	*1008*
Tillard, Rev. R. M. (Rugby)		
Obituary	1916	*210*
Tilley, E. W. (Leicestershire)		
Obituary	1979	*1092*
Timms, B. S. V. (Hampshire; Warwickshire)		
Photograph	1969	*423*
Timms, J. E. (Wellingborough; Northamptonshire)		
Obituary	1981	*1150*
Tindall, E. (New South Wales)		
Obituary	1927/I	*292*
Tindall, Rev. H. C. L. (Kent)		
Obituary	1941	*402*
Tindall, R. A. E. (Surrey)		
Photographs	1962	*581*
	1964	*548*
Tindall, Capt. R. G. (Winchester; Oxford University; Dorset)		
Obituary	1943	*367*
Tindall, S. M. (Lancashire; London County)		
Obituary	1923/I	*305*
Tinley, Capt. N. L. (Harvard University)		
Obituary	1919	*191*
Tinley, R. C. (Nottinghamshire)		
Benefit Match	1876	*156*
Obituary	1901	*lxiii*
Tinley, W. E. (Assistant Secretary Nottinghamshire)		
Obituary	1878	*202*
Tinling, Lieut. C. B. (Highfield School, Ontario)		
Obituary	1920/I	*158*
Tinsley, A. (Lancashire; Staffordshire; Yorkshire)		
Obituary	1934/I	*277*
Tiplady, H. (Yorkshire Club Cricketer)		
Obituary	1927/I	*297*
Titchmarsh, C. H. (Bishop's Stortford College; Hertfordshire)		
Obituary	1931/I	*267*
Titchmarsh, V. A. (Hertfordshire; Umpire)		
Benefit Match	1907	*206*
Obituary	1908/I	*154*

Titley, Flt/Lt. E. G. (Uppingham; Free Foresters)
   Obituary   1944   *308*
Titley, U. A. (Journalist)
   Obituary   1975   *1083*
Titmus, F. J. (Middlesex; Surrey; Orange Free State; England)
   Benefit Match   1964   *486*
   Cricketer of the Year   1963   *170*
   Photographs   1954   *459*
                           1955   *435*
                           1956   *465*
                           1960   *482*
                           1963   *158*
                                          521
   'Talk of the Double' Book Review   1965   *1022*
   Titmus moves to Surrey Note on   1977   *114*
Tobago and Trinidad Schools in England 1977   1978   *841*
Tobin, F. (Rugby)
   Obituary   1928/I   *300*
Tobin, Rev. F. (Rugby; Cambridge University)
   Obituary   1915/I   *242*
Tobin, M. J. (Cornwall)
   Obituary   1982   *210*
Tobin, W. A. (Stonyhurst College; Victoria)
   Obituary   1905   *ci*
Tod, Lt-Col. A. A. (Eton)
   Obituary   1947   *695*
Tod, B. R. (Edinburgh Academy; Scotland)
   Schools Notes   1928/I   *320,341*
   75 wkts Schools Averages   1928/II   *605*
Todd, Lieut. A. F. (Mill Hill School; Berkshire)
   Obituary   1916   *210*
Todd, Rev. J. D. (Winchester)
   Obituary   1913/I   *200*
Todd, L. J. (Kent; London Counties; R.A.F.)
   Benefit Match   1948   *353*
   Obituary   1968   *1008*
Todd, P. A. (Nottinghamshire)
   Photographs   1977   *52*
                           1980   *52*
Tolchard, R. W. (Malvern; Devon; Leicestershire; England)
   Career Figures   1984   *1256*
   Photographs   1968   *48*
                           1971   *43*
                           1978   *45*
   Schools Note   1965   *74*
Tolhurst, E. K. (Victoria)
   Obituary   1983   *1257*

Tollemache, Hon. M. G. (Eton; Cheshire; Suffolk)
  Obituary   1951   *928*

Tolley, R. (Nottinghamshire)
  Obituary   1902   *lxxi*

Tomasson, Sir W. H. (Secretary; Treasurer Nottinghamshire)
  Obituary   1923/I   *306*

Tomblin, Rev. A. C. (Uppingham; Cambridge University)
  Obituary   1912/I   *182*

Tom Brown Centenary Match   1942   *22*
  The Match in Progress
  Photograph   1942   *26*
  Team Portraits   1942   *25*

Tombs, 2nd Lieut. J. S. M. (Loretto)
  Obituary   1916   *211*

Tomkins, E. F. (Northamptonshire)
  Obituary   1983   *1257*

Tomkinson, Sir G. S. (Winchester; Worcestershire)
  Obituaries   1964   *952*
                                      1965   *973*

Tomkinson, H. R. (Rugby)
  Obituary   1908/I   *156*

Tomkinson, Rt. Hon. J. (Rugby)
  Obituary   1911/I   *157*

Tomlin, 2nd Lieut. C. G. (Uppingham)
  Obituary   1917   *217*

Tomlin, W. (Leicestershire)
  Obituary   1911/I   *158*

Tomlinson, R. (Coach Loretto)
  Obituary   1931/I   *268*

Tomlinson, R. G. (Derbyshire)
  Obituary   1951   *930*

Tompkin, M. (Leicestershire)
  Benefit Match   1955   *431*
  Obituary   1957   *949*
  Photographs   1954   *439*
                                      1956   *445*

'Tonbridge Nursery' Capt. W. McCanlis   1907   *xcvi*

Tong, D. (Elland C.C.)
  Obituary   1917   *266*

Tonge, J. N. (Cheltenham; Kent)
  Obituary   1904   *lxxxiii*

Tonge, Lt-Col. W. C. (Cheltenham; Gloucestershire; Norfolk)
  Obituary   1944   *325*

Toogood, T. (Gloucestershire)
  Obituary   1955   *938*

Toomer, Lt-Col. C. R. (Northumberland; Wiltshire; Durham)
    Obituary   1927/I   297
Toone, Sir F. C. (Secretary Leicestershire and Yorkshire)
    'Australian Tours and their Management'   1930/I   270
    Obituary   1931/I   268
Toone, J. W. (Jamaica)
    Obituary   1928/I   300
Topham, Rev. H. G. (Repton; Derbyshire; Cambridge University)
    Obituary   1926/I   284
Toppin, C. (Sedbergh; Cambridge University; Cumberland; Worcestershire)
    'Modern Batting'   1922/I   242
    Obituary   1929/I   260
Toppin, C. G. (Malvern; Worcestershire)
    Obituary   1973   1014
Toppin, J. F. T. (Winchester; Worcestershire)
    Obituary   1966   973
Toronto Zingari in England 1910   1911/II   468
Torquay Plan of County Ground   1956   694
Torre, H. J. (Harrow; Oxford University)
    Obituary   1905   cii
Torrens, Capt. A. (Harrow)
    Obituary   1904   lxxix
Torrens, Major A. A. (Harrow)
    Obituary   1917   217
Torrens, W. (Writer)
    'Queensland Cricket and Cricketers 1862-1981'
    Book Review   1983   1298
Torrens, W. M. (Harrow; Kent)
    Obituary   1932/I   253
Tosetti, Major D. (Essex)
    Obituary   1919   191
Tosetti, G. (Essex)
    Obituary   1924/I   270
Toss Note on   1954   83
    Photograph of P. B. H. May and J. R. Reid   1959   37
Tosswill, A. C. (Rugby; Devon)
    Obituary   1927/I   292
Toulmin, E. M. O. (King's Canterbury; Essex)
    Obituary   1946   447
'Touring, Joy Of' H. Blofeld   1975   120
Tours–Dual Note on   1968   91
    Too Many Note on   1949   119
Towell, E. F. (Northamptonshire)
    Obituary   1975   1083
Townend, Capt. F. W. (Army; Bombay Presidency)
    Obituary   1916   211

Townley, R. C. (Tasmania)
  Obituary   1984   *1209*
Townsend, A. (Warwickshire)
  Benefit Match   1961   *595*
Townsend, C. L. (Clifton; Gloucestershire; London County; England)
  Obituary   1959   *938*
  Portrait and Biography   1899   *lix*
  Schools Notes   1894   *lvi, lviii*
  85 wkts Schools Averages   1895   *323*
Townsend, D. C. H. (Winchester; Oxford University; Durham; England)
  Schools Note   1932/I   *285*
Townsend, F. (Gloucestershire)
  Obituary   1921/I   *242*
Townsend, F. N. (Blair Lodge School; Gloucestershire)
  Obituary   1902   *lxxii*
Townsend, H. N. (Staten Island)
  Obituary   1928/I   *300*
Townsend, L. F. (Derbyshire; Northumberland; England; Auckland)
  Portrait and Biography   1934/I   *286*
Townshend, Rev. Canon W. (Rossall; Oxford University; Herefordshire; Leicestershire)
  Obituary   1924/I   *270*
Toynbee, Capt. G. P. R. (Winchester)
  Obituary   1915/I   *242*
Tozer, Dr. C. J. (New South Wales)
  Obituary   1921/I   *238*
Tracey, W. (New South Wales)
  Obituary   1913/I   *200*
Trafford, Hon. C. E. De (Lancashire; Leicestershire)
  Obituary   1952   *964*
Traill, W. F. (Merchant Taylors; Oxford University; Kent)
  Obituary   1906   *c*
Transfer System Note on   1968   *87*
Trasenter, Major H. A. (Winchester; Cambridge University)
  Obituary   1951   *930*
Trask, Surg. Capt. J. E. (Somerset)
  Obituary   1897   *xl*
Trask, W. (Sherborne; Somerset)
  Obituary   1950   *914*
Travers, B. (Playwright)
  Obituary   1982   *1210*
  '94 Declared : Cricket Reminscences'
  Book Review   1982   *1270*
Travers, F. G. (Bombay)
  Obituary   1951   *929*

Travers, 2nd Lieut. H. E. K. (Regina C.C., Canada)
Obituary   1917   *217*
Travis, Lieut. C. W. (St. Andrews College, Toronto)
Obituary   1920/I   *158*
Trayes, 2nd Lieut. F. K. J. (Aldenham)
Obituary   1919   *191*
Treadgold, J. P. (Yorkshire Club Cricket)
Obituary   1928/I   *300*
Tregar, D. H. (Middlesex)
Obituary   1952   *964*
Treglown, Lt-Col. C. J. H. (Essex; Norfolk)
Obituary   1981   *1150*
Tremantle, T. F. (See under Cottesloe, 2nd Baron)
Tremellan, 2nd Lieut. D. H. (Highgate School)
Obituary   1918   *207*
Tremlett, Major-Gen. E. A. E. (M.C.C.)
Obituary   1984   *1209*
Tremlett, M. F. (Somerset; Central Districts; England)
Benefit Match   1957   *525*
Photograph   1952   *487*
     1953   *508*
     1956   *525*
     1958   *523*
Record of Service   1961   *652*
Tremlett, T. M. (Hampshire)
Photograph   1982   *430*
Tremlin, B. (Essex)
Obituary   1937/I   *283*
Trench, Sgt. A. R. R. (Staten Island C.C.)
Obituary   1919   *191*
Trenehard, 2nd Lieut. J. W. (Mill Hill School)
Obituary   1918   *207*
Trenerry, W. L. (Australian Imperial Forces)
Obituary   1976   *1103*
Trent Bridge
'Centenary of Trent Bridge' A. W. Shelton   1938   *461*
England Team at: Photographs   1954   1955   *60*
     1957   1958   *48*
     1965   1966   *56*
     1967   1968   *61*
     1969   1970   *51*
     1970   1971   *66*
Note on   1952   *96*
Plan of Ground   1950   *461*
     ad passim
Queen Elizabeth II at Photograph   1978   *81*

Scoreboard Photograph	1952	*71*
Tresawana, H. (Cornwall)		
Obituary	1969	*988*
Tresider, P. (Writer)		
'Captains on a See-Saw' Book Review	1970	*1070*
Trestrail, Major A. E. Y. (Somerset)		
Obituary	1937/I	*289*
Trevelyan, W. B. (Harrow; Cambridge University)		
Obituary	1895	*xlii*
Trevilian, E. B. C. (Winchester)		
Obituary	1915/I	*243*
Trevor, A. H. (Winchester; Oxford University; Sussex)		
Obituary	1925/I	*282*
Trevor, Rev. E. W. (Durham School)		
Obituary	1917	*217*
Trevor, Major-Gen. F. C. (Auditor M.C.C.)		
Obituary	1915/I	*243*
Trevor, F. G. B. (Marlborough)		
Obituary	1926/I	*284*
Trevor, Col. P. C. W. (Journalist)		
Obituary	1933/I	*259*
Trevor, Canon Rev. Preb. T. W. (Marlborough)		
Obituary	1925/I	*283*
Trew, Capt. V. P. (Harrow)		
Obituary	1945	*342*
'Trials of a County Secretary' R. V. Ryder	1936/I	*257*
Triangular Tournament 1912	1913/II	*1*
Tribe, G. E. (Northamptonshire; Victoria, Australia)		
Career Figures	1960	*143*
Cricketer of the Year	1955	*75*
'Five Stalwarts Retire' Sir N. Cardus	1960	*142*
Photographs	1953	*471*
	1954	*478*
	1955	*67*
	1956	*485*
	1958	*482*
Trickett, Hon. W. J. (President New South Wales Cricket Association)		
Obituary	1917	*266*
Trim, J. (British Guiana; West Indies)		
Obituary	1961	*952*
Trimmer, Capt. A. S. (Ridley College, Ontario)		
Obituary	1919	*201*
Trinidad Rioters Photograph	1961	*90*
Trinidad and Tobago Schools in England 1977	1978	*841*
Tristram, H. B. (Loretto; Oxford University; Durham)		
Obituary	1947	*696*

Tristram, Lt-Col M. H. (Eton)
Obituary 1953 *950*
Tritton, E. W. (Eton; Oxford University; Surrey; Middlesex)
Obituary 1902 *lxx*
Tritton, W. F. (Eton)
Obituary 1931/I *269*
Trollope, W. S. (Westminster; Surrey)
Obituary 1896 *xlii*
Trotman, Canon E. F. (Winchester)
Obituary 1911/I *158*
Trott, A. E. (Victoria; Middlesex; England; Australia; Umpire)
Benefit Match 1908/II *134*
Obituary 1915/I *243*
Portrait and Biography 1899 *lviii*
Record by 1941 *65*
Trott, F. (Middlesex; Peebles County)
Obituary 1922.I *270*
Trott, G. H. S. (Victoria; Australia)
Obituary 1918 *235*
Portrait and Biography 1894 *xli*
Trotter, Lieut. C. H. (Galway Grammar School)
Obituary 1919 *191*
Trotter, D. N. (Ireland)
Obituary 1913/I *200*
Trotter, J. J. (Scotland)
Obituary 1918 *236*
Trotter, Lieut. S. F. (St.Dunstans; Winnipeg C.C.)
Obituary 1918 *207*
Troughton, H. C. (Writer)
'Recollections of W. Caffyn' 1920/I *168*
Troughton, Lt-Col. L. H. W. (Dulwich; Kent)
Obituary 1934/I *277*
Troughton, M. A. (Kent)
Obituary 1913/I *200*
Trouncer, C. A. (Surrey)
Obituary 1939 *918*
Troup, Capt. F. C. (Cheltenham; Gloucestershire)
Obituary 1925/I *283*
Troup, Major. W. (Gloucestershire)
Obituary 1942 *364*
Trower, Rev. H. W. (Buckinghamshire)
Obituary 1919 *212*
Trubshaw, E. (Glamorgan)
Obituary 1911/I *158*
Truell, Rev. W. H. A. (Cheltenham)
Obituary 1935/I *274*

Trueman, Lt-Col. A. P. H. (Military Cricket)
Obituary	1919	*191*

Trueman, F. S. (Yorkshire; Derbyshire; England)
'Ball of Fire' Book Review	1977	*1100*
Benefit Match	1963	*683*
Career Statistics	1970	*99*
Cricketer of the Year	1953	*66*
'Fast Fury' Book Review	1962	*1042*
'Fred: Portrait of a Fast Bowler'		
J. Arlott Book Review	1972	*1109*
Lone Spearhead Note on	1964	*92*
Photographs	1953	*60*
	1955	*588*
	1962	*138*
	1970	*93*
Retirement Note	1969	*93*
'Statham and Trueman; 'An Appreciation'		
J. M. Kilburn	1962	*134*
Statistics	1962	*142*
Tribute to Sir F. Worrell	1968	*122*
Trueman Arrives Note on	1953	*77*
Trueman joins Derbyshire Note on	1972	*124*
'F. S. Trueman: Fiery Fred' W. E. Bowes	1970	*92*
Trueman's Match Photograph	1962	*89*
Trueman's Record Photograph	1964	*85*
'The Freddie Trueman Story'		
Book Review	1966	*1020*
Trueman's World Record Photograph	1965	*69*
300 Test Wickets List of	1965	*399*

Trueman, G (New South Wales)
Obituary	1982	*1210*

Truman, L. (Treasurer Western Australia Cricket Association)
Obituary	1974	1081

Truman, 2nd Lieut. T. A. (Gloucestershire)
Obituary	1919	*191*

Trumble, H. (Victoria; Australia)
Obituary	1939	*918*
Portrait and Biography	1897/I	*1*

Trumble, J. W. (Victoria; Australia)
Cricket Reform	1927/I	*348*
Obituary	1945	*342*

Trumble, W. (Father of H. and J. W.)
Obituary	1910/I	*152*

Trumper, V. T. (New South Wales; Australia)
Benefit Match	1914/II	*512*

Fastest Hundred in Test Cricket
Note on 1983 *107*
'Giant of the Wisden Century'
Sir N. Cardus 1963 *102*
'The Immortal Victor Trumper'
J. Fingleton Book Review 1979 *1128*
In the Cricket Field 1916 *133*
Photograph 1963 *104*
Portrait and Biography 1903 *lxxxvii*
Special Memoir of (Obituary) 1916 *131*
'Victor Trumper' V Raiji
Book Review 1965 *1023*
'Victor Trumper and the 1902 Australians'
L. H. Brown Book Review 1982 *1271*
Trumper, V. (Junior) (New South Wales)
Obituary 1983 *1257*
Tryon, Lieut. (Northamptonshire)
Obituary 1902 *lxxi*
Obituary Correction 1903 *lxxxii*
Tubb, H. (Rugby; Oxfordshire)
Obituary 1925/I *283*
Tubbs, Capt. S. B. (Harrow)
Obituary 1918 *207*
Tubbs, Sir S. W. B. (Highgate School; President Gloucestershire)
Obituary 1942 *364*
Tuck, Rev. A. J. (Master l/c Uppingham)
Obituary 1919 *214*
Tuck, G. H. (Eton; Cambridge University; Norfolk)
Obituary 1921/I *238*
Tuck, Col. J. J. (Winchester)
Obituary 1936/I *293*
Tuck, Capt. W. S. (Upper Canada College)
Obituary 1918 *217*
Tucker, Sgt. G. S. (Trinity College, Port Hope)
Obituary 1918 *218*
Tucker, K. H. (Wellington, New Zealand)
Obituary 1940 *846*
Tucker, Rev. W. H. (Eton)
Obituary 1902 *lxxi*
Tuckett, L. R. (Orange Free State; South Africa)
Obituary 1965 *973*
Tuckwell, A. J. (Winnipeg C.C.)
Obituary 1912/I *182*
Tuckwell, B. J. (Victoria; Otago; Wellington)
Obituary 1944 *325*

554

Tudor, Brig. C. L. St.J. (Eastbourne College; Sussex)
Obituary   1978   *1082*
Tudor, Lt-Col R. G. (Eastbourne College; Sussex)
Obituary   1974   *1081*
Tudway, Lieut. H. R. C. (Household Brigade C.C.)
Obituary   1915/I   *245*
Tuff, Capt. C. T. (Kent Club Cricketer)
Obituary   1916   *211*
Tuff, 2nd Lieut. F. N. (Malvern; Oxford University)
Obituary   1916   *211*
Tufnell, C. F. (Coopers Hill School; Kent)
Obituary   1941   *402*
Tufnell, 2nd Lieut. C. W. (Eton)
Obituary   1915/I   *245*
Tufnell, Col. N. C. (Eton; Cambridge University; Surrey; England)
Obituary   1952   *964*
Schools Notes   1906   *cxx*
    1907   *cxxxviii*
    cxxxix

Tufton, Sir H. J. (See under Hothfield, 1st Lord)
Tufton, J. S. R. (See under Hothfield, 2nd Baron)
Tuke, 2nd Lieut. A. H. S. (Sherborne)
Obituary   1916   *212*
Tuke, 2nd Lieut A. H. S. (Sherborne)
Obituary   1916   *212*
Tuke, Dr. C. M. (Middlesex)
Obituary   1926/I   *284*
Tuke, Rev. F. H. (Herefordshire)
Obituary   1917   *217*
Tunbridge Wells Neville Ground
Plan of County Ground   1953   *396*
    ad passim
Tunnicliffe, C. J. (Derbyshire)
Career Figures   1984   *1250*
Photograph   1978   *356*
Tunicliffe, G. (Secretary Gloucestershire)
Obituary   1968   *1008*
Tunicliffe, J. (Yorkshire)
Benefit Match   1904   *53*
In First Class Cricket   1908/I   *167*
Obituary   1949   *870*
Portrait and Biography   1901   *lxx*
Turnbull, C. C. (Cheltenham)
Obituary   1911/I   *158*
Turnbull, M. J. (Downside; Cambridge University; Glamorgan; England)
'Memoir of' (Obituary) J. C. Clay   1945   *41*

Memorial Match	1946	*228*
Photograph	1945	*40*
Portrait and Biography	1931/I	*291*
Schools Notes	1924/I	*313*
	1925/I	*298,323*
	1926/I	*301,302*
		305,325,326
1323 runs Schools Averages	1926/II	*552*
'Study in Greatness' B. Easterbrook	1978	*157*
Turnbull, Pte. T. L. G. (Harrow)		
Obituary	1916	*212*
Turner, Pte. A. (Galt C.C., Ontario)		
Obituary	1918	*207*
Turner, Rt. Rev. A. B. (Marlborough)		
Obituary	1911/I	*158*
Turner, Brig. A. J. (Bedford Modern School; Bedfordshire; Essex)		
Obituary	1953	*950*
Turner, A. N. (Cheshire)		
Obituary	1907	*cxvi*
Turner, C. (Yorkshire)		
Obituary	1969	*988*
Turner, Major C. (Secretary Berkshire)		
Obituary	1927/I	*293*
Turner, C. T. B. (New South Wales; Australia)		
Benefit Match	1911/II	*519*
Obituary	1945	*342*
Portrait and Biography	1889	*xxviii*
Turner, D. R. (Hampshire; Western Province)		
Photographs	1970	*421*
	1976	*425*
Turner, E. (Melbourne C.C.)		
Obituary	1894	*xxxv*
Turner, Lieut. E. N. (Sandhurst; Scotland)		
Obituary	1909/I	*147*
Turner, 2nd Lieut. E. W. C. (St.Johns, Leatherhead)		
Obituary	1917	*217*
Turner, Lieut. F. H. (Sedbergh; Oxford University)		
Obituary	1916	*212*
Turner, Capt. G. (Fettes; Sandhurst)		
Obituary	1916	*212*
Turner, G. M. (Otago; Worcestershire; Northern Districts; New Zealand)		
Career Figures	1983	*96*
Cricketer of the Year	1971	*82*
Hundredth Hundred	1983	*628*
'My Way' Book Review	1976	*1150*

Photographs	1969	*620*
	1971	*71*
	1974	*82*
	1981	*596*
	1983	*94*
'Glen Turner's Century of Centuries' R. Cairns		
Book Review	1984	*1268*
'Glen Turner joins the Elite: 1000 runs by End of May'		
B. Easterbrook	1974	*80*
'Turner Marches on' N. Harris	1983	*93*
Turner, H. (Scorer Yorkshire)		
Obituary	1900	*lv*
Turner, H. (Treasurer Middlesex)		
Obituary	1911/I	*159*
Turner, H. (Scorer Oxford University; Journalist)		
Obituary	1942	*364*
Views on Second Class Counties and the		
L.B.W. Rule	1903	*lxv*
Turner, H. (Secretary Nottinghamshire)		
Obituary	1920/I	*187*
Turner, J. A. (Uppingham; Cambridge University; Leicestershire)		
Obituary	1926/I	*288*
Turner, J. R. F. (Cricket Coach)		
Obituary	1945	*344*
Turner, Dr. J. W. C. (Worcestershire)		
Obituary	1969	*988*
Turner, M. (Cheltenham; Middlesex)		
Obituary	1909/I	*147*
Turner, Capt. N. V. C. (Repton; Nottinghamshire)		
Obituary	1942	*364*
Turner, R. E. (Worcestershire)		
Obituary	1968	*1008*
Turner, Major R. H. (Repton; Nottinghamshire)		
Obituary	1948	*788*
Turner, S. (Essex; Natal)		
Photographs	1971	*335*
	1975	*380*
Turner, Lt-Col. W. M. F. (Wellington; Essex)		
Obituary	1949	*870*
Turton, E. E. (Canadian Club Cricketer)		
Obituary	1936/I	*289*
Tuthill, C. V. (New York Veterans Cricketers' Association)		
Obituary	1923/I	*306*

Tutt, A. J. (Groundsman Hastings)
Obituary 1945 *344*
Tutton, C. E. (Durban High School)
Obituary 1979 *1088*
Twemlow, Col. F. R. (Winchester; Cheshire; Staffordshire)
Obituary 1928/I *300*
'Twenty Years of Indian Test Cricket'
V. M. Merchant 1952 *110*
Twigg, Capt. F. W. (Repton; Staffordshire)
Obituary 1919 *192*
Twigg, W. H. (Staffordshire)
Obituary 1964 *952*
Twining, R. H. (Eton; Oxford University; Middlesex; President M.C.C.)
Obituary 1980 *1158*
Twisleton-Wykeham-Fienne's, Rev. Hon. W. S. (Winchester; Oxford University; Oxfordshire; Herefordshire)
Obituary 1924/I *271*
'Two Elevens, The – A Bygone Phase of Cricket'
S. H. Pardon 1925/I *229*
Twyman, G. (Kent)
Obituary 1921/I *244*
Twynam, Corpl. W. H. (Canadian Club Cricketer)
Obituary 1916 *213*
Tye, J. (Derbyshire; Nottinghamshire)
Obituary 1906 *ci*
Tyers, H. (U.S.A. Club Cricketer)
Obituary 1922/I *270*
Tyldesley, E. (Lancashire; England)
Benefit Matches 1925/II *160*
1934/II *209*
Hundredth Hundred 1935/II *378*
Obituary 1963 *1036*
Portrait and Biography 1920/I *255*
Tyldesley, H. (Lancashire)
Obituary 1936/I *289*
Tyldesley, J. D. (Lancashire)
Obituary 1924/I *271*
Tyldesley, J. T. (Lancashire; England)
Benefit Match 1907 *87*
In the Cricket Field Major R. O. Edwards 1923/I *273*
Obituary 1931/I *269*
Portrait and Biography 1902 *lxxxi*
Tyldesley, R. K. (Lancashire; England)

Benefit Match	1931/II	*144*
Obituary	1944	*326*
Portrait and Biography	1925/I	*294*
Tyldesley, Lieut. W. K. (Lancashire)		
Obituary	1919	*192*
Tylecote, C. B. L. (Clifton; Oxford University)		
Obituary	1936/I	*289*
Tylecote, E. F. S. (Clifton; Oxford University; Kent; Bedfordshire)		
Obituary	1939	*919*
Tylecote, H. G. (Clifton; Oxford University; Bedfordshire; Hertfordshire)		
Obituary	1936/I	*290*
Tylecote, Rev. T. B. (Bedfordshire)		
Obituary	1930/I	*264*
Tyler, E. J. (Somerset; Worcestershire; England)		
Benefit Match	1900	*224*
Obituary	1918	*237*
Tyler, F. (Northamptonshire)		
Obituary	1931/I	*270*
Tyler, 2nd Lieut. J. E .S .(Radley; IZingari)		
Obituary	1946	*435*
Tyndall, Lt-Col. W. E. M. (Bradfield)		
Obituary	1917	*217*
Tyrwhitt-Drake, Sir G. (Mayor of Maidstone)		
Obituary	1965	*971*
Tyson, C. (Yorkshire)		
Obituary	1941/I	*402*
Tyson, F. H. (Northamptonshire; England; Author; Broadcaster)		
'The Centenary Test' Book Review	1978	*1117*
Cricketer of the Year	1956	*60*
'The Hapless Hookers' Book Review	1977	*1094*
Photographs	1955	*454*
	1956	*53*
	1977	*117*
'Test of Nerves' Book Review	1976	*1145*
'A Typhoon Called Tyson' Book Review	1962	*1042*
Tyson's Coaching Manual Note on	1977	*113*
Tyssen, Rev. C. A. D. (Harrow)		
Obituary	1942	*366*
Ubsdell, G. (Hampshire)		
Obituary	1906	*ci*
Udal, G. F. (Middlesex; Leicestershire)		
Obituary	1982	*1210*
Udal, J. S. (Bromsgrove School; Dorset; Somerset)		
Obituary	1926/I	*284*

Udal, N. R. (Winchester; Oxford University)
  Obituary   1965   *972*
Ullathorne, C. E. (Yorkshire)
  Obituary   1905   *ciii*
Ullathorne, T. (Northumberland)
  Obituary   1927/I   *293*
Ulyett, G. (Yorkshire; England)
  Benefit Match   1888   *93*
  Obituary   1899   xlv
Umney, J. C. (Crystal Palace C.C.)
  Obituary   1920/I   *187*
'Umpires Association' A. Riley   1963   *784*
'Umpires Decisions, Lord Harris and'   1923/I   *231*
'Umpires – First-Class Photograph   1984   *Plate*
Umpires Notes on   1951   *119*
                                                1964   *90*
                                                1976   *63*
                                                1981   *93*
                                                1983   *77*
                                                1984   *50*
'Umpire's Point of View, The' F. Chester   1933/I   *302*
'Umpiring' T. Smith   1960   *103*
Under 25 Competition Note on   1972   *888*
Underhill, T. (Beverley C.C.)
  Obituary   1928/I   *300*
Underwood, D. L. (Kent; England)
  'Beating the Bat' Book Review   1976   *1150*
  Cricketer of the Year   1969   *63*
  'Deadly Down Under' Book Review   1981   *1198*
  Photographs   1964   *429*
                                                  1967   *441*
                                                  1969   *62*
                                                  1973   *109*
                                                  1980   442
Underwood, W. (Devonshire)
  Obituary   1915/I   *246*
Unique Individual Records Notes   1941   *61*
United States of America – U.S.A.
  Cricket Association – Formation   1962   *882*
  in England 1968 Note on   1968   *95*
                                                    1969   *709*
University Blues   1827-1939   1940   *557*
                       Correction   1941   *61*
                       1946-1983   1984   *636*

'Universities, The, in the Wisden Century'
  R. G. Marlar   1963   *697*
Upcher, Canon A. R. (Rossall)
  Obituary   1931/I   *273*
Upcher, H. B. (Repton)
  Obituary   1918   *238*
Upcher, H. M. (Harrow)
  Obituary   1922/I   *270*
Upham, E. F. (Wellington, New Zealand)
  Obituary   1936/I   *291*
'Ups and Downs on the Veld' L. Duffus   1951   *104*
Upton, Lieut/Adjt. J. A. E. (Forest School; Shropshire)
  Obituary   1917   *218*
Upton, 2nd Lieut. R. H. W. (Haileybury)
  Obituary   1918   *207*
Ure, Capt. I. (Loretto)
  Obituary   1919   *192*
Ussher, Capt. B. (Buckinghamshire)
  Obituary   1916   *213*
Utley, Rev. R. P. H. (Ampleforth; Hampshire; R.A.F.)
  Obituary   1969   *988*
Uzielli, Col. T. J. (Marlborough)
  Obituary   1935/I   *274*
Vaidya, S. (Writer)
  'Vinoo Mankad' Book Review   1971   *1078*
Vale, C. (Staffordshire)
  Obituary   1902   *lxxiv*
Vale, H. (Secretary East Melbourne C.C.)
  Obituary   1907   *cxvi*
Valentine, A. L. (Jamaica; West Indies)
  Cricketer of the Year   1951   *73*
  Photograph   1951   *64*
Valentine, B. H. (Repton; Cambridge University; Kent; England)
  Obituary   1984   *1210*
  Schools Notes   1925/I   *313*
                                                      1926/I   *302,316*
                                                      1927/I   *324*
Valentine, E. (Cumberland)
  Obituary   1952   *964*
Vallance, H. I. A. (Marlborough)
  Obituary   1924/I   *272*
Van Allen, K. M. (Trinity College, Port Hope)
  Obituary   1920/I   *158*
Van Cuylenburg, R. (Royal College, Ceylon; Broadcaster)
  Obituary   1974   *1085*

Van Der Bijl, P. G. V. (Oxford University; Western Province; South Africa)
  Obituary 1974 *1081*
Van Der Bijl, V. A. P. (South African Universities; Natal; Middlesex)
  Cricketer of the Year 1981 *87*
  Photograph 1981 *75*
Van Der Byl, V. A. W. (Western Province)
  Obituary 1943 *387*
Vane, Flt/Sgt. J. A. (King's Canterbury)
  Obituary 1945 *325*
Vane-Tempest, Lieut. C. S. (Eton)
  Obituary 1918 *207*
Van Geloven, J. (Yorkshire; Leicestershire)
  Photographs 1958 *444*
    1963 *503*
    1965 *472*
Van Geyzel, C. T. (Ceylon)
  Obituary 1972 *1056*
Van Manew, H. (Holland)
  Obituary 1984 *1210*
Vann, D. W. A. (Northamptonshire)
  Obituary 1962 *993*
Van Rensburg, M. (Beroni C.C., South Africa)
  Obituary 1969 *988*
Van Zyl, Major G. B. (Cape Town)
  Obituary 1957 *949*
Varachia, R. (President South African Cricket Union)
  Obituary 1983 *1258*
Vassall, G. C. (Charterhouse; Somerset)
  Obituary 1942 *364*
Vassall, H. H. (Bedford Grammar School)
  Obituary 1950 *914*
Vaughan, Inst. Comdr. D. B. (Devon)
  Obituary 1978 *1083*
Vaughan-Roberts, Lieut. R. W. (Northern C.C.)
  Obituary 1917 *218*
Vaughton, R. W. (South Australia)
  Obituary 1980 *1158*
Vaulkhard, D. H. (Nottinghamshire)
  Obituary 1983 *1258*
Veal, Major C. L. (Repton; Glamorgan)
  Obituary 1930/I *264*
Vears, A. W. (Committee Gloucestershire)
  Obituary 1918 *238*
Vehicle and General Test Awards Note on 1969 *655*
Veitch, 2nd Lieut. D. G. Le D. (Westminster)
  Obituary 1917 *218*

Venables, Lieut. G. R. (Gentlemen of Shropshire)
    Obituary   1918   *218*
Venables, R. G. (Rugby)
    Obituary   1921/I   *239*
Venkataraghavan, S. (Tamil Nadu; Derbyshire; India)
    Note on   1973   *372*
Venn, W. H. (Warwickshire)
    Obituary   1954   *929*
Ventry, 5th Lord (Harrow)
    Obituary   1925/I   *290*
Verelst, H. W. (Rugby; Yorkshire)
    Obituary   1919   *212*
Verity, H. (Yorkshire; England)
    Appreciation of (Sir D. Bradman)   1944   *50*
    Appreciation of (A. B. Sellers)   1944   *51*
    Benefit Match for Dependents   1946   *269*
    Bowling (1930-1939)   1941   *40*
    Memoir of (Obituary)
    R. C. Robertson-Glasgow   1944   *41*
    Memorial Match – Team Portraits   1945   *35*
    Notes on   1944   *192*
                                          1945   *205*
    Photograph   1944   *40*
    Portrait and Biography   1932/I   *273*
    Records by   1941   *65*
    'H. Verity' S. Davis Book Review   1953   *1001*
Verley, B. L. (Jamaica)
    Obituary   1908/I   *154*
Vernon, A. L. (Essex; Suffolk; Staffordshire)
    Obituary   1927/I   *297*
Vernon, B. W. (Supporter Northamptonshire)
    Obituary   1917   *266*
Vernon, G. F. (Rugby; Middlesex; England)
    Obituary   1903   *lxxv*
    Team in Australia 1887-88   1889   *286*
    Team in India 1889-90   1891   *323*
Vernon, Rev. Canon J. E. (Huntingdonshire)
    Obituary   1929/I   *260*
Vernou, Col. C. A. (Philadelphia; U.S.A.)
    Obituary   1921/I   *244*
Vials, G. A. T. (Wellingborough; Northamptonshire)
    Obituary   1975   *1083*
Vibart, R. F. (Harrow; Cornwall)
    Obituary   1936/I   *294*
Vick, His Hon. Judge Sir G. R. (Leys School)
    Obituary   1959   *939*

Vickers, Capt. C. G. (Repton)
  Obituary   1919   *201*

Vickers, W. W. (Canada)
  Obituary   1929/I   *262*

Vickery, Lieut. G. (St. Michael's C.C., Calgary)
  Obituary   1918   *207*

Vickery, J. C. (Devon)
  Obituary   1972   *1056*

Victory Calypso Photograph   1951   *57*

Victory Tests Note   1946   *62*

Vidal, 2nd Lieut. L. A. (Malvern)
  Obituary   1916   *213*

Vidler, J. L. S. (Repton; Oxford University; Oxfordshire; Sussex)
  Obituary   1968   *1008*

'Views and Values' R. C. Robertson-Glasgow   1945   *46*

Vigar, F. H. (Essex)
  Benefit Match   1954   *329*

Vigar, J. E. (Trinity School, Croydon)
  Schools Notes   1982   *864*
  1,103 runs Schools Averages   1982   *897*

Vigers, 2nd Lieut. R. S. G. (Uppingham)
  Obituary   1918   *207*

Viljoen, K. G. (Western Province; Orange Free State; Griqualand West; South Africa)
  Obituary   1975   *1083*

Village Cricket Championship   1972   *1001*

Vincent, Sir H. G. (Haileybury; Cambridge University)
  Obituary   1982   *1211*

Vincent, R. (Treasurer New Zealand Cricket Council)
  Obituary   1916   *222*

Vincent, Major R. B. (Journalist)
  Obituary   1959   *939*

Vine, J. (Sussex; England)
  Benefit Match   1914/II   *137*
  Obituary   1947   *696*
  Portrait and Biography   1906   *cix*

Vint, W. (North of Ireland C.C.)
  Obituary   1898   *xliii*

Vint, Capt. W. P. (Bedford Grammar School)
  Obituary   1919   *192*

Vintcent, C. H. (Charterhouse; Griqualand West; Transvaal; South Africa)
  Obituary   1944   *326*

Violence Note on   1970   *78*

Viret, J. (British Guiana; U.S.A. Club Cricketer)
  Obituary   1937/I   *283*

Virgin, R. T. (Somerset; Northamptonshire)

Cricketer of the Year	1971	*85*
Photograph	1966	*534*
	1968	*549*
	1971	*72*
	1972	*546*
	1975	*502*

Vivian, H. G. (Auckland; New Zealand)

Obituary	1984	*1210*

Vizianagram, Maharaj Sir Vijaya (see entry under **Anand Majaraj Kumur**)

Voce, W. (Nottinghamshire; England)

Benefit Match	1940	*416*
Bradford League Note	1944	*286*
Portrait and Biography	1933/I	*269*

Vockins, M. D. (Writer)
Worcester County Cricket Club – A Pictorial History'

Book Review	1981	*1193*

Vogler, A. E. (Middlesex; Natal; Eastern Province; Transvaal; Aberdeenshire; South Africa)

Obituary	1947	*696*
Portrait and Biography	1908/I	*166*

Voller, Pte. S. F. (West Surrey Club Cricketer)

Obituary	1916	*213*

Von Donop, Lt-Col. P. G. (Woolwich Garrison)

Obituary	1922/I	*270*

Von Poellnitz, Major H. W. (Repton; Sandhurst)

Obituary	1919	*192*

Von Winckler, Lieut. M. W. (St.Paul's)

Obituary	1918	*207*

Vorrath, W. (Otago, New Zealand)

Obituary	1935/I	*274*

Voss, R. (Surrey)

Obituary	1901	*lxv*

Voules, Rev. S. C. (Marlborough; Oxford University)

Obituary	1924/I	*272*

Waad, R. (Junior) (American Club Cricketer)

Obituary	1927/I	*293*

Wace, H. (Shrewsbury)

Obituary	1949	*873*

Waddington, A. (Yorkshire; England)

Obituary	1960	*957*

Waddy, Rev. E. F. (New South Wales; Warwickshire)

Obituary	1959	*939*

Waddy, Canon P. S. (New South Wales; Oxford University)

Obituary	1938	*946*

Wade, H. F. (Natal; South Africa)
Obituary   1982   *1211*
Wade, S. (Yorkshire)
Obituary   1933/I   *265*
Wade, T. H. (Essex)
Benefit Match   1949   *309*
Wade-Gery, Capt. R. H. (Army)
Obituary   1917   *218*
Wadekar, A. (Bombay; India)
'My Cricketing Years' Book Review   1973   *1059*
Wadham, Midshipman N. C. (Eton)
Obituary   1954   *930*
Wadlow, Major H. (Malvern)
Obituary   1917   *218*
Wadsworth, Lieut. D' A. R. (Toronto C.C.; Upper Canada College)
Obituary   1917   *218*
Wadsworth, K. J. (Nelson; Central Districts; Canterbury; New Zealand)
Obituary   1977   *1050*
Testimonial Match   1978   *947*
Wadsworth, W. R. (Canada)
Obituary   1931/I   *270*
Waduragala, M. (Combined Services, Ceylon)
Obituary   1971   *1032*
Waghorn, H. T. (Student of the Game)
Obituary   1931/I   *270*
Wainwright, E. (Yorkshire; England)
Benefit Match   1899   *17*
In the Cricket Field   1898   *xci*
Obituary   1920/I   *187*
Portrait and Biography   1894   *xlv*
Wainwright, 2nd Lieut. G. C. (Wellington)
Obituary   1916   *222*
Wait, Lieut. H. A. V. (Oakham)
Obituary   1919   *201*
Wait, O. J. (Dulwich; Cambridge University; Surrey)
Obituary   1982   *1211*
Waite, J. C. (Emanuel School)
Schools Notes   1981   *856*
1056 runs Schools Averages   1981   *877*
Waite, J. H. B. (Eastern Province; Transvaal; South Africa)
'Perchance to Bowl' Book Review   1962   *1042*
Wake, Sir H. 12th Bart. (Supporter Northamptonshire)
Obituary   1917   *266*
Wake, W. R. (Yorkshire)
Obituary   1897   *xxxix*

Wakefield, J. (Charterhouse)
   Obituary   1949   *870*

Wakefield, W. H. (West Indies Tour 1895)
   Obituary   1923/I   *306*

Wakeman, E. M. (Eton; Shropshire; Worcestershire)
   Obituary   1927/I   *293*

Wakley, J. B. (Writer)
   'Bradman the Great' Book Review   1960   *1002*

Walcot, Lieut. J. H. L. (Christ's Hospital)
   Obituary   1915/I   *246*

Walcott, C. L. (Barbados; British Guiana; West Indies)
   Cricketer of the Year   1958   *57*
   'Island Cricketers' Book Review   1959   *990*
   Photograph   1958   *56*

Waldegrave, 2nd Lieut. E. J. (Marlborough)
   Obituary   1919   *192*

Walden, F. I. (Northamptonshire; Umpire)
   Benefit Match   1928/II   *366*
   Obituary   1950   *914*

Waldcock, F. A. (Uppingham; Oxford University; Ceylon)
   Obituary   1960   *957*

Waldcock, H. F. (Uppingham)
   Obituary   1924/I   *273*

Waleran, 1st Baron of Uffculme (Eton; Devon)
   Obituary   1926/I   *285*

Walford, Major G. H. (Rugby)
   Obituary   1916   *213*

Walford, Capt. H. S. (Tonbridge)
   Obituary   1919   *192*

Walford, Rev. O. S. (Charterhouse)
   Obituary   1931/I   *271*

Walkden, G. G. (Derbyshire)
   Obituary   1924/I   *273*

Walker, A. (Westminster; Cambridge University; Yorkshire; Staffordshire; Ceylon)
   Obituary   1928/I   *300*

Walker, Preb. A. (Westminster)
   Obituary   1920/I   *194*

Walker, Capt. A. J. (Wellingborough Grammar School)
   Obituary   1916   *213*

Walker, Rev. C. H. (Harrow)
   Obituary   1911   *163*

Walker, C. W. (South Australia)
   Obituary   1946   *435*

Walker, Flt/Lt. D. F. (King's College, Wimbledon; Hampshire)
   Obituary   1942   *351*

Walker, Flt/Lt. D. F. (Uppingham; Oxford University; Norfolk)
Obituary   1943   *367*

Walker, Lieut. D. F. G. (Magdalen College School; Lincolnshire)
Obituary   1944   *308*

Walker, Rev. F. (St.George C.C., Canada)
Obituary   1911/I   *159*

Walker, Capt. F. D. (IZingari)
Obituary   1914/I   *196*

Walker, Sir G. C. (Winchester)
Obituary   1926/I   *285*

Walker, G. G. (Derbyshire)
Obituary   1909/I   *147*

Walker, Capt. H. J. I. (Military Cricket)
Obituary   1916   *214*

Walker, H. L. (Scorer Yorkshire)
Obituary   1966   *973*

Walker, I. D. (Harrow; Middlesex)
Special Memoir of (Obituary)   1899   *li*
Views on the L.B.W. Rule   1888   *356*
Views on Reforms of 1889   1890   *xxxvii*
Views on Some Questions of the Day   1890   *xlii*
Views on Throwing   1895   *liii*

Walker, J. (Kent)
Obituary   1969   *988*

Walker, J. B. (Scotland)
Obituary   1955   *938*

Walker, Lieut. J. C. (Trinity College, Port Hope)
Obituary   1918   *208*

Walker, J. C. (Malden Wanderers C.C.)
Obituary   1964   *953*

Walker, J. G. (Loretto; Oxford University; Middlesex)
Obituary   1924/I   *273*

Walker, Sgt. J. P. (East Melbourne C.C.)
Obituary   1918   *218*

Walker, Capt. J. S. D. (Sydney University)
Obituary   1919   *192*

Walker, Rev. J. S. M. (Lancing)
Obituary   1954   *930*

Walker, L. (London County; Surrey)
Obituary   1941   *402*

Walker, M. H. N. (Victoria; Australia)
'Tangles' Book Review   1978   *1126*

Walker, Lieut. M. J. L. (Uppingham)
Obituary   1918   *208*

Walker, Capt. N. A. M. (Derbyshire)
Obituary   1961   *952*

Walker, N. S. (U.S.A. Club Cricketer)
Obituary   1932/I   *253*
Walker, P. M. (Glamorgan; Transvaal; Western Province; England)
Benefit Match   1967   *398*
Photographs   1960   *376*
                                                  1962   *389*
                                                  1969   *383*
'Peter Walker Benefit Brochure' Book Review   1967   *1020*
Walker, R. (Lancashire)
Obituary   1920/I   *189*
Walker, Capt. R. B. (Wellington)
Obituary   1919   *192*
Walker, R. D. (Harrow; Oxford University; Middlesex)
Appreciatrion of R. A. H. Mitchell   1906   *lxxxiii*
Obituary   1923/I   *306*
Walker, R. St.G. (Junior) (Staten Island C.C.)
Obituary   1920/I   *158*
Walker, Capt. S. (Hillhurst C.C., Calgary)
Obituary   1918   *218*
Walker, T. (Yorkshire)
Obituary   1926/I   *285*
Walker, V. E. (Harrow; Middlesex; President M.C.C.)
Obituary   1907   *ci*
Memoir of (Obituary) Old Friend   1907   *lxxxiii*
Views on High Scoring and the L.B.W Rule   1899   *lxxi*
Views on the L.B.W. Rule   1888   *355*
Views on Throwing   1895   *liii*
Walker, W. (Groundsman Trent Bridge)
Obituary   1912/I   *183*
Walker, W. (Nottinghamshire)
Benefit Match   1934/II   *272*
Walker, W. A. (Secretary Sussex)
Obituary   1955   *937*
Walker, Capt. W. G. J. (Epsom College)
Obituary   1918   *208*
Walker-Coren, E. (Cheltenham)
Obituary   1916   *214*
Wall, T. W. (South Australia; Australia)
Obituary   1982   *1211*
Wall, W. (Lancashire)
Obituary   1923/I   *308*
Wall, W. H. (Gloucestershire)
Obituary   1915/I   *246*
Wallace, Sgt. A. (New Zealand Club Cricket)
Obituary   1918   *218*

Wallace, Dr. A. (Winchester; Oxford University)
Obituary 1900 *liv*
Wallace, C. I. S. (Cricket Book Collector)
Obituary 1970 *1026*
Wallace, F. (President Flintshire C.C.C.)
Obituary 1968 *1009*
Wallace, Capt. Dr. G. H. (St. Andrews, Toronto)
Obituary 1920/I *159*
Wallace, 2nd Lieut. H. S. H. (Fettes)
Obituary 1917 *218*
Wallace, Col. N. W. (Rugby; Club Cricketer)
Obituary 1932/I *253*
Wallace, Lieut. W. M. (Edinburgh Academy)
Obituary 1916 *214*
Wallach, B. (London County; Transvaal)
Obituary 1936/I *291*
Waller, C. E. (Surrey; Sussex)
Photograph 1978 *554*
Waller, Very Rev. C. K. (Felsted)
Obituary 1952 *964*
Waller, Capt. Sir F. E. 4th Bart. (Warwickshire)
Obituary 1916 *222*
Waller, G. (Yorkshire)
Obituary 1938 *946*
Waller, Lieut. J. C. (Trinity College, Port Hope)
Obituary 1918 *208*
Wallington, Sir E. W. (Sherborne; Oxford University; Dorset; Wiltshire)
Obituary 1934/I *278*
Wallington, Capt./Adjt. G. S. (Eton)
Obituary 1918 *208*
Wallington, Sir J. W. (Gentlemen of Hampshire)
Obituary 1911/I *159*
Wallis, P. (Vice President Derbyshire)
Obituary 1906 *ci*
Wallroth, C. A. (Harrow; Oxford University; Kent; Derbyshire)
Obituary 1927/I *293*
Walmisley, Major W. M. (Famous Cricket Family)
Obituary 1916 *214*
Walmsley, E. (London County)
Obituary 1949 *871*
Walmsley, W. T. (Tasmania; Queensland)
Obituary 1979 *1088*
Walpole, Lieut. H. S. (Kent)
Obituary 1919 *192*
Walpole, R. C. (Radley)
Obituary 1929/I *260*

570

Valrond, S. H. (Rugby)
Obituary   1931   *271*

Valsh, G. (Lancashire)
Obituary   1905   *ciii*

Valsh, J. E. (New South Wales; Leicestershire)
Benefit Match   1956   *449*
Obituary   1981   *1150*
Photograph   1950   *410*
    1951   *415*
    1953   *433*

Valsingham, Baron (Eton; Cambridge University; Norfolk)
Obituary   1920/I   *189*

Valter, A. F. (Eton; Oxford University)
Obituary   1911/I   *159*

Valter, Rev. H. M. (Eton)
Obituary   1933/I   *265*

Valters, C. (Oxfordshire)
Obituary   1972   *1056*

Valters, C. F. (Worcestershire; Glamorgan; England)
Portrait and Biography   1934/I   *283*

Valters, Rev. E. (Broadcaster)
Obituary   1975   *1084*

Valters, Rev. E. W. R. (Ardingly; Northumberland)
Obituary   1906   *ci*

Valters, F. H. (Victoria; New South Wales; Australia)
Obituary   1923/I   *308*

Valters, J. (Derbyshire)
Photograph   1981   *371*

Valters, K. D. (New South Wales; Australia)
'Looking for Runs' Book Review   1972   *1101*

Valton, Sgt. W. A. (Ferguslie C.C.)
Obituary   1917   *218*

Vanklyn, D. (New Zealand Cricket Council)
Obituary   1955   *937*

Vanklyn, W. G. (Writer)
'Derief Taylor—the Natural Coach'   1977   *154*

Vanostrocht, N. ('Felix')
'Felix on the Bat' G. Brodribb Book Review   1963   *1102*
Obituary   1877   *109*

Varburton, F. (Lancashire League Cricketer)
Obituary   1950   *916*

Varburton, F. G. (American Club Cricketer)
Obituary   1908/I   *154*

Vard, A. (Yorkshire; Lancashire; England)
Benefit Match   1903   *97*
Obituary   1940   *846*

Portrait and Biography	1890	*xxvii*
Ward, A. (Derbyshire; Border; Leicestershire; England)		
Photograph	1972	36
Ward, A. S. (Eton)		
Obituary	1951	92
Ward, B. (Essex)		
Photograph	1970	37
Ward, Rt. Rev. Monsignor B. (Grandson of W. Ward)		
Obituary	1921/I	23
Ward, Rev. C. G. (Hampshire; Lincolnshire; Hertfordshire)		
Obituary	1955	93
Ward, Rev. E. E. H. (Bury St. Edmunds Grammar School; Cambridge University Suffolk)		
Obituary	1941	40
Ward, E. P. (British Columbia Club Cricketer)		
Obituary	1917	26
Ward, E. R. (Journalist)		
Obituary	1935/I	27
Ward, F. A. (South Australia; Australia)		
Obituary	1975	108
Ward, Sgt. G. (Balmain C.C., New South Wales)		
Obituary	1917	22
Ward, Lieut. Hon. G. E. F. (Eton; Gloucestershire)		
Obituary	1918	21
Ward, G. R. (Secretary Buckinghamshire)		
Obituary	1908/I	15
Ward, H. F. (Hampshire)		
Obituary	1898	xl
Ward, H. P. (Shrewsbury; Oxford University; Yorkshire)		
Obituary	1947	69
Ward, K. (Writer)		
'Put Lock On' Book Review	1973	105
Ward, L. M. (Warwickshire)		
Obituary	1982	121
Ward, Capt. M. A. (St. Paul's)		
Obituary	1919	1
Ward, M. De. S. C. (Eton; Hampshire)		
Obituary	1982	121
Ward, Capt. Hon. R. A. (Eton)		
Obituary	1943	3
Ward, T. A. (Transvaal; South Africa)		
Obituary	1937/I	28
Ward, 2nd Lieut. T. P. (Rugby House Matches)		
Obituary	1918	20
Ward, W. (Warwickshire)		
Obituary	1962	9

Ward, Capt. W. D. (Blundells)
Obituary   1919   *192*

Wardell, T. A. (Yorkshire)
Obituary   1933/I   *260*

Warden J. S. (Parsis; All India)
Obituary   1929/I   *261*

Wardill, Major B. J. (Victoria)
Obituary   1918   *239*

Wardle, J. H. (Yorkshire; Cambridgeshire; England)
Benefit Match   1958   *1016*
Career Figures   1959   *112*
'Cricketer of the Year'   1954   *75*
'Happy Go Johnny' Book Review   1958   *1016*
Notes on   1947   *528*
   1956   *71*
Photographs   1950   *571*
   1951   *587*
   1953   *611*
   1954   *62*
   1956   *632*
'The Wardle Case' N. Preston   1959   *111*

Wardley, Lieut. G. C. N. (Trinity College, Cambridge)
Obituary   1917   *218*

Wareham, C. (Wellington, New Zealand)
Obituary   1943   *368*

Waring, S. (Yorkshire)
Obituary   1920/I   *190*

Warman, Lieut. E. L. (Bradfield)
Obituary   1919   *193*

Warne, T. S. (Victoria)
Benefit Match   1912/II   *537*

Warner, G. T. (Cricket Enthusiast)
Obituary   1917   *266*

Warner, H. (New York Club Cricketer)
Obituary   1911/I   *159*

Warner, H. W. (Writer)
'The Story of Canterbury Cricket Week'
Book Review   1961   *992*

Warner, O. (Writer)
'Frank Woolley' Book Review   1953   *1001*

Warner, Sir P. F. (Rugby; Oxford University; Middlesex; President M.C.C.; England)
At Lord's and the Oval   1917   *268*
'The Book of Cricket' Advert Review   1946   *4*
'Cricket Between Two Wars' Advert Review   1946   *2*
'Cricket in West Indies and America'   1898   *lxx*

'Long Innings' Book Review		1952	101
Notes on		1947	20
		1951	12
		1955	9
Obituary (Note on)		1964	9
'Our Young Cricketers'		1911/I	11
Photographs		1921/I	24
		1964	12
Portrait and Biography		1904	xc
Presentation to		1944	16
Schools Notes		1891	30
		1892	27
		1893	30
Special Article on		1921/I	24
Team in U.S.A.	1897	1898	40
Team in U.S.A./Canada	1898	1899	41
Tributes to: C. S. Caine		1934/I	2
C. B. Fry		1957	11
Sir S. Jackson		1948	7
D. R. Jardine		1959	93
G. Jessop		1956	97
S. H. Pardon		1926/I	3
A. J. Webbe		1942	35
Views on Growing Pains of Cricket		1956	8
'Sir P. F. Warner' A. W. Langford (Obituary)		1964	12
'Plum Warner' L. Meynell Book Review		1952	101
'Plum Warner's Last Season' R. Mason Book Review		1971	106
The Warner Stand Note on		1959	8
'The West Indian Tour'		1901	xc
Warner, R. S. A. (Trinidad)			
Obituary		1945	34
Warr, J. J. (Ealing Grammar School; Cambridge University; Middlesex; England)			
Photographs		1957	45
		1960	48
Warre, Rev. Dr. E. (Headmaster Eton)			
Obituary		1921/I	2
Warren, A. R. (Derbyshire; England)			
Obituary		1952	9
Warren, Rev. C. (Oakham; Cambridge University)			
Obituary		1920/I	1
Warren, Pte. H. S. (West Herts C.C.)			
Obituary		1918	2
Warren, Capt/Ass. Adjt. T. (Upper Canada College)			
Obituary		1917	2

Warren, 2nd Lieut. T. S. W. (Monkton Combe School)

Obituary	1917	*219*

Warsop, B. (Cricket Bat Maker)

Obituary	1926/I	*285*

Warsop, W. (Cricket Bat Maker)

Obituaries	1950	*914*
	1951	*930*

'Wartime, Cricket in' H. S. Altham

	1940	*43*

Warton, Major R. (See under **Wharton, Major, R. G.**)

Warwickshire County Cricket Club

County Badge	1950/I	*533*
	ad passim	
In First Class Cricket	1912/I	*194*
Notes on	1952	*93*
	1960	*120*
'The Story of Warwickshire Cricket'		
L. Duckworth Book Review	1975	*1116*
Team Portraits		

County Champions	1951	1952	*68*
Championship Runners-up	1964	1965	*73*
County Champions	1972	1973	*65*
	1974	1975	*585*
	1975	1976	*588*
	1976	1977	*591*
	1977	1978	*573*
	1978	1979	*565*
	1979	1980	*591*
	1980	1981	*583*
	1981	1982	*590*
	1982	1983	*608*
	1983	1984	*568*

'Trials of a County Secretary'

R. V. Ryder	1936/I	*257*

'Warwickshire County Cricketers 1843-1973'

R. Brooke Book Review	1974	*1118*

'Warwickshire Cricket Record Book'

R. Brooke Book Review	1983	*1302*

'Warwickshire – the Unpredictable'

R. Ryder	1968	*124*

'Warwickshire's Ups and Downs'

M. F. K. Fraser	1950	*88*
'The Warwickshire Way' R. Ryder	1973	*127*
Warwickshire Win Gillette Cup Photograph	1969	*57*
Warwickshire's World Record Photograph	1975	*71*
(J. A. Jameson, R. ,B. Kanhai)		

Washbrook, C. (Lancashire; England)
Benefit Match	1949	249
Career Figures	1960	143
Cricketer of the Year	1947	53
'Cricket: The Silver Lining' Book Review	1951	99
'Five Stalwarts Retire' Sir N. Cardus	1960	139
'Hutton and Washbrook' A. A. Thomson		
Book Review	1964	100
Photographs	1947	4
	1950	39
	1951	39
	1955	40
	1958	42
Tribute to: G. Duckworth	1967	96

Washer, A. (Canterbury)
Obituary	1912/I	18

Washer, G. W. (Journalist; Writer; Scorer Sussex)
'A Complete Record of Sussex Cricket'
Book Review	1959	98
Obituary	1976	110

Washington, Lieut. H. H. (DHamilton C.C., Ontario)
Obituary	1918	23

Washington, W. A. I. (Yorkshire)
Obituary	1928/I	30

Wasim Bari (Pakistan International Airways; Pakistan)
Wasim Bari Equals a Test Record – Photograph	1972	6

Wass, T. G. (Nottinghamshire)
Obituary	1954	93
Portrait and Biography	1908/I	16

Wassell, A. (Hampshire)
Photograph	1963	44

Wassell, A. (Warwickshire)
Obituary	1977	105

Wassell, T. E. (Vice President Derbyshire)
Obituary	1966	97

Waterman, L. W. (Queensland)
Obituary	1953	95

Water Orton Photograph of Ground 1980 5

Wathen, A. C. (Kent)
Obituary	1938	94

Wathen, W. H. (Kent)
Obituary	1915/I	24

Watkins, Pte. A. H. (Hillhurst C.C.; Calgary)
Obituary	1917	21

Watkins, A. J. (Glamorgan; England)
Benefit Match	1956	34

Photographs	1952	*327*
	1954	*344*
	1955	*329*
	1956	*343*
Watkins, B. T. L. (Gloucestershire)		
Obituary	1984	*1211*
Watkins, Wing-Comdr. D. H. (Secretary Devon)		
Obituary	1970	*1026*
Watkins, Lieut. M. H. (Monmouth Grammar School)		
Obituary	1919	*193*
Watling, W. H. (South Australia)		
Obituary	1930/I	*269*
Watney, A. G. (Winchester)		
Obituary	1929/I	*262*
Watson, A. (Lancashire)		
Benefit Match	1886	*174*
Obituary	1921/I	*239*
Watson, Rev. A. (Cambridge University)		
Obituary	1921/I	*241*
Watson, Capt. A. C. (York C.C.)		
Obituary	1917	*219*
Watson, Lt-Col. A. C. (Uppingham; Sussex; Essex)		
Obituary	1953	*951*
Watson, Hon. A. G. (Grange C.C., Scotland)		
Obituary	1949	*872*
Watson, Rev. A. H. (Lincolnshire; Suffolk)		
Obituary	1953	*951*
Watson, D. (Rugby; Sussex)		
Obituary	1966	*976*
Watson, Lieut. D. J. F. (Sedbergh; Oxford University)		
Obituary	1944	*308*
Watson, F. (Lancashire)		
Obituary	1977	*1050*
Watson, G. (Scarborough C.C.)		
Obituary	1939	*921*
Watson, G. S. (Shrewsbury; Kent; Leicestershire)		
Obituary	1975	*1084*
Watson, 2nd Lieut. H. (Lancashire Club Cricketer)		
Obituary	1917	*219*
Watson, H. (Norfolk)		
Obituary	1970	*1026*
Watson, H. D. (Harrow; Oxford University)		
Obituary	1948	*788*
Watson, Dr. J. R. (Harrogate C.C.)		
Obituary	1916	*214*

Watson, Lt-Col. O. C. S. (St.Paul's)
Obituary   1919   *193*
Watson, R. F. (Campbell College, Belfast)
75 wkts Schools Averages   1936/II   *586*
Watson, Rev. T. H. (St.Bees; Cambridge University; Warwickshire)
Obituary   1945   *345*
Watson, W. (Yorkshire; Leicestershire; England)
Benefit Match   1957   *631*
Career Record   1963   *1042*
Cricketer of the Year   1954   *73*
'Double International' Book Review   1957   *1001*
Photographs   1954   *63*
                                                     1957   *620*
                                                     1960   *464*
Test Selector Photograph   1963   *150*
Watson, W. G. (Writer)
Obituary   1926/I   *285*
Watson, Capt. W. G. D. (Annan C.C.)
Obituary   1918   *208*
Watt, A. E. (Kent)
Obituary   1975   *1084*
Watt, J. (Tasmania)
Obituary   1920/I   *195*
Watt, Lieut. P. B. (Watson's College)
Obituary   1919   *193*
Watt, Lieut. P. D. (Watson's College)
Obituary   1919   *193*
Watts, E. A. (Surrey)
Benefit Match   1950   *511*
Obituary   1983   *1258*
Watts, F. M. I. (Devon)
Obituary   1968   *1009*
Watts, G. H. (Surrey; Cambridgeshire)
Obituary   1950   *915*
Watts, 2nd Lieut. H. V. I. (Newton College; Devon)
Obituary   1918   *208*
Watts, J. A. I. (Newton College)
93 wkts Schools Averages   1913/II   *510*
Watts, P. D. (Northamptonshire; Nottinghamshire)
Photograph   1963   *538*
Watts, P. J. (Northamptonshire)
Benefit Match   1975   *713*

Photographs	1963	*538*
	1966	*500*
	1972	*514*
	1974	*496*
	1981	*505*
Watts, 2nd Lieut. R. K. (Military Cricket)		
Obituary	1919	*193*
Watts, W. (Cambridgeshire)		
Obituary	1911/I	*159*
Waude, Lieut. S. (Hillhunt C.C., Calgary)		
Obituary	1919	*201*
Waugh, A. (Novelist)		
Obituary	1982	*1212*
Waugh, Capt. A. J. (Forest School)		
Obituary	1917	*219*
Waugh, H. P. (Essex; Suffolk)		
Obituary	1956	*978*
Waymouth, Major E. G. (R.A.XI)		
Obituary	1918	*208*
Wazir Ali, Major S. (Southern Punjab; India)		
Obituary	1951	*929*
Weatherby, C. T. (Winchester)		
Obituary	1914/I	*196*
Weatherby, J. H. (Winchester)		
Obituary	1949	*872*
Weatherby, Capt. T. (Winchester)		
Obituary	1916	*214*
Weaver, F. C. (Gloucestershire)		
Obituary	1950	*915*
Weaver, Sub-Lt. F. C. (Metropolitan Club Cricket)		
Obituary	1917	*219*
Weaver-Adams, Dr. E. (Buckinghamshire)		
Obituary	1932/I	*254*
Weaver-Adams, Dr. E. R. (Buckinghamshire)		
Obituary	1966	*973*
Webb, A. (Hampshire)		
Benefit Match	1905	*249*
Webb, Lt-Comdr. A. G. C. (Kent; Leicestershire)		
Obituary	1982	*1212*
Webb, Rev. C. J. B. (Radley; Middlesex; Dorset)		
Obituary	1965	*973*
Webb, G. (Wellington, New Zealand)		
Obituary	1935/I	*275*
Webb, Lt-Col. H. L. (Winchester)		
Obituary	1950	*915*

Webb, Capt. J. P. (Bristol Grammar School)
  Obituary   1919   *193*
Webb, S. (Middlesex; Lancashire)
  Obituary   1924/I   *273*
Webb, S. G. (Australian Board of Control)
  Obituary   1977   *1050*
Webb, W. T. (Scorer Somerset)
  Obituary   1905   *cv*
Webbe, A. J. (Harrow; Oxford University; Middlesex; England)
  Special Memoir of (Obituary)   1942   *352*
  Tributes to: C. S. Caine   1934/I   *28*
                S. H. Pardon   1926/I   *30*
Webbe, Capt. G. A. (Dorset)
  Obituary   1926/I   *285*
Webber, Lieut. H. (Tonbridge)
  Obituary   1917   *219*
Webber, R. (Journalist; Statistician; Writer)
  with C. White 'The Ashes Go Home'
  Book Review   1960   *1000*
  'The Ashes Retained'
  Book Review   1957   *999*
  'England Keep the Ashes'
  Book Review   1956   *1028*
  with J. Arlott; H. S. Altham; D. Eagar
  'Hampshire County Cricket' Book Review   1958   *1023*
  Obituary   1963   *1037*
Webster, Capt. J. R. (Taplow C.C.)
  Obituary   1917   *219*
Webster, R. E. (See under Alverstone, 1st Viscount)
Webster, T. (Cartoonist)
  Reproduction of Cartoon by   1941   *25*
Wedd, 2nd Lieut. H. (Rossall)
  Obituary   1918   *208*
Wedel, G. (Gloucestershire)
  Obituary   1982   *1212*
Weeding, Major T. (Army)
  Obituary   1918   *208*
Weeding, T. W. (Marlborough; Surrey)
  Obituary   1931/I   *274*
Weedon, B. R. (King's Canterbury)
  Schools Note   1971   *790*
  1084 runs Schools Averages   1971   *815*
Weekes, E. D. (Barbados; West Indies)
  Cricketer of the Year   1951   *75*
  Photograph   1951   *67*

Weigall, A. (The Cricket Society)
Obituary   1978   *1083*
Weigall, G. J. V. (Wellington; Cambridge University; Kent)
Obituary   1945   *345*
Weighell, Rev, W. B. (Bedford Grammar School; Cambridge University; Norfolk; Sussex)
Obituary   1907   *cxviii*
Welby, Lieut. R. W. G. (Grantham C.C.)
Obituary   1918   *218*
Welch, T. H. G. (Northamptonshire)
Obituary   1938   *949*
Welch, Lieut. W. M. (Harrow)
Obituary   1942   *351*
Weld-Blundell, Lieut. R. S. (Pembroke College, Oxford)
Obituary   1918   *218*
Welford, J. W. (Durham; Warwickshire)
Obituary   1946   *447*
Wellard, A. W. (Somerset; England)
Benefit Match   1940   *439*
Obituary   1982   *1212*
Portrait and Biography   1936/I   *301*
Welldon, J. T. (Tonbridge; Kent)
Obituary   1928/I   *301*
Welldron, Rev. M. E. (Tonbridge)
Obituary   1952   *966*
Wellicome, Sgt. W. C. (Marlow C.C.)
Obituary   1917   *220*
Wellingborough School
Plans of County Ground   1971   *467*
     1978   *492*
Wellings, E. M. (Cheltenham; Oxford University; Surrey; Writer, especially on Public School Cricket)
'The Ashes Retained' Book Review   1956   *1027*
'The Ashes Thrown Away' Book Review   1960   *1000*
'Dexter v Benaud' Book Review   1964   *1000*
'Googly Bowlers and Captains Retire'   1958   *94*
'The Greatest Test Match'   1961   *105*
'Lower Standards'   1980   *103*
'Middlesex' Book Review   1973   *1052*
'No Ashes for England' Book Review   1952   *1015*
'Seeing Cricket After Four Years'   1945   *54*
'Simpson's Australians: the England Tour of 1964'
Book Review   1965   *1020*
'Stars of the Tests'   1963   *115*
Wells, Lieut. A. S. (Ripon Grammar School)
Obituary   1917   *220*

Wells, B. D. (Gloucestershire; Nottinghamshire)

Photograph	1956	*362*
'Wells, Wells, Wells' Book Review	1982	*1271*

Wells, Lieut. C. D. (Gresham's School, Holt)

Obituary	1919	*193*

Wells, C. M. (Dulwich; Cambridge University; Surrey; Middlesex)

Obituary	1964	*953*
Views on 'The Follow On'	1894	*lii*

Wells, C. M. (Sussex; Border)

Photograph	1981	*566*

Wells, G. (Sussex; Middlesex)

Obituary	1982	*xxxi*

Wells, J. (Kent)

Obituary	1911/I	*160*

Wells, L. S. (Middlesex; London County)

Obituary	1929/I	*261*

Wells, W. (Northamptonshire)

Obituary	1940	*847*

Wells, W. B. (Canadian Club Cricketer)

Obituary	1931/I	*271*

Wells-Cole, G. C. (Lincolnshire)

Obituary	1976	*1105*

Wells-Cole, G. F. (Winchester; Lincolnshire)

Obituary	1918	*239*

Wells-Cole, Major N. W. (Winchester; Woolwich M.A.; Lincolnshire)

Obituary	1919	*193*

Wellman, F. T. (Somerset; Middlesex)

Obituary	1933/I	*265*

Welsby, Lieut. S. W. H. (Malvern)

Obituary	1918	*208*

Welsh, S. (Philadelphia; U.S.A.)

Obituary	1908/I	*155*

Wenlock, 3rd Lord (President M.C.C.)

Obituary	1913/I	*200*

Wenman, W. (Kent)

Obituary	1923/I	*311*

Wensley, A. F. (Sussex)

Benefit Match	1937/II	*377*
Obituary	1971	*1032*

Wenyon, H. J. (Middlesex)

Obituary	1945	*345*

Wescott, E. J. (Northumberland; Cumberland)

Obituary	1964	*953*

Wessels, K. C. (Orange Free State; Western Province; Northern Transvaal; Sussex; Queensland; Australia)

Photograph	1980	*572*

Photograph ('The Helmet')	1981	*124*
West, Capt. A. E. L. (Mountjoy School, Dublin)		
Obituary	1918	*209*
West, Rev. A. G. B. (Tonbridge; Lincolnshire)		
Obituary	1953	*951*
West, Lieut. A. H. M. (Oundle)		
Obituary	1919	*193*
West, G. H. (Editor of Wisden 1880-1886; Journalist)		
Obituary	1897	*xli*
West, J. (Yorkshire)		
Benefit Match for Family of	1891	*203*
West, J. E. (Middlesex; Umpire)		
Benefit Match	1910/II	*170*
Obituary	1921/I	*241*
West, L. H. (Essex)		
Obituary	1983	*1258*
West, P. (Broadcaster; Writer)		
'The Fight for the Ashes 1953' Book Review	1954	*983*
'The Fight for the Ashes 1956' Book Review	1957	*998*
West, L/Cpl. W. (Brantford C.C., Canada)		
Obituary	1918	*218*
West, W. (Member Surrey)		
Obituary	1951	*929*
West, W. A. J. (Northamptonshire; Warwickshire; Umpire)		
Obituary	1939	*919*
Westbrook, K. R. (Tasmania)		
Obituary	1984	*1211*
Westcliff – Chalkwell Park		
Plan of County Ground	1967	*371*
Westell, T. (Hertfordshire)		
Obituary	1907	*cxvi*
Westell, W. (Hertfordshire)		
Obituary	1902	*lxxi*
Westell, W. T. (Hertfordshire)		
Obituary	1925/I	*283*
West Indies		
In Australia 1930 – 31	1932/II	*665*
and New Zealand 1951–52	1953	*813*
'Cricket Crusader' H. Dale Book Review	1953	*998*
'Straight Hit' K. R. Miller and R. S. Whitington		
Book Review	1953	*997*
'With the West Indies in Australia 1951–52'		
A. G. Moyes Book Review	1953	*997*
1960–61	1962	*832*
Note on	1961	*120*

'A.B.C. Cricket Book–West Indies Tour 1960–61'			
Book Review		1961	*993*
'Cricket's Brightest Summer'			
L. D. Roberts Book Review		1962	*1038*
'Cricket in the Sun' G. S. Sobers			
and J. S. Barker Book Review		1968	*1046*
'The Greatest Test Match'			
E. M. Wellings		1961	*105*
'The Greatest Test of All'			
J. Fingleton Book Review		1962	*1038*
'A Tale of Two Tests' R. Benaud			
Book Review		1968	*1108*
'With the West Indies in Australia'			
A. G. Moyes Book Review		1962	*1037*
and New Zealand 1968–69		1970	*880*
'Captains on a See-Saw'			
P. Tresider Book Review		1970	*1070*
'Fours Galore' R. S. Whitington and			
K. Miller Book Review		1970	*1070*
	1975–76	1977	*871*
'Frindall's Scorebook: Australia v			
West Indies' W. Frindall Book Review		1977	*1094*
'The Hapless Hookers'			
F. H. Tyson Book Review		1977	*1094*
'Meet the West Indies'			
Book Review		1977	*1102*
and New Zealand 1979–80		1981	*942*
'Cricket Contest 1979–80: The Post			
Packer Tests' C. Martin-Jenkins			
Book Review		1981	*1198*
'Frindall's Scorebook: Australia v			
West Indies and England 1979 – 80'			
W. Frindall Book Review		1981	*1196*
	1981–82	1983	*989*
In Canada and U.S.A.	1886	1887	*299*
In England	1900	1901	*426*
	1906	1907	*440*
	1923	1924/II	*422*
	1928	1929/II	*1*
	1933	1934/II	*1*
	1939	1940	*174*
Team Portrait	1939	1940	*33*
	1950	1951	*207*
Team Portrait	1950	1951	*58*
'Days at the Cricket'			

J. Arlott Book Review		1952	*1022*
	1957	1958	*227*
Team Portrait	1957	1958	*49*
Note on		1957	*72*
'Cricketers from the West Indies'			
G. Ross Book Review		1958	*1014*
'West Indies Cricket Challenge'			
B. Harris Book Review		1958	*1014*
	1963	1964	*269*
Team Portrait	1963	1964	*62*
Pen Portrait		1963	*89*
Welcome		1963	*136*
Worrell's Men Celebrate		1964	*875*
'Cricketers from the West Indies'			
G. Ross Book Review		1964	*1006*
'Cricket Lovely Cricket'			
I. Wooldridge Book Review		1964	*1001*
'Cricket with A Swing'			
J. Clarke Book Review		1964	*1000*
'Rothmans Test Cricket Almanack'			
G. Ross Book Review		1964	*1006*
'Summer Spectacular' J. S. Barker			
Book Review		1964	*1000*
'West Indies Cricket Tour 1963'			
I. Rosenwater Book Review		1964	*1006*
'The West Indies at Lord's'			
A. Ross Book Review		1964	*1000*
	1966	1967	*279*
Team Portrait	1966	1967	*62*
West Indies Retain Wisden Trophy			
Photograph		1967	*61*
West Indies Retain Wisden Trophy			
G. Ross Book Review		1967	*1021*
'Everything that's Cricket'			
B. Scovell Book Review		1967	*1016*
'King Cricket' G. Sobers			
Book Review		1968	*1054*
'Rothmans Test Cricket Almanack:			
England v West Indies 1966' Book Review		1967	*1021*
	1969	1970	*289*
Team Portrait	1969	1970	*52*
'Rothmans Cricket Almanack 1969'			
Book Review		1970	*1074*
	1973	1974	*327*
Team Portrait	1973	1974	*45*
World Cup Tournament	1975	1976	*300*

West Indies World Cup Champions

Team Portrait		1976	*36*
	1976	1977	*306*
Team Portrait	1976	1977	*84*
'Frindall's Scorebook: England v West Indies' W. Frindall Book Review		1977	*1096*
World Cup Tournament	1979	1980	*297*
West Indies win the Prudential Cup Photograph		1980	*60*
Team Portrait	1979	1980	*298*
	1980	1981	*313*
Team Portrait	1980	1981	*312*
Note on		1981	*91*
World Cup Tournament	1983	1984	*293*
In India	1948 – 49	1950	*795*
and Pakistan	1958 – 59	1960	*852*
and Sri Lanka	1966 – 67	1968	*855*
and Pakistan, Sri Lanka	1974 – 75	1976	*958*
and Sri Lanka	1978 – 79	1980	*980*
In New Zealand			
and Australia	1951 – 52	1953	*818*
	1955 – 56	1957	*829*
and Australia	1968 – 69	1970	*903*
'Scoreboard 69' R. T. Brittenden Book Review		1971	*1081*
and Australia	1979 – 80	1981	*957*
In Pakistan			
and India	1958 – 59	1960	*852*
and India, Sri Lanka	1974 – 75	1976	*958*
	1980 – 81	1982	*927*
In South Africa (Rebel Tour)	1982 – 83	1984	*1057*
In Sri Lanka	1967	1968	*869*
India and Pakistan	1974 – 75	1976	*958*
and India	1978 – 79	1980	*980*
In U.S.A.	1958	1959	*865*
and Canada	1886	1887	*299*
West Indies Women in England	1979	1980	*1108*
West Indies Young Cricketers in England	1982	1983	*891*
West Indies Under 19 in England	1978	1979	*638*
West Indies Youngsters in England	1970	1971	*844*
Young West Indies in Zimbabwe	1981	1983	*1181*

List of Articles and Notes:
'Cricket in West Indies and America'

Sir P. F. Warner	1898	*lxx*
'How West Indies Cricket Grew Up		
Sir L. Constantine	1957	*99*
Notable Dates and Other Memorabilia in West Indian Cricket History'		
R. Bowen	1969	*151*
Notes on	1951	*114*
	1954	*80*
Test Statistics	1966	*92*
Victory Calypso Photograph	1951	*70*
Victory Flowers Photograph	1954	*80*
'Welcome West Indies' H. Blofeld	1976	*71*
'The West Indian Cricket Team'		
Sir P. F. Warner	1901	*xciv*
'West Indies in Test Cricket' J. Anderson	1950	*119*
and World Series Cricket Note on	1979	*966*
Western Province Willows in England 1966	1967	*807*
Westlake, Lieut. A. N. (Shrewsbury)		
Obituary	1919	*193*
Westley, R. B. (Lancaster Grammar School; Oxford University)		
Obituary	1983	*1258*
Westmorland, 13th Earl of (Northamptonshire)		
Obituary	1923/I	*309*
Weston, G. N. (Writer; Collector)		
'W. G. Grace – the Great Cricketer'		
Book Review	1976	*1148*
'My Cricket World and Cricket Literature'		
Book Review	1976	*1144*
Weston, Sir J. W. 1st Bart. (Rugby)		
Obituary	1927/I	*293*
Weston-Super-Mare Plan of County Ground	1956	*526*
	ad passim	
Westray, F. W. (Uppingham)		
Obituary	1952	*966*
Westray, T. (Uppingham)		
Obituary	1952	*965*
Wetherall, C. R. (Northamptonshire)		
Obituary	1956	*977*
Wettest Summer 1958		
Note on	1959	*78*
Whale, Pte. A. (Shrewsbury)		
Obituary	1917	*220*
Whalley-Tooker, E. (Hambledon C.C.)		
Obituary	1941	*404*

Wharmby, J. (Leicestershire Club Cricketer)
    Obituary   1921/I   *241*
Wharton, A. (Lancashire; Leicestershire; England)
    Benefit Match   1959   *423*
    Photographs   1957   *422*
                                              1960   *447*
Wharton, Lieut. G. F. (Charterhouse)
    Obituary   1916   *215*
Wharton, J. F. (Bound Brook C.C., New Jersey)
    Obituary   1921/I   *241*
Wharton, Major R. G. (Patron)
    Team in South Africa 1888-89   1890   *257*
Wharton, W. B. (Manhattan C.C.)
    Obituary   1916   *215*
Whatford, Capt. G. L. (Sussex)
    Obituary   1916   *215*
Whatley, Major E. G. (Eton; Hertfordshire; Somerset)
    Obituary   1970   *1027*
Whatley, F/O. W. D. (Clifton)
    Obituary   1943   *368*
Whatman, Major A. D. (Suffolk)
    Obituary   1966   *973*
Wheat, A. B. (Nottinghamshire)
    Obituary   1974   *1081*
Wheatley, J. (Canterbury)
    Obituary   1963   *1037*
Wheatley, J. B. (St.Paul's; Middlesex)
    Obituary   1983   *1258*
Wheatley, O. S. (King Edward's Birmingham; Cambridge University; Glamorgan; Warwickshire)
    Cricketer of the Year   1969   *71*
    Photographs   1962   *389*
                                                1966   *381*
                                                1969   *60*
Wheatley, 2nd Lieut. R. V. (Elston C.C.)
    Obituary   1918   *209*
Wheeler, A. (Surrey)
    Obituary   1908/I   *155*
Wheeler, C. (Warwickshire)
    Obituary   1931/I   *271*
Wheeler, J. (Leicestershire; Nottinghamshire)
    Benefit Match   1894   *232*
    Obituary   1909/I   *148*
Wheeler, T. (Secretary Wiltshire)
    Views on Second Class Counties and the
    L.B.W. Rule   1903   *lxix*

Wheeler, W. H. (Metropolitan Club Cricket)
  Obituary   1933/I   260
Wheldon, G. F. (Worcestershire)
  Obituary   1925/I   284
Whetherley, Major R. E. (Harrow)
  Obituary   1944   308
Whewell, W. T. (Cambridgeshire)
  Obituary   1941   390
Whichelow, H. (Berkshire)
  Obituary   1914/I   197
Whinney, Major E. (Haywards Heath C.C.)
  Obituary   1917   220
Whipp, A. (Scorer B.B.C.)
  Obituary   1969   988
Whistler, Gen. Sir L. G. (Harrow)
  Obituary   1964   953
Whistler, Capt. R. A. F. (King's Bruton; Army)
  Obituary   1918   209
Whitaker, E. H. (Editor Wisden 1940-1943)
  Obituary   1983   1258
Whitaker, Lieut. H. A. (Calgary C.C., Alberta)
  Obituary   1918   219
Whitbread, S. H. (President Bedfordshire)
  Obituary   1945   345
Whitbread Scholarships List of   1983   472
Whitby, H. O. (Leamington College; Oxford University; Warwickshire)
  Obituary   1935/I   275
White, A. A. (Umpire)
  Obituary   1921/I   241
White, A. V. (Marlborough)
  Obituary   1928/I   301
White, Sir A. W. 4th Bart. (Wellington; Yorkshire)
  Obituary   1946   447
White, C. (Journalist; Writer)
  with R. Webber 'The Ashes Go Home'
  Book Review   1960   1000
  with R. Webber 'The Ashes Retained'
  Book Review   1957   999
  with R. Webber 'England Keeps the Ashes'
  Book Review   1956   1028
  'The England Victory' Book Review   1954   984
White, D. W. (Hampshire; Glamorgan; England)
  Photographs   1961   410
                                                          1964   411
                                                          1967   424

White, E. A. (Kent)
   Obituary   1923/I   309
White, F. C. (Sussex Cricket Club Welfare Association)
   Obituary   1956   977
White, G. C. (Transvaal; South Africa)
   Obituary   1919   193
White, Brig G. W. (Winchester)
   Obituary   1978   1083
White, H. (Hertfordshire; Lord's Groundsman)
   Obituary   1944   327
White, Rev. H. (Denstone; Oxford University; Northumberland)
   Obituary   1966   974
White, J. (Bury and West Suffolk C.C.)
   Obituary   1917   266
White, J. (Wellingborough; Cambridge University; Surrey)
   Obituary   1969   988
White, J. C. (Taunton School; Somerset; England)
   Obituary   1962   993
   Portrait and Biography   1929/I   269
   Record by   1941   65
   'Study in Greatness' B. Easterbrook   1978   159
White, 2nd Lieut. J. G. (Edingburgh Academy)
   Obituary   1918   209
White, Capt. J. V. (Southport C.C.)
   Obituary   1917   220
White, Lt-Col. L. A. (Kent)
   Obituary   1920/I   195
White, M. E. (Worcestershire)
   Obituary   1971   1033
White, N. (Writer)
   with G. Headley 'George Atlas Headley'
   Book Review   1976   1150
White, R. A. (Middlesex; Nottinghamshire)
   Career Figures   1983   711
   Photographs   1964   480
                                             1971   482
                                             1975   517
White, Brig. W. M. (Malvern; Hampshire)
   Obituary   1953   951
Whitehead, 2nd Lieut. G. N. (Shrewsbury)
   Obituary   1918   209
Whitehead, Lieut. G. W. E. (Clifton; Kent)
   Obituary   1919   194
Whitehead, H. (Leicestershire)
   Benefit Match   1915/II   237
   Obituary   1945   345

Whitehead, H. H. (Yorkshire)
  Obituary 1970 *1027*
Whitehead, J. G. (Western Province; Griqualand West)
  Obituary 1943 *387*
Whitehead, 2nd Lieut. J. H. E. (Clifton; Kent)
  Obituary 1920/I *159*
Whitehead, L. (Yorkshire)
  Obituary 1914/I *197*
Whitehead, Capt. P. N. (Charterhouse)
  Obituary 1919 *195*
Whitehead, S. J. (Warwickshire)
  Obituary 1905 *ciii*
Whitehouse, J. (Warwickshire)
  Photographs 1976 *585*
                        1978 *570*
Whitehouse, Lieut. P. M. W. (Marlborough; Oxford University; Kent)
  Obituary 1944 *309*
Whitelaw, Lieut. R. H .L. (Glenalmond, Grange C.C.)
  Obituary 1918 *209*
Whiteman, 2nd Lieut. G. W. (Bedford Modern School)
  Obituary 1918 *209*
Whiteside, J. P. (Lancashire; Leicestershire)
  Benefit Match 1903 *182*
  Obituary 1947 *697*
Whitesides, T. (Tasmania)
  Obituary 1920/I *191*
White-Thomson, R. W. (King's College, Cambridge)
  Obituary 1917 *267*
Whitfeld, F. B. (IZingari)
  Obituary 1925/I *284*
Whitfeld, G. S. (IZingari)
  Obituary 1946 *447*
Whitfield, H. (Eton; Cambridge University; Sussex)
  Obituary 1910/I *148*
Whitfield, H. E. P. (South Australia)
  Obituary 1938 *946*
Whiting, A. O. (Sherborne; Oxford University)
  Obituary 1933/I *265*
Whiting, C. P. (Yorkshire)
  Obituary 1960 *957*
Whitington, R. S. (South Australia; Writer; Journalist)
  'Bradman, Benaud and Goddards Cinderellas'
  Book Review 1965 *1018*
  with K. R. Miller 'Bumper' Book Review 1954 *976*
  'Captain Outrageous' Book Review 1973 *1056*
  with K. R. Miller 'Cricket Caravan'
  Book Review 1952 *1012*

591

with K. R. Miller 'Cricket Typhoon'

Book Review	1956	*1025*
with K. R. Miller 'Fours Galore'		
Book Review	1970	*1070*
with K. R. Miller 'Gods or Flannelled Fools'		
Book Review	1955	*994*
'Keith Miller – The Golden Nuggett'		
Book Review	1983	*1310*
'The Quiet Australian' Book Review	1970	*1067*
'John Reids Kiwis' Book Review	1963	*1108*
with K. R. Miller 'Straight Hit'		
Book Review	1953	*997*
'Time of the Tiger: The Bill O'Reilly Story'		
Book Review	1971	*1080*
Whitmore, W. W. (Eton)		
Obituary	1926/I	*286*
Whitridge, W. O. (South Australia)		
Obituary	1920/I	*190*
Whittaker, D. (Lancashire)		
Obituary	1902	*lxxii*
Whittaker, G. J. (Surrey)		
Photograph	1952	*505*
Whittaker, Capt. R. D'A. (Burrand C.C., Vancouver)		
Obituary	1918	*219*
Whitting, F. (President Cambridge University C.C.)		
Obituary	1912/I	*183*
Whittingham, N. B. (Nottinghamshire)		
Photograph	1964	*513*
Whittington, T. A. L. (Glamorgan)		
Obituary	1945	*346*
Whitty, W. J. (New South Wales; South Australia; Australia)		
Obituary	1975	*1085*
Whitwell, J. F. (Uppingham; Yorkshire; Durham)		
Obituary	1933/I	*260*
Views on Second Class Counties and the		
L.B.W. Rule	1903/I	*lxix*
Whitwell, W. F. (Uppingham; Yorkshire; Durham)		
Obituary	1943	*384*
Whybrew, A. (British Guiana)		
Obituary	1926/I	*289*
Whympner, W. (Surbiton C.C.)		
Obituary	1917	*267*
Whynne-Thomas, P. (Writer; Statistician)		
'A Complete Register of Cricketers to Represent Nottingham Old Clubs and Nottinghamshire County Cricket from 1821 to 1965'		
Book Review	1967	*1011*

'England on Tour' Book Review	1983	*1298*
'Milestones of Nottinghamshire Cricket' Book Review	1982	*1255*
'Nottinghamshire Cricketers 1821-1914' Book Review	1972	*1091*

Whysall, W. W. (Nottinghamshire; England)

Benefit Match	1927/II	*184*
Obituary	1931/I	*271*
Portrait and Biography	1925/I	*293*

Whyte, Lieut. R. (Dollar Academy)

Obituary	1919	*195*

'Wicket Covering in England, A History of'

I. Rosenwater	1970	*131*

'Wicket Keepers, The Great – From T. Sueter to
A. Knott' R. Ryder | 1972 | *137*

Wicket Keepers

Note on	1980	*85*
Test Appearances	1972	*144*

Wickets Fast Note on | 1944 | *66*

Wickham, Preb. A. P. (Marlborough; Oxford University; Norfolk; Somerset)

Obituary	1936/I	*291*

Wickham, Rev. H. J. (Winchester)

Obituary	1915/I	*246*

Widdop, Lieut. A. N. (Lancaster Grammar School)

Obituary	1919	*195*

Widdowson, S. W. (Nottinghamshire)

Obituary	1928/I	*301*

Wiener, L. De V. (South African College, Cape Town)

Obituary	1920/I	*153*

Wigan, D. G. (Eton)

Obituary	1959	*939*

Wigginton, S. H. (Wyggeston School; Leicestershire)

Obituary	1978	*1083*

Wigley, J. W. (Trenton C.C., U.S.A.)

Obituary	1914/I	*197*

Wigram, Lord Clive (Winchester)

Obituary	1961	*952*

Wigram, Gen. Sir K. (Winchester)

Obituary	1950	*915*

Wilby, A. (Wissahickon C.C., U.S.A.)

Obituary	1920/I	*191*

Wilcock, G. (Yorkshire)

Obituary	1954	*931*

Wilcock, H. G. (Worcestershire)

Photographs	1973	*573*
	1975	*598*

Wilcox, C. R. (St.Paul C.C., Minnesota)
Obituary   1908/I   *155*

Wilcox, D. R. (Dulwich; Cambridge University; Essex)
Obituary   1954   *931*
Schools Note   1930/I   *283-287,296*
1025 runs Schools Averages   1930/II   *627*

Wilcox, Lieut. K. T. D. (Westminster)
Obituary   1917   *226*

Wild, F. (Nottinghamshire)
Obituary   1894   *xxxv*

Wild, F. (U.S.A. Club Cricket)
Obituary   1918   *240*

Wild, H. (Derbyshire)
Obituary   1978   *1083*

Wildbore, B. O. (Surrey Colts)
Obituary   1945   *326*

Wiley, Lieut. E. O. S. (Bedford Modern School)
Obituary   1919   *195*

Wilkie, D. (Victoria)
Obituary   1918   *240*

Wilkins, A. H. (Glamorgan; Gloucestershire; Northern Transvaal)
Photograph   1980   *395*

Wilkins, Pte. C. (Brantford C.C., Ontario)
Obituary   1918   *219*

Wilkins, C. P. (Derbyshire; Eastern Province; Natal)
Photograph   1971   *319*

Wilkins, H. (Cricket Coach Eton)
Obituary   1962   *993*

Wilkins, H. E. B. (Forest Hill C.C.)
Obituary   1966   *974*

Wilkins-Leir, Rev. E. J. P. (Marlborough; Cambridge University)
Obituary   1922/I   *271*

Wilkinson, A. J. A. (Shrewsbury; Yorkshire; Middlesex)
Obituary   1907   *cxviii*

Wilkinson, C. T. A. (Blundells; Surrey)
Obituary   1971   *1033*

Wilkinson, H. O. (U.S.A. Club Cricketer)
Obituary   1922/I   *271*

Wilkinson, J. (Worcestershire)
Obituary   1968   *1009*

Wilkinson, Brig-Gen. M. G. (Harrow)
Obituary   1945   *347*

Wilkinson, W. (Yorkshire)
Obituary   1969   *988*

Wilkinson, Col. W. A. C. (Eton; Oxford University)
Obituary   1984   *1211*

Wilkinson, Dr. W. C. (Middlesex)
  Obituary   1947   *697*
Wilkinson, W. H. (Yorkshire)
  Obituary   1962   *993*
Wilkinson, W. O. (Haarlem C.C., New York)
  Obituary   1909/I   *149*
Will, Lieut. J. G. (Merchant Taylors)
  Obituary   1918   *209*
Willatt, G. L. (Repton; Cambridge University; Derbyshire; Nottinghamshire)
  Photograph   1953   *297*
Willcocks, Major H. F. (Radley; Berkshire)
  Obituary   1920/I   *191*
Willes, Rev. E. H. L. (Winchester; Oxford University; Kent)
  Obituary   1897   *xl*
Willett, B. H. (Westminster)
  Obituary   1950   *915*
Willett, M. D. (Surrey)
  Photograph   1965   *554*
Willey, P. (Northamptonshire; Leicestershire; Eastern Province; England)
  Benefit Match   1982   *769*
  Photographs   1974   *496*
                                            1979   *482*
  Unlucky Willey Note   1977   *112*
Williams, A. B. (Wellington)
  Obituary   1930/I   *265*
Williams, Capt. A. I. M. (Highgate School)
  Obituary   1919   *195*
Williams, B. H. (Rhodesia)
  Obituary   1979   *1088*
Williams, Rev. B. H. M. (Marlborough; Monmouthshire)
  Obituary   1930/I   *265*
Williams, C. D. (Harrow)
  Obituary   1953   *951*
Williams, Lieut. C. E. (King's Bruton)
  Obituary   1918   *209*
Williams, C. H. (Vice President Lancashire)
  Obituary   1943   *384*
Williams, Lt-Col. D. B. (Glamorgan)
  Obituary   1923/I   *309*
Williams, D. W. (Winchester)
  Obituary   1907   *cxvii*
Williams, Brig. E. S. B. (Winchester; Devon; Army)
  Obituary   1978   *1083*
Williams, 2nd Lieut. F. C. D. (St.Edmund's, Canterbury)
  Obituary   1917   *220*

Williams, F. V. (Harrow)
  Obituary   1916   *215*
Williams, G. T. (New York)
  Obituary   1906   *ciii*
Williams, H. (Secretary Thames Ditton C.C.)
  Obituary   1914/I   *197*
Williams, H. R. H. (Charterhouse; Essex)
  Obituary   1976   *1105*
Williams, J. (Sydney Club Cricket)
  Obituary   1917   *267*
Williams, Pte. J. (Bromsborough C.C.)
  Obituary   1917   *220*
Williams, Pte. J. N. (South Auckland)
  Obituary   1916   *215*
Williams, Lieut. J. W. (Quebec)
  Obituary   1920/I   *159*
Williams, 2nd Lieut. L. A. (Kingswood School, Bath)
  Obituary   1917   *220*
Williams, L. E. W. (Oratory; Glamorgan)
  Obituary   1975   *1085*
Williams, M. (Auctioneer; Journalist)
  'Philatelic Cricket'   1984   *72*
Williams, M. B. (Ireland)
  Obituary   1974   *1082*
Williams, O. C. (Victoria)
  Obituary   1919   *212*
Williams, Rev. P. (Winchester; Oxford University; Nottinghamshire)
  Obituary   1901   *lxvi*
Williams, Lieut. P. C. (Brighton College)
  Obituary   1916   *216*
Williams, Sir P. F. C. Bart. (Eton; Oxfordshire; Gloucestershire)
  Obituary   1959   *939*
Williams, P. V. (Winchester; Sussex)
  Obituary   1972   *1056*
Williams, R. G. (Northamptonshire)
  Photograph   1981   *505*
Williams, R. G. (Australian Services)
  Obituary   1980   *1161*
Williams, R. H. (Journalist)
  Obituary   1970   *1027*
Williams, R. H. (Worcestershire)
  Obituary   1984   *1211*
Williams, Lieut. R. L. (Bedford Grammar School)
  Obituary   1919   *195*
Williams, R. M. C. (Epsom College)
  Schools Note   1983   *901*

1013 runs Schools Averages	1983	*918*
Williams, T. C. (Ireland)		
Obituary	1984	*1211*
Williams, W. (Middlesex)		
Obituary	1952	*965*
Williamson, Pte. A. (Havaimo C.C., British Columbia)		
Obituary	1919	*201*
Williamson, C. R. (Writer)		
'The Yorkshire Connection'	1983	*110*
Williamson, 2nd Lieut. H. G. (St.Edwards, Oxford)		
Obituary	1917	*220*
Williamson, I. H. (Dewsbury, Savile C.C.)		
Obituary	1913/I	*201*
Williamson, 2nd Lieut. J. M. (Leys School)		
Obituary	1916	*216*
Williamson, Fl/Lt. R. H. (Uppingham; Surrey)		
Obituary	1944	*309*
Willingdon, Marquess of (Eton; Cambridge University; Sussex)		
Obituary	1942	*365*
Willis, C. B. (Victoria; Australian Imperial Forces)		
Obituary	1931/I	*272*
Willis, H. (Surrey)		
Obituary	1927/I	*294*
Willis, R. G. D. (Surrey; Warwickshire; Northern Transvaal; England)		
'The Captain's Diary' Book Review	1984	*1268*
Controversial Bouncer by – Photograph	1979	*63*
Cricketer of the Year	1978	*93*
'Diary of a Cricket Season' Book Review	1980	*1212*
Photographs	1971	*515*
	1973	*558*
	1978	*92*
	1981	*581*
	1983	*plate*
Willis – New England Captain Note	1983	*77*
Willis Performs Vital Hat-Trick Photograph	1973	*66*
Wills, A. C. L. (Harrow; Northamptonshire)		
Obituary	1979	*1088*
Wills, C. (Journalist)		
Obituary	1965	*972*
Wills, C. P. (Harrow)		
Obituary	1932/I	*254*
Wills, Rev. G. F. (Devon Club Cricket)		
Obituary	1928/I	*301*
Wills, S. G. (Gloucestershire)		
Obituary	1979	*1092*
Willsher, E. (Kent; All England XI)		
Benefit Match	1872	*45,152*

Biography	1870	*98*
Willson, Lieut. F. J. (Kelly College, Tavistock)		
Obituary	1918	*209*
Wilmot, W. (Derbyshire)		
Obituary	1958	*965*
Wilson, A. (Rugby; Oxford University)		
Obituary	1909/I	*149*
Wilson, A. (Lancashire)		
Benefit Match	1963	*490*
Wilson, A. (Secretary Derbyshire)		
Obituary	1907	*cxvi*
Wilson, A. C. (Canterbury)		
Obituary	1912/I	*183*
Wilson, A. E. (Middlesex; Gloucestershire)		
Benefit Match	1954	*370*
Wilson, Pte. A. J. (Glenalmond)		
Obituary	1919	*201*
Wilson, A. K. (Brighton College; Sussex)		
Obituary	1978	*1083*
Wilson, B. B. (Yorkshire)		
Obituary	1958	*965*
Wilson, C. (Lincolnshire)		
Obituary	1950	*915*
Wilson, Major C. (Somerset)		
Obituary	1928/I	*302*
Wilson, Rt. Rev. C. (Tonbridge; Cambridge University; Kent)		
Obituary	1942	*365*
Wilson, Rev. Preb. C. E. M. (Uppingham; Cambridge University; Yorkshire; England)		
Obituary	1945	*346*
Wilson, C. G. (Victoria; Wellington; Otago; South Island)		
Obituary	1953	*951*
Wilson, C. P. (Marlborough; Cambridge University; Norfolk)		
Obituary	1939	*920*
Wilson, C. R. (Committee Yorkshire)		
Obituary	1946	*447*
Wilson, C. S. (Suffolk)		
Obituary	1966	*974*
Wilson, D. (Yorkshire; England)		
Benefit Match	1973	*593*
Photographs	1966	*624*
	1969	*637*
Wilson, Capt. D'A. B. (Rugby)		
Obituary	1933	*1259*
Wilson, E. F. (Surrey)		
Obituary	1983	*1259*

Wilson, E. R. (Rugby; Cambridge University; Yorkshire; England)
 Obituary   1958   *966*

Wilson, 2nd Lieut. E. W. (Fettes)
 Obituary   1918   *209*

Wilson, Col. F. (Committee Sussex)
 Obituary   1970   *1027*

Wilson, F. B. (Harrow; Cambridge University; London County; Journalist)
 Obituary   1933/I   *260*

Wilson, F. du B. (Hurstpierpoint)
 Obituary   1930/I   *265*

Wilson, 2nd Lieut. F. T. A. (Felsted)
 Obituary   1920/I   *159*

Wilson, Lt-Col F. T. D. (Suffolk)
 Obituary   1965   *972*

Wilson, G. (Harrow; Cambridge University; Yorkshire)
 Obituary   1961   *952*

Wilson, G. A. (Worcestershire)
 Obituary   1963   *1037*

Wilson, G. L. (Brighton College; Oxford University; Sussex)
 Obituary   1921/I   *242*

Wilson, G. P. (Rossall)
 Obituary   1935/I   *276*

Wilson, H. (Worcestershire)
 Obituary   1907   *cxvii*

Wilson, H. G. (Canada)
 Obituary   1926/I   *286*

Wilson, H. H. (Weymouth College)
 Obituary   1919   *195*

Wilson, Capt. Adjt. H. I. (King's, Canterbury)
 Obituary   1918   *209*

Wilson, H. L. (Suffolk; Sussex)
 Obituary   1938   *947*

Wilson, Lieut. H. M. (Ridley College, Ontario)
 Obituary   1917   *220*

Wilson, J. (Yorkshire)
 Obituary   1933/I   *265*

Wilson, Major J. P. (Yorkshire)
 Obituary   1960   *957*

Wilson, J. V. (Yorkshire)
 Benefit Match   1959   *619*
 Career Record   1963   *1042*
 Cricketer of the Year   1961   *102*
 Photographs   1952   *586*
               1955   *588*
               1961   *94*
 'Vic Wilson Benefit Book' Book Review   1959   *993*

Wilson, K. P. (Rossall)
Obituary   1950   *915*

Wilson, L. (Tonbridge; Kent)
Obituary   1945   *346*

Wilson, P. (Journalist)
Obituary   1983   *1259*

Wilson, Canon R. A. (Brother C. E. M. and E. R.)
Obituary   1961   *953*

Wilson, R. C. (Kent)
Benefit Match   1965   *448*
Photographs   1956   *404*
    1958   *403*
    1960   *429*
    1963   *466*
    1965   *436*

Wilson, Group Capt. R. G. (Secretary Nottinghamshire)
Obituary   1981   *1151*

Wilson, 2nd. Lieut. T. B. (Harrow)
Obituaries   1918   *209*
    1919   *195*

Wilson, T. F. (Durham)
Obituary   1919   *212*

Wilson, T. S. B. (Bath College; Oxford University; Monmouthshire)
Obituary   1942   *365*

Wilson, T. W. (Repton; Cambridge University; Lincolnshire; Norfolk; Dorset)
Obituary   1925/I   *284*

Win Without Hitting the Ball Note on   1980   *636*

Winch, R. F. (Northamptonshire)
Obituary   1928/I   *302*

Windsor, G. (Metropolitan Club Cricketer)
Obituary   1926/I   *286*

Windsor-Clive, Lieut. Hon. A. (Eton; Glamorgan)
Obituary   1915/I   *247*

Wingfield, Rev. W. (Rossall; Cambridge University; Shropshire)
Obituary   1914/I   *197*

Wingham, G. (Northumberland)
Obituary   1922/I   *271*

Wingham, G. C. (Kent)
Obituary   1914/I   *197*

Winlaw, Sqd. Ldr. R. de W. K. (Winchester; Cambridge University; Surrey; Bedfordshire)
Obituary   1943   *368*

Winnington, Lt-Col. J. F. S. (Gentlemen of Worcestershire)
Obituary   1919   *195*

Winrow, H. F. (Nottinghamshire; Umpire)
Obituary   1974   *1082*

Winslow, Dr. L. F. (Cricket Supporter)
Obituary	1914/I	*197*

Winslow, O. E. (Sussex)
Obituary	1897	*xlii*

Winston, J. H. E. (Guys Hospital)
Obituary	1956	*977*

Winstone, A. (Gloucestershire)
Obituary	1964	*953*

Winter, Rev. A. H. (Westminster; Cambridge University; Middlesex)
Obituary	1938	*947*

Winter, C. E. (Uppingham; Cambridge University)
Obituary	1965	*972*

Winter, C. H. (Philadelphia; U.S.A.)
Obituary	1970	*1027*

Winter, Canon G. A. (Marlborough)
Obituary	1934/I	*278*

Winter, G. E. (Winchester; Cambridge University; Middlesex)
Obituary	1924/I	*274*

Winter, W. (Westminster; Incogniti)
Obituary	1906	*ci*

Winterbotham, J. P. (Marlborough; Oxford University; Gloucestershire)
Obituary	1926/I	*286*

Winterburn, G. E. (New England C.C.)
Obituary	1918	*240*

Winterflood, T. (Committee Surrey)
Obituary	1901	*lxv*

Winterton, 5th Earl of (E. Turnour) (Eton; Sussex; Norfolk)
Obituary	1908/I	*155*

Winthorp, B. (Harrow)
Obituary	1903	*lxxiii*

Wiren, A. F. (Wellington, New Zealand)
Obituary	1944	*327*

Wisden, J. (Sussex; Kent; Middlesex; founder John Wisden and Co. and Wisden's Cricketers' Almanack)
Obituary	1885	*4*
Personal Recollections of	1913/I	*122*
Photographs	1913/I	*122*
	1963	*iv*

'John Wisden's New Century'
Rt. Hon. Lord De L'Isle and Dudley	1951	*126*

Wisden Centenary Note on
	1964	*87*

'Wisden Century' J. Hadfield
Book Review	1951	*989*

Wisden Cricketers' Almanacks Prices
	1981	*126*

Wisden Editors of (see under Editors of Wisden)

'Wisden–Giants of the Wisden Century'
Sir N. Cardus   1963   *92*
'Wisden – A History of' L. S. Gutteridge   1963   *74*
Wisden – Occasions Notes on   1972   *160*
                                       1979   *83*
'Wisden – Pleasures of Reading' R. Ryder   1965   *95*
Wisden Trophy Photographs   1963   *89*
                                       1964   *89*
                                       1966   *84*
                                       1967   *61*
                                       1969   *101*
                                       1974   *43*
                                       1976   *68*

Wise, A. J. (Ripon C.C.)
    Obituary   1918   *238*
Wise, Capt. A. V. D. (Cheltenham; Woolwich R.M.A.)
    Obituary   1918   *210*
Wise, N. (Secretary Cumberland C.C.C.)
    Obituary   1984   *1211*
Wishart, J. (South African Club Cricketer)
    Obituary   1915/I   *247*
Wishart, K. L. (British Guiana; West Indies)
    Obituary   1973   *1014*
Wister, A. W. (Germantown C.C.)
    Obituary   1932/I   *254*
Wister, Col. F. (Germantown C.C.)
    Obituary   1907   *cxviii*
Wister, J. (U.S.A. Club Cricket)
    Obituaries   1918   *238*
                                       1919   *214*
Wister, L. W. (Germantown C.C.)
    Obituary   1920/I   *191*
Wister, R. (Young America C.C.)
    Obituary   1914/I   *198*
Wister, W. R. (Philadelphia; U.S.A.)
    Obituary   1912/I   *183*
Witherington, Sgt. Pilot A. J. (Leys School)
    Obituary   1943   *369*
Witherington, D. M. (Leys School; Cambridge University)
    Obituary   1945   *325*
Withington, D. (President Paterson C.C., New Jersey)
    Obituary   1910/I   *149*
Witt, J. G. (Eton)
    Obituary   1907   *cxvii*
Wodehouse, Major E. C. (Gentlemen of Worcestershire)
    Obituary   1916   *216*

Wodehouse, Rt. Hon. E. R. (Eton)
Obituary	1915/I	*247*

Wodehouse, Sir P. G. (Dulwich; Author)
Obituary	1976	*1103*
'P. G. Wodehouse: A Literary Biography'		
B. Green Book Review	1982	*1271*

Wolfe-Murray, Brig.–Gen. A. A. (Sandhurst)
Obituary	1920/I	*159*

Wolfson, A. C. (Marlborough)
Obituary	1981	*1151*

Wollaston, S. S. (Marlborough)
Obituary	1925/I	*284*

Wolstencroft, 2nd. Lieut. W. H. B. (Hurstpierpoint)
Obituary	1919	*195*

Wolstenholme, Capt. R. F. (Stubbington House, Fareham)
Obituary	1917	*220*

Wolton, A. V. (Warwickshire)
Benefit Match	1960	*596*
Photographs	1955	*549*
	1957	*578*

Women's Cricket 1938 onwards
Women Play at Lord's Photograph	1977	*89*
Women's Cricket Coaches Note on	1963	*924*

Wonderful 1947 Season Note on
	1948	*82*

Womersley, D. (Marlborough; Essex)
Obituary	1943	*385*

Womersley, L. D. (Marlborough; Essex)
Obituary	1972	*1056*

Wood, A. (Yorkshire; England)
Benefit Match	1940	*524*
Obituary	1974	*1082*
Portrait and Biography	1939	*40*
Record by	1941	*65*

Wood, A. H. (Hampshire)
Obituary	1934/I	*278*

Wood, A. M. (Nottinghamshire; Derbyshire; Gentlemen of Philadelphia)
Obituary	1949	*873*

Wood, B. (Lancashire; Yorkshire; Derbyshire; England)
Career Figures	1984	*1250*
Photographs	1971	*417*
	1975	*456*
	1980	*458*
	1982	*372*

Wood, C. J. B. (Wellingborough; Leicestershire; Northamptonshire)
Obituary	1961	*952*
Record by	1941	*65*

Wood, Capt. C. S. (Tonbridge)
  Obituary   1915/I   *247*
Wood, Lt-Col. D. (Military Cricket)
  Obituary   1917   *221*
Wood, D. J. (Sussex)
  Benefit Match   1956   *580*
  Photograph   1953   *549*
  Retirement   1956   *567*
Wood, Sgt. Navg. E. I. (Tonbridge)
  Obituary   1943   *369*
Wood, Lieut. E. R. G. (Radley)
  Obituary   1919   *195*
Wood, G. A. (Toronto Cricket Clubs)
  Obituary   1921/I   *242*
Wood, Lieut. G. D. (Cheltenham)
  Obituary   1916   *216*
Wood, G. E. C. (Cheltenham; Cambridge University; Kent; England)
  Obituary   1972   *1056*
  Schools Notes   1911/I   *127*
                                                1913/I   *213*
Wood, H. (Kent; Surrey; England)
  Benefit Match   1895   *292*
  Obituary   1920/I   *191*
  Portrait and Biography   1891   *xxxvi*
Wood, Rev. H. (Sheffield Collegiate School; Cambridge University; Yorkshire)
  Obituary   1942   *365*
Wood, Sir J. B. (Marlborough; Oxford University; Warwickshire)
  Obituary   1934/I   *278*
Wood, J. J. H. (Author; Writer)
  Obituary   1914/I   *198*
Wood, L. C. K. (Staten Island C.C.)
  Obituary   1941   *404*
Wood, Lieut. P. B. S. (Rossall)
  Obituary   1919   *196*
Woodall, Lieut. J. F. (Ellesmere College; Shropshire)
  Obituary   1918   *210*
Woodburn, Dr. W. Y. (Berkshire)
  Obituary   1946   *447*
Woodcock, A. (Leicestershire)
  Benefit Match   1904   *231*
  Obituary   1911/I   *160*
Woodcock, J. (Journalist; Editor of Wisden 1981-)
  'The Ashes 1956' Book Review   1957   *998*
  'T. E. Bailey – Resolute and Impenitent'   1969   *129*
  'Ken Barrington – The Accumulator'   1970   *106*
  'John Edrich M.B.E.'   1978   *133*

'M. J. Smith Lays Down His Bat'	1976	*111*
Tribute to C. Taylor	1978	*1082*

Woodcock, R. G. (Worcester, Royal Grammar School; Oxford University)

Schools Notes	1952	*697*
	1954	*726*
93 wkts Schools Averages	1952	*758*
103 wkts Schools Averages	1954	*779*

Woodfull, W. M. (Victoria; Australia)

Obituary	1966	*974*
Portrait and Biography	1927/I	*305*
Record By	1941	*65*
Testimonial Match	1936/II	*650*

Woodhams, Capt. G. (Christ's Hospital)

Obituary	1918	*219*

Woodhead, F. E. (Loretto; Yorkshire)

Obituary	1944	*327*

Woodhouse, L. (Haileybury; Journalist)

Obituary	1944	*327*

Woodhouse, T. (Writer)
with R. Yeomans 'Yorkshire Cricket: A Pictorial Survey'

Book Review	1975	*1116*

Woodhouse, W. H. (Yorkshire)

Obituary	1939	*920*

Woodin, W. C. B. (President South African Cricket Association)

Obituary	1978	*1083*

Woodman, R. G. (Gloucestershire)

Obituary	1983	*1259*

Woodroffe, 2nd Lieut. K. H. C. (Marlborough; Cambridge University; Hampshire; Sussex)

Obituary	1916	*216*

Woodroffe, Capt. L. (Marlborough)

Obituary	1917	*221*

Woodroffe, 2nd Lieut. S. C. (Marlborough)

Obituary	1916	*217*

Woods, A. P. (Bobby) (Natal)

Obituary	1951	*929*

Woods, E. M. N. (British Columbia Club Cricketer)

Obituary	1921/I	*244*

Woods, Capt. H. D. L. (New South Wales Club Cricketer)

Obituary	1918	*238*

Woods, Capt. J. R. (Upper Canada College; Toronto C.C.)

Obituary	1918	*210*

Woods, S. M .J. (Brighton College; Cambridge University; Somerset; Australia; England)

Obituary	1932/I	*254*

Portrait and Biography	1889	*xxix*
Views on Reforms of 1889	1890	*xxxviii*
Views on Some Questions of the Day	1890	*xlv*
Views on Throwing	1895	*lv*
Woodward, J. (Warwickshire; Worcestershire)		
Obituary	1928/I	*303*
Woodward, K. A. (Harrow; Oxford University; Hereford; Derbyshire)		
Obituary	1952	*966*
Woof, W. A. (Gloucestershire)		
Obituary	1938	*947*
Woolcott, Sgt. R. J. (Balmain C.C., New South Wales)		
Obituary	1917	*226*
Wooldridge, I. (Journalist; Writer)		
'Cricket Lovely Cricket' Book Review	1964	*1001*
'Travelling Reserve' Book Review	1983	*1311*
Wooler, 2nd Lieut. C. A. (Sedbergh)		
Obituary	1917	*221*
Wooler, 2nd Lieut. H. S. (Sedbergh)		
Obituary	1917	*221*
Woolf, L. S. (Victoria)		
Obituary	1943	*385*
Wooller, W. (Groundsman Eastbourne)		
Obituary	1977	*1050*
Wooller, W. (Rydal; Cambridge University; Glamorgan)		
'Glamorgan' Book Review	1972	*1095*
Photographs	1954	*344*
	1955	*329*
	1957	*344*
Record of Service	1961	*652*
Views on Growing Pains of Cricket	1956	*88*
Woolley, C. N. (Gloucestershire; Northamptonshire)		
Benefit Match	1929/II	*374*
Obituary	1963	*1038*
Woolley, F. E. (Kent; England)		
Benefit Match	1929/II	*140*
Career Figures	1979	*108*
'Early Memoirs of Frank Woolley'		
M. Woolley Book Review	1977	*1100*
Hundredth Hundred	1930/II	*270*
'In First Class Cricket'	1939	*59*
'My Happy Cricket Life'	1939	*53*
Photographs	1939	*54*
	1979	*105*
Portrait and Biography	1911/I	*171*
Records by	1941	*65*

Tributes to: C. B. Fry	1957	*116*
Sir J. Hobbs	1964	*104*
'F. Woolley' O. Warner Book Review	1953	*1001*
'Frank Woolley' (Obituary) N. Preston;		
R. L. Arrowsmith	1979	*104*
'Woolley: The Pride of Kent' I. A. R Peebles		
Book Review	1970	*1070*
Woolley, G. (Philadelphia)		
Obituary	1939	*920*
Woolley, Martha		
'Early Memoirs of Frank Woolley'		
Book Review	1977	*1100*
Woolmer, R. A. (Kent; Natal; Western Province; England)		
Cricketer of the Year	1976	*56*
Photographs	1972	*448*
	1975	*441*
	1976	*45*
	1980	*442*
Woolrych, Rev. H. R. (Rossall)		
Obituary	1918	*240*
Woolwich Garrison 1945	1946	*200*
Woosnam, M. (Winchester; Cambridge University)		
Obituary	1966	*975*
Wootton, G. (Nottinghamshire)		
Benefit Match	1874	*26*
Obituary	1925/I	*284*
Wootton, J. (Kent; Hampshire)		
Benefit Match	1895	*72*
Obituary	1942	*366*
Wootton, Pte. R. (Prestwick C.C.)		
Obituary	1917	*221*
Worcester		
Photograph of Ground and Scoreboard	1955	*59*
Plan of County Ground	1950	*552*
	ad passim	
Worcestershire County Cricket Club		
County Badge	1950	*551*
	ad passim	
'A History of the Worcestershire County Cricket Club'		
W. R. Chignell Book Review	1952	*1016*
in Jamaica 1966	1967	*847*
Notes on	1952	*95*
	1965	*105*
	1966	*80*
'The Rise of Worcestershire' N. Stone	1963	*124*

Team Portraits:

Runners-Up	1962	1963	*155*
County Champions	1964	1965	*72*
County Champions	1965	1966	*59*
Gillette Cup Winners	1966	1967	*67*
John Player League Champions	1971	1972	*61*
County Champions	1974	1975	*601*
	1975	1976	*605*
	1976	1977	*608*
	1977	1978	*588*
	1978	1979	*580*
	1979	1980	*606*
	1980	1981	*599*
	1981	1982	*605*
	1982	1983	*624*
	1983	1984	*586*

'Worcestershire' R. Genders Book Review 1953 *1000*
'Worcestershire County Cricket Club: A Pictorial History'
M. D. Vockins Book Review 1981 *1193*
'Worcestershire Cricket 1750-1968'
W. R. Chignell Book Review 1969 *1024*
'Worcestershire Cricket' P. Thorn Book Review 1975 *1116*
World Tour 1965 1966 *847*
Wordsworth, Rt. Rev. C. (Winchester; Cambridge University)
Obituary 1893 *xxxvi*
Wordsworth, R. W. (Winchester)
Obituary 1915/I *247*
Work, M. C. (Pennsylvania University)
Obituary 1935/I *276*
Workman, J. A. (South Australia)
Obituary 1971 *1033*
World Champions – Note on 1968 *93*
World Cricket Growth of Note on 1953 *83*
World Cup Cricket 1966 1967 *345*
World Cup – Prudential

in England	1975	1976	*300*
	1979	1980	*297*
	1983	1984	*293*

'Cricket World Cup '83' D. Hodgson
Book Review 1984 *1262*
World Record Opening Partnership 1978 *1024*
World Series Cricket – Passing of
Note on 1981 *94*
World Team in Australia 1971-72 1973 *899*
Worm, C. A. (American Club Cricketer)
Obituary 1937/I *289*

Wormald, Capt. G. (Eton)
Obituary 1917 *221*
Wormald, Major J. (Eton; Middlesex; Norfolk)
Obituary 1958 *966*
Worrall, J. (Victoria; Australia)
Obituary 1938 *948*
Worrell, Sir F. M. M. (Barbados; Jamaica; West Indies)
Cricketer of the Year 1951 *77*
'Cricket Punch' Book Review 1960 *1003*
In First-Class Cricket 1968 *122*
Knighthood Note on 1964 *88*
Memorial Fund Match 1969 *916*
Notes on 1945 *310*
1964 *875*
Photographs 1951 *66*
1968 *117*
with Queen Elizabeth II at Lord's Photograph 1964 *61*
'Frank Worrell: The Career of a Great Cricketer'
E. Eytle Book Review 1964 *1004*
'Sir Frank Worrell' (Obituary Tribute)
Sir L. N. Constantine 1968 *116*
'Sir Frank Worrell' U. Guiseppe Book Review 1970 *1070*
Worsley, A. E. (Malvern; Northamptonshire)
Obituary 1970 *1027*
Worsley, D. R. (Bolton School; Lancashire; Oxford University)
Photograph 1965 *453*
Worsley, F. (Glamorgan)
Obituary 1950 *915*
Worsley, H. (Canadian Club Cricketer)
Obituary 1913/I *201*
Worsley, T. C. (Marlborough; Cambridge University)
Obituary 1978 *1083*
Worsley, W. (Lancashire)
Obituary 1919 *213*
Worsley, Col. Sir W. A. Bt. (Eton; Yorkshire)
Obituary 1974 *1082*
Worster, Capt. F. C. (Whitgift Grammar School)
Obituary 1919 *196*
Worst Start in Test Cricket
Photograph 1953 *58*
Worthington Prof. A. M. (Trinity College, Oxford)
Obituary 1917 *267*
Worthington, Capt. R. F. (Tonbridge)
Obituary 1918 *210*
Worthington, T. S. (Derbyshire; Northumberland; England)
Career Figures 1974 *1083*

Obituary	1974	*1082*
Portrait and Biography	1937/I	*292*
Wostinholm, J. B. (Secretary Yorkshire)		
Obituary	1910/I	*149*
Wrathall, H. (Gloucestershire; Northumberland)		
Benefit Match	1906	*233*
Wreford-Brown, C. (Charterhouse; Oxford University; Gloucestershire)		
Obituary	1952	*965*
Wreford-Brown, Capt. O. E. (Charterhouse; Gloucestershire)		
Obituary	1917	*221*
Wright, A. C. (Kent)		
Obituary	1960	*958*
Wright, A. H. (Journalist)		
Obituary	1906	*cii*
Wright, C. W. (Charterhouse; Cambridge University; Nottinghamshire; England)		
Obituary	1937/I	*284*
Views on 'The Follow On'	1894	*li*
Views on Throwing	1895	*lvi*
Wright, D. V. P. (Kent; England)		
Benefit Matches	1951	*391*
	1958	*417*
Career Figures	1958	*97*
Photographs	1950	*376*
	1951	*378*
	1953	*395*
	1954	*401*
	1955	*385*
Portrait and Biography	1940	*38*
Tribute to A. P. Freeman	1966	*965*
Views on Growing Pains of Cricket	1956	*89*
Wright, E. C. (Clergy Orphan School, Canterbury; Oxford University; Kent; Gloucestershire)		
Obituary	1948	*788*
Wright, Capt. E. L. (Malvern; Herefordshire)		
Obituary	1917	*221*
Wright, Capt/Major E. L. (Winchester; Oxford University)		
Obituary	1919	*196*
Wright, E. V. (Wellingborough; Northamptonshire)		
Obituary	1979	*1092*
Wright, Rev. F. W. (Rossall; Oxford University; Lancashire)		
Obituary	1925/I	*285*
Wright, G. (U.S.A.)		
Obituary	1938	*948*
Wright, Major G. B. (Quebec)		
Obituary	1920/I	*159*

Wright, Capt. H. (Mill Hill School; Leicestershire)
  Obituary   1916   *217*

Wright, H. (U.S.A.)
  Obituary   1896   *xlii*

Wright, Pte. H. (St. Barnabas C.C., Toronto)
  Obituary   1917   *221*

Wright, H. (North of England C.C.; Groundsman Bramall Lane, Sheffield)
  Obituary   1894   *xxxviii*

Wright, H. F. (Eton; Derbyshire)
  Obituary   1948   *788*

Wright, Lieut. H. R. L. (St. Andrews College, Toronto)
  Obituary   1919   *196*

Wright, J. (Derbyshire)
  Obituary   1962   *994*

Wright, J. (Cheshire)
  Obituary   1913/I   *201*

Wright, J. G. (Derbyshire; Northern Districts; New Zealand)
  Photograph   1978   *356*

Wright, L. (Worcestershire)
  Obituary   1957   *950*

Wright, L. G. (Derbyshire)
  Obituary   1954   *931*
  Portrait and Biography   1906   *cx*
  'Scraps from a Cricketer's Memory' F. G. Peach
  Book Review   1981   *1206*

Wright, N. E. (Wellingborough; Northamptonshire)
  Obituary   1975   *1085*

Wright, O. J. (Leicestershire Committee)
  Obituary   1946   *447*

Wright, P. A. (Wellingborough; Cambridge University; Northamptonshire)
  Obituary   1969   *989*

Wright, Capt. R. (Leigh C.C.)
  Obituary   1918   *210*

Wright, Rev. R. L. G. (Lincolnshire)
  Obituary   1966   *975*

Wright, Col. T. Y. (Ceylon)
  Obituary   1965   *972*

Wright, 2nd Lieut. V. A. (Birmingham Club Cricketer)
  Obituary   1919   *196*

Wright, W. (Nottinghamshire; Kent; Umpire)
  Obituary   1941   *404*

Wright, W. (Secretary Nottinghamshire)
  Obituary   1901   *lxv*

Wrigley, A. (B.B.C. Scorer; Statistician)
  Obituary   1966   *975*

Wrigley, S. (Northamptonshire)
Obituary   1928/I   *302*
Wrigley Cricket Crusade Note on   1981   *534*
Wrigley Foundation Notes on   1974   *71*
                1977   *113*
                1980   *91*
Wrigley, Six-A-Side Indoor Finals 1982 1983   *454*
Wrottesley, A. 3rd Baron (Rugby)
Obituary   1912/I   *184*
Wroughton, Lieut. M. C. (Christ's College, Oxford)
Obituary   1918   *219*
Wroughton, W. M. (Harrow)
Obituary   1930/I   *269*
Wyatt, C. G. A. (U.S.A. Club Cricketer)
Obituary   1922/I   *271*
Wyatt, Col. F. J. C. (Glenalmond; Hampshire; Orange Free State)
Obituary   1972   *1057*
Wyatt, G. N. (Cheltenham; Sandhurst; Gloucestershire; Surrey; Sussex)
Obituary   1927/I   *294*
Wyattt, Lieut. G. W. P. (Winchester)
Obituary   1917   *221*
Wyatt, Lt-Col. M. T. H. (Oxford University; Cheshire)
Obituary   1910/I   *149*
Wyatt, R. E. S. (King Henry VIII School, Coventry; Warwickshire;
Worcestershire; England)
 'Last Over' Note on   1946   *65*
 Portrait and Biography   1930/I   *278*
 'Three Straight Sticks' Book Review 1952   *1018*
 Views on Growing Pains of Cricket 1956   *86*
 Views on L.B.W. Experiment   1936/I   *344*
Wyatt-Smith, 2nd Lieut. J. D. (Sherborne)
Obituary   1919   *196*
Wyld, Capt. W. H. (Marlborough)
Obituary   1934/I   *279*
Wyllie, Capt. A. (Edinburgh Academy)
Obituary   1918   *210*
Wynne, Capt. E. E. (Uppingham)
Obituary   1918   *210*
Wynne, O. E. (Transvaal; Western Province; South Africa)
Obituary   1976   *1103*
Wynne-Finch, E. H. (Cambridge University)
Obituary   1915/I   *248*
Wynyard, Major E. G. (Charterhouse; Hampshire; Army; England)
Obituary   1937/I   *284*
Wynyard, W. T. (Wellington; Auckland)
Obituary   1939   *920*

Yalland, Lieut. S. W. (Gloucestershire)
Obituary ..... 1915/I *248*
Yardley, N. W. D. (St.Peter's, York; Cambridge University; Yorkshire; England)
Cricket Campaigns' Book Review ..... 1951 ..... *995*
Cricketer of the Year ..... 1948 ..... *55*
Photographs ..... 1948 ..... *41*
..... 1950 ..... *571*
..... 1952 ..... *586*
Schools Notes ..... 1932/I *295*
..... 1933/I *298*
..... 1934/I *295*
..... 1935/I *293,312*
Yardley Retires Note on ..... 1956 ..... *567*
Yardley, W. (Rugby; Cambridge University; Kent)
Benefit Match for the Family of ..... 1902 ..... *366*
Obituary ..... 1901 ..... *lxv*
Yarnold, H. (Worcestershire)
Benefit Match ..... 1955 ..... *578*
Obituary ..... 1975 ..... *1085*
Photographs ..... 1950 ..... *551*
..... 1952 ..... *69*
Yates, H. R. (Brantford, C.C., Ontario)
Obituary ..... 1919 ..... *213*
Yates, Major H. W. G. (Hampshire)
Obituary ..... 1957 ..... *950*
Yates, J. M. (Westminster; Cambridge University)
Obituary ..... 1917 ..... *267*
Yatman, W. H. (Winchester)
Obituary ..... 1914/I *198*
Yeabsley, D. I. (Exeter School; Devon)
Schools Notes ..... 1960 ..... *749*
86 wkts Schools Averages ..... 1960 ..... *765*
Yeadon, J. (Yorkshire)
Obituary ..... 1915/I *248*
'Year to Remember – 1884' S. Green ..... 1984 ..... *81*
Yearwood, Hon. L. (Barbados; West Indies Board of Control)
Obituary ..... 1943 ..... *385*
'Ye Olde Game of Cricket' ..... 1972 ..... *645*
Yeoman, W. F. (Western Province)
Obituary ..... 1945 ..... *346*
Yeomans, R. (St.Peters, York; Journalist)
'The Cricket Society Movement' ..... 1979 ..... *127*
Obituary ..... 1981 ..... *1151*
with T. Woodhouse 'Yorkshire Cricket: A Pictorial Survey'
Book Review ..... 1975 ..... *1116*

Yonge, G. E. (Eton; Oxford University; Berkshire)
Obituary 1906 *ciii*
Yorke, G. J. (Eton; Gloucestershire)
Obituary 1984 *1212*
Yorke, J. R. (Eton)
Obituary 1913/I *201*
Yorkshire County Cricket Club
in Bermuda 1964 1965 860
in Canada 1964 1965 860
'A Century of Yorkshire County Cricket Club at
Park Avenue, Bradford 1881-1981'
D. Maude Book Review 1982 *1258*
'A Century of Yorkshire Cricket' J. M. Kilburn
Book Review 1964 997
County Badge 1950 571
ad passim
'Farewell Bramall Lane' K. Farnsworth 1974 *135*
'Fifty Years of Yorkshire Cricket'
Lord Hawke 1932/I *257*
'Half a Century of Yorkshire Cricket'
D. Boothroyd Book Review 1982 *1255*
'A History of Yorkshire County Cricket 1924-1949
J. M. Kilburn Book Review 1951 989
'A History of Yorkshire Cricket' J. M. Kilburn
Book Review 1971 *1070*
in Jamaica 1936 1937/II 691
Lowest Score Note on 1966 78
More Trouble in Yorkshire Note on 1982 89
Notes on 1960 120
1967 92

'Over 100 Years of Scarborough Festivities'
J. M. Kilburn 1977 *151*
'Rebuilding Yorkshire Cricket' A. B. Sellars 1948 71
Special General Meeting Note on 1979 597
'The Story of Cricket at Bramall Lane'
K. Farnsworth Book Review 1974 *1118*
'The Story of Yorkshire' J. M. Kilburn 1955 105
Team Portraits
County Champions 1938 1939 63
County Champions 1946 1947 33
Joint Champions 1949 1950 69
County Champions 1959 1960 94
County Champions 1960 1961 91
County Champions 1962 1963 *154*
County Champions 1963 1964 66
Gillette Cup Champions 1965 1966 53

County Champions	1966	1967	*66*
County Champions	1967	1968	*65*
County Champions	1968	1969	*56*
Gillette Cup Champions	1969	1970	*49*
	1974	1975	*617*
	1975	1976	*623*
	1976	1977	*624*
	1978	1979	*598*
	1979	1980	*624*
	1980	1981	*614*
	1981	1982	*621*
	1982	1983	*641*
	1983	1984	*603*
Three Yorkshire Centurions Photograph in U.S.A.	1978 1964	1965	*142* *860*
'The Wardle Case' N. Preston		1959	*111*
'Yorkshire' M. Stevenson Book Review		1973	*1052*
Yorkshire – Centenary		1963	*141*
'Yorkshire – A Century of Championship Cricket' Yorkshire Post Book Review		1974	*1117*
'The Yorkshire Connection' C. R. Williamson		1983	*110*
'Yorkshire Cricket: A Pictorial Survey' T. Woodhouse and R. Yeomans Book Review		1975	*1116*
'Yorkshire Cricketers 1839-1939' P. Thomas Book Review		1974	*1118*
'Yorkshire – The Top County. Their Post War History' J. Bapty		1969	*134*
'Yorkshire's Twenty Two Championships 1893-1946' E. L. Roberts Book Review		1950	*974*
Yorkshire Cricket Council			
Views on Laws		1957	*86*
Young, A. (Somerset)			
Benefit Match		1931/II	*394*
Obituary		1937/I	*286*
Young, A. J. (Croydon Amateurs C.C.)			
Obituary		1957	*950*
Young, Sir A. K. (Kent)			
Obituary		1943	*385*
Young, Major A. W. (Derbyshire Friars)			
Obituary		1916	*217*
Young, D. M. (Worcestershire; Gloucestershire)			
Benefit Match		1964	*406*
Photographs		1956	*362*
		1959	*360*
		1960	*393*
Young, Major G. E. S. (Bradfield)			
Obituary		1918	*210*

Young, H. A. (New York Cricket Association)
Obituary   1924/I   *274*
Young, H. I. (Essex; England; Umpire)
Benefit Match   1926/II   *190*
Obituary   1970   *1027*
Young, J. A. (Middlesex; England)
Benefit Match   1953   *459*
Photographs   1950   *426*
         1951   *434*
         1952   *434*
Young, J. H. (Derbyshire)
Obituary   1914/I   *198*
Young, J. V. (Eastbourne College; Sussex)
Obituary   1961   *953*
Young, 2nd Lieut. N. C. de B. (Trinity College School, Port Hope)
Obituary   1917   *227*
Young, R. A. (Repton; Cambridge University; Sussex; England)
Obituary   1969   *989*
Schools Notes   1903   *cviii, cix*
         1905   *cxxxiv*
Young, S. (Philadelphia C.C.)
Obituary   1925/I   *286*
Young, Rev. W. A. R. (Harrow; Somerset)
Obituary   1948   *788*
Young, Sir W. M. (Eton)
Obituary   1925/I   *286*
Young England in West Indies 1976   1977   *866*
Younger, Lieut. C. F. (Winchester; Clackmannan County)
Obituary   1918   *210*
Younis Ahmed (Pakistan International Airways; Surrey; Worcestershire; South Australia; Pakistan)
Photographs   1970   *542*
         1975   *549*
         1980   *603*
Younis Ahmed's Great Season Photograph   1980   *63*
Younis Ahmed's Transformation   1980   *86*
Youth Cricket Association
'Cricket Thrives Here' H. S. Altham   1961   *154*
Notes on   1952   *1002*
         1955   *79*
         1976   *65*
Youths Defy Weather Photograph   1955   *62*
Zaheer Abbas (Gloucestershire; Pakistan International Airways; Pakistan)
Batsman of the Summer 1981 Photograph   1982   *69*
Cricketer of the Year   1972   *74*
Gloucestershire's Star Batsman Photograph   1977   *83*
Hundredth Hundred   1984   *928*

List of Hundreds	1984	*79*
Photographs	1972	*67*
	1973	*402*
	1976	*408*
	1984	*78*
'Zaheer Abbas – A Flourishing Talent: Twentieth Batsman to reach 100		
Hundreds' D. M. Green	1984	*76*
'Zed: Zaheer Abbas' Book Review	1984	*1270*
Zahid Cockar (Nairobi)		
Obituary	1974	*1084*
Zambia in England 1967	1968	*827*
Zimbabwe Winners of the I.C.C. Trophy 1982		
Photograph	1983	*348*
Zulch, J. W. (Senior) (Father of J. W.)		
Obituary	1913/I	*201*
Zulch, J. W. (Junior) (Transvaal; South Africa)		
Obituary	1925/I	*287*
Zulfiqar Ali (Lahore Board of Control)		
Obituary	1969	*989*

APPENDIX A

Photographs in Wisden (Excluding Individual Photographs in County Sections and County Team Photographs in the County Sections)

1889	C. T. B. Turner, J. J. Ferris, S. M. J. Woods, G. A. Lohmann, R. Peel, J. Briggs.	*xxviii*
1890	A. Ward, M. Read, R. Henderson, W. Gunn, A. Shrewsbury, W. Barnes, L. Hall, F. H. Sugg, R. Abel	*xxviii*
1891	R. Pilling, M. Sherwin, J. M. Blackham, G. McGregor, H. Wood	*xxxiii*
1892	J. T. Hearne, F. Martin, W. Attewell, J. W. Sharpe, A. Mold	*xxxvi*
1893	S. W. Scott, A. E. Stoddart, W. W. Read, L. C. H. Palairet, H. T. Hewett.	*xxxviii*
1894	G. Giffen, G. H. S. Trott, F. S. Jackson, A. Hearne, E. Wainwright	*xl*
1895	A. C. MacLaren, C. B. Fry, W. Brockwell, J. T. Brown, T. Hayward	*xliv*
1896	W. G. Grace	*xlvii*
1897	A. A. Lilley, T. Richardson, K. S. Ranjitsinhji, H. Trumble, S. E. Gregory	*xlv*
1898	J. R. Mason, N. F. Druce, G. L. Jessop, F. G. Bull, W. R. Cuttell	*xlix*
1899	W. Storer, A. Trott, C. L. Townsend, W. Rhodes, W. H. Lockwood	*lvii*
1900	J. Darling, M. A. Noble, R. M. Poore, C. Hill, A. O. Jones	*lix*
1901	R. E. Foster, J. Tunnicliffe, T. L. Taylor, G. H. Hurst, S. Haigh	*lxix*
1902	F. Mitchell, C. McGahey, J. T. Tyldesley, L. C. Braund, W. G. Quaife	*lxxvii*
1903	C. J. Burnup, W. W. Armstrong, V. Trumper, J. Iremonger, J. J. Kelly	*lxxxv*
1904	P. F. Warner, A. E. Knight, J. Gunn, W. Mead, C. Blythe	*xci*
1905	R. H. Spooner, P. A. Perrin, B. J. T. Bosasnquet, E. A. Halliwell, J. Hallows	*cix*
1906	J. Vine, L. G. Wright, D. Denton, W. Lees, G. J. Thompson	*cix*
1907	J. N. Crawford, E. G. Hayes, K. L. Hutchings, N. A. Knox, A. Fielder	*cxxiii*
1908	T. Wass, A. W. Hallam, F. A. Tarrant, R. O. Schwarz, A. E. Vogler	*I/161*
1909	J. B. Hobbs, A. Marshal, Lord Hawke, J. T. Newstead, W. Brearley	*I/157*
1910	W. Bardsley, V. S. Ransford, S. F. Barnes, D. W. Carr, A. P. Day	*I/157*
1911	H. K. Foster, A. Hartley, W. C. Smith, F. E. Woolley, C. B. Llewellyn	*I/167*
1912	S. P. Kinneir, C. P. Mead, F. R. Foster, H. Strudwick, J. W. Hearne	*I/189*
1913	John Wisden	*I/122*
1914	G. Gunn, A. E. Relf, Hon. L. H. Tennyson, W. Booth, J. W. Hitch	*I/233*

1915	P. G. H. Fender, D. J. Knight, J. W. H. T. Douglas, S. G. Smith, H. T. W. Hardinge	I/199
1916	No Photographs	
1917	No Photographs	
1918	G. T. S. Stevens, J. E. D'E. Firth, C. H. Gibson, G. A. Rotherham, H. L. Calder	150
1919	A. C. Gore, A. P. F. Chapman, N. E. Partridge, P. W. Adams, L. P. Hedges	150
1920	P. Holmes, H. Sutcliffe, E. Hendren, A. Ducat, E. Tyldesley	I/252
1921	P. F. Warner	I/245
1922	E. A. McDonald, J. M. Gregory, C. G. Macartney, H. Ashton, J. L. Bryan	I/274
1923	A. W. Carr, A. Sandham, C. Parker, A. C. Russell, A. P. Freeman	I/312
1924	R. Kilner, C. G. Macaulay, M. W. Tate, A. E. R. Gilligan, C. H. Parkin	I/277
1925	H. W. Taylor, R. H. Catterall, J. C. W. Macbryan, W. W. Whysall, R. Tyldesley	I/291
1926	J. B. Hobbs	I/291
1927	W. M. Woodfull, W. A. Oldfield, H. Larwood, G. Geary, J. Mercer	I/305
1928	W. R. Hammond, C. Hallows, W. W. C. Jupp, D. R. Jardine, R. C. Blunt	I/309
1929	J. C. White, G. Duckworth, L. E. G. Ames, S. J. Staples, M. Leyland	I/269
1930	K. S. Duleepsinhji, E. H. Bowley, R. E. S. Wyatt, H. G. Owen-Smith, R. W. V. Robins	I/275
1931	D. G. Bradman, C. V. Grimmett, I. A. R. Peebles, B. H. Lyon M. J. Turnbull	I/283
1932	Nawab of Pataudi (Senior), James Langridge, C. S. Dempster, H. Verity, W. E. Bowes	I/269
1933	F. R. Brown, C. K. Nayudu, W. Voce, W. E. Astill, A. S. Kennedy	I/266
	Lord Harris	I/229
1934	A. H. Bakewell, C. F. Walters, G. A. Headley, L. F. Townsend, M. S. Nichols	I/281
1935	W. H. Ponsford, S. J. McCabe, W. J. O'Reilly, G. A. E. Paine, C. I. J. Smith	I/279
1936	H. B. Cameron, B. Mitchell, E. R. T. Holmes, D. Smith, A. Wellard	I/295
1937	A. R. Gover, W. H. Copson, T. S. Worthington, Vijay Merchant, C. J. Barnett	I/296
1938	New Zealand Team in England 1937	33
	T. W. J. Goddard	34
	J. Hardstaff	35
	L. Hutton	37

	J. H. Parks	*38*
	E. Paynter	*39*
	A. P. Freeman	*41*
	Leg-Break Grip	*42*
	Top Spinner Grip	*43*
	Googly Grip	*44*
	E. Hendren	*47*
	G. O. Allen	*52*
	D. G. Bradman	*59*
1939	Australian Team in England 1938	*33*
	H. T. Bartlett	*34*
	W. A. Brown	*35*
	D. C. S. Compton	*37*
	K. Farnes	*38*
	A. Wood	*41*
	D. G. Bradman	*42*
	Sydney Scoreboard	*46*
	Oval Scoreboard	*47*
	A. E. R. Gilligan	*48*
	F. E. Woolley	*54*
	Yorkshire C.C.	*63*
	Lord Hawke	*64*
1940	West Indies Team in England 1939	*33*
	L. N. Constantine	*34*
	W. J. Edrich	*36*
	D. V. P. Wright	*38*
	A. B. Sellers	*39*
	W. Keeton	*41*
1941	Cricket And The War Effort Cartoon	*25*
	Capt. J. W. A. Stephenson's XI v British Empire XI in 1940 Team Portraits	*26*
	Slough v London Counties in 1940 Team Portraits	*27*
	M. A. Noble	*28*
	Herbert Sutcliffe in Action	*32*
1942	Tom Brown Centenary Group	*25*
	A View of the Tom Brown Centenary Match played at Rugby on 17th June 1941	*26*
	London Counties and British Empire XI 1941 Team Portraits	*27*
	The Army 1941	*28*
	Royal Air Force 1941	*29*
	Bradford League 1941	*30*
	Haileybury College 1941	*31*
	Walter Hammond	*32*
1943	The Army 1942	*25*
	Royal Air Force 1942	*26*
	Public Schools XI at Lord's 1942	*27*

620

	Dulwich College 1942	28
	Andrew Ducat	29
	Maurice Leyland	30
1944	Civil Defence 1943	33
	England XI v Dominions 1943	34
	Dominions XI 1943	35
	British Empire XI 1943	36
	Northern Cricket XI (C. Leatherbarrow's Empire XI)	37
	Cambridge University 1943	38
	Eton College XI 1943	39
	Hedley Verity	40
1945	Flying Bomb Stops Cricket	33
	Royal Australian Air Force	34
	Hedley Verity Memorial Match	35
	Royal Navy	36
	West of England XI	37
	North of England XI	38
	Northamptonshire	39
	Maurice Joseph Turnbull	40
1946	Old Trafford of the Future	33
	Oval Prison Cage	34
	Kennington Oval in 1945	35
	England's Victory Team 1945	36
	Australia's Victory Team 1945	37
	Central Mediterranean Force	38
	Desert Air Force	39
	Edward Paynter	40
1947	Yorkshire Champion County 1946	33
	England Team v India at the Oval	34
	1946 Indian Team in England	35
	The King (George VI) at the Oval	36
	Surrey Centenary Match – The Old England XI	37
	Last Wicket Records at the Oval (C. T. Sarwate and S. Banerjee)	38
	Indians at Hove (First four batsmen hit centuries)	39
	A. V. Bedser	40
	L. B. Fishlock	41
	V. Mankad	42
	P. Smith	43
	C. Washbrook	44
1948	The Great Middlesex Pair (Compton and Edrich)	33
	Middlesex Champion County 1947	34
	Gloucestershire – Runners up 1947	35
	1947 South African Team in England	36
	Bruce Mitchell Defies England	37
	Smithson Leaves the Mines	38

621

	The Edrich Family Team	39
	A. Melville	40
	N. W. D. Yardley	41
	M. P. Donnelly	42
	A. D. Nourse	43
	J. D. Robertson	44
1949	Australians at Balmoral	65
	England Team at Lord's 1948	66
	1948 Australian team in England	67
	Bradman's Last Test Appearance	68
	Barnes injured at Manchester	69
	Glamorgan Champion County 1948	70
	A. L. Hassett	71
	A. R. Morris	72
	R. R. Lindwall	73
	D. Tallon	74
	W. A. Johnston	75
	Don Bradman's Farewell	76
1950	A Notable First Ball (Duke of Edinburgh Bowling)	65
	England Team at the Oval 1949	66
	1949 New Zealand Team in England	67
	Middlesex – Joint Champions	68
	Yorkshire – Joint Champions	69
	A Remarkable Catch (by T. G. Evans)	70
	Three Records for 18 Year Old (D. B. Close)	71
	T. E. Bailey	72
	R. O. Jenkins	73
	B. Sutcliffe	74
	R. T. Simpson	75
	John Langridge	76
1951	Victory Calypso (West Indies supporters at Lord's)	57
	1950 West Indies Team in England	58
	England Team at Manchester 1950	59
	Hutton at his Best	60
	Compton with the Schoolboys	61
	Lancashire – Joint Champions	62
	Surrey – Joint Champions	63
	A. L. Valentine	64
	S. Ramadhin	65
	F. M. Worrell	66
	E. Weekes	67
	T. G. Evans	68
	L. E. G. Ames	90
1952	The Ideal Fielder	65
	England Team at Oval	66
	1951 South African Team in England	67

	Warwickshire County Champions	68
	The Art of Stumping (H. Yarnold)	69
	When Glamorgan Beat the South Africans	70
	The Nottingham Scoreboard (Trent Bridge)	71
	E. A. Rowan	72
	R. Appleyard	73
	H. E. Dollery	74
	J. C. Laker	75
	P. B. H. May	76
	F. R. Brown	102
1953	The Queen at Lord's (with Indian Team)	53
	England Team at Oval	54
	Indian Team in England	55
	Surrey – County Champions 1952	56
	England's New Captain in action (L. Hutton)	57
	The worst start in Test Cricket (India at Headingley)	58
	An exciting moment in the Oval Test	59
	F. S. Trueman	60
	D. S. Sheppard	61
	H. Gimblett	62
	W. S. Surridge	63
	T. W. Graveney	64
	A. V. Bedser	98
1954	The Victorious Captain (L. Hutton on the Oval balcony)	53
	England's Winning Team at the Oval	54
	Australians in England 1953	55
	Test Match Saving Stand at Lord's (T. E. Bailey Batting)	56
	Tense Moment at the Oval	57
	Another Record for A. V. Bedser	58
	Surrey County Champions 1953	59
	K. R. Miller	60
	R. N. Harvey	61
	J. H. Wardle	62
	W. Watson	63
	G. A. R. Lock	64
	A. L. Hassett	92
1955	Champions Again (W. S. Surridge and P. B. H. May)	57
	Surrey County Champions 1954	58
	Supporters Help Counties (Worcester Scoreboard)	59
	England's Winning Team at Nottingham 1954	60
	Pakistan in England 1954	61
	Youths Defy the Weather	62
	Hot Tempered Test Crowd (Georgetown West Indies Rioters)	63
	Fazal Mahmood	64
	E. Hollies	65

	B. Dooland	66
	G. E. Tribe	67
	J. B. Statham	68
1956	The Queen Meets the Champions (Surrey)	45
	Surrey – County Champions 1955	46
	South Africans in England 1955	47
	M.C.C. Australasian Team 1954-55	48
	World's Smallest Test Score (Auckland Scoreboard)	49
	Vital Test Catch for South Africa	50
	Imperial Cricket Conference	51
	D. J. Insole	52
	F. H. Tyson	53
	D. J. McGlew	54
	H. J. Tayfield	55
	M. C. Cowdrey	56
	Ray Lindwall and Keith Miller	108
1957	Presentation to J. C. Laker	45
	England Team at Kennington Oval	46
	1956 Australian Team in England	47
	Surrey – County Champions for the Fifth Successive Year	48
	Laker Completes his Bowling Record	49
	Lucky Escape for England	50
	A Catch in Laker's Leg Trap	51
	J. W. Burke	52
	G. R. A. Langley	53
	D. Brookes	54
	M. J. Hilton	55
	P. E. Richardson	56
	C. B. Fry	112
1958	Old Timers at Lord's	45
	Test Cricket at Edgbaston Again	46
	England's Record Partnership (M. C. Cowdrey and P. B. H. May)	47
	England Team at Trent Bridge 1957	48
	1957 West Indies Team at England	49
	Surrey County Champions for the Sixth Successive Season	50
	Surrey's Lively Close Fielding	51
	P. J. Loader	52
	A. J. W. McIntyre	53
	M. J. Stewart	54
	O. G. Smith	55
	C. L. Walcott	56
1959	The Toss (P. B. H. May and J. R. Reid)	37
	England Team at Edgbaston 1958	38
	Another Wicket for Lock	39
	1958 New Zealand Team in England	40

624

	Milton's Anxious Moment	*41*
	Surrey – County Champions for Seventh Successive Year	*42*
	Hampshire – The Runners Up	*43*
	J. R. Reid	*44*
	H. L. Jackson	*45*
	C. A. Milton	*46*
	D. Shackleton	*47*
	R. E. Marshall	*48*
1960	M. J. Smith	*85*
	K. F. Barrington	*86*
	R. Illingworth	*87*
	G. Pullar	*88*
	D. B. Carr	*89*
	Godfrey Evans in his Last Test	*90*
	England Team at Old Trafford	*91*
	A Maiden Test Hundred (A. A. Baig)	*92*
	1959 Indian Team in England	*93*
	Yorkshire County Champions	*94*
	Gloucestershire – Runners up	*95*
	The Drag (G. Rorke)	*96*
1961	The Queen at Lord's (with South Africa)	*85*
	1960 South African Team in England	*86*
	Imperial Cricket Conference	*88*
	The Throwing Controversy (G. Griffin)	*89*
	Firemen Disperse Trinidad Rioters	*90*
	Yorkshire County Champions	*91*
	R. A. McClean	*92*
	R. Subba Row	*93*
	J. V. Wilson	*94*
	N. A. T. Adcock	*95*
	E. R. Dexter	*96*
	Alec Bedser	*143*
1962	Queen at Lord's (with Australia)	*85*
	1961 Australia Team in England	*86*
	England Team at Edgbaston	*87*
	A. W. T. Grout's Wicket Keeping Record	*88*
	Trueman's Match	*89*
	Hampshire County Champions	*90*
	Richard Hutton's Prize (with Archbishop of Canterbury)	*91*
	N. C. O'Neill	*92*
	A. K. Davidson	*93*
	W. E. Alley	*94*
	R. Benaud	*95*
	W. M. Lawry	*96*
	J. B. Statham	*136*
	F. S. Trueman	*138*

1963	John Wisden	*Frontispiece*
	Rt. Hon. Sir Robert Menzies	66
	S. H. Pardon	77
	Wisden Trophy	89
	W. G. Grace	93
	Sir Jack Hobbs	96
	Tom Richardson	100
	Victor Trumper	104
	S. F. Barnes	107
	Sir Donald Bradman	112
	Two Chiefs at Lord's (Duke of Norfolk and S. C. Griffith)	149
	The England Selectors (at Nottingham)	150
	England Team at Edgbaston	151
	A Fine Catch at Lord's (M.C. Cowdrey)	152
	1962 Pakistan Team in England	153
	Yorkshire County Champions	154
	Worcestershire Runners up	155
	P. J. Sharpe	156
	Mushtaq Mohammad	157
	F. J. Titmus	158
	P. H. Parfitt	159
	D. Kenyon	160
1964	The Queen and the Captain (West Indies at Lord's)	61
	1963 West Indies Team in England	62
	England Team at Lord's	64
	Injured Cowdrey Saves England	64
	Trueman's Reward	65
	Yorkshire County Champions	66
	Four Stumps in Lord's Experiment	67
	D. B. Close	68
	C. C. Griffith	69
	C. C. Hunte	70
	R. B. Kanhai	71
	G. S. Sobers	72
	Wisden Trophy (Lord Nugent and Sir Frank Worrell)	89
	Sir Jack Hobbs	96, 101,
	Sir Pelham Warner	120
1965	Trueman's World Record	69
	1964 Australian Team in England	70
	England Team at Leeds	71
	Worcestershire – County Champions 1964	72
	Warwickshire – Championship Runners up 1964	73
	A Brilliant Slip Catch (R. B. Simpson)	74
	Dexter's Broken Bat	75
	G. Boycott	76
	G. D. McKenzie	77

	P. J. Burge	78
	J. A. Flavell	79
	R. B. Simpson	80
	T. W. Graveney	112
	Neville Cardus	120
1966	Yorkshire Win Gillette Cup	53
	New Zealand Team in England 1965	54
	South African Team in England 1965	55
	England Team at Trent Bridge 1965 (v South Africa)	56
	Brian Statham Awarded C.B.E.	57
	The Nightwatchman – Fails	58
	Worcestershire – County Champions 1965	59
	R. G. Pollock	60
	P. M. Pollock	61
	K. C. Bland	62
	R. C. Motz	63
	J. H. Edrich	64
	Wisden Trophy	84
	Walter Reginald Hammond	115,119
1967	West Indies Retain the Wisden Trophy (with G. S. Sobers)	61
	West Indies Team in England 1966	62
	England Team at the Oval 1966	63
	Tom Graveney's Happy Return	64
	Ken Higgs – The Persistent Attacker	65
	Yorkshire County Champions 1966	66
	Warwickshire – Gillette Cup Winners 1966	67
	C. Milburn	68
	S. M. Nurse	69
	B. D'Oliviera	70
	J. T. Murray	71
	R. W. Barber	72
	G. S. Sobers	127,129,131
1968	The Queen at Lord's (with Pakistan)	59
	Kent Win Gillette Cup (A. Douglas-Home Presents Cup to M. C. Cowdrey)	60
	England Team at Trent Bridge (v Pakistan)	61
	Indian Team in England 1967	62
	Pakistan Team in England 1967	63
	Alan Knott's First Test Victim	64
	Yorkshire County Champions 1967	65
	J. M. Parkes	66
	K. Higgs	67
	Hanif Mohammad	68
	Asif Iqbal	69
	Nawab of Pataudi (Junior)	70
	Denis Compton	96

627

	S. F. Barnes	*111*
	Sir Frank Worrell	*117*
1969	Prince Charles Executes the Sweep	*51*
	Desolate Test Scene (Oval flooded with M. C. Cowdrey)	*52*
	The Moment of Triumph	*53*
	England's Victorious Team (at the Oval)	*54*
	Australians in England 1968	*55*
	Yorkshire County Champions 1968	*56*
	Warwickshire Win Gillette Cup	*57*
	(Presentation to A. C. Smith by A. E. R. Gilligan)	
	B. A. Richards	*58*
	J. G. Binks	*59*
	O. S. Wheatley	*60*
	D. M. Green	*61*
	D. L. Underwood	*62*
	M. C. Cowdrey	*98*
	M. C. Cowdrey Displays the Wisden Trophy	*101*
	J. B. Statham – Gentleman George	*115*
1970	Yorkshire Win the Gillette Cup	*49*
	Glamorgan County Champions 1969	*50*
	England Team at Trent Bridge 1969	*51*
	West Indies Team in England 1969	*52*
	New Zealand Team in England 1969	*53*
	Lancashire win Player's Sunday League	*54*
	Sharpe Takes Another Slip Catch	*55*
	B. F. Butcher	*56*
	M. J. Procter	*57*
	Majid Jahangair Khan	*58*
	D. J. Shepherd	*59*
	A. P. E. Knott	*60*
	Emmott Robinson	*83*
	F. S. Trueman	*93*
	K. F. Barrington	*107*
	Enid Bakewell	*120*
	Gilligan Leads the England Team on to the field Against South Africa at Edgbaston in 1924	*126*
1971	Tom Graveney's Farewell	*63*
	Kent County Champions 1970	*64*
	Lancashire – John Player and Gillette Cup Winners	*65*
	England Team at Trent Bridge 1970	*66*
	Rest of the World Team at Lord's	*67*
	Hero Worship at the Oval (G. Pollock and G. Sobers leaving the field)	*68*
	Barlow's Four Wickets in Five Balls	*69*
	B. W. Luckhurst	*70*
	G. M. Turner	*71*

	R. T. Virgin	72
	C. H. Lloyd	73
	J. D. Bond	74
	Peter May	102
	H. Strudwick	115
	Syd Buller and Frank Lee	119
	1877 Gloucestershire Team – County Champions	143
1972	England Recapture The Ashes	
	(England in Australia 1970-71)	59
	Surrey County Champions 1971	60
	Worcestershire – John Player League Champions	61
	Lancashire Retain the Gillette Cup 1971	62
	Wasim Bari Equals a Test Record	63
	Pakistan Team in England 1971	64
	Indian Team in England 1971	65
	B. S. Chandrasekhar	66
	Zaheer Abbas	67
	Brian Taylor	68
	G. G. Arnold	69
	L. R. Gibbs	70
	A. Sandham with J. B. Hobbs	115
	Learie Constantine	126
	P. Holmes with H. Sutcliffe	131
1973	Clive Lloyd's Thrilling Century	61
	Australians in England 1972	62
	England Team in First Test 1972	63
	Lancashire Triple Winners of the Gillette Cup	64
	Warwickshire County Champions 1972	65
	Willis Performs Vital Hat Trick	66
	Leicestershire Win Benson and Hedges Trophy	67
	D. K. Lillee	68
	G. S. Chappell	69
	R. A. L. Massie	70
	K. R. Stackpole	71
	J. A. Snow	72
	Sir Compton Mackenzie	104
	Ray Illingworth with Ian Chappell and Derek Underwood	109
	Leslie Deakins with David and Winnie Blackmore the	
	Money Spinners of Edgbaston	128
1974	West Indies Regain Wisden Trophy (with R. B. Kanhai)	43
	New Zealanders in England 1973	44
	West Indies in England 1973	45
	Hampshire County Champions 1973	46
	Kent – Dual Champions	47
	Gloucestershire Gillette Cup Winners	48
	Howarth Traps Boycott	49

	B. E. Congdon	50
	P. J. Sainsbury	51
	R. C. Fredericks	52
	K. D. Boyce	53
	K. W. R. Fletcher	54
	Colin Cowdrey Completes 100 Hundreds	75
	Glen Turner off for a Single after Cutting the Ball	82
	Wilfred Rhodes from a Painting by Ernest Moore 1923	93
	Jack Gregory – Cricketer in Excelsis	114
	Scene during Last County Cricket Match at Bramall Lane 1973	136
1975	H. R. H. Duke of Edinburgh	66
	The Duke of Edinburgh Bowling for the Duke of Norfolk's XI at Arundel in 1953	69
	Warwickshire's World Record (J. Jameson and R. B. Kanhai)	71
	England Team at Headingley 1974 (v Pakistan)	72
	Pakistan Team in Final Test (at the Oval)	73
	Sadiq Mohammad in Dashing Mood	74
	Narrow escape for Dennis Amiss	75
	Tony Greig's Daring Position	76
	David Lloyd's Double Century	77
	A. W. Greig	78
	Norman Gifford	79
	M. H. Denness	80
	A. M. E. Roberts	81
	D. L. Amiss	82
	Sobers Displays the Wisden Trophy in 1966	108
	Gilbert Jessop	138
1976	Clive Lloyd Displays the Cup (World Cup)	35
	West Indies – The World Cup Champions	36
	Australia – World Cup Runners up	37
	England Test Team 1975	38
	Rodney Marshe's Great Catch	39
	Snow Prevents Play at Buxton	40
	Kallicharan Hooks the Bouncer	41
	I. M. Chappell	42
	R. B. McCosker	43
	P. G. Lee	44
	R. A. Woolmer	45
	D. S. Steele	46
	R. B. Kanhai with the Wisden Trophy	68
	Sir Neville Cardus	108
	M. J. K. Smith leaves the field	113
	J. T. Murray	121
	F. R. Foster	135

	Bert Lock	145
	New Zealand World Cup Team	301
	Pakistan World Cup Team	302
	Indian World Cup Team	303
	East African World Cup Team	304
	Sri Lankan World Cup Team	305
1977	Zaheer Abbas – Gloucestershire's Star Batsman	83
	West Indies Take the Wisden Trophy	84
	The England Team at Lord's	85
	Close takes the Body Blows	86
	Holding's Oval Record	87
	Alan Knott at his Best	88
	Women Play at Lord's	89
	J. M. Brearley	90
	R. W. Taylor	91
	M. A. Holding	92
	C. G. Greenidge	93
	I. V. A. Richards	94
	Frank Tyson	117
	Dennis Lillee	119
	G. O. Allen	123
	Arthur Gilligan	131
	W. A. Oldfield	135
	London County v Cambridge University 1901	139
1978	The Queen at Trent Bridge (with England)	81
	England Team that Won Back The Ashes	82
	Australian Team 1977	83
	Full House for Jubilee Test at Lord's	84
	England's Brilliant Fielding	85
	Gloucestershire Win Benson and Hedges Cup	86
	Gillette Cup Goes to Middlesex	87
	K. S. McEwan	88
	M. Hendrick	89
	I. T. Botham	90
	Alan Jones	91
	R. G. D. Willis	92
	John Edrich M.B.E. (Family Group)	134
	Geoffrey Boycott	141
	The Three Yorkshire Centurions (G. Boycott, L. Hutton, H. Sutcliffe)	142
1979	The Helmet and Dennis Amiss	57
	England Team at Edgbaston	58
	Pakistan in England 1978	59
	New Zealand in England 1978	60
	Brilliant England Fielding	61
	Ian Botham's Dramatic Run Out	62

	The Controversial Bouncer By Willis	63
	J. K. Lever	64
	C. T. Radley	65
	C. M. Old	66
	J. N. Shepherd	67
	D. I. Gower	68
	Norman Preston (with G. Ross, D. B. Carr)	83
	Herbert Sutcliffe	97
	Frank Woolley	105
	John Langridge	116
1980	The Grass Roots of Cricket (Water Orton Ground)	59
	West Indies Win the Prudential Cup (with C. Lloyd)	60
	Sri Lanka Take the I.C.C. Trophy	61
	England Regain The Ashes in Australia (1978-79)	62
	Younis Ahmed's Great Season	63
	A Typical Randall Effort	64
	Botham's Thrilling Knock at Headingley	65
	D. W. Randall	66
	Joel Garner	67
	G. A. Gooch	68
	B. C. Rose	69
	S. M. Gavaskar	70
	E. J. (Tiger) Smith	97
	'Tiger' Smith	100
	Charles William Alcock	107
	West Indies World Champions	298
	1979 Indian Touring Team	333
1981	Unbridled Dissent (M. Holding Kicks Stumps)	67
	'Police Protection at Lord's	68
	The Long Walk, the Long Wait (M. Holding's Run up)	69
	England's Centenary Test Team	70
	The Australians in England 1980	71
	Somerset's Test Match Contribution (K. E. Palmer,	
	I. V. A. Richards, B. C. Rose, J. Garner, I. Botham, W. E. Alley)	72
	England Captain's Fitness Test (I. Botham)	73
	R. D. Jackman	74
	V. A. P Van Der Bijl	75
	A. J. Lamb	76
	C. E. B. Rice	77
	K. J. Hughes	78
	Hubert Preston, Norman Preston	101
	Clarrie Grimmett and Bill O'Reilly	105
	Centenary Test Group at Lord's	110
	John Arlott with Keith Miller	115
	1948 Fiji Team	121
	The Helmet (Kepler Wessels)	124

	West Indies in England 1980	*312*
1982	Using the Crease (C. Croft)	*63*
	The Leaving of Guyana	*64*
	Sneaky Chappell (T. Chappell's Underarm Delivery)	*65*
	Turning Point at Edgbaston	*66*
	England's Fourth Test Team	*67*
	Botham – in the Image of Jessop	*68*
	Batsman of the Summer (Zaheer Abbas)	*69*
	R. J. Hadlee	*70*
	T. M. Alderman	*71*
	Javed Miandad	*72*
	R. W. Marsh	*73*
	A. R. Border	*74*
	Ken Barrington	*92*
	Mike Procter	*98,101*
	Mike Brearley – Using and Keeping his Head	*110*
	Madras Test Scene	*116*
	Cyril Coote	*122*
	The Australians in England 1981	*308*
1983	Eastern Magic (Abdul Qadir)	*Plate*
	'O' Tempora! O' Mores!	*Plate*
	Near to Death (D. Bairstow)	*Plate*
	Out of Bounds (G. Boycott, G. Gooch)	*Plate*
	England's Team v India at Lord's	*Plate*
	Rising Passions (Appealing)	*Plate*
	Captains Face the Camera (R. Willis, Imran Khan, with P. West)	*Plate*
	M. D. Marshall, T. E. Jesty, Kapil Dev, A. E. Kallicharran, Imran Khan	*Plate*
	Brearley Takes his Leave	*86*
	The Milestone Achieved (Glen Turner	*94*
	Indians in England 1982	*300*
	Pakistan in England 1982	*322*
	Zimbabwe – Winners of the I.C.C. Trophy 1982	*348*
1984	Moment of Triumph (Kapil Dev with World Cup)	*Plate*
	Selectors at Work	*Plate*
	England's Team v New Zealand at the Oval	*Plate*
	History at Headingley – (Jeremy Coney makes the Winning Hit and New Zealand Celebrate)	*Plate*
	A Trusty Servant (A. L. Jones)	*Plate*
	Violence in the Outfield (T. Alderman Carried Off Injured at Perth)	*Plate*
	The First Class Umpires 1983	*Plate*
	M. W. Gatting, C. L. Smith, M. Amarnath, J. V. Coney, J. E. Emburey	*Plate*
	Petition handed in at Lord's	*66*

Cricket Stamps   73
Zaheer Abbas – Twentieth Batsman to Reach 100 Hundreds   78
New Zealanders in England 1983   273
Indian World Cup Party 1983   294

APPENDIX B

Chronological List of Special Articles Excluding Portraits and Biographies and Five Cricketers of the Year. Where no author is given for an Article it will usually be the work of the Editor of *Wisden*.

1869	'Individual Innings of 200 or More Runs' W. H. Knight	98
1874	'Qualifications for a County Cricketer' (Discussion)	93
	'Thomas Humphrey'	123
1875	'Mr Charles Absolon in 1874'	15
	John Lillywhite	173
1888	'County Cricket'	xxiii
	'Formation of a County Cricket Council'	345
	'The L.B.W. Discussion – Expert Opinion'	354
1889	'A Few Jottings' R. Thoms	xxxv
	Meeting of the County Cricket Council	
	The L.B.W. Question	339
	General Meeting of the Marleybone Club – The L.B.W. Question	343
1890	'The Reforms of 1889'	xxxvi
	'Some Questions of the Day' (Discussion)	xl
	'Bowling' G. Lohmann	xlvii
	'More Jottings' R. Thoms	xlviii
1891	'In Memoriam: C. F. Pardon'	xi
	'Cambridge Memories' A. G. Steel	xxxvii
1892	'The Development of Cricket' Hon. R. H. Lyttelton	xlii
	'The Bibliography of Cricket' A. J. Gaston	xlviii
1893	'Hints from the Press Box' C. S. Caine	xliv
	'A Few Words on Fielding' G. Lohmann	xlix
1894	'The Follow On' (Discussion)	xlvi
	'Cricket Bibliography' A. J. Gaston	lxiii
	'George Lohmann in First Class Cricket'	lxviii
1895	Throwing in First Class Cricket (Discussion)	li
	'Cricketers past and present' – An Old Cambridge Captain	lix
	Robert Peel in the Cricket Field	lxix
1896	'W. G. Grace'	xlvii
	'Personal Recollections of W. G. Grace'	
	i) Lord Harris	xlix
	ii) A. G. Steel	liii
	W. G. Grace – Statistics	lvii
	Mr A. C. Maclaren	lxx
1897	K. S. Ranjitsinhji Scores in First Class Matches in 1896	liii
	'Mr W. G. Grace and the Surrey Club'	liv
	'Some Current Topics'	lv

	'The Batsman of One Thousand Runs' A. J. Gaston	lxix
1898	'Throwing: A Note by the Editor'	lvii
	Concerning 'Throwing and the Follow On Rule' F. R. Spofforth	lvii
	'The Oldest Living Cricketer – H. Jenner-Fust'	lix
	Cricket in the West Indies and America' P. F. Warner	lxx
	'Richardson's, Briggs's and Wainwright's Performances'	lxxxix
1899	'The Late I. D. Walker'	li
	High Scoring and the Law of Leg-Before-Wicket' (Discussion)	lxv
	'Throwing – A Note by the Editor'	xc
	'Mr R. A. H. Mitchell and Eton Cricket'	xci
	'England v Australia'	xciii
	'The Bowlers of 100 Wickets' A. J. Gaston	xcvii
1900	'Suggested Reforms' Lord Harris, A. G. Steel.	lxvii
	E. M. Grace in the Cricket Field	lxxxvi
	'Bibliography of Cricket' A. J. Gaston	xc
	'The Highest Individual Score on Record'	xcvi
	'Cricket Centuries and L.B.W.'	xcvii
1901	'Fielding in 1900' D. L. A. Jephson	lxxvii
	'The West Indian Cricket Team' P. F. Warner	xciv
	Ranjitsinhji in Eleven-A-Side Matches	xcviii
1902	'George Lohmann' (Obituary)	liii
	'Leg Break Bowling in 1901' D. L. A. Jephson	lxxxvi
	Mr C. B. Fry in First Class Cricket	cvii
1903	'The Second Class Counties and Leg-Before-Wicket' (Discussion)	lxii
	Mr W. G. Grace's Hundreds	xciii
1904	'Schoolboys' Bowling' F. R. Spofforth	lxvi
	'Play Back' D. L. A. Jephson	lxviii
	'Arthur Shrewsbury in First Class Cricket'	xcviii
1905	'M.C.C. in Australia' B. J. T. Bosanquet	lxxi
	'On the Preparation of Wickets' A. C. Maclaren	lxxviii
	Robert Abel in First Class Cricket	cxvii
1906	The Late R. A. H. Mitchell – An Appreciation	
	i) Lord Harris	lxxviii
	ii) R. D. Walker	lxxxiii
	Thomas Hayward in First Class Cricket	cxv
1907	'V. E. Walker' – An old Friend	lxxxiii
	'A Short History of Kent Cricket for the Past 30 Years and More' G. Marsham	lxxxv
	'The Tonbridge Nursery' Capt W. McCanlis	xcvi
	'W. G. Grace in Gentlemen v Players Matches'	cxxx
	'W. W. Read'	clxxiv
1908	'South African Bowling' R. E. Foster	I/106
	'John Tunnicliffe in First Class Cricket'	I/167
1909	'Cricket in the Sixties and at the Present Day' A. Lubbock	I/109
	K. S. Ranjitsinhji in First Class Cricket	I/165
1910	'Modern Batting' Lord Harris	I/113

	'G. H. Hirst in First-Class Cricket'	I/165
1911	'Our Young Cricketers' P. F. Warner	I/114
	'Lord Hawke in the Cricket Field'	I/174
1912	'Mr Archibald Campbell Maclaren in First Class Cricket'	I/156
	'Warwickshire in First Class Cricket' R. O. Edwards	I/194
1913	'John Wisden – Personal Recollections of'	
	i) Sir K. Digby	I/122
	ii) Sir Spencer Ponsonby-Fane	I/123
	iii) Canon McCormick	I/124
	iv) Rev. H. B. Biron	I/125
	v) Sir H. M. Plowden	I/126
	Wisden's Chief Scores and Bowling Performances	I/127
	'J. R. Mason in the Cricket Field'	I/169
	'R. E. Foster in the Cricket Field'	I/176
1914	'Hayward's Hundreds'	I/125
	Schofield Haigh in First Class Cricket	I/170
	'A Tribute to Alfred Lyttelton' Earl of Darnley	I/200
1915	'A Tribute to Allan Gibson Steel' Hon R. H. Lyttelton	I/171
1916	'W. G. Grace – A Tribute' Lord Harris	68
	'W. G. Grace in the Cricket Field'	84
	'A. E. Stoddart in the Cricket Field'	123
	'Victor Thomas Trumper in the Cricket Field'	131
	'Sir Spencer Ponsonby-Fane'	138
1917	'P. Warner at Lord's and the Oval'	268
	'A Great Bowling Feat'	270
1920	'Tribute to Gregor MacGregor' D. L. A. Jephson	I/247
1921	'Modern Batting and the Law of Leg-Before-Wicket'	
	Hon. R. H. Lyttelton	I/216
	'P. F. Warner'	I/245
	'Tom Hayward in the Cricket Field' Major R. O. Edwards	I/264
1922	'England v Australia: A Survey of 104 Test Matches'	
	F. S. Ashley-Cooper	I/227
	'Modern Batting' C. Toppin I	242
1923	'George Hirst in the Cricket Field' Major R. O. Edwards	I/308
	'Lord Harris and Umpire's Decisions'	I/231
	'Bibliography of Cricket' A. J. Gaston	I/255
	'J. T. Tyldesley and D. Denton in the Cricket Field'	
	Major R. O. Edwards	I/273
	'E. Hendren at Lord's since the War'	I/281
1924	'England v South Africa: A Survey of the 34 Matches'	
	F. S. Ashley Cooper	I/219
1925	'The Googly' B. J. T. Bosanquet	I/225
	'A Bygone Phase of Cricket; the Two Elevens'	I/229
1926	'Sydney H. Pardon' C. S. Caine	I/28
	'Jack Hobbs'	I/291
1927	'Recollections of Mr F. R. Spofforth' Lord Harris, Earl of Darnley;	

	C. I. Thornton	I/299
	'Cricket Reform' J. W. Trumble	I/348
1928	'Oxford Memories' Lord Harris	I/305
1929	'My Years at Cambridge' G. H. Longman	I/263
1930	'Australian Tours and their Management' Sir F. Toone	I/270
	C. I. Thornton; Lord Harris	I/316
1931	'Lord's and the M.C.C.: Thirty Years of History' Sir F. Lacey	I/275
	Wilfred Rhodes	I/331
1932	'Fifty Years of Yorkshire County Cricket' Lord Hawke	I/257
1933	'The Late Lord Harris' Lord Hawke; W. Findlay; C. S. Caine	I/229
	'F. S. Ashley Cooper'	I/237
	'The Umpire's Point of View' F. Chester	I/302
	'Grange C. C. Centenary' W. Reid	II/639
1934	'P. Holmes (Yorkshire) 1913-1933'	I/245
	'The Late Jan Saheb of Nawanagar (K. S. Ranjitsinhji)'	
	Sir F. S. Jackson	I/251
	'The Bowling Controversy'	I/328
1935	'The Hobbs Era' J. Hobbs	I/247
	'Australian Cricket; its Control and Management'	
	Hon. Justice H. V. Evatt	I/255
	'Settlement of the Bowling Controversy'	I/325
1936	'Sydney James Southerton'	I/27
	'Trials of a County Secretary' R. V. Ryder	I/257
	'J. B. Hobbs – Twenty Five Years of Triumph 1905-1934'	
	J. A. H. Catton	I/263
	'Direct Attack and L.B.W.'	I/339
	'The Success of the L.B.W. Experiment' (Discussion)	I/341
1937	'Recollections of Oxford Cricket' H. G. D. Leveson Gower	I/249
	'A. P. Freeman in the Cricket Field' F. J. C. Gustard	I/257
1938	'Spin Bowling' A. P. Freeman	41
	'Reflections' E. Hendren	47
	'A Case for more National Wickets' G. O. Allen	52
	'D. G. Bradman 1927-1937' Hon Justice H. V. Evatt	57
	'Centenary of Trent Bridge' A. W. Shelton	461
1939	'Cricket at the Crossroads' D. G. Bradman	42
	'Cricket Conundrums' A. E. R. Gilligan	48
	'My Happy Cricket Life' F. E. Woolley	53
	'F. E. Woolley in First Class Cricket' E. L. Roberts	59
	'The Late Lord Hawke' Sir F. S. Jackson; Sir F. Lacey; H. Preston	65
1940	'Cricket in War Time' H. S. Altham	43
	'Notes on the 1939 Season' R. C. Robertson-Glasgow	49
1941	'M. A. Noble' H. Preston	29
	'Herbert Sutcliffe in First Class Cricket'	33
	Verity's Bowling 1930-1939'	40
	'Some Dates in the History of Cricket' H. S. Altham	42

'Some Dates in the Evolution of the Laws of Cricket'
H. S. Altham   48
'Notes on the 1940 Season' R. C. Robertson-Glasgow   55
'County Ranking list with Batsmen and Bowlers
1919-1939'   66
1942 **'W. R. Hammond in First Class Cricket'**
R. C. Robertson-Glasgow   33
'County Championship Reviewed' H. Preston   48
'Notes' R. C. Robertson-Glasgow   58
'Hobb's Hundreds in All Matches' J. B. Hobbs   90
'The Late A. J. Webbe'   352
1943 'Maurice Leyland in First Class Cricket'
R. C. Robertson-Glasgow   31
'Andrew Ducat' H. Preston   42
'Notes on Season 1942' R. C. Robertson-Glasgow   48
Planning Post War Cricket' N. Preston   62
1944 'Hedley Verity' R. C. Robertson-Glasgow   41
'The Best Fast Bowler' Sir Stanley Jackson   53
'Australians in English Club Cricket' Ft/Lt Bruce Andrew   56
1945 'Maurice Turnbull' J. C. Clay   41
'Views and Values' R. C. Robertson-Glasgow   46
'Australian Survey' A. G. Moyes   50
'Seeing Cricket after Four Years' E. M. Wellings   54
'Cricketers of the Year' A. S. Dixon   349
1946 'Edward Paynter' R. C. Robertson-Glasgow   41
'Cricket under the Japs' E. W. Swanton   48
'Hundred Years of Surrey Cricket'
H. D. Leveson Gower   52
1947 'South Africa and England' R. C. Robertson Glasgow   55
1948 'Compton and Edrich' R. C. Robertson-Glasgow   45
'No Magic in Fast Bowling' C. J. Kortright   67
'Sir Stanley Jackson' H. Preston   74
'Australia and England Sidelights on the Tests'
V. G. J. Jenkins   90
1949 'Sir Donald Bradman' R. C. Robertson-Glasgow   77
'W. G. Grace Centenary' H. Preston   101
'Glamorgan's March of Progress' J. H. Morgan   107
'Cricket and the British Commonwealth'
Rt. Hon. H. V. Evatt   111
'Growth of New Zealand Cricket' A. H. H. Gilligan   125
1950 'Warwickshire's Ups and Downs' M. F. K. Fraser   88
'Tribute to Hutton' V. G. J. Jenkins   93
'Coaching the Schoolboy' J. D. Eggar   103
M. P. Donnelly – R. C. Robertson-Glasgow   106
'West Indies in Test Cricket' J. Anderson   119
1951 'Fifty Years of Lancashire Cricket' N. Cardus   80

639

	'Then and Now' R. C. Robertson-Glasgow	87
	'Leslie Ames – A Century of Centuries' V. G. J. Jenkins	91
	'Ups and Downs on the Veld' L. Duffus	104
	'John Wisden's New Century' Lord De L'Isle	126
1952	'Modern County Cricket' Col. R. S. Rait Kerr	84
	'A Call for Culture' N. Cardus	88
	'F. R. Brown – Leader of Man' V. G. J. Jenkins	100
	'How Test Players are Raised' L. Hassett	107
	'Twenty Years of Indian Test Cricket' V. M. Merchant	110
	'Growth of Hampshire Cricket' E. D. R. Eagar	117
	'Tom Goddard Retires' D. Moore	123
1953	'Australia Throws Down the Gauntlet' N. Cardus	84
	'A. V. Bedser – A Giant Among Bowlers' R. C. Robertson-Glasgow	95
	'History of Derbyshire Cricket' W. T. Taylor	104
	'Dates in Cricket History' H. S. Altham	115
1954	'Batsmen must be Bold' F. R. Brown	87
	'A. L. Hassett – A Born Cricketer' N. Cardus	93
	'Growth of Pakistan Cricket' A. H. Kardar	97
	'Thirty Years an Umpire' (F. Chester) V. G. J. Jenkins	103
	'Sussex through the Years' A. E. R. Gilligan	108
1955	'South Africa Offers Serious Challenge' N. Cardus	88
	'Twilight Reflections' Sir Pelham Warner	95
	'The Story of Yorkshire' J. M. Kilburn	105
1956	'The Growing Pains of Cricket' W. E. Bowes	76
	'Len Hutton – The Master' N. Cardus	91
	'Two Eras of Australian Pace' I. A. R. Peebles	109
	'Centenary of Free Foresters' Col. K. B. Stanley	126
1957	'Reviving First Class Cricket' M.C.C. Report	73
	'Don't Tamper with the Laws' W. E. Bowes	79
	'Stuart Surridge: Surrey's Inspiration' D. R. Jardine	88
	'Laker's Wonderful Year' N. Cardus	91
	'How West Indies Cricket Grew Up' L. N. Constantine	99
	'The Great Men of Gloucestershire' H. F. Hutt	104
	'C. B. Fry' N. Cardus	111
	'Old Trafford Centenary' A. W. Ledbrooke	117
1958	'The Love of Cricket' Rt. Hon. Lord Birkett	68
	'Denis Compton – The Cavalier' N. Cardus	78
	'Googly Bowlers and Captains Retire' E. M. Wellings	94
	'The Story of New Zealand Cricket' C. Bray	98
	'Ups and Downs of Northamptonshire' J. D. Coldham	103
	M.C.C. Examine Amateur Status – M.C.C.	111

1959	'From Dr Grace to Peter May' H. Strudwick	61
	'India be Bold' V. Merchant	82
	'Charles Macartney and George Gunn' N. Cardus	87
	'The Early County Champions' R. Bowen	91
	'The Story of Somerset' E. Hill	99
	'The Wardle Case' N. Preston	111
1960	'Throw and Drag' H. Gee	97
	'Umpiring' Tom Smith	103
	'Essex 1876 - 1960' C. Bray	128
	'Five Stalwarts Retire' N. Cardus	137
	'The Early County Champions – A Postscript' R. Bowen	992
1961	'The Greatest Test Match' E. M. Wellings	105
	'The Throwing Controversy' L. Smith	111
	'Cricket Alive Again' J. Fingleton	127
	'Bowling For Surrey and England' A. V. Bedser	142
	'Cricket Thrives Here' H. S. Altham	154
	'Hubert Preston' N. Cardus	157
1962	'My Seven Year Stretch' G. O. Allen	118
	'An Enjoyable Visit to England' J. Fingleton	126
	'Statham and Trueman' J. M. Kilburn	134
	'Happy Hampshire' H. L. V. Day	143
	'Cricket Inquiry – Interim Report' M.C.C.	149
	'Evolution of the Laws of Cricket' H. S. Altham	153
1963	'Cricket – An Enduring Art' Sir R. Menzies	67
	'The History of Wisden' L. E. S. Gutteridge	75
	'Six Giants of the Wisden Century' N. Cardus	92
	'Stars of the Tests' E. M. Wellings	115
	'The Rise of Worcestershire' N. Stone	124
	'Through the Crystal Ball' J. Solan	145
	'The Joy of Cricket' R. C. Robertson-Glasgow	173
	'The County Championship in the Wisden Century' R. Bowen	366
	'The Universities in the Wisden Century' R. Marlar	697
	'Umpires' Associations' A. Riley	784
	'Public School Cricket in the Wisden Century' D. Eagar	787
	'Cricket Literature of the Wisden Century' J. Arlott	1077
1964	'Sir J. B. Hobbs' N. Cardus	97
	'Sir Pelham Warner' A. W. T. Langford	121
	'The Gift of Captaincy' N. Cardus	134
	'Following Leicestershire' B. Chapman	150
1965	'The Pleasures of Reading Wisden' R. Ryder	95
	'Cricket – An Art not a Science' Sir L. N. Constantine	108

	'Tom Graveney – A Century of Centuries' N. Cardus	*113*
	'Neville Cardus' J. Arlott	*121*
	'A Middlesex Century' I. A. R. Peebles	*128*
	'Cricket in the 17th and 18th Centuries' R. Bowen	*135*
1966	'Welcome West Indies – World Cup Cricket Champions'	
	Sir L. Constantine	*85*
	'Walter Reginald Hammond' N. Cardus	*113*
	'Cricket – a Game – Not a Subject' A. D. G. Mathews	*133*
	'The Great years and the Great Players of Kent' R. L. Arrowsmith	*138*
1967	'Counties Reject the Clark Plan' C. Bray	*96*
	The Two David Clark Reports	*101*
	The Throwing Report	*114*
	'My Favourite Summer' A. A. Thomson	*118*
	'Sobers – The Lion of Cricket' Sir N. Cardus	*126*
	'Nottinghamshire's Notable part in the Growth of Cricket'	
	R. T. Simpson	*134*
	'Indian Cricket – Its Problems and Players'	
	Dicky Rutnagur	*143*
	'The Rise of Cricket in Pakistan'	
	Ghulam Mustafa Khan	*153*
1968	'Batsmen Must Hit the Ball Again' D. Compton	*96*
	'The Googly Summer' A. A. Thomson	*102*
	'Sydney Francis Barnes' Sir N. Cardus	*110*
	'Sir Frank Worrell' Sir L. Constantine	*116*
	'Warwickshire the Unpredictable' Rowland Ryder	*124*
	'The Modern Golden Age' Sir N. Cardus	*131*
	'Notable Dates in Australian Cricket History'	
	Rowland Bowen	*144*
1969	'The D'Oliveira Case' M. Melford	*74*
	'Watery Reflections from Australia' J. Fingleton	*80*
	'M. C. Cowdrey – Centurian and Captain Courteous'	
	J. Arlott	*97*
	'J. B. Statham – Gentleman George' Sir N. Cardus	*114*
	'T. E. Bailey – Resolute and Impenitent'	
	J. Woodcock	*129*
	'Yorkshire – The Top County' J. Bapty	*134*
	'The Heritage of Our Cricket Grounds'	
	B. Easterbrook	*142*
	'Notable Dates in West Indies Cricket History'	
	R. Bowen	*151*
1970	'Emmott Robinson' Sir N. Cardus	*82*
	'Glamorgan – A Peep into the Past' J. H. Morgan	*86*
	'F. S. Trueman – Fiery Fred' W. E. Bowes	*92*
	'Ken Barrington – The Accumulator' J. Woodcock	*106*
	'Enid Bakewell – Champion Woman Cricketer'	
	Netta Rheinberg	*119*

	'And Gilligan Led Them Out' R. Ryder	124
	'A History of Wicket Covering' Irving Rosenwater	131
	'Ups and Downs of the Springboks' M. Melford	147
	'Notable Dates in South African Cricket History' R. Bowen	153
1971	'Reshaping Lancashire Cricket' J. Kay	93
	'Peter May – the Complete Master' J. Woodcock	101
	'Herbert Strudwick' Sir N. Cardus	114
	'Syd Buller' Frank Lee	118
	'The Thills of Sunday Cricket' Jim Laker	122
	'The South African Tour Dispute' Irving Rosenwater	128
	'The Midwinter File' Graham Parker	142
	'The Dreaded Cypher' Basil Easterbrook	152
1972	'Welcome Australia' E. R. Dexter	91
	'Sir Donald Bradman – Selector' Irving Rosenwater	108
	'A Lifetime with Surrey' Archer Sandham	114
	'Lord Constantine' John Arlott	125
	'Percy Holmes' Sir N. Cardus	130
	'The Great Wicket-Keepers' R. Ryder	137
	'Compton's Record Season' B. Easterbrook	146
1973	'Skills and Controversy' Richie Benaud	97
	'Shillings for W. G.' Sir Compton Mackenzie	103
	'Ray Illingworth C.B.E.' T. Bailey	108
	'The Warwickshire Way' R. Ryder	127
	'Norfolk and the Edrich Clan' B. Easterbrook	135
	'County Championship "Mosts"' E. L. Peake	356
1974	'Cricket Fever Hits Australia' Richie Benaud	39
	'Kent's Triumphant Revival' Dudley Moore	74
	'Glen Turner Joins the Elite' B. Easterbrook	80
	'Wilfred Rhodes – Yorkshire Personified' Sir N. Cardus	92
	'Jack Gregory – Cricketer in Excelsis' Sir N. Cardus	113
	'The Glorious Uncertainty' R. Ryder	117
	'A Century in the Fiji Islands' P. A. Snow	123
	'When Three Day Cricket was Worthwhile' C. T. Bennett	130
	'Farewell Bramall Lane' K. Farnsworth	135
	'Cricket's Strongest Wind of Change' Gordon Ross	140
1975	'The Pleasures of Cricket' H. R. H. Duke of Edinburgh	66
	'Old Trafford Humiliated' Sir N. Cardus	101
	'Sir Garfield Sobers – Cricket's most Versatile Performer' J. Arlott	106
	'The Joy of Touring' Henry Blofeld	120
	'200 Years of Laws' Gordon Ross	128
	'Gilbert Jessop – The Most Exciting Cricketer' R. Ryder	137

	'Buying Back One's Past' J. I. Marder	*143*
	'Willing Workhorses of Cricket' B. Easterbrook	*150*
	'Cricket in Israel' Hon. T. Prittie	*157*
1976	'Eleven West Indies of My Time' R. Benaud	*67*
	'Welcome West Indies' H. Blofeld	*71*
	'England v West Indies Statistics' S. Conder	*79*
	'The Greatest Centenary of Them All' Gordon Ross	*96*
	'Sir Neville Cardus C. B. E.' Alan Gibson	*107*
	'M. J. K. Smith Lays Down His Bat' John Woodcock	*111*
	'John Murray – Champion Keeper' J. M. Brearley	*120*
	'The Greatly-Praised Hanif and his Brothers' B. Easterbrook	*127*
	'F. R. Foster – A Prince of the Golden Age' R. Ryder	*134*
	'Bert Lock – King of Groundsmen' A, Bannister	*141*
1977	'From Spofforth to Lillee' R. Benaud	*116*
	'G. O. Allen – Mr Cricket' I. Peebles	*122*
	'Arthur Gilligan' R. L. Arrowsmith	*130*
	'W. A. Oldfield – Star Keeper' R. Ryder	*134*
	'Tales of W. G. Grace' J. Arlidge	*138*
	'The Cricket Rhymester' B. Easterbrook	*142*
	'Over 100 years of Scarborough Festivities' J. M. Kilburn	*151*
	'Derief Taylor – The National Coach' W. G. Wanklyn	*154*
	'The Gillette Cup Spans the World' G. Ross	*156*
1978	'The Packer Case' G. Ross	*123*
	'Judge Hits Cricket Ban for Six'	*128*
	'The Centenary Test' R. Hayter	*130*
	'Centurions of 1977: The'	
	'J. H. Edrich' – J. Woodcock	*133*
	'G. Boycott' – T. Brindle	*140*
	'Effects of the Bumper – Hasn't Ruined Batsmanship' R. Benaud	*148*
	'100 Years of Leicestershire Cricket' E. E. Snow	*151*
	'Three Studies in Greatness – W. E. Astill; M. J. Turnbull; J. C. White' B. Easterbrook	*156*
1979	'Captaincy' A. R. Lewis	*84*
	'The Packer Case' G. Ross	*88*
	'Herbert Sutcliffe' J. M. Kilburn	*96*
	'Frank Woolley' N. Preston	*104*
	'John Langridge – Golden Jubilee' J. Arlidge	*115*
	'Three More Studies in Greatness – T. Goddard; W. H. Copson; K. Farnes' B. Easterbrook	*121*
	'The Cricket Society Movement' R. Yeomans	*127*
1980	'How Essex Rose to Glory' Tony Lewis	*93*
	'E. J. ("Tiger") Smith' R. Ryder	*96*
	'Lower Standards' E. M. Wellings	*103*

	'The Man who made All Seasons' B. Easterbrook	*106*
	'My Life Reporting Cricket' Alex Bannister	*113*
	'The Packer Case' Gordon Ross	*121*
1981	'Norman Preston M.B.E.' John Woodcock	*100*
	'Clarrie Grimmett' W. J. O'Reilly	*103*
	'Fifty Years On' G. O. Allen	*107*
	'Radio Reflections' E. W. Swanton	*114*
	'Cricket in the Pacific' Scyld Berry	*119*
	'The Helmet' T. E. Bailey	*123*
	'Cricketana – A Bull Market' David Frith	*127*
1982	'Ken Barrington – An Appreciation' Robin Marlar	*93*
	'Mike Procter – A Great All Rounder' Alan Gibson	*99*
	'The Escalating Effects of Politics on Cricket' W. A. Hadlee	*106*
	'Some Thoughts about Modern Captaincy' J. M. Brearley	*109*
	'India 1932 – 1982' Michael Melford	*117*
	'Cyril Coote – A Cambridge Legend' J. G. W. Davies	*123*
	'The Career Figures of W. G. Grace' M. Fordham	*127*
1983	'J. M. Brearley – Success through Perceptiveness' J. Arlott	*87*
	'Turner Marches on' N. Harris	*93*
	'The Continuing Struggle for Survival' P. G. Carling	*100*
	'South Africa: Progress Towards Non-Racial Cricket' G. Johnson	*104*
	'The Fastest Hundreds in Test Cricket' G. Brodribb	*106*
	'The Yorkshire Connection' C. R. Williamson	*110*
1984	'M.C.C. and South Africa' M. Engel	*65*
	'Australia – A New Era' R. J. Parish	*69*
	'Philatelic Cricket' M. Williams	*74*
	'Zaheer Abbas – A Flourishing Talent' D. Green	*76*
	'1884 – A Year to Remember' S. Green	*81*